W9-BRM-537

NOVA SCOTIA
NEW BRUNSWICK & PRINCE EDWARD ISLAND

ANDREW HEMPSTEAD

NEW BRUNSWICK

PRINCE EDWARD ISLAND

Tignish

Mont-Carmel

CHARLOTTETO

FREDERICTON

Grand Lake

Moncton

Cape Tormentine

Tidnish

Northumberlan Strait

Pugwash

Sussex

Amherst

Balmoral Mills

Joggins

Chignecto Bay

Cape Chignecto Provincial Park

Parrsboro

Cape d'Or

Blomidon Provincial Park

Minas Basin

Cobequid Bay

Truro

Saint John

Bay of Fundy

Canning

Kentville

Wolfville

Windsor

Shubenac

Annapolis Royal

Digby

Digby Neck

Brier Island

Meteghan

Kejimkujik National Park

Mahone Bay

Chester

Peggy's Cove

Lunenburg

Ovens Natural Park

HALIFAX

Dartmouth

Lawrence town

Musquodoboit Harbour

Bridgewater

Lake Rossignol

Mavillette

Liverpool

Port Joli

Shelburne

Kejimkujik National Park Seaside Adjunct

Yarmouth

Ferry to Portland, Maine

Bartington

ATLANTIC

Contents

DISCOVER

Nova Scotia, New Brunswick & Prince Edward Island

The ocean is a defining feature of Canada's Maritime provinces. It permeates all aspects of life here, as it has for centuries.

Enticing Nova Scotia is a like a picture-book painting, a spacious canvas splashed with brightly colored fishing villages, richly historic towns, and uncluttered parks. Combine historic attractions such as imposing Citadel Hill with walks through coastal parks and feasts of seafood fresh from local waters. Hike through national parks, bike along back roads, kayak the coast, and admire famously photogenic lighthouses. But the options don't end with the ordinary: It's also a place where you can feel the excitement of white-water rafting on a tidal bore, get up close and personal with the world's rarest whales, or feel the fresh salt air on your face as you set sail aboard a famous racing schooner.

Nova Scotia is almost an island, but is connected by a slender, 15-kilometer-long border with New Brunswick, where you'll find elegant resort towns, pristine beaches, the phenomenal Fundy tides—and a distinct Acadian culture. Canada's smallest province, Prince Edward Island, is an easy excursion. It boasts the country's smallest capitol, Charlottetown, as well as charming villages and a photogenic landscape.

Clockwise from top left: Shelburne Historic District; Mahone Bay; Lunenburg Harbour; Halifax waterfront; Acadian church; whale watching.

As a visitor, you will be encouraged to immerse yourself in the Maritimes' cultural melting pot. Join in the dancing at a *ceilidh* (Celtic dance), taste rappie pie, and watch artisans at work. Like they have for centuries, the vast majority of the inhabitants continue to live an unpretentious and resourceful lifestyle, yet they are welcoming to visitors and generous to a fault. Conversation comes easily and humor abounds, especially over a few drinks. These are the friendliest folk you're ever likely to meet.

The Martimes' charms may reveal themselves slowly, but your greatest memories will be far from ordinary—ones that go beyond the scope of what a guidebook can recommend and instead revolve around adventures of your own making.

Clockwise from top left: Shelburne waterfront; downtown Lunenberg; lighthouse at Peggy's Cove; kayaking in the Bay of Fundy.

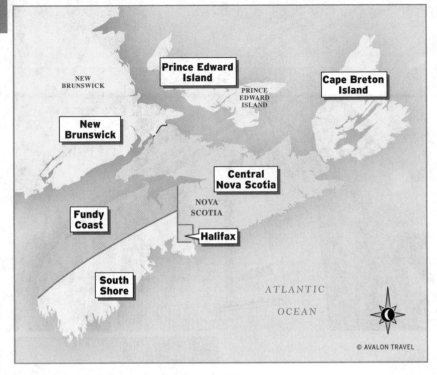

New Brunswick

New Brunswick

Prince Edward Island

PRINCE EDWARD ISLAND

Cape Breton Island

Central Nova Scotia

NOVA SCOTIA

Fundy Coast

Halifax

South Shore

ATLANTIC

OCEAN

© AVALON TRAVEL

Planning Your Trip

Where to Go

Nova Scotia

Nova Scotia typifies Atlantic Canada, with a dramatic, 7,459-kilometer-long coastline notched with innumerable coves and bays holding scores of picturesque fishing villages. It would be easy to spend an entire vacation exploring Nova Scotia, yet still leave feeling you hadn't seen everything. The cosmopolitan streets of **Halifax,** the colorful port of **Lunenburg,** the historical ambience of **Annapolis Royal,** and the wilds of **Cape Breton Island** are just a taste of what you can expect in this diverse province.

New Brunswick

New Brunswick is the largest of the Maritime provinces, but is the least known to outsiders. Although the province is mostly forested, it is its coastline and fertile **Saint John River valley** that attract the most attention. Here you'll find the elegant resort town of **St. Andrews,** the phenomenal **Fundy tides,** and **pristine beaches** such as **Parlee.** These attractions, along with the three main cities—**Fredericton, Saint John,** and **Moncton**—and a distinct Acadian flavor to the north coast, create a destination with something for everyone.

Prince Edward Island

Little PEI ranks as Canada's smallest province, as well as its most densely populated, most cultivated, most ribboned with roads, and most bereft of original wilderness. PEI also has the country's smallest provincial capital—Charlottetown, with a population of just 33,000. Tourism revolves around Cavendish, but the island's low-key charm is found elsewhere, along rural roads that end at the ocean and drift through neat villages that have changed little over the last century.

Know Before You Go

When to Go

Summer revolves around outdoor activities such as hiking, biking, swimming, canoeing and kayaking, fishing, surfing, and just about anything you can do outdoors. July and August are especially busy. This is the time of year when school is out and the parks come alive with campers, anglers, swimmers, and sunbathers. If you're traveling during this time, you should book lodging as far in advance as possible.

Spring and fall are excellent times to visit Nova Scotia, New Brunswick, and PEI. While May-June is considered a shoulder season, in many ways the provinces are at their blooming best in spring. After the first weekend in September, there is a substantial decrease in travelers across the region. But early fall (Sept.-Oct.) provides pleasant daytime temperatures, reduced room rates, and uncrowded attractions. By late September, fall colors are at their peak (Cape Breton Island is a major destination this time of year), creating a mini-surge in visitors.

Officially, winter extends from late December into March, but in reality most attractions and visitor information centers, as well as accommodations in resort towns, start closing in mid-October.

Passports and Visas

To enter Canada, a passport is required of citizens and permanent residents of the United States. For further information, see the website http://travel.state.gov/travel. For current entry requirements to Canada, check the Citizenship and Immigration Canada website (www.cic.gc.ca).

All other foreign visitors must have a valid passport and may need a visa or visitors permit, depending on their country of residence and the vagaries of international politics. At present, visas are not required for citizens of the United States, the British Commonwealth, or Western Europe. The standard entry permit is for six months, and you may be asked to show onward tickets or proof of sufficient funds to last you through your intended stay.

Transportation

Visitors to Nova Scotia, New Brunswick, and PEI have the option of arriving by road, rail, ferry, or air. The main gateway city for flights from North America and Europe is the capital of Nova Scotia. Ferries cross to Yarmouth from Maine, while the main rail line enters the region from Quebec and terminates at Halifax. Driving, whether in your own vehicle or a rental car, is by far the best way to get around, although major towns are served by bus. It is possible to visit Nova Scotia, New Brunswick, and PEI without your own vehicle (or a rental), but you'll be confining yourself to the cities and then relying on public transportation and guided tours to travel farther afield. Driving is more practical, especially if you plan to tour all three provinces and pursue outdoor endeavors.

The Best of Nova Scotia

Hitting all the highlights of Nova Scotia in one week is possible, but you're not going to see everything. In fact, you'll be covering so much ground, it may not seem like a vacation at all. This itinerary balances a little bit of everything—Halifax, the prettiest coastal villages, the two national parks, and the main historic sites—with time out for enjoying a glass of Nova Scotian wine over a feast of local seafood. The itinerary, like those that follow, assumes you rent a vehicle or have your own.

Day 1

Check in for a two-night stay at a downtown **Halifax** accommodation such as The Halliburton, a historic lodging within walking distance of Halifax's harbor front. Rather than start ticking off attractions, settle into the city by walking along the waterfront and soaking up the sights and sounds of the busy harbor. You'll see all manner of vessels tied up at the docks, and plenty of places where you may want to eat dinner at an outdoor table.

Citadel Hill

Day 2

Start at the top, literally, by visiting **Halifax Citadel National Historic Site** and then take a stroll through Halifax's formal **Public Gardens.** It's now lunchtime, and the Italian Gourmet is ideally situated en route to downtown. Take a tour of **Alexander Keith's Brewery** on your way to the *Titanic* exhibit at the **Maritime Museum of the Atlantic.** Dine at the Economy Shoe Shop.

Day 3

Rise early for the one-hour drive to **Peggy's Cove,** famous for its photogenic lighthouse. Continue south to **Mahone Bay** for an early lunch and a walk through the many shops lining the main street of this busy waterfront town. **Lunenburg** is your overnight stop, and there's plenty of colorful seafaring history to soak up along the harbor of this town that UNESCO has dedicated as a World Heritage Site. Grand Banker Bar & Grill is within walking distance of your room at the Spinnaker Inn (both have water views).

The *Bluenose*

A Family Affair

The most important thing to remember when traveling with children is not to try to fit too much in. Instead, sacrifice covering great distances for enjoying specific sights and towns for extended periods of time, and try to fit as many of these family-friendly attractions and activities into your itinerary as possible:

- **Harbour Hopper Tours,** Halifax, Nova Scotia

- **Museum of Natural History,** Halifax, Nova Scotia

- **Shubenacadie Wildlife Park,** near Truro, Nova Scotia

- **Hector Heritage Quay,** Pictou, Nova Scotia

- **Hopewell Rocks,** Fundy Coast, New Brunswick

- **Historic Garrison District,** Fredericton, New Brunswick

Green Gables Heritage Place

- **Magnetic Hill,** Moncton, New Brunswick

- **Parlee Beach,** Shediac, New Brunswick

- **Anne of Green Gables attractions,** Cavendish, Prince Edward Island

- **Prince Edward Island National Park,** Prince Edward Island

- **Attend a lobster supper,** Prince Edward Island

Day 4

Take Highway 8 to **Kejimkujik National Park,** which protects a large chunk of the forested interior. Rent a canoe for a paddle on the protected waterways. Continue to **Annapolis Royal,** where **Port-Royal National Historic Site** protects one of North America's oldest settlements. After dinner, watch the sun set across the Annapolis Basin from the grounds of **Fort Anne National Historic Site.** With reservations at the inviting Garrison House, you'll be within walking distance of everything.

Day 5

Drive through the apple orchards of the Annapolis Valley to Truro and take the TransCanada Highway across to **Cape Breton Island** and overnight lodgings at Baddeck's restored Telegraph House. The **Alexander Graham Bell National Historic Site** is the main attraction, but the town also has a picturesque lakefront area and a good choice of stylish eateries.

Day 6

Today's destination is **Ingonish,** along the **Cabot Trail.** You drive the long way around, but that's a good thing, because the rugged coastal scenery between Chéticamp and Ingonish is more beautiful than you could ever imagine. (Though this also means that the 200-kilometer drive will take longer than you imagine.) Plan on feasting on seafood at the Chowder House in Neil's Harbour and staying the night at Glenghorm Beach Resort.

Day 7

It takes a little more than five hours to reach Halifax International Airport from Ingonish. If you're on an afternoon flight, there's enough time to spend an hour or two in Ingonish. To play the revered **Highlands Links** golf course, you'll need to tee off early and fly out in the evening.

The Maritime Tour

It's possible to touch down in all three provinces in one week. This itinerary assumes you have your own vehicle or a rental.

For lodging, choose The Halliburton for historic charm or the Prince George Hotel for modern conveniences.

Day 1

Arrive in **Halifax** and spend the afternoon exploring the downtown precinct; include a visit to the **Maritime Museum of the Atlantic** and a tour of **Alexander Keith's Brewery.** Enjoy your first evening in the city by tucking into seafood at an outdoor waterfront restaurant such as Salty's.

Day 2

Rise early to beat the crowd to **Peggy's Cove,** then follow the scenic coastal route through **Chester** to **Mahone Bay.** After lunch, spend time admiring the local arts and crafts scene and walk along the waterfront to view the trio of waterfront churches. At nearby **Lunenburg,**

Ingonish Beach

While most visitors who choose Atlantic Canada for their vacations do so for the outdoors, there are a number of appealing cultural attractions to enjoy.

NOVA SCOTIA

- Take a tour of **Alexander Keith's Brewery,** Halifax.
- Explore the colorful architecture of **Lunenburg.**
- Wander along one of North America's best-preserved pre-1800s streets at **Annapolis Royal.**
- Soak up historic luxury at the **Keltic Lodge** on Cape Breton Island.

NEW BRUNSWICK

- Enjoy strolling along the historic **Prince William** and **Germain Streets** in Saint John.
- Take in the sights and smells of **Kingsbrae Garden,** St. Andrews.
- Immerse yourself in Acadian culture at **Le Pays de la Sagouine.**
- Step back in time at **Village Historique** Acadian.

Historic buildings line Prince William and Germain Streets.

PRINCE EDWARD ISLAND

- Learn about Canada's political beginnings at **Providence House,** Charlottetown.
- Step into the fictional shoes of Anne of Green Gables at **Cavendish.**

you'll find enough time for a sunset harbor cruise before turning in for the night at the Spinnaker Inn.

Day 3

Drive across southwestern Nova Scotia to **Annapolis Royal** and spend the afternoon exploring North America's oldest downtown street as well as attractions like **Port-Royal National Historic Site.** Guest rooms at the Garrison House reflect the town's gracious past.

Day 4

Catch the ferry from Digby to Saint John and drive down the coast to **St. Andrews,** where you can do what visitors have done for over a century—browse through the boutiques, enjoy **Kingsbrae Garden,** and dine on seafood. Have a room reserved at Seaside Beach Resort, unless it's a special occasion, in which case you'll want to spend the night at the Kingsbrae Arms.

Best Scenic Drives

A great way to see Atlantic Canada is to hop in your car (or rental car) and explore. Scenic drives can be wonderful family vacation activities, too.

- **South Shore** (Nova Scotia, page 84). We devote an entire chapter to the South Shore of Nova Scotia, a scenic drive of epic proportions that extends between Halifax and Shelburne in 210 kilometers via Highway 103, but highlights such as Mahone Bay, Lunenburg, Crescent Beach, and numerous coastal provincial parks require detours—and at least two or three days.

- **Bras D'Or Lakes** (Nova Scotia, page 158). The two-hour drive from Canso Causeway to Sydney on Highway 105 gives travelers a taste of the Bras D'Or Lakes, but to fully appreciate the expansive water, plan on detouring to Iona and as far as Big Pond, adding an extra three hours driving time. Baddeck is a good base for exploring this area.

- **Cabot Trail** (Nova Scotia, page 169). For its stunning coastal scenery and abundant wildlife, the 311-kilometer Cabot Trail, which loops around the top end of Cape Breton Island, is generally regarded as one of the world's most scenic drives. You could make the loop in five or six hours, but two or three days are needed to fully appreciate the beauty of the region.

- **Saint John River Valley** (New Brunswick, page 234). The TransCanada Highway zooms up the Saint John River between Fredericton and Edmundston in 270 kilometers (three hours), but travel upriver along the backroads and you'll pass through delightful villages such as Hartland, Bath, and Beechwood.

- **Strait Coast** (New Brunswick, page 253). Named for Northumberland Strait, which separates Prince Edward Island from the mainland, the two-hour drive between Cape Tormentine and Miramichi is notable for warm swimming beaches, French-influenced attractions such as Le Pays de la Sagouine, and the barrier islands of Kouchibouguac National Park.

- **North Cape** (Prince Edward Island, page 317). On the western portion of Prince Edward Island, all routes lead north to North Cape, but I suggest taking the coastal road (Highway 14) via West Point and Miminegash to the end of the road, where you enjoy sweeping ocean views, hiking trails, and even a restaurant. With scenic stops, allow a full day from Summerside for the 300-kilometer round-trip.

Day 5

Drive along the Fundy Coast to **Fundy National Park.** Plan on at least one hike (Dickson Falls is an easy walk), and time your early afternoon departure for low tide at **Hopewell Rocks,** where you can "walk on the ocean floor." Continue north across the Confederation Bridge to the Shipwright Inn in **Charlottetown.**

Day 6

Spend some time in the island capital, where **Province House** is a highlight, but also head north to **Cavendish** to soak up the story of Anne of Green Gables at **Green Gables Heritage Place** and explore the beachfront national park. Either way, the last ferry of the day departs Wood Islands at 7:30 pm, and you'll need to be on it to reach **Pictou** and your room at the waterfront Consulate Inn.

Day 7

Drive to Halifax. If time allows, fit in a few more city sights. The **Halifax Citadel National Historic Site** and the **Public Gardens** should be at the top of your list.

Nova Scotia

Halifax

Halifax (pop. 390,000), the 250-year-old provincial capital, presents Nova Scotia's strikingly modern face wrapped around a historic soul.

It's one of the most vibrant cities in Canada, with an exuberant cultural life and cosmopolitan population. The tourist's Halifax is tidily compact, concentrated on the manageable, boot-shaped peninsula the city inhabits. Its prettiest parts are clustered between the bustling waterfront and the short, steep hillside that the early British developed two centuries ago. In these areas you'll find handsomely historic old districts meshed with stylishly chic, new glass-sheathed buildings.

Halifax is more than a city, more than a seaport, and more than a provincial capital. Halifax is a harbor with a city attached, as the Haligonians say. Events in the harbor have shaped Nova Scotia's history. The savvy British military immediately grasped its potential when they first sailed in centuries ago. In fact, Halifax's founding as a settlement in 1749 was incidental to the harbor's development. From the first, the British used the 26-kilometer-long harbor as a watery warehouse of almost unlimited ship-holding capacity. The ships that defeated the French at Louisbourg in 1758—and ultimately conquered this part of Atlantic Canada—were launched from Halifax Harbour. A few years later, the Royal Navy sped from the harbor to harass the rebellious colonies on the Eastern Seaboard during the American Revolution. Ships from Halifax ran the blockades on the South's side during the American Civil War. And during World Wars I and II, the harbor bulged with troop convoys destined for Europe.

PLANNING YOUR TIME

Everyone has his or her own idea of how best to spend time in Halifax. History buffs will want to spend an entire week exploring the city's oldest corners, while outdoorsy types will want to hit the highlights before moving through to the rest of the province. Halifax has three attractions no one will want to miss, even if you have just one day. The first of these is the **Historic Properties,** a group of waterfront warehouses converted to restaurants

---

Highlights

★ **Historic Properties:** The oldest waterfront warehouses in Canada have been brought to life with an impressive restoration project and are now filled with bustling boutiques, cafés, and a brewery (page 28).

★ **Maritime Museum of the Atlantic:** If you visit just one museum in Nova Scotia, make it this one, which tells the many stories of the region's links to the ocean, from the *Titanic* tragedy to fishing the Grand Banks (page 28).

★ **Alexander Keith's Brewery:** Tours of North America's oldest working brewery go beyond describing the beer-making process, delving deep into Halifax's history and its most colorful characters (page 29).

★ **Point Pleasant Park:** On the southern tip of the Halifax Peninsula, this urban park is a favorite for walking and biking (page 31).

★ **Halifax Citadel National Historic Site:** Canada's most visited historic site lies atop downtown Halifax's highest point. It provides a glimpse into the city's past as well as sweeping harbor views (page 32).

★ **Public Gardens:** Strolling through these formal Victorian gardens is a morning rite for many locals (page 33).

★ **Fairview Cemetery:** Varying from three-digit numbers to moving family messages, the inscriptions on the headstones of more than 100 *Titanic* victims make this suburban cemetery a poignant place to visit (page 35).

© AVALON TRAVEL

★ **Fisherman's Cove:** If you're not planning to travel beyond Halifax, a visit to this historic fishing village will give you a taste of what you'll be missing farther afield (page 38).

Halifax

To Halifax International Airport, Atlantic Canada Aviation Museum, and Uniacke Estate Museum Park

CHERRY BROOK

DARTMOUTH

Lake Charles

SHUBIE PARK

Shubie Park

Micmac Lake

TRAVELERS MOTEL

ESQUIRE MOTEL

Hemlock Ravine Park

CLEARWATER

Bedford Basin

BEDFORD INSTITUTE OF OCEANOGRAPHY

Birch Cove Lakes

FOREST HILLS PKWY

Seaview Park

COLE HARBOUR HERITAGE FARM MUSEUM

Fort Needham Memorial Park

HALIFAX CITADEL NATIONAL HISTORIC SITE

PUBLIC GARDENS

COLE HARBOUR RD

BAYVIEW MOTOR INN

MARITIME COMMAND MUSEUM

HISTORIC PROPERTIES

FAIRVIEW CEMETERY

ST. GEORGE'S ROUND CHURCH

MARITIME MUSEUM OF THE ATLANTIC

BARRINGTON ST

ALEXANDER KEITH'S BREWERY

HALIFAX

CFB SHEARWATER

MUSEUM OF NATURAL HISTORY

SEE "DOWNTOWN HALIFAX" MAP

SHEARWATER AVIATION MUSEUM

Deadman's Island Park

DINGLE TOWER

Long Lake Regional Park

Sir Sandford Fleming Park

POINT PLEASANT PARK

FORT IVES

Eastern Passage

FISHERMAN'S COVE

Long Lake

Mcnabs Island

FORT MCNAB

To Peggy's Cove

0   1 mi
0   1 km

To York Redoubt National Historic Site

© AVALON TRAVEL

and boutiques, while the nearby **Maritime Museum of the Atlantic** is the place to learn about the city's seafaring traditions. The third is **Halifax Citadel National Historic Site.** These three attractions, along with time exploring the waterfront, could fill one day, but you'd be missing one of Halifax's best known attractions—its **pubs and breweries,** including **Alexander Keith's Brewery,** North America's oldest, which is open daily for tours.

Since it's both a gateway for air travelers and the hub of three highways, chances are you'll be passing through Halifax more than once on your travels through Nova Scotia. This allows you to break up your sightseeing and to plan your schedule around the weather. If, for example, the sun is shining when you first arrive, plan to visit **Point Pleasant Park,** the **Public Gardens,** and **Fairview Cemetery.** These spots and

historic downtown attractions should fill two full days.

Across the harbor from downtown is the city of Dartmouth, where a seafood lunch at the fishing village of **Fisherman's Cove** makes a perfect getaway from the city.

HISTORY

The French learned about the area in the early 1700s, when local Mi'kmaq Indians escorted the French governor on a tour of what they called Chebuctook, the "Great Long Harbor," and adjacent waterways. But it was the British who saw the site's potential: In 1749, Colonel Edward Cornwallis arrived with about 2,500 settlers on 13 ships and founded Halifax along what is now Barrington Street. The settlement was named for Lord Halifax, then president of Britain's Board of Trade and Plantations. Early Halifax was a stockaded settlement backed by

The *Titanic* Tragedy

"My God, the *Titanic* has struck a berg." With these fateful words, uttered on April 14, 1912, by wireless operator Jack Goodwin of Cape Race, Newfoundland, the outside world first heard about what would develop into the world's best-known maritime disaster—the sinking of the unsinkable ship on its maiden voyage between Southampton, England, and New York City. On board were 2,227 passengers and crew.

At the time of the wireless transmission, the vessel was 800 kilometers east of Halifax. Three Halifax ships were promptly chartered to search for the foundering vessel. By the time the first had arrived, the *Titanic* was lying on the bottom of the Atlantic Ocean. More than 1,500 passengers and crew perished while 702 lucky souls, mostly women and children, were rescued. Bodies were brought ashore at Karlsen's Wharf (2089 Upper Wharf St.) and Coaling Wharf No. 4 (north of the MacDonald Bridge), neither of which is open to the public. They were then transported in coffins to a variety of locations, including a curling rink (now an army surplus store, at 2660 Agricola

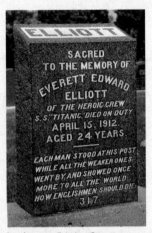

headstone at Fairview Cemetery

St.) and **Snow's Funeral Home** (1750 Argyle St.), which is now a seafood restaurant. Some bodies were claimed by families, but most were buried in three local cemeteries. The largest concentration is in a plot donated by the White Star Line within **Fairview Cemetery** (corner of Connaught and Chisholm Aves.). Most of the black headstones simply note the date of the tragedy and a number that relates to the order in which bodies were pulled from the ocean. Others have moving tributes to the bravery of loved ones. John Clarke, a band member famous for continuing to play as the ship was sinking, is buried at **Mount Olivet Cemetery** (Mumford Rd., off Joseph Howe Dr.).

The *Titanic*'s owners, the White Star Line, maintained an office in Halifax at 1682 Hollis Street that still stands. It became a hive of activity when the bodies began arriving, as staff members were an important link between the victims and their families from around the world.

Funerals and services were held at a number of downtown churches, including **St. George's Anglican Church** (222 Brunswick St.), **St. Paul's Anglican Church** (1749 Argyle St.), and **St. Mary's Catholic Church** (corner of Spring Garden Rd. and Barrington St.).

The best place to learn about the tragedy is the **Maritime Museum of the Atlantic** (1675 Lower Water St., 902/424-7490, http://maritimemuseum.novascotia.ca, Mon.-Sat. 9:30am-5:30pm, Sun. 1pm-5:30pm), which has a dedicated display area with artifacts, such as the only deck chair recovered from the vessel. For archival records, including travel documents, photos, and correspondence related to *Titanic* passengers, visit the **Nova Scotia Archives** (6016 University Ave., 902/424-6060, Mon.-Fri. 8:30am-4:30pm, Sat. 9am-5pm, free).

the Grand Parade, the town green where the militia drilled. More English settlers arrived in 1750, and by 1807 the city's population topped 60,000. A proper government setting—the sandstone Colonial Building (now Province House)—opened in 1819, followed by a number of noteworthy academic institutions. The harbor front acquired commercial

legitimacy when native Haligonian Samuel Cunard, rich from lumbering, whaling, and banking, turned his interests to shipping. By 1838 the Cunard Steamship Company handled the British and North American Royal Mail, and by 1840 Cunard's four ships provided the first regular transport between the two continents. The seaport's incorporation in 1841 ushered in a prosperous mercantile era. Granville Street, with its stylish shops, became, in its day, Atlantic Canada's Fifth Avenue. Less stylish brothels and taverns lined Brunswick, Market, and Barrack Streets, and the military police swept through the area often, breaking up drunken fistfights and re-establishing order.

By the 1960s, Halifax looked like a hoary victim of the centuries, somewhat the worse for wear. Massive federal, provincial, and private investment, however, restored the harbor to its early luster, with its warehouses groomed as the handsome Historic Properties. The city continued to polish its image, as sandblasting renewed the exterior of architectural treasures such as Province House. The Art Gallery of Nova Scotia moved from cramped quarters near the Public Archives and settled within the stunningly renovated former Dominion Building. Municipal guidelines sought to control the city's growth. The unobstructed view on George Street between the harbor and the Citadel was secured with a municipal mandate, and the height of the hillside's high-rise buildings was also restricted to preserve the cityscape. During this time, the waterfront evolved into a bustling tourist precinct, one that is also enjoyed by locals.

ORIENTATION

The layout of Halifax is easy to grasp. **Downtown** lines the western side of **Halifax Harbour.** Lower and Upper Water Streets and Barrington Street run through downtown parallel to the water. This is the core of the city, chock-full of historic attractions, the city's finest accommodations, and a wonderful choice of restaurants. The waterfront itself bustles day and night. From Historic Properties' wharves at the waterfront, sightseeing boats explore the harbor. The splendid Maritime Museum and Art Gallery of Nova Scotia are close by.

A series of short streets rise like ramps from the waterfront, past the grassy Grand Parade and up **Citadel Hill.** Around the hill, a great swath of green space provides a welcome break from residential and commercial sprawl. Laid out by the city's original surveyor, **Central Common,** on the west side of the hill, marks a meeting of roads. Major thoroughfares merge here (Robie Street running north-south, Bell Road running southeast, and Cogswell Street running east-west). Locals refer to everything south of the commons as the South End, everything to the north the North End, and to the west the West End.

In the South End is the city's **academic area,** site of Dalhousie University, University of King's College, St. Mary's University, and the Atlantic School of Theology. At the southern tip of the downtown peninsula is **Point Pleasant Park,** an oasis of green surrounded by the grays of sprawling loading docks to the north and the surrounding sparkling blue waters of Halifax Harbour.

The **Northwest Arm** of Halifax Harbour nearly cuts the downtown area off from the rest of the city. At the head of this waterway is the **Armdale Rotary,** from where Herring Cove Road spurs south to **Purcells Cove Road,** which passes yacht-filled marinas, Sir Sandford Fleming Park, and York Redoubt National Historic Site.

Across Halifax Harbour from downtown is the city of **Dartmouth.** Linked to downtown by ferry and bridge, this commercial and residential area has a smattering of sights and is also worth visiting for the views back across to Halifax. Beyond the two bridges spanning Halifax Harbour is Bedford Basin, a large body of water surrounded by development. At the head of the basin is the residential area of Bedford and suburbs, including Lower Sackville and Waverly. Traveling down Highway 102 from Truro and **Halifax International Airport** (38 kilometers north of downtown), you'll pass exits for these and other towns.

A Long Weekend in Halifax

Halifax is a major destination for conventioneers (modern facilities, well-priced accommodations, centrally located for delegates from both North America and Europe), and in this regard, you may find yourself wanting to hang around for a few days when the last meeting wraps up on Friday. Or, for leisure travelers, many flights to other parts of Atlantic Canada are routed through Halifax, so it will cost little or nothing to have a stopover before continuing to Newfoundland, Prince Edward Island, or elsewhere. This itinerary covers both scenarios, and you don't have to worry about driving.

DAY 1
You've been staying at an upscale downtown Halifax hotel such as Four Points by Sheraton Halifax, and suddenly it's not business anymore. No worries; rates drop dramatically come the weekend, so you won't break the bank by staying another two nights. Join the after-work crowd at the **Seahorse Tavern,** and then plan on dining next door at the **Economy Shoe Shop.**

DAY 2
Visit **Halifax Citadel National Historic Site** to get a feel for the city's colorful history, then walk over to the **Public Gardens.** After lunch, learn about the *Titanic* tragedy at the **Maritime Museum of the Atlantic** before visiting the graves of some of the victims at **Fairview Cemetery.** For a casual seafood dinner with a sublime view, walk along the waterfront to **Salty's.**

DAY 3
The local tour company Ambassatours operates an excellent full-day trip along the South Shore. It hits the highlights—scenic **Peggy's Cove** and the beautiful waterfront **churches of Mahone Bay**—while also allowing time to wander through the historic streets of downtown **Lunenburg,** where there's time for shopping and lunch. You'll be back in Halifax in time for dinner at **Chives Canadian Bistro,** which features lots of fresh seasonal produce.

DAY 4
Check the sailing schedule of the *Bluenose II* and make reservations for a morning cruise if this grand old lady is in port. Otherwise, you could start out with breakfast at the **Italian Market,** followed by shopping at downtown stores as varied as **Nova Scotian Crystal** and **Rum Runners Rum Cake Factory.** Golfers may want to squeeze in a tee time at **Glen Arbour Golf Course,** which is on the way out to the airport.

Sights

Halifax is packed with attractions, all reasonably priced or absolutely free. The biggest concentration is within walking distance of the waterfront precinct and many accommodations. Beyond the downtown core are a number of interesting sights that are easy to miss but easy to reach by public transportation. Whatever your interests—searching out *Titanic*-related sights or exploring coastal parks—you will find plenty to do and see in the capital.

DOWNTOWN
The following sights are within walking distance of each other from the waterfront. You could easily spend a full day exploring this part of the city, taking time out to lunch at an outdoor harbor-front restaurant.

Downtown Halifax

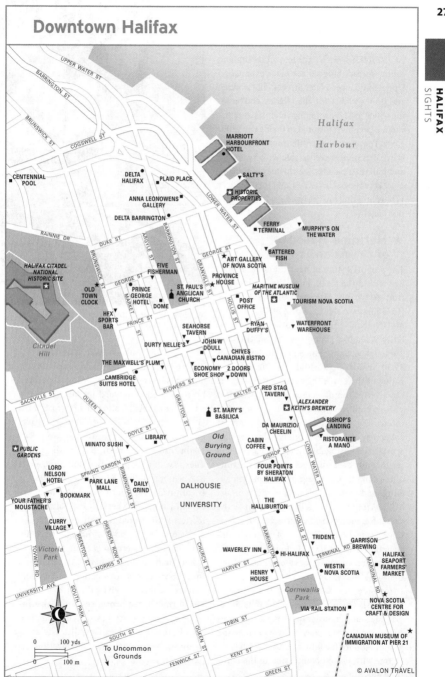

UPPER WATER ST

BARRINGTON ST

BRUNSWICK ST

COGSWELL ST

Halifax Harbour

CENTENNIAL POOL

DELTA HALIFAX

PLAID PLACE

MARRIOTT HARBOURFRONT HOTEL

SALTY'S

HISTORIC PROPERTIES

ANNA LEONOWENS GALLERY

DELTA BARRINGTON

LOWER WATER ST

FERRY TERMINAL

MURPHY'S ON THE WATER

RAINNIE DR

DUKE ST

BRUNSWICK ST

ARGYLE ST

GRANVILLE ST

GEORGE ST

BATTERED FISH

HALIFAX CITADEL NATIONAL HISTORIC SITE

GEORGE ST

FIVE FISHERMAN

ART GALLERY OF NOVA SCOTIA

PROVINCE HOUSE

OLD TOWN CLOCK

PRINCE GEORGE HOTEL

ST. PAUL'S ANGLICAN CHURCH

MARITIME MUSEUM OF THE ATLANTIC

TOURISM NOVA SCOTIA

MARKET ST

DOME

HOLLIS ST

POST OFFICE

Citadel Hill

HFX SPORTS BAR

PRINCE ST

RYAN DUFFY'S

WATERFRONT WAREHOUSE

SEAHORSE TAVERN

JOHN W DOULL

DURTY NELLIE'S

CHIVES CANADIAN BISTRO

THE MAXWELL'S PLUM

ECONOMY SHOE SHOP

2 DOORS DOWN

CAMBRIDGE SUITES HOTEL

BLOWERS ST

GRAFTON ST

SALTER ST

RED STAG TAVERN

SACKVILLE ST

QUEEN ST

ST. MARY'S BASILICA

ALEXANDER KEITH'S BREWERY

DOYLE ST

LIBRARY

Old Burying Ground

DA MAURIZIO/ CHEELIN

BISHOP'S LANDING

PUBLIC GARDENS

MINATO SUSHI

CABIN COFFEE

BISHOP ST

RISTORANTE A MANO

LOWER WATER ST

LORD NELSON HOTEL

SPRING GARDEN RD

PARK LANE MALL

DAILY GRIND

FOUR POINTS BY SHERATON HALIFAX

BIRMINGHAM ST

DALHOUSIE UNIVERSITY

YOUR FATHER'S MOUSTACHE

BOOKMARK

DRESDEN ROW

THE HALLIBURTON

CURRY VILLAGE

CLYDE ST

BRENTON ST

CHURCH ST

BARRINGTON ST

TRIDENT

GARRISON RD

GARRISON BREWING

Victoria Park

MORRIS ST

WAVERLEY INN

HI-HALIFAX

TERMINAL RD

HALIFAX SEAPORT FARMERS' MARKET

TOWER RD

UNIVERSITY AVE

SOUTH PARK ST

HARVEY ST

HENRY HOUSE

WESTIN NOVA SCOTIA

MARGINAL RD

HOLLIS ST

Cornwallis Park

NOVA SCOTIA CENTRE FOR CRAFT & DESIGN

VIA RAIL STATION

SOUTH ST

0   100 yds
0   100 m

To Uncommon Grounds

TOBIN ST

QUEEN ST

KENT ST

CANADIAN MUSEUM OF IMMIGRATION AT PIER 21

FENWICK ST

GREEN ST

© AVALON TRAVEL

★ Historic Properties

Canada's oldest surviving group of waterfront warehouses is also one of the city's main tourist attractions, with excellent shopping and dining spread along a three-block expanse on Upper and Lower Water Streets. The wooden and stone warehouses, chandleries, and buildings once used by shipping interests and privateers have been restored to their early 1800s glory. They now house restaurants, shops, and other sites impressively styled with Victorian and Italianate facades. The history of the precinct is cataloged halfway along the Privateer Wharf building (on the inside) with interpretive panels.

★ Maritime Museum of the Atlantic

The seaport's store of nautical memorabilia lies within the sleek, burnished-red waterfront **Maritime Museum of the Atlantic** (1675 Lower Water St., 902/424-7490, http://maritimemuseum.novascotia.ca, summer daily 9:30am-5:30pm, the rest of the year Tues.-Sat. 9:30am-5pm, Sun. 1pm-5pm, adult $9.50, senior $8.50, child $5). The museum is one of the crowning achievements of the city's Waterfront Development Project. Most visitors find the *Titanic* display room most interesting. It contains the world's largest collection of artifacts from the floating palace deemed unsinkable by its owners; you will see the only deck chair recovered at the time of the sinking, a cribbage board, lounge paneling, and more. Also on display is a model of the *Titanic,* the wireless log taken as the vessel foundered, and a variety of information boards that tell the story of the ship's construction. *Titanic 3D,* a National Geographic documentary created from footage taken from the wreck, shows continuously.

Outside, the **CSS** *Acadia* is tied up at the wharf. This sturdy vessel spent its life as Canada's first hydrographic vessel, its crew surveying the east coast using sextants and graphing shoreline features. Admission is $2, or free with proof of admission to the maritime museum.

Maritime Museum of the Atlantic

Art Gallery of Nova Scotia

Atlantic Canada's largest and finest art collection is housed in two buildings separated by a cobbled courtyard just up from the harbor at the **Art Gallery of Nova Scotia** (1723 Hollis St., 902/424-5280, www.artgalleryofnovascotia.ca, summer Mon.-Sat. 10am-5pm, Sun. noon-5pm, fall-spring Tues.-Sat. 10am-5pm, Sun. noon-5pm, adult $12, senior $10, child $5). The main entrance is within Gallery South (also home to an excellent café). The vast majority of the collection is displayed in Gallery North, the sandstone Dominion Building. Some 2,000 works in oils, watercolors, stone, wood, and other media are exhibited throughout its four floors of spacious galleries. The permanent collections give priority to current and former Nova Scotia residents and include works by Mary Pratt, Arthur Lismer, Carol Fraser, and Alex Colville. The mezzanine-level regional folk-art collection is a particular delight.

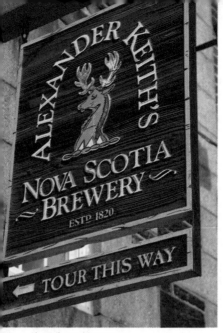

Alexander Keith's Brewery

it is the oldest surviving building in Halifax and was the first Anglican church in Canada. The interior is full of memorials to Halifax's early residents. Notice the bit of metal embedded above the door at the back of the north wall—it's a piece of shrapnel hurled from the *Mont Blanc,* two kilometers away, during the Halifax Explosion. The church is between Barrington and Argyle Streets at the edge of the Grand Parade; look for the square belfry topped by an octagonal cupola.

Old Burying Ground

Designated a national historic site in 1991, the **Old Burying Ground cemetery** (June-Sept. daily 9am-5pm, free) sits opposite Government House at Barrington Street and Spring Garden Road. Its history goes back to the city's founding. The first customer, so to speak, was interred just one day after the arrival of the original convoy of English settlers in 1749. Also among the thicket of age-darkened, hand-carved, old-fashioned headstones is the 1754 grave of John Connor, the settlement's first ferry captain. The most recent burial took place more than 160 years ago, in 1844.

St. Mary's Cathedral Basilica

Two popes and hundreds of thousands of parishioners have filed through the doors of the Gothic Revival **St. Mary's Cathedral Basilica** (1508 Barrington St., 902/429-9800, www.halifaxyarmouth.org/cathedral), whose spires cast an afternoon shadow over the Old Burying Ground. It was built in 1860; the title "Basilica" was bestowed during a visit by Pope Pius XII in 1950. The stained-glass windows, replaced after the originals were destroyed by the 1917 Halifax Explosion, are particularly impressive.

★ Alexander Keith's Brewery

At the south end of downtown and one block back from the water, **Alexander Keith's Brewery** (1496 Lower Water St., 902/455-1474, http://keiths.ca, tours June-Oct. Mon.-Sat. noon-8pm, Sun. noon-5pm, Nov.-May

Province House

The seat of the provincial government, **Province House** (1726 Hollis St., 902/424-4661, July-Aug. Mon.-Fri. 9am-5pm, Sat.-Sun. 10am-4pm, the rest of the year Mon.-Fri. 9am-4pm, free) was completed in 1819. It's the smallest and oldest provincial legislature building in the country and features a fine Georgian exterior and splendid interior, resembling a rural English mansion more than an official residence. On his visit to modest but dignified Province House in 1842, author Charles Dickens remarked, "It was like looking at Westminster through the wrong end of a telescope . . . a gem of Georgian architecture."

St. Paul's Anglican Church

The stately white wooden **St. Paul's Anglican Church** (1749 Argyle St., 902/429-2240, www.stpaulshalifax.org, tours July-Aug. Mon.-Sat. 9am-4pm, free) was styled after the Palladian St. Peter's Church on Vere Street in London, England. Dating to 1749,

Halifax Harbour

From a maritime standpoint, Halifax Harbour is a jewel, the world's second-largest natural harbor (after Sydney Harbour in Australia). High rocky bluffs notched with coves rim the wide entrance where the harbor meets the frothy Atlantic. McNabs Island is spread across the harbor's mouth and is so large that it almost clogs the entrance. Many an unwary ship has foundered on the island's shallow, treacherous Eastern Passage coastline.

On the western side of McNabs Island, the harbor is split in two by Halifax's peninsula. The Northwest Arm, a fjord-like sliver of sea, cuts off to one side and wraps around the city's back side. Along its banks are the long lawns of parks, estates, yacht clubs, and several university campuses. The main channel continues inland, shouldered by uptown Halifax on one side and its sister city of Dartmouth on the other.

THE TOURIST'S HARBOUR

The harbor puts on its best show directly in front of downtown. White-hulled cruise ships nose into port and dock alongside Halifax's Point Pleasant Park at the peninsula's southern tip. Freighters, tugs, tour boats, and sailboats skim the choppy waters, and ferries cut through the sea traffic, scurrying back and forth between the two cities with their loads of commuters and sightseers.

The scene has a transfixing quality about it. Tourist season unofficially starts and ends when the harbor-front Halifax Sheraton hotel sets tables and chairs for alfresco dining on the waterfront promenade. Stiff summer breezes usually accompany lunch, but the view is worth it. Less hardy diners jostle for tables with a harbor view at Salty's, the nearby restaurant with its enviable wide-windowed dining room overlooking the same scene.

Beyond the tourist's realm and the two cities' harbor fronts, the spacious harbor compresses itself into the Narrows. Two high-flung steel expressways—the MacDonald and MacKay Bridges—cross the Narrows at either end. The MacDonald Bridge permits pedestrians and provides an aerial view of the Maritime Command and Her Majesty's Canadian Dockyard along the Halifax side.

The slender Narrows then opens into 40-square-kilometer Bedford Basin, 16 kilometers long and as capacious as a small inland sea. Sailboats cruise its waters now, but the expanse has seen a parade of ships cross its waters through the years—from the white-sailed British warships of centuries ago to the steel-hulled vessels of the Allies during both world wars.

HALIFAX HARBOUR FROM VARIED ANGLES

Halifax Harbour reveals itself in different views. Its pulse can be probed from one of the ferries or from the harbor front in either city. The approach from the Atlantic can be seen best from the historic fort at York Redoubt on Purcells Cove Road. You'll get a good view of the Northwest Arm's ritzy estate and university scene from Fleming Park's Memorial Tower on the same road. Africville Park beneath the MacKay Bridge overlooks the Narrows where that slender strait meets Bedford Basin.

Fri. 5pm-8pm, Sat. noon-8pm, Sun. noon-5pm, adult $23, senior $20, child $10) is North America's oldest operating brewery. Keith arrived in Halifax in 1795, bringing with him brewing techniques from his English homeland and finding a ready market among the soldiers and sailors living in the city. Although main brewing operations have been moved to the Oland Brewery, north of downtown, the original brewery, an impressive stone and granite edifice extending along an entire block, produces seasonal brews using traditional techniques. Tours are led by costumed guides, ending with a traditional toast to the "Father of Great Beer."

Canadian Museum of Immigration at Pier 21

As you continue south along Lower Water Street from the brewery (take the Harbourwalk for the full effect), beyond the statue of Samuel Cunard, the waterfront is dominated by Halifax's massive cruise-ship terminal. This 3,900-square-meter structure has a long and colorful history of welcoming foreigners in its original capacity as an "immigration shed," where more than a million immigrants, refugees, and war brides first set foot on Canadian soil between 1928 and 1971. It was also the main departure point for 500,000 Canadians who fought in World War II. Upstairs within the building is the **Canadian Museum of Immigration at Pier 21** (1055 Marginal Rd., 902/425-7770, www.pier21.ca, May-Nov. daily 9:30am-5:30pm, Dec.-Apr. Wed.-Sun. 10am-5pm, adult $11, senior $8.50, child $7). This vast immigration museum does a wonderful job of bringing to life the stories of those who traveled across the ocean to make a new home in Canada. The firsthand accounts begin with the decision to leave home, then go through voyage and arrival to describe onward journeys by rail across Canada. Allow time to view *Oceans of Hope*, a 30-minute film narrated by a fictional immigration officer.

Beside the street-level reception area is the **Research Centre,** which can be used by individuals whose families arrived in Canada through Pier 21. It contains a wide variety of documents, passenger logs, and historic images of passenger vessels.

Nova Scotia Centre for Craft and Design

Beside the Canadian Museum of Immigration, provincial crafts development and innovation are nurtured at the **Nova Scotia Centre for Craft and Design** (1061 Marginal Rd., 902/492-2522, www.craft-design.ns.ca, Tues.-Fri. 9am-5pm, Sat.-Sun. 11am-4pm, free), a workshop ensconced in the cruise-ship terminal geared to weaving, woodworking, metal, and multimedia production.

★ Point Pleasant Park

Before dawn on September 29, 2003, Hurricane Juan hit Halifax like no other storm in living memory. Seventy-five-hectare **Point Pleasant Park** (5718 Point Pleasant Dr., www.pointpleasantpark.ca, daily 6am-midnight), at the southern tip of the Halifax peninsula, took the full brunt of the storm.

the Martello Tower, Point Pleasant Park

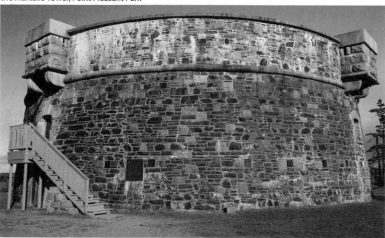

By daybreak the next morning, the full extent of the damage was first seen—more than 75,000 of the park's 100,000 trees had been destroyed, and the park's ecology had been changed forever. After the cleanup, a massive rejuvenation project that continues to this day began.

Although much of the forest may be gone, the park is still well worth visiting. To get to the main entrance, take South Park Street south from Sackville Street. South Park becomes Young Avenue, a tree-lined boulevard graced by magnificent mansions; turn left on Point Pleasant Drive. Marginal Road from downtown also terminates at the same waterside entrance. Views from the parking lot sweep across the harbor, with container terminals on one side and green space on the other. Forty kilometers of trails, many paved, allow for hiking, jogging, and cross-country skiing in winter. Bikes are allowed only Monday-Friday. Most of the main trails have reopened since the storm, allowing access to all corners of the spread, with terns, gulls, and ospreys winging overhead. A bit of real-estate trivia: The park is still rented from the British government, on a 999-year lease, for one shilling per year.

Point Pleasant's military significance is evidenced by the 1796 **Prince of Wales Martello Tower** (July-early Sept. daily 10am-6pm, free) and Fort Ogilvie, built in 1862, both part of Halifax's defensive system. The former, a thick-walled round tower based on those the British were building at the time to repel Napoleon's forces, was the first of its kind to be built in North America.

CITADEL HILL AND VICINITY

Walk up George Street from the harbor front to reach Citadel Hill. You'll know you're on the right street by the **Old Town Clock,** framed by the buildings of George Street at the base of Citadel Hill. Originally constructed as the official timekeeper for Halifax, the four-faced clock tower was completed in 1803 by order of the compulsively punctual Prince Edward. It is not open to the public but instead stands as a city landmark.

★ Halifax Citadel National Historic Site

Halifax's premier landmark, the **Citadel National Historic Site** (5425 Sackville St., 902-426-5080, www.pc.gc.ca, July-Aug. daily 9am-6pm, Sept.-June daily 9am-5pm, adult

Halifax Citadel National Historic Site

$12, senior $10.50, child $6, parking $3.15) is also the most visited national historic site in Canada. The Citadel crowns the hill at the top of George Street, commanding the strategic high ground above the city and harbor, with magnificent views of the entire area. This star-shaped, dressed-granite fortress, the fourth military works built on the site, was completed in 1856. In its heyday, the Citadel represented the pinnacle of defensive military technology, though its design was never tested by an attack.

In summer, students in period uniforms portray soldiers of the 78th Highlanders and the Royal Artillery, demonstrating military drills, powder magazine operation, changing of the sentries, and piping. At the stroke of noon each day, they load and fire a cannon with due military precision and ceremony, a shot heard round the city. Most of the fortress is open for exploration; exhibits include a museum, barrack rooms, a powder magazine, and a 50-minute audiovisual presentation on the fort's history. Guided tours are included in the admission price, while within the grounds are a gift shop and café.

The grounds are open year-round, but no services are offered November-April.

Museum of Natural History

The rather plain exterior of the **Museum of Natural History** (1747 Summer St., 902/424-7353, http://naturalhistory.novascotia.ca, mid-May-Oct. daily 9am-5pm, Nov.-mid-May Tues.-Sun. 9am-5pm, adult $6.50, senior $5.70, child $4.05) belies a treasure trove of exhibits that bring the province's natural world to life. Opposite the ticket desk is a kid-friendly nature center with small critters in enclosures and tanks, and staff on hand to answer any questions. Beyond this point are exhibits that tell the story of Nova Scotia's first human inhabitants, Paleo Indians, who moved into the region 11,000 years ago. The dinosaur displays are a major draw for young and old. You'll also learn about modern-day creatures in a room full of stuffed animals and a large hall dominated by a pilot whale skeleton. Other highlights include a gem and mineral display and artifacts from Acadian culture. The museum is a five-minute walk from Citadel Hill, but it also has plenty of its own parking.

★ Public Gardens

South across Sackville Street from the Citadel grounds, the **Public Gardens** (www.halifaxpublicgardens.ca, May-mid-Oct. daily

the Public Gardens

Halifax Explosion

On the morning of Thursday, December 6, 1917, Halifax experienced a catastrophic explosion—at the time the largest human-created explosion in history, unrivaled until the detonation of the first atomic bomb. On that fateful morning, Halifax Harbour was busy with warships transporting troops, munitions, and other supplies bound for the war in Europe. A French ship, the *Mont Blanc*, filled to the gunwales with explosives—including 400,000 pounds of TNT—was heading through the Narrows toward the harbor mouth when it was struck by a larger vessel, the *Imo*, which was steaming in the opposite direction, and caught fire. The terrified crew of the *Mont Blanc* took immediately to the lifeboats as the burning ship drifted close to the Halifax shore.

A short time later, at 9:05am, the *Mont Blanc* cargo blew up, instantly killing an estimated 2,000 people, wounding another 10,000, and obliterating about 130 hectares of the North End of downtown Halifax. So colossal was the explosion that windows were shattered 80 kilometers away, and the shock wave rocked Sydney on Cape Breton, 430 kilometers northeast. The barrel of one of the *Mont Blanc*'s cannons was hurled 5.5 kilometers, while its half-ton anchor shank landed more than 3 kilometers away in the opposite direction.

Serving as a memorial to the tragedy is **Fort Needham Memorial Park,** along Gottingen Street north from downtown. Here, a 14-bell carillon is on a high point of land from which the site of the original explosion can be seen. While the harbor-front **Maritime Museum of the Atlantic** has an exhibit dedicated to the explosion, one of the most interesting reminders is up the hill at **St. Paul's Anglican Church** (1749 Argyle St.), where a chunk of metal from the doomed *Mont Blanc* is embedded in the north-facing wall.

8am-dusk) are an irresistibly attractive oasis spread over seven hectares in the heart of the city. Bordered by Spring Garden Road, South Park Street, Summer Street, and Sackville Street, what started in 1753 as a private garden is reminiscent of the handsome parks of Europe and now considered one of the loveliest formal gardens in North America.

Inside the wrought-iron fence (main entrance at the corner of South Park Street and Spring Garden Road), the setting revels in tulips that flower late May-early June, followed by rhododendrons, roses, and perennials through summer. Other highlights are the exotic and native trees, fountains, and lily ponds where ducks and geese make their homes. The ornate bandstand dates from Queen Victoria's Golden Jubilee and is the site of free Sunday afternoon concerts in July and August. Also during the summer, vendors of arts and crafts hawk their wares outside the gardens along Spring Garden Road.

NORTH OF DOWNTOWN

The following sights are north of Cogswell Street. It's a two-kilometer walk from downtown to Fort Needham Memorial Park. Fairview Cemetery is not within walking distance.

St. George's Round Church

Architect William Hughes designed the unusual and charming timber-frame **St. George's Round Church** (Cornwallis and Brunswick Sts., www.roundchurch.ca, tours July-Aug. Mon.-Fri. 11am-4pm, free), which at once accommodated the overflow of parishioners from the nearby Dutch Church on Brunswick Street and satisfied Prince Edward's penchant for round buildings. The cornerstone was laid in 1800, and the chancel and front porch were added later. A fire in 1994 destroyed the dome, but it has since been replaced. St. George's is a few blocks north of downtown.

Maritime Command Museum

On the grounds of Canadian Forces Base Halifax, the **Maritime Command Museum** (Gottingen St. between North St. and Russell St., 902/721-8250, http://psphalifax.ca/marcommuseum, Mon.-Fri. 9am-3:30pm, free) is ensconced in the 30-room Admiralty House, built in the 1840s as a residence for the base's admiral. Exhibits include presentation swords, memorabilia from the World War II Battle of the Atlantic, a military gun collection, uniforms, ship models, and other artifacts relating to the history of the Canadian Maritime Military Forces.

Fort Needham Memorial Park

Continue north along Gottingen Street from the Maritime Command Museum and veer right onto Dartmouth Street to reach the **Fort Needham Memorial Park,** a high point of land with views across the head of Halifax Harbour. The park's most distinctive feature is a 14-bell carillon, a monument to the Halifax Explosion of 1917, at the time the largest human-created explosion the world had ever known. Stand in the break between the memorial's two halves to get views through a clearing to the harbor and the actual site of the explosion.

Africville Park

Halifax's peninsula is bookended by a pair of expansive green spaces. **Africville Park** is at the north end, overlooking Bedford Basin from the foot of the A. Murray MacKay Bridge. This was once the site of Africville, a community of Black Haligonians established in the 1840s but since demolished. The importance of the settlement is reflected in its designation as a national historic site. The only physical remainder of its history is a replica of the African United Church. As you head north from downtown along Barrington Street, access is along Service Road. A boat launch provides the only water access.

★ Fairview Cemetery

Take Windsor Street north from Quinpool Road to reach **Fairview Cemetery** (daily dawn-dusk), the final resting place of 121 *Titanic* victims. When the bodies were pulled from the Atlantic Ocean, they were given a number. These numbers, along with the date of the disaster, April 15, 1912 (it is assumed no one could have survived any longer than a day in the frigid ocean), adorn a majority of the simple black headstones paid for by the White Star Line, owners of the *Titanic*. Where identification was possible, a name accompanies the number (such as victim 227, J. Dawson, inspiration for the character Jack Dawson, played by Leonardo DiCaprio, in the movie *Titanic*). Some headstones are engraved with moving tributes, such as that to Everett Edward Elliott, aged 24, which reads, "Each man stood at his port while all the weaker ones went by, and showed once more to all the world how Englishmen should die."

The turn into the cemetery is easy to miss; get in the left lane by Connaught Avenue and turn against oncoming traffic to reach the cemetery's main entrance. The other option is to take Connaught Avenue off Windsor Street and park at the end of Chisholm Avenue. Once you're at the cemetery, the plot is well signposted, with an interpretive board describing the events leading up to identifying victims, even long after they were buried.

Hemlock Ravine Park

The rugged tract of forest known as **Hemlock Ravine Park** lies beside the western side of Bedford Basin between the busy Bedford and Bicentennial highways—but you'd never know urban civilization is so close as you walk along the five interconnecting walking trails. The park's namesake ravine, with its towering hemlocks, takes about 20 minutes to reach from the main parking lot, at the end of Kent Avenue, which branches off the Bedford Highway (Highway 2) one kilometer north of the Kearney Lake Road intersection. Beside the parking lot is a heart-shaped pond designed by Prince

Edward, who spent his summers here with his companion Julie St. Laurent.

Uniacke Estate Museum Park

The splendid 930-hectare **Uniacke Estate Museum Park** (758 Main Rd., Mount Uniacke, 902/866-0032, http://uniacke.novascotia.ca, June-Sept. Tues.-Sat. 10am-5pm, Sun. 11:30am-5pm, adult $4, senior and child $3) is along Highway 1 beyond the city limits, 20 kilometers northwest from the intersection of Highway 102. The easiest way to get there is to take exit 3 from Highway 101. The home's interior features original furnishings, including four-poster beds and family portraits. The grounds offer seven hiking trails.

Atlantic Canada Aviation Museum

Across the highway from the airport (take Exit 6 from Hwy. 102), the **Atlantic Canada Aviation Museum** (20 Sky Blvd., 902/873-3773, www.atlanticcanadaaviationmuseum.com, May-Sept. daily 9am-5pm, adult $5) is a good place to visit on the way north to Truro or before your flight home. On display are about 30 aircraft—everything from fighter planes to a homemade helicopter—and a couple of simulators.

WEST SIDE OF NORTHWEST ARM

Carefully make your way onto the Armdale Rotary at the west end of Quinpool Road and take the Herring Cove Road exit. A short distance south along this road, Purcells Cove Road veers off to the left. This winding road hugs the Northwest Arm for nine kilometers to the fishing village of Herring Cove. Along the way are two yacht clubs filled with glistening white sailboats.

Sir Sandford Fleming Park

A 38-hectare grassy spread, the delightful **Sir Sandford Fleming Park** (daily 8am-dusk) is mostly forested, sloping to a seawall promenade fringing a quiet waterway. The land was donated by the Scottish-born Fleming, best known for establishing time zones. It is said a missed train led the enterprising Fleming to begin formulating a plan that would see the entire world operate on a 24-hour clock with time zones that related to longitude. Fleming, who also designed Canada's first postage stamp, lived in Halifax from the 1880s until his death in 1915.

On a slight rise above the bay is the 10-story **Dingle Tower** (June-Aug. daily 9am-5pm).

Atlantic Canada Aviation Museum

A stairway winds up the interior of this stone edifice, presenting great views from the top.

The main entrance is off Purcells Cove Road; Dingle Road leads down through the wooded park to the waterfront.

York Redoubt National Historic Site

Set on a bluff high above the harbor entrance, **York Redoubt National Historic Site** (Purcells Cove Rd., 902/426-5080, www.pc.gc. ca, grounds mid-May-Oct. daily 9am-6pm, buildings mid-June-Aug. daily 10am-6pm, free) is six kilometers south of downtown. The setting draws visitors with walking paths that lead down the steep incline to picnic tables and protected coves. Up top are strategic fortifications dating to 1793, when Britain went to war with the French. Most of the fort is from later times, including massive muzzle-loading guns that were designed to fire nine-inch shells capable of piercing armored vessels.

MCNABS ISLAND

Whatever your interests, the five-kilometer-long **McNabs Island,** at the entrance to Halifax Harbour, is a wonderful place to spend a day. The island is mostly wooded, its forests filled with birdlife and its shoreline dotted with beaches and tidal pools. Archaeological evidence points to habitation by the Mi'kmaq at least 1,600 years ago, but the most obvious signs of human development are more recent, including two forts and the remains of a number of residences (including the summer home of Frederick Perrin, of Lea & Perrins Worcestershire sauce fame). Although many of the early residences have disappeared, signs of their formal gardens remain; look for ash, oak, and apple trees.

Recreation

Most visitors come to the island to go hiking. Ferries land at Garrison Pier, from which trails radiate in all directions. The top of Jenkin's Hill, easily reached in 10 minutes, is a good place to get oriented while also enjoying sweeping harbor views. At the 1864 **Fort Ives,** an easy 30-minute walk from the pier, cannons are still in place. **Fort McNab,** a similar distance south of the pier, was built in 1889 and is protected as a national historic site. Sandy **Mauger's Beach,** just south of Garrison Pier, is the best and most accessible of many island beaches.

Getting There

Year-round access to the island is provided by **McNabs Island Ferry** (902/465-4563, www. mcnabsisland.com, adult round-trip $20, senior and child round-trip $15), which departs on demand from Fisherman's Cove on the Dartmouth side of the harbor. The crossing takes less than 10 minutes. No services are available on the island, so bring your own food and drink and be prepared for changeable weather by bringing a rain jacket.

DARTMOUTH

Dartmouth is a large residential, commercial, and industrial area across the harbor from Halifax. The two cities are joined by a bridge and Metro Transit's Halifax-Dartmouth ferry from the foot of downtown's George Street to the Alderney Gate complex in Dartmouth. Ferries operate year-round Monday-Saturday 6:30am-midnight, and daily in summer. The fare is adult $2.50, senior and child $1.75 each way. The ferry arrives within walking distance of Dartmouth Heritage Museum properties and various shops and restaurants.

Dartmouth Heritage Museum

The **Dartmouth Heritage Museum** (www. dartmouthheritagemuseum.ns.ca) comprises two historic homes within walking distance of Alderney Gate. The 1867 **Evergreen House** (26 Newcastle St., 902/464-2300, summer Tues.-Sat. 10am-5pm, the rest of the year Tues.-Fri. 10am-5pm, adult $5), filled with period antiques, is the grander of the two. Built by a cooper (barrel maker) in 1785, **Quaker House** (57 Ochterloney St., 902/464-5823, summer Tues.-Sun. 10am-1pm and 2pm-5pm, adult $5) is one of Dartmouth's oldest residences. In addition to period furnishings, exhibits tell the story of the Quakers, who were drawn to Nova Scotia for its abundance of whales.

Bedford Institute of Oceanography

The government-run **Bedford Institute of Oceanography** (Baffin Blvd., 902/426-4306, www.bio.gc.ca, guided tours by appointment only May-Aug. Mon.-Fri. 9am-4pm, free) has a mandate that includes everything from helping maintain Canada's sovereignty to federal fisheries, but it is best known for its work on the sunken *Titanic*. On the guided tour, you'll get to learn about all this work, as well as step aboard a simulated ship's bridge and get up close and personal at the Touch Tank. To get there from downtown Halifax, cross the Narrows and take the Shannon Park exit from the MacKay Bridge (immediately after the toll gates); turn right and then left onto Baffin Boulevard, which crosses under the bridge to the institute.

Shubie Park

In 1858, construction began on an ambitious canal system that linked Halifax Harbour with the Bay of Fundy via a string of lakes and the Shubenacadie River. The canal was abandoned just 12 years later. The canal between Lake Micmac and Lake Charles has been restored, complete with one of nine original locks. **Shubie Park** is laced with hiking and biking trails, but many visitors take to the water in canoes, kayaks, and paddleboards, paddling from the main day-use area to Lake Charles. Access is signposted from Braemar Drive, which branches north from Exit 6 of Highway 111.

Cole Harbour Heritage Farm Museum

Surrounded by a residential subdivision, the outdoor **Cole Harbour Heritage Farm Museum** (471 Poplar Dr., 902/434-0222, http://coleharbourfarmmuseum.ca, mid-May-mid-Oct. daily 10am-4pm, donation) is a great place for children. Buildings include a

200-year-old farmhouse, a blacksmith shop, various barns, and a tearoom, while garden plots represent early crops, with the produce used in the tearoom. Livestock is fenced, but rabbits, geese, and ducks roam free.

EASTERN PASSAGE

The Eastern Passage is a narrow waterway running between the Dartmouth side of Halifax Harbour and McNabs Island. From downtown Dartmouth, take Pleasant Street south to Highway 322. This route passes oil refineries and Canadian Forces Base Shearwater before reaching the delightful Fisherman's Cove. Beyond this point, Highway 322 continues through an oceanfront residential area to Southeast Passage Provincial Park.

Shearwater Aviation Museum

At the entrance to Canadian Forces Base Shearwater, the **Shearwater Aviation Museum** (12 Wing Gate, Pleasant St., 902/720-1083, www.shearwateraviationmuseum.ns.ca, June-Aug. Mon.-Fri. 10am-5pm, Sat.-Sun. noon-4pm, Apr.-May and Sept.-Nov. Tues.-Fri. 10am-5pm, Sat. noon-4pm, free) is home to 10 restored aircraft and an impressive collection of air force memorabilia. The museum is off Pleasant Street (Highway 322); turn left at the first set of lights beyond the Imperial oil refinery.

★ Fisherman's Cove

Fisherman's Cove is no different from the hundreds of picturesque fishing villages that dot the Nova Scotia coastline, with one exception—it's within the city limits of the capital. Lying along the Eastern Passage, two kilometers southeast of Dartmouth along Highway 322, the cove mixes the needs of working fishing vessels with a constant flow of curious visitors. You can drive along Government Wharf Road, which spurs right at the traffic lights in Eastern Passage, onto the main dock area, but it's much more enjoyable to explore the area on foot from the parking lot just beyond the cove's main entrance.

Recreation

WALKING AND HIKING

Even if you're not feeling overly energetic, plan to take a stroll along the downtown waterfront. A seawall promenade winds past docks filled with all manner of boats (tall ships, tugboats, and visiting yachts), harborfront restaurants, the Maritime Museum of the Atlantic, Historic Properties, and south to Pier 21. While it's possible to do all your downtown sightseeing on foot, an easier option is to catch a cab to Citadel Hill, from which it's downhill all the way back to the harbor. At Citadel Hill, take the time not only to visit the fort but also to walk around the perimeter, and then cross Sackville Street to the Public Gardens, a delightful place for a flower-filled stroll.

McNabs Island is a popular destination for day-tripping hikers.

Point Pleasant Park, 2.5 kilometers south of downtown, off Young Avenue, is laced with hiking and biking trails. The obvious choice is to stick to the water, along a two-kilometer (one-way) trail that hugs the shoreline, passing Point Pleasant itself before winding around to the Northwest Arm. Other trails lead inland to historic fortifications and through the remains of forests devastated by Hurricane Juan in 2003.

Across the Northwest Arm from downtown, Sir Sandford Fleming Park flanks the water in an upscale neighborhood. Again, it's the seawall walk that is most popular, but another pleasant trail leads up through the forest to Frog Lake.

Take the Bedford Highway north from downtown and then one kilometer north of the Kearney Lake Road junction and watch for Kent Avenue (to the left), which leads into a dense old-growth forest protected as Hemlock Ravine Park. From the pond and picnic area, a world away from surrounding development, five trails branch off into the forest. Some are short and perfect for younger and older walkers, while others, including the trail to the hemlock-filled ravine, are steeper and can be slippery after rain.

BICYCLING

The local municipality, with its many lakes and harbor-side coves, has put considerable effort into making the city as bike-friendly as possible. The Halifax Regional Municipality website (www.halifax.ca) has a PDF bike map, or pick one up at the information center. A centrally located source for rentals and advice is Ideal Bikes (1678 Barrington St., 902/444-7433, Mon.-Fri. 10am-6pm, Sat. 10am-5pm). Standard bikes cost from $25 for two hours or $50 for a full day.

Freewheeling Adventures (902/857-3600 or 800/672-0775, www.freewheeling.ca, from $2,400 per person) is a local tour company that runs recommended guided bike trips along the South Shore, starting from Hubbards, just south of the city. Guests ride for up to six hours per day, stay in cottages or B&Bs, and have all meals included.

WATER SPORTS
Swimming and Sunbathing

In addition to indoor pools at most major downtown hotels, municipal swimming pools include the centrally located, 50-meter-long Centennial Pool (1970 Gottingen St., 902/490-7219, daily 7:45am-8:30pm), which has lots of times set aside for public swims, and Needham Pool (3372 Devonshire Ave., 902/490-4633, Mon.-Fri. 8:30am-6pm, Sun. 1:30pm-6:30pm).

Crystal Crescent Beach Provincial Park lies a half hour south of Halifax, off Highway 349, and is the locals' favorite Atlantic beach. Its sand is fine, and the sea is usually cold, but summer crowds heat up the action. Nature lovers will enjoy the 10-kilometer trail to remote Pennant Point, while naturists will want to gravitate to the farthest of the park's three beaches—one of Canada's few official nude beaches.

If you're visiting Fisherman's Cove, head east for eight kilometers along Cow Bay Road to reach **Rainbow Haven Provincial Park.** The park protects wetlands at the mouth of Cole Harbour and an ocean-facing beach. The beach is often windy (it's not uncommon to see people sunbathing back in the dunes), but on calm days it's a delightful place to soak up some rays and maybe, if you're brave, take a dip in the water. At the end of the park access road are changing rooms and a concession selling beachy food (ice cream and hot dogs).

Canoeing and Kayaking

Based on the Northwest Arm, **Saint Mary's Boat Club** (1641 Fairfield Rd., 902/490-4688, June-Sept. Sat.-Sun. 11am-7pm) rents canoes at no cost on a limited basis through summer. If you're interested in kayaking, call ahead for a schedule of evening events, which often include tours on Northwest Arm for $15 per person.

GOLFING

Halifax and the surrounding area are home to more than a dozen courses, varying from 9-hole public courses to exclusive 18-holers. The **Nova Scotia Golf Association** website (www.nsga.ns.ca) has links to all provincial courses.

The Courses

Glen Arbour Golf Course (Glen Arbour Way, off Hammonds Plains Rd., 1 km west of Bedford, 902/835-4653) is one of Canada's finest links. Choose from five sets of tees, to a maximum of 6,800 yards. The course has abundant water hazards, 90 bunkers, and fairways lined by hardwood forests. Greens fees top out at $115 in midsummer, dropping as low as $60 for twilight golf in October.

Lost Creek Golf Club (310 Kinsac Rd., 902/865-4653) enjoys the same forested environment as Glen Arbour, but without the valet parking and high greens fees

(golfing is just $48). To get there, take Exit 2 from Highway 101 and follow Beaverbank Road north for 10 kilometers; turn right on Kinsac Road and then left on William Nelson Drive.

One of the region's most enjoyable layouts is **Granite Springs** (25 km west of downtown, off Hwy. 333 at 4441 Prospect Rd., Bayside, 902/852-4653). This challenging course winds through 120 hectares of mature forest, with distant ocean views. Greens fees are $60 ($40 twilight).

WINTER SPORTS

In winter, walking paths become **cross-country ski trails** at Point Pleasant Park, Sir Sandford Fleming Park, and Hemlock Ravine. Dartmouth maintains groomed surfaces at Lake Charles, and several lakes in Halifax are great for skating.

Skiing and Snowboarding

The closest downhill skiing and boarding is at **Ski Martock** (902/798-9501, www.martock. com, in season daily 9am-9pm, day passes adult $40, child $30), an hour's drive northwest of Halifax off Highway 101 (signposted from Exit 5). It's a popular family hill, with mostly beginner runs accessible by two lifts rising 180 vertical meters. Snowmaking covers the entire resort, while lights keep runs open nightly until 10pm.

Hockey

Through the long winter, when outside activities are curtailed by the weather, there is much interest in ice hockey (known in Canada simply as "hockey"). When they're not watching the National Hockey League on television (the closest teams are in Boston, Montréal, and Toronto), local fans flock to the Halifax Metro Centre to cheer on their own **Halifax Mooseheads** (5284 Duke St., 902/429-3267, www.halifaxmooseheads.ca, tickets from adult $19, senior $16, child $10), who play mid-September-mid-March in the Québec Major Junior Hockey League.

HARBOR CRUISES AND LAND TOURS

If you don't have a lot of time to explore Halifax or just want an introduction to the city, consider one of the many tours available—they'll maximize your time and get you to the highlights with minimum stress.

Bluenose II

The harbor front's premier attraction, the magnificent schooner *Bluenose II* (http://bluenose.novascotia.ca) divides her summer between Halifax, her home port of Lunenburg, and goodwill tours to other Canadian ports. The vessel is an exact replica of the famous *Bluenose*. The schooner is operated by the Lunenburg Marine Museum Society on behalf of the Province of Nova Scotia. When in Halifax, two-hour **harbor tours** (902/634-4794 or 800/763-1963, daily 9:30am and 1pm, adult $55, child $32) are available from the Maritime Museum of the Atlantic's wharf. Each sailing has 75 spots—40 spots can be reserved by calling, with the remaining 35 going on sale 90 minutes before departure. Without a reservation, expect to line up for a spot.

Harbour Hopper Tours

Harbour Hopper Tours (902/490-8687, www.mtcw.ca, adult $35, senior $32, child $20) picks up passengers from the north side of the maritime museum for a quick trip around the historic streets of Halifax. Then the fun really starts, as the company's distinctive green and yellow amphibious vehicles plunge into the water for a cruise around the harbor. The trip lasts around one hour, with up to 20 departures daily May-October (9am-9:30pm). The ticket kiosk is on the waterfront just north of the maritime museum.

Other Harbor Cruises

Many other sightseeing craft also offer harbor tours. **Murphy's on the Water** (Cable Wharf, 1751 Lower Water St., 902/420-1015, www.mtcw.ca) operates several vessels through a sailing season that runs mid-May-late October. The 23-meter wooden sailing ketch *Mar* departs up to six times daily (adult $35, senior $32, child $19). The *Harbour Queen I* is a 200-passenger paddle wheeler offering a narrated harbor cruise (adult $35, senior $32, child $19) and a variety of lunch and dinner cruises ($72 for dinner).

Bus Tours

Ambassatours (902/423-6242 or 800/565-9662) has the local Grayline franchise. The

downtown harbor front

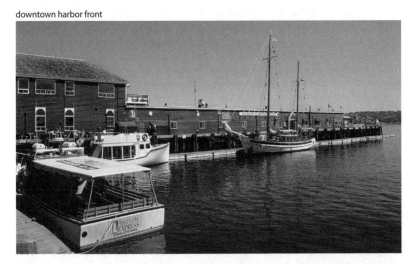

three-hour Deluxe Historic Halifax City Tour includes stops at the Public Gardens, Halifax Citadel National Historic Site, and Fairview Cemetery. The tour also passes all major downtown attractions, working precincts of the harbor, and various university campuses. This tour departs June-mid-October daily at 9am and 1pm (adult $52, senior $49, child $30). Another option with Ambassatours is a downtown loop tour aboard an old British double-decker bus (mid-June-mid-Oct., adult $54, child $26).

You can get on and off as you please at any of the 17 stops on two loops, and tickets are valid for two days (a good plan is to ride the entire loop once, and then plan your stops for the second go-round). This same company also has a three-hour trip to Peggy's Cove (departs June-mid-Oct. Tues., Thurs., and Sun. 1pm, adult $49, senior $46, child $34) and a full-day trip that combines a stop in Mahone Bay with time in Lunenburg (departs June-Oct. Mon., Wed., Fri., and Sat. 9am, adult $85, senior $76, child $60).

Entertainment and Events

Halifax has a reputation as a party town, partly because of its large population of students. The city has dozens of pubs, many with local brews on tap and Celtic-inspired bands performing to small but raucous crowds. Most pubs close around midnight. The city also has a notable performing arts community. Although most seasons run through the cooler months, many companies put on events especially for summer crowds.

For complete listings of all that's happening around Halifax, pick up the free *Coast* (www.thecoast.ca). Friday and weekend editions of the *Chronicle Herald* (http://thechronicleherald.ca) also offer comprehensive entertainment listings.

PUBS AND BREWERIES

Halifax is renowned for its pubs and its great selection of locally brewed beers. Pubs range from historic homes to waterfront decks, but all are friendly and most also offer a good selection of food.

If you're going to have just one beer in Halifax, quaff it at the **Red Stag Tavern** (1496 Lower Water St., 902/422-0275, Sun.-Thurs. 11:30am-11pm, Fri.-Sat. 11:30am-10:30pm), part of the Keith's Brewery complex. Best known as North America's oldest working brewery, Keith's still uses traditional British brewing techniques. Its famous India Pale Ale is widely available on draught and in bottles

across the country, but it's best enjoyed in the Red Stag, surrounded by a convivial atmosphere and with traditional Maritime music in the background.

Henry House (1222 Barrington St., 902/423-5660, daily from 11am) is ensconced in a historic 1834 stone building a couple of blocks back from Alexander Keith's Brewery. The pub attracts a slightly older crowd of well-dressed locals and has a wide-ranging menu of food and beer, including gluten-free options.

In the harbor-front Historic Properties complex, **Gahan House** (1869 Upper Water St., 902/407-4278, daily 11am-midnight) is a big, bright room, with lots of outside waterfront seating. It has its own small brewery and offers a range of other local brews. The food here is also notable, ranging from traditional (lobster rolls) to modern (maple curry penne). Adjacent to Gahan House, live music at the **Lower Deck** (Upper Water St., 902/425-1501, daily from 11:30am) keeps the crowds humming nightly at this waterfront pub within the historic Privateers Warehouse.

The Maxwell's Plum (1600 Grafton St., 902/423-5090, Sun.-Wed. 11am-midnight, Thurs.-Sat. 11am-2am) has an excellent selection of imported draft beers (notably Beamish Irish Stout, John Courage, and Newcastle Brown Ale) and single-malt scotches. That alone may be reason enough to visit, but it's

Granite Brewery

also a good venue for straight-ahead jazz, including Sunday afternoon jam sessions.

Best known for its rooftop patio, **Your Father's Moustache** (5686 Spring Garden Rd., 902/423-6766, Mon.-Fri. 10:30am-midnight, Sat.-Sun. 10am-midnight) puts on excellent live, usually local, music most evenings. On Saturday afternoon, it hosts the popular Blues Matinee.

Aside from sidling up to the bar at the above pubs, beer connoisseurs visiting Halifax can buy directly from a number of small breweries scattered around the city. Generally, you can buy regular bottles, "growlers" (one- or two-liter jugs), or kegs up to 50 liters. **Garrison Brewing** (1149 Marginal Rd., 902/453-5343, Sun.-Fri. 10am-8pm, Sat. 7am-9pm) is in a touristy location south of downtown near the farmers market and Pier 21, but that doesn't stop the brewmaster from producing a wonderful range of ales. Garrison also has a large shop and tasting area.

Northwest of downtown, the **Granite Brewery** (6054 Stairs St., 902/422-4954,

Mon.-Thurs. 10am-7pm, Fri.-Sat. 10am-8pm, Sun. noon-6pm) is tucked away between Robie and Kempt Streets, but it's well worth searching out for its excellent English-style ales that are sold to go.

NIGHTLIFE
Bars

In the basement of the Marquee Ballroom north of downtown is the **Seahorse Tavern** (2037 Gottingen St., 902/423-7200, Thurs.-Fri. 9pm-2am, Sat. 6pm-2am), which has been around since 1948 (although it has moved from its original location). Horsepower Beer, produced by the local Propeller Brewery, is available on tap only at the Seahorse, but most patrons are here for the music, with live performances Thursday-Saturday. Part of the same complex is the **Economy Shoe Shop** (1663 Argyle St., 902/423-8845, Mon.-Thurs. 11am-midnight, Fri.-Sun. 11am-2am), a drinking and dining venue incorporating three restaurants and the Belgian Bar, with a gaudy but appealing tropical vibe.

HFX Sports Bar (1721 Brunswick St., 902/404-1404, Sun.-Fri. 4pm-2am, Sat. 11am-2am) is a cavernous sports bar anchored by a two-story wall of TV screens. It's arguably the best place in the city to go for U.S. sports, but you can also watch British-oriented sports such as cricket and rugby. Food is typical pub fare, but is well priced.

Stayner's Wharf Pub & Grill (5075 George St., 902/492-1800, Sun.-Thurs. 11am-11pm, Fri.-Sat. 11am-2am) is in the heart of the tourist district, but since it's a smaller place, the casual visitor often misses this bar, which remains quiet until local jazz and blues bands hit the stage Wednesday-Sunday.

Nightclubs

Around midnight, when the pubs start closing their doors, the crowds move on to nightclubs spread through downtown.

The **Dome** (1726 Argyle St., 902/422-6907, Thurs.-Sat. 11pm-3:30am) is a mass of young heaving bodies who dance the night away in sync to one of Canada's most dynamic sound and light systems. It's also a bit of a pickup place. Under the same roof is **Cheers** (902/421-1655, daily 10pm-3:30am), which attracts an older crowd. Another multi-venue nightclub is **Pacifico** (corner of Barrington and Salter Sts., 902/422-3633, Thurs.-Sat. 9pm-2am), where **CraveBar** attracts serious dancers and the **Capitol** hosts a martini bar.

Starting out as a gay bar and then making a move to a new location in late 2014, **Reflections** (5187 Salter St., 902/422-2957, Thurs.-Mon. 10pm-4am) now attracts an eclectic mix of locals of all persuasions. The biggest crowds are on weekends, when the resident DJ spins tunes until 4am.

Jazz and Blues

The **Seahorse Tavern** (2037 Gottingen St., 902/423-7200, Thurs.-Fri. 9pm-2am, Sat. 6pm-2am) hosts a blues jam every Thursday night. The Belgian Bar, within the **Economy Shoe Shop** (1663 Argyle St., 902/423-8845, daily 11am-2am) features no-charge Monday evening jazz.

Economy Shoe Shop

The best blues bar in town is **Bearly's House of Blues and Ribs** (1269 Barrington St., 902/423-2526, daily 11am-midnight). As the name suggests, ribs ($14 for a half rack) are the dining specialty, but it is the music that draws an enthusiastic crowd. Weekends feature local talent, while weekdays except Monday and Wednesday the stage is turned over to traveling talent. On Saturday afternoons through winter, bluegrass musicians strum their stuff.

PERFORMING ARTS

Haligonians have a sweet and sometimes bittersweet Canadian sense of humor (somewhat like the British), and local theater revels in their brand of fun. A $47 admission will get you into dinner-theater musical productions at **Grafton Street Dinner Theatre** (1741 Grafton St., 902/425-1961), which operates daily except Monday in summer and Friday and Saturday only through the rest of the year.

The **Neptune Theatre** (1593 Argyle St., 902/429-7070, mid-Sept.-late May) underwent a huge renovation in the 1990s, during which time the original 1915 auditorium was saved and renovated, while the surrounding structure was rebuilt. Today the theater hosts musicals, comedies, and Canadian premieres.

FESTIVALS AND EVENTS

Halifax hosts a number of well-known events that visitors plan their trips around, as well as many you probably haven't heard of but that are well worth attending if the dates correspond with your own travels. The most popular festivals are held outdoors and in summer, but the cooler months are the season for performing arts. For exact dates of festivals, check the event's website or **Tourism Nova Scotia** (www.novascotia.com).

Spring

The **Scotia Festival of Music** centers on the **Music Room** (6181 Lady Hammond Rd., 902/429-9467, www.scotiafestival.ns.ca) for two weeks from the last weekend

Booths and Burgers

Beyond the white linens and perfectly presented seafood of Halifax's finer restaurants are a smattering of old-style diners. The following are my favorites—one downtown, another overlooking the city's most notorious intersection, and another handy for those traveling into downtown from the north.

In the heart of the central business district, the venerable **Bluenose II** (1824 Hollis St., 902/425-5092, Mon.-Fri. 7:30am-9pm, Sat.-Sun. 8am-9pm, $9-16) is named for the famous schooner that calls Halifax home on a part-time basis. The booths fill with an eclectic crowd of locals for breakfast, but the space is bright and welcoming, and many regulars are families. Eggs Benedict is $8, steak and eggs $9.50, while the rest-of-the-day choices vary from a lobster sandwich ($11) to Greek specialties ($9-16).

Overlooking the confusing-even-for-the-locals Armdale Rotary is **Armview Restaurant** (7156 Chebucto Rd., 902/455-4395, Mon.-Wed. 11am-10pm, Thurs.-Sun. 8:30am-11pm, $8-21), which has been in business since the 1960s, which makes it one of Halifax's oldest restaurants. Although it's undergone renovations and the menu has been expanded to include options like mango halibut salad, you can still order no-frills breakfasts and burgers for around $10.

On Monday, Tuesday, and Wednesday, coupon-clipping retirees fill **Esquire Restaurant** (772 Bedford Hwy., 902/835-9033, daily 7:30am-8 pm, $9-16) for specials such as home-style pork dinners for $10. The restaurant is across from the Bedford Basin, and there's plenty of parking, or, if you're staying across the road at the Esquire Motel, you need only to negotiate traffic zooming along the busy Bedford Highway.

in May. Chamber musicians present piano, cello, and violin recitals in a dignified yet casual atmosphere.

The **Nova Scotia Multicultural Festival** (Halifax Seaport, 945 Marginal Rd., 902/423-6534, www.multifest.ca) fills the waterfront precinct with the sounds, sights, and smells of various cultures the middle weekend of June. You can feast on barbecued Korean short ribs while watching Polish folk dancing or tap your feet to Celtic Highland dancers while juggling a plate of German sausages.

Summer

Nothing reflects Halifax's long military heritage better than the **Royal Nova Scotia International Tattoo** (902/420-1114, www.nstattoo.ca), held annually for 10 days at the beginning of July at the Scotiabank Centre (5284 Duke St.). A "tattoo" is an outdoor military exercise presented as entertainment. Here it involves competitions, military bands, dancers, gymnasts, and choirs. The event has grown to be regarded as one of the world's greatest indoor events, bringing together

thousands of performers from around the world. You can buy tickets (around $32-54) through the **Scotiabank Centre Box Office** (902/451-1221, www.scotiabank-centre.com).

In mid-July, jazz fans descend on Halifax for the **Halifax Jazz Festival** (902/492-2225, www.halifaxjazzfestival.ca), the largest music festival east of Montréal. In addition to performing in a large tent set up on the waterfront along Lower Water Street at Salter Street, more than 400 musicians from around the world gather at venues as unique as a tugboat and as character-filled as local churches to perform traditional and contemporary jazz.

Halifax and Dartmouth come together to celebrate their birthdays with a civic holiday known as **Natal Day** (www.natalday.org) on the first Monday of every August. Events take place through the entire weekend, including a Saturday parade, talent shows, sporting events, and a grand finale fireworks presentation on the harbor Monday night.

Street performers fill five stages spread along the downtown waterfront for 11 days in early August during the Halifax International Busker Festival (www.buskers.ca).

Summer finishes with the Atlantic Fringe Festival (902/423-4653, www.atlanticfringe.ca), featuring over 50 shows at various downtown venues through the first week of September.

Fall

The mid-September Atlantic Film Festival (902/422-3456, www.atlanticfilm.com) has been wowing moviegoers for more than 35 years. It features the very best films from around the world, but the emphasis is on local and Canadian productions. Venues are mostly downtown theaters.

Celebrate Alexander Keith's birthday (902/455-1474, www.keiths.ca) on October 5 with hundreds of enthusiastic locals. Or pull up a barstool at any local pub and raise a toast of India Pale Ale to "The Great Man of Beer," who began brewing beer in Halifax in 1820. The brewery (check the website for locations) is the epicenter of celebrations, with plenty of foot-stomping, beer-drinking east coast music.

For four days in early October, the country comes to the city for the Atlantic Agricultural Fall Fair (Halifax Exhibition Centre, 200 Prospect Rd., 902/876-1811, www.atlanticfair.com). It has everything a fall fair should—a crafts marketplace, agricultural competitions, equestrian competitions, live music, and a midway. Exhibition Centre is off Highway 333, the main road to Peggy's Cove.

Winter

The middle weekend of November, the Christmas Craft Village (www.christmascraftvillage.com) fills Exhibition Park with hundreds of crafty booths selling everything from homemade preserves to self-published books to coastal antiques.

Shopping

Shopping in Halifax—the type visitors to the city will enjoy—centers on the downtown waterfront, with the exception being the boutiques and quirky shops along Spring Garden Road. Expect to find everything from lighthouse Christmas decorations made in China to original oil paintings, and everything in between.

Most shops and all major department stores are generally open Monday-Saturday 9:30am-5:30pm. Stores along the touristy harbor front usually have longer hours and are also open Sunday.

Arts and Crafts

The city's art galleries are superb, and most are located downtown. The newest fine arts trends are on exhibit at Nova Scotia College of Art and Design's Anna Leonowens Gallery (1891 Granville St., 902/494-8223, Mon.-Fri. 11am-5pm, Sat. noon-4pm). The gallery displays and sells the work of Nova Scotia College of Art and Design students. This downtown university, one of North America's oldest cultural institutions, was founded by the gallery's namesake, Anna Leonowens, in 1887. Leonowens, a one-time English teacher who was governess to the King of Siam in the 1860s, spent 20 years in Halifax, during which time she established NSCAD.

The capital's definitive crafts source is Jennifer's of Nova Scotia (5635 Spring Garden Rd., 902/425-3119, Wed.-Fri. 9am-9pm, Sat. and Mon.-Tues. 9am-6pm, Sun. 11am-5pm), an outlet for 120 provincial producers of handicrafts such as patchwork quilts, pottery, and soaps.

The Gallery Shop at street level of the Art Gallery of Nova Scotia (1723 Hollis St., 902/424-7542, Mon.-Sat. 10am-5pm, Sun. noon-5pm) is an inspiring room filled with the cream of provincial arts and crafts, as well as prints by folk artist Maude Lewis, books, cards, and other assorted arty gifts. Walking west down Hollis Street from the gallery is **Studio 21 Fine Art** (1273 Hollis St., 902/420-1852, Tues.-Fri. 11am-6pm, Sat. 10am-5pm), a good source of contemporary paintings by local artists.

For a unique combination of hand-built furniture and oddities such as porcelain dog dishes, head to **Bellissimo** (2743 Agricola St., 902/423-6014, Tues.-Sat. 10am-5pm).

Crystal

Canada's only traditional glassworks is **Nova Scotian Crystal** (5080 George St., 902/492-0416, Mon.-Fri. 9am-6pm, Sat. 10am-6pm, Sun. 10am-5pm), which is ensconced in a waterfront building that contains a showroom and workshop. You can watch master craftspeople at work every day, but Tuesday, Thursday, and Saturday are the days you won't want to miss—this is when the actual glassblowing takes place. Rather than taking a tour, interested folks crowd around open factory doors to watch the goings-on inside. The shop sells pieces such as Christmas ornaments, stemware, toasting flutes, candleholders, and bowls, many with Nova Scotian-inspired designs.

Clothing

Hundreds of clan fabrics and tartans in kilts, skirts, vests, ties, and other apparel are stocked at **Plaid Place** (1903 Barrington St., 902/429-6872, Mon.-Fri. 9:30am-5:30pm, Sat. 10am-5pm). For something a little less traditional, stop by the **Marine Heritage Store** (1675 Lower Water St., 902/423-9787, summer daily 9:30am-5:30pm, the rest of the year Tues.-Sat. 9:30am-5pm, Sun. 1pm-5pm), where you'll find casual clothing in a bright, subtly nautical-themed setting. Starting out by selling shirts from a log church, this local company has grown into a 30-store chain with outlets across Atlantic Canada. The downtown Halifax store is in the Maritime Museum of the Atlantic; another is at Halifax International Airport.

Markets

Halifax Seaport Farmers' Market (Pier 20, 1209 Marginal Rd., 902/492-4043, Mon.-Fri. 10am-5pm, Sat. 10am-3pm, Sun. 9am-3pm), North America's oldest such market (although the location is new), fills a massive waterfront building with local produce and handmade arts and crafts that make the perfect memento of your time in Nova Scotia.

In the same vicinity, **Pavilion 22** (1031 Marginal Rd., 902/426-8222, May-Oct. when cruise ships have docked, see www.cruisehalifax.ca for a schedule) is designed as a market-style shopping experience for cruise-ship visitors, but is also worth stopping by if you are at this end of town.

Local Delicacies

You'll no doubt eat a lot of seafood while in Nova Scotia, but it can also make a great souvenir to take home for friends and family. Or plan a get-together upon your return and impress everyone with a Nova Scotian feast.

Clearwater (757 Bedford Hwy., 902/443-0333, daily 9am-7pm) is a high-profile supplier with a huge shopfront along the Bedford Highway waterfront. The outlet is anchored by a massive lobster tank divided into sections that make choosing the right-size lobster easy (from $10 per pound). You can also pick up cooked crab legs to go, attend cooking demonstrations, and buy all manner of seafood cookbooks. Better still for those departing Halifax International Airport, Clearwater has an airport location (902/873-4509, daily 5am-8pm) with a lobster tank. For an additional fee, live lobsters can be packaged for air travel. Clearwater also sells crabs, scallops, clams, and shrimp.

The days of Prohibition, when smuggling rum into the United States was a way to make a living for seafaring Nova Scotians, may be a distant memory, but at the **Rum Runners Rum Cake Factory** (Bishop's Landing, 1479 Lower Water St., 902/421-6079, mid-Apr.-late Dec. daily 10am-dusk), you can buy rum cakes from a rum-running family's recipe.

The cakes are deliciously rich and sweet, and they travel well.

Outdoor and Camping Gear

Halifax's largest outdoor equipment store is **Mountain Equipment Co-op** (1550 Granville St., 902/421-2667, Mon.-Wed. 9:30am-7pm, Thurs.-Fri. 9:30am-9pm, Sat. 10am-6pm, Sun. 11am-5pm). This is a cooperative owned by its members; to make a purchase, you must be a member (a one-time $5 charge). The store holds a massive selection of clothing, climbing and mountaineering equipment, tents, backpacks, sleeping bags, books, and other accessories. To obtain a copy of the mail-order catalog, call 800/663-2667 or go online to www.mec.ca.

The Trail Shop (6210 Quinpool Rd., 902/423-8736, Mon.-Sat. 9am-6pm, Sun noon-5pm) has been a Halifax staple in the outfitting business since 1967. The selection of camping equipment, footwear, and field guides is particularly strong.

Food

Halifax may not have a reputation as a gastronomical wonderland, but the dining scene has improved greatly during the last decade. Not only is the standard of food high in many of the better restaurants, but prices are generally reasonable, with mains in even the very best restaurants rarely more than $35.

Naturally, seafood dominates many menus—especially lobster, crab, mussels, scallops, shrimp, halibut, and salmon, all of which are harvested in Nova Scotia. Some of the best seafood is found in the touristy waterfront precinct. You can also buy it fresh from trawlers at Fisherman's Cove and even pick up live lobsters packed for flying out at the airport.

DOWNTOWN
Cafés

You can get a caffeine hit at outlets of Second Cup and Tim Hortons spread throughout the city, but the absence of coffeehouse chains in downtown Halifax is refreshing.

In the waterfront Historic Properties, **Two if by Sea** (1869 Upper Water St., 902/492-4600, Mon.-Fri. 7:30am-5pm, Sat. 8am-5pm, lunches $6-9), known as TIBS to regulars, roast their own coffee, but are best known for buttery croissants that melt in your mouth.

The refined European vibe at **Pavia Espresso Bar & Cafe** (1273 Hollis St, 902/407-4008, Mon.-Fri. 8am-5pm, Sat.-Sun. 9am-6pm, lunches $7-10) is fitting for this café's location within the Art Gallery of Nova Scotia. The coffee is sourced by a well-known Italian roaster—and the baristas get their training in Florence—so you know this place is serious about pouring excellent coffee. The food is also notable, with choices such as an artichoke heart and pesto sourdough panini.

Step inside **Cabin Coffee** (1554 Hollis St., 902/422-8130, Mon.-Fri. 6:30am-6pm, Sat.-Sun. 9am-5pm, lunches $6-9) and you'll be surprised by the relaxed and friendly ambience of this smaller café in the heart of downtown. In addition to top-notch coffee, the wraps, sandwiches, cinnamon buns, and muffins are all tasty and well priced.

Head down Bishop Street from Cabin Coffee to Bishop's Landing and you'll find ★ **Smiling Goat** (1475 Lower Water St., 902/446-3366, Mon. 7am-8pm, Tues.-Sat. 7am-9pm, Sun. 8am-8pm, lunches $6-9), a stylish espresso bar, serving some of the very best coffee in Halifax. Either order it to go and enjoy along the adjacent waterfront or relax in the paved courtyard.

On the south side of downtown, **Trident** (1256 Hollis St., 902/423-7100, Mon.-Fri. 8am-5pm, Sat. 8:30am-5pm, lunches $6-10) is a secondhand bookstore on one side and an old-fashioned café with leather-backed chairs on the other—the perfect place to relax with a newly bought literary treasure, or to take advantage of the free wireless Internet.

Seafood Along the Waterfront

The least expensive way to enjoy seafood along the waterfront is by ordering fish-and-chips from **Battered Fish** (1751 Lower Water St., 902/491-3474, May-Oct. daily 11am-dusk, $9-14), where the haddock is fresh and the quality very good. The deep-fried clams and scallops are also worth trying.

In the Historic Properties, **Salty's** (1869 Lower Water St., 902/423-6818, daily 11:30am-10pm, $17-29) mixes seafood with succulent meat dishes in a sublime setting. Kick back with a margarita and watch the boats in the harbor. Sit indoors or out to enjoy some of the city's best food in a casual atmosphere, and don't miss the scrumptious desserts. The upstairs dining room is slightly more formal, with a menu and prices to match. Here, mains such as scallops roasted in red Thai curry and butter-poached halibut are in the $25-36 range.

Diners at **Murphy's on the Water** (1751 Lower Water St., 902/420-1015, daily 9am-10pm, $15-24) also enjoy panoramic harbor views, although it is slightly more touristy than Salty's. This restaurant fills a converted warehouse, with outside tables at the end of the pier. The emphasis is on seafood, such as lobster dip and fish cakes as starters and a unique lobster burger (a meat pattie topped with lobster meat).

Waterfront Warehouse (1549 Lower Water St., 902/425-7610, May-Oct. daily 11:30am-10pm, $17-44) is exactly that—a converted waterfront warehouse where tugboats were once repaired. The setting is casual yet refined, with white linens, nautical-themed furnishings, and an oversized fireplace. The seafood chowder is a hearty starter, while seafood-oriented mains include grilled salmon, seafood crepes, and the Seafood Tower to share.

Other Seafood Restaurants

★ **Five Fishermen** (1740 Argyle St., 902/422-4421, Mon.-Fri. 11:30am-10pm, Sat.-Sun. 4pm-10pm, $24-40) occupies one of Halifax's oldest buildings—it was built in 1816 and once used by famed governess Anna Leonowens (of *Anna and the King* fame) for her Victorian School of Art and Design. The restaurant is popular with seafood-loving Haligonians for its large-dish menu, which includes shellfish tagliatelle, pan-seared halibut, PEI oysters, and lobster-stuffed Digby scallops, as well as Alberta beef.

Pub Dining

Durty Nelly's (1660 Argyle St., 902/406-7640, Mon.-Fri. 11:30am-2am, Sat.-Sun. 10:30am-2am, $11-18) is Irish in more than name. All furnishings in the traditionally stylish room were actually built in Ireland and transported across the Atlantic. The menu includes traditional treats such as lamb shank braised in Guinness, cottage pie, and bangers and mash, as well as local seafood.

It's a little away from the tourist precinct, but ★ **Henry House** (1222 Barrington St., 902/423-5660, daily 11:30am-12:30am, $17-29) offers excellent food in an intimate pub setting. Melt-in-your-mouth baby back ribs are a house specialty, or choose healthy options such as salmon baked in crushed cashews.

Contemporary

Chives Canadian Bistro (1537 Barrington St., 902/420-9626, daily 5pm-9:30pm, $20-29) is well worth searching out, and even though it's away from the touristy waterfront, you'll need a reservation. The menu revolves around seasonal ingredients and produce sourced from throughout Nova Scotia. Add immaculate presentation to fresh and healthy cooking styles, and you have a meal to remember. Mains such as cauliflower curry are all delicious and well presented. Save room for the lemon tart.

The unusual name, **2 Doors Down** (1533 Barrington St., 902/422-4224, daily 11am-10pm, $15-26), comes from its location relative to the aforementioned Chives, which is part of the same ownership group. The 2 Doors Down space is unpretentious and simply decorated, leaving diners to focus on dishes that, like Chives, use local and seasonal ingredients, all sourced personally by the chef. Dishes such as arctic char smothered in corn sauce and the butter chicken burger are simple yet tasty. Rounding out an excellent choice for a well-priced dinner is a wine list that includes many Nova Scotian bottles.

A Halifax Original

The stretch of Argyle Street between Sackville and Blowers Streets has emerged as a dining hot spot, with the utterly original ★ **Economy Shoe Shop** (1663 Argyle St., 902/423-8845, daily 11:30am-2am, $11-25) anchoring the strip. The unusual name originated when one of the owners was starting out in the restaurant business; with little cash to spare, he found an old neon sign bearing the name and hung it out front. The original space has grown to encompass three very different restaurants and a bar—one a bohemian-themed space, another a glass-roofed room enclosing a rainforest that adds a tropical vibe even in the dead of winter. On offer is everything from run-of-the-mill hamburgers to baked halibut and scallops Mornay. Throw entertaining servers into the mix and you get a unique dining experience without spending a fortune.

Steakhouses

For carnivorous cravings, prepare to splurge at **Ryan Duffy's** (1650 Bedford Row, 902/421-1116, daily 11:30am-2pm and 5pm-10pm, $20-55). Some cuts, such as the signature strip loin, are wheeled to your table by a waitperson, who asks how much of the loin you'd like before carving the cut and telling you the price. Back in the kitchen, it is cooked exactly the way you ordered it over charcoal coals. You'll be charged extra for accompanying vegetables.

Henry House

Italian

A truly traditional Italian restaurant in downtown Halifax is ★ **Ristorante a Mano** (Bishop's Landing, 1477 Lower Water St., 902/423-6266, www.ristorantemano.ca, Mon.-Sat. 11:30am-10pm, $15-26), a bustling space with typical Italian trattoria food at very reasonable prices. The menu changes regularly, but one staple is pasta and pizza handmade daily.

In the vicinity of Ristorante a Mano but more upscale, **Da Maurizio** (1496 Lower Water St., 902/423-0859 Mon.-Sat. 5pm-10pm, $25-39) is a character-filled room within the historic Keith's Brewery building. Decorated in mellow hues, its walls are lined with Italian art, the wine rack filled with thoughtfully selected bottles from around the world, and the linen-draped tables highlighted by vases of fresh flowers. The menu represents the best of northern Italian cooking, with mains such as veal delicately sautéed with lobster in a brandy and cream sauce.

Spring Garden Road

SPRING GARDEN ROAD AND VICINITY

This restaurant-lined thoroughfare begins at Barrington Street and heads uphill past the main library and the Sexton Campus of Dalhousie University to the Public Gardens. Downstairs in **Spring Garden Place** is one of the city's better food courts.

Cafés

Serious coffee-lovers gravitate to a restored Victorian-era home that houses **Just Us!** (5876 Spring Garden Rd., 902/423-0856, Mon.-Fri. 7am-6pm, Sat.-Sun. 10am-5pm, lunches $7-10), which does an admirable job of sourcing fair-trade coffee from throughout Central America.

Within Halifax Central Library, **Pavia Espresso Bar & Cafe** (5440 Spring Garden Rd., 902/407-4008, Mon.-Thurs. 8am-9pm, Fri.-Sun. 9am-6pm, lunches $7-9) offers locally roasted, Italian-style coffee, along with delicious soups and salads, and grilled paninis on sourdough bread.

Just off the busy strip is **Daily Grind** (1479 Birmingham St., 902/429-6397, daily 9am-5pm, lunches $7-10), a longtime favorite with locals looking to avoid the chains. Cooked breakfasts are small, but the sandwiches, hot dishes such as quiche, and muffins are all delicious.

South of Spring Garden Road a few blocks, **Uncommon Grounds** (1030 S. Park St., 902/404-3124, daily 7am-10pm, lunches $6-10) is a very popular spot—both for its excellent coffee and university district vibe.

Casual Dining

Your Father's Moustache (5686 Spring Garden Rd., 902/423-6766, Mon.-Fri. 10:30am-midnight, Sat.-Sun. 10am-midnight, $15-24) is a casual favorite with a reasonably priced menu of seafood, steaks, and pasta, and a popular brunch is served Sunday 11am-3pm. The beer-battered fish is also excellent. A huge patio and inexpensive kids' menu (everything $6) are also notable.

Asian

Throughout downtown you'll find a smattering of good Asian restaurants. One of the best is **Cheelin** (1496 Lower Water St., 902/422-2252, Mon.-Sat. 11:30am-2:30pm and 5pm-10pm, Sun. 5pm-10pm, $11-24), within the Alexander Keith's Brewery complex. The atmosphere is informal, with chefs in an open kitchen churning out flavorful Chinese favorites. The steamed salmon with black bean sauce is a unique treat.

Hamachi Steakhouse (Bishop's Landing, 1477 Lower Water St., 902/422-1600, Mon.-Sat. 11:30am-10pm, Sun. 4pm-10pm, $23-45) is a contemporary Japanese restaurant specializing in *teppan* cooking. In the center of communal tables are grills; chefs slice, dice, and then grill your choice of a beef, chicken, or seafood main as you sample starters such as *niku balu* (tenderloin meatballs with pineapple-chili dipping sauce). For dessert, the Mount Fuji (a combination of brownie, ice cream, cream, and chocolate sauce) is an easy choice.

Asian

My favorite Indian restaurant in Halifax is **Curry Village** (1569 Dresden Row, 902/429-5010, daily 10am-9:30pm, $15-22), on the north side of Spring Garden Road, toward the Citadel. This place prepares chicken tandoori, *biryanis,* lamb *vindaloo,* and other Indian dishes to order.

For no-frills Japanese and Korean cooking at reasonable prices, consider a meal at **Minato Sushi** (1520 Queen St., 902/420-0331, Mon.-Sat. 11:30am-9pm, $12-20). Dishes such as sautéed scallops and mushrooms in butter sauce are all under $20, and *bulkokee* (sweet beef teriyaki), a Korean dish, is $17.

NORTH OF DOWNTOWN
Cafés

A few blocks northwest of the Citadel, **Java Blend** (6027 North St., 902/423-6144, Mon.-Fri. 6:30am-6pm, Sat. 7:30am-5pm, Sun. 9am-4:30pm), in business as a coffee roaster since 1938, is well worth searching out if you appreciate coffee and its origins. Today, they roast over 30 blends of coffee—and many locals will tell you it's the best in town.

Delis

Well worth searching out, ★ **Italian Market** (6061 Young St., 902/455-6124, Mon.-Sat. 8am-7pm, Sun. 10am-6pm, lunch $7-11) is an absolute delight. Along one side is a deli counter with premade dishes, while another side is home to desserts and drinks. The shelves are lined with goodies imported from around the world. Choose from cabbage rolls, quiche, meatloaf meatballs, sun-dried tomato-crusted chicken breasts, smoked salmon pâté, and more. Prices are reasonable, and there are a few tables at which to eat.

DARTMOUTH AND VICINITY

Ask a local where to go for the best fish-and-chips, and many will send you to **John's Lunch** (352 Pleasant St., 902/469-3074, daily 10am-9pm, $7.50-18), a simple diner within walking distance of the ferry terminal that has been dishing up popular seafood dishes since 1969. Not much has changed since—seating choices include stools at the counter, vinyl booths, or picnic tables out front. Haddock is the fish of choice and is sourced daily at the market, but the deep-fried clams are also tasty. It's also remarkably

Head to Uncommon Grounds for great coffee.

inexpensive—fish (one piece) and chips is just $7.50, and a cup of coffee is $1.

From **Wooden Monkey** (88 Alderney Dr., 902/466-3100, Sun.-Thurs. 11:30am-9pm, Fri.-Sat. 11:30am-11pm, $22-28), views extend back across Halifax Harbour to downtown, a real treat when the nighttime lights of downtown are sparkling across the water. The menu is dominated by simple yet stylish dishes that will please all tastes, including vegetarians and vegans, all reasonably priced and well presented. The bacon-wrapped scallops are a good starter to share, while seafood chowder is a tasty yet inexpensive main. Wooden Monkey is on the upper floor of the Alderney Gate complex, where ferries from Halifax terminate. With ferries running until midnight, there's plenty of time to enjoy a meal before returning to your downtown accommodation.

Fisherman's Cove

At this historic fishing village, two kilometers southeast of Dartmouth alongside the Eastern Passage, it's no surprise that seafood dominates local menus. The most obvious place to eat is **Boondocks** (200 Government Wharf Rd., 902/465-3474, daily 11am-9pm, $12-24), a big, red-roofed building with a pleasant oceanfront patio. The menu offers the usual collection of seafood, including an excellent seafood chowder filled with Digby scallops, haddock tacos, pan-seared halibut and chips, and a decadently rich lobster stew.

For a more authentic atmosphere, visit smaller places such as **Fish Basket** (100 Government Wharf Rd., 902/465-5902, Mon.-Fri. 9am-6pm, Sat. 11am-6pm, $9-14), which is primarily in business selling fresh seafood but also sells lobster sandwiches for $9.50.

Accommodations and Camping

Accommodations in Halifax vary from a hostel and budget-priced roadside motels to luxurious B&Bs. Downtown is home to a number of full-service hotels catering to top-end travelers and business conventions. In general, these properties offer drastically reduced rates on weekends—Friday and Saturday nights might be half the regular room rate. No matter when you plan to visit, arriving in Halifax without a reservation is unwise, but it's especially so in the summer, when gaggles of tourists compete for a relative paucity of rooms.

All rates quoted are for a double room in summer.

DOWNTOWN
Under $50

Also known as the Halifax Heritage House Hostel, **HI-Halifax** (1253 Barrington St., 902/422-3863, www.hihostels.ca) has 75 beds two blocks from the harbor and a 15-minute walk to attractions such as the Maritime Museum of the Atlantic and Citadel Hill. Facilities include a communal kitchen, a laundry room, television in the common room, and a storeroom for bikes. Beds in four- to eight-bed dorms are $34 per night ($39 for nonmembers), while those in private rooms are $62-74 s or d ($68-82 for nonmembers).

$150-200

Oscar Wilde and P. T. Barnum both slept (not together) at the **Waverley Inn** (1266 Barrington St., 902/423-9346 or 800/565-9346, www.waverleyinn.com, $135-235 s, $175-235 d), which, at its completion in 1866, was one of the city's grandest residences. Rates for the 34 rooms include a cooked breakfast and wireless Internet, and tea, coffee, and snacks are offered all day and evening in the hospitality suite. Rooms are furnished with Victorian-era antiques, and deluxe rooms contain whirlpool tubs and feather beds. The least expensive single rooms are very small, while the deluxe twins are spacious and extravagantly luxurious.

★ **Cambridge Suites Hotel** (1583 Brunswick St., 902/420-0555 or 800/565-1263, www.cambridgesuiteshalifax.com, $185-235 s or d) is a modern, centrally located, all-suite hotel with 200 rooms. A few units are studios, but most have one or two separate bedrooms, and continental breakfast is included in the rates. Rooms are packed with amenities, including wireless Internet, beautiful bathrooms, lounge and work areas, and basic cooking facilities. The rooftop patio and a fitness center are pluses. Ask about rates that include free parking, full breakfast, and extras for traveling families.

★ **The Halliburton** (5184 Morris St., 902/420-0658 or 888/512-3344, www.thehalliburton.com, from $195 s or d) is a beautiful heritage property transformed into a boutique hotel. The 29 rooms come with super-comfortable beds topped with goose-down duvets and luxurious en suite bathrooms. Rates include continental breakfast, and wireless Internet is available throughout the building. The intimate in-house dining room, Stories, is open nightly (except Mon.) for dinner.

Halifax is home to two Delta properties. **Delta Barrington** (1875 Barrington St., 902/429-7410 or 888/236-2427, www.marriott.com, from $195 s or d) shares space with Barrington Place Mall in the historic area and has 200 comfortable rooms. Amenities include a fitness room, an indoor pool, a business center, a street-side café (with a summer seafood menu), and a lounge bar. Rack rates are around $190 s or d midweek and $160 on weekends. Nearby, the **Delta Halifax** (1990 Barrington St., 902/425-6700 or 888/236-2427, www.marriott.com, $195 s or d) was one of the city's first grande dame hotels, and the old girl's still a handsome dowager. A highlight is the lavish indoor pool complex, complete with whirlpools and a sauna as well as an adjacent fitness room.

$200-250

In any other Canadian capital, you'd pay a lot more for a room of similar standard as those at the full-service **Prince George Hotel** (1725 Market St., 902/425-1986 or 800/565-1567, www.princegeorgehotel.com, from $235 s or d), one block below the Halifax Citadel and seven blocks uphill from the harbor. The rooms feature contemporary furnishings, and amenities include a midsize indoor pool, a business center with Internet access, a restaurant, a lounge, and quiet public areas off the main lobby. Although rack rates start at over $200, check the website for weekend specials or upgrade to the Crown Service rooms for an extra $40.

Waverley Inn

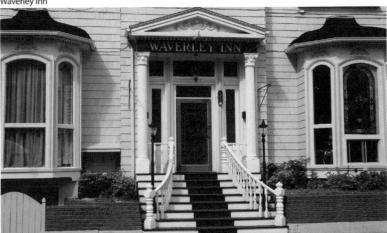

Part of the Casino Nova Scotia complex, **Marriott Harbourfront Hotel** (1919 Upper Water St., 902/421-1700 or 800/943-6760, www.marriott.com, $245 s or d) is a modern edifice designed to resemble the garrison that once occupied the waterfront. Although many guests are from Atlantic Canada and are staying especially to play the tables, the hotel is also a convenient choice for leisure travelers. In addition to the casino, there is an upscale restaurant with harbor views, a stylish English pub, and live entertainment. Almost no one pays rack rates; check the website for a world of options starting at $149 s or d.

Over $250

If you're after modern accommodations, consider **Four Points by Sheraton Halifax** (1496 Hollis St., 902/423-4444, www.fourpointshalifax.com, from $260 s or d), one block back from the harbor. The 177 guest rooms are filled with modern conveniences (free wireless Internet, 27-inch TVs, multiple phones, and well-designed work areas), while other facilities include an indoor pool and fitness room. Disregard the rack rates and book online, and you'll pay as little as $175 s or d, even in midsummer.

Opened in 1930 to coincide with the arrival of the first passenger trains to Halifax, the station's adjacent **Westin Nova Scotian** (1181 Hollis St., 902/421-1000 or 888/627-8553, www.thewestinnovascotian.com, from $285 s or d) has been extensively renovated throughout. Linked to the railway station—many guests are still rail passengers—it oozes old-world charm throughout the public areas (poke your head into the Atlantic Ballroom) and the 300 guest rooms. Amenities include a fine-dining restaurant featuring contemporary cooking, a fitness room, an indoor pool, spa services, and a shuttle to the central business district (one kilometer away).

CITADEL HILL AND VICINITY

The following accommodations are in the vicinity of Citadel Hill, from which it's downhill all the way to the harbor. Even the fittest visitors may not feel like tramping back up to the Citadel Hill area after a full day of sightseeing or a big meal at a downtown restaurant. No worries; a cab will cost around $7.

$50-100

A rambling old house directly opposite North Common has been renovated as **Fountain View Guest House** (2138 Robie

A big draw at the Prince George Hotel is the indoor pool.

St., between Williams St. and Compton Ave., 902/422-4169 or 800/565-4877, $35 s, $50 d), where the price is reflective of the rooms and services offered. The seven rooms share bathrooms, there is no kitchen or laundry, and parking is limited to what you can find on the street.

$100-150

Across North Common from Citadel Hill is the **Commons Inn** (5780 West St., 902/484-3466 or 877/797-7999, www.commonsinn.ca, $105-150 s or d), an older three-story building with 40 basic guest rooms. The rooms are on the small side, but they are smartly outfitted with comfortable beds, en suite bathrooms, free local calls, cable TV, and wireless Internet. The spacious suite, complete with a separate sitting area and jetted tub, is an excellent value. Other pluses are free parking, two rooftop patios, and a continental breakfast buffet.

$200-250

The grandiose ★ **Lord Nelson Hotel** (1515 S. Park St., 902/423-5130 or 800/565-2020, www.lordnelsonhotel.com, from $215 s or d) presides over a busy Spring Garden Road intersection and overlooks the famous Public Gardens. Originally opened in 1928, the Lord Nelson underwent a transformation in the late 1990s, reopening as one of the city's finest hotels. It is probably a little too far for some to walk to and from downtown, but location aside, it is one of Halifax's best and best-value accommodations. Beyond the extravagant marble-floored lobby are 260 elegantly furnished rooms, each with a large bathroom, wireless Internet access, a coffeemaker, and an iron. Other amenities include a fitness room, a restaurant and English-style pub, and room service. Parking is $18 per night. Check the website for specials under the "Our Packages" link.

BEDFORD HIGHWAY

Running along the western edge of the Bedford Basin, the Bedford Highway (Highway 2) is the original route north from downtown to the airport and beyond. A few motels from pre-bypass days exist, providing inexpensive accommodations a 10-minute (or quicker) drive from the city center. If you make this part of the city your base, you'll need a vehicle or be prepared to ride transit buses. To get there from the north, take Exit 3 from Highway 102 and follow the signs toward downtown.

$50-100

Nestled in wooded grounds on the harbor side of the Bedford Highway is the **Travelers Motel** (773 Bedford Hwy., 902/835-3367 or 800/565-3367, www.travelersmotel.ca, $85-125). It is a classic 1950s park-at-the-door roadside motel, where rates start at $89 for smallish rooms with dated decor, cable TVs, and phones. Summer-only cabins with TV but no phones are $60-95 s or d. This place is surprisingly busy, so you'll need reservations in summer.

Over the rise toward the city, opposite a busy diner of the same name, is the **Esquire Motel** (771 Bedford Hwy., 902/835-3367 or 800/565-3367, www.esquiremotel.ca, $85-155 s or d). Amenities are similar to its neighbor, the cheaper Travelers Motel, with the only real difference being a small outdoor pool and free local calls. Outside of summer, rates drop as low as $75.

NEAR THE AIRPORT

From the airport, it's only 40 minutes to downtown on the Airporter. Here are a few options just in case you must stay in the vicinity.

$100-150

Across the highway from the airport and linked by free shuttle is the **Quality Inn Halifax Airport Hotel** (60 Sky Blvd., 902/873-3000 or 800/667-3333, www.airporthotelhalifax.com, $130 s or d), which has regularly revamped rooms, indoor and outdoor pools, wireless Internet, a fitness room, and a restaurant where guests enjoy complimentary breakfast.

The ALT Hotel is at the airport.

★ **ALT Hotel** (40 Silver Dart Dr., 902/334-0136 or 855/258-5775, www.althotels.ca, $154 s or d) is a no-frills hotel located right at the airport. The rooms are simply decorated in a modern chic theme, while downstairs is a café filled with "grab and go" meals, and a smallish indoor pool. There's no room service or valet parking; in return there are no seasonal price adjustments.

$150-200

Four kilometers south of the airport, **Hilton Garden Inn** (200 Pratt & Whitney Dr., Enfield, 902/873-1400, www.hilton.com, from $199 s or d) offers 24-hour shuttle service for guests. It's a newer property with a high standard of guest rooms, as well as a restaurant and a fitness room.

About halfway between the airport and downtown is **Inn on the Lake** (3009 Hwy. 2, Fall River, 902/861-3480 or 800/463-6465, www.innonthelake.com, from $179 s or d), which is a full-blown resort, complete with multiple dining rooms, recreational opportunities spread over two hectares of landscaped lakefront, and even a sandy beach.

FISHERMAN'S COVE

If you don't need to be right downtown, consider the following oceanfront accommodation—it's both an excellent value and a world away from the bustle of the city.

$100-150

Overlooking the historic fishing village, the ★ **Inn at Fisherman's Cove** (1531 Shore Rd., Eastern Passage, 902/465-3455 or 866/725-3455, www.theinnatfishermanscove.com, $115-165 s or d) is a modern three-story building with its own private dock on the "crick" that has been chock-full of fishing boats for more than 200 years. Each room has an en suite bathroom and TV, while downstairs is a breakfast room that opens to the dock. Four of the eight guest rooms face the water and have private balconies. Rates include a light breakfast.

CAMPGROUNDS

A few commercial campgrounds lie within a 30-minute drive of downtown. Farther out are two provincial parks that offer camping without hookups.

Dartmouth

The closest camping to downtown is at ★ **Shubie Park Campground** (Jaybee Dr., Dartmouth, 902/435-8328, www.shubiecampground.com, mid-May-mid-Oct., tents $35, hookups $40-55). Facilities such as washrooms are clean and modern, while wireless Internet access and colorful landscaping add to the appeal. The adjacent beach on Lake Charles comes with supervised swimming, and the campground is linked to walking trails along the Shubenacadie Canal. On the downside, sites offer little privacy.

West

Woodhaven RV Park (1757 Hammonds Plains Rd., 902/835-2271, www.woodhaven-rvpark.com, May-mid-Oct., $30-48) is 18 kilometers southwest from downtown and handy for an early morning start out to the South Shore. Facilities include 200 sites, coin-operated showers, two launderettes, a swimming pool, a playground, a games room, and wireless Internet access.

Halifax West KOA (3070 Hwy. 1, Upper Sackville, 902/865-4342, www.koa.com, mid-May-mid-Oct., campsites $36-58, cabins with shared bathrooms $68) is northwest of the city, farther out than Woodhaven and a 45-minute drive from downtown.

North

Laurie Provincial Park (coming from the north, take Exit 7 south to Highway 2, mid-June-early September, $27) lies on the southern shore of Grand Lake. Here, 71 sites are spread around a tree-lined loop. Each site has a picnic table and fire pit, while park amenities include toilets, a short walking trail, and a day-use area, but no showers or hookups.

Dollar Lake Provincial Park (mid-June-mid-Oct., $27) is farther from the city than Laurie Provincial Park, but it has showers and a concession, as well as a nicer beach, with swimming, boating, walking trails, and a playground. Sites are spread around three loops, with Loop A closest to the water.

Information and Services

For information on Halifax, contact **Destination Halifax** (902/422-9334 or 877/422-9334, www.destinationhalifax.com). The **Halifax Regional Municipality** website (www.halifax.ca) has general information about the city, such as festivals and events, transportation, and park programs.

TOURIST INFORMATION
Downtown

Tourism Nova Scotia (1655 Lower Water St., 902/424-4248, daily 8:30am-6pm) operates an information center along the downtown waterfront at Sackville Landing. Its shelves are filled with province-wide information, so this is the place to get help planning your travels beyond the capital.

Airport

After retrieving your bags from the luggage carousels, you'll pass right by the **Airport Visitor Information Centre** (902/873-1223, daily 9am-9pm), which is a provincially operated facility. Most questions thrown its way relate to Halifax, but the center represents the entire province.

EMERGENCY SERVICES

The city's hospital services are coordinated under the auspices of the **Queen Elizabeth II Hospital** (1796 Summer St., 902/473-3383).

Municipal **police** are assigned to Halifax and Dartmouth; in emergencies, dial 911, and for nonemergency business, call 902/490-5026. The **Royal Canadian Mounted Police (RCMP)** can be reached by calling 911 or 902/426-1323.

ACCESS FOR TRAVELERS WITH DISABILITIES

The good news about Halifax is that its major attractions, as well as a small percentage of rooms in most major hotels, are wheelchair-accessible. Theaters and performing arts venues are also usually wheelchair-accessible. Halifax's public transit system, Metro Transit, has low-floor buses along all major routes as well as the **Access-A-Bus** program, providing wheelchair-accessible transportation on a door-to-door basis. Register at 902/490-6681.

BANKS

As Nova Scotia's capital, Halifax has banks by the dozens. **Scotiabank** (Mon.-Fri. 10am-5pm) has branches throughout the city and does not charge to convert foreign currency to Canadian dollars. The fee for cashing travelers checks is $2, so it pays to convert several checks at one time.

Hotel desks also exchange currency, but rates are more favorable at the banks.

Getting There

CAR

From Truro, it's 100 kilometers (a one-hour drive) south to Halifax along wide, divided Highway 102. From Digby, the 230-kilometer drive takes under three hours along Highway 101, which enters Halifax from the northwest. If you are planning on catching the ferry from Maine to Yarmouth, it is 310 kilometers north along the South Shore (Highway 103) to Halifax (allow four hours). From Sydney, on Cape Breton Island, it's an easy five-hour drive to cover the 408 kilometers south to Halifax.

From other Canadian provinces, you will enter Nova Scotia along the TransCanada Highway east of Sackville. From Sackville, it's around 200 kilometers (two hours) into downtown Halifax via Truro. From Charlottetown, on Prince Edward Island, allow four hours for the 330-kilometer drive to Halifax via the Confederation Bridge ($46 toll).

It's 260 kilometers (three hours) to Halifax from Moncton along Highway 104 then 102. It's 410 kilometers (4.5 hours) from Saint John on Highway 1 then 104 and 102; the alternative to driving around the Bay of Fundy is to catch the Saint John-Digby ferry, although this takes longer and is more expensive. It's 430 kilometers (4.5 hours) from Fredericton on Highways 2, 104, and 102. It's 1,230 kilometers (12 hours) from Montreal on the TransCanada Highway. It's 1,800 kilometers (18 hours) from Toronto on the TransCanada Highway.

From the United States, you can either travel up I-95 through Bangor, Maine, to New Brunswick via Moncton (480 kilometers, 4.5 hours) or catch the ferry from Portland, Maine, to Yarmouth (11 hours sailing time, adult $139, vehicle $119, children free), from where it's 310 kilometers (four-hour drive) to Halifax along Highway 103.

AIR

Halifax International Airport (YHZ, www.flyhalifax.com) is beside Highway 102, 38 kilometers north of Halifax. It is Atlantic Canada's busiest airport, handling more than 3.7 million passengers annually.

Beyond the baggage carousels are the car rental desks and an information counter specifically for helping out with airport transportation. The arrivals area is linked to the rest of the terminal by a short concourse. In between is the main concentration of food and retail shops, including a currency exchange (daily 7am-9pm); **Clearwater Seafood** (902/873-4509, daily 5am-8pm), which plucks live lobsters from a tank and packs them for air travel; a bookstore; and a variety of locally themed souvenir shops. There are also a play area and wireless Internet hotspots.

The airport's website has lots of information about the airport itself, as well as general travel-planning information and a nifty virtual flight map that tracks flights in real time as they arrive and depart from Halifax.

Airport Transportation

The **Halifax Airport Express** (902/429-2029, www.maritimebus.com/halifax-airport-shuttle) runs between the airport and major downtown hotels ($22 one-way, $40 return) at least once every hour between 5am and 1am. You need reservations only when returning to the airport from your hotel.

Taxi and limousine services are available curbside in the domestic arrivals area for all arriving flights. A one-way trip to Halifax city center is $56 by taxi or limousine.

Airport Car Rental

Once you've picked up your bags from the baggage carousels, you'll find a row of check-in desks for major car rental companies immediately behind you. Airport phone numbers are **Avis** (902/429-0963), **Budget** (902/492-7553), **Enterprise** (902/873-4700), **Hertz** (902/873-2273), **National/Alamo** (902/873-3505), and **Thrifty** (902/873-3527).

Along the airport access road is a **Petro Canada** gas station, so you can avoid outrageous charges for not returning the vehicle with a full tank of gas.

Parking

Short-term covered airport parking within walking distance of the terminal costs $6 per hour, to a maximum of $21 per day and $105 per week. For long-term parking, nearby **Park 'N Fly** (668 Barnes Dr., 902/873-4574, www. parknfly.ca) charges $15 per day and $75 per week, inclusive of a free ride to and from the airport. (Check the Park'N Fly website for a discount coupon.)

RAIL

Halifax is served by **VIA Rail** (416/366-8411 or 888/842-7245, www.viarail.ca) passenger trains from Montréal (22-24 hours, $175 pp). Trains run up to three times a week.

The **VIA Rail Station** is one kilometer south of downtown at the corner of Barrington and Cornwallis Streets. It's a classic old terminal with a colonnaded facade, high ceiling, and tiled floors, but it is only ever busy when a train rolls in. **Hertz** has a desk at the terminal, and a concourse links the terminal to the grand Westin hotel.

BUS

Long-distance bus services arrive and depart from the **VIA Rail Station** (corner of Barrington and Cornwallis Sts.), one kilometer south of downtown and within walking distance of HI-Halifax. The main carrier is **Maritime Bus** (902/429-2029, www.maritimebus.com), which has departures from Halifax to points throughout the province and beyond, including daily service to Wolfville (1.5 hours, $22), Moncton (4 hours, $54), and Sydney (7 hours, $78). Maritime runs as far as Québec, from where connections can be made to Greyhound buses.

Getting Around

PUBLIC TRANSPORTATION

Metro Transit (902/490-4000, www.halifax.ca/metrotransit) buses saturate city streets; charge adult $2.50, senior and child $1.75 (exact change only) with free transfers; and operate daily 6am-midnight. Main bus stops are on Water, Barrington, Cornwallis, Cogswell, and Duke Streets, Spring Garden Road, and Gottingen Street, with service to Quinpool Road and Bayers Street. If you're at a stop waiting for a bus, dial 465 followed by the four-digit route number (marked in red at every stop) for real-time information on when the next bus will be arriving.

Ferries

Metro Transit runs the **Halifax-Dartmouth ferry** from the foot of George Street (beside Historic Properties) to Alderney Drive in Dartmouth. It is the oldest saltwater passenger service in North America, having transported its first passengers by rowboat more than 200 years ago. Today, three modern vessels ply the route in just 12 minutes. The service runs year-round Monday-Saturday 6:30am-midnight, and June-September also on Sunday 6:30am-midnight. The one-way fare is the same as by bus—adult $2.50, senior and child $1.75.

Taxi

Cabs are easiest to flag outside major hotels or transportation hubs, such as the VIA Rail Station. All rides start at $3.50, with an additional $2.65 charged for each kilometer plus $0.60 for each additional person. Taxi fares within downtown usually run around $10, while the trip between the airport and downtown is set at $53. The two main companies are **Casino Taxi** (902/429-6666) and **Yellow Cab** (902/420-0000).

DRIVING

Getting into the city is made easy by a number of major arteries that spill right into downtown. Once in the commercial core, Haligonians are painstakingly careful and slow drivers—a wise way to go, as hillside streets are steep and many roads are posted for one-way traffic. Pedestrians have the right-of-way on crosswalks. Two **bridges** link Halifax and Dartmouth, the A. Murray MacKay and the Angus L. MacDonald; the toll is $1 one-way for vehicles, free for bicyclists and pedestrians.

Downtown Parking

Metered parking costs $1.50-2 per hour but is difficult to find during business hours. Most major hotels have underground public parking, and a few multistory parking lots are scattered throughout the city core. The most convenient parking lots are along Lower Water Street, at the foot of Prince and Salter Streets, but these are also the most costly ($5 per hour). If you're staying at a downtown hotel, expect to pay up to $24 per day for parking (ask about free parking for weekend reservations).

Car Rental

Each of the major car rental companies is represented at the airport and downtown. As always, book as far in advance as possible, and use the Internet to find the best deals. Vehicles rented from downtown are generally the same price as out at the airport, but the final bill comes with fewer taxes.

South Shore

Nova Scotians must have had this region in mind when they coined the province's motto, "So Much to Sea."

The crashing Atlantic lays itself out in foaming breakers along the deeply scored Atlantic coastline that extends from Lunenburg to Yarmouth. It's a three-hour drive between these two towns, but you'll want at least two days and preferably more to explore the hidden corners of this quintessential corner of Nova Scotia. The seaports and towns follow one another, like a series of glossy, life-size picture postcards. There are those that outsiders will know by name—Peggy's Cove, Mahone Bay, and Lunenburg—but one of the joys of touring the South Shore is discovering your own Peggy's Cove.

The South Shore ends at Yarmouth, where the Atlantic meets the Bay of Fundy. Locals say the Vikings came ashore a thousand years ago and inscribed the boulder that now sits at the Yarmouth County Museum's front door. Yarmouth's ragged coastline impressed early explorer Samuel de Champlain, who named the seaport's outermost peninsula Cap Forchu ("Forked Cape"). Like the Vikings, Champlain arrived and departed, as do thousands of visitors driving around the South Shore.

PLANNING YOUR TIME

It is possible to visit the best-known towns along this stretch of coast in a day and return to Halifax, but don't. More realistically, plan a day in each place that interests you. As elsewhere in Nova Scotia, dining at its best is superb, and the region's specialty is its abundance of top-notch country inns with public dining rooms. Many lodgings are in historic houses and mansions converted to country inns and in categories best described as better, best, and beautiful. But it is the towns themselves that are this region's highlight. Even with just one week to explore the entire province, plan to spend at least one night in **Mahone Bay** or **Lunenburg,** the former recognized for its three waterfront churches and the latter a UNESCO World Heritage Site. While the detour to **Peggy's Cove** is almost de rigueur, you should work into your itinerary less publicized villages, such as **Blue Rocks,** near Lunenburg. Taking part in one of the highlights of the South Shore involves some planning—a sailing trip on the *Bluenose II* requires searching out the boat's schedule and making reservations well in advance.

Previous: Peggy's Cove; Blue Rocks. **Above:** Fisheries Museum of the Atlantic.

Highlights

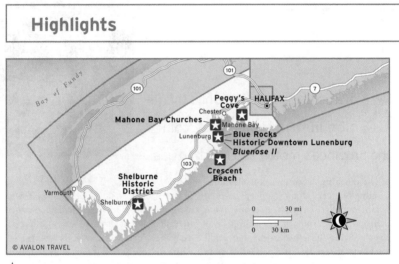

© AVALON TRAVEL

★ **Peggy's Cove:** Nova Scotia's most famous village is a photogenic gem you won't want to miss (page 66).

★ **Mahone Bay Churches:** Lining up along the waterfront, three historic churches reflect across the waters of charming Mahone Bay (page 71).

★ **Historic Downtown Lunenburg:** Designated a World Heritage Site by UNESCO, Lunenburg is as interesting as it is charming (page 76).

★ **Blue Rocks:** A world away from the crowds of Peggy's Cove, this picture-perfect

fishing village clings to the shore of a rocky harbor (page 77).

★ *Bluenose II:* Lunenburg is a wooden-ships kind of town, and what better way to tour the harbor than aboard one (page 78)?

★ **Crescent Beach:** Just a short detour from the busy South Shore highway, this is my favorite beach among many choices south of Halifax (page 84).

★ **Shelburne Historic District:** A wonderful collection of 200-year-old wooden buildings brings the shipbuilding era to life (page 88).

South Shore

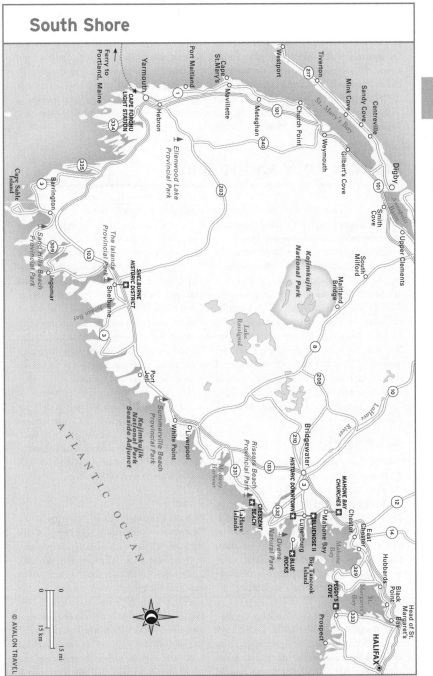

ATLANTIC OCEAN

© AVALON TRAVEL

Ferry to
Portland, Maine

Yarmouth
CAPE FORCHU
LIGHT STATION
Hebron
Port Maitland
Cape
St. Mary's
Mavillette
Meteghan
Church Point
Weymouth
Gilbert's Cove
Smith
Cove
South
Milford
Upper Clements
Digby
Westport
Tiverton
Mink Cove
Sandy Cove
Centreville
St. Mary's Bay

Ellenwood Lake
Provincial Park

Cape Sable
Island
Barrington
Ingomar
Sand Hills Beach
Provincial Park

The Islands
Provincial Park
SHELBURNE
HISTORIC DISTRICT
Shelburne

Jordan Bay

Port
Joli
Summerville Beach
Provincial Park
White Point
Liverpool
Kejimkujik
National Park
Seaside Adjunct

Medway Harbour

Kejimkujik
National Park

Lake
Rossignol

Maitland
Bridge

LaHave
River

Bridgewater
HISTORIC DOWNTOWN
Risser's Beach
Provincial Park
LaHave
Islands
CRESCENT
BEACH
Ovens
Natural Park
BLUE
ROCKS
Lunenburg
BLUENOSE II
Mahone Bay
MAHONE BAY
CHURCHES
Big Tancook
Island
Chester
East
Chester
Hubbards
Black
Point
Head of St.
Margaret's
Bay
PEGGY'S
COVE
Prospect
HALIFAX

Mahone
Bay

St.
Margaret's
Bay

0   15 km
0   15 mi

Travelers on a tight schedule make Lunenburg a turnaround point, but the rest of the South Shore is well worth exploring and sets you up for exploring the Fundy Coast. This stretch of coast is dotted with coastal provincial parks and hideaways such as **Crescent Beach,** which is a long stretch of white sand. The major historic attraction between Lunenburg and Yarmouth is the **Shelburne Historic District.** If you are planning to circumnavigate southwestern Nova Scotia, Shelburne is an ideal location for an overnight stay. Couple that with a night in Lunenburg or Mahone Bay to give yourself three days for the South Shore—not enough time to see everything, but a chance to spend quality time visiting each of the highlights.

Halifax to Mahone Bay

From downtown Halifax, it's 105 kilometers (1.5 hours) along Highway 103 to Lunenburg, but for the most scenic views and interesting insights, forget the expressway and drive the secondary coastal routes. The best-known village in all of Nova Scotia is Peggy's Cove, a 40-minute drive southwest from downtown Halifax along Highway 333. Meanwhile, Highway 103 takes a direct route across to St. Margaret's Bay, from where secondary Highway 3 passes the charming towns set around Mahone Bay and its islands. One of these, Oak Island, looms large in the world of treasure-hunting legends—pirates are believed to have buried incalculable booty on it in the 1500s.

★ PEGGY'S COVE

Atlantic Canada's most photographed site is a 40-minute drive southwest from Halifax, and the place is everything its fans say it is. With the houses of the tiny fishing village clinging like mussels to weathered granite boulders at the edge of St. Margaret's Bay, the Atlantic lathering against the boulder-bound coast, the fishing boats moored in the small cove, and the white octagonal lighthouse overlooking it all, the scene is the quintessence of the Nova Scotia coast.

Sightseers clog the village during the daytime (to miss the worst of the crowds, get there before 9am or after 5pm), wandering along the wharves and around the weathered granite boulders surrounding the photogenic lighthouse. Peggy's Cove has a population of just 60 souls, so don't come expecting the services of a tourist town. The village has just one B&B, a restaurant, and the **deGarthe Gallery** (109 Peggy's Point Rd., 902/823-2256, May-Oct. daily 9am-5pm, free). The latter, along the main road through town, displays the work of Finnish-born artist William deGarthe, whose stunning nautically themed oil paintings grace galleries the world over. Behind the gallery, deGarthe sculpted a 30-meter-long frieze on a granite outcropping. It depicts 32 of the seaside village's fishermen and families.

The town received worldwide attention in September 1998, when a Swissair MD-11 jetliner bound from New York City to Geneva crashed in shallow waters off the coast here, killing all 229 people aboard. A small memorial overlooks the ocean along Highway 333, two kilometers west of the village.

Food

The road through the village ends at the **Sou'wester Restaurant** (178 Peggy's Point Rd., 902/823-2561, June-Aug. daily 8am-8:30pm, Sept.-May daily 9am-8pm, $12-28), a cavernous room with a menu designed to appeal to the tourist crowd. And as the only place in town to eat, attract them it does—try to plan your meal before 10am or after 5pm. The menu does have a distinct maritime flavor, with dishes such as fish cakes, pickled beets, and eggs offered in the morning. The rest of the day, seafood continues to dominate,

Halifax to Mahone Bay

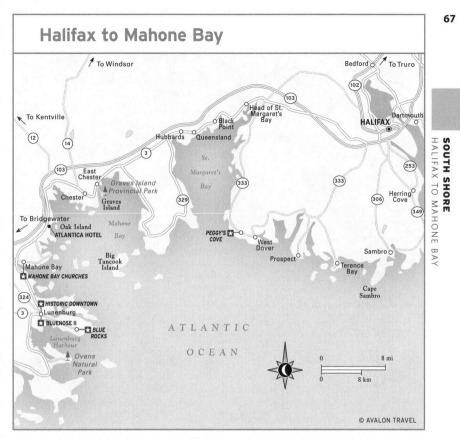

To Windsor
Bedford
To Truro
102
103
Head of St.
Margaret's
Bay
To Kentville
Black
Point
Dartmouth
HALIFAX
Hubbards
Queensland
12
14
253
3
St.
103
East
Chester
Margaret's
333
333
Bay
Graves Island
Provincial Park
329
Herring
Cove
306
Chester
Graves
Island
349
To Bridgewater
Mahone
Oak Island
ATLANTICA HOTEL
Bay
**PEGGY'S
COVE**
West
Dover
Sambro
Big
Tancook
Island
Prospect
Mahone Bay
Terence
Bay
MAHONE BAY CHURCHES
Cape
Sambro
324
HISTORIC DOWNTOWN
3
Lunenburg
A T L A N T I C
BLUENOSE II
**BLUE
ROCKS**
*Lunenburg
Harbour*
O C E A N
0   8 mi
Ovens
Natural
Park
0   8 km

© AVALON TRAVEL

with haddock and chips for $15 and a full lobster supper under $30.

Accommodations

The only accommodation has just five guest rooms, so book well ahead if you'd like to stay overnight in this delightful village. At the head of the actual cove, ★ **Peggy's Cove Bed and Breakfast** (17 Church Rd., 902/823-2265 or 877/725-8732, www.peggyscovebb.com, Apr.-Oct., $155 s or d including breakfast) has well-furnished guest rooms with wireless Internet, a living area, a dining room, and a deck promising magnificent views across the cove.

Getting There

Peggy's Cove is about 45 kilometers southwest of Halifax on Highway 333. The drive takes about 40 minutes.

PEGGY'S COVE TO CHESTER

Highway 333 beyond Peggy's Cove winds north past a string of small fishing villages before reaching Highway 3 (Highway 103, the divided highway along the South Shore, takes an inland route, so turn at the older Highway 3). Rather than promising places at which you simply must stop, this route that lazily rounds St. Margaret's Bay is simply an enjoyable drive.

Continue west to **Hubbards,** where the ★ **Trellis Café** (22 Main St., 902/857-1188, daily 8am-9pm, $18-29) is a casual restaurant with colorful decor and

Chester

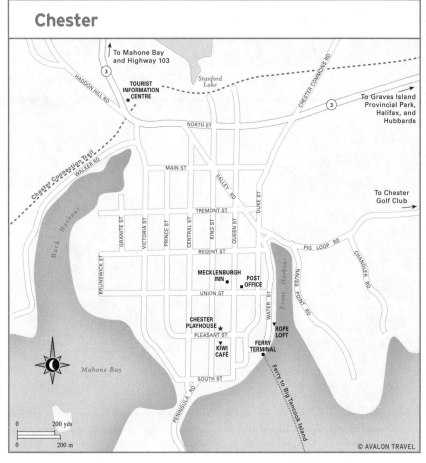

occasional live entertainment on weekends. The namesake trellised deck is a good spot on warmer days. The morning starts out with great coffee and above-average breakfasts that include local specialties such as fish cakes. Lunch choices such as a lobster roll and a vegetarian coconut curry are all under $20. Dinner mains are generally less than $25, but you can spend less by ordering a combination of starters, such as seafood chowder and Caesar salad.

Beyond Hubbards, **Queensland Beach** is a popular stretch of sand with safe but chilly swimming and a freshwater lagoon that attracts lots of birdlife.

CHESTER AND VICINITY

The bayside town of Chester, first settled by New Englanders in 1759, lies at the northern head of Mahone Bay. Its first hotel was built in 1827, and the town, with its ideal sailing conditions and many vacation homes, has been a popular summer retreat ever since. Getting oriented beyond the downtown core can be confusing, so start your visit at the **Tourist Information Centre** (20 Smith Rd., 902/275-4616, May-early Oct. daily 10am-5pm), which is in a 1905 railway station on the Mahone Bay side of town (coming into town from Halifax, continue up the hill to the right of the downtown turnoff).

Broadway-style revues, comedy improv, puppet shows, and children's programs.

Food

In downtown Chester, the **Kiwi Café** (19 Pleasant St., 902/275-1492, daily 8am-5pm, lunches $8-25) offers simple and healthy breakfasts and lunches along with a wide range of hot drinks, including chai tea and creamy hot chocolate; the lobster and haddock chowder is a lunchtime highlight. It's painted a cheery blue and kiwifruit green, with outside tables down one side.

The combination of excellent haddock chowder and stunning water views make **Rope Loft** (36 Water St., 902/275-3430, daily 11:30am-10pm, $14-30) the best choice in town for dinner. Housed in a 200-year-old waterfront building, the Rope Loft has a downstairs pub, but it is the upstairs restaurant with its wide deck that is the best place to dine. Beyond the chowder, expect the usual array of seafood and burger choices.

Accommodations and Camping

The most noteworthy of Chester's inns is ★ **Mecklenburgh Inn** (78 Queen St., 902/275-4638, www.mecklenburghinn.ca, May-Dec., $115-155 s, $125-155 d), a 120-year-old sea captain's home that has been given a bohemian-chic look. Guests tend to gather on the wide veranda to watch the world of Chester go by, and then, after dinner at a local restaurant, gravitate to the comfortable couches set around two fireplaces in the living room. Three of the four rooms have en suite bathrooms with claw-foot tubs, while the fourth has a private bathroom down the hall. A big breakfast of pancakes or smoked salmon eggs Benedict will set you up for a day of sightseeing.

Signposted from Highway 3, three kilometers northeast of Chester, **Graves Island Provincial Park** (mid-May-mid-Sept., $29) covers a small island connected to the mainland by a causeway. An open

The bright and cheery Kiwi Café is a great place for a light meal in Chester.

Recreation and Entertainment

Most visitors to Chester are content to browse through downtown shops and wander lazily along the Front Harbour waterfront.

An easy excursion is to **Big Tancook Island** (adult $6 round-trip, cash only) via ferries departing regularly from Front Harbour. Big Tancook is mostly residential, but it's a pleasant trip across, and walking paths lace the island.

Dating to 1914, **Chester Golf Club** (Golf Course Rd., Prescott Point, 902/275-4543) is an old-style golf course that opens up along the oceanfront to offer sweeping views on holes lapped by the water. Greens fees are a good value at $68.

Chester Playhouse (22 Pleasant St., 902/275-3933 or 800/363-7529, www.chesterplayhouse.ca) hosts some form of live entertainment weekly between March and December. Its Summer Theatre Festival draws professional talents in July and August. Past seasons have included musicals, area at a high point of the island allows for pull-through RVs, while tent sites are scattered around the surrounding forest. If you're just visiting for the day, plan on a picnic at the waterfront day-use area just across the causeway.

Chester is just off Highway 103 (take Exit 8), about 70 kilometers (45 minutes) from Halifax. It's around 70 kilometers from Peggy's Cove via Highway 333 and Highway 103.

Mahone Bay

The town of Mahone Bay (pop. 1,000), on the island-speckled bay of the same name, is one of the most charming in all of Nova Scotia. The town's prosperous past is mirrored in its architecture, with Gothic Revival, Classic Revival, and Italianate styles in evidence. Many of these buildings have been converted to restaurants specializing in seafood and shops selling the work of local artisans. The distinctive bayside trio of 19th-century churches reflected in the still water here has become one of the most photographed scenes in Nova Scotia.

SIGHTS AND EVENTS

Most visitors to Mahone Bay are quite happy to spend their time admiring the architecture, browsing through the shops, and enjoying lunch at one of the many cafés. If you are interested in the town's architectural highlights, ask for the three walking-tour brochures at the museum.

Mahone Bay Museum

Inside a 150-year-old wooden house, the **Mahone Bay Museum** (578 Main St., 902/624-6263, http://mahonebaymuseum. com, June-Sept. daily 10am-4pm, donation) describes the town's 250-year history. One room is dedicated to settlement of the area in the mid-1700s by German, French, and Swiss Protestants and the story of how they were enticed by the British government's offer of free land, farm equipment, and a year's "victuals." You'll also learn about the importance of shipbuilding to the area, which thrived in a dozen

Mahone Bay's photogenic churches

Mahone Bay

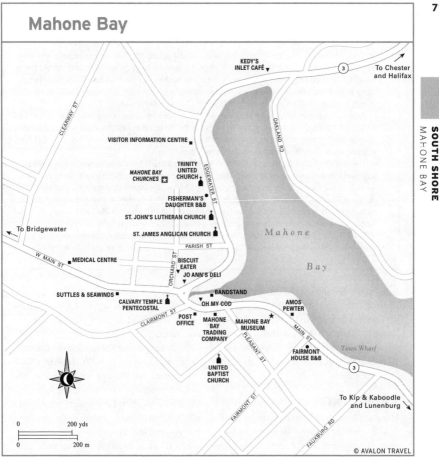

VISITOR INFORMATION CENTRE

MAHONE BAY CHURCHES

TRINITY UNITED CHURCH

FISHERMAN'S DAUGHTER B&B

ST. JOHN'S LUTHERAN CHURCH

ST. JAMES ANGLICAN CHURCH

KEDY'S INLET CAFÉ

To Chester and Halifax

OAKLAND RD

EDGEWATER ST

CLEARWAY ST

To Bridgewater

W MAIN ST

MEDICAL CENTRE

PARISH ST

ORCHARD ST

BISCUIT EATER

JO ANN'S DELI

Mahone Bay

SUTTLES & SEAWINDS

CALVARY TEMPLE PENTECOSTAL

CLAIRMONT ST

BANDSTAND

OH MY COD

POST OFFICE

MAHONE BAY TRADING COMPANY

MAHONE BAY MUSEUM

AMOS PEWTER

MAIN ST

PLEASANT ST

FAIRMONT HOUSE B&B

Town Wharf

UNITED BAPTIST CHURCH

FAIRMONT ST

To Kip & Kaboodle and Lunenburg

FAUXBURG RD

0   200 yds
0   200 m

© AVALON TRAVEL

shipyards from the 1850s to the early part of the 20th century, and you can admire historic arts and crafts.

★ Mahone Bay Churches

From the flower-bedecked bandstand on Main Street, three churches can be seen shoulder to shoulder across the water. The oldest (and farthest from this viewpoint) is the **Trinity United Church** (Edgewater St., 902/624-9287), which dates to 1861 and was dragged by oxen to its current site in 1885. **St. John's Lutheran** (Edgewater St., 902/624-9660) is a symmetrical wooden structure standing in the middle of the three. Right on the corner is the Gothic Revival **St. James Anglican Church** (Edgewater St., 902/624-8614). This is the only one of the three open for tours (July-Aug. Thurs.-Sat. 11am-3pm).

Music at the Three Churches (www.threechurches.com, adult $20, child 12 and under free) is a series of classical music concerts hosted by the churches on select Friday nights through summer. Visit the website or check with the information center for a schedule and pay at the door.

If you walk along the waterfront beyond the information center, you'll see a different angle on the churches, as well as two others. Completed in 1875, the white spire you see

The Mystery of Oak Island

In 1795, on Oak Island, a small island in Mahone Bay, a young man came upon an area where the forest had been cut away. Besides the stumps, he found a large forked limb with an old tackle block and a "treenail," and the ground nearby was sunken in a pit. His first thought would have been buried treasure, as the bay was a known haunt for pirates such as "Captain" William Kidd, Sir Henry Morgan, and Edward "Blackbeard" Teach 100 years previously.

After hours of digging, Daniel McGinnis and two farmer friends reached a depth of 10 feet and hit wood. It turned out, however, not to be the rotted lid of a treasure chest but rather a platform of logs. So the men pressed on, convinced that the treasure lay just below. At a depth of 25 feet, digging became difficult, and they abandoned the effort.

The first organized dig occurred in 1804, when a boat loaded with equipment arrived. Another log platform was uncovered at the 30-foot level, and others 40 and then 50 feet from the surface. At 60 feet, the men uncovered a layer of coconut fiber, which hinted at cargo from warmer climes. At the 90-foot level, a large slab of granite (which was later verified as being from Europe) was uncovered. The next morning, the men returned to the pit to find it had filled with water. They had no success pumping the water out, so the search was halted until the following spring.

In 1805 a second shaft was dug, and at the 100-foot mark a horizontal tunnel was dug in the hope of reaching the treasure, but this search too was abandoned. It would be another 40 years

rising above the trees is the **United Baptist Church** (56 Maple St., 902/624-9124), open for services Sunday at 11am. The **Calvary Temple Pentecostal** (at the traffic circle where Main and Edgewater Sts. meet, 902/624-8420) opens its doors Sunday at 7pm for hymn singing.

SHOPPING

Many artists are attracted to Mahone Bay for its scenic setting, and the main street has developed into a hub for shoppers. Most shops are open late spring-Christmas.

At **Amos Pewter** (589 Main St., 902/624-9547, summer Mon.-Sat. 9am-7pm, Sun. 10am-7pm, shorter hours and closed Sun. the rest of the year), you can watch artists at work as they cast, spin, and finish pewter pieces. Tea connoisseurs will be in their element at the **Tea Brewery** (525 Main St., 902/624-0566, Mon.-Fri. 10am-5:30 pm, Sat.-Sun. 11am-5:30pm), while up the hill from the Tea Brewery, **Suttles and Seawinds** (466 Main St., 902/624-8375, Mon.-Sat. 10am-5:30pm, Sun. 11am-5pm) sells stylish but colorful clothing.

FOOD

Mahone Bay's main street has a smattering of cafés, but most close in the late afternoon.

With a bag of carrots serving as a counterweight on the front door, ★ **Jo Ann's Deli** (9 Edgewater St., 902/624-6305, late May-late Oct. daily 9am-7pm) is a welcoming food shop filled with goodies. Locals come for organic produce, but everyone comes out with something—gourmet sandwiches, filled bagels, oatmeal cakes, brownies, homemade jams and preserves, ice cream, and more. If you're planning a picnic, this is the place to get everything together.

Away from the main street but worth the effort to find is the **Biscuit Eater** (16 Orchard St., 902/624-2665, Wed.-Mon. 9:30am-4pm, lunches $7-12), ensconced in a renovated 1775 residence (Mahone Bay's oldest building) and with a quiet patio surrounded by greenery. Lots of local ingredients and seasonal produce are used in a menu that ranges from a traditional ploughman's platter to creative sandwiches such as bacon, avocado, blue cheese, and fried egg on a ciabatta bun.

Oh My Cod (567 Main St., 902/531-2600, daily 8am-8pm, $12-18) is in the before the next serious attempt was made to retrieve whatever lay deep below Oak Island. While the secondary shafts filled with water only when linked to the original pit, it was noted that the level of water in all three shafts rose and fell with the tide. This deepened the mystery even further, but what the men found next amazed everyone present. Along the adjacent bay, just below the low-tide mark, were five drains that, it was later found, converged on a single tunnel. While it was understood that this simple man-made flooding system had been put in place after the treasure pit had been dug, this didn't help solve the mystery. Nor did it help the next round of investors, who spent the summer of 1863 in a futile attempt to reach below the 100-foot level, or the numerous other treasure seekers who attempted to get to the bottom of the pit during the next 140 years.

The saga has cost six lives, left many investors broke, and created numerous feuds between island property owners. Two treasure hunters, Dan Blankenship and Fred Nolan, spent a combined 100 years trying to outsmart those who designed the "Money Pit" many centuries ago. In 2005, Blankenship, who had sole road access to the island via a causeway, sold his share of the island to the government of Nova Scotia in the hopes that it would be opened to tourism. Incredibly, one of the world's great mysteries and longest treasure hunts continues to this day.

heart of the tourist precinct, and the food is surprisingly good at reasonable prices. The fish-and-chips comes with your choice of cod or haddock, while other options include a huge bowl of seafood chowder (that includes lobster), mussels by the pound, and scallop skewers. You can dine inside, but if the weather is nice, choose one of the two outside decks—one facing the street is good for people-watching while the other overlooks the water.

More of a restaurant than a café, ★ **Kedy's Inlet Cafe** (249 Edgewater St., 902/531-3030, Mon.-Thurs. 11:30am-3pm, Fri.-Sun. 11:30am-8pm, $11-27) sits at the head of the bay, a 10-minute waterfront walk from downtown, with a classic view of all five Mahone Bay churches. Tables are set out on a stone patio, perfect for warmer weather. Most mains are under $20, including almond-crusted salmon and a wide range of pastas. Leave room for a slice of the delicious mud cake.

ACCOMMODATIONS

Through summer, especially on weekends, demand is high for a limited number of rooms, so plan accordingly and book as far in advance as possible.

$50-100

Mahone Bay is home to one of Nova Scotia's only privately operated backpacker lodges, ★ **Kip and Kaboodle** (9466 Hwy. 3, Mader's Cove, 902/531-5494 or 866/549-4522, www.kiwikaboodle.com, dorms $30, $69 s or d), which is three kilometers from the center of town toward Lunenburg. It's small, with facilities to match, but everything is well maintained, including a communal kitchen, living area, and outdoor pool. Other amenities include a barbecue and wireless Internet access. Rates include linens and a light breakfast.

$100-200

Opposite the town wharf, you can sit on the veranda of **Fairmont House B&B** (654 Main St., 902/624-8089, www.fairmonthouse. com, $115-175 s or d) and watch the world of Mahone Bay go by. A local shipbuilder built this Gothic Revival home in 1857, and it was converted to a B&B in 1991. In the ensuing years, its exterior has been given a coat of stately blue paint, and three guest rooms have been outfitted in stylish colored themes. All rooms have en suite bathrooms, air-conditioning, and niceties such as hair dryers and irons. Downstairs is a library with board games and a TV. Rates include a continental breakfast.

Nestled amid the famous three churches is ★ **Fisherman's Daughter B&B** (97 Edgewater St., 902/624-0660, www.fishermans-daughter.com, $135-145 s or d). Built in 1840 by a local shipbuilder, the home is understated but shows a restrained Gothic Revival style. A couple of the four guest rooms have funky layouts (such as beds nestled under the eaves), but this adds to the charm. Throw in a host of modern amenities and a full breakfast to make this place an excellent choice.

A few kilometers north of Mahone Bay back toward Chester, **Atlantica Oak Island Resort** (off Hwy. 103 at 36 Treasure Dr., 800/565-5075, www.atlanticaoakisland.com, $179-350 s or d) is one of the province's only full-service resorts. Located right on the water and overlooking mystery-filled Oak Island, it offers indoor and outdoor pools, kayak rentals, boat tours, tennis courts, mini-golf, a children's program (summer only), and a restaurant with tables that spill out onto a huge ocean-facing deck. The main building holds standard guest rooms (some with balconies and ocean views), modern condos overlook the marina, and down a gravel road are two-bedroom cottages. The latter are right on the ocean, and each has a fire pit and picnic table out front.

INFORMATION AND SERVICES

The **Visitor Information Centre** (165 Edgewater St., 902/624-6151, summer Mon.-Sat. 9am-5pm, Sun. 11am-5pm) is in a small building just before you reach the first church.

GETTING THERE

Mahone Bay is about 30 kilometers (20 minutes) from Chester. You can get there via Highway 103 or Highway 3. From Halifax, follow Highway 103 to Exit 10. From there, Mahone Bay is a short drive south. Allow just over an hour for this 80-kilometer trip.

Atlantica Oak Island Resort

Lunenburg

Lunenburg (pop. 2,300) lies about equidistant between Halifax and Shelburne off Highway 103. Sited on a hilly peninsula between two harbors, this is one of the most attractive towns in Nova Scotia, with a wealth of beautiful homes painted in a crayon box of bold primary colors. In 1991, Lunenburg's Old Town was designated a national historic district, and in December 1995 the town received the ultimate honor when UNESCO designated it a World Heritage Site—one of only two cities in North America to enjoy that status (the other is Québec City). More recently, in 2005, the provincial government stepped in and bought a chunk of waterfront buildings and wharves, saving them from development that would have taken away from the town's well-preserved history.

History

To understand what the fuss is all about, you have to go back in time a couple of centuries. Protestant German, Swiss, and French immigrants, recruited by the British to help stabilize their new dominion, settled the town in 1753; their influence is still apparent in the town's architectural details. With its excellent harbor—a protected inner arm of the Atlantic embraced by two long, curving peninsulas—Lunenburg became one of Nova Scotia's premier fishing ports and shipbuilding centers in the 19th century. In 1921, the famous schooner *Bluenose* was built here. The 49-meter fishing vessel won the International Fisherman's Trophy race that same year, and for the next 18 years it remained the undefeated champion of the Atlantic fleets. The ship has become the proud symbol of the province, and its image is embossed on the back of the Canadian dime.

Today, the fishing industry that fostered the town's growth and boatbuilding reputation is comatose, and the Atlantic fisheries are mere shadows of their former selves. But here in Lunenburg, the townspeople carry on the shipbuilding and shipfitting skills of their ancestors. The port is still known as a tall ship mecca, and big multimasted sailing ships, old and new alike from around the world, continue to put in here for repairs, shipfitting, or

Lunenburg's Old Town is a UNESCO World Heritage Site.

Lunenburg

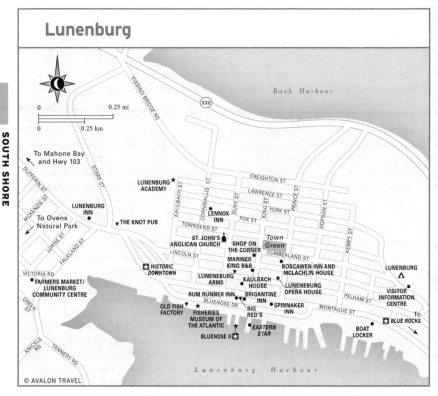

provisions—whatever excuse the owners can come up with. Underneath the tourist glitz, the community pride in this tradition runs strong and deep, and the town's international reputation among mariners remains formidable. Strike up a conversation with a local about sailing ships and see what happens.

★ HISTORIC DOWNTOWN

The port's oldest part is set on the hillside overlooking the harbor. The nine blocks of Old Town, designated a World Heritage Site by UNESCO, rise steeply from the water, and the village green spreads across the center. Bluenose Drive, the narrow lane along the harbor, and Montague Street, a block uphill, define the main sightseeing area. A mesh of one-way streets connects Old Town with the newer area built with shipbuilding profits. One of the pleasures of Lunenburg is strolling the residential and commercial streets, admiring the town's many meticulously preserved architectural gems. At the northern end of the harbor is the **Scotia Trawler Shipyard,** where the *Bluenose* was built. This shipyard, 16 other properties, and most of the wharves are off-limits, but the long-term plan is that the holdings will be opened to the public.

Fisheries Museum of the Atlantic

The spacious, bright red **Fisheries Museum of the Atlantic** (68 Bluenose Dr., 902/634-4794, mid-May-mid-Oct. daily 9:30am-5:30pm, adult $12, senior $8, child $3.50) boasts a trove of artifacts and exhibits on shipbuilding, seafaring, rum running, and marine biology. This thoroughly fascinating museum engages the visitor with demonstrations of fish filleting, lobster-trap construction, dory building, net mending, and other maritime arts. Inside are aquariums, tanks of touchable marine life, a gallery of ship models, full-size fishing vessels from around Atlantic Canada, a theater, a restaurant, and a gift shop. Tied up at the wharf outside are the fishing schooner *Theresa E. Connor,* built in Lunenburg in 1938; the steel-hulled trawler *Cape Sable,* an example of the sort of vessel that made the former obsolete; the *Royal Wave,* a Digby scallop dragger; and, when it's in its home port, the *Bluenose II.* All the vessels can be boarded and explored.

St. John's Anglican Church

St. John's Anglican Church (Cumberland and Cornwallis Sts., 902/634-4994, early June-Sept. daily 11am-7pm, free) stood for almost 250 years. In 2001, at the time the second-oldest church in Canada, it was destroyed by fire. It has now been rebuilt and can be visited on volunteer-led tours.

Lunenburg Academy

High above the port and surrounded by parkland, the imposing **Lunenburg Academy** (97 Kaulbach St.) is easily spotted from afar. Dating to 1885, this black-and-white wooden building, with its mansard roof and worn

wooden stairways, was originally a prestigious high school. Today, it is the local elementary school, but it remains one of the oldest academies in Canada.

OTHER SIGHTS
★ Blue Rocks

Follow any of Lunenburg's downtown streets eastbound to link with a road that leads eight kilometers to **Blue Rocks,** toward the end of the peninsula. This tiny fishing village is set along a jagged coastline wrapped with blue-gray slate and sandstone, and the combination of color and texture will inspire photographers. Blue Rocks has no official attractions or services. Instead, drive to the end of the road, from where you need to explore on foot to get the full effect of a part of Nova Scotia far removed from touristy Lunenburg and Peggy's Cove. The shoreline is littered with boats and fishing gear, such as nets and traps in various states of repair, while simple but colorful homes cling to the rocky foreshore.

Ovens Natural Park

A 15-minute drive south of Lunenburg on Highway 332, spectacular sea caves have been scooped out of the coastal cliffs. Early prospectors discovered veins of gold embedded in

Blue Rocks

the slate and white quartz cliffs, sparking a small gold rush in 1861. During the following several decades, the cliffs surrendered 15,500 grams of the precious metal, while the Cunard family, of shipping fame, had the beach sand transported to England to retrieve the gold. Today, **Ovens Natural Park** (902/766-4621, adult $10, senior and child $5) is privately owned, combining camping, cabins, hiking trails, and a restaurant on a 75-hectare site. Below the main parking lot, visitors can try their hand at panning for gold along Cunard's Beach. A trail leads along the sea cliffs and into one of the "ovens," and you can jump aboard an inflatable boat to get a sea-level view of the caves.

RECREATION
★ Bluenose II

To immerse yourself fully in the Lunenburg experience, set sail aboard the *Bluenose II* (902/634-8483 or 877/441-0347, www.bluenose.novascotia.ca), an exact replica of the famous sailing ship. She underwent multiyear restorations from 2010 through 2014 to return to her former glory.

When not in Halifax or visiting other Canadian ports, the *Bluenose II* can be found here at her home berth, outside the Fisheries Museum of the Atlantic. Rather than separating you from the maritime experience with cushy reclining seats, acrylic windows, and a cocktail lounge, the *Bluenose II* takes you to sea as a sailor. Cruising out of the harbor under a fresh breeze—the sails snapping taut and the hull slicing through the chilly waters—you'll begin to understand and actually feel the history and lifeblood of Lunenburg.

When in Lunenburg, she departs twice daily (9:30am and 1pm, adult $55, child $32.50) for a two-hour harbor cruise. A total of 75 spots are offered on each sailing. Of these, 40 can be reserved through the phone numbers or website. The remaining 35 are offered on a first-come, first-served basis from the booth at the entrance to the Fisheries Museum, 90 minutes before departure. Tickets are always in high demand, so making a reservation well in advance is essential.

Other Boat Tours

The *Bluenose II* isn't always in port, and when she is, tickets sell fast. An excellent alternative is the *Eastern Star,* operated by **Star Charters** (waterfront, 902/634-3535, www.novascotiasailing.com, adult $37, child $18). The *Eastern Star* is a character-imbued 48-foot wooden ketch tended by an amiable and knowledgeable crew intent on perpetuating the seafaring tradition that put Lunenburg on the map. The *Eastern Star* makes four 90-minute cruises per day June-October, with a two-hour sunset cruise added in July and August.

Lunenburg Whale Watching Tours (902/527-7175, adult $58, child $35) depart Government Wharf May-October four times daily. While whales are definitely the highlight, regular sightings are also made of sunfish, turtles, dolphins, seals, and puffins.

ENTERTAINMENT AND EVENTS
Nightlife

The seaport is usually quiet evenings and Sundays. Locals frequent **The Knot Pub** (4 Dufferin St., 902/634-3334, daily noon-11pm), a comfortable and lively place where you can get "knotwurst" and kraut with your draft beer. Up from the harbor, the **Lunenburg Arms** (94 Pelham St., 902/640-4040, daily 11am-close) has a lounge bar with tables that spill out onto a quiet patio.

Performing Arts

South Shore Players (www.southshoreplayers.com), the local theater troupe, uses a variety of venues for its performances, including the Central United Church Hall on Lincoln Street. **Lunenburg Opera House** (290 Lincoln St., 902/640-6500, www.lunenburgoperahouse.com) hosts gigs by musicians from throughout Atlantic Canada. Cover charges range up to $20, and a schedule is posted on its website.

The Famous *Bluenose*

Featured on Nova Scotian license plates and the back of the Canadian dime, the original *Bluenose* was launched from Lunenburg in 1921. Built as a fishing schooner, she was designed specifically for competing in the International Fisherman's Trophy, a racing series that pitted working ships from Canada and the United States against one another. Much to the joy of Canadians, the *Bluenose* won every racing competition she entered, while also serving as a working fishing boat. But by 1942, the era of the sail-powered fishing industry was giving way to that of modern steel-hulled trawlers, and the great *Bluenose* was sold to carry freight in the West Indies. Four years later, she foundered and was lost on a Haitian reef.

The ship herself was black. The name is thought to have originated from local fishermen, who, when conditions were cold and wet, would wipe their noses with their blue mittens, causing the dye to run.

In July 1963, the *Bluenose II* was re-created from the plans of the original and launched at Lunenburg. Some of the same craftspeople who had built the first *Bluenose* even participated in her construction.

Lunenburg Folk Harbour Festival

For four days from the second Thursday in August, a roster of traditional, roots, and contemporary folk musicians come together for the **Lunenburg Folk Harbour Festival** (902/634-3180, www.folkharbour.com). They perform under a tent atop Blockhouse Hill, at the Lunenburg Opera House, in the downtown bandstand, and out on the wharf. Many performances are free, with big-name acts under the big tent costing $20.

SHOPPING

The **farmers market** at Lunenburg Community Centre (corner of Victoria Rd. and Green St., July-Oct. Thurs. 8am-noon) lures crowds for fresh produce, smoked meats, and crafts at the former railroad depot grounds; wares are high quality and priced accordingly.

Nautical gifts are available at the **Boat Locker** (280 Montague St., 902/640-3202, Mon.-Fri. 9am-5pm, Sun. 10am-4pm), which is also a full-service marine-supply center, and at the nonprofit *Bluenose II* **Company Store** (121 Bluenose Dr., 902/634-8483, mid-May-Oct. daily 9:30am-5pm), which sells all manner of *Bluenose* clothing, gifts, and art to support preservation of the vessel.

FOOD

Lunenburg has a great number of restaurants, nearly all serving seafood in a casual setting. Local specialties appearing on some menus include Solomon Gundy (pickled herring, usually served with sour cream), Lunenburg pudding (pork sausage), and fish cakes topped with rhubarb relish.

A couple of blocks uphill from the waterfront, **Shop on the Corner** (263 Lincoln St., 902/634-3434, Mon.-Fri. 8:30am-5pm, Sat. 9am-5pm, Sun. 10am-5pm, lunches $7-10) is an untouristy place that combines kitchen giftware with a small café offering a wide range of teas and the locally roasted, delightfully named Laughing Whale coffee.

Seafood

In the big red building down on the water, the **Old Fish Factory** (68 Bluenose Dr., 902/634-3333, mid-May-mid-Oct. daily 11am-9pm, $15-31) is a large restaurant in a converted fish storehouse. Specialties include creamy seafood chowder, beer-battered haddock, and fish baked on a cedar plank. After the Solomon Gundy, a sour-tasting local specialty, you'll be ready for Blueberry Grunt, sweet dumplings floating in a blueberry compote and topped with whipped cream. Non-seafood dishes with a Canadian twist are also offered, such as maple-glazed chicken. Lunch features similar offerings, but with lower prices.

One block back from the harbor, several restaurants line Montague Street. All have decks or floor-to-ceiling windows facing the water. **Big Red's** (80 Montague St., 902/634-3554, daily 10am-9pm, $14-28) is exactly that—a cavernous, family-friendly restaurant with a standard seafood menu and lots of pizza choices. Portions are generous and prices reasonable.

Grand Banker Bar & Grill (82 Montague St., 902/634-3300, daily 11am-midnight, $14-26) offers similarly great views from an enclosed dining room and serves a wide-ranging menu of seafood, salads, pastas, and sandwiches. The food is well prepared and the atmosphere pleasant and relaxed. Mains include crab cakes, Acadian seafood stew, and maple-pecan glazed salmon. A half dozen good beers and a couple of Nova Scotia wines are available. The Grand Banker puts on a fine brunch (Sat.-Sun. 11am-2:30pm, $10-18) that includes lobster eggs Benedict.

ACCOMMODATIONS AND CAMPING

Whatever Mahone Bay may lack in accommodations is more than made up for in Lunenburg, where more than 60 B&Bs—even more than Halifax, which has over 100 times the population—clog the historic streets. You should still try to make reservations ahead of time in summer, but be prepared for an answering machine in winter, when many lodgings are closed.

$50-100

Many of the B&Bs in the $100-150 range have rooms under $100 outside of summer, but in July and August, your choices are limited. One of the best is the ★ **Lennox Inn** (69 Fox St., 902/521-0214 or 888/379-7605, Apr.-Dec., $95-120 s or d), which dates to 1791, making it Canada's oldest inn. The owners breathed life into the building through a meticulous restoration using the original plans. Two guest rooms share a single bathroom, and the other two are en suite. Breakfast in what was originally the tavern is included in the rates.

Incorporating two (circa 1888 and 1905) buildings, the **Boscawen Inn and McLachlan House** (150 Cumberland St., 902/634-3325 or 800/354-5009, www.boscawen.ca, $99-225 s or d) also has a couple of rooms under $100, but most are higher-priced. This European-style hotel occupies a scenic perch above the harbor and is surrounded by gardens. The five guest rooms in McLachlan House are less expensive than those across the road at what was originally known as the Boscawen Manor, but all guests enjoy a light breakfast included in the rates. Other amenities include a formal dining room and sun-soaked terrace, both open to the public for meals.

$100-150

Right downtown, above the Grand Banker restaurant, the tidy **Brigantine Inn and Suites** (82 Montague St., 902/634-3300 or 800/360-1181, www.brigantineinn.com, $105-190 s or d) provides excellent value. The inn offers seven nautically themed rooms, each with a private bathroom and named for a famous sailing ship. The smallest of the rooms is the brightly decorated Cutty Sark room, while the much larger Brigantine Romance room features a jetted tub on a glass-enclosed balcony overlooking the harbor. Part of the inn is a complex of seven suites one block from the main building. These have separate bedrooms, as well as sitting areas, coffeemakers, microwaves, and fridges.

Kaulbach House (75 Pelham St., 902/634-8818 or 800/568-8818, www.kaulbachhouse.com, $115-165 s or d) is one of Lunenburg's many historic treasures (circa 1880) converted to an inn, complete with the unique "Lunenburg bump," an enlarged dormer that extends past a building's eaves. Two blocks up from the harbor but with partial water views, the six antiques-filled rooms have en suite or private bathrooms, flat-screen TVs, air-conditioning, and wireless Internet. A full breakfast is included in the rates.

With rooms and suites spread through three buildings on King Street, the ornately detailed **Mariner King B&B** (15 King St., 902/634-8509 or 800/565-8509, www.marinerking.com, $115-225 s or d) is also right downtown. Its cheaper rooms are a little more threadbare than those at Kaulbach House, but the character-filled Attic Suite is a gem. It even has its own rooftop patio.

Rum Runner Inn (66 Montague St., 902/634-9200 or 888/778-6786, www.rumrunnerinn.com, $119-179 s or d) is right along the busy restaurant strip opposite the waterfront. It's a historic building, but the 13 rooms are thoroughly modernized and look no different from a regular upscale motel. Each has a coffeemaker, a fridge, air-conditioning, and Internet connections. The most expensive rooms have a king bed and glassed-in veranda. A light breakfast is included.

If you're looking to stay in a historic building with a modern feel, consider the centrally situated ★ **Spinnaker Inn** (126 Montague St., 902/634-4543 or 888/634-8973, www.spinnakerinn.com, $150-195 s or d). Overlooking the harbor, all four guest rooms have polished hardwood floors and antique-style beds. Two are split-level with jetted tubs in the en suite bathrooms and harbor views.

The **Lunenburg Inn** (26 Dufferin St., 902/634-9419 or 800/565-3963, www.lunenburginn.com, Apr.-Oct., $149-189 s or d) is an elaborate Victorian home that has been taking in guests since 1924. It underwent serious renovations in the mid-1990s and now provides some of the nicest rooms in town, with rates including a full breakfast. If I had a choice, I'd stay in one of the two suites, which each have a sitting area with a TV, a jetted tub in the en suite bathroom, and a private entrance from the veranda. Guests enjoy a sitting room with a fireplace, a private bar, and wireless Internet.

Lunenburg Inn

Campgrounds

The **Lunenburg Campground** (Blockhouse Hill Rd., 902/634-8100, May-late Oct., $28-42) sits on Blockhouse Hill, high above downtown and beside the information center. It's on the small side (55 sites), but the facilities are adequate (showers, views, Internet access).

A lot more than a campground, ★ **Ovens Natural Park** (off Hwy. 332, 902/766-4621, www.ovenspark.com, mid-May-mid-Oct.) has campsites (tents $35, hookups $50-75) and cabins varying from those with shared bathrooms (from $60 s or d) to self-contained two-bedroom chalets ($190). Amenities include lawn games, a playground, evening bonfires, a restaurant, and a gift shop. Stephen Chapin, younger brother of Harry Chapin (of "Cat's in the Cradle" fame) owns and operates the property with his family, making the evening sing-alongs a real treat. The middle weekend of August, the entire Chapin family comes together as a tribute to the singer, with everyone welcome to join in the fun.

INFORMATION AND SERVICES

Lunenburg Visitor Information Centre (Blockhouse Hill Rd., 902/634-8100, www. lunenburgns.com, May-June and Sept.-Oct. daily 9am-6pm, July-Aug. daily 9am-8pm) stocks locally written, informative literature about the port's historic architecture. Staff will help those without reservations find accommodations. The office can be a little hard to find. As you enter town, stay on Lincoln Street as it passes the signs for the waterfront, and you'll soon find yourself on Blockhouse Hill.

Fishermen's Memorial Hospital (14 High St., 902/634-8801) is between Dufferin and Green Streets. For the **RCMP,** call 902/634-8674.

GETTING THERE AND AROUND

Along divided Highway 103, it takes a little more than one hour to reach Lunenburg from Halifax (100 kilometers), taking Exit 10 via Mahone Bay for the final stretch.

If you're in Halifax without a vehicle, consider a six-hour tour with **Ambassatours** (902/423-6242 or 800/565-7173). These depart June-October Wednesday, Friday, and Saturday at 8:30am.

Lunenburg to Shelburne

Beyond Lunenburg, the divided highway continues south to Bridgewater, but the crowds thin out quickly. This is one of the best reasons to continue south—the rugged coastline is dotted with Peggy's Cove-like villages steeped in history but unaffected by tourism, and parks with designated hiking trails and sandy beaches beckon.

The 140-kilometer drive between Lunenburg and Shelburne takes less than two hours nonstop. As accommodations are limited along this stretch of coast, a sensible schedule is to plan to leave Lunenburg after breakfast, spend the day exploring the following parks and towns, and have a room booked in Shelburne for the night.

BRIDGEWATER

Situated on the LaHave River, west of Lunenburg, Bridgewater (pop. 8,200) is the main service town of the South Shore. Industry revolves around a Michelin tire plant, and if you're traveling south, this is the last place to fill up on fast food and do your mall shopping.

Sights

The 1860 **Wile Carding Mill** (242 Victoria Rd., 902/543-8233, June-mid-Sept. Mon.-Sat. 9:30am-5:30pm, Sun. 1pm-5:30pm, adult $3.50, senior $2.25, child $2) was once a wool-processing mill. The wool was carded for spinning and weaving or made into batts for quilts. The original machinery is still in operation, powered by a waterwheel, and now demonstrates old carding methods. It's on the south side of the river (take Exit 13 from Highway 103).

Surrounded by parkland on the south side of downtown off King Street, **DesBrisay Museum** (130 Jubilee Rd., 902/543-4033, June-Aug. Tues.-Sat. 9am-5pm, Sun. 1pm-5pm, Sept.-May Wed.-Sun. 1pm-5pm, adult $3.50, senior $2.50, child $2) looks unappealing from the outside, but inside displays tell the story of Bridgewater's first European settlers and the importance of local industries. Highlights include Mi'kmaq quilting and a wooden plough dating to 1800.

Food and Accommodations

Bridgewater's premier bed and breakfast is **River Reflections** (225 King St., 902/527-2682 or 888/527-2682, www.riverreflections.ca, $100-125 s or d), a gracious wooden building that dates to 1906. It has been beautifully restored, now with three simple guest rooms furnished with antiques. Rates include a full breakfast and the luxury of relaxing on a covered porch overlooking the LaHave River. To get there from Highway 103, take Exit 13 and follow Victoria Road to King Street in the heart of downtown.

About six kilometers east of town along Highway 331 on the south side of the LaHave River is the **Lighthouse Motel** (13 Conradin Dr., Conquerall Bank, 902/543-8151, www.lighthousemotel.ca, May-Oct., $85-110 s or d). It occupies a prime riverside location, and guests have access to a private beach, a picnic area, and a playground.

Waves Seafood Grill (Eastside Plaza, 28 Davison Dr., 902/543-2020, Mon.-Fri. 11am-9pm, Sat.-Sun. 8am-9pm, $10-18) is open for the usual breakfast choices weekends only, but where this place really shines is with its inexpensive fish-and-chips, such as two pieces and chips for $14.

Getting There

Bridgewater is about 20 kilometers west of Lunenburg via Highway 3. It's 110 kilometers (1.5 hours) southwest of Halifax.

Bridgewater and the LaHave River

HIGHWAY 331 TO LIVERPOOL

Highway 331, which begins in downtown Bridgewater as King Street, follows the LaHave River to its mouth and then winds along the coast to Exit 17 of Highway 103. It adds just 30 minutes to the trip between Bridgewater and Liverpool, but you'll want to allow longer—it's a beautiful introduction to the untouristy South Shore beyond Lunenburg.

★ Crescent Beach

Around 20 minutes southeast of Bridgewater is **Crescent Beach,** a beautiful two-kilometer stretch of finely ground quartz sand that links the mainland to the LaHave Islands. Like the rest of Nova Scotia, the water is cool, but on a hot summer's day, many people dive in for a swim. But it is the beach itself that is the draw, with sand dunes up to two meters high separating the beach from a shallow bay popular with kite surfers.

Crescent Beach is day-use only, but adjacent **Rissers Beach Provincial Park** boasts the same white sand and an area of pristine salt marsh laced with boardwalks. The park **campground** (902/688-2034, mid-May-mid-Oct., $29) fills every weekend through summer, but midweek even sites close to the sandy beach may remain empty. The park is just south of the turnoff to Crescent Beach.

GETTING THERE

Crescent Beach is about 30 kilometers (30 minutes) southeast of Bridgewater via Highway 331. It's 140 kilometers south of Halifax on Highways 103 and 331 (just under two hours).

LaHave Islands

The causeway along Crescent Beach crosses to **Bush Island,** from where quirky old iron bridges provide access to **Bell Island** and **LaHave Island.** Just three of dozens of islands in the group, they are dotted with old fishing cottages inhabited by those who have escaped the rat race. On Bell Island, a museum filled with local history is in the church, while Bush Island Provincial Park is little more than a boat launch, but the rugged scenery and funky fishing cottages make the drive to the end of the road a delightful detour from the main South Shore tourist route.

LIVERPOOL

This historic town, at the mouth of the Mersey River, about 50 kilometers south of

Crescent Beach

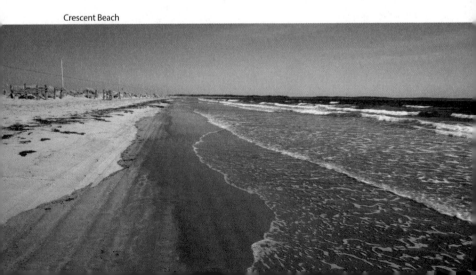

Bridgewater, doesn't get as much attention as it deserves. Throughout the compact downtown core are a number of interesting attractions, while Privateer Days (late June) provide a lively glimpse of the town's colorful past.

Sights and Events
THE PORT OF PRIVATEERS

Privateers were government-sanctioned pirates who had permission to capture enemy vessels. American privateers found their way to Nova Scotia during the American Revolution, but the British responded by attacking American boats. Privateers were required by law to take captured vessels to Halifax's Privateers Wharf, where the boats and cargo were auctioned off, a portion of which was handed back to the privateer and his crew. Liverpool local Simeon Perkins had a share in a privateering boat, along with dozens of others who used Liverpool as their home port. The most prolific of the privateer vessels was the *Liverpool Packet* captained by Joseph Barss, which captured an estimated 200 vessels during its lifetime. With plundered goods from a single vessel selling for up to $1 million at auction, Liverpool became a wealthy town, and many of the grand homes still standing were financed by privateering.

OTHER SIGHTS

Well-known Canadian photographer Sherman Hines injected his own resources into developing the **Rossignol Cultural Centre** (205 Church St., 902/354-3067, July-Aug. Mon.-Sat. 10am-5:30pm, Sun. noon-5:30pm, adult $5, child $3) in a school building once slated for demolition. One block south of Main Street along Old Bridge Street, it encompasses multiple small museums, including one devoted to outhouses (Hines is known for his outhouse photography), and others to folk art, the Mi'kmaq, and wildlife.

Built by infamous privateer Simeon Perkins, **Perkins House** (105 Main St.) is a classic example of a New England planter's adaptation to Nova Scotia. Built in 1766, it is furnished with antiques and displays that tell the story of Perkins's colorful life on the high seas. At the time of publication, the home was closed due to structural issues, but due to its age and interesting former owner, it is still worth viewing from the surrounding gardens.

Country music legend Hank Snow, who sold 70 million records, was born in nearby Brooklyn. Between Highway 103 and downtown, a railway station has been converted to the **Hank Snow Home Town Museum** (148 Bristol St., 902/354-4675, Mon.-Fri. 9am-5pm, plus Sat.-Sun. 9am-5pm in summer, adult $5, senior $4, children free) in his memory. Displays catalog his life, from the earliest performances in Halifax through details of his seven number-one hits from 120 albums, to his Grand Ole Opry performances, his role in introducing Elvis Presley to the entertainment world, and, finally, the huge collection of awards accumulated through six decades of performing.

PRIVATEER DAYS

There's no better place to immerse yourself in the colorful history of Nova Scotia's privateers than **Privateer Days** (902/354-4500, www.privateerdays.ca), a Liverpool tradition held annually in late June. Walking tours led by locals in period dress and a re-creation of when two American privateer boats once invaded the town are highlights, but events go on all week, culminating with a bang during the final night's fireworks.

Food and Accommodations

Once home to a privateer, **Lane's Privateer Inn** (27 Bristol Ave., 902/354-3456 or 800/794-3332, www.lanesprivateerinn.com, $115-170 s, $135-190 d) has everything you need for an overnight stay under one roof. The 27 rooms all have en suite bathrooms and air-conditioning, while some have king beds and balconies overlooking the Mersey River. Downstairs is an excellent restaurant. Breakfast includes all the usual options, with Nova Scotian specialties such as smoked salmon sausage as a substitute for bacon. The lunch and dinner includes a lamb burger for $15, a lobster roll for $17, and roasted halibut for $27.

Getting There

Liverpool is about 50 kilometers south of Bridgewater via Highway 103. It's 160 kilometers (two hours) south of Halifax, also via Highway 103.

LIVERPOOL TO PORT JOLI

If you've left Highway 103 to explore Liverpool, continue south through town along the older Highway 3 to reach White Point before rejoining the main route south at Summerville.

White Point

Activities at **White Point Beach Resort** (White Point Beach, 902/354-2711 or 800/565-5068, www.whitepoint.com) make this lodging a destination in itself. Stretching along a wide swath of white sand, it has indoor and outdoor pools, swimming in a freshwater lake, surfboard and kayak rentals, tennis courts, a nine-hole golf course, a games room, two restaurants, and nightly entertainment in the lounge. Most guests are families, many returning annually for summer vacation. Comfortable motel-like rooms are $175-210 s or d depending on the view, and cottages are $295-355.

Continuing along Highway 3 from White Point to Hunts Point, you'll come to **Hunts Point Beach Cottages** (Hwy. 3, 902/683-2077, www.huntspointbeach.com, mid-May-Sept., $145-165 s or d), a much quieter spot, where guests laze their time away on the grassy grounds, which extend to the beach. The newly renovated cottages have one or two bedrooms, kitchens, covered decks, and living rooms with TVs.

GETTING THERE

White Point is less than 10 kilometers (10 minutes) south of Liverpool via Highway 3. It's 170 kilometers (two hours) south of Halifax via Highways 103 and 3.

White Point Beach

Summerville Beach Provincial Park

Just before Highway 3 rejoins Highway 103, a short gravel road leads along the back of the small **Summerville Beach Provincial Park,** which protects a spit of sand jutting across Port Mouton. It's a day-use park with picnic tables and plenty of room to spread your towel on the beach.

Kejimkujik National Park Seaside Adjunct

About 25 kilometers southwest of Liverpool is one of the largest remaining undisturbed areas of Nova Scotian coastline. Affiliated with the inland Kejimkujik National Park (along Highway 8 between Liverpool and Annapolis Royal), the **Kejimkujik National Park Seaside Adjunct** encompasses unspoiled beaches and offshore isles. The park is accessible only on foot. The main access is along an easy three-kilometer trail beginning at the parking lot on St. Catherine's Road (turn off in Port Joli) and ending at the southwest end of St. Catherine's River Beach. Some sections of this beach close late April-late July to protect piping plover nesting sites. The Seaside Adjunct has no visitor facilities, and camping is not permitted.

PORT JOLI

Port Joli is a picturesque coastal village with a seaside park that gets busy only on the hottest of summer weekends.

Thomas Raddall Provincial Park

This gem known as **Thomas Raddall Provincial Park** protects rock formations that suggest it was the point where the Gondwana and North American continents collided many millions of years ago. But for most, the beaches are the main draw. Left behind by the retreating ice cap at the end of the last ice age, banks of sand have washed ashore, forming beautiful stretches of beach now protected by the park.

The park has an 11-kilometer trail system, half of which is paved and set aside for both cyclists and walkers. The most popular destination is Sandy Bay, a short beach bookended by rocky headlands. If you can pull yourself away from the beach, follow the **Sandy Bay Trail** over the northern headland to the **Herring Rock Trail,** where the remains of a 1700s fishing station can be seen. Take both these trails and you'll be back on your beach towel within an hour. In the north of the park, beaches are lapped by the protected waters of Port Joli Harbour. Starting from the top end of the campground, the **Port Joli Trail** (one kilometer each way) winds south past interpretive panels to Scotch Point Beach. To the north, a string of beaches spread out well beyond the park boundary.

The park **campground** (902/683-2664, mid-May-mid-Oct., $29) has 82 large sites, including a few designated for tents. Each site has a picnic table and fire pit, while other amenities include washrooms with showers, a playground, and firewood sales.

To get to the park, continue along Highway 103 south from Port Joli and turn south on East Port L'Herbert Road; it's three kilometers from the highway.

Getting There

Port Joli is 25 kilometers (15 minutes) south of Liverpool along Highway 103. It's 185 kilometers (over two hours) south of Halifax via Highway 103.

Shelburne and Vicinity

Like Lunenburg, 140 kilometers to the northeast, Shelburne (pop. 1,700) sits at the innermost end of a long harbor formed between two peninsulas. The seaport was established in 1783 when Loyalists fleeing the newly independent American colonies settled here by the thousands, establishing shipbuilding and fish processing businesses. But eventually the seaport began to show its age. Then Hollywood came to town. In 1992, the motley collection of historic buildings along the waterfront was used as a setting for Fairfield, Connecticut, circa 1780, in the American Revolution movie *Mary Silliman's War.* In 1995, Shelburne again hit the big screen as the setting for 1600s Boston in *The Scarlet Letter,* an adaptation of Nathaniel Hawthorne's novel. Demi Moore and Robert Duvall may be long gone, but the two movies created an impetus for preservation. While some "historic" buildings were added to the mix, many original buildings were spruced up, power lines were buried, and generally the town came together to promote its past.

★ SHELBURNE HISTORIC DISTRICT

Dock Street is dotted with some of Canada's oldest wooden buildings. The local historical society has done a wonderful job of breathing life into the **Shelburne Historic District,** while businesses such as a cooperage and boatbuilder help bring its history to life. In between are grassy areas, a waterfront pathway, and kayak rentals. Admission to each of the buildings is $4, or buy a ticket for $10 to visit all three.

Shelburne County Museum

The **Shelburne County Museum** (8 Maiden Ln., 902/875-3219, June-mid-Oct. daily 9:30am-5:30pm, mid-Oct.-May Tues.-Sat. 2pm-5pm) is the best place to make your first stop. It contains exhibits covering Shelburne's Loyalist heritage and shipbuilding history. One highlight is the 250-year-old fire engine, believed to be the oldest in Canada.

Dory Shop Museum

First used in the mid-1800s, dories were small, skifflike wooden boats that were essential to the success of fishing the Grand Banks. Rather than fishing from the mother vessel, a dozen or more dories would be transported to the fishing grounds, allowing hundreds of hooks to be laid out at once. Adding to their usability, they were inexpensive to make and stackable. On the waterfront across from the county museum, the **Dory Shop Museum** (11 Dock St., June-mid-Oct. daily 9:30am-5:30pm) is the last of seven once-thriving boat factories in town. The seven shops turned out thousands of handcrafted wooden fishing dories between 1880 and 1970. The shop now houses interpretive displays and gives demonstrations of the dying art.

Ross-Thomson House and Store Museum

The **Ross-Thomson House and Store Museum** (9 Charlotte Ln., 902/875-3141, June-mid-Oct. daily 9:30am-5:30pm) was built in 1785 as a Loyalist store. The last example of its kind today in Nova Scotia, it depicts the period setting with sample wares such as lumber and salted codfish, which were traded for tobacco, molasses, and dry goods. Upstairs is a military display, and outside, the garden has been planted as it would have been in the late 1700s.

Muir-Cox Shipyard

At the far south end of Dock Street, the small **Muir-Cox Shipyard** was closed at the time of publication. If it reopens in the near future,

Shelburne Historic District

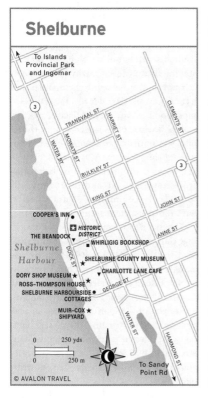

Shelburne

an established reputation for fine dining. Its Swiss owner-chef, Roland Glauser, specializes in local seafood prepared with cooking techniques from around the world. The seafood chowder is one of the best I've tasted.

ACCOMMODATIONS AND CAMPING

Shelburne Harbourside Cottages (10 George St., 902/875-4555, www.shelburneharboursidecottages.com, $105 s or d) is an excellent lodging value. Each of its two modern cottages enjoys harbor views and has cooking facilities, a separate bedroom, a TV, and a deck. Extras include bike rentals and kayak rentals; the latter can be launched right from the cottages.

Cooper's Inn (36 Dock St., 902/875-4656 or 800/688-2011, www.thecoopersinn.com, Apr.-Oct., $130-220 s or d) is a two-story colonial beauty overlooking the harbor and next to the tourist bureau and museum. Built in 1784 by a merchant and restored and opened in 1988, the lodging has six rooms, all with private baths ($130-180), and a large top-floor suite with water views ($220). Rates include a full breakfast in the cheery dining room.

★ **Whispering Waves Cottages** (Black Point Rd., Ingomar, 902/637-3535 or 866/470-9283, www.novascotiacottages.info, $165 s or d) may be out of town, but an overnight stay at this welcoming waterfront property is as enjoyable as one could imagine. The modern cottages are stylishly furnished in wilderness, nautical, or romance themes, and each has a separate bedroom, kitchen, lounge room with a fireplace, and a deck with ocean views. A lobster dinner, delivered to your cottage door, is a delicious extra.

Campgrounds

Rustic and pretty, **The Islands Provincial Park** (off Hwy. 3, 5 km west of Shelburne, 902/875-4304, mid-May-early Sept., $29) faces the town across the upper harbor. It offers 64 unserviced sites with table shelters and grills, pit toilets, running water, and a spacious modern shower room.

expect to see local men building traditional boats. It operated continuously between the 1820s and 1980s, launching square-rigged barques in its earliest days and wooden racing yachts in more modern times.

FOOD

If you're touring the historic waterfront precinct, you'll pass right by **Beandock** (32 Dock St., 902/875-1302, Mon.-Thurs. 8:30am-8pm, Fri. 8:30am-5pm, Sat. 10am-4pm, Sun. 10am-2pm, lunches $6-9), in a rambling old wooden building with outdoor chairs that offer stunning water views. It's the best place in town for coffee, with food offerings including sandwiches, wraps, and desserts.

The bright and cheery ★ **Charlotte Lane Café** (13 Charlotte Ln., 902/875-3314, Tues.-Sat. 11:30am-2:30pm and 5pm-8pm, $19-33), between Water and Dock Streets, has

INFORMATION AND SERVICES

While Dock Street is the historic heart of Shelburne, Water Street, running parallel one block to the west, is lined with all the services of a small town, including banks and the post office. **Whirligig Book Shop** (135 Water St., 902/875-1117, Tues.-Fri. 10am-5pm, Sat. 10am-1pm) stocks a good selection of local and Nova Scotian literature.

GETTING THERE

Shelburne is 140 kilometers from Lunenburg along Highway 103. The drive takes less than two hours nonstop. It's 220 kilometers (almost three hours) from Halifax via Highway 103.

SHELBURNE TO YARMOUTH
Barrington and Vicinity

Highway 103 takes a mainly inland route between Shelburne and Yarmouth. One place it does come in contact with the ocean is near Barrington, just off the main highway along Highway 3, where coastal views are exquisite. In Barrington itself, the **Old Meeting House Museum** (2408 Hwy. 3, 902/637-2185, June-Sept. Mon.-Sat. 9:30am-5:30pm, Sun. 1pm-5:30pm, donation) is a variation on planter life. Built by 50 Cape Cod families in 1765, the New England-style church is Canada's oldest nonconformist house of worship.

Beyond Barrington, at Villagedale, is **Sand Hills Beach Provincial Park,** so named for a complex dune system where wide tidal flats extend into the ocean. Time your arrival for high tide; the water is warm enough for swimming—in summer only, of course.

GETTING THERE

Barrington is about 35 kilometers (25 minutes) southwest of Shelburne on Highway 103. It's 255 kilometers (three hours) from Halifax via Highway 103.

Cape Sable Island

At Barrington West, Cape Sable Island is well worth the detour, although there are limited services on the island, so plan on staying or dining in nearby Shelburne or Yarmouth. Connected to the mainland by a causeway, the island forms the southernmost point in Nova Scotia. Feared by early sailors because of its jagged shores, the island was settled by brick-making Acadians during the 17th century. The island also served as a summer base for fishermen from New England, and fishing prevails today as the community's main industry, with tourism a close second.

The island's four main beaches offer surfing, clam digging, swimming, fishing, and bird-watching. At **Hawk Beach,** on the eastern side (turn at Lower Clark's Harbour at Hawk Road and go left), you can see the **Cape Lighthouse** on a small nearby sandbar. The original tower, built in 1861, was Canada's first eight-sided structure; the present lighthouse, a protected heritage building, was constructed in 1923. At low tide on Hawk Beach, you can also see the remains of a 1,500-year-old forest.

Causeway Beach (turn right at the Corbett Heights subdivision) is a prime sunbathing and fishing (mackerel) spot. **Stoney Island Beach,** as the name implies, is not as popular with sunbathers as it is with seals, which like to sun themselves on the rocks. **South Side Beach** (turn on Daniel's Head Rd. in South Side) is also popular as a seal-watching and beachcombing locale.

GETTING THERE

Cape Sable Island is about 50 kilometers southwest of Shelburne along Highway 103, continuing on Highway 3 through Barrington. Allow 40 minutes. From Halifax, allow at least three hours for the 270-kilometer drive down Highway 103 and 3.

Yarmouth

Yarmouth (pop. 6,700) was the center of a shipbuilding empire during Canada's Great Age of Sail, when it ranked as the world's fourth-largest port of registry. Still the region's largest seaport, the town is a prosperous and orderly place supported by shipping—primarily lumber products, Irish moss, and Christmas trees—and fishing. Yarmouth's herring fleet is a major contributor to the local economy. The fleet sails at night and anchors with all its lights blazing farther up the Fundy coast, creating a sight known as "herring city."

SIGHTS

If historic architecture interests you, take a leisurely walk along Main Street, where the commercial buildings demonstrate late 19th-century Classic Revival, Queen Anne Revival, Georgian, and Italianate styles. At the tourist information center on Forest Street, pick up the *Walking Tour of Yarmouth* brochure, which details about two dozen points of architectural and historical interest on a self-guided four-kilometer walk.

Firefighters' Museum of Nova Scotia

The **Firefighters' Museum of Nova Scotia** (451 Main St., 902/742-5525, June and Sept. Mon.-Sat. 9am-5pm, July-Aug. Mon.-Sat. 9am-9pm, Sun. 10am-5pm, adult $4, senior $3, child $2) is a museum dedicated solely to firefighting equipment. Among the extensive vintage collection is an 1819 Hopwood and Tilley hand pump and other sparkling tools.

Yarmouth County Museum

An enjoyable walk from downtown through a tree-lined residential area east of Main Street leads to **Yarmouth County Museum** (22 Collins St., 902/742-5539, June-Sept. Mon.-Sat. 9am-5pm, Oct.-May Tues.-Sat. 2pm-5pm, adult $3, senior $2.50, child $1). It showcases Canada's largest ship-portrait collection and exhibits a trove of seafaring lore, musical instruments, ship models, furniture, and more. The research library and archives store extensive records and genealogical materials.

Cape Forchu

The most scenic destination in the vicinity of Yarmouth is Cape Forchu, 10 kilometers south of town via Highway 304, where the red-and-white **Cape Forchu Light Station** guides ships into the harbor. Follow Main Street north and turn left at Vancouver Street. Just past the hospital complex, turn left on Grove Road. The Faith Memorial Baptist Church marks the site where the famous Yarmouth runic stone, believed to have been inscribed by Leif Eriksson's men, was found. Next you come to the lighthouse (July-Aug. daily 11:30am-7pm, free) perched on a stone promontory. The actual lighthouse is open to climb, and you get good views from the top. Below the lighthouse, a paved walking trail leads from the parking lot down to **Leif Ericson Picnic Park,** overlooking the rocky coast.

FOOD

Locals and visitors alike looking for quality tea and coffee in a refined setting gravitate to **Sip Cafe** (1 Collins St., 902/742-3579, Mon.-Fri. 7am-8pm, Sat. 9am-8pm, Sun. 10am-5pm), which has indoor and outdoor seating, free Wi-Fi, and a range of sweet and savory pastries.

Rudder's (96 Water St., 902/742-7311, daily 10am-11pm, $16-30) is a large brew-pub set right on the water. It's a big room that manages to maintain a warm atmosphere, with even more tables spread across a veranda facing the harbor. The menu blends traditional pub food with Nova Scotian specialties—think maple-glazed salmon baked on a cedar plank, lobster and scallop crepes, and steak and lobster. The lobster dinner is a major draw.

ACCOMMODATIONS AND CAMPING

North of downtown, where Vancouver Street crosses the head of Yarmouth Harbour, is the **Lakelawn Motel** (641 Main St., 902/742-3588 or 877/664-0664, www.lakelawnmotel.com, from $109-149 s or d). The centerpiece of this lodging is a grand 1864 mansion that holds a breakfast room and four upstairs B&B rooms. Spread around its perimeter is a U-shaped wing of 27 motel rooms that are a little worn but still a good value.

Churchill Mansion Country Inn (44 Old Post Rd., Darlings Lake, 902/649-2818 or 888/453-5565, www.churchillmansion.com,

May-mid-Nov., $175-235 s or d) was the hilltop summer home of Aaron Flint Churchill, who made his fortune in the shipping trade after establishing the Churchill Line out of Savannah, Georgia. Overlooking a lake and with distant ocean views, the house was converted to an inn in the 1980s. All the beautifully restored rooms are super spacious. The most expensive is Churchill's master bedroom, with a balcony overlooking the lake. A gourmet breakfast and evening snacks are included in the rates, while dinner is available for an extra charge in the restaurant. The town of Darlings Lake is 15 kilometers north of Yarmouth.

Campgrounds

The closest campground to Yarmouth is **Campers' Haven** (5 km east of Yarmouth, off Hwy. 3 in Arcadia, 902/742-4848, www.campershavencampground.com, mid-May–mid-Oct., campsites $24-45, cottage $65). The lakeside campground offers more than 200 sites, as well as canoe rentals, a pool, a camp store, a launderette, and a recreation hall with a fireplace.

For a wilderness experience, travel a little farther out to **Ellenwood Lake Provincial Park** (mid-June–mid-Oct., $29), which has a beach with swimming, a short hiking trail through a mixed forest typical of the southwest region, showers, and a playground. To get there, drive 19 kilometers north of Yarmouth on Highway 101, take Exit 34, and follow the signs along Highway 340 for seven kilometers.

INFORMATION AND SERVICES

Greeting visitors as they arrive in town is the cavernous **Nova Scotia Visitor Information Centre** (228 Main St. at Forest St., 902/742-5033, May-June and Sept.-Oct. daily 8am-5pm, July-Aug. daily 8am-7pm), where you'll find literature and information on just about everything imaginable in the city and the province. In advance of your visit, visit www.yarmouthandacadianshores.com.

The **Regional Health Centre** (902/742-1540) is at 50 Vancouver Street. For the **RCMP,** call 902/742-8777.

GETTING THERE

Yarmouth is 310 kilometers from Halifax via the South Shore (Highway 103) and 330 kilometers via the Annapolis Valley (Highway 101); allow at least four hours for either route.

Ferries from Portland, Maine, dock downtown in Yarmouth. The **CAT** (877/762-7245, www.ferries.ca) operates this service between mid-June and October, charging adult $107, senior $102, child $65, vehicle under 6.6 feet $199. The crossing takes 5.5 hours, with departures from Portland daily at 2:30pm and departures from Yarmouth daily at 8:30am.

sunset over Cape Forchu

Fundy Coast

The natural beauty of Nova Scotia's Fundy Coast is sublime. Sea breezes bathe the shore in crisp salt air, and the sun illuminates the seascape colors with a clarity that defies a painter's palette.

Wildflowers bloom with abandon, nourished by the moist coastal air. And fog, thick as cotton, sometimes envelops the region during the summer. This is the Fundy Coast, which stretches from Yarmouth in the west to the farthest reaches of the Bay of Fundy in the east. Quietly and relentlessly, twice a day, a tidal surge that has its beginnings far away pours into the bay, creating the highest tides on the planet. Fishing boats are lifted from the muddy seafloor, and whales in pursuit of silvery herring hurry along the summertime currents, their mammoth bulks buoyed by the 100 billion tons of seawater that gush into the long bay between Nova Scotia and New Brunswick. The cycle from low to high tide takes a mere six hours. The tide peaks, in places high enough to swamp a four-story building, and then begins to retreat. As the sea level drops, coastal peninsulas and rocky islets emerge

from the froth, veiled in seaweed. The seafloor reappears, shiny as shellac and littered with sea urchins, periwinkles, and shells. Where no one walked just hours ago, local children run and skip on the beaches, pausing to retrieve tidal treasures. Locals take the Fundy tides for granted. For visitors, it's an astounding show.

To a great extent, the history of the province's Fundy Coast is the story of all of Nova Scotia, and this is reflected in the region's wealth of historic and cultural wonders. France's colonial ambitions began at Port-Royal and clashed head-on with England's quest for New World dominance, and multiple national historic sites along the coast lie in testament to these troubled times. The trim Acadian villages of La Côte Acadienne, the historic streetscape of Annapolis Royal, and the gracious towns of Wolfville and Windsor add to the appeal.

Previous: Annapolis Royal; whale-watching off Brier Island. **Above:** Grand Pré National Historic Site.

Highlights

★ **Église de Sainte-Marie:** You may strain your neck viewing the tallest wooden church in North America located on the charming Acadian Coast (page 99).

★ **Balancing Rock:** Out on Digby Neck, a short trail suddenly emerges at the Bay of Fundy—and this stunning pillar balanced precariously over the water (page 105).

★ **Whale-Watching on the Bay of Fundy:** Use Digby Neck and the adjacent islands as a base for whale-watching trips into the Bay of Fundy (page 106).

★ **Fort Anne National Historic Site:** After centuries of changing hands between the British and the French, this onetime capital of Nova Scotia is now managed by the government as a tourist attraction (page 107).

★ **Port-Royal National Historic Site:** The oldest European settlement north of St. Augustine, Florida, has been re-created here (page 108).

★ **Grand Pré National Historic Site:** This outdoor museum brings to life Longfellow's story of Evangeline, a young girl caught up in the Acadian deportation (page 120).

Fundy Coast

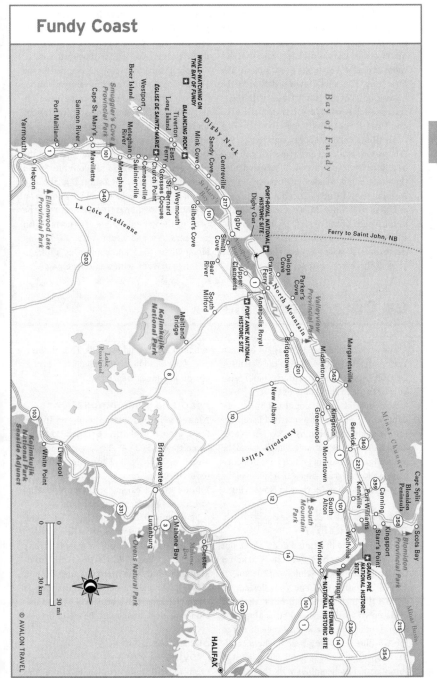

© AVALON TRAVEL

PLANNING YOUR TIME

You can drive between Yarmouth and Halifax in a single day, but you should allow a minimum of two days, which lets you reserve a room at one of Annapolis Royal's many historic inns. This small town is definitely the historic heart of the Fundy Coast, with sights such as **Fort Anne National Historic Site** and **Port-Royal National Historic Site** easily filling out a full day of sightseeing. For this reason, two days and two nights should be allotted for exploring the Fundy Coast. At the western end, the detour through La Côte Acadienne and stops at Acadian icons such as **Église de Sainte-Marie** add only slightly to the length of the drive. The most impressive Acadian attraction, **Grand Pré National Historic Site,** is farther east, and it deserves at least three hours of your time. At some point during your travels through the region you'll want to focus on the Bay of Fundy (digging into a plate of plump Digby scallops doesn't count). Taking the above into consideration, if you have two nights planned for the Fundy Coast, and you are traveling east from Yarmouth, spend the first morning meandering along La Côte Acadienne, order scallops for lunch in Digby, and continue to Annapolis Royal. Spend the rest of the afternoon and the first part of the next morning exploring the town before moving on to Wolfville. Spend the night, rise early for a short hike through Blomidon Provincial Park, and then move on to Grand Pré National Historic Site. You'll be back in the capital by late afternoon. With an extra day and night, plan on driving along Digby Neck and combining a hike to **Balancing Rock** with whale-watching.

La Côte Acadienne

Those who zoom along Highway 101 between Yarmouth and Digby will miss the charming La Côte Acadienne (Acadian Coast), also known as the Municipality of Clare, a 50-kilometer coastal stretch populated by descendants of the French who resettled here after the Acadian expulsion of 1755. The place-names, the soaring Catholic churches, and the proud Acadian flags (a French tricolor with a single yellow star) announce that you're in the largest Francophone enclave in Nova Scotia.

MAVILLETTE AND VICINITY

For a look at the dynamic Fundy, check out **Mavillette Beach Provincial Park,** on the south side of Cap Sainte-Marie (Cape St. Mary's). The sign for Cape View Restaurant signals the turn from Highway 1; the road peels down to the sea and runs alongside high dunes. Boardwalks cross the dunes to the 1.5-kilometer-long beach, where sandbars trap water in warm pools at low tide. On sunny days, beachcombers walk the expanse and hunt for unusual seashells. Though this is one of the finest beaches in all of Nova Scotia, crowds are nonexistent.

Food and Accommodations

Along the beach access road you'll find **Cape View Motel and Cottages** (124 John Doucette Rd., 902/645-2258, www.capeview-motel.ca, May-Oct.). The motel's 10 basic rooms ($90-145 s or d) and five cottages ($110-140) are set on expansive grounds overlooking sand dunes and the provincial park.

Across the road from the Cape View Motel and with wonderful views of the beach and its stunning sunsets is **Cape View Restaurant** (157 John Doucette Rd., 902/645-2519, mid-May-Oct. daily for breakfast and dinner, $15-27), which dishes up breakfasts such as scrambled eggs with lobster ($14.50) and seafood with an Acadian twist the rest of the day.

Smuggler's Cove Provincial Park

From Mavillette Beach, it's 16 kilometers

north to **Smuggler's Cove Provincial Park.** Walkways here lead to great blufftop views of the coast and down steep, tree-lined steps to the rocky shoreline. The coastal cliffs in this area are notched with caves, which were used by Prohibition-era rum runners. Some of the caves can be explored at low tide. The park also holds numerous picnic tables (making it an ideal lunch stop), but no campsites.

Getting There
Mavillette is just over 30 kilometers (25 minutes) north of Yarmouth via Highway 1. From Halifax, the quickest way to reach Mavillette is via Highway 101 along the Bay of Fundy (300 kilometers, 3.5 hours).

METEGHAN TO POINTE DE L'EGLISE
I recommend staying on the coastal route (Highway 1) between Meteghan and Pointe de L'Eglise (20 km/20 minutes), rather than the much faster inland Highway 101.

Although the seaport of Meteghan, 15 kilometers north of Mavillette, has few tourist facilities, it's worth stopping and taking a look around the dock area, as the main wharf is a hive of activity throughout the day, with local fishermen hauling up mostly lobster and scallops. The area was settled by a number of Acadian families in 1785 and is now the district's commercial hub, although the population still numbers fewer than 1,000. Although currently not open to the public, one of the oldest homes in town is **La Vieille Maison,** built by the founding Robicheau family in the late 1700s.

Food
A seafood cornucopia is brought in daily by the seaport's scallop draggers, herring seiners, and lobster boats. **Seashore Restaurant** (8467 Hwy. 1, 902/645-3453, daily 9am-7pm, $12-19) is a good place for seafood dining, and on a warm summer evening, enjoying dinner on the outdoor deck overlooking the water is priceless.

Getting There
Meteghan is 45 kilometers (35 minutes) north of Yarmouth along Highway 1. It's 280 kilometers (3.5 hours) west of Halifax along Highway 101.

North from Meteghan
The village of **Meteghan River,** about two kilometers north of Meteghan, is Nova Scotia's largest wooden ship-building center. One of the nicest lodgings along La Côte Acadienne is **Au Havre du Capitaine** (9118 Hwy. 1, 902/769-2001, www.havreducapitaine.ca, $105-135 s or d), a country-style inn with hardwood floors and a sitting area set around a large stone fireplace. Choose from rooms with private baths and TVs or larger suites with whirlpool tubs. The inn's licensed dining room is open daily for breakfast, lunch, and dinner.

Also in Meteghan River, lobster lovers should stop in at **Riverside Lobster** (9089 Hwy. 1, 902/769-3340, Mon.-Fri. 9am-6pm), where you can buy live lobsters kept in flow-through crates at the large warehouse—perfect if you're camping or if your accommodation has cooking facilities.

Comeauville
The village of Comeauville, around eight kilometers north of Meteghan River, is notable for **La Galerie Comeau** (761 Hwy. 1, 902/769-2650, call for hours), where artist Denise Comeau displays and sells her folksy watercolors that reflect the region and its Acadian roots.

POINTE DE L'ÉGLISE (CHURCH POINT)
This aptly named community is the last major Acadian community for northbound travelers, but it's also the most interesting.

★ Église de Sainte-Marie
Built between 1903 and 1905, the enormous **Église de Sainte-Marie** (St. Mary's Church), the largest and tallest wooden church in North America, dominates this

village of 490 inhabitants. The building is laid out in the shape of a cross, and its soaring 56-meter steeple has been ballasted with 40 tons of rock to withstand the winter wind. Inside, **Le Musée Sainte-Marie** (902/769-2808, mid-May-mid-Oct. daily 9am-5pm, adult $2, child free) exhibits religious artifacts and historical documents and photos. Mass takes place Sunday at 10:30am.

Food

Through town to the south is ★ **Rapure Acadienne** (1443 Hwy. 1, 902/769-2172, Mon.-Sat. 8am-5:30pm), the most authentic place in all of Nova Scotia to try rappie pie, a traditional Acadian chicken dish with a rather unusually textured potato filling. The pies are massive (and also come with beef and clam fillings) and cost $9, including a side of butter or molasses. Order at the inside window (where you can peek through at the big ovens) and eat at the one indoor table or the picnic tables outside.

Église de Sainte-Marie

Camping

Campers can head to the full-service **Belle Baie Park** (Hwy. 1, 902/769-3160, www.bellebaiepark.ca, May-late Sept., tents $30, hookups $40-55), an oceanfront campground with its own beach, an outdoor pool, a playground, Internet access, and a launderette.

Getting There

Pointe de l'Église is just over 60 kilometers north of Yarmouth on Highway 1.

NORTH TO DIGBY
Grosses Coques

The last of the Acadian communities is **Grosses Coques,** a small village immediately north of Pointe de l'Église that takes its

name from the huge bar clams harvested here on the tidal flats, an important food source for early settlers.

Grosses Coques is almost 65 kilometers north of Yarmouth via Highway 1.

Gilbert's Cove

A short, unpaved road leads from Highway 101 to **Gilbert's Cove Lighthouse** (Hwy. 101, July-Aug. Mon.-Sat. 10am-4pm, Sun. noon-4pm, donation). Built in 1904 to help vessels navigate the upper reaches of St. Mary's Bay, it has been restored and is open to the public in July and August, but the site can be visited any time of the year.

Gilbert's Cove is on Highway 101. It's about 85 kilometers north of Yarmouth via Highway 101. Allow about 70 minutes.

Digby and Vicinity

The port of Digby (pop. 2,100), 105 kilometers northeast of Yarmouth and 235 kilometers west of Halifax, is the terminus for the ferry from Saint John (New Brunswick) and home for the world's largest scallop fleet. The Mi'kmaq name for the area is Te'Wapskik, meaning "flowing between high rocks," a reference to Digby Gut, a narrow opening in the Annapolis Basin to the north of town. Digby derived its English name from Admiral Robert Digby, who sailed up the Fundy in 1793 and settled the place with 1,500 Loyalists from New England. The scallop fleet ties up off Fishermen's Wharf off Water Street; be there at sunset when the pastel-painted draggers lie at anchor in a semicircle, backlit by the intense setting sun.

SIGHTS AND RECREATION

A couple of worthwhile attractions are scattered through town, but the highlights are farther afield—Digby Neck and Kejimkujik National Park, both covered in this section.

Admiral Digby Museum

Digby's place in history is on display at the harbor-front **Admiral Digby Museum** (95 Montague Row, 902/245-6322, mid-June-Aug. Mon.-Sat. 9am-5pm, the rest of the year Wed. and Fri. 9:30am-4:30pm, donation), housed in a trim two-story Georgian-era residence with exhibits of old photographs, interesting maps, and maritime artifacts.

Bear River

Calling itself the "Switzerland of Nova Scotia" may be a stretch, but the small village of **Bear River,** straddling the waterway of the same name, eight kilometers south of Digby, is nestled in a delightful little valley, where the trees turn glorious colors in late September. Along the main street are a motley collection of wooden buildings in various states of repair, many built on stilts above the river far below. Those that have been restored now hold craft shops.

Digby is home to the world's largest fleet of scallop trawlers.

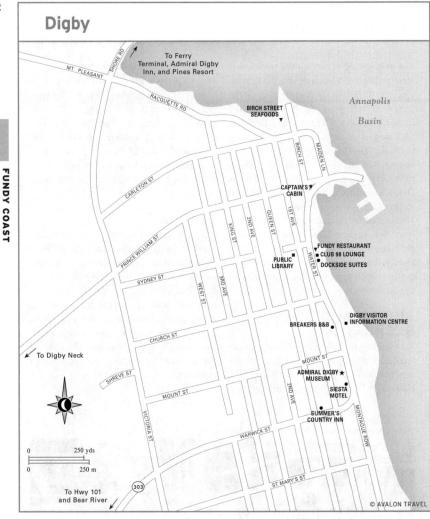

ENTERTAINMENT AND EVENTS

Montague Row to Water Street is the place for people-watching, especially at sunset. **Club 98** (28 Water St., 902/245-4950, 10am-midnight) in the Fundy Restaurant has a band (cover charge) or disc jockey Friday-Saturday. The lounge at the **Pines Resort** (103 Shore Rd., 902/245-2511, Mon.-Sat.) is known for tamer pursuits, low lighting, a comfortable ambience, and finely tuned mixed drinks.

The port's famed scallops attract appropriate fanfare the second week of every August during **Digby Scallop Days** (www.digbyscallopdays.com), with a parade, scallop-shucking competitions, scallop barbecues, street vendors, the crowning of the Scallop Queen and Princesses, music, fireworks, and a parade of the scallop fleet.

Digging into Digby Scallops

Digby is known for its scallops, so there is no better place to try them than this small Fundy Coast port. Unlike other bivalves (such as clams), scallops do not bury themselves in the sand. Instead, they live on the bottom of the Bay of Fundy and "swim" by quickly opening and closing their shells. The fishermen of Digby harvest scallops by dragging large wire baskets over the seafloor. They are shucked (opened) immediately and put on ice until reaching the shore.

The water temperature in the Bay of Fundy varies only slightly through the year, which, combined with the tides' creating lots of nutrient movement, creates ideal conditions for the scallops. The result is the plumpest yet most delicate and succulent meat you could imagine. As a bonus, scallops are low in fat and full of protein.

Across Nova Scotia and beyond, Digby scallops appear on menus by name. In better dining rooms they are sautéed in butter with light spices or combined in seafood casseroles or dishes such as bouillabaisse. Local eateries such as the **Fundy Restaurant** (34 Water St., 902/245-4950, daily 10am-10pm), which has views of the fishing fleet, get creative with scallop omelets, scallop chowder, and scallop fettuccine. At **Birch Street Seafoods** (35 Birch St., 902/245-6551, Mon.-Fri. 9am-5:30pm, Sat. 9am-noon), you can buy them fresh from the trawler (if the weather is bad, the boats don't go out, and they may not have any stock) and prepare them as you please back at your kitchen-equipped accommodation. Expect to pay around $20 per pound.

FOOD

Right downtown, **Fundy Restaurant** (34 Water St., 902/245-4950, daily 10am-10pm, $13-25) is a large, casual restaurant overlooking the scallop fleet. Seating is inside in a main dining room, in a solarium, or out on the balcony. Digby scallops are the specialty, prepared any way you'd like them or in combination with other seafood—the Fundy (scallop) omelet is an interesting breakfast choice, while the rest of the day, dishes such as scallop chowder and a platter of scallops cooked in various styles are good ways to sample this tasty treat.

One block back from the water, **Captain's Cabin** (2 Birch St., 902/245-4868, daily 11am-9pm, $11-18) is a locals' hangout, but it still specializes in seafood. Dishes are a little less creative, but the scallops are just as fresh and delicious.

Check out ★ **Birch Street Seafoods** (35 Birch St., 902/245-6551, Mon.-Fri. 9am-5:30pm, Sat. 9am-noon) for fresh seafood for those staying somewhere with cooking facilities. Naturally scallops are the main draw, but you can also order seasonal catches such as halibut, haddock, and flounder by the pound, as well as Digby chicks (smoked herring).

ACCOMMODATIONS AND CAMPING
$50-100

Digby has a few motel rooms under $100, including the **Siesta Motel** (81 Montague Row, 902/245-2568, www.siestamotel.org, $75-95 s or d), but there are no real bargains in town. The rooms do have wireless Internet and there is a pleasant garden out front.

$100-150

Two blocks from the waterfront, **Summer's Country Inn** (16 Warwick St., 902/245-2250, www.summerscountryinn.ca, May-Oct., $109-129 s or d) has nine guest rooms in an 1830s home and attached annex. Each room has a private bath and comfortable bed, although the decorations are bright—in some a little too flowery for my taste. Rates include a delicious cooked breakfast.

The **Admiral Digby Inn** (441 Shore Rd., 902/245-2531 or 800/465-6262, www.digby-hotels.com, early Apr.-Oct., $119-249 s or d) is across the road from the Annapolis Basin, halfway between town and the ferry terminal. Better-than-average motel rooms start at $121 s or d, and for $160 you get a balcony with water views. Cottages with one and two bedrooms are $179 and $249, respectively. All rates include a light breakfast. Amenities include a restaurant, a lounge, an indoor pool, and a laundry.

Breakers Bed and Breakfast (5 Water St., 902/245-4643 or 866/333-5773, www.the-breakersbb.com, May-Oct., $169-189 s or d, including full breakfast) is an 1853 two-story home across from the waterfront. The three guest rooms are extra-large and furnished in keeping with a heritage theme. A covered front porch with water views and the book-filled sitting room add to the charm.

Dockside Suites (26 Water St., 902/245-4950, www.fundyrestaurant.com, $159-189 s or d) is part of the Fundy Restaurant complex. Each of the 11 modern units is air-conditioned and has a balcony with harbor views and a separate bedroom. Other in-room amenities include a TV/DVD combo and wireless Internet.

Over $200

Appealing to visitors looking for an old-fashioned resort experience, the baronial **Pines Resort** (103 Shore Rd., 902/245-2511 or 800/667-4637, www.digbypines.ca, mid-May-mid-Oct., from $239 s or d) peers down over the port from the brow of a hill on the town's outskirts. The French-Norman manor of stucco and stone was built in 1903 and served as a Canadian Pacific Railway hotel until the province bought it in 1965. The accommodations include more than 80 contemporary rooms in the manor and 30 cottages shaded by spruce, fir, and pine trees. The hotel offers a dining room of provincial renown, an 18-hole golf course (greens fee $69), an outdoor pool, a fitness center, a day spa, tennis courts, hiking trails, and afternoon tea. Most guests stay as part of a package.

Campgrounds

Close to town is **Digby Campground** (Smith's Cove, 230 Victoria St., 902/245-1985, mid-May-mid-Oct., $24-40). To get there, take Exit 26 from Highway 101 and follow the signs toward the ferry for three kilometers. Within walking distance of downtown, it has an outdoor pool, a launderette, and hookups.

INFORMATION

Downtown, the **Digby Visitor Information Centre** (110 Montague Row, 902/245-5714) is open June-early October daily 9am-5pm.

Breakers Bed and Breakfast

Balancing Rock

GETTING THERE

Lying outside the area's main roads, Digby is easily bypassed. Digby is 105 kilometers (1.5 hours) northeast of Yarmouth via Highway 101. It's 230 kilometers (2.5-3 hours) west of Halifax on Highway 101.

The terminus of the ferry from Saint John, *Princess of Acadia,* is through town near the mouth of the Annapolis Basin. Operated by **Bay Ferries** (902-245-2116 or 888/249-7245, www.ferries.ca), the large vessel plies the Bay of Fundy between Saint John (New Brunswick) and Digby (Nova Scotia) one or two times daily throughout the year. High-season one-way fares are adult $46, senior and youth $36, vehicle $92 plus a $20 fuel surcharge. The crossing takes 3.5 hours, and reservations are essential if you're traveling with a vehicle.

DIGBY NECK

The Digby Neck is a long, spindly peninsula reaching like an antenna for almost 80 kilometers back down the Bay of Fundy from Digby. Beyond the end of the peninsula are two small islands. Off the main tourist path, the peninsula will appeal to those interested in nature and spending time in tiny coastal villages where the pace of life is much slower than elsewhere along the Fundy Coast.

From Digby, Highway 217 runs down the center of Digby Neck, through the villages of **Centreville, Sandy Cove,** and **Mink Cove.** At picturesque Sandy Cove, houses cling to the shoreline, while a nearby trail leads to Nova Scotia's highest waterfall. At East Ferry, a ferry departs every 30 minutes on the half hour for **Long Island.** The trip across takes just five minutes and costs $5 per vehicle, including passengers.

★ Balancing Rock

Beyond Tiverton, the main town on Long Island, a two-kilometer (30-minute) each-way trail leads through a forest dotted with marshes, then descends over 200 stairs to a wooden platform where the natural wonder of **Balancing Rock** presents itself in all its glory. This towering basalt column balances precariously above St. Mary's Bay, looking as if it will topple at any time.

Brier Island

A second ferry (also $5) connects Long Island to Brier Island, Nova Scotia's westernmost extremity. The island has a bustling little fishing port at **Westport** and a tourism business that revolves around spring wildflowers, summer whale-watching, and year-round bird-watching. The island's most famous inhabitant was Joshua Slocum (the two vehicle ferries are named for him and his famous sailing boat, *Spray*), who spent his childhood on the island before taking to the high seas and becoming the first person to sail around the world solo. A small monument on a headland south of Westport commemorates the feat.

★ Whale-Watching on the Bay of Fundy

Digby Neck is the base for a thriving whale-watching community. Companies generally offer half-day excursions between mid-June and early October, with regular sightings of finback, right, humpback, and minke whales, as well as Atlantic white-sided dolphins and porpoises. **Ocean Explorations,** based on Long Island at Tiverton (902/839-2417 or 877/654-2341, www.oceanex-plorations.ca, adult $70, child $50), is notable for guide Tom Goodwin, a well-known biologist who takes interested visitors out into the bay aboard high-speed but stable inflatable Zodiac boats. In addition to the most common species, Goodwin searches out North Atlantic right whales when they gather in the middle of the bay (usually Aug.). Estimated to number fewer than 300, these are the world's rarest whales, so named because they were the "right" whales to hunt. Other operators with similar prices include **Brier Island Whale and Seabird Cruises** (Westport, Brier Island, 902/839-2995 or 800/656-3660, www.brierislandwhalewatch.com) and **Mariner Cruises** (Westport, Brier Island, 902/839-2346 or 800/239-2189, www.novascotiawhalewatching.ca).

whale-watching off Brier Island

Food and Accommodations

Between the ferry and Westport (one km from each), **Brier Island Lodge** (Northern Point Rd., 902/839-2300 or 800/662-8355, www. brierisland.com, May-early Oct., $109-169 s or d) sits on a bluff overlooking the sea. The 40 motel-style rooms are spacious and bright; most have water views, and some have king beds. The lodge's homey pine-paneled restaurant (breakfast and dinner daily) is my favorite island dining room. You can order old-fashioned roast turkey dinner or local specialties such as smoked pollock chowder and steamed periwinkles.

Annapolis Royal

The history of Annapolis Royal (pop. 500) spans four centuries, with much of the past preserved along a main street that is lined with the finest collection of pre-1800 buildings in Canada. The town and surrounding area has 150 registered historic buildings, three national historic sites, and Canada's oldest wooden building. Add to the mix one of the world's only tidal power-generating plants, Nova Scotia's largest fun park and its smallest pub, and a selection of gracious accommodations, and you find a town like no other in the province.

History

In 1605, Samuel de Champlain and the survivors of the bitter winter in New Brunswick moved across the Bay of Fundy

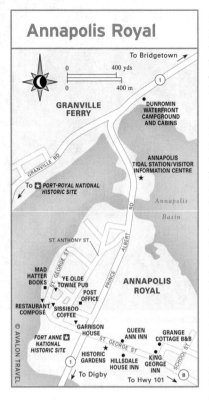

Annapolis Royal

To Bridgetown

0   400 yds
0   400 m

GRANVILLE FERRY

DUNROMIN WATERFRONT CAMPGROUND AND CABINS

GRANVILLE RD

ANNAPOLIS TIDAL STATION/VISITOR INFORMATION CENTRE

To PORT-ROYAL NATIONAL HISTORIC SITE

Annapolis Basin

ST. ANTHONY ST.

MAD HATTER BOOKS
YE OLDE TOWNE PUB
POST OFFICE

ST. GEORGE ST.
PRINCE
ALBERT RD

ANNAPOLIS ROYAL

RESTAURANT COMPOSÉ
SISSIBOO COFFEE

GARRISON HOUSE
QUEEN ANN INN
GRANGE COTTAGE B&B

FORT ANNE NATIONAL HISTORIC SITE
ST. GEORGE ST.

HISTORIC GARDENS
HILLSDALE HOUSE INN
KING GEORGE INN

SCHOOL ST.

To Digby
To Hwy 101

© AVALON TRAVEL

SIGHTS

It's easy to spend a half day wandering through Fort Anne National Historic Site and the adjacent St. George Street, which curves downhill to the waterfront. For Annapolis Royal's other attractions, you'll need a vehicle.

Annapolis Tidal Station

It may not be the town's oldest attraction, but it contains the local tourist information center, so it makes a sensible starting place for your visit. Near the head of Annapolis Basin, signposted to the right as you come into town off Highways 1 or 101, the **Annapolis Tidal Station** (236 Prince Albert Rd., 902/532-0502, May-June and Sept.-mid-Oct. daily 9am-5pm, July-Aug. daily 9am-8pm, free) is the only facility in North America that generates electricity from the tides. Originally built as an experiment, the plant still operates and is capable of generating 20 kilowatts of electricity (enough to power 4,000 homes). The facility harnesses the energy of the massive Fundy tides, which fill a head pond twice daily and then pass through a turbine as they flow back out toward the ocean. The plant's top floor is dedicated to describing the process, with windows allowing views of the head pond and down the bay.

★ Fort Anne National Historic Site

An 18th-century fort and grounds and Canada's first national historic site, **Fort Anne** (St. George St., 902/532-2397, June and Sept. Tues.-Sat. 9am-5:30pm, July-Aug. daily 9am-5:30pm, adult $4, senior $3.50, child $2), overlooks Annapolis Basin from the heart of Annapolis Royal. Considered the key stronghold for possession of Nova Scotia, as the British knew the region—it was Acadie to the French—the site had particular importance to both parties. It has been fortified on at least eight occasions since Scots built Fort Charles in 1629. The earliest French fort, dating to 1630, was designed with a star-shaped layout. Earthwork from the French fort of 1702 remains today, impressively banked

and established the fortified Port-Royal across Annapolis Basin from modern-day Annapolis Royal. It was the first permanent European settlement north of St. Augustine, Florida. After eight years, the settlement came to an abrupt end when it was attacked and destroyed by New Englanders. In the 1630s, the French governor Charles de Menou d'Aulnay built a new Port-Royal on the south shore of the Annapolis Basin, attracting French settlers who came to be known as Acadians. The site would remain the capital of Acadie for the next eight decades. The British captured the fort in 1710, renaming it Fort Anne and rechristening the town Annapolis Royal, in honor of their queen. It would serve as Nova Scotia's first capital until 1749, when it was succeeded by the new town of Halifax.

with sweeping verdant lawns, which are open to the public year-round. Interpretive boards describe features such as a parade ground, chapel site, and restored powder magazine. The British added an officers' garrison in 1797. This whitewashed building now houses a museum that tells the long and colorful story of the fort.

Historic Gardens

The **Historic Gardens** (441 St. George St., 902/532-7018, May-June and Sept.-Oct. daily 9am-5pm, July-Aug. daily 9am-8pm, adult $13, senior $11, child $3) comprise four hectares of theme gardens, a restaurant, and a gift shop. The gardens are undeniably beautiful, but they are also interesting. The Acadian Garden, complete with an Acadian house and outdoor oven, replicates that of the earliest European settlers. Vegetables such as beets, carrots, parsnips, onions, and cabbages are surrounded by a hedge to keep out wild animals, and off to one side is a hedge-encircled orchard of apple and pear trees. Other highlights include the Knot Garden, styled after a hedge garden of the Middle Ages; the Governor's Garden, laid out as a formal garden from the 1750s, when Annapolis Royal was the capital; and a striking Rose Garden with more than 200 varieties, including early English and modern hybrids. The gardens are at their most spectacular in summer, with roses peaking mid-July-September.

★ Port-Royal National Historic Site

The first lasting settlement north of Florida, the 1605 fort at the **Port-Royal National Historic Site** (902/532-2898, mid-May-mid-Oct. daily 9am-5:30pm, adult $4, senior $3.50, child $2) has been reconstructed at what is believed to be the original location. The original French settlement has been rebuilt from Samuel de Champlain's plan using 17th-century construction techniques; the rustic buildings—governor's house, priest's dwelling, bakery, guardroom, and others, furnished with period reproductions—form a rectangle

cannon at Fort Anne

around a courtyard within the palisaded compound. The original outpost boasted many historic firsts: Canada's first play, *Le Théâtre de Neptune,* was written and produced here by the young Parisian lawyer Marc Lescarbot; the continent's first social club, l'Ordre de Bon Temps (the Order of Good Cheer) was founded here in 1606; and the New World's first grain mill was built here to grind meal from the first cereal crops. The story of all this is brought to life by knowledgeable staff dressed in period costume. To get to Port-Royal, cross Annapolis Basin by the generating station and turn left at Granville Ferry. It's 10 kilometers along the road (2 kilometers beyond Melanson Settlement National Historic Site).

RECREATION
Hiking

Delaps Cove, 24 kilometers west of Annapolis Royal (cross Annapolis Basin, head south toward Port-Royal for 8 kilometers, and turn right on the unpaved road that ends at the Bay

the Historic Gardens of Annapolis Royal

of Fundy), is a small fishing village that is the start of the **Delap's Cove Wilderness Trail,** one of the few longer hiking trails along this stretch of coast. From the wharf at the end of the road, the trail meanders southwest along the coast for 15 kilometers. It takes about eight hours round-trip, but you can hike for just an hour or so before turning around if time is an issue.

Amusement Parks

Upper Clements Parks (2931 Hwy. 1, Upper Clements, 902/532-7557, mid-June-early Sept. daily 11am-7pm, entry $11, $5 per ride) is Nova Scotia's largest theme park. Its style is thoroughly Nova Scotian, featuring a train ride on a historical replica, a mini-golf course designed as a map of the province, and the re-creation of a fishing village. The park also has a roller coaster, a flume ride, a carousel, pedal boats, live entertainment, dinner theater Friday-Saturday evenings, a crafts area with demonstrations and a shop, and dining rooms. The adjacent **Adventure**

Park, featuring 14 ziplines, obstacle courses, and suspended bridges, costs $34.50 for a full-day pass.

FOOD

St. George Street has many dining choices, including diner-style cafés and fine-dining restaurants. For surprisingly good coffee, roasted locally, head to **Sissiboo Coffee** (262 St. George St., 902/286-3010, Mon.-Sat. 7:30am-4pm, Sun. 9pm-5pm), which shares a space in a gallery with a local photographer. In addition to coffee, Sissiboo has locally produced apple cider and a limited menu of cakes and pastries.

Facing Annapolis Basin from behind the main row of shops, **Restaurant Composé** (235 St. George St., 902/532-1251, Mon.-Sat. 11am-8pm, Sun. 1pm-8pm, $20-34) is easy to miss. This European-style eatery has evolved from a café into a popular restaurant, with the menu blending local seafood (namely scallops and lobster) with Continental cooking styles. The best place to enjoy the view is in the water-facing solarium. The apple strudel is a great way to finish your meal.

Locals gather for afternoon beer and pub grub on the outdoor patio or for nightcaps in the cozy interior of English-style **Ye Olde Towne Pub** (9 Church St., 902/532-2244, Mon.-Sat. 11am-11pm, Sun. noon-8pm, $11-21), beside the outdoor farmers market at the bottom end of St. George Street. Built in 1884 as a bank and reputed to be the smallest bar in Nova Scotia, its meals are typical pub fare, but the portions are generous. Look to the blackboard for seafood specials.

★ **Garrison House** (350 St. George St., 902/532-5501, daily from 6pm, $21-32) is a refined restaurant spread through three connected rooms of an 1854 inn. The chef is renowned for sourcing seasonal produce, while year-round specialties include fish cakes and Acadian jambalaya. With its impressive wine list and professional service, this is the best place in town for fine dining.

If you're staying at a campground or have chosen an accommodation with cooking facilities, head over North Mountain to Parker's Cove and pick up fresh seafood such as scallops, lobster, mussels, halibut, and haddock from **Nautical Seafoods** (Shore Rd. W., 902/532-2212, summer daily 11am-7pm). You can also order seafood chowder, boiled lobsters, and lobster rolls to eat at the picnic tables out front.

ACCOMMODATIONS AND CAMPING
$50-100

Aside from the cabins at Dunromin Waterfront Campground and Cabins, few places offer rooms for less than $100 in July and August. One option is **Grange Cottage** (102 Richie St., 902/532-7993, $85 s, $95 d), where the three guest rooms share one bathroom. The rear deck has river views, and the front porch is a relaxing place to cool off on hot afternoons. Rates include a full breakfast.

King George Inn (548 Upper St. George St., 902/532-5286, www.kinggeorgeinn.20m. com, mid-May-mid-Nov., $99-139 s or d) is a grandiose ship captain's home, built circa 1868 and furnished with Victorian-era antiques. It offers eight luxurious guest rooms, including a two-room family suite. Amenities include a library, pianos, free use of bicycles, and evening tea and coffee.

$100-150

The closest of the historic bed-and-breakfasts to downtown is **Garrison House** (350 St. George St., 902/532-5750 or 866/532-5750, www.garrisonhouse.ca, mid-Apr.-Oct., $139-179 s or d), which is across the road from Fort Anne. Built in 1854 as a hotel, this gracious building holds seven guest rooms of varying configurations, as well as a downstairs restaurant open daily for dinner.

Hillsdale House Inn (519 St. George St., 902/532-2345 or 877/839-2821, www.hillsdale-houseinn.ca, May-Oct., $120-170 s or d) is on a six-hectare estate that has been graced by kings and prime ministers. The main house has 11 air-conditioned guest rooms, and the adjacent coach house another four. Antiques

Queen Anne Inn

fill public areas, including a cozy lounge. A cooked breakfast is included in the rates.

Set on two hectares of landscaped grounds, ★ **Queen Anne Inn** (494 Upper St. George St., 902/532-7850 or 877/536-0403, www. queenanneinn.ns.ca, May-Oct., $149-249 s or d) is a restored 1865 Victorian mansion with a grand mahogany staircase that sweeps upstairs to 10 guest rooms outfitted with period furnishings. Room 10 is significantly smaller than the remaining nine, which are extra large. Behind the main house, the carriage house contains two two-bedroom units, perfect for two couples traveling together or a family. Rates include a full three-course breakfast and afternoon tea.

Swimming, hiking, wagon rides, canoeing, and lawn games fill the day at **Mountain Top Cottages** (888 Parker Mountain Rd., 902/532-2564 or 877/885-1185, www.mountaintopcottages.com, May-Oct., $124-154 s or d), in a forested setting atop North Mountain. Seventeen simple cottages with one or two bedrooms overlook a private lake. Each has a microwave and fridge as well as wireless Internet. To get there, cross Annapolis Basin at the tidal power plant, follow Highway 1 through Granville Ferry, and take Parker Mountain Road off to the north.

Campgrounds

Running right down to a private beach on the Annapolis Basin, **Dunromin Waterfront Campground and Cabins** (902/532-2808, www.dunromincampground.ca, mid-May-mid-Oct., campsites $32-46) is the perfect place for families. With a fort-themed playground, an outdoor pool, mini-golf, lawn games, canoe rentals, and a café, the biggest problem will be dragging the children off for a day of sightseeing. The campground has 165 sites, most of them serviced. Canvas tepees with shared bathrooms are $50 s or d, and cabins range from $78 with shared bathroom to $125 for a two-bedroom waterfront cottage.

INFORMATION AND SERVICES

Annapolis Royal Visitor Information Centre (Hwy. 1, 902/532-5769, May-June and Sept.-mid-Oct. daily 9am-5pm, July-Aug. daily 9am-8pm, free) is at the tidal power plant, on the north side of downtown. Coming into town from Exit 22 along Highway 101, turn right before the historic main street.

GETTING THERE

Annapolis Royal is 35 kilometers (30 minutes) from Digby along Highway 101. It's 200 kilometers (2.5 hours) west of Halifax on Highway 101.

Kejimkujik National Park

Deep in the interior of southwestern Nova Scotia, **Kejimkujik** (kedji-muh-KOO-jick, or "Keji" or "Kedge" for short) **National Park** (www.pc.gc.ca) lies off Highway 8, about midway between Liverpool and Annapolis Royal. Encompassing 381 square kilometers of drumlins (rounded glacial hills), island-dotted lakes (legacies of the last ice age), and hardwood and conifer forests, the park and the adjacent Tobeatic Game Sanctuary are an important refuge for native wildlife and town-weary Nova Scotians.

Wildlife enthusiasts visit the park for birdwatching (including barred owls, pileated woodpeckers, scarlet tanagers, great crested flycatchers, and loons and other waterfowl) and may also spot black bears, white-tailed deer, bobcats, porcupines, and beavers. The many lakes and connecting rivers attract canoeists and swimmers in warm weather, as well as anglers (particularly for perch and brook trout). Hikers can choose from a network of trails, some leading to backcountry campgrounds; some of the campgrounds are also accessible by canoe. In winter, cross-country skiers take over the hiking trails.

RECREATION

The two most popular park activities are hiking and canoeing. The **Beech Grove Trail,** a two-kilometer loop, starts at the visitors center and wends along the Mersey River, where it climbs a drumlin hilltop swathed in an almost-pure beech grove. The **Farmlands Trail** is another drumlin variation, and the 45-minute hike makes its way up a drumlin to an abandoned farm on the hilltop. A little farther south along the park access road is the trailhead for the one-kilometer **Rogers Brook** loop, which passes through a forest of red maple and hemlock trees.

You can rent canoes, rowboats, and bicycles ($5 per hour, $24 per day) at Jakes Landing, on the northeast side of large Kejimkujik Lake; the adjacent stretch of the Mersey River is placid and suitable for beginning paddlers.

Kejimkujik National Park

0   4 mi

0   4 km

To South Milford and Annapolis Royal

Big Dam Lake

Frozen Ocean Lake

8 Maitland Bridge

VISITOR RECEPTION CENTRE ■

JEREMY'S BAY △

To Liverpool

JAKE'S LANDING ■

West River

Kejimkujik National Park

Kejimkujik Lake

McGinty Lake

Peskawa Lake

Mountain Lake

Mersey River

Peskowesk Lake

© AVALON TRAVEL

ACCOMMODATIONS AND CAMPING

Within the park, **Jeremy's Bay Campground** (mid-May-mid-Oct., $27.50-31.50), on the north side of Kejimkujik Lake, has 360 sites, some with power hookups, as well as washrooms and showers, fire pits and firewood ($8), a playground, picnic areas, and an interpretive program. Another 46 wilderness sites ($18) are scattered in the woodlands and offer toilets, tables, grills, and firewood. A percentage of sites can be booked through the **Parks Canada Campground Reservation Service** (519/826-5391 or 877/737-3783, www.reservation.pc.gc.ca) for $12 per reservation.

Milford House (902/532-2617, www.milfordhouse.ca, from $155 s or d) is in South Milford, about 20 kilometers north of the park toward Annapolis Royal. The resort features a main lodge (rebuilt after it was destroyed by fire in 2014) and 28 lakeside cabins. All cabins have separate bedrooms, a wood-burning fireplace, and a full bathroom. Four hiking trails radiate out from the resort, some leading to lakes where canoes are available free of charge. Dinner and breakfast is a very reasonable adult $35, child $25, per day.

INFORMATION

The **Visitor Reception Centre** (902/682-2772, mid-June-Aug. daily 8:30am-8pm, Sept.-mid-June daily 8:30am-4pm) is just beyond the park entrance. This is the place to buy day passes (adult $6, senior $5, child $3) and fishing licenses ($10 per day, $35 annual) and pick up literature on the park, including hiking trail descriptions.

a foggy morning in Kejimkujik National Park

GETTING THERE

Although the park is just 50 kilometers from Annapolis Royal along Highway 8, allow about an hour to reach the entrance, as the road is narrow and winding.

From Halifax, take Highway 101 along the South Shore to Liverpool and then Highway 8 north. The total distance from Halifax to the park is 170 kilometers (two hours).

Annapolis Valley

The Annapolis Valley, which spreads along the Annapolis River east from Annapolis Royal, is a haze of white when its apple orchards bloom in late May-early June. The valley, extending northeast from Annapolis Royal, supports more than magnificent apple orchards, however; if you look closely, you'll also see hectares of strawberries, plums, peaches, pears, and cherries, as well as crops of hay, grain, and tobacco.

The Annapolis Valley has a legion of fans, among them the Mi'kmaq, who first settled this region. According to Mi'kmaq legend, Glooscap, a deity taking the form of a giant man, roamed the upper Fundy. He made his home atop the basalt cliffs of the peninsula—the lofty hook-shaped cape that finishes in sea stacks at Cape Split—and buried jewels on the Fundy beaches. (Today's tides still claw at the coastline to reveal agate, amethyst, and zeolite from Hall's Harbour to Cape Split's tip.)

ANNAPOLIS ROYAL TO CANNING

From Annapolis Royal, Highway 101 heads northeast, crossing the Annapolis River near Bridgetown and continuing east for 100 kilometers to Wolfville. You don't see a great deal from the highway, so plan to travel Highway 1 (cross the Annapolis Basin at Annapolis Royal to get going). Along this route, you pass through the villages and apple orchards now bypassed by Highway 101.

Bridgetown

This town has wide streets lined with grand old homes and stately trees. **James House Museum** (12 Queen St., 902/665-4530,

June-Aug. Tues.-Sat. 10am-5pm, free) is an 1835 residence sandwiched between modern shops along the main street.

Take Church Street north out of town and you reach **Valleyview Provincial Park** after five kilometers. This small park sits atop North Mountain, an ancient ridge of lava that forms a cap over softer shale and sandstone that has been gouged away to the south, forming the Annapolis Valley. From the park, views extend across the valley to the province's remote interior. The park campground (mid-June-mid-Oct., $29) has just 30 sites, but it only ever fills on summer weekends. It has toilets and drinking water but no showers.

GETTING THERE

Bridgetown is 24 kilometers (20 minutes) northeast of Annapolis Royal along Highway 101. From Halifax, Bridgetown is 170 kilometers (two hours) west on Highway 101.

Kentville

The commercial hub of the Annapolis Valley is Kentville (pop. 6,100). The town is on the north side of Highway 101 and at the junction of Highway 12, which cuts south through the Nova Scotia interior to Mahone Bay and Lunenburg. In the historic heart of town is **King's County Museum** (37 Cornwallis Ave., 902/678-6237, Mon.-Fri. 9am-4pm, free), which contains a predictable collection of pioneer artifacts, as well as many interesting historical photographs within a two-story 1903 red-brick courthouse.

On the outskirts of town, you'll find a couple of inexpensive motels, including **Allen's Motel** (384 Park St., 902/678-2683, www.allensmotel.ns.ca, mid-Mar.-mid-Dec., $76-162 s or d), two kilometers west of downtown. Here, 10 rooms are separated from the highway by well-tended gardens and a picnic area with a gas barbecue; larger units have separate bedrooms and full kitchens.

South Mountain Park (Hwy. 12, South Alton, 902/678-0152 or 866/860-6092, www.southmountainparkcampground.com, campsites $39-47, cabins $80) fills with holidaying families through its mid-May-mid-October season. A few kilometers south of Kentville, it's not really set up for quick overnight stays. But if you have children and are looking for a break from touring, it's a great place to kick back for a few days. The activities offered could easily fill a week of fun—everything from fishing to tennis to wagon rides to walking paths. Amenities include a par-3 golf course, a games room, a TV room, a library with wireless Internet access, a large outdoor pool, and lots more. On the downside, campsites offer little privacy.

GETTING THERE
Kentville is about 95 kilometers (just over an hour) northeast of Annapolis Royal via Highway 101. It's 100 kilometers (1.5 hours) northwest of Halifax on Highway 101 and 100 kilometers (1 hour) northwest from Halifax, also via Highway 101.

Starr's Point
Prescott House Museum (1633 Starr's Point Rd., 902/542-3984, June-Sept. Mon.-Sat. 10am-5pm, Sun. 1pm-5pm, adult $4, senior $3) harks back to the valley's orchard beginnings, when horticulturist Charles Ramage Prescott imported species to add to the provincial store of fruit trees. His profits built this Georgian-style homestead. The restored mansion, constructed circa 1812, displays period furnishings and sits amid beautiful gardens. Its special events celebrate the fall harvest. It's along Highway 358, which leads north from Greenwich.

GETTING THERE
Starr's Point is about 110 kilometers (1.5 hours) northeast from Annapolis Royal via Highway 101.

Canning
The east end of the Annapolis Valley has a smattering of emerging boutique wineries, including **Blomidon Estate Winery** (10318 Hwy. 221, 902/582-7565, June-Oct. Mon.-Sat. 10am-6pm, Sun. 11am-6pm). This winery was the first in Nova Scotia to produce classic varietals such as chardonnay, pinot noir, and shiraz. Tours depart daily at 1pm and 3pm, ending with a tasting session ($10 per person). You can also order meat and cheese platters, accompanied by a glass of wine of course, and enjoy them on the patio. The winery is two kilometers east of Canning along Highway 221.

GETTING THERE
Canning is about 115 kilometers (1.5 hours) northeast of Annapolis Royal along Highway 101. It's 105 kilometers northwest of Halifax on Highway 101.

BLOMIDON PENINSULA
The Blomidon Peninsula is at the northern end of North Mountain. Extending into the Minas Channel and with Minas Basin to its back, it features more fantastic Fundy scenery and a couple of good campgrounds.

The Look-Off
On the north side of Canning, **Look-Off Family Camping** (Hwy. 358, 902/582-3022, www.lookoffcamping.com, mid-May-late Sept., campsites $30-36, cabins $70-100 s or d) lives up to its name with a long list of activities—think hayrides, bingo, and fitness classes—and workshops such as kite-making and cookie painting. Other facilities include a café open daily at 9am, a playground, a pool, and a launderette. The namesake Look-Off (a Nova Scotian term for a lookout) is across the road and has wonderful views across the bucolic Annapolis Valley.

Blomidon Provincial Park

The dramatically positioned 759-hectare **Blomidon Provincial Park** (902/582-7319) is along the eastern side of the Blomidon Peninsula, facing Minas Basin. To get there, turn off Highway 358 three kilometers north of the Look-Off and follow the secondary road north for 14 kilometers. The red shale and sandstone that make the park so striking were laid down millions of years ago and then eroded by glacial and water action to form 180-meter-high bluffs that are topped by coastal forest. Fundy tides sweep up to the cliff face twice daily, but as the water recedes, you can walk along the red-sand beach, searching for semiprecious stones such as amethyst and agate. The uplands area is covered in forests of sugar maple, beech, and birch, yet also present are alpine plants such as maidenhair.

The best place for a walk is along the beach, but check at the park office or information boards for tide times. Four official trails wind their way through the park. The best views are from the **Look-Off Trail,** an easy 1-kilometer walk to a lookout high atop the cliffs. The 5.6-kilometer **Jodrey Trail** fringes the cliffs, while the **Interpretive Trail** passes information boards describing the forest and its inhabitants. The main day-use area is where the access road enters the park. It's one of the few places along the Fundy Coast where the water gets warm enough for swimming.

Beyond the day-use area, the access road climbs to the **campground** (early June-early Oct., $26), where sites are spread through the forest on two short loops. Facilities include showers, a playground, and drinking water.

To Cape Split

At the tip of the Blomidon Peninsula is Cape Split. To get there, continue north on Highway 358 from the Look-Off to Scots Bay, where there's a small day-use-only provincial park with a pebbly beach fronting Minas Channel. The road ends just beyond Scots Bay, from where it's 13 kilometers on foot to Cape Split. It's a long way to walk (and make the return trek) in one day, but there is no elevation gain and the rewards are total wilderness and sweeping views from the cliff top at the end of the trail.

Getting There

The Blomidon Peninsula is about 130 kilometers (1.5 hours) northeast of Annapolis Royal along Highway 101, and about 20 kilometers (20 minutes) north of Canning.

FUNDY COAST
ANNAPOLIS VALLEY

Blomidon Provincial Park is notable for its high sea cliffs.

Wolfville and Vicinity

At the eastern end of the Annapolis Valley, the genteel town of Wolfville (pop. 4,200) began with the name Mud Creek, an ignoble tribute from the founding New England planters who wrestled with the Fundy coastal area once farmed by early Acadians. Now the town sits in the lushest part of the Annapolis Valley, and you won't want to miss it. Highway 1 runs through town as Main Street, where large houses with bay windows and ample porches sit comfortably beneath stately trees. Acadia University's ivy-covered buildings and manicured lawns lie along Main and University Avenue.

The town, just six blocks deep, has an uncomplicated layout alongside Highway 1 and Highway 101.

SIGHTS
Main Street

Wolville's refined nature is apparent to anyone walking along Main Street, which is dotted with grand stone buildings and, at the eastern end, stately trees.

Randall House Museum (259 Main St., 902/542-9775, June-late Aug. Tues.-Sat. 10am-5pm, Sun. 1:30pm-5pm, donation) is an 1815 historic home with period furnishings and local artifacts from the 1760s to the 20th century.

Acadia University Art Gallery (Beveridge Arts Centre, 10 Highland Ave., 902/585-1373, Tues.-Sun. noon-4pm, free) has a fine-arts collection of local and regional works, highlighted by Alex Colville's oils and serigraphs.

Waterfront

Most visitors miss Wolfville's waterfront, but the town does have one, one block north of Main Street across Front Street. Trails and a small park have been developed at the mouth of the Cornwallis River, which was once lined with busy shipyards. Views extend across the

Minas Basin to the red cliffs of Blomidon Provincial Park.

Along Front Street to the west is **Robie Tufts Nature Centre,** which is a series of covered interpretive boards describing the flora and fauna native to the area. The main purpose of the structure is to provide a dwelling for chimney swifts, which make their home in the red-brick chimney rising through the roof.

SHOPPING

The **Harvest Gallery** (462 Main St., 902/542-7093, July-Oct. Mon.-Sat. 10am-5pm, Sun. noon-5pm, closed Mon. the rest of the year) displays the work of local artists. Especially eye-catching are the colorful oil paintings of Jeanne Aisthorpe-Smith.

Although apples get most of the glory, lots of other farming happens in the Annapolis Valley. **Gaspereau Valley Fibres** (830 Gaspereau River Rd., 902/542-2656, www.gaspereauvalleyfibres.ca, Tues.-Fri. 10am-5pm, Sat.-Sun. 11am-4pm) highlights the local wool industries, with knitting, weaving, and spinning, as well as raw materials sold as-is. The shop is on a farm on the south side of Highway 101; to get there from town, take Gaspereau Road south.

FOOD

For a small town, Wolfville has a surprising number of eateries, but my suggestion if you're in town on a Wednesday or Saturday is to head to ★ **Wolfville Farmers Market** (24 Elm St., 902/697-3344, May-Dec. Wed. 4pm-7pm, year-round Sat. 8:30am-1pm), which has a mouthwatering selection of choices from local producers, including many choices cooked on the spot, such as Harbourville Schnitzelhaus, which sells authentic German dishes using lots of local produce. Many stalls sell items to go, such as baked goods, preserves, smoked meats, and wine.

Wolfville

Just Us! (450 Main St., 902/542-7731, Mon.-Fri. 7:30am-7pm, Sat. 8am-7pm, Sun. 9am-6pm, lunches $5-8) pours organic coffees and a wide range of teas from the front of a historic theater building, with seating spread through the lobby. Meals are very inexpensive ($6.50 for soup and sandwich), and the muffins are baked fresh daily.

Tucked away between Main Street and the farmers market, ★ **Troy Restaurant** (12 Elm St., 902/542-4425, Sun.-Thurs. noon-8pm, Fri.-Sat. noon-9pm, $16-26) specializes in Mediterranean cuisine, with the emphasis on Turkish favorites. The room itself is spacious and airy, with wooden floors and red-brick walls creating a background

for hanging rugs and brightly painted light shades. The menu is relatively inexpensive, with kebabs under $20 and a roasted lamb shank for just $25.

The dining rooms at the local inns are good bets for meals. One of the best of the dining rooms associated with local accommodations is the **Acadian Room** (Old Orchard Inn, 153 Greenwich Rd., 902/542-5751, daily 7am-9pm, $17-29), which draws diners to its large restaurant with stunning views and good food. Before 11am, the French toast with whipped cream and blueberry sauce is a delight. Local fare such as cedar-plank salmon basted with dark rum and maple syrup is an evening standout. Most dinner mains are less than

$20. The wine list allows the opportunity to taste Nova Scotian wine by the glass.

ACCOMMODATIONS

Most Wolfville accommodations are grand heritage homes, so there are few bargains.

$100-150

Roselawn Lodging (32 Main St., 902/542-3420, www.roselawnlodging.ca, $100-195 s or d) is a modest motel on the east side of downtown. Facilities include an outdoor pool, a launderette, barbecues and picnic tables, a tennis court, and a playground. The 28 motel rooms are clean and comfortable, and 12 adjacent cottages come with kitchens.

On the hill behind the information center, **Blue Shutters Bed and Breakfast** (7 Blomidon Terr., 902/542-3363, www.blueshuttersbnb.ns.ca, $100-120 s, $110-130 d) has three well-equipped guest rooms. Each has an en suite bathroom, a TV/DVD combo, wireless Internet, and an electric fireplace. Rates include a full breakfast.

If you're a garden lover, you won't want to leave the expansive grounds of ★ **Blomidon Inn** (195 Main St., 902/542-2291 or 800/565-2291, www.blomidon.ns.ca, $139-269 s or d), which is surrounded by more than one hectare of cacti, roses, rhododendrons, azaleas, ponds, a croquet lawn, and a terraced vegetable garden that doubles as an outdoor eating area. The home itself, built in 1882 by a shipbuilder, reflects the wealth of its original owner. Mahogany and teak dominate, and local antiques are found throughout public areas and the 29 guest rooms. The least expensive rooms are on the small side, but all have en suite bathrooms. Rates include a continental breakfast and afternoon tea. Tennis courts, a restaurant open daily for dinner, and a lounge round out this elegant accommodation.

A registered historic property built in 1893, **Victoria's Historic Inn and Carriage House** (600 Main St., 902/542-5744 or 800/556-5744, www.victoriashistoricinn.com, $149-189 s or d) combines a grand Victorian house with an adjacent carriage house. Rooms vary greatly in character; my favorite is the Hunt Room ($149 s or d), on the upper floor of the carriage house, which has a smart green and burgundy color theme and a vaulted cathedral ceiling. Like the other rooms, it has an en suite four-piece bathroom, TV, telephone, bathrobes, and a CD player. Rates include a cooked breakfast and afternoon tea.

Wolfville Farmers Market

Dating to 1874 and within walking distance of downtown, **Tattingstone Inn** (630 Main St., 902/542-7696 or 800/565-7696, www.tattingstoneinn.com, $128-178 s or d) is casually formal, with nine guest rooms spread through the main house and adjacent carriage house. All are decorated with antiques, and some have whirlpool tubs. The inn also offers a music room, a dining room, a steam room and heated outdoor pool, and a tennis court. Rates include a cooked breakfast.

The **Old Orchard Inn** (153 Greenwich Rd., 902/542-5751 or 800/561-8090, www.oldorchardinn.com) is a sprawling resort near Exit 11 of Highway 101. It comprises more than 100 motel-style guest rooms ($125-175 s or d) and 29 cabins (May-Oct., $175-245 s or d) spread through the forest. Tennis courts, an indoor pool, saunas, spa services, hiking trails, and a stone patio with sweeping valley views add to the appeal. The resort also has a dining room and lounge.

INFORMATION AND SERVICES

In Willow Park at the east end of town is the **Wolfville Visitor Centre** (11 Willow Ave., 902/542-7000, www.wolfville.ca, May-Oct. daily 9am-6pm).

Eastern Kings Memorial Hospital (902/542-2266) is at 23 Earnscliffe Avenue. Call the **police** at 902/542-3817 or the **RCMP** at 902/679-5555.

GETTING THERE

Wolfville is 120 kilometers (1.5 hours) east of Annapolis Royal along Highway 101. It's 90 kilometers (just over an hour) northwest of Halifax on Highway 101.

GRAND PRÉ

This small village was the epicenter of one of the most tragic events in Canadian history, the expulsion of the Acadians from their homeland. First settled in 1680 by an Acadian family who moved from the confines of nearby Port-Royal, Grand Pré grew to become the largest Acadian settlement in Nova Scotia. The main attraction is Grand Pré National Historic Site, but also worth visiting is **Grand Pré Wines** (Hwy. 1, 902/542-1753, July-mid-Oct. Mon.-Sat. 10am-6pm, Sun. 11am-6pm, mid-Oct.-Dec. Wed.-Sun. 11am-5pm), where grapes are grown on 60 hectares of former Acadian farmland. In the main building you'll find a restaurant (summer, Mon.-Sat. 10am-6pm, Sun. 11am-6pm), wine shop, and

Blomidon Inn

crafts corner. Free winery tours are offered through summer (daily 11am, 3pm, and 5pm).

★ **Grand Pré**
National Historic Site

Commemorating the Acadian deportation, the **Grand Pré National Historic Site** (2242 Grand Pré Rd., 902/542-3631, mid-May-mid-Oct. daily 9am-5pm, adult $7.80, senior $6.60, child $4) brings Acadian history and the deportation to life. It wasn't until Henry Wadsworth Longfellow wrote the poem *Evangeline* in 1847 that the English-speaking world became aware of the expulsion, but by then nothing remained of Grand-Pré (Great Meadow), the setting for the story of the Acadian heroine separated from her lover by the deportation.

In 1922, an interested benefactor with Acadian roots built a small stone church on the presumed site of Grand Pré, and this became the foundation for the historic site of today. Visitors enter through a large museum complex, where there's a bookstore and gift shop, along with information panels describing Acadian life, the deportation, and the return of Acadians to Nova Scotia. Outside are sprawling grounds crisscrossed by pathways that lead to vegetable gardens, a blacksmith shop, an orchard, a lookout over the diked farmland, and a statue of Henry Wadsworth Longfellow. In the middle of the site is a statue of Evangeline. Directly behind the statue is the 1922 church. It houses an exhibit of paintings that showcase the history of the people and a copy of the original expulsion order that was read to a congregation within the original church, as well as stained-glass windows with a story to tell. Guided tours of the grounds (included with admission) are highly recommended. A guide is also stationed within Église Saint-Charles to lead you through the story of each painting.

Food and Accommodations

The best choice of accommodations are in nearby Wolfville, but the centrally located **Evangeline Inn and Motel** (11668 Hwy. 1, 902/542-2703 or 888/542-2703, www.evangelineinncafe.com, May-Oct., $125-145 s or d) provides comfortable accommodations right at the turnoff to the historic site. Choose from motel units or five guest rooms in the adjacent boyhood home of Sir Robert Borden, prime minister of Canada for nine years in the early 20th century. All guests have use of the swimming pool. Also on the grounds is

Grand Pré National Historic Site

Holy Pumpkins!

Windsor may be famous as the birthplace of hockey, but no attraction is bigger than the pumpkins grown on the south side of town at **Howard Dill Enterprises** (400 College Rd., 902/798-2728, Mon.-Fri. 9am-4pm). The Dill family is renowned in the giant pumpkin-growing business for developing seeds that go on to produce some of the world's largest pumpkins, some of which swell to over 700 kilograms.

You won't find the pumpkins grown from Dill's seeds on grocery store shelves. They are used for fall fairs and pumpkin-growing competitions, and as jack-o-lanterns by folks with strong porches. Most of the company's business is done online; at www. howarddill.com you can order the precious seeds and books such as *How to Grow World Class Giant Pumpkins* as well as download growing tips. At the Dill farm, visitors are encouraged to drop by and see Dill's own pumpkin patch, where even the smallest pumpkins are in the 180- to 230-kilogram range leading up to the late September-early October harvest.

---

a modern **restaurant** (May-Oct. daily 8am-7pm), where cooked breakfasts are less than $7, and dishes such as haddock chowder with a warmed scone on the side are $6-10.

Stop at the headquarters of locally owned **Just Us!** (11865 Hwy. 1, 902/697-4225; Mon.-Wed. 7am-5pm, Thurs.-Fri. 7am-6pm, Sat. 8am-6pm, Sun. 9am-6pm). Here, on the north side of the historic site, you'll find a roaster, a shop selling a thoughtful collection of coffee-related items, and a small museum (free) explaining the owners' dedication to free trade coffee and why it's important. Out back is a garden that visitors are free to wander through.

Getting There

To get to Grand Pré from Wolfville, head east on Highway 1 for about five kilometers, or take Exit 10 from Highway 101. From Halifax, head north on Highway 101 for 85 kilometers (one hour).

WINDSOR

If you've toured along the South Shore and then traveled along the Fundy Coast, the temptation may be to stay on the highway and give Windsor, just 60 kilometers northwest of Halifax, a miss. But this gracious town on the banks of the Avon River is worth the short detour from busy Highway 101. To get there from the main highway, take Exit 6, which leads into downtown. Before town is a small **information center** (902/798-2690, mid-May-mid-Oct. daily 9am-5pm).

Fort Edward National Historic Site

Dating to 1750, **Fort Edward National Historic Site** (King St., 902/542-3631, mid-June-late Sept. daily 10am-6pm, free) preserves the last 18th-century blockhouse in Nova Scotia. Fort Edward was one of the main assembly points for the deportation of the Acadians from the province in 1755. Although the building is open only during summer, touring the grounds will give a good feel for the location of the fort and the chance to see earthen mounds where the rest of the fort once stood.

Historic Homes

Sprawling **Haliburton House** (414 Clifton Ave., 902/798-5619, June-Sept. Mon.-Sat. 10am-5pm, Sun. 1pm-5pm, adult $4, senior and student $3) was owned by 19th-century author, humorist, historian, and judge Thomas Chandler Haliburton, who was born in Windsor in 1796. Among the sayings that originated in Haliburton's writings are "It's raining cats and dogs," "barking up the wrong tree," "facts are stranger than fiction," and "quick as a wink." The Victorian mansion on 10 hectares is open to the public, as are the surrounding gardens. For hockey fans, Haliburton's written memories of childhood have special meaning. In them, he reminisced about children "playing ball on ice" behind Haliburton House, which is the earliest mention of the game of ice hockey.

On Ferry Hill, **Shand House** (389 Avon St.) is another vintage beauty and marks the wealthy Shand family's prominence in Windsor. When it was built in the early 1890s, the Queen Anne-style mansion was one of the first residences in the area fitted with electric lights and indoor plumbing. Currently, there is no public access, but the grandeur can be admired from the grounds.

Getting There

Windsor is southeast of Wolfville, about 30 kilometers (25 minutes) away via Highway 1 or Highway 101. Windsor is about 60 kilometers (45 minutes) northwest of Halifax via Highway 101.

Central Nova Scotia

Look for ★ to find recommended sights, activities, dining, and lodging.

Highlights

★ **Riding the Tidal Bore:** This phenomenon occurs in only a few places in the world. Locals call it the Total Bore, and while admittedly it's not exactly exciting to watch from the sidelines, riding the wave on a raft is a once-in-a-lifetime experience (page 127).

★ **Balmoral Grist Mill:** The reflection of this bright red building in an adjacent pond creates a scene of tranquility (page 138).

★ **Hector Heritage Quay:** Step aboard a full-size replica of the *Hector*, upon which Pictou's first settlers arrived, to get a taste of the hardships that they endured crossing the Atlantic Ocean (page 139).

★ **Arisaig:** Unassuming cliffs are filled with fossils that have helped scientists understand the evolution of life on earth 400 million years ago (page 143).

★ **Taylor Head Provincial Park:** Marine Drive passes dozens of protected areas, but Taylor Head stands out for its ease of access and interesting geology (page 147).

★ **Sherbrooke Village:** History comes alive at this living museum. For the full effect, join the Hands on History program and dress up in period costume (page 149).

★ **Canso Islands National Historic Site:** The focus of this attraction is Grassy Island, once home to a thriving fishing community in the early 1700s. But the best part for budget-conscious travelers is the price—which includes a boat trip (page 151).

Perfect for those looking for low-key attractions as varied as ancient fossils, beautiful beaches, and remote park,

Central Nova Scotia extends north from Halifax to Truro (the geographical center of the province) and then west to the New Brunswick border and east to the causeway leading to Cape Breton Island.

The region can be divided roughly into manageable sections—each very different in look and feel. The TransCanada Highway slices through the region's northwest corner and extends to Cape Breton Island in the east. But this route promises little besides uninterrupted speed. Detour south to explore an area that was once the realm of Glooscap, the mythical Mi'kmaq god who roamed this part of Nova Scotia in the form of a man as large as Gulliver among the Lilliputians. According to legend, Glooscap slept stretched out over the region's northern portion and used Prince Edward Island as his pillow. While the Northumberland Strait has long been the domain of vacationing locals—attracted by warm water and long stretches of beautiful beach—other visitors on a fast track often see the region as a flash of landscape from the TransCanada Highway. The other option for reaching Cape Breton Island from

Halifax is to drive along the Eastern Shore, which is as rugged as the Northumberland Strait shore is tame. This super-scenic road unfurls itself at a leisurely pace, and it's worth slowing down and taking two or three days to travel its length. Passing tiny fishing ports reminiscent of seafaring life of decades ago, and rock-bound coves where the forest grows right down to the sea, the road's services are few and far between (Canso, with a population of 950, is the largest town), so plan ahead by making accommodations reservations and keeping your gas tank full.

PLANNING YOUR TIME

Central Nova Scotia is not a destination like Cape Breton Island, where you would plan your visit around an itinerary that lasted a certain length of time. Instead, you will surely find yourself passing through central Nova Scotia on more than one occasion—for example, driving from New Brunswick through to Halifax and then again on the way to Cape Breton Island. If you've been touring through New Brunswick, you'll already be well aware of the massive Fundy tides. In central Nova

---

Previous: Waterside Beach; historic boat at dock. **Above:** Balmoral Grist Mill.

Central Nova Scotia

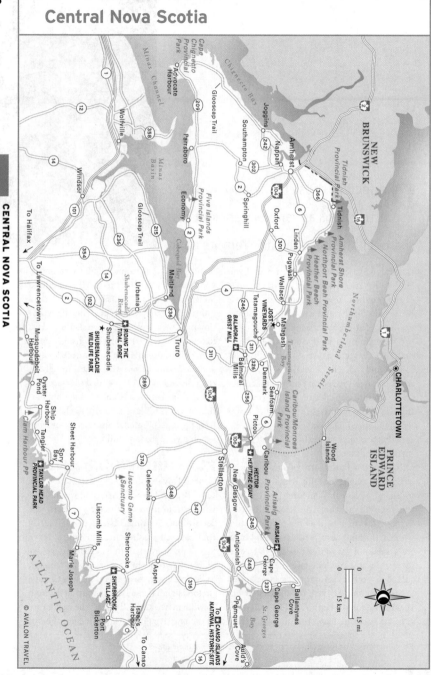

© AVALON TRAVEL

Scotia, you can **ride the tidal bore** on the Shubenacadie River. Along Northumberland Strait, beaches lapped by warm water will tempt you to linger, while historic attractions such as **Balmoral Grist Mill** and Pictou's **Hector Heritage Quay Museum** keep the past alive. From Halifax, you could plan on spending two days reaching Cape Breton Island via the above-mentioned attractions, which would also allow time for a detour to **Arisaig,** a fossil hot spot protected by a small provincial park. If you have an extra day or two, consider taking Marine Drive to or from Cape Breton Island. The distance (320 kilometers from Dartmouth to Canso) is deceiving when planning how long the drive will take. Add a ferry trip to a winding, often narrow road that passes through dozens of small townships, and you should expect the journey to take six hours, without stops. From Canso, it will take another 90 minutes to reach Port Hastings, the gateway to Cape Breton Island. But of course, this estimate of 7.5 hours to complete the Marine Drive is sans stops, and if you're only interested in reaching Cape Breton Island from Halifax, the Highway 102/104 route via Truro takes about half as long. Leaving Halifax in the morning, an ideal scenario would be to spend one night en route and to plan on reaching Cape Breton Island later the following day. This would allow time to explore **Taylor Head Provincial Park,** to step back in time at **Sherbrooke Village,** and to take the boat trip to **Canso Islands National Historic Site.**

Halifax to Truro

As you head north from Halifax, suburbia is quickly left behind, as divided Highway 102 speeds north to Truro, which is easily reached in an hour from downtown. Highway 2, the original route between these two cities, may look appealing on the map, but the scenery is no different from what you'll see from Highway 102—it simply takes around 30 minutes longer.

SHUBENACADIE

If you're willing to try something new, or you have an animal-loving family, there are two good reasons to visit Shubenacadie.

★ Riding the Tidal Bore

The **Shubenacadie River,** which drains into the Bay of Fundy at Cobequid Bay, is not just a good place to view the tidal bore but also to *ride* it. **Tidal Bore Rafting Resort** (Hwy. 215, Urbania, 902/758-4032 or 800/565-7238, www.raftingcanada.ca) operates two- and four-hour Zodiac raft excursions May-September. You board the rafts at low tide and head downstream, just in time to catch the tidal bore back upriver. The driver rides the wave, then doubles back to blast through its face, finding rapids along the way to keep the adrenaline pumping. Rates for the two-hour tour range $60-70 depending on the extremity of the tide. Departures are dependent on the tides; check the website for times.

Shubenacadie Wildlife Park

Families will enjoy **Shubenacadie Wildlife Park** (149 Creighton Rd., 902/758-2040, mid-May-mid-Oct. daily 9am-6:30pm, mid-Oct.-mid-May Sat.-Sun. 9am-3pm, adult $4.75, child $2), a provincially operated zoo well signposted from Highway 102 (take Exit 10 or 11). Throughout the spacious grounds are Canadian animals you are unlikely to see in the wild (fishers, otters, and more), ones that you don't want to meet face to face (bears, cougars, wolves, and lynx), and those you'll see only at Christmas (reindeer). The Sable Island horses may look like regular horses, but they are one of the world's few wild horse populations.

Accommodations and Camping

★ **Rafters Ridge Cottages** (Hwy. 215, Urbania, 902/758-4032 or 800/565-7238, www.raftingcanada.ca, $160-203 s or d) is part of the Tidal Bore Rafting Resort complex, so it's no surprise that many guests come for the rafting (rooms are discounted when a rafting package is purchased). In the riverside location, you can also rent canoes or hang out around the outdoor pool. Lodging is in one- and two-bedroom cottages. The cottages have decks, barbecues, and pleasant views across a tree-sprinkled hillside. The facility also has a restaurant open daily for breakfast and dinner.

In the vicinity of the rafting park and also right on the Shubenacadie River is **Wide Open Wilderness Campground** (Urbania, 902/261-2228 or 866/811-2267, www.wowcamping.com, mid-May-Sept., campsites $30-38, cabins $90 s or d). You can watch the tidal bore, walk marked hiking trails, relax around the pool, try your hand at the horseshoe pits, or join in the many scheduled activities.

Getting There

To get to Shubenacadie from Halifax, take Exit 10 from Highway 102. It's a 60-kilometer, 45-minute drive.

MAITLAND

Maitland, at the mouth of the Shubenacadie River, was where Canada's largest wooden ship, the three-masted *William D. Lawrence,* was built. Documentaries, ship portraits, and memorabilia are kept at the shipbuilder's former homestead, the **Lawrence House Museum** (8660 Hwy. 215, 902/261-2628, June-Sept. Tues.-Sat. 10am-5pm, adult $3.90, senior and child $2.80), which overlooks Cobequid Bay. The actual 1874 launching is commemorated on the middle Saturday of each September with a parade of period-dressed locals, a symbolic launch, and seafood suppers hosted throughout the village.

peacock at Shubenacadie Wildlife Park

Getting There

To get to Maitland from Halifax, it's a 90-kilometer, 70-minute drive starting with Highway 118 and ending with Highway 215.

If you've been moseying eastbound along the Bay of Fundy and don't particularly want to detour back through Halifax, turn at Windsor (take Exit 5 from Highway 101) and follow Highway 215 along the edge of Minas Basin to Maitland, crossing the Shubenacadie River to meet busy Highway 102 at Truro. Between Windsor and Truro it's 90 kilometers (1.5 hours)—you won't save any time, but the scenery is better than via Halifax (120 kilometers, 1.5 hours).

TRURO

Situated at the convergence of the province's major expressways and served by VIA Rail, Truro (pop. 12,000) is called the hub of Nova Scotia. It is the province's third-largest population center, with an economy based on shipping, dairy products, and the manufacture of clothing, carpets, plastic products, and wines.

Truro

Truro's academic side includes a teachers' college in town and an agricultural college on the outskirts.

Sights

The access road leading into 400-hectare **Victoria Park** (corner of Brunswick St. and Park Rd.) ends at a wide-open day-use area where beds of tulips flower through June, a colorful highlight of the town. At other times of the year, the park is still worth visiting—forests of spruce, hemlock, and white pine are spliced with hiking trails that lead along a deep canyon and past two waterfalls.

In a quiet residential area, the **Colchester Historeum** (29 Young St., 902/895-6284,

June-Aug. Mon.-Sat. 10am-5pm, shorter hours Sept.-May, adult $5, senior $4, child $1) does a fine job entwining exhibits on Fundy eccentricities and the area's natural history.

WATCHING THE TIDAL BORE

Tidal bores only occur in a few places in the world, and one of the most accessible is at the **Salmon River**, which flows through Truro. Best described as a small wave, the bore is particularly high along the Salmon River, as it is at the head of Cobequid Bay, where the incoming tide pushing up the Bay of Fundy is forced into a narrow funnel. At Truro, the lead wave travels up the river as it pushes toward town beneath the Highway 102 overpass.

If you want a close-up look at the tidal bore, take Robie Street west out of town beyond Highway 102 (or, from Hwy. 102 take Exit 14) and take the signed road that leads to the Tidal Bore Observation Deck. Tidal bore arrival times are listed at the deck, in the *Truro Daily News*, and at the Truro Welcome Centre (Commercial St.).

Food

NovelTea (622 Prince St., 902/895-8329, Mon.-Fri. 8:30am-6pm, Sat. 9:30am-5:30pm, Sun. noon-5pm, lunches $7-10) combines a wide selection of teas, excellent coffee, and a secondhand bookstore. Part of the appeal is the setting—a surprisingly bright space filled with comfortable couches and colorful local artwork.

In a nondescript strip mall near the heart of downtown, ★ **Murphy's** (88 Esplanade, 902/895-1275, Mon.-Sat. 11am-7pm, $9-18) serves some of the best-priced seafood anywhere in this part of the province. I had the deep-fried haddock and chips—cooked to perfection—for just $11. A variety of fish is offered—pan-fried, poached, or "Texas style"—amid bright nautical-themed decor.

Another favorite is **Nook and Cranny** (627 Prince St., 902/895-0779, Mon. 11am-10pm,

Tues.-Thurs. 11am-11pm, Fri. 11am-1am, Sat. 9am-11pm, Sun. 9am-11pm, $10-22). While locals often stop by just for a craft beer on the outdoor tables, the lunch and dinner menu provides good value (I'm yet to find another place in Nova Scotia where a filet mignon is under $20), with most dishes featuring local produce and game.

Accommodations

Lodgings in Truro are plentiful and reasonably priced. Motels line all the main routes into town, and you shouldn't have a problem finding a room at short notice.

The standout for value is the **Willow Bend Motel** (277 Willow St., 902/895-5325 or 888/594-5569, www.willowbendmotel. com, $105-149 s or d) along Highway 2, which feeds into downtown from the south. From the highway, it doesn't look that impressive, but the guest rooms have been given a major modern overhaul, creating the impression that you are spending a lot more money than you really are. The beds are super comfortable and the bathrooms a delight. Adding to the appeal is a heated outdoor pool and landscaped surrounds.

As usual, the **Super 8** (85 Treaty Trail, 902/895-8884 or 877/508-7666, www.

looking out from the Tidal Bore Observation Deck

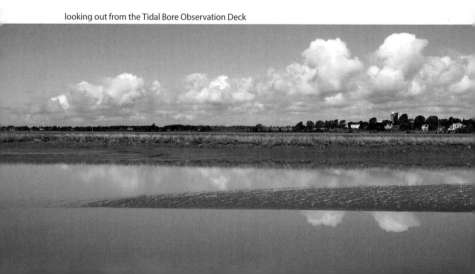

super8truro.com, $155 s or d) is close to a main artery and is filled with clean, comfortable air-conditioned rooms packed with amenities. Here you also get an indoor pool with a waterslide and hot tub. A light breakfast is included, and you are within walking distance of restaurants for dinner. Call for last-minute specials.

Information

The **Truro Welcome Centre** (Commercial St., 902/893-2922, mid-May-June and Sept.-mid-Oct. daily 9am-5pm, July-Aug. daily 8:30am-7:30pm) is at the heart of downtown overlooking Victoria Square; ask for a map of the tree-trunk sculptures scattered through town, and check your email using the free wireless Internet.

Getting There

True to its nickname, the "Hub of Nova Scotia," Truro is centrally located within the province at the junction of Highways 102 and 104. It's an easy one-hour run between Halifax and Truro (100 km apart), and even less from Halifax Airport (66 km south). Baddeck on Cape Breton Island is 252 kilometers to the northeast (allow three hours), and Moncton, New Brunswick, is 172 kilometers (90 minutes) to the west.

Glooscap Trail

Named for the mighty Glooscap, a mythical Mi'kmaq figure who controlled the tides, this region is far enough from the main highway that it is missed by most visitors. It's a shame, because it is dotted with interesting seaside villages, has beaches that occasionally give up precious gemstones, and has been the site of some amazing dinosaur discoveries. The Glooscap Trail extends along the Bay of Fundy from as far west as Windsor; this section covers the best of Highway 2, which follows the coast west from Truro to Cape Chignecto and then north to Amherst.

TRURO TO PARRSBORO

Take Exit 14A from Highway 102, and you'll quickly find yourself on Highway 2, heading west along Cobequid Bay. En route to Parrsboro are a string of small fishing villages, lookout points, and a couple of spots where beach access is possible at low tide.

Five Islands Provincial Park

As the name suggests, **Five Islands Provincial Park** does protect five islands, but it also encompasses more than 600 hectares of the mainland between Economy and Parrsboro. Among the park's coastal extremes are high cliffs and beaches, the latter revealing gems such as agate, amethyst, and jasper as the huge Fundy tides sweep across the bay. The five-kilometer (round-trip; allow 90 minutes) **Red Head Trail** reaches almost a dozen lookouts, including the Old Wife, a point of land that enjoys views across to the five islands.

PARRSBORO

The sea's erosive force has opened a window on the ancient world here along the coastlines of Chignecto Bay and Minas Basin. Archaeological digs have yielded 100,000 fossilized bone fragments of ancient dinosaurs, crocodiles, lizards, sharks, and primitive fish.

Sights

FUNDY GEOLOGICAL MUSEUM

Cross the bridge from downtown via Two Islands Road to reach **Fundy Geological Museum** (162 Two Islands Rd., 902/254-3814, mid-May-mid-Oct. daily 10am-5pm, adult $8.25, senior $6.75, child $4.75). It highlights the Bay of Fundy, with displays describing how the tides have eroded the bedrock to expose numerous geological wonders, such as precious gemstones and

Glooscap Trail

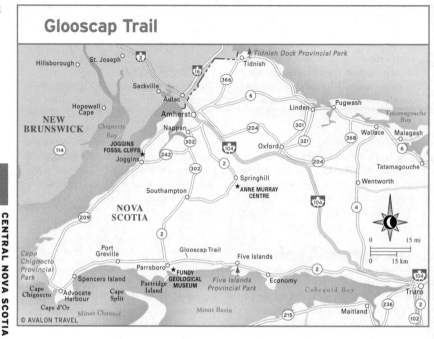

the fossilized remains of dinosaurs. It also holds the collection of Eldon George, a local man who spent 60 years collecting fossils from around the world., including some of the world's smallest dinosaur tracks, which he uncovered in the Parrsboro region.

OTTAWA HOUSE MUSEUM
Through town, beyond the mineral shop, is **Ottawa House By The Sea Museum** (902/254-2376, June-Sept. daily 10am-6pm, adult $2.50), a 21-bedroom waterfront home dating to 1775. All that remains on the beach in front of the home are broken-down pylons, so it's hard to believe that this was once an important shipbuilding port. Now cared for by the local historical society, Ottawa House has two floors of historical displays and a tearoom.

Linked to the mainland by a narrow strip of rocky beach that begins below Ottawa House, you'll find Partridge Island; archaeological evidence points to Mi'kmaq occupation of the island 10,000 years ago. A rough

road ends just before the island, from where a hiking trail winds to the summit and allows views across the Minas Basin to Cape Split (30 minutes round-trip).

Food
As you cruise the main street, **Glooscap Restaurant** (758 Upper Main St., 902/254-3488, daily breakfast, lunch, and dinner, $12-19) is obvious, but a better choice is the **Harbour View Restaurant** (476 Pier Rd., 902/254-3507, summer daily 7am-9pm, $14-27), which has uninterrupted water views off Two Island Road. It's a friendly place, with all the usual seafood choices, including daily specials that are sourced from seasonal catches. The lobster dinner is a favorite.

Accommodations
Riverview Cottages (3575 Eastern Ave., 902/254-2388 or 877/254-2388, www.riverviewcottages.ca, mid-May-mid-Oct., $60-105 s or d) lies along the Farrells River on the east side of town. The cabins are older, and only

a few have cooking facilities such as funky woodstoves, but canoes are available for guest use, and the price is right.

Within walking distance of downtown, the ★ **Maple Inn** (2358 Western Ave., 902/254-3735, www.mapleinn.ca, $99-169) smoothly combines two historic homes into an accommodation with 11 regular rooms and a spacious two-bedroom suite. The building was originally a hospital, so the inn has special meaning to those visitors returning to the town where they were born (Room 1 was the delivery room). The inn is surrounded by well-tended gardens, while inside is a lounge with a TV and a library of books. Rates include a full breakfast served in a cheery dining room.

The guest rooms at **Gillespie House Inn** (358 Main St., 902/254-3196 or 877/901-3196, www.gillespiehouseinn.com, May-Oct., $129-149 s or d) ooze old-world charm, and each has an en suite bathroom. The Elderkin Room has a wooden sleigh bed and looks over the front garden, which catches the morning sun.

Getting There

Parrsboro is just over 90 kilometers (1.5 hours) west from Truro via Highway 2. It's 180 kilometers (2.5 hours) from Halifax via Highways 102 and 2 through Truro.

WEST TO CAPE CHIGNECTO

At Parrsboro, most travelers head north to Springhill on Highway 2, but Highway 209 along Minas Channel makes for a pleasant drive. It's 50 kilometers to the last village of any consequence, Advocate Harbour. At the halfway mark is Port Greville, once home to four shipbuilding companies. Today, you can take Wagstaff Street to the cliff edge and peer down at the river mouth that 100 years ago would have been filled with ships in various stages of construction. Across the water, Cape Split is plainly visible.

Advocate Harbour

At Spencers Island, Highway 209 turns inland to **Advocate Harbour,** a quiet corner of the province first visited by Europeans in 1604, when Samuel de Champlain came ashore. Just before town, take the signposted road to Cape d'Or, where a light-keeper's residence has been converted into ★ **The Lighthouse at Cape d'Or** (902/670-0534, www.capedor.ca, May-mid-Oct., $80-110 s or d). Perched on high cliffs overlooking the Bay of Fundy, this four-room lodge is a wonderful place to kick back and do absolutely nothing at all. One room has an en suite bathroom, while the other three share two bathrooms, and the common room is stocked with books and board games. The attached restaurant (closed Wed.; cash only) serves light lunches and creative dinners ($12-30).

Cape Chignecto Provincial Park

As the crow flies, **Cape Chignecto Provincial Park** isn't far from the TransCanada Highway or the city of Saint John (New Brunswick), but it is a world away from civilization, protecting an arrow-shaped headland jutting into the Bay of Fundy. Cliffs up to 185 meters high are lapped by the world's highest tides, which pour into Chignecto Bay on one side and Minas Basin on the other. No roads penetrate the park. Instead, from the end of the road at Red Rocks, just beyond the village of West Advocate and 46 kilometers from Parrsboro, a hiking trail leads around the cape and loops back through the forested interior. Most backpackers complete the circuit in three days, packing their own food and water and pitching their tents at backcountry campgrounds. Cabins along the way at Arch Gulch and Eatonville provide an alternative to camping (call 902/392-2085 for reservations). All hikers should be experienced in backcountry travel and totally self-sufficient.

JOGGINS

This town on the Chignecto Bay coast is 40 kilometers southwest of Amherst.

Joggins Fossil Cliffs

Declared a UNESCO World Heritage Site in 2008, Joggins Fossil Cliffs have yielded thousands of fossils from the Carboniferous period (350-280 million years ago). Plants are most common, but a forest of upright petrified tree stumps is what the site is best known for. First noted in the 1850s, the hollow stumps contained the fossilized remains of *Hylonomus,* the earliest reptile ever discovered. It is supposed that these 30-centimeter-long critters fell inside and were unable to escape. The site has also revealed a two-meter-long arthropod with 30 sets of legs, as well as dinosaur footprints.

In conjunction with the UNESCO designation, the location of the Joggins Fossil Centre (100 Main St., off Hwy. 302, 902/251-2727, mid-Apr.-June and Sept.-Oct. daily 10am-4pm, July-Aug. daily 9:30am-5:30pm, adult $8, senior and child $6) on the site of an abandoned coal mine at the top of the cliffs provides the perfect setting to learn about the importance of the site. In addition to displays of ferns, fish scales, reptile footprints, and gastropods, visitors can watch lab technicians at work. To fully immerse yourself in the experience, plan on joining a guided tour. Departing daily from the interpretive center, they are tide-dependent; options include an easy 30-minute stroll (adult $10.50, senior $10), a more in-depth two-hour tour (adult $25, senior $23.50), and a strenuous four-hour outing (adult $75, senior $65). All tours include admission to the center, and guests joining the four-hour tour are supplied with a picnic lunch.

Getting There

From Parrsboro, take Highway 2 north to Southampton and then follow Highways 302 and 242 north and then west for 40 kilometers (40 minutes) until you reach Joggins. From Halifax, take Highway 102 north to Truro, then Highway 104 west to Amherst, where Highways 302 and 242 lead to Joggins. Allow 2.5 hours for the 225-kilometer drive from Halifax.

SPRINGHILL

The sultry voice of crooner Anne Murray is known the world over, but the folks in the small town of Springhill, on a slight rise just off Highway 104, take special pride in this local girl who has gone on to sell 50 million albums and win more awards than any other female vocalist.

Anne Murray Centre

You probably already guessed that Springhill would provide a home for the Anne Murray Centre (36 Main St., 902/597-8614, mid-May-mid-Oct. daily 9am-4:30pm, adult $9, senior and student $8). The museum pays tribute to the beloved local warbler who hit the Top 40 in the 1970s with "Snow Bird" and is still going strong. Exhibits include photos, clothing, and other memorabilia, and an audiovisual display catalogs Murray's career.

Getting There

Springhill is 45 kilometers (45 minutes) northeast of Parrsboro via Highway 2. It's 180 kilometers (two hours) north then west of Halifax via Highways 102 and 104.

AMHERST AND VICINITY

Amherst (pop. 9,500) is built on high ground above Amherst Marsh—part of the larger 200-square-kilometer Tantramar Marshes—on the isthmus joining Nova Scotia to the mainland of Canada. The fertile marshes were first diked and farmed by the Acadians in the 1600s and are still productive today, mainly as hayfields.

Sights

Amherst is at its architectural best along Victoria Street, where the profits of industry and trade were translated into gracious houses, commercial buildings, and churches garnished in Tudor, Gothic, and Queen

Anne Revival styles (the red sandstone **First Baptist Church** on Victoria Street in the heart of downtown is particularly impressive). A few blocks south of the historic district, **Cumberland County Museum** (150 Church St., 902/667-2561, Feb.-Dec. Tues.-Fri. 9am-5pm, Sat. noon-5pm, adult $3) is in an 1838 residence. The museum does an impressive job of tracking the past, with exhibits on early Acadian settlements, Amherst's Anglo background, and spicy tidbits relating to Russian revolutionary Leon Trotsky, who was interned in an Amherst POW camp in 1917.

Amherst Point Migratory Bird Sanctuary, a few kilometers from town at the end of Victoria Street, spreads out over 190 hectares with trails through woodlands, fields, and marshes and around ponds. The sediment-rich Cumberland Basin lures 200 bird species, including Eurasian kestrels, bald eagles, hawks, and snowy owls.

Food and Accommodations

Amherst Wandlyn Inn (Victoria St., off Hwy. 104 at Exit 3, 902/667-3331 or 800/561-0000, www.wandlyninns.com, from $115 s or d), the town's largest lodging, has 88 air-conditioned rooms with wireless Internet and an indoor pool. Guests enjoy a free continental buffet breakfast.

Information

The **Nova Scotia Visitor Information Centre** (90 Cumberland Loop, 902/667-8429, July-Aug. daily 8am-8pm, Sept.-June daily 8:30am-4:30pm) is a large complex well signposted from Highway 102 as you enter the province from New Brunswick to the west. Adjacent is a promenade describing driving routes through the province, with picnic tables overlooking Tantramar Marshes. In a rail carriage on the same side of town, the **Amherst Tourist Bureau** (51 La Planche St., 902/667-0696, www.amherst.ca, May-Aug. Mon.-Sat. 10am-6pm) specializes in the region, with lots of information for those heading south to the Glooscap Trail.

Getting There

Staying on Highway 2, Amherst is 25 kilometers (20 minutes) northwest of Springhill. Taking Highway 102 then Highway 104, Amherst is 200 kilometers (two hours) northwest of Halifax.

CENTRAL NOVA SCOTIA
GLOOSCAP TRAIL

Amherst's First Baptist Church

Sunrise Coast to Pictou

The quickest way to reach Pictou from Amherst is to take Highway 104 via Truro, but Highway 6 is more scenic. Throughout the region, the land dips and sweeps in manicured farmlands extending to the red beaches and cliffs of Northumberland Strait. The villages are small, and the backcountry roads are scenic. This is rural Nova Scotia at its best. Allow three hours, plus stops.

TIDNISH AND VICINITY

Highway 366 branches off Highway 6 a few kilometers northeast of Amherst and reaches the Northumberland Strait at Tidnish, which lies right on the provincial border between Nova Scotia and New Brunswick.

Tidnish Dock Provincial Park

Across the Tidnish River from town is **Tidnish Dock Provincial Park.** This small day-use park protects the northern terminus of an ambitious railway construction project that was designed to transport vessels across the isthmus between the Bay of Fundy and Northumberland Strait. The initial proposal had been for a canal link, but the government decided that constructing a rail line would be easier. The plan called for the construction of hydraulic presses at either end to lift the boats into cradles that were to be pulled across the 28-kilometer rail line by locomotives. In 1891, nearing completion, the entire project was abandoned; the dock and a short length of the rail bed remain.

Continuing East Along Highway 366

Head east from Tidnish to **Amherst Shore Provincial Park.** From the day-use area, a short trail follows Annebelles Brook to a short beach, while on the other side of the highway is a **campground** (mid-May-mid-Sept., $29) with flush toilets, showers, and fire pits. Continue east for seven kilometers

to **Northport Beach Provincial Park,** renowned for its excellent beach and water warmed by shallow sandbars. Next up, and equally popular for swimming, is **Heather Beach Provincial Park.**

Getting There

Tidnish is about 30 kilometers (30 minutes) northeast of Amherst. From Highway 6, take Highway 366 until you reach Tidnish. From Halifax, Tidnish is 215 kilometers (2.5 hours) northwest via Highways 102, 104, 6, then 366.

PUGWASH

Recognized mostly for its delightful name, Pugwash (from the Mi'kmaq word *pagweak,* meaning "shallow water") lies at the mouth of Pugwash Basin, 50 kilometers east of Amherst. Durham Street (Hwy. 6) is the main drag. Here you'll find a summer-only information center and the usual array of small-town businesses. Across the water to the south of downtown is a salt mine. Current production is 90,000 tons annually (10 percent of Nova Scotia's total mineral value). The best opportunity to get an idea of the operation's scope is to watch the freighters being loaded at the downtown dock.

Food and Accommodations

Downtown, the vaguely Irish-themed **Inn the Elms** (10340 Durham St., 902/243-2885, www.inntheelms.com, June-mid-Oct., $98 s or d) has a distinctive green and red exterior and four guest rooms with older furnishings. The dining room is open Wed.-Sun. 9am-2:30pm; breakfast is included for all paying guests. It also opens Friday evening for dinner until 8pm with simple mains all under $20.

    Sheryl's Bakery & Café (10480 Durham St., 902/243-2156, Mon.-Fri. 7am-4:30pm, Sat. 9am-4pm, lunches $5-8) is a friendly little place where you are guaranteed soup made

Thinker's Lodge

Recognized mostly for its delightful name, Pugwash (from the Mi'kmaq word *pagweak,* meaning "shallow water"), 50 kilometers east of Amherst, is best known as the origin of the **Pugwash Conferences on Science and World Affairs** (www.pugwash.org). The first of these took place in 1955 in Pugwash after Albert Einstein called for a meeting to discuss the dangers of a nuclear war. Cyrus Eaton, who had made his fortune in the United States as an industrialist, offered to sponsor the event on the condition it was held in his hometown. And so in 1957 it came to be that 13 Cold War nuclear scientists, including three from the USSR, met at what became known as the Thinker's Lodge, a large but otherwise unremarkable residence on the Pugwash foreshore. It was the first of many such gatherings, which now take place annually in London, Washington, Rome, Tokyo, and even still in Pugwash. Weapons of mass destruction are still discussed, but topics have broadened to include breaking down international borders, the environment, and economic prosperity. To get to **Thinker's Lodge** (249 Water St., info@ thinkerslodge.org, tours July-Aug. Tues.-Sun. 10am-5pm, free), follow Durham Street to its eastern end and turn right down Water Street.

in-house each day and the sweetest, stickiest, most delicious cinnamon buns imaginable.

Getting There

Pugwash is 50 kilometers (45 minutes) east of Amherst via Highway 6. It's 40 kilometers (40 minutes) from Tidnish to Pugwash, for those traveling along Highway 366. From Halifax, it's a 200-kilometer, 2.5-hour drive northwest.

PUGWASH TO PICTOU

It's 110 kilometers (1.5 hours) between Pugwash and Pictou along Highway 6, but there are many worthwhile detours; the first, Gulf Shore Road, starts from downtown Pugwash.

Along Gulf Shore Road

From downtown's Durham Street, Gulf Shore Road spurs north and then follows the edge of Northumberland Strait in an easterly direction before rejoining Highway 6 at Wallace. About four kilometers from Pugwash is **Gulf Shore Picnic Park,** a day-use area with fireplaces and picnic tables spread across a grassed area that slopes to a red-sand beach.

Near where Gulf Shore Road loops south to Wallace is **Fox Harb'r Golf Resort and Spa** (1337 Fox Harbour Rd., 902/257-1801 or 866/257-1801, www.foxharbr.com). While

the resort and its facilities wouldn't look out of place in Arizona or on the Atlantic Coast, it's certainly unique in rural Nova Scotia. At $225 for a round of golf, the greens fee is high, but it's a beautiful course. Other facilities include an Olympic-size indoor pool, spa services, guided kayaking, and formal dining (jacket required) in the Great Room. Guests soak up pure luxury in suites (from $475 s or d) contained within chalets that line the fairways and look out over Northumberland Strait.

Jost Vineyards

About 34 kilometers west of Pugwash, **Jost Vineyards** (48 Vintage Ln., 902/257-2636, mid-June-mid-Sept. daily 9am-6pm, the rest of the year daily 10am-5pm) is signposted off Highway 6. The creation of the Jost (pronounced "yost") family from Europe's Rhineland and now part of Devonian Coast Wineries, this 40-hectare vineyard produces fine white wines that are sold throughout the province, including at many better restaurants. The best-known blends are the Jost ice wines. To produce this style, grapes are left on the vines until after the first frost, then gently pressed to produce just a few drops of concentrated juice from each grape. The result is an intensely sweet wine that is perfect as an after-dinner treat. Free guided tours are given daily in summer at noon and 3pm.

★ Balmoral Grist Mill

Best known for its 1864 gristmill, the town of Balmoral Mills lies along Highway 311, 10 kilometers south of Tatamagouche and 38 kilometers north of Truro. Nestled at the base of a wooded vale, bright red **Balmoral Grist Mill** (660 Matheson Brook Rd., 902/657-3016, June-early Oct. Mon.-Sat. 10am-5pm, Sun. 1pm-5pm, adult $4, senior and child $2.80) is a photographer's ideal setting. Wheat, oats, and barley are still ground using 19th-century methods at this historic gristmill-cum-museum built in 1874. Milling demonstrations are at 10am and 2pm. The mill is busiest the first Sunday in October—an Open Day drawing a crowd of hundreds with activities such as milling demonstrations and popular taste-testing of oatmeal cakes.

Seafoam

At the coastal village of **Seafoam,** 24 kilometers east of Tatamagouche, you'll find the ★ **Seafoam Campground** (Harris Ave., 902/351-3122, www.seafoamcampground.ca, mid-May-Sept., $32-39), a large facility with direct access to the beach and warm swimming water. Amenities include lawn games, a playground, showers, and a laundry. On the west side of the campground, a side road leads to an abandoned dock, where a concrete wall has created a barrier for shifting sand. The result is a wide stretch of beach, perfect for lazing away a few hours on a warm summer day.

Balmoral Grist Mill

Pictou

Pictou (PIC-toe), 160 kilometers east of Amherst and 14 kilometers north of Exit 22 from Highway 104, is a historic port town of 3,500 on Northumberland Strait. It is also the ferry gateway to Prince Edward Island, meaning plenty of traffic passes through.

Nearly everything in Pictou happens at the waterfront, which is home to the main museum, restaurants, and historic accommodations. Some of the older buildings have a distinct Scottish vernacular style, designed to reflect local lineage. The residential streets also have numerous fancier styles; you'll see examples of stone Gothic and Second Empire designs along Water, Front, and Church Streets.

History

In 1773, 33 families and 25 unmarried men arrived from the Scottish Highlands aboard the *Hector,* and Pictou quickly became known as the "birthplace of New Scotland." The flamboyant Presbyterian minister and doctor Thomas McCulloch, en route to ministerial duties on Prince Edward Island, arrived here with his family by accident in 1803 when a storm blew his ship into Pictou Harbour. Local immigrants asked him to stay, and McCulloch agreed. In addition to providing medical care to the immigrants, McCulloch tried to reform the province's backward educational system.

SIGHTS
★ Hector Heritage Quay

At the heart of the downtown waterfront, **Hector Heritage Quay** (33 Caladh Ave., 902/485-4371, May-June daily 11am-5pm, July-Aug. daily 9am-7pm, Sept.-Oct. daily 10am-4pm, adult $7, senior and student $6, child $3) is home to a three-floor interpretive center detailing the Scottish immigrants' arrival and early years. An elevated outdoor walkway overlooks the harbor. Admission includes access to the *Hector,* a replica of the sailing ship that transported Scottish settlers from across the Atlantic.

Take time to look over the *Hector.* The three-masted black-and-off-white replica is a splendid vessel, wide-hulled and

Climb aboard this replica of the *Hector.*

Pictou

round-ended. From the shape of the ship, though, you'll easily see that the voyage from Scotland was not so splendid. The ship's hull is unusually wide, and indeed the *Hector,* owned by the Dutch and chartered by the Scots for the voyage, was built as a freighter and modified only slightly to carry human cargo. Remarkably, the 200-plus immigrants from the Highlands survived, and Nova Scotia owes its Scottish heritage to those seaworthy voyagers.

Northumberland Fisheries Museum

The fascinating **Northumberland Fisheries Museum** (71 Front St., 902/485-4972, mid-June-Sept. daily 10am-6pm, adult $5, senior $4, child $2) is within a red-brick railway station, away from the redeveloped waterfront precinct and easy to miss. Displays tell the story of the local fishing industry through a vintage lobster boat, an aquarium holding local marine species, a mock fisherman's bunkhouse, period photos, and other memorabilia.

McCulloch Heritage Centre

The next worthwhile attraction is east of downtown along Old Haliburton Road. The main building at **McCulloch Heritage Centre** (86 Old Haliburton Rd., 902/485-4563, June-mid-Oct. Mon.-Sat. 9am-5pm, adult $5) showcases fine arts as part of the national arts exhibit circuit. The site is also one of the province's best genealogical libraries. A path leads uphill from the main building to McCulloch House, the early 1800s home of Thomas McCulloch. With distant water views, it holds period antiques and a small library. The print of a Labrador falcon downstairs was a gift to McCulloch from artist-naturalist John James Audubon.

ENTERTAINMENT

The local performing arts scene is based at **deCoste** (85 Water St., 902/485-8848, https://decostecentre.ca), a modern waterfront entertainment complex that puts on upwards of 100 shows each year. In July and August, the center hosts the Summer Sounds of Nova Scotia series. These concerts highlight top Celtic

the Customs House Inn

11:30am-8pm, $15-24) is owned and operated by a longtime local family. As the name suggests, the menu is inspired by the ocean, with lots of traditional choices such as haddock cakes and, of course, lobster dinners.

Five kilometers out of town, the dining room at the ★ **Pictou Lodge Beach Resort** (172 Braeshore Rd., 902/485-4322, mid-May-mid-Oct. daily 7am-9pm, $18-31) is a woodsy, old-fashioned space. You'll enjoy strait views from an intimate setting, with tables centered around a massive stone fireplace. The menu features entrées such as Indian-spiced lamb shank, cedar-planked salmon, and smoked maple pork belly with grilled scallops. Sunday brunch (11am-2pm) attracts locals for a buffet that includes everything from sushi to smoothies.

ACCOMMODATIONS AND CAMPING

Pictou has a wonderful choice of historic lodgings, many within walking distance of the waterfront and all well priced.

$50-100

In the heart of downtown and close to the waterfront, the 1865 **Auberge Walker Inn** (34 Coleraine St., 902/485-1433 or 800/370-5553, www.walkerinn.com, $99-139 s or d) has 11 guest rooms, some with harbor views, and a dining room where guests gather for a light breakfast each morning.

$100-150

Right on the water and within walking distance of downtown, the ★ **Customs House Inn** (38 Depot St., 902/485-4546, www.customshouseinn.ca, $129-159 s or d) dates to 1870. It's a historic building overlooking the harbor constructed of red brick and sandstone that was, as the name suggests, originally a customs house. The restored inn has eight guest rooms, all air-conditioned and some with exposed brickwork and water views. Rates include Internet access and a light breakfast.

dancers, singers, and fiddlers, who hit the stage Tuesday-Thursday at 8pm. Tickets are generally under $20.

FOOD

Pictou doesn't have any standout coffee joints, although **Canape Bakery** (31 Front St., 902/382-3002, Mon.-Wed. 8am-3pm, Thurs.-Fri. 8am-4pm, lunches $6-9) is a popular morning hangout for locals, with cooked breakfasts all under $8. The rest of the day, it's simple soups and sandwiches, as well as breads and pastries baked on-site.

The vibe at **Sharon's Place** (12 Front St., 902/485-4669, Mon.-Fri. 10am-7pm, Sat.-Sun. 9am-6pm, $8-16) is similar to the nearby Canape Bakery, with the difference being that Sharon's is also open for dinner. The cooking is simple (think burgers or fish-and-chips) and inexpensive, with friendly staff and delicious desserts adding to the appeal.

Across the road from the harbor, **Lobster Bar Restaurant** (50 Caladh Ave., 902/382-8527, Tues. 4:30pm-8pm, Wed.-Sun.

Dating to the 1920s, **Pictou Lodge Beach Resort** (172 Braeshore Rd., 5 km east of town, 902/485-4322 or 800/495-6343, www.pictou-lodge.com, mid-May-mid-Oct., $145-445 s or d) sits on a 67-hectare oceanfront estate overlooking Northumberland Strait. The roomy lodge has been restored with rustic comforts and features a long outside porch, dining in the high-ceilinged rotunda, and a nearby pond with canoes. Lodging choices include oceanfront villas, three-bedroom chalets, suites of various sizes and configurations, and standard motel rooms. All units have private baths, and many have fireplaces, kitchens, and separate living rooms. Resort amenities include canoe rentals, an outdoor pool, and a playground.

Camping

Caribou/Munroes Island Provincial Park (mid-June-mid-Oct., $29) has 87 campsites (Loop B is closest to the beach), cooking shelters, flush toilets, and fire pits. It fronts a long red-sand beach, which at low tide links Munroes Island to the mainland. The park is six kilometers west of town, signposted from Highway 6.

INFORMATION AND SERVICES

Pictou's **Visitor Information Centre** (902/485-6213, May-Sept. daily 9am-5pm), west of downtown beside the Rotary (where Highway 106 meets Highway 6) was operated by the province for decades, but closed in 2015. At the time of publication, its future was unknown, although in the 2016 season it was operated by local volunteers. The website www.townofpictou.com may also help you plan your trip to the town.

Sutherland-Harris Hospital is at 1059 Haliburton Road (902/485-4324). Locals do their banking in style at the architecturally resplendent **Bank of Nova Scotia,** in a Second Empire-style building at the corner of Front and Colerain Streets (902/485-4378). The **post office** is at 49 Front Street.

GETTING THERE

If you're combining your travels through Nova Scotia with a visit to Prince Edward Island, you have the choice of driving across the Confederation Bridge or catching the ferry. From Caribou, a short drive north of Pictou, **Northumberland Ferries** (902/566-3838 or 800/565-0201, www.ferries.ca) operates 5-9 sailings May-mid-December daily to the eastern side of Prince Edward Island. The trip takes just over an hour, and the fare is $71 round-trip per vehicle, regardless of the number of passengers (you pay when leaving the island).

From the west, it's 110 kilometers (1.5 hours) along Highway 6 to Pictou from Pugwash. Heading north from Halifax, Pictou is 165 kilometers (two hours) along Highways 102, 104, and 106.

Pictou to Cape Breton Island

The TransCanada Highway promises little besides uninterrupted speed on its route across the northeastern mainland. The best vistas, beaches, camping, and other attractions lie off the expressway, along the strait's coastal roads between Tatamagouche and Cape Breton. Shallow pools of seawater among sandbars turn warm in the sun, making for comfortable wading and swimming at Rushton's Beach Provincial Park, Tatamagouche Bay, and Melmerby Beach Provincial Park, east of Pictou.

CAPE GEORGE SCENIC DRIVE

The route to fossil hunting at Arisaig and Cape George's ruggedly beautiful eastern coastline lies along Highways 245 and 337 between New Glasgow and Antigonish, via a 110-kilometer, two-hour drive. From Exit 27

Arisaig

were buried. As ocean levels dropped, cliffs were formed along the shoreline, and as erosion broke the sediment down further, fossils from the Silurian period were exposed, perfectly preserved in bands of rock that represent specific time periods all those millions of years ago. Added to the mix is the upper cliff face, which is topped with up to four meters of sand and gravel left behind when glaciers retreated across the area at the end of the last ice age. Geologists have studied the site since the mid-1800s, and as the erosion process continues and more fossils are uncovered, interest continues.

You can walk to the cliffs from the harbor at Arisaig, but the official access is from **Arisaig Provincial Park,** on the west side of the town. The advantage of using the park access is that there are interpretive panels beside the parking lot, which help visitors appreciate the geology down at sea level. From these panels, steps descend to the beach far below, from where it's a short stroll westward along the beach to Arisaig Brook, where the largest concentration of fossils is found. It is illegal to dig at the cliff face, but scavenging through fallen rock is permitted.

Cape George

At Malignant Cove, Highway 337 branches north from Highway 245 and climbs steadily before peaking at an elevation of 190 meters at Cape George. The setting is a bicyclist's favorite scene and a just reward after the steep coastal climb. The panorama from the lighthouse at the cape's tip takes in the manicured farmlands of the Pictou-Antigonish highlands to the south as well as the misty vision of Prince Edward Island across the strait.

Along Cape George's eastern side, Highway 337 peels down from the peak alongside St. George's Bay. Nestled below the cape is **Ballantynes Cove.** From the town wharf, a rough walking trail climbs back to the lighthouse. The 1.8-kilometer route takes less than an hour each way and makes reaching the cape more satisfying than simply driving to its summit.

east of New Glasgow, allow half a day to reach Antigonish, which is enough time to visit the sights detailed here.

This is a sparsely populated region—there are no tourist services, such as accommodations or restaurants, so plan accordingly.

★ Arisaig

Like many other places in Nova Scotia, Arisaig, 57 kilometers northeast of New Glasgow, is an unassuming place that is much more interesting than the casual visitor might imagine. The cliffs on the west side of the village tell the story of a 4-million-year period of life on earth 400 million years ago—one of the only places in the world where such a long period of time is exposed in a single layered cliff line. This area was a shallow sea 400 hundred million years ago, and as the layers of sediment built up on its floor, brachiopods (shells), nautiloids (related to squid), trilobites (ancient crabs), crinoids (filter-feeders that attached themselves to the seabed), and bryozoans (coral)

ANTIGONISH

First impressions of Antigonish (an-tee-guh-NISH), from a Mi'kmaq name meaning "place where the branches are torn off by bears gathering beechnuts," are not promising. As it passes through town, the highway is a thicket of fast-food restaurants and service stations—but the town is not without its charms. Dig deeper and you'll find a bustling university town with nearby beaches and hiking trails, a good choice of places to stay and eat, and two popular festivals.

Sights

In a 1908 red-brick railway building on the north side of downtown, the **Antigonish Heritage Museum** (20 E. Main St., 902/863-6160, July-Aug. Mon.-Sat. 10am-5pm, Sept.-June. Mon.-Fri. 10am-noon and 1pm-5pm, free) tells the town's story through donated items and historical photographs. Back toward the historic heart of town is the **County Courthouse** (168 Main St.), still in use even though it has been designated a national historic site. Although no tours are offered, the landscaped grounds of gracious **St. Francis Xavier University** (take Exit 32 north from Highway 104) are pleasant for a stroll, especially in summer when the campus is deserted.

Festivals and Events

The first week of July, the town hosts the **Antigonish Highland Games** (902/863-4275, www.antigonishhighlandgames.ca)—the longest-running in North America, celebrated since 1863. Highlights include Celtic music, pipe bands, dancing, heavy sports such as caber tossing, and a kilted golf tournament. Throughout July and August, the **Festival Antigonish** (902/867-3333 or 800/563-7529, www.festivalantigonish.com), Nova Scotia's largest and most successful professional summer theater program, features a variety of drama, musicals, comedies, cutting-edge improv, and children's entertainment at the university campus.

Food

Antigonish offers a surprising number of good dining options along the main street. If you're looking for good coffee or a quick bite to eat, search out **Tall and Small** (342 Main St., 902/863-4682, Mon.-Wed. 7am-6pm, Thurs.-Fri. 7am-9pm, Sat. 8am-9pm, lunches $6-9), a modern space brightened by local artwork on the walls. It has the usual array of soup and sandwiches, as well as muffins and pastries.

At first glance, **Little Christo's** (332 Main St., 902/867-4992, Mon.-Thurs. 11am-9:30pm, Fri. 11am-10:30pm, Sat. 10am-10:30pm, Sun. 11am-8:30pm, $11-19) may look like just another pizza joint, but the food is made from scratch each morning, very creative, and most importantly, well priced. The pizzas are the highlight, but there are also Mediterranean-inspired platters to share, vegetarian and gluten-free options, and entrées such as a lamb burger topped with pomegranate yoghurt sauce. The attached patio is in high demand on warmer evenings.

Being close to the university, **Piper's Pub** (33 College St., 902/863-2590, Mon.-Sat. 10am-2am, Sun. 11am-2am, $12-18) is a popular student hangout. The typical pub grub is well priced, and bands play Saturday night.

Accommodations

Maritime Inn Antigonish (158 Main St., 902/863-4001 or 888/662-7484, www.maritimeinns.com, $130-185) is open year-round. It has 32 modern units, free Internet, free daily newspapers, and a restaurant open daily for breakfast, lunch, and dinner. Directly across the road, **Antigonish Victorian Inn** (149 Main St., 902/863-1103 or 800/706-5558, www.antigonishvictorianinn.ca, $130-175 s or d) is a splendid bed-and-breakfast occupying a dark burgundy-colored William Critchlow Harris-designed Queen Anne-style mansion. Each of the 12 guest rooms has a private bath and TV. Rates include a full cooked breakfast.

Getting There

The most direct route to Antigonish from New Glasgow is along Highway 104, about

60 kilometers (40 minutes). Via the Cape George scenic drive, it's about 110 kilometers (two hours) from New Glasgow to Antigonish. Antigonish is 215 kilometers (2.5 hours) north then east from Halifax via Highways 102 and 104.

Marine Drive

Marine Drive extends 320 kilometers along the Eastern Shore from Dartmouth to Canso, at the eastern tip of mainland Nova Scotia. From Canso, it's another 80 kilometers to the Canso Causeway, gateway to Cape Breton Island. The Marine Drive is a scenic alternative to Highways 102 and 104 via Truro. It's longer (allow 5-6 hours, not counting stops) and beyond the main tourist path, but it features delightful bays, sandy beaches, and interesting fishing villages around every bend.

LAWRENCETOWN

Begin the Marine Drive by following Cole Harbour Road from Exit 7 of Highway 111 in Dartmouth to **Lawrencetown Beach,** one of Canada's best-known surf spots. Easily reached in 30 minutes from Dartmouth, this long stretch of sand backed by high dunes is an enjoyable stop even if you don't plan to take to the water.

Surfing

The waves of "L-town," as it's known to locals, break along the length of the beach and off a rocky headland that breaks the main beach in two. They are best November-May, when winter swells provide large and consistent waves. These waves also coincide with the coldest ocean temperatures. But even with water temperatures of 0°C (32°F) and air temperatures that drop to -20°C (-4°F), it's not unusual to see footprints leading down a snow-covered beach to the breakers beyond. Summer is not devoid of waves. They are just likely to be smaller and less consistent. Hardy locals swim in the ocean in the warmer months, when water temperatures rise to 15°C (59°F), but for surfing, be prepared with a wetsuit.

The beach's southern headland provides an ideal vantage point for watching the action. **Kannon Beach Wind & Surf** (4144 Lawrencetown Rd., 902/471-0025, Mon.-Sat. 9am-6pm, Sun. 10am-4pm) is a full-service surf shop in a renovated house on the hill between Lawrencetown and Stoney Beaches. Surfboard and wetsuit rental packages (complete with gloves and booties) are $40 per day, and stand-up paddleboard rentals cost $50 per day. **East Coast Surf School** (902/434-3040, July-early Sept. daily 9am-6pm), which bases itself at the beach itself each summer day, offers lessons for $75 per day, which includes a rental board and wetsuit.

Accommodations

Ocean views from **Moonlight Beach Suites** (Hwy. 207, north end of Lawrencetown Beach, 902/827-2712, www.moonlightbeachinn.com, $139-350 s or d) are nothing short of stunning. The three guest rooms are decorated in a nautical theme, and each has a private deck, jetted tub, and TV/DVD combo, while thoughtful extras include binoculars and beach towels. The largest of the three rooms is massive and has a huge private deck with sweeping water views. Rates include a full breakfast.

Getting There

Lawrencetown is about 15 kilometers (20 minutes) east of Dartmouth (a suburb of Halifax) via Highway 207.

MUSQUODOBOIT HARBOUR TO SHERBROOKE

From Musquodoboit Harbour, 50 kilometers (40 minutes) from Halifax via Highway 107, it's a further 150 kilometers east along

Fabled Sable Island

Just under 200 kilometers off Nova Scotia's eastern coastline is a 40-kilometer-long sliver of sand that was known to generations of seafarers as the "Graveyard of the Atlantic." Protected today as a national park, **Sable Island** is inhabited by a herd of horses that have taken on almost mythical proportions.

The island is made up entirely of sand. The sand is part of a terminal moraine left behind by the receding ice cap at the end of the last ice age 11,000 years ago. Hardy marram grass stabilizes the central part of the island, while seals and birds are also native. The island's most famous residents are horses; they were introduced in the late 1700s. Some say it was to feed shipwreck victims, while others claim they were aboard ships that came to grief. Today, Sable Island is home to about 400 horses. They are of special interest since they are one of the world's few truly wild horse populations, without feral intruders (such as domestic horses gone wild), and they are free to roam, feed, and reproduce without human interference.

Since Sable Island was first mapped in the late 1500s, more than 350 vessels have been wrecked along its fog-shrouded shore (the last was a small yacht, the *Merrimac,* in 1999). In 1801 a station

---

the Marine Drive to Sherbrooke. The journey takes around two hours, but there are many worthwhile stops and a couple of good accommodations options, which I've recommended below.

Musquodoboit Harbour

With just 900 people, Musquodoboit Harbour is nevertheless the largest community between Dartmouth and Canso. The only real attraction in town is the **Musquodoboit Harbour Railway Museum** (7897 Hwy. 7, 902/889-2689, June-Aug. daily 9am-4pm, free), housed within a 1918 railway station and three vintage rail cars. The **tourist information center** is in the same building. Ten kilometers south of Musquodoboit Harbour on East Petpeswick Road, **Martinique Beach Provincial Park** protects the southern end of Nova Scotia's longest beach. The beach is often windy, but it's still a relaxing place for a long, easy walk.

Salmon River Bridge

Cross the bridge for which the village of Salmon River Bridge, 13 kilometers east of Musquodoboit Harbour, is named and you reach a neat little lodge nestled between a forested hill and the river. Dating to 1850 and operating as a guesthouse since 1920, **Salmon River Country Inn** (9931 Hwy. 7,

902/889-3353, www.salmonrivercountryinn. ca, $95-130 s or d) has seven guest rooms, all with en suite bathrooms and some with water views, and a riverfront cottage with a fireplace. Part of the inn is a seafood **restaurant** (Apr.-mid-Oct. daily 8am-9pm, $12-28), with seats that spill outside to a large riverfront deck. Lobsters kept in the tank are often larger than three pounds, but there's a wide choice of less-expensive seafood, including delicious fish-and-chips.

Drive three kilometers beyond Salmon River Bridge and then four kilometers north to reach ★ **Webber's Lakeside Park** (738 Upper Lakeville Rd., 902/845-2340 or 800/589-2282, www.webberslakesideresort.com), which is filled with opportunities for activities that include lake swimming with a floating dock, canoe and boat rentals, a playground, and a games room with table tennis. The two-bedroom cottages ($150 s or d) have kitchens and wide decks, and the campground (mid-May-mid-Oct., $33-43) has full hookups and hot showers. Being just an hour's drive from Halifax, this place fills up every summer weekend, so you'll need reservations.

Oyster Pond

Turn south off Highway 7 just beyond Salmon River Bridge to visit the small but interesting manned with a lifesaving crew was established on the island. This government-operated service soon expanded to five stations and continued until 1958. Today the island has a year-round population of fewer than 20 people—mostly scientists who study the weather and monitor the island's environment.

Only about 200 intrepid travelers visit Sable Island each year, most arriving by air charter or private vessel and staying for just the day. The season runs June-October, but June and July are often foggy. If you'd like to visit, the first step is to register with Parks Canada (902/426-5080, www.pc.gc.ca/sable). You will then need to arrange fixed-wing air charters from Halifax through **Sable Aviation** (902/499-7941, www.sableaviation.ca), which charges $6,200 for the round-trip, inclusive of taxes; Parks Canada also charges a $500 per flight landing fee (collected by the airline). These flights take up to seven passengers, so the best way to reduce costs is to check the company website for a link to a Facebook page dedicated to sharing costs of reaching the island. The best source of island information is the website of the **Friends of Sable Island Society** (www.sableislandfriends.ca).

Fisherman's Life Museum (58 Navy Pool Loop, 902/889-4209, June-Sept. Mon.-Fri. 8am-4pm, adult $4, senior and child $2.80). Rather than a collection of artifacts, this museum within a small homestead re-creates the simple, self-sufficient lifestyle of a fisherman, his wife, and their 13 children.

Clam Harbour Provincial Park and Vicinity

Clam Harbour Provincial Park, along the south-facing side of Clam Bay, protects a long stretch of hard white sand. The beach has supervised swimming in summer, as well as changing rooms and picnic areas, but no camping. (From the end of the access road, turn right to reach the nicest picnic area, where tables are nestled in windswept coastal forest.)

Members of the Murphy family have lived in Murphy Cove for seven generations, and have been involved through time in everything from rum running to fishing. Now they operate ★ **Murphy's Camping on the Ocean** (308 Murphy's Rd., 902/772-2700, www.murphyscamping.ca, mid-May-mid-Oct., $27-39), which sprawls across a grassy headland. The campground has all the usual facilities—showers, boat and kayak rentals, a laundry, a playground, and more—but it's

Brian's evening storytelling, boat tours (two hours for $23), clam-digging trips, and mussel bakes that make this place stand apart.

Kayaking at Tangier

Tangier, 85 kilometers (1.5 hours) east of Dartmouth via Highway 7, is the base for **Coastal Adventures** (84 Mason's Point Rd., 902/772-2774, www.coastaladventures.com), which pushes off into the cove on full-day kayak excursions ($110 pp, including lunch) that include a visit to uninhabited islands. Kayak rentals are $70 per day for a single and $90 for a double. The same people operate ★ **Paddler's Retreat Bed and Breakfast** ($65-85 s or d), which is an excellent spot to spend one or more nights. Most guests staying in this restored 1860s fisherman's home do so as part of a kayaking instruction package or before or after participating in a day trip. Three of the four rooms share bathrooms, while the fourth has an en suite bathroom and private entrance. Rates include a full breakfast.

★ Taylor Head Provincial Park

Turn off at Spry Bay, 15 kilometers beyond Tangier, to reach the interesting oceanside **Taylor Head Provincial Park,** which protects a narrow peninsula extending 6 kilometers to Taylor Head. The west-facing side of the spit is rugged and windswept, with stunted white spruce trees clinging precariously to the rocky ground, while the east side is characterized by sandy coves lapped by calm waters. A five-kilometer unpaved road from Highway 7 hugs the west side of the peninsula before crossing to protected **Psyche Cove.** At the end of the road is a series of small parking lots with beach access. You can walk along the beach back toward the mainland to Bob Bluff or head in the opposite direction to a headland with sweeping views up and down the peninsula and of island-dotted Mushaboom Harbour. Taylor Head itself is 4 kilometers by hiking trail from the end of the road. If you return via rocky Spry Bay, you'll have walked 10 kilometers (allow four hours).

Spry Bay to Liscomb Mills

Marine Drive between Spry Bay and Liscomb Mills passes a string of fishing villages with delightful names such as Ecum Secum (a Mi'kmaq word of unknown origin) and Spanish Ship Bay (named for a nearby headland that resembles a Spanish galleon). Linked to Highway 7 by a short bridge, Sober Island's name has a more cynical origin (the first residents bemoaned the lack of alcohol).

In Liscomb Mills, **Liscombe Lodge Resort** (2884 Hwy. 7, 902/779-2307 or 877/375-6343, www.liscombelodge.ca, mid-May-mid-Oct., from $180 s or d) boasts an idyllic setting along the Liscomb River. Amenities include an indoor pool, a sauna, hot tubs, a fitness center, hiking trails, tennis courts, a small marina with boat, canoe, and fishing-equipment rentals, and a comfortable dining room overlooking the river (where children eat free).

SHERBROOKE

Highway 7 leaves the coast at Liscomb, turning north to Sherbrooke, from which it continues north to Antigonish and the Marine Drive spurs east, continuing along the Eastern Shore as Highway 316. Sherbrooke (pop. 400) was founded at the farthest navigable point of the St. Mary's River in the early 1800s. By 1869 gold had been discovered in the area, and the town was booming. In addition to mining, mills were established to process lumber for export, and local farms depended on the town for services. By 1890 the gold rush was over, and the population began slipping away.

Liscombe Lodge Resort

★ Sherbrooke Village

By the late 1960s, Sherbrooke was a shadow of its former self. Gold rush-era buildings remained in varying states of disrepair, but the only visitors were anglers chasing salmon along the river. At this point, a local trust stepped in, and under the guidance of the Nova Scotia Museum, an ambitious restoration project took place. Today, **Sherbrooke Village** (42 Main St., 902/522-2400, June-early Oct. daily 9:30am-5pm, adult $14, senior $11, child $5) comprises more than 80 restored buildings that are integrated with the town itself. About 20 buildings are open to the public, including an ambrotype photography studio, the colonnaded courthouse, a jail, a water-powered sawmill, the Sherbrooke Hotel, a drugstore, a blacksmith shop, a church, and a farmyard. The site is brought alive by costumed interpreters who wander the village streets, tend to their crops, and go about operating each business as folks would have done in the late 1800s.

To fully immerse yourself in the experience, consider participating in the Hands on History program (July-Aug. only, $99 per family), where the costume department will dress you in period clothing and you can spend the day helping in the kitchens, trying

your hand at pottery, or learning skills from the blacksmith. The Courthouse Concert Series ($10 per person) takes place 2-3 nights a week through the summer season; entertainment varies from traditional Celtic ceilidhs to musical comedies. Starting time is usually around 7:30pm. The main parking lot and entrance are off Court Street (turn left at the end of the modern-day main street).

Food and Accommodations

For overnight stays, Sherbrooke offers several choices. **St. Mary's River Lodge** (21 Main St., 902/522-2177, www.riverlodge.ca, Apr.-Dec., $76-106 s or d) is across the road from the river and steps from Sherbrooke Village. It has five guest rooms, each with an en suite bathroom. A cooked breakfast is included in the rates. On the east side of town, a 10-minute walk from the village, is **Sherbrooke Village Inn** (7975 Hwy. 7, 902/522-2235 or 866/522-3818, www.sherbrookevillageinn.ca, May-Oct., $125-159 s or d). The medium-size motel rooms are plain but comfortable, the pine-paneled cabins have kitchens, and the on-site restaurant is open daily 7am-7pm.

In the Sherbrooke Hotel, within the historical village, the ★ **What Cheer Tea Room** (June-mid-Oct. daily 9:30am-5pm, lunches

Sherbrooke Village

$7-14) is a countrified restaurant with friendly staff and basic but tasty dishes that will set you up for more historical sightseeing. You can try traditional rural dishes such as fish cakes with a side of homemade baked beans. **Sherbrooke Village Inn Restaurant** (7975 Hwy. 7, 902/522-2235, May-Oct. daily 7am-7pm, $15-26) is a small wood-paneled restaurant on the east (Halifax) side of town. The emphasis is on simple presentations of local seafood. You could start with fish chowder and then choose between dishes such as deep-fried scallops and strip loin or a lobster from the tank. Save room for the homemade pie with ice cream.

GETTING THERE

Sherbrooke is about 200 kilometers (three hours) east of Dartmouth along Highway 7.

SHERBROOKE TO CANSO

It's only a little more than 100 kilometers between Sherbrooke and Canso, but the drive will take at least two hours, plus any time you wait for the ferry at Country Harbour.

Port Bickerton Lighthouse

There could be no better location for a lighthouse display than in a restored light-keeper's home at the end of a windswept, often fog-enshrouded peninsula—which is exactly where the **Port Bickerton Lighthouse** (Lighthouse Rd., Port Bickerton, 902/364-2000, mid-June-mid-Sept. daily 10am-5pm, adult $3) is situated. Built in 1901 and deactivated in 1962, the two-building complex now holds a display describing the lonely life of Nova Scotian light-keepers and their families, the original foghorn, and a directory of Nova Scotia's lighthouses. Stairs lead to an observation tower. Outside, a trail leads past clumps of tasty blueberries and cranberries to a sandy beach. From the turnoff in Port Bickerton, 25 kilometers beyond Sherbrooke and 7 kilometers before the ferry across Country Harbour, it's 3 kilometers to the interpretive center, the last 2 kilometers along an unpaved road.

Country Harbour

The **Country Harbour ferry,** along Highway 316, seven kilometers north of Port Bickerton, departs from the east side (Halifax side) of the bay on the half hour and the west side on the hour. During the laughably named "rush hour" (9am-10am and 5pm-6pm), ferries operate more frequently. The ferry has room for just 12 passenger vehicles or a limited number of trucks and RVs, and the fare is $7 (cash only), which is paid to the attendant upon loading. From the west side of the bay, it's 86 kilometers to Canso. Aside from the short detour to Tor Bay, it's worth slowing down to admire the village of Isaacs Harbour, which on a calm day is reflected across the bay of the same name from Goldboro.

Tor Bay

Named for granite knolls that dot the region, Tor Bay is lined by three small communities established by Acadians after their deportation by the English in 1755. For visitors, the highlight is **Tor Bay Provincial Park,** on an isthmus along a peninsula that forms the southern boundary of the bay. This small day-use park has one of the few sandy beaches this far east along the Marine Drive. A boardwalk leads to the beach, from where a short trail leads to a rocky headland where covered interpretive boards describe the geology that led to the creation of the beach.

CANSO

The remote town of Canso, 320 kilometers along Marine Drive from Halifax, is the jumping-off point to an interesting historic site that protects Canada's oldest fishing village. In more recent times, Canso was an important link in trans-Atlantic communications. The most striking reminder of this era is the 1884 **Hazel Hill Cable Station,** just outside town. It was from here that the distress signal from the sinking *Titanic* and news of the 1929 stock market crash were transmitted to the rest of the world.

★ Canso Islands National Historic Site

Archaeological digs point to European settlement as early as the 1500s on the small island that comprises the **Canso Islands National Historic Site,** one kilometer offshore from Canso. These visitors' time on the island was only temporary, and no obvious signs of this era remain today. Two hundred years later, the French and British were fighting for control of North America, with ownership of the Canso Islands in dispute even after the signing of the Treaty of Utrecht in 1713. In 1718 the French were displaced, and the same year, fearing a reprisal attack by the French, the British built a small fort on Grassy Island to protect access to cod stocks that were being harvested at the amazing rate of 10 million pounds per year. Grassy Island grew into a prosperous community, complete with wealthy merchants who built solid stone homes. The village was destroyed by a French invasion from Louisbourg in 1744 and was never rebuilt.

The site comprises a **visitors center** (Union St., 902/366-3136, July-Aug. daily 10am-6pm, $5 donation) on the Canso waterfront and the island itself. Mainland exhibits include a scale model of the settlement, fragments of French pottery dated to the early 1700s, and a short documentary film. Boats run on demand between the visitors center and the island. Once safety regulations are described, the small craft is off, and you'll be on the island within 15 minutes. A mowed trail passes eight information boards describing the settlement and what remains—cellar pits, mounds of rubble from residences, and terraced vegetable plots—before looping back down to the dock. Allow about 30 minutes to walk the trail. If visitation is slow, the boat will be waiting at the wharf for your return; otherwise, expect a wait of up to 30 minutes while it transports more visitors across. The only services on the island are pit toilets and a shelter, so bring warm clothes and water. The suggested donation at the visitors center includes the boat ride to the island.

Stan Rogers Folk Festival

On the first weekend of July, the population of Canso increases 10 times as music fans descend on the town for **"Stanfest"** (888/554-7826, www.stanfest.com), a folk-music festival of 50 acts from around the world performing on six stages. In addition to the music, the festival features a food fair, craft show, and beer garden. Most visitors camp at the Acoustic Campground, set

CENTRAL NOVA SCOTIA
MARINE DRIVE

Canso Islands National Historic Site

up by the organizers within walking distance of the main stage. Other temporary campgrounds take the overflow, with shuttle buses running to the grounds and to showers at the local high school. A camping pass is $70-90, and entry to the concert is $125 for the entire weekend.

Accommodations and Camping

Canso is most definitely not a tourist town. The **Last Port Motel** (Hwy. 16, 902/366-2400, www.lastportmotel.ca, $95-110) is just before town. It offers 13 basic rooms with wireless Internet access, as well as a restaurant open daily at 7am. A better option for those looking for a memorable stay is ★ **DesBarres Manor Inn** (90 Church St., 902/533-2099, www.desbarresmanor.com, $199-259 s or d), 56 kilometers east in Guysborough. Dating to 1837, the three-story inn has been beautifully restored, and the grounds remain in immaculate shape. The 10 guest rooms are stylish and come with niceties like 600-thread-count sheets on super-comfortable mattresses, plus luxurious bathrooms. Rates include a gourmet cooked breakfast, with dinner available with many of the packages offered online.

Ten kilometers west of Canso along Highway 16 is **Seabreeze Campground and Cottages** (230 Fox Island Rd., Fox Island, 902/366-2352, www.seabreezecampground.com, mid-May-mid-Oct., campsites $27-37, cottages $100-110 s or d), where modern facilities, full hookups, and views across Chedabucto Bay keep the 51 campsites full through July and August. One- and two-bedroom cottages have basic cooking facilities, a lounge area with TV, and separate bedrooms. Other resort amenities include coin-operated showers, a laundry, firewood sales, a playground, canoe rentals, and even a lobster pound, where you can buy live lobster.

Information

Whitman House (1297 Union St., 902/366-2170, June-Sept. daily 9am-5pm, donation), a handsome three-story 1885 house with displays illustrating local history, doubles as an information center.

Getting There

Canso is about 320 kilometers (5-6 hours) east of Dartmouth, a suburb of Halifax, via Highway 7.

Cape Breton Island

Look for ★ to find recommended sights, activities, dining, and lodging.

Highlights

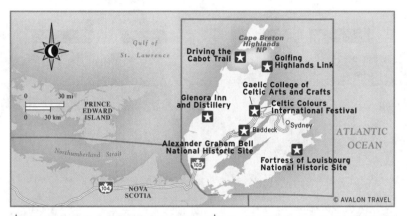

★ **Glenora Inn and Distillery:** Tucked into a quiet glen along the remote west coast is North America's only single-malt whiskey distillery, complete with a restaurant and guest rooms (page 159).

★ **Alexander Graham Bell National Historic Site:** Dedicated to one of the world's most prolific inventors, this museum will interest all ages (page 161).

★ **Driving the Cabot Trail:** This 300-kilometer circuit traversing varying landscapes—including Cape Breton Highlands National Park—is one of the world's great scenic drives (page 169).

★ **Golfing Highlands Links:** Walk the fairways of one of the world's finest golf courses, knowing that what you've paid to play is less than at many regular city courses (page 173).

★ **Gaelic College of Celtic Arts and Crafts:** No, you don't need to sign up for a course. Instead, take in music recitals and demonstrations such as weaving (page 175).

★ **Celtic Colours International Festival:** This October festival draws crowds who enjoy traditional music while soaking up the colors of fall (page 176).

★ **Fortress of Louisbourg National Historic Site:** Sprawling across 10 hectares of a remote headland is this reconstruction of a French town destroyed by the British 250 years ago (page 178).

Alexander Graham Bell, perhaps Cape Breton Island's most renowned transplant, once wrote, "I have seen the Canadian and American Rockies, the Andes and the Alps, and the Highlands of Scotland; but for simple beauty, Cape Breton outrivals them all."

Linked to the mainland by a two-lane causeway, nearly every coastal and inland backcountry road on the western half of the island leads eventually to the Cabot Trail, the scenic highway rimming the unforgettable landscape of northwestern Cape Breton. The dramatic coastal scenery alone qualifies the Cabot Trail as one of the world's great drives, but you can also spend time soaking up local Acadian culture, hiking through pristine forests of the Cape Breton Highlands, or simply relaxing on white-sand beaches. The most spectacular section of the route is in the far northern part of the island, through magnificent Cape Breton Highlands National Park, which stretches from coast to coast and is as wild and remote as the Highlands of Scotland. Green, steeply pitched highlands begin at the sea in the south and sweep north, cut by salmon-filled rivers. As the elevation increases, the Acadian and boreal forests give way to a taiga tableland of stunted, windswept trees.

The Northumberland Strait opens into the Gulf of St. Lawrence on the western coast, while the Atlantic washes the opposite shore. The 1,098-square-kilometer Bras d'Or Lakes forms the island's heart. The saltwater "Arm of Gold," though barely influenced by tidal cycles, is an inland arm of the Atlantic consisting of a sapphire-blue main lake with numerous peripheral channels, straits, and bays.

PLANNING YOUR TIME

Although you can fly into the airport at Sydney, most visitors drive to Cape Breton from Halifax, reaching the causeway linking the island to the mainland in less than four hours. From the causeway, a choice of routes present themselves, including the little-traveled route up the west coast, which passes the **Glenora Inn and Distillery.** The geographic and tourist hub is Baddeck. Plan to

Previous: Keltic Lodge; Cabot Links. **Above:** Le Bloc Beach.

Cape Breton Island

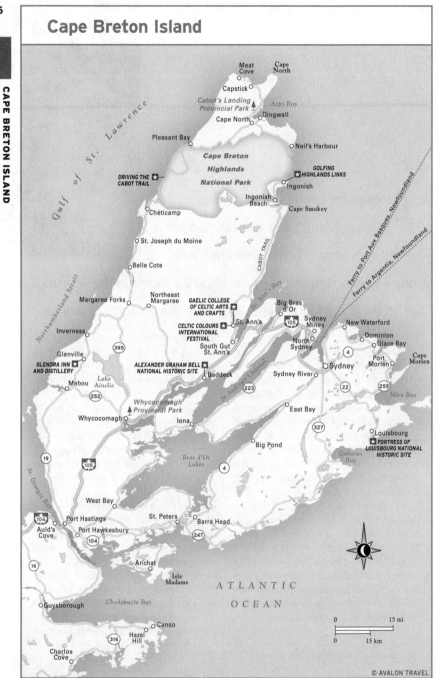

Meat Cove
Cape North
Capstick
Cabot's Landing Provincial Park
Dingwall
Aspy Bay
Cape North
Pleasant Bay
Neil's Harbour
Cape Breton Highlands National Park
DRIVING THE CABOT TRAIL
GOLFING HIGHLANDS LINKS
Ingonish
Ingonish Beach
Chéticamp
Cape Smokey
St. Joseph du Moine
Belle Cote
Northeast Margaree
GAELIC COLLEGE OF CELTIC ARTS AND CRAFTS
Big Bras d'Or
Margaree Forks
CELTIC COLOURS INTERNATIONAL FESTIVAL
St. Ann's
Sydney Mines
New Waterford
Inverness
South Gut St. Ann's
North Sydney
Dominion
Glace Bay
Glenville
ALEXANDER GRAHAM BELL NATIONAL HISTORIC SITE
Baddeck
Sydney
Port Morien
Cape Morien
GLENORA INN AND DISTILLERY
Mabou
Lake Ainslie
Sydney River
Whycocomagh Provincial Park
East Bay
Mira Bay
Whycocomagh
Iona
Louisbourg
FORTRESS OF LOUISBOURG NATIONAL HISTORIC SITE
Big Pond
Gabarus Bay
Bras d'Or Lakes
West Bay
St. Peters
Barra Head
Port Hastings
Port Hawkesbury
Auld's Cove
Arichat
Isle Madame
ATLANTIC OCEAN
Guysborough
Chedabucto Bay
Canso
Hazel Hill
Charlos Cove

Gulf of St. Lawrence
Northumberland Strait
St. George's Bay
St. Andrews Channel
St. Ann's Bay
CABOT TRAIL
Ferry to Port Aux Basques, Newfoundland
Ferry to Argentia, Newfoundland

0   15 mi
0   15 km

© AVALON TRAVEL

spend at least one full day at this resort town, which is enough time to visit the **Alexander Graham Bell National Historic Site** and take to the waters of Bras d'Or Lakes. Baddeck is also a good starting point for beginning the **Cabot Trail,** a 311-kilometer highway that loops through the wilderness of **Cape Breton Highlands National Park.** The park scenery is the highlight of the drive, but along the way, plan on browsing the **arts and crafts of Chéticamp** and **golfing** at Cabot Links and Highlands Links. If your travels correspond with the October **Celtic Colours International Festival,** plan on taking in as many concerts as you can. At other times of the year, St. Ann's **Gaelic College of Celtic Arts and Crafts** is the place to immerse yourself in Celtic culture. To hit all the highlights mentioned above, you should allow yourself at the very least three days from Halifax, but preferably four or five. The main reason for veering from the Cabot Trail is to visit the **Fortress of Louisbourg,** a lesser-known but impressive attraction that re-creates a French town from the mid-1700s.

Port Hastings to Baddeck

Canso Causeway, easily reached in four hours from Halifax, links Cape Breton to the mainland. From this point, Highways 104 and 105 (the TransCanada) and Highway 19 fan out across the island. Highway 19 follows the west coast up to Mabou and Inverness, and then links up with the Cabot Trail in the Margaree Valley. The TransCanada Highway lies straight ahead, leading through the center of the island to Baddeck and on to Sydney. The endless stream of buses packed with tourists makes a beeline along this route, connecting with the Cabot Trail at Baddeck. Highway 4 branches off to the east (or take the more direct Highway 104 for the first 28 kilometers), passing the turnoff to Isle Madame and then following Bras d'Or Lakes, en route to Sydney.

PORT HASTINGS

The main reason to stop in Port Hastings, the gateway town to Cape Breton Island, is to load up with brochures at the well-stocked **Nova Scotia Visitor Information Centre** (902/625-4201, May-June and Sept.-Dec. daily 9am-5pm, July-Aug. daily 9am-8:30pm), on the right as the TransCanada Highway crosses to the island. Behind the center, views extend back across to the mainland, and information boards describe the processes involved in constructing the causeway.

Accommodations

Through town toward Port Hawkesbury, **Hearthstone Inn** (388 Hwy. 4, 902/625-0621 or 800/867-2212, www.hearthstonehospitality. ca, Apr.-late Dec., $109-159 s or d) has air-conditioned rooms, each with comfortable beds, coffeemaker, and wireless Internet. Bonuses include a small indoor pool and a small on-site restaurant.

Getting There

Port Hastings is 60 kilometers (45 minutes) east of Antigonish via Highway 104. It's 275 kilometers (three hours) north then east from Halifax via Highways 102 and 104.

ISLE MADAME

Settled by French fishermen in the early 1700s, this was one of the first parts of the province to be settled, and it's one of the oldest fishing ports in North America. Isle Madame has four main communities—Arichat, West Arichat, Petit Grat, and D'Escousse.

The wooded island is a popular weekend getaway, with two provincial parks (**Lennox Passage** to the north and **Pondville Beach** on the east side) and plenty of picnicking, swimming, and vista spots. In Arichat, on the waterfront, **LeNoir Forge Museum** (708 Veteran's Memorial Dr., 902/226-9364,

June-Aug. daily 10am-6pm, donation) is a restored working 18th-century forge open to visitors.

L'Auberge Acadienne Inn (2375 Hwy. 206, Arichat, 902/226-2200, www.acadienne. com) is designed as a 19th-century Acadian-style inn, with eight inviting rooms, one with a jetted tub, in the main building ($105 s, $115 d) and nine adjacent motel units ($85 s, $95 d). The dining room serves Acadian breakfast and dinner dishes in a casual, country-style atmosphere; accommodations, dinner, and breakfast for two people is $185.

Getting There

Take Highway 104 for 30 kilometers (30 minutes) east from Port Hastings, and then Highway 320 south over Lennox Passage Bridge to reach this 43-square-kilometer island.

BRAS D'OR LAKES SCENIC DRIVE

The most direct route between the Canso Causeway and Sydney is Highway 105 through Baddeck, a total distance of 130 kilometers (allow 90 minutes). This route hugs the northwestern shore of Bras d'Or Lakes, but I recommend the slightly longer **Bras d'Or Lakes scenic drive,** which traces the southern shore, passing through the villages of St. Peters and Big Pond via Highway 4, a total distance of 148 kilometers (two hours).

Highway 4 steers away from the water until passing St. Peters, but a short detour to West Bay and then east along West Bay Road will bring you to **Dundee Resort** (368 Shore Rd., Baddeck, 902/295-3500 or 800/565-5660, www.capebretonresorts.com, May-Oct.), a destination in itself. The resort, 12 kilometers from Highway 4, is set on 223 hectares overlooking Bras d'Or Lakes. It features an 18-hole golf course (greens fee $68), an outdoor pool, a marina with all manner of watercraft for rent, an arcade activities center, summer programs for the kids, and a restaurant. Motel rooms, most with balconies, range $159-219, while cottages with limited cooking facilities and up to three bedrooms are $159-259.

St. Peters and Vicinity

The first town reached along the Bras d'Or scenic drive is St. Peters, where photography buffs should check out the **MacAskill House Museum** (7 MacAskill Dr., 902/535-2531, mid-June-Aug. daily 9:30am-5:30pm, donation), in the restored childhood home of Wallace MacAskill, one of the world's preeminent marine photographers. The museum exhibits a collection of his best photographs as well as historic cameras.

Overlooking Bras d'Or Lakes, 1.5 kilometers east of St. Peters, **Joyce's Motel and Cottages** (902/535-2404, www.joyces-motel.com, mid-May-Oct., $69-105 s or d) offers the choice of regular motel rooms or larger but dated one-bedroom cottages. The motel offers extensive landscaped grounds, water views, an outdoor swimming pool, and a laundry. **Battery Provincial Park** (off Hwy. 4, 1 km east of town, 902/535-3094, mid-June-early Sept.) has hiking trails and ocean views. The 52 open, wooded, unserviced campsites rent for $29.

GETTING THERE

The village of St. Peters lies along the Bras d'Or scenic drive, 12 kilometers (10 minutes) beyond the turnoff to Isle Madame and 55 kilometers (40 minutes) from the Canso Causeway. St. Peters is 320 kilometers (3.5 hours) from Halifax via Highways 102 and 104.

Big Pond

From St. Peters, the run to Sydney takes a little more than an hour, with Highway 4 paralleling Bras d'Or Lakes for much of the way. A good halfway-point lunch stop is **Rita's Tea Room** (902/828-2667, summer daily 10am-5pm, lunch $8-12), in a converted schoolhouse at Big Pond. Opened by well-known folk singer Rita MacNeil, who grew up in Big Pond and who continued to promote Cape Breton Island around the world until her death in 2013, the café serves specially blended teas, sandwiches, and salads

Fiddling the Night Away

A ceilidh (KAY-lee) was originally an informal gathering, usually on a Friday or Saturday night, that would bring together young people to dance the night away to lively Celtic music in a local hall. These social gatherings originated in Gaelic-speaking regions of Scotland and Ireland, with the tradition introduced to the New World by immigrants in the 1700s. Although nightclubs and pubs may have replaced the ceilidh in popularity in the city, along the west coast of Cape Breton Island and in other rural areas they remain an important part of the social scene. Most important, the music has retained its original roots, with progressive dancing in which the woman moves along a ring from man to man or everyone dancing in formation (similar to line dancing). The most skilled dancers break away from the formations to step dance.

Highway 19 is known as the Ceilidh Trail, and for good reason, as ceilidhs take place in towns and villages along the route year-round. Everyone is welcome, with many of the summer events especially tailored for visitors. At Mabou, the Mabou Community Hall fills with the sound of fiddle music every Tuesday through summer, while the following night, the foot-stomping fun happens down the road at the local museum. Passing through on Thursday? Plan for a lively evening of entertainment at the Inverness Fire Hall ceilidh.

in a country setting. An adjacent room is devoted to her distinguished career.

GETTING THERE

Big Pond is 50 kilometers (45 minutes) northeast of St. Peters along Highway 4 and 370 kilometers (four hours) from Halifax via Highways 102, 104, and 4.

HIGHWAY 19: THE CEILIDH TRAIL

The least traveled of the three routes north from the Canso Causeway, Highway 19 hugs the coastline and passes many small villages that haven't changed much in decades. This stretch of coastline is a bastion of Celtic music, hence the nickname Ceilidh Trail. Natalie MacMaster and the Rankins, as well as a new generation of stars headed by Chrissy Crowley, were all born and raised in the area.

Mabou

The town of Mabou (pop. 400) is the center of Gaelic education in Nova Scotia (the language is taught in the local school) and the location of Our Lady of Seven Sorrows Pioneers Shrine. The Mabou Gaelic and Historical Society Museum, or **An Drochaid** (902/945-2311, July-Aug. Tues.-Sun. 9am-5pm, donation),

housed in a former general store, focuses on crafts, local music and poetry, genealogical research, and Gaelic culture.

The Mabou Mines area, near the coast, has some excellent hiking trails into a roadless section of the **Mabou Highlands.**

GETTING THERE

Mabou is a 60-kilometer (40-minute) drive north up Highway 19 from the Canso Causeway. It's 335 kilometers (3.5 hours) from Halifax via Highways 102, 104, and 19.

★ Glenora Inn and Distillery

The **Glenora Inn and Distillery** (Hwy. 19, Glenville, 902/258-2662 or 800/839-0491, www.glenoradistillery.com, tours May-Oct. daily 9am-5pm, adult $7) is North America's only single-malt whiskey distillery. (It can't be called Scotch whiskey, as it's not from Scotland.) The final product is marketed as Glen Breton Rare, with 250,000 liters distilled annually. Built in 1990 using impressive post-and-beam construction and traditional copper pots for the distilling process, the complex is open for tours daily on the hour 9am-5pm. Better still, it's also a country inn with nine comfortable rooms ($189-199 s or d) and six spacious log chalets ($235-345) that sleep up to six people. Also at the distillery is **Glenora**

Dining Room and Washback Pub (May-Oct. daily 11am-11pm, $17-39), which serves hearty lunches and dinners accompanied by live Celtic music.

GETTING THERE

Glenville is 12 kilometers north of Mabou on Highway 19.

Inverness

Golfers know this Scottish settlement (pop. 1,300), the largest town along Highway 19, for **Cabot Links** (Beach Rd. #2, 902/258-4653, greens fee $275), one of North America's few links courses and rated one of the world's top 100 golf courses, and the equally spectacular **Cabot Links,** which opened to rave reviews in 2016 (same contact information and greens fee). Located between the town and the ocean, the location alone makes the effort to reach Inverness worthwhile. Overlooking the original course, **Cabot Links Lodge** (Beach Rd. #2, 902/258-4653, www.cabotlinks.com, May-Oct., $295-435 s or d) features 72 modern hotel-style rooms in five configurations, as well as a restaurant and lounge. If you're not a golfer, spend your time beyond the course, walking along the seemingly endless sandy beach below the golf course. Back up the hill

in town, the **Ned Macdonald Museum** (62 Lower Railway St., 902/258-3291, June-Oct. daily 10am-6pm, adult $1) focuses on the region's mining history and pioneer families.

Ten kilometers north of Inverness on Highway 19 is ★ **MacLeod's Beach Campsite** (Dunvegan, 902/258-2433, www.macleods.com, June 15-Oct. 15, campsites $37-40, cottages $170-190 s or d), which slopes down to a delightful beach that rarely gets crowded. Amenities include washrooms, showers, fire pits, a store, a launderette, a games room, volleyball, basketball, horseshoes, and more.

GETTING THERE

Inverness is about 20 kilometers north of Mabou on Highway 19.

HIGHWAY 105 TO BADDECK

From the Canso Causeway, it's 90 kilometers to Baddeck along Highway 105 (the TransCanada Highway). This is the main route north to Sydney and the Cabot Trail.

Iona

Where it intersects with Highway 105, Highway 223 crosses Little Narrows to

Glenora Inn and Distillery

Iona, then follows the shoreline of St. Andrews Channel all the way to Sydney. It's the least traveled of the many up-island highways, but no less interesting than the other options. The route is posted as Bras d'Or Lakes Drive.

Set on 16 hectares overlooking the narrow body of water between Bras d'Or Lakes and St. Andrews Channel, Iona's **Highland Village Museum** (Hwy. 223, 902/725-2272, June-mid-Oct. daily 10am-5pm, adult $11, senior $9, child $5) tells the story of the island's Gaelic heritage through features such as 10 historic buildings as well as many examples of working farm equipment.

GETTING THERE

From the intersection of Highway 105 and Highway 223, it's 25 kilometers to Iona along Highway 223.

Baddeck and Vicinity

Baddeck (from *abadak,* or "place near an island," as the Mi'kmaq called it, referring to Kidston Island just offshore) is a picturesque town of 900 that lies on the misty wooded shore of St. Patrick's Channel, a long inlet of Bras d'Or Lakes. Baddeck also marks the traditional beginning and ending point for the Cabot Trail.

SIGHTS AND RECREATION

Many visitors plan a stop in Baddeck for its heritage accommodations and fine dining, but there are also a few things to see and do, including a national historic site that everyone should visit.

★ Alexander Graham Bell National Historic Site

At the east end of Baddeck (within walking distance of downtown) is the **Alexander Graham Bell National Historic Site** (902/295-2069, late May-Oct. daily 9am-5pm, adult $7.80, senior $6.55, child $3.90), a tremendously satisfying museum with displays on Bell's life, his family, and his seemingly inexhaustible curiosity about science. The multimedia exhibits include working models of Bell's first telephones and a full-size reproduction of his speed-record-setting HD-4 hydrofoil, but some of the most interesting displays are information panels describing how Bell's interest in teaching the

deaf to speak led to the invention of the telephone. The inventor always had a soft spot for children, and his love of the younger generation is reflected in the museum's Children's Corner, a large space where kids of all ages can make and decorate kites, do experiments, and generally have fun in an educational environment. Allow at least two hours, more if you have children.

Kidston Island

A free ferry runs from Government Wharf (Jones St.) out to **Kidston Island,** just 200 meters from the mainland, which has a beach with supervised swimming. The wooded island also has numerous short walking trails, including one that leads to a lighthouse that has been guiding vessels on Bras d'Or Lakes for more than a century. The ferry operates every 20 minutes July-August (Mon.-Fri. 10am-6pm, Sat.-Sun. noon-6pm). The trip takes less than five minutes.

Boat Tours

The *Amoeba* (902/295-7780, June-mid-Oct., adult $25, child $10), a 67-foot concrete-hulled yacht built by the owner's father during a 10-year period, provides an inexpensive way to enjoy the Bras d'Or Lakes. Ninety-minute trips depart from Government Wharf at the end of Jones Street three or four times daily through the summer season. In addition to enjoying the lake, you'll pass Alexander

Baddeck

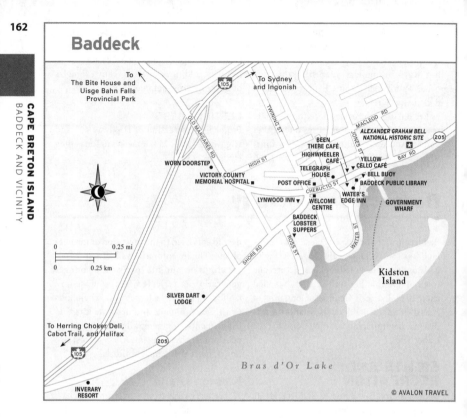

To
The Bite House and
Uisge Bahn Falls
Provincial Park

To Sydney
and Ingonish

To Herring Choker Deli,
Cabot Trail, and Halifax

INVERARY
RESORT

SILVER DART
LODGE

SHORE RD

ROSS ST

BADDECK
LOBSTER
SUPPERS

LYNWOOD INN

WELCOME
CENTRE

WATER'S
EDGE INN

POST OFFICE

TELEGRAPH
HOUSE

BADDECK PUBLIC LIBRARY

BELL BUOY

YELLOW
CELLO CAFÉ

HIGHWHEELER
CAFÉ

BEEN
THERE CAFÉ

WORN DOORSTEP

VICTORY COUNTY
MEMORIAL HOSPITAL

HIGH ST

TWINING ST

OLD MARGAREE RD

CHEBUCTO ST

WATER ST

JONES ST

MACLEOD RD

BAY RD

ALEXANDER GRAHAM BELL
NATIONAL HISTORIC SITE

GOVERNMENT
WHARF

Kidston
Island

Bras d'Or Lake

0   0.25 mi

0   0.25 km

© AVALON TRAVEL

Graham Bell's estate and can often spot bald eagles perched atop shoreline trees.

FOOD

Cafés and restaurants line Baddeck's main street, but most are open only through the warmer months, and by mid-October, choices become very limited.

Casual Dining

For breakfast, sandwiches, pizzas, and light meals, the **Yellow Cello Cafe** (525 Chebucto St., 902/295-2303, May-mid-Oct. daily 8am-11pm, $12-20) is centrally located and well priced, with an indoor dining room and veranda in front. The calzones are delicious, the beer selection is good, and the people-watching can't be beat.

For the best coffee in town, head to the **Highwheeler Café** (484 Chebucto St., 902/295-3006, May-mid-Oct. Tues.-Sun. 7am-6pm, lunches $8-12). This café has an in-house bakery, so you know everything is fresh, including daily soup specials and healthy sandwiches made to order.

Across the road from the Highwheeler, **Bean There Cafe** (503 Chebucto St., 902/295-1634, Mon.-Sat. 6:30am-4pm, Sun. 7am-4pm) is another decent place for coffee, with a few outdoor tables good for watching the world of Baddeck pass by.

With a welcoming, woodsy ambience, ★ **Herring Choker Deli** (Hwy. 105, 902/295-2275, daily 9am-5pm, lunches $9-15) overlooks the water from 11 kilometers west of town. Instead of greasy cooked breakfasts, tuck into a scrambled egg, ham, and cheese panini ($8). The lunchtime highlight: thick gourmet sandwiches packed with goodies on bread baked each morning. The

Alexander Graham Bell

Once a major shipbuilding center, Baddeck claims as its most famous resident not a sailor but an inventor—Alexander Graham Bell. The landscape, language, and people all reminded the Scotsman of his native land. He built a grand summer home, Beinn Bhreagh (pronounced Ben Vreeah), across the inlet from Baddeck (it is still owned by his descendants and is not open to the public). While the telephone is his most famous invention, Bell possessed an intellectual curiosity that is almost impossible to comprehend in today's world.

At Beinn Bhreagh, he studied heredity by breeding sheep and seeking to increase twin births. Even when separated from the rest of the world at Baddeck, he maintained friendships in high places—after the attempted assassination of President Garfield in 1881, Bell was hastily commissioned to invent an electromagnetic device to find the bullet. When his son died after experiencing breathing problems, he developed a breathing device that was the prototype of the iron lungs used to help polio victims. More than anything else, Bell was cap-

Alexander Bell National Historic Site

tivated by flight. He tested propeller-driven kits as early as the 1890s, and in 1909, four years after the Wright brothers' famous flight, the great inventor took to the air over Bras d'Or Lakes in the **Silver Dart.** But he wasn't done yet: In 1919, at the age of 72, Bell and his estate manager, Casey Baldwin, invented the hydrofoil, which set a water-speed record of more than 70 miles per hour. Bell died three years later and was buried at Beinn Bhreagh.

coffee is also excellent, and there is a wide selection of meats and cheeses to go.

Lobster Supper

Lobster suppers originated as local gatherings held in church basements and community halls. Today, they have become a little more commercialized, but they are still a fun and inexpensive way to enjoy this succulent seafood treat. One of the few regularly scheduled in Nova Scotia (Prince Edward Island is a hotbed of lobster suppers) is **Baddeck Lobster Suppers** (17 Ross St., 902/295-3307, early June-mid-Oct. daily 4pm-9pm), held in a community hall just off Main Street. A 1- to 1.5-pound lobster with all-you-can-eat chowder, mussels, trimmings, dessert, and nonalcoholic drinks costs $42 per person. If you're not a lobster fan, substitute salmon, crab, or steak at the same price.

Other Restaurants

The most unique dining experience in Baddeck—and arguably one of the most unique in all of Nova Scotia—can be enjoyed at ★ **The Bite House** (1471 Westside Rd., eat@thebitehouse.com, May-Dec. Wed.-Sat. 6pm-9pm, $60). Here, in a century-old farmhouse, chef Bryan Picard cooks for 12 lucky diners each night. The five-course tasting menu he offers comprises solely locally grown, sourced, and even foraged ingredients, all prepared simply yet presented perfectly. Wine and beer are available. Reservations well in advance are a must, and can be made by email.

Watching the sun set over Bras d'Or Lakes from a window table at the **Bell Buoy Restaurant** (536 Chebucto St., 902/295-2581, mid-May-June daily 4pm-9pm, July-mid-Oct. daily 11:30am-9pm, $16-30) is worth the price of dinner alone. A menu highlight is the seafood chowder, which comes chock-full of haddock, salmon, mussels, and even lobster, as well as a slab of homemade oatmeal bread as a side. Mains vary from pastas to whole lobsters, with a number of vegetarian and gluten-free options also offered.

Of many local lodges with dining rooms that welcome nonguests, none is better than the **Lynwood Inn** (24 Shore Rd., 902/295-1995, mid-May-mid-Oct. noon-8:30pm, $16-32), a grand 1868 home that has been converted into an inn and restaurant. The smallish dining room is tastefully decorated in Victorian-era style. The menu is less expensive than you may imagine.

ACCOMMODATIONS AND CAMPING
$50-100

A 10-minute walk from town and the Alexander Graham Bell National Historic Site, the ★ **Worn Doorstep** (43 Old Margaree Rd., 902/295-1997, $90 s or d) has four delightful en suite rooms, each with its own private entrance, air-conditioning, basic cooking facilities such as a microwave and toaster, and a TV. All guests share a rooftop patio with sweeping views across Bras d'Or Lakes.

Owned by the same family for five generations, **Telegraph House** (479 Chebucto St., 902/295-1100, www.baddeckhotel.com, $100-135 s or d) combines 18 basic rooms in the grandly historic original 1861 home with a row of 13 modern motel units. The lodge has two historic links of note—it was once home to a telegraph office that sent some of the first transatlantic messages, and Alexander Graham Bell was a frequent guest. The room that Bell called his own looks exactly like it would have in the 1880s ($130 s or d); others have been given a modern look while retaining the historical feel through antique furnishings. Amenities include a library, a sitting room, and a dining room open daily for breakfast, lunch, and dinner. Telegraph House is also one of the few downtown accommodations open year-round.

Over $100

Direct water access is a major draw at **Inverary Resort** (Exit 8 from Hwy. 105, 902/295-3500 or 800/565-5660, www.capebretonresorts.com, May-Nov., $150-405), a large complex that offers accommodations varying from homey B&B-style rooms to modern two-bedroom suites. Down on the waterfront, you can rent canoes and kayaks from the activity

Inverary Resort

center. Elsewhere on the grounds are an indoor pool, game rooms, a playground, spa services, two dining rooms, and a pub.

Named for Alexander Graham Bell's famous airplane, **Silver Dart Lodge** (257 Shore Rd., 902/295-2340 or 888/662-7484, www.maritimeinns.com, mid-May-mid-Oct., $145-230 s or d) sits on a 40-hectare hillside overlooking the lake. Amenities include a heated outdoor pool and playground, as well as free use of bikes, a small stretch of private beach, and hiking trails. Large windows in the restaurant allow diners to take full advantage of the water views, but the food is also good, including a large buffet breakfast ($15 pp), prepacked picnic lunches, and dinner mains ($21-30) such as maple whiskey salmon.

★ **Water's Edge Inn** (22 Water St., 902/295-3600 or 866/439-2528, www.thewatersedgeinn.com, June-mid-Oct., $155-185 s or d) is across the road from the lake and also within easy walking distance of downtown restaurants. Four of the six rooms have lake views and private balconies. All six are heritage-themed yet stylishly outfitted with modern touches such as air-conditioning and TV/DVD combos. A nice touch is the downstairs gallery, which is filled with regional art.

Campgrounds

Bras d'Or Lakes Campground (5 km west of Baddeck on Hwy. 105, 902/295-2329, www.brasdorlakescampground.com, mid-June-Sept., campsites $32-61, cabins $59-89 s or d) has almost 100 unserviced and hookup sites. The only local campground actually on the lake, it has showers, washrooms, a launderette, wireless Internet throughout, an outdoor swimming pool, a book exchange, and free coffee each morning. You'll need to bring your own linens for the cabins, and they do share bathrooms, but for families they provide excellent value.

In the vicinity, **Adventures East Campground** (between Exits 7 and 8 of Hwy. 105, 902/295-2417 or 800/507-2228, www.adventureseast.ca, early June-mid-Oct., campsites $31-40, cabins $125-165 s or d) also has all the necessary amenities for an overnight or longer stay—showers, a laundry, and an outdoor pool.

INFORMATION AND SERVICES

At the east end of the main street, the **Baddeck Welcome Centre** (corner of Chebucto St. and Shore Rd., 902/295-1911, www.visitbaddeck.com, June-Sept. daily 9am-5pm) is indeed welcoming. Friendly staff will help out with finding accommodations and, as always, love handing out maps and brochures.

For emergencies, dial 911 or **Victoria County Memorial Hospital** (902/295-2112).

GETTING THERE

Halfway between the Canso Causeway and Sydney, Baddeck is 350 kilometers northeast from Halifax (allow at least four hours driving time).

MARGAREE RIVER VALLEY

Eight kilometers west of Baddeck, the Cabot Trail branches off the TransCanada Highway northwest through the hills and into the valley of the Margaree River, a renowned salmon-fishing stream and the namesake of seven small communities.

The peak time for fishing is mid-June-mid-July and September-mid-October; many guides are available locally. Near North East Margaree, **Margaree Salmon Museum** (60 E. Big Intervale Rd., 902/248-2848, mid-June-mid-Oct. daily 9am-5pm, adult $2, child $1) tells the story of the river and its fishy inhabitants.

Accommodations

Even though it's away from the ocean, the Margaree River Valley is a popular spot to get away from it all. Near the village of Margaree Valley, **Normaway Inn** (691 Egypt Rd., 902/248-2987 or 800/565-9463, www.thenormawayinn.com, $99-169 s or d) is typical of the many accommodations options. This elegantly rustic 1920s resort is nestled on 100

Cabot Trail: Planning Your Drive

Looping around the northern end of Cape Breton Island by driving the 311-kilometer **Cabot Trail** is always a highlight of my travels through Nova Scotia, but understanding the route is key to making the most of your travel time. It is possible to drive the entire Cabot Trail in less than five hours—but don't. Instead, plan on immersing yourself in the destination for at least two full days. Offering a mix of historic and resort-style accommodations and dining options, Baddeck is an ideal base. Those equipped for camping will appreciate the numerous campgrounds through Cape Breton Highlands National Park, or for unequalled historical ambience, make reservations at the Keltic Lodge, which is perched high above the ocean overlooking Ingonish Beach.

Unlike every other highway in the province, the Cabot Trail does not have a specific number designation; instead it is a combination of numbered highways (also called "routes" by the locals). Nor does the Cabot Trail have an official start or finish point, although many start their journey by veering off Highway 105 at Whycocomagh, 50 kilometers north of the Canso Causeway, and heading north on Highway 395. From Whycocomagh, key driving distances (and minimum driving times) are:

· **Whycocomagh to Margaree Forks:** 48 kilometers (50 minutes). Highway 395 from Whycocomagh leads north through lush valleys and prime angling territory.

· **Margaree Forks to Cheticamp:** 39 kilometers (30 minutes). Heading north from Margaree Forks, the Cabot Trail follows the Margaree River to the Gulf of St. Lawrence, then hugs the ocean to the Acadian village of Cheticamp.

· **Cheticamp to Ingonish:** 105 kilometers (80 minutes). This section through Cape Breton Highlands National Park is the highlight of the Cabot Trail, with seeming endless ocean views before crossing the rugged interior to emerge at the white-sand beaches of Ingonish.

· **Ingonish to St. Anns:** 73 kilometers (90 minutes). It's only 85 kilometers from Ingonish south to St. Anns, but the road is narrow and there are many tight corners, so allow at least 90 minutes, plus any time spent at the numerous lookouts en route.

· **St. Anns to Baddeck:** 21 kilometers (30 minutes). Heading south from St. Anns, the Cabot Trail is extremely narrow and winding. At South Haven, you reach the main island highway and can head south to Baddeck or north to Sydney.

· **Baddeck to Whycocomagh:** 25 kilometers (20 minutes). The final leg of the Cabot Trail is along Highway 105, the main route up-island to Sydney.

hectares in the hills. The main lodge has eight guest rooms, and the grounds hold 19 one- and two-bedroom cabins. Activities include nightly films or traditional musical entertainment, tennis, walking trails, bicycling, weekly barn dances, and fiddling contests. The dining room (open for breakfast and dinner) serves dishes of Atlantic salmon, lamb, scallops, and fresh fruits and vegetables. The Normaway is about 30 kilometers along the Cabot Trail from Highway 105, and then three kilometers along Egypt Road.

On Lake O'Law, **The Lakes Resort** (902/248-2360 or 888/722-2112, www.thelakesresort.com, May-Oct., campsites $26-29, cottages $125-145 s or d) comprises treed campsites and eight two-bedroom cottages overlooking the lake. Each cottage has a bathroom, microwave, living area, and outdoor barbecue. Recreational opportunities include boating, fishing, canoeing, mini-golf, and go-karting, while the resort restaurant offers well-priced, simple cooking, including lobster dinners. To get there, turn off the Cabot Trail at North East Margaree.

Getting There

The Margaree River Valley is about 50 kilometers northwest of Baddeck via the southern portion of the Cabot Trail.

Chéticamp

Along the Cabot Trail, Chéticamp is an Acadian fishing village (pop. 1,000) set along a protected waterway that opens to the Gulf of St. Lawrence. Deep-sea fishing and whale-watching charter boats leave from the central Government Wharf, and the entrance to Cape Breton Highlands National Park is five kilometers north of town.

The village was first settled by Acadians expelled from the Nova Scotia mainland in the 18th century. Today, the weeklong **Festival de l'Escaouette,** in early August, celebrates aspects of Acadian culture with a parade, arts and crafts, and music.

SIGHTS

The first stones for **St. Pierre Catholic Church** were laid in 1893, but it took almost 20 years to finish. Its tower pierces the sky at a height of more than 50 meters and can be seen from far up and down the coast. On the south side of town, the **Acadian Museum** (744 Main St., 902/224-2170, May-June and Sept.-Oct. daily 9am-5pm, July-Aug. daily 8am-9pm, donation) displays artifacts from early settler days, with an emphasis on the area's sheepherding past, including weaving, spinning, and rug-hooking demonstrations.

RECREATION

Along the boardwalk opposite the Irving gas station, **Seaside Whale & Nature Cruises** (902/224-2899, adult $55, child $32.50) takes guests out on two-hour whale-watching trips two or three times daily June-mid-October.

One of the major cottage industries of this area is the production of hooked rugs, a craft developed by Acadians centuries ago. In the late 1930s, a group of Chéticamp women formed a rug-hooking cooperative that still thrives. The Co-op Artisanale de Chéticamp gives demonstrations and displays its wares at the Acadian Museum. You can also see beautiful hooked rugs and tapestries at **Les Trois**

Pignons (15584 Main St., 902/224-2642, mid-May-mid-Oct. daily 8:30am-5pm, adult $5, senior and child $4), in a striking red-roofed building at the northern end of Chéticamp. The building also houses the visitor information center.

A number of galleries and shops hereabouts also sell locally produced folk arts—brightly colored, whimsical carvings and paintings of fish, seabirds, fishermen, boats, or whatever strikes the artists' fancy. One kilometer north of the visitors center, the **Sunset Art Gallery** (15856 Cabot Trail, 902/224-1831, mid-May-mid-Oct. daily 9am-5:30pm) features the colorfully painted woodcarvings of William Roach.

FOOD

At the north end of town, **Hometown Kitchen** (15559 Main St., 902/224-3888, summer daily 8am- 8pm, $13-21) has a few outdoor tables with water views. The food is simple but tasty and a good value.

Dine at the ★ **Restaurant Acadien** (774 Main St., 902/224-3207, May-Oct. daily 11am-7pm, summer 7am-10pm, $14-23) for authentic Acadian food: *fricot* (souplike stew), meat pies, fresh fish, blood pudding, and butterscotch pie. **Evangeline** (15150 Main St., 902/224-2044, daily 7am-9pm, $12-20) is a family restaurant specializing in homemade soups and meat pies.

ACCOMMODATIONS

If you're traveling on a budget, a choice of older, inexpensive motels along the main street makes Chéticamp a good base for day trips into Cape Breton Highlands National Park. Best of the bunch is **Albert's Motel** (15086 Cabot Trail, 902/224-2077, mid-May-mid-Oct., $70-85 s or d), which has remarkably comfortable rooms for the price.

Overlooking the ocean a few kilometers south of town, ★ **Chéticamp Outfitters**

Inn B&B (13938 Cabot Trail, Point Cross, 902/224-2776, www.cheticampoutfitters.com, Apr.-mid-Dec., $100-150 s or d) is a large, modern home with six guest rooms and common areas that include a deck with sweeping ocean views. The less-expensive rooms share two bathrooms, while all rates include a full breakfast. The hosts operate a charter fishing business, so this is a good base for anglers.

At the north end of the main street, ★ **Ocean View Chalets** (15569 Cabot Trail, 902/224-2313 or 877/743-4404, www.oceanviewchalets.com, motel rooms $125-140 s or d, cabins $150-190 s or d) has a delightful oceanfront setting, with a wide strip of green space separating the cabins from the water. Each unit has a kitchen, a separate bedroom, and a wood barbecue out front.

Behind the main street and linked to the local golf course by a short trail, **Cabot Trail Sea and Golf Chalets** (902/224-1777 or 877/244-1777, www.seagolfchalets.com, mid-May-mid-Oct., $159-299 for up to four people) is a complex of spacious and modern freestanding units, each with a bathroom, kitchen, deck, and barbecue.

INFORMATION

On the north side of town, **Chéticamp Visitor Information Centre** (15584 Main St., 902/224-2642, mid-May-mid-Oct. daily 8:30am-5pm) has information on tours, accommodations, and campgrounds. For national park information, continue north through town to the large visitors center complex.

GETTING THERE

Chéticamp is 90 kilometers (just over an hour) northwest of Baddeck via the Cabot Trail. The trip northeast from Halifax is 400 kilometers and takes five hours.

Cape Breton Highlands National Park

Protecting a swath of wilderness at the northern tip of Cape Breton Island, this national park is one of the finest in Canada. While outdoor enthusiasts are attracted by opportunities to hike and bike, anyone can enjoy the most spectacular scenery simply by driving the Cabot Trail, which spans the length of the park from Chéticamp in the west to Ingonish in the east.

The Landscape

Heath bogs, a dry rocky plateau, and a high taiga 400 meters above sea level mark the interior of the 950-square-kilometer park. Rugged cliffs characterize the seacoast on the west side, where the mountains kneel into the Gulf of St. Lawrence, and gentler but still wildly beautiful shores define the eastern side. Nova Scotia's highest point, 532-meter White Hill, is simply a windswept hump, far from the nearest road and with no formal access trail reaching it.

Typical Acadian forest, a combination of hardwoods and conifers, carpets much of the region. Wild orchids bloom under the shade of thick spruce, balsam fir, and paper birch. The **Grand Anse River** gorge near MacKenzie Mountain is the Acadian forest's showpiece. Its terrain—with sugar maples, yellow birches, and rare alpine-arctic plants—has been designated an international biological preserve. The park is also a wildlife sanctuary for white-tailed deer, black bears, beavers, lynx, mink, red foxes, snowshoe hares, and more than 200 bird species, including eagles and red-tailed hawks.

Park Entry

Cape Breton Highlands National Park is open year-round, though campgrounds and the two information centers operate only mid-May-October. A **National Parks Day Pass** (adult $7.80, senior $6.80, child $3.90, maximum of $19.60 per vehicle) is valid until 4pm the

Cape Breton Highlands National Park

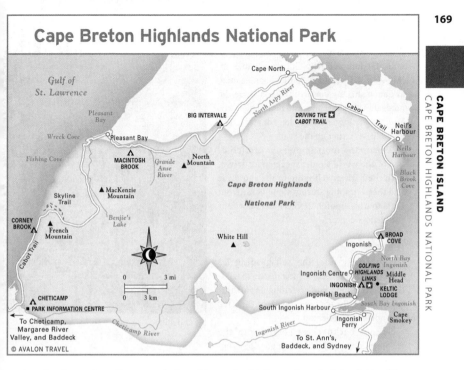

© AVALON TRAVEL

day after its purchase. Passes can be bought at both park information centers, Chéticamp and Ingonish Campgrounds, or at the two park gates.

★ DRIVING THE CABOT TRAIL

The Cabot Trail extends well beyond park boundaries along its 311-kilometer length, but the most spectacular stretch is undoubtedly the 110 kilometers through the park between Chéticamp and Ingonish. By allowing a full day for the drive, you will have time to walk a trail or two, stop at the best lookouts, and even head out on a whale-watching trip. This section describes the drive itself, with recreational opportunities discussed next. You can of course follow the Cabot Trail in either direction, but I've laid out the drive from Chéticamp to Ingonish (clockwise), meaning you pass the main park information center at the beginning of the drive and

you're driving on the safer inland side of the road the entire way.

Thousands of outdoor enthusiasts tackle the Cabot Trail under pedal power each summer. The trip is not particularly long, but it is very strenuous in sections, and lack of a wide shoulder can make for some hair-raising moments.

Hiking is a major attraction for visitors of all fitness levels. The park offers 26 established hiking trails, varying from simple strolls shorter than half a kilometer to challenging treks leading to campgrounds more than 20 kilometers away. Many of the trails are level; a few climb to awesome viewpoints. Some hug the rocky shoreline; others explore river valleys. No matter what your abilities may be, you'll be able to enjoy the park at your own speed. For details on hiking in the park, browse the many books sold at Les Amis du Plein Air, the bookstore within the Cheticamp Visitor Centre.

Chéticamp to Pleasant Bay

Make your first stop inside the park at the **Cheticamp Visitor Centre** (902/224-2306, mid-May-June and Sept.-Oct. daily 9am-5pm, July-Aug. daily 8:30am-7pm). Pick up a map, ask about hiking opportunities, browse the natural history displays, and hit the highway. You can pay for park entry here or at the toll-gate a little farther up the road.

This is the most impressive stretch of one of the world's most spectacular drives, with the highway clinging to the shoreline and then climbing steeply along oceanfront cliffs to a viewpoint 18 kilometers north of the visitors center.

HIKING

On the light side, the self-guiding **Le Buttereau Trail** leads 1.9 kilometers to wild-flowers and good bird-watching opportunities. The trailhead is just north of the park gate north of Chéticamp.

Serious backpackers gravitate to the **Fishing Cove Trail** (16 km round-trip), a rugged journey to a campground and beach. You can reach the end of the trail in two hours, but allow at least three for the strenuous return trip back up to the highway. The trailhead is just south of Pleasant Bay.

WHALE-WATCHING

From Pleasant Bay, one of two whale-watching spots in Nova Scotia (the other is the Bay of Fundy), a number of operators depart daily through summer. The region boasts a high success rate when it comes to spotting pilot, humpback, and minke whales, simply because of the high numbers close to the coastline. **Captain Mark's** (902/224-1316 or 888/754-5112) is easily recognized down at the harbor by his booth shaped like a lighthouse. This company offers the option of stable ex-fishing boats (adult $45, senior $40, child $20) and rigid-hulled Zodiacs (adult $55, senior $50, child $30). The advantage with the latter is that the whales are reached much more quickly. You should book by phone in advance for July and August sailings.

the Cabot Trail

Continuing Around the Cape

From Pleasant Bay, the park's northwestern corner, the highway turns inland and wraps upward to 455-meter-high **French Mountain.** From this point, a level stretch barrels across a narrow ridge overlooking deeply scooped valleys. The road climbs again, this time to **MacKenzie Mountain,** at 372 meters, and then switchbacks down a 10-12 percent grade. Another ascent, to **North Mountain,** formed more than a billion years ago, peaks at 445 meters on a three-kilometer summit. The lookout opens up views of a deep gorge and the North Aspy River.

HIKING

For fit and energetic visitors, the seven-kilometer (two hours one-way) **Skyline Loop** climbs a headland, from which the lucky can spot pilot whales; along the way, look for bald eagles, deer, and bears. The trail begins where the Cabot Trail heads inland at French Mountain.

waterfalls at the north end of Black Brook Cove

On overcast or wet days, the much easier **Benjie's Lake Trail** provides an ideal break from driving. From a trailhead six kilometers east of the start of the Skyline Loop Trail, this easy walk takes about 30 minutes each way.

Cape North and Vicinity
The northernmost point on the Cabot Trail is Cape North, the name of a small service town (as well as a geographical feature to the north). Here a spur road leads 22 kilometers north to Meat Cove. Although outside the park, this road traverses complete wilderness before reaching the open ocean at St. Lawrence Bay. En route, **Cabot's Landing Provincial Park,** the supposed landing site of English explorer John Cabot, offers a sandy beach on Aspy Bay (good for clam digging) and a picnic area, and marks the starting point for hikes up 442-meter-high Sugar Loaf Mountain.

The East Coast to Ingonish
From Cape North, it's 45 kilometers east and then south to the resort town of Ingonish.

Aside from tucking into a seafood feast at Neil's Harbour, you should make time for a stop at **Black Brook Cove.** Backed by a short stretch of beach, the cove is an extremely popular spot for picnicking and swimming. To escape the summertime crowd, walk to the north end of the beach and follow the Jack Pine Loop through open coastal forest.

ACCOMMODATIONS AND CAMPING
Since it's a national park, there are no hotel accommodations within the park boundary. Instead, visitors stay at Chéticamp for its Acadian heritage, at Ingonish for its beaches and golfing, or at one of the following choices in between the two.

Under $50
HI-Cabot Trail Hostel (23349 Cabot Trail, 902/224-1976, www.cabottrailhostel.com, dorm $26, $58 s or d) is within walking distance of Pleasant Bay, 38 kilometers north of Chéticamp on the park's western side. The facility is small but friendly and comfortable, with 18 dorm beds in two rooms and an adjacent bunkhouse. Guests have use of communal washrooms, two kitchens, a deck with a barbecue, and wireless Internet access.

$100-150
Just more than 40 kilometers north of Chéticamp, the Cabot Trail exits the park for a short distance at Pleasant Bay. Here, the distinctively salmon-pink **Midtrail Motel & Inn** (23475 Cabot Trail, 902/224-2529 or 800/215-0411, www.midtrail.com, mid-May-Oct., $105-125 s or d) offers 20 bright but basic motel rooms, some with ocean views, as well as a family-friendly seafood restaurant, a launderette, and a couple of Adirondack chairs perched high above the motel on a knob of land offering sweeping ocean views.

Set on 25 hectares of oceanfront property, **Markland Beach Cottages** (802 Dingwall Rd., Dingwall, 902/383-2246, www.themarkland.com, May-mid-Oct., $165-300 s or d) is 52 kilometers north of Ingonish (signposted off the Cabot Trail between Cape North and South Harbour). Although it is a resort, the emphasis is on the outdoors, with most guests spending their time on the adjacent beach or lazing around the outdoor pool. The cottages (from $200 s or d) are an excellent value. The resort restaurant features the freshest of fresh seafood combined with seasonal produce such as fiddleheads and wild mint.

Campgrounds

Cape Breton Highlands National Park is the most popular camping destination in Nova Scotia. Parks Canada operates seven campgrounds within the park.

Chéticamp Campground (5 km north of Chéticamp) is behind the main park visitors center. Amenities include showers, flush toilets, kitchen shelters, playgrounds, and an outdoor theater hosting a summer interpretive program. Only some sites have fire pits. Tent sites are $25.50 per night, serviced sites $38.20. Chéticamp Campground is the park's only campground that accepts reservations. Sites can be reserved through the **Parks Canada Campground Reservation Service** (519/826-5391 or 877/737-3783, www.pccamping.ca) for $12 per reservation. If you're traveling in the height of summer and require hookups, this booking system is highly recommended.

Continue north from the park gate for 10 kilometers to ★ **Corney Brook Campground** (mid-May-early Oct., $23.50), which is not much more than a parking lot with 20 designated sites, but incredible ocean

views more than make up for a lack of facilities. Beyond Pleasant Bay, the 10 sites at **MacIntosh Brook Campground** (mid-May-early Oct., $21.50) fill quickly. Ten kilometers farther east is **Big Intervale Campground** (mid-May-early Oct., $18), also with 10 sites. Neither of these two campgrounds has drinking water. With 256 sites, **Broad Cove Campground** (mid-May-early Oct., $25.50), on the ocean just north of Ingonish, is the park's largest campground. Campers have use of showers, flush toilets, kitchen shelters, playgrounds, and an outdoor theater. **Ingonish Campground** (late June-early Sept., $25.50) is within a finger of the park that extends to the ocean along the Ingonish coastline. Although it's close to the resort town of Ingonish, the wooded setting is quiet and private and within walking distance of a sandy beach with safe swimming. It has showers, flush toilets, and kitchen shelters.

INFORMATION

Turn right as soon as you cross into the park north of Cheticamp for the excellent **Cheticamp Visitor Centre** (902/224-2306, mid-May-June and Sept.-Oct. daily 9am-5pm, July-Aug. daily 8:30am-7pm). It features natural-history exhibits, weather reports, an activities schedule, and helpful staff.

Parks Canada also operates a smaller information center in Ingonish (mid-May-June and Sept.-Oct. daily 9am-5pm, July-Aug. daily 8:30am-7pm) for those entering the park from the east. It's located along the Cabot Trail beside Freshwater Lake.

Ingonish and Vicinity

Ingonish (pop. 1,100), 110 kilometers east of Chéticamp and 100 kilometers north of Baddeck, is a busy resort center at the eastern entrance to Cape Breton Highlands National Park. The town is a lot more than somewhere simply to rest your head: It is fringed by beautiful beaches, has one of Canada's premier golf courses, and offers a delightful choice of seafood restaurants. If you are allowing yourself some rest time on your Nova Scotia travels, this is the place to book two or more nights in the same accommodation.

SIGHTS AND RECREATION

Ingonish has no official attractions as such. Instead, beach lovers gather on **Ingonish Beach,** where a lifeguard watches over swimmers splashing around in the shallow water that reaches enjoyable temperatures July-August.

Drag yourself away from one of Canada's finest beaches and you'll find the **Freshwater Lake Loop,** a two-kilometer circuit that encircles a shallow lake where beavers can often be seen hard at work in the evening. The trailhead is the parking lot at Ingonish Beach.

Even if you're not a guest at the **Keltic Lodge,** the grounds are a pleasant place for a stroll. Beyond the end of the lodge access road, a walking trail leads two kilometers to the end of Middle Head Peninsula.

★ Highlands Links

Highlands Links (3 km north of Ingonish Beach, 902/285-2600 or 800/441-1118) is generally regarded as one of the world's top 100 golf courses, and relative to other courses of similar reputation, the greens fees are a steal—$125 in high season, with twilight rates from just $65. Power carts are an additional $39. The course, which opened in 1939, was designed by Stanley Thompson, the same

architect commissioned to design famous courses in Banff and Jasper National Parks.

FOOD

Occupying a weathered wooden building on the high headland at Neil's Harbour is the ★ **Chowder House** (90 Lighthouse Rd., 902/336-2463, June-Sept. daily 11am-6pm, later hours July-Aug., $12-22). Order at the inside window and wait for your number to be called. Then tuck into creamy clam chowder ($6), fish-and-chips ($10), a lobster burger ($12), or a full crab ($22). Dollar for dollar, you're doing well if you find better value than the food at this always-busy establishment.

Keltic Lodge

The **Keltic Lodge** (Middle Head Peninsula, 902/285-2880) is home to two very different restaurants. Along the access road is the **Atlantic Restaurant** (mid-May-mid-Oct. daily 11am-9pm, $16-34), a big family-style restaurant with seafood for all tastes and budgets: beer-battered fish-and-chips, grilled salmon, and lobster. An excellent add-on is the salad bar ($12). The tables along the east side have stunning ocean views. The smart-casual **Purple Thistle Dining Room** (late May-mid-Oct. daily 7am-10am and 6pm-9pm) has one of Nova Scotia's finest reputations, especially in seafood. Meals are five courses (about $65) rather than à la carte, with an emphasis on lobster in varied creations and other seafood. If you're tooling along Cabot Trail and hope to stop here for dinner, reservations are very wise.

ACCOMMODATIONS

Accommodations are spread along the Ingonish coastline, but demand is high in July and August, so book well ahead. Also note the given open dates, as very few places are open year-round.

$100-150

Sea Breeze Cottages and Motel (8 km north of the east park gate, 902/285-2879 or 888/743-4443, www.seabreezecottagesand-motel.com, mid-Apr.-mid-Dec.) overlooks the ocean and boasts a playground that children will love. Accommodations options include basic motel rooms ($115 s or d) or cottages scattered through a forested area ($135-185 s or d).

Open year-round, **Ingonish Chalets** (36784 Cabot Trail, Ingonish Beach, 902/285-2008 or 888/505-0552, www.ingonishchalets.com, $125-205 s or d) has access to the beach and hiking trails. Nine two-bedroom log chalets start at $175, while five motel-style rooms cost $125. The rooms are furnished in a very woodsy way, with pine paneling extending from the handcrafted furniture to the wall linings. These units also come with basic cooking facilities—microwave, kettle, and so on.

It would be difficult to claim boredom at ★ **Glenghorm Beach Resort** (36743 Cabot Trail, Ingonish, 902/285-2049 or 855/285-4631, www.glenghorm.net, May-Oct., $140-410 s or d), a sprawling complex that extends from the Cabot Trail to a long arc of sandy beach. Things to do include walking along the beach, relaxing around the outdoor pool, renting kayaks and paddling through calm offshore waters, or working out in the fitness room. There are also lawn games, tennis, volleyball, and bike rentals. At the end of the day, you can relax with a glass of wine in one of the shoreline Adirondack chairs or try a Nova Scotian brew at the resort pub. Accommodations options are motel rooms up by the highway, older-style cottages (some right by the ocean), and my favorite rooms in all of Cape Breton Island—casual but stylish kitchen-equipped suites with private balconies.

Over $200

The Cabot Trail has its devoted fans, and so does the **Keltic Lodge** (902/285-2880 or 800/565-0444, www.kelticlodge.ca, mid-May-mid-Oct., from $255 s or d), on Middle

Keltic Lodge sits atop high cliffs.

Head Peninsula. The access lane from the Cabot Trail meanders through thick stands of white birches and finishes at the lodge. The long, low, wood-sided lodge—painted bright white and topped with a bright red roof—is as picturesque as a lord's manor in the Highlands of Scotland. The main lodge has 32 rustic rooms off a comfortable lobby that is furnished with overstuffed chairs and sofas arranged before a massive stone fireplace. Another 40 rooms are in the adjacent newer White Birch Inn. In addition, nine cottages with suite-style layouts (nice for families) are scattered across the grounds. Well-marked hiking trails meander through the adjacent national park woodlands and ribbon the coastal peninsula. An outdoor pool, tennis courts, and a spa facility are also available.

Affiliated with one of the region's finest restaurants, ★ **Seascape Coastal Retreat** (36083 Cabot Trail, Ingonish, 902/285-3003 or 866/385-3003, www.seascapecoastal-retreat.com, Apr.-Oct., $239-259 s or d) is suited to couples looking for a quiet getaway in romantic surroundings. Within the walls of this very private resort are 10 wooden cottages, each air-conditioned and with a private deck overlooking the ocean and a separate bedroom. Bathrobes, jetted tubs, and TV/DVD combos add to the appeal. Outside, paths lead through landscaped gardens to an herb garden and courtyard where guests gather in the evening. Rates include a full breakfast, and dinner is available with advance reservations in a smart, stylish dining room overlooking the ocean. A three-course meal is $45 per person.

GETTING THERE

Ingonish lies on the Cabot Trail 110 kilometers (1.5 hours) east of Chéticamp and 100 kilometers (1.5 hours) north of Baddeck. To get to Ingonish from Halifax, it's 440 kilometers (five hours) northeast.

SOUTH FROM INGONISH

South of Ingonish Beach, the Cabot Trail descends hairpin turns. Stop at 366-meter-high **Cape Smokey** for a picnic or hiking along the cliff top, which has wonderful views. The steep and twisting road finishes in a coastal glide with views of the offshore Bird Islands. Lying off the northwest side of the cape at the mouth of St. Ann's Bay, these two islands are the nesting site of a multitude of seabird species.

ST. ANN'S

During the 1850s, about 900 of St. Ann's residents, dissatisfied with Cape Breton, sailed away to Australia and eventually settled in New Zealand, where their descendants today make up a good part of the Scottish population. Despite this loss of nearly half its population, St. Ann's, 80 kilometers south of Ingonish and 30 kilometers north of Baddeck, is today the center of Cape Breton's Gaelic culture.

A good place to eat in this area is the **Lobster Galley** (51943 Cabot Trail, 902/295-3100, daily 11am-8pm, until 10pm in summer, $13-30), at the head of St. Ann's Harbour. Fish cakes and Caesar salad are just $12, a filled lobster roll $18; or try the full lobster dinner for $30.

★ Gaelic College of Celtic Arts and Crafts

The only institution of its kind in North America, the **Gaelic College of Celtic Arts and Crafts** (51779 Cabot Trail, 902/295-3411) was established in 1938. Programs include Highland dancing, fiddling, piping, Gaelic

Gaelic College of Celtic Arts and Crafts

language, weaving, and other subjects. The summer session attracts Gaelophiles from around the world. The **Great Hall of the Clans** (July-Aug. daily 9am-5pm, free), on the campus, examines the course of Scottish culture and history, including the migrations that brought Highlanders to Cape Breton. Activities include weaving and instrument-making demonstrations, as well as music and dance performances (July-Aug. Mon.-Fri.). The campus gift shop sells a predictable collection of kilts and tartans.

★ Celtic Colours International Festival

The popular **Celtic Colours International Festival** (902/567-3000 or 888/355-7744, www.celtic-colours.com) takes place the second full week of October. It celebrates Cape Breton's Gaelic heritage through concerts held at venues around the island, but the Gaelic College of Celtic Arts and Crafts is a focal point, especially for its nightly Festival Club, where musicians get together for an unofficial jam after performing elsewhere. The festival proper features six or seven concerts nightly, usually in small town halls, with visitors enjoying the brilliant colors of fall as they travel from venue to venue.

Getting There

St. Ann's is 80 kilometers (over an hour) south of Ingonish and 30 kilometers (25 minutes) north of Baddeck. To get to St. Ann's from Halifax, it's 400 kilometers (five hours) northeast.

The Northeast

SYDNEY

Cape Breton Island's only city is Sydney (pop. 31,000), set around a large harbor on the island's northeast corner. In the early 1800s, it was the capital of the colony of Cape Breton. At the turn of the 20th century the Sydney area boomed, ranking as one of Canada's major steel production centers.

Sights

Historic buildings constructed of stone quarried at nearby Louisbourg dot the streets north of downtown. One of these, the 1828 **St. Patrick's Church Museum** (87 Esplanade, July-Aug. Tues.-Sat. 9am-5pm, donation), is Cape Breton's oldest Roman Catholic sanctuary. **Cossit House** (75 Charlotte St., 902/539-7973, mid-June-Oct. Mon.-Sat. 9am-4pm, adult $2, senior and child $1) is almost as old as Sydney itself. The 1787 manse has been restored to its original condition.

Food

The best coffee in town is poured at **Wentworth Perk** (697 George St., 902/270-3355, Mon.-Sat. 7:30am-8pm, Sun. 11am-5pm, lunches $7-10), a modern café with the usual range of drink choices as well as wraps, sandwiches, and pastries. It's located in a converted residence on the south side of downtown.

★ **Trio** (Cambridge Suites Hotel, 380 Esplanade, 902/563-7009, daily 6:30am-10am and 5pm-10pm, $16-28) stands out as the best place in town for a healthy, well-priced meal in contemporary surroundings. Breakfast is served buffet-style, while in the evening tasty temptations include blackened haddock, an East Coast hot pot, and rib eye steak.

Away from the hotel dining scene, **Governor's Pub & Eatery** (233 Esplanade, 902/562-7646, daily 11am-11pm, $14-30) has two bustling patios, a pub-style room, and a restaurant. The food is surprisingly good, with seafood and steak the specialties. You could start with maple mandarin salad and then choose from mains such as beer-battered fish-and-chips with hand-cut fries or slow-cooked pork back ribs.

Sydney

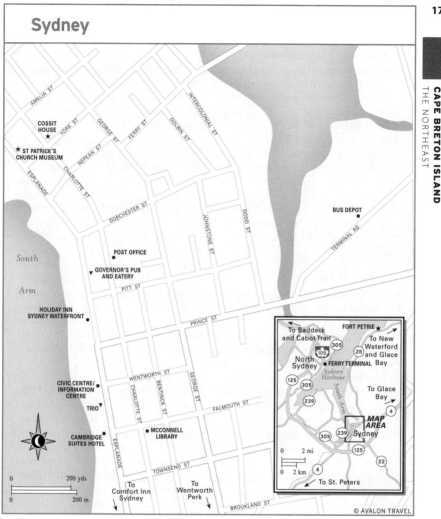

© AVALON TRAVEL

Accommodations

Motel rooms in Sydney are generally more expensive than they should be. Use the websites to search out package rates or wait until the last minute and start calling around for deals.

Comfort Inn Sydney (368 Kings Rd., 902/562-0200, www.comfortinn.com, $130-150 s or d) overlooks the waterfront two kilometers south of downtown. The midsize rooms have contemporary style and modern necessities such as high-speed Internet access.

My pick in Sydney is the modern **Cambridge Suites Hotel** (380 Esplanade, 902/562-6500 or 800/565-9466, www.cambridgesuitessydney.com, $175 s or d), which comprises 150 spacious self-contained units, each with a kitchen and wireless Internet access. On the roof level are a pool, sauna, exercise room, and sundeck.

Right downtown, **Holiday Inn Sydney Waterfront** (300 Esplanade, 902/562-7500 or 877/660-8550, www.ihg.com, $200 s or d) is a well-designed, comfortable high-rise with more than 150 rooms, a restaurant with water views, an indoor pool and waterslide, a whirlpool and sauna, an exercise room, and a gift shop. The rack rates of $200 are too high, but the $150 I was quoted for a water-view room in early June seemed about right.

Information and Services

Sydney Visitor Information Centre is well signposted as you enter town from the south (20 Keltic Dr., Sydney River, 902/539-9876, www.cbisland.com, June-mid-Oct. Mon.-Fri. 8:30am-5pm).

Cape Breton Regional Hospital (902/567-8000) is at 1482 George Street. For the **RCMP,** call 564-7171, or 911 in emergencies.

Getting There and Around

It's just more than 400 kilometers between Halifax and Sydney—easily driven in under five hours.

The main reason to fly in would be the ease of getting to Cape Breton Highlands National Park, a two-hour drive northeast of town. **Sydney Airport** (YQY, 280 Silver Dart Way, 902/564-7720, http://sydneyairport.ca) is 14 kilometers northeast of the city center. A taxi to town costs $22, or rent a car through Avis, Budget, Hertz, or National, all of which have rental desks at the airport. Sydney is served by **Air Canada** (902/539-7501 or 888/247-2262) with daily direct flights (40 minutes) from Halifax.

HIGHWAY 28 TO GLACE BAY

From Sydney, the New Waterford Highway (Highway 28) spurs north off Prince Street and follows the eastern side of Sydney Harbour for 26 kilometers to the industrial town of New Waterford. Along the way is **Fort Petrie** (3479 Hwy. 28, 902/862-8367, May-Nov. 10am-6pm, free), one of seven such forts constructed to protect local coal and steel production facilities from attack during World War II. Not much remains, but an interpretive

display tells the story of the fort, and views of the harbor make the stop worthwhile.

Glace Bay

At Glace Bay, 21 kilometers northeast of Sydney, **Cape Breton Miners' Museum** (17 Museum St., 902/849-4522, June-Aug. daily 10am-6pm, Sept.-May Mon.-Fri. 9am-4pm, adult $13, child $10) is the main attraction for visitors. Retired miners guide you on an underground tour of a real mine, the Ocean Deeps Colliery, to show the rough working conditions under which workers manually extracted coal. Above the mine is an exhibit gallery where the highlight is a simulated, multimedia trip into the workings of a modern mine, using laser-disc projection and other special effects. On selected Tuesday evenings through summer (usually at 8pm), the Men of the Deeps, a local singing group composed of miners dressed in their coveralls, gives concerts at the museum. Also in the main building is **Miners' Village Restaurant** (May-Sept. daily 11am-8pm), where the food is both tasty and well priced.

LOUISBOURG

This small fishing town (pop. 1,200), 32 kilometers southeast of Sydney, is famous for its historic links to France and for its reconstruction of an entire walled town. Louisbourg may be well off the main Baddeck-Cape Breton Highlands National Park itinerary of many visitors, but it gets a steady flow of visitors through summer and has limited accommodations, so plan accordingly.

★ Fortress of Louisbourg National Historic Site

The **Fortress of Louisbourg National Historic Site** (259 Park Service Rd., 902/733-3552, mid-May-Oct. daily 9:30am-5pm, adult $17.60, senior $15, child $8.80) is a fantastic re-creation of the original French fort. Parks Canada has reconstructed 50 of the original 80 buildings, right down to the last window, nail, and shingle, based on historical records.

Louisbourg reveals itself slowly. The seaport covers 10 hectares, and you can spend the better part of a day exploring. From the Visitor Reception Centre, it's a brief bus ride across fields and marsh to the back of the fortress. The reconstructed fortress and town open a window on New France; they are designed to reflect Louisbourg on a spring day in 1744, the year preceding England's first attack, when the seaport hummed with activity. The houses, fortifications, ramparts, and other structures—as authentically 18th-century French as anything you will find in France—were conceived as a statement of grandeur and power in the New World. The fancy houses lining cobbled lanes belonged to the elite, who ate sumptuous meals on fine china and drank the finest French wines. The simpler houses are the rustic cottages of the working class. Guides and reenactors—portraying soldiers, merchants, workers, and craftspeople—are on hand to answer questions and demonstrate military exercises, blacksmithing, lace making, and other skills. The historical feel flows through to three dining rooms. Hungry visitors can feast on a slice of heavy bread and a chunk of cheese at the **King's Bakery;** at **Hotel de la Marine** servers dish up simple fare in big wooden bowls; while over in **Grandchamps Inn** the "wealthy" can dine on exquisite European cuisine served up on the finest china.

The site is open and fully staffed June-mid-October. In May and through the last two weeks of October, access is by guided tour only (departs daily 10am and 2pm). There are no services during these periods, and so admission is reduced (adult $7.50, senior $6.25, child $4.25). The grounds are closed the rest of the year.

Be prepared for walking, and bring a sweater or jacket in case of breezy or wet weather. Louisbourg's reconstructed buildings stretch from the bus stop to the harbor. Remaining ruins lying beyond the re-creation are marked by trails. You can wander on your own or join a tour—usually 10am and 2pm for English tours and 1pm for the French-language tour.

Food

Wander Louisbourg's main street and you'll find numerous dining choices. My favorite is ★ **Grubstake Restaurant** (7499 Main St., 902/733-2308, daily noon-8pm, $13-25), which has been open since the 1970s but offers an up-to-date menu of seafood, with such offerings as linguine

the Fortress of Louisbourg National Historic Site

topped with shrimp, scallops, haddock, and salmon in a cream sauce. If you want to take a break from seafood, this is the place to do so—the meatloaf with mashed potatoes and vegetables is delicious.

Accommodations and Camping

Accommodations in Louisbourg are limited, so it's wise to make reservations.

Overlooking the harbor is **Stacey House** (7438 Main St., 902/733-2317 or 866/924-2242, June-mid-Oct., $75-105 s or d). It offers four rooms, two with private baths, and an antiques-filled parlor, all within walking distance of town. Rates include a cooked breakfast.

Perfectly situated on a headland with sweeping views of the fortress, ★ **Point of View Suites** (15 Commercial St., 902/733-2080 or 888/374-8439, www.louisbourgpointofview.com, mid-May-Oct., $125-199 s or d) is Louisbourg's finest accommodation. The sun-filled suites (some with ocean views) and much larger apartments look as if they are straight out of a glossy architectural magazine with their crisp color schemes, hardwood floors, and sliding doors that open to balconies with ocean views. At the edge of the property is a private beach, and each evening at 6pm guests are invited to a Beggar's Banquet in the adjacent restaurant.

Riverdale RV Park (9 Riverdale St., 902/733-2531, mid-May-mid-Oct., campsites $25-35, cottages $110) enjoys a quiet setting within walking distance of the fort. Amenities include showers, 30-amp hookups, and a laundry.

The wilderness camping nearest to Louisbourg is at **Mira River Provincial Park** (mid-June-early Sept., $29), 17 kilometers before town off Highway 22. The park has showers, fire pits and firewood sales, and canoe rentals. Sites are scattered through the forest or along the river.

Getting There

Louisbourg is 30 kilometers (25 minutes) southeast of Sydney along Highway 22. It's 440 kilometers northeast from Halifax.

New Brunswick

Saint John and the Fundy Coast

Imagine the scene: A pervasive unearthly stillness. Seabirds wheel and dart across the horizon.

Suddenly, the birds cry out in a chorus as the incoming tide approaches. The tidal surge, which began halfway around the world in the southern Indian Ocean, quietly and relentlessly pours into the Fundy's mouth, creating the highest tides on the planet. Fishing boats are lifted from the muddy seafloor, and whales in pursuit of silvery herring hurry along the summertime currents, their mammoth hulks buoyed by the 100 billion tons of seawater that gush into the long bay between New Brunswick and Nova Scotia.

The cycle from low to high tide takes a mere six hours. The tide peaks, in places high enough to swamp a four-story building, and then begins to retreat. As the sea level drops, coastal peninsulas and rocky islets emerge from the froth, veiled in seaweed. The seafloor reappears, shiny as shellac and littered with sea urchins, periwinkles, and shells. Where no one walked just hours ago, local children run and skip on the beaches, pausing to retrieve tidal treasures. New Brunswickers take the Fundy tides for granted. For visitors, it's an astounding show.

The Fundy Coast is a paradox: It's at once the most- and least-developed part of the province. Saint John—the province's largest city and major port—sits at the midpoint. To either side, the coastline is remotely settled and wonderfully wild. The region is best considered as two distinct areas, with Saint John interposed between them. The Lower Fundy, situated at the bay's southwestern end, includes St. Andrews—the province's definitive resort town on sheltered Passamaquoddy Bay—and the Fundy Isles, the archipelago (made up of Grand Manan, Deer, Campobello, and White Islands) that dangles into the sea alongside Maine's northernmost coast. The Upper Fundy area, situated at the coast's northeastern end, takes in Fundy National Park and several coastal bird sanctuaries.

PLANNING YOUR TIME

New Brunswick's 250-kilometer-long Fundy coastline is central to all of mainland Atlantic Canada, with the port city of Saint John roughly halfway between the U.S. border and the head of the bay. This is the place to explore historic **Prince William and**

Previous: Swallowtail Lighthouse on Grand Manan Island; St. Andrews Harbour. **Above:** great blue heron along the Fundy Coast.

Look for ★ to find recommended sights, activities, dining, and lodging.

Highlights

★ **Prince William and Germain Streets:** Downtown Saint John oozes history at every corner, but nowhere is it as concentrated as along these two streets (page 190).

★ **Irving Nature Park:** Nature is left to its own devices within this oceanfront park, but what makes it remarkable is its vicinity to a major shipping port (page 193).

★ **St. Andrews National Historic District:** Yes, wandering along the main street of St. Andrews seems to be all about shopping and dining, but there is a wealth of history behind the bright facades (page 202).

★ **Kingsbrae Garden:** Blending formal gardens with trails through Acadian coastal forest, Kingsbrae will soothe your senses (page 203).

★ **Grand Manan Island:** Catch the ferry over to this Bay of Fundy island to watch the abundance of seabirds that gather each spring and fall (page 209).

★ **Fundy National Park:** Protecting a huge swath of coastline, this park offers plenty of chances to get back to nature—or, if you prefer, to go golfing and feast on fresh seafood (page 212).

★ **Hopewell Rocks:** This attraction, where you can "walk on the ocean floor," is a wonderful natural phenomenon helped along by the massive Fundy tides (page 216).

Saint John and the Fundy Coast

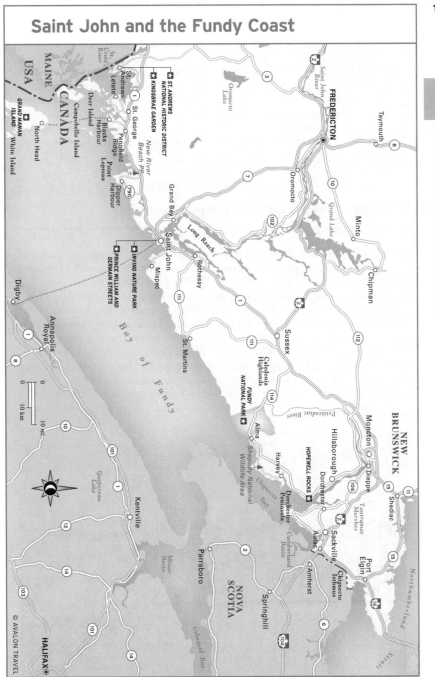

© AVALON TRAVEL

Germain Streets, get a taste of nature at **Irving Nature Park,** and take advantage of fine lodgings and restaurants. Everywhere else is within day-tripping distance of Saint John, but then you'd miss out on soaking up the old-fashioned resort atmosphere of **St. Andrews.** So plan on spending at least one night there, which will also allow time to wander through the **St. Andrews National Historic District** and visit **Kingsbrae Garden.** If you're driving up through Maine to Atlantic Canada, St. Andrews makes an ideal first stop. If you've rented a vehicle in Halifax, St. Andrews marks your turnaround point on a loop that incorporates a ferry trip from Digby to Saint John. Either way, on the north side of Saint John, plan on stops at **Fundy National Park** and **Hopewell Rocks** as you follow the Fundy Coast north to Moncton. By virtue of their location, the Fundy Isles require some extra time to reach, especially **Grand Manan Island,** but nature lovers will be rewarded with a magnificent display of birds, whales, and seals.

Saint John and Vicinity

Saint John (pop. 68,000), 110 kilometers south of Fredericton and 155 kilometers southwest of Moncton, ranks as New Brunswick's largest city, its major port, and its principal industrial center. It is also Canada's largest city in terms of area, sprawling across 321 square kilometers. The city perches on steep hills, laid out southwest to northeast across two peninsulas that almost mesh, like two hands about to meet in a handshake. The setting is among Atlantic Canada's most unusual—Saint John looks east across the spacious Saint John Harbour to the Bay of Fundy and is backed on the west by the confluence of the Saint John River and Kennebecasis Bay.

Saint John began as a collection of small Loyalist settlements. Today these settlements maintain their identities in the form of neighborhoods within greater Saint John. This accounts for numerous street-name duplications, a confusing fact of life when sightseeing across the oddly laid-out city. One Charlotte Street, for example, runs through the city's historic part, while another Charlotte Street is

Saint John skyline

Saint John

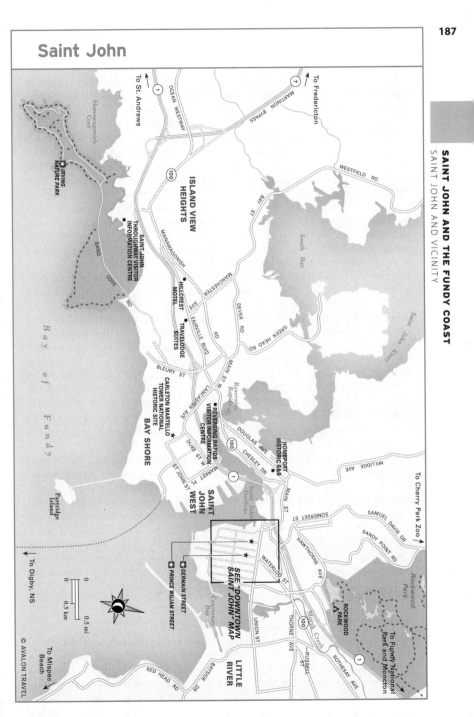

To St. Andrews

To Frederickton

OCEAN WESTWAY

MARITHON BYPASS

WESTFIELD RD

Manawagonish Cove

IRVING NATURE PARK

ISLAND VIEW HEIGHTS

BAY ST

South Bay

Saint John River

SAND COVE RD

SAINT JOHN THROUGHWAY VISITOR INFORMATION CENTRE

MANAWAGONISH AVE

MANCHESTER

DEVER RD

GREEN HEAD RD

HILLCREST MOTEL

FAIRVILLE BLVD

TRAVELODGE SUITES

MAIN ST W

LANCASTER AVE

BLEURY ST

CARLETON MARTELLO TOWER NATIONAL HISTORIC SITE

Reversing Rapids

REVERSING RAPIDS VISITOR INFORMATION CENTRE

DOUGLAS AVE

CHESLEY DR

HOMEPORT HISTORIC B&B

MILLIDGE AVE

To Cherry Park Zoo

Bay of Fundy

BAY SHORE

DUKE ST W

ST JOHN ST

MARKET PL

SAINT JOHN WEST

Saint John Harbour

MAIN ST

SOMERSET ST

SAMUEL DAVIS DR

SANDY POINT RD

Partridge Island

HAWTHORNE AVE

SEE "DOWNTOWN SAINT JOHN MAP"

WATERLOO ST

To Digby NS

0   0.5 km
0   0.5 mi

GERMAIN STREET

PRINCE WILLIAM STREET

Courtenay Bay

THORNE AVE

Rockwood Park

ROCKWOOD PARK

To Fundy National Park and Moncton

To Mispec Beach

© AVALON TRAVEL

UNION ST

BAYSIDE DR

RED HEAD RD

LITTLE RIVER

BISSELL ST

ROTHESAY AVE

Marsh Creek

found in western Saint John. It helps to keep a map handy, or to just ask: The locals are sympathetic to the visitor's confusion.

Locals and visitors alike take full advantage of a revitalized waterfront precinct that includes the provincial museum, dining and shopping in Market Square, live outdoor entertainment, and the 2.3-kilometer Harbour Passage, a walking and biking trail that rims the waterfront.

HISTORY

Saint John's history as an Anglo settlement began with 14,000 Loyalists, who arrived by ship in 1783. The refugees quickly settled the fledgling town and spread out to found Carleton west of the harbor and Parrtown to the east. The city was incorporated in 1785, making it Canada's oldest. The city's next great wave of immigrants brought the Irish, who were fleeing poverty and persecution at home. Saint John's reputation as Canada's most Irish city began with a trickle of Irish in 1815; before the wave subsided in 1850, the city's 150,000 Irish outnumbered the Loyalists, and Saint John's religious complexion changed from Protestant to Roman Catholic.

Despite its early social woes, Saint John strode ahead economically, and by the 1850s was ranked third worldwide as a wooden ship builder. After steel-hulled steam vessels began to replace the great sailing ships in the 1860s, the city plunged into a decline, which was deepened by the Great Fire of 1877. Undaunted, Saint John replaced the damage with more elaborate, sturdier brick and stone buildings designed in the ornate Victorian style, which remain in place to this day.

ORIENTATION

On a map, Saint John looks large and somewhat unmanageable, almost intimidating. Forget about Saint John's unusual shape and the soaring bridges that connect the city's parts. Instead, concentrate on the main highways: The closely aligned Highway 1 and Highway 100, which parallel each other in most parts, are often the best routes for getting from one section of the city to another.

Tackle Saint John by areas. Most sightseeing is on the eastern peninsula in **uptown Saint John.** Access is easiest from Highway 1's Exits 121 or 125; the access roads peel down into the heart of downtown, centered on Market Square. The surrounding area is **Trinity Royal,** a national heritage preservation area protecting the original 20 blocks laid out by the Loyalists. You'll also know you've arrived by the street names: The early Loyalists called the area Parrtown, and the avenues were royally named as King, Princess, Queen, Prince William, and Charlotte Streets. This precinct is easily identified by distinctive blue and gold street signs.

Northern Saint John (the North End) lies on the highways' other side. **Rockwood Park,** one of Canada's largest municipal parks, dominates the area, with 870 wooded hectares speckled with lakes and an 18-hole golf course; numerous roads off Highway 1 feed into the park. This part of the city is also known to offer Saint John Harbour's best views; for a sublime overview, drive up to the **Fort Howe Lookout,** where timber blockhouses perch atop a rocky outcrop on Highway 1's northern side. Worthy hotels are nearby.

Western Saint John lies across the highway bridges on the western peninsula. Here you'll find some of the newer motels and a shopping mall along Highway 100, the area's commercial row, while Highway 1 heads west to St. Andrews. The residential area, which has several interesting B&Bs, spreads out closer to the water, while the Bay Ferries ferry terminal (with service to Digby, Nova Scotia) is at the harbor's edge.

SIGHTS
Downtown

Hills aside, the following attractions are all within walking distance of one another. If the steep streets look daunting, flag a cab in front of the Hilton Saint John and ask the driver to drop you at King's Square ($5 with tip).

Downtown Saint John

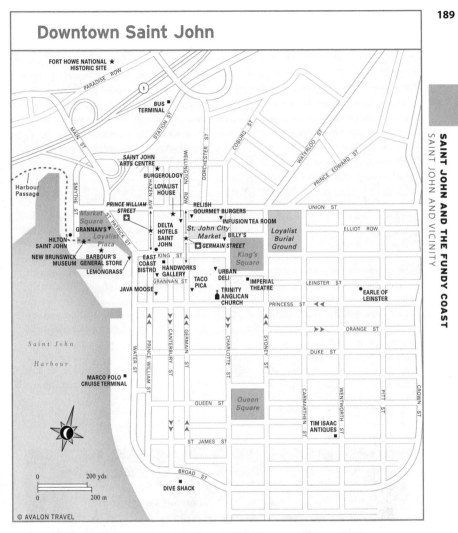

Downtown sightseeing starts at **Loyalist Plaza,** an outdoor strip filled with plants and seating that ends at the waterfront. It's a good place to get oriented by visiting the information center (in Market Square) and taking the **Harbour Passage** waterfront promenade around the head of the harbor. This paved walking/biking trail leads 2.3 kilometers to a pavilion, from which views extend back across to downtown.

NEW BRUNSWICK MUSEUM

The province's prime resource for fine arts and natural history lore, the **New Brunswick Museum** (St. Patrick St., 506/643-2300, Mon.-Fri. 9am-5pm, Sat. 10am-5pm, Sun. noon-5pm, adult $10, senior $8, child $6) is inside Market Square. One of Canada's oldest museums, its displays are spread through three floors packed with elegant ship models, shipbuilding tools, war memorabilia, stuffed birds and beasts, agricultural and domestic implements, you name it. There's a hands-on Discovery Centre for kids and a bookstore that stocks a good selection of literature about the province.

BARBOUR'S GENERAL STORE

Across Loyalist Plaza from Market Square, the essence of old-time New Brunswick is re-created at the restored **Barbour's General Store** (10 Market Square, 506/642-2242, May-Oct. Mon.-Sat. noon-6pm, Sun. 9am-6pm, free), which was moved from upriver at Sheffield. Inside are 2,000 artifacts typical of the period 1840-1940, information and tour services, and a gift shop. Next door, peek into the bright red schoolhouse, which was also moved to the site from rural New Brunswick.

★ PRINCE WILLIAM AND GERMAIN STREETS

A block up from Market Square, the parallel **Prince William and Germain Streets** delineate the commercial heart of old Saint John. Following a devastating fire in June 1877, the city hurried to rebuild itself in even grander style. The stone and brick edifices along Prince William Street are a splendid farrago of architectural styles, incorporating Italianate facades, Corinthian columns, Queen Anne Revival elements, scowling gargoyles, and other decorative details. One of the country's finest surviving examples of 19th-century streetscape, this was the first "national historic street" in Canada. Some good art galleries and craft shops are ensconced here among other businesses. Two blocks east, Germain Street is the more residential counterpoint, proffering a number of opulent townhouses.

LOYALIST HOUSE NATIONAL HISTORIC SITE

The simple, white clapboard Georgian-style **Loyalist House National Historic Site** (120 Union St., 506/652-3590, mid-May-June Mon.-Fri. 10am-5pm, July-mid-Sept. daily 10am-5pm, adult $5, child $2) was built between 1810 and 1817 by pioneer David Merrit, and it remained in his family for five generations. Having survived the 1877 fire and now meticulously restored, it's the oldest unaltered building in the city. The original front door with brass knocker opens into an authentic evocation of the early Loyalist years, furnished with Sheraton, Empire, and Duncan Phyfe antiques.

The Harbour Passage leads along the waterfront.

SAINT JOHN ARTS CENTRE

One block west of the Jewish museum, the grandiose former Carnegie Library is now a cultural complex, the **Saint John Arts Centre** (20 Hazen Ave., 506/633-4870, June-early Sept. daily 10am-5pm, early Sept.-May Tues.-Sat. 9am-5pm, free). Inside, six galleries (including the City of Saint John Gallery) hold frequently changing fine arts and photography exhibits.

SAINT JOHN CITY MARKET

For a visual and culinary treat, spend some time at **Saint John City Market** (47 Charlotte St., 506/658-2820, Mon.-Fri. 7:30am-6pm, Sat. 7:30am-5pm, free), spanning a whole city block between Charlotte and Germain Streets. The setting is impressive. The original ornate iron gates stand at each entrance, and there's usually a busker or two working the crowd. Inside the airy stone building, local shipbuilders framed the expansive ceiling in the form of an inverted ship's hull. "Market Street," the market's central, widest aisle, divides the space in half; alongside the adjacent aisles, the bustling stalls stand cheek-by-jowl, their tables groaning with wares. Notice the building's pitched floor, a convenient arrangement on the slanted hillside that makes hosing the floor easier after the market closes each day.

The market is a great venue for people-watching and for sampling freshly baked goods, cheeses, seafood, meat, and produce. If you haven't yet tried dulse, a leather-tough purple seaweed that's harvested from the Bay of Fundy, then dried and sold in little packages for a dollar or two, here's your chance. Splendid, reasonably priced crafts have a sizable niche here, too.

KING'S SQUARE AND THE LOYALIST BURIAL GROUND

Across Charlotte Street from the City Market are two maple-shaded, vest-pocket green spaces situated on separate kitty-corner blocks. At **King's Square,** the walkways are laid out like the stripes on the British Union Jack, radiating from the 1908 bandstand, the site of summertime concerts.

Across Sydney Street is the **Loyalist Burial Ground,** a surprisingly cheerful place with benches and flower gardens, scattered with old-style headstones dating back to 1784.

As busy as the square and burial ground are—alive with schoolchildren on field trips, bantering seniors, and moms with

Historic buildings line Prince William and Germain Streets.

strollers—**Queen's Square,** three blocks south, is virtually deserted.

TRINITY ANGLICAN CHURCH

A victim of the city's historic fires, the handsome Loyalist **Trinity Anglican Church** (115 Charlotte St., 506/693-8558, Mon.-Fri. 9am-3pm, free) was built in 1791, rebuilt in 1856, and rebuilt again in 1880 after the Great Fire. The sanctuary's famed treasure is the House of Hanover Royal Coat of Arms from the reign of George I, which was rescued by fleeing Loyalists from the Boston Council Chamber in 1783 and rescued again from the 1877 runaway fire.

West of Downtown
FORT HOWE NATIONAL HISTORIC SITE LOOKOUT

Fort Howe, the blockhouse of 1777, did double duty as harbor defense and city jail. The structure itself is a replica, but the rocky promontory **lookout site** on Magazine Street nonetheless offers an excellent panoramic view of the city and harbor. To get there from downtown, cross the highway along Main Street.

REVERSING RAPIDS

If ever there were a contest for Most Overhyped Tourist Attraction, **Reversing Rapids** would win the grand prize. Tour buses and out-of-province license plates pack the parking lot, disgorging gaggles of camera-toting visitors to see . . . what? At low tide, the Bay of Fundy lies 4.4 meters below the Saint John River, and the river flows out to sea across a small falls (more like a rapids) here. During the slack tide, the sea and the river levels are equal and the rapids disappear. Then, as the slack tide grows to high tide, the waters of the rising sea enter Saint John Harbour, muscling the river inland for 100 kilometers and creating some turbulent rapids. It's an unspectacular sight, and even the minimal physical science interest can't be appreciated unless you're willing to hang around for 12

hours and watch the tide go through a full cycle. Nevertheless, throngs of visitors line up here for the requisite photo opportunity. To get there from downtown, cross Highway 1 via Main Street and turn left on Clesley Drive. The complex is on the far side of the bridge spanning the river.

For a reverse angle on Reversing Rapids, go to **Fallsview Park,** which overlooks the spectacle from the east side of the river, off Douglas Avenue.

CARLETON MARTELLO TOWER NATIONAL HISTORIC SITE

The massive circular stone **Carleton Martello Tower** (Fundy Dr. at Whipple St., Saint John West, 506/636-4011, June-early Oct. daily 10am-5pm, adult $4, senior $3.50, child $2) served as a harbor defense outpost from 1812 and was declared a national historic site in 1924. The superstructure above it was a military intelligence center during World War II. Within, stone staircases connect the restored quarters and powder magazine. The observation decks provide splendid views of the harbor.

PARTRIDGE ISLAND

Near the mouth of Saint John Harbour, a national and provincial historic site and now a coast guard light station, **Partridge Island** was a quarantine station for almost a million arriving immigrants during the 19th and 20th centuries, many of whom arrived sick with cholera, typhus, and smallpox. Some 2,000 newcomers who never made it any farther are buried here in six graveyards. A Celtic cross was erected for the Irish refugees, and a memorial stone commemorates Jewish immigrants. From the early 1800s up to 1947, the island was used as a military fortification. Most of the old wooden buildings have now been destroyed, and the island is off-limits to the public. If you're catching the ferry to Digby (Nova Scotia), stand on the starboard (right) side as the vessel pulls away from the terminal and you'll get a great view of the island.

RECREATION

A visit to Saint John is about soaking up history and enjoying the services affiliated with a city, but there are a few things to keep you busy beyond sightseeing. The two parks detailed below have good walking trails, **Rockwood Park Golf Course** (1255 Sandy Point Rd., 506/634-0090, greens fee $45) offers a challenging tree-lined layout, and there are water sports to try.

Parks

ROCKWOOD PARK

The huge woodland **Rockwood Park** (506/658-2883, daily dawn-dusk), speckled with 13 lakes and laced with foot and horse trails, is across Highway 1 from downtown, with access from Exits 123, 125, and 128. In spring, yellow lady's slipper and colorful wild orchid varieties bloom on the forest floor, and the gardens and arboretum are in their full glory. Activities in summer include fishing, boating, swimming, bird-watching, hiking, horseback riding, golfing at the 18-hole course, picnicking at lakeside tables, and camping. In winter, the ice skaters come out and the trails are taken over by cross-country skiers.

Cherry Brook Zoo (901 Foster Thurston Rd., 506/634-1440, Mon.-Fri. 10am-4pm, Sat.-Sun. 10am-6pm, adult $10.50, senior $8.50, child $5.50), at the park's northern end, off Sandy Point Road, is stocked with lions, leopards, zebras, and other exotic animals. The zoo includes Vanished Kingdom Park, where you'll find replicas of extinct animals.

★ IRVING NATURE PARK

Irving Nature Park occupies an unlikely setting. The forested reserve encompasses an entire peninsula dangling into Saint John Harbour, the province's busiest port. At the harbor's northeastern corner rises the skyline of New Brunswick's largest city. Across the harbor's center, oceangoing vessels enter and leave the port. Yet at the harbor's western corner, this expanse of natural terrain remains as undeveloped as it was when the city's founding Loyalists arrived centuries ago.

To get there, take Highway 1 out of the city to western Saint John and watch for the Catherwood Street turnoff (Exit 119). The narrow road angles south off the highway, takes a jog to the right (west), descends through a residential area, and then lopes across an undeveloped marshland to the 225-hectare reserve. A long beach backed by the Saints Rest Marsh is near the park's

Irving Nature Park

entrance. Many visitors park at the bottom of the hill and continue on foot. It is also possible to continue by road into the park, to a parking lot 500 meters from the beach, or to follow a one-way road that encircles the entire headland. Trails probe the park's interior and also wander off to parallel the water.

The reserve's mixed ecosystem offers interesting trekking terrain and draws songbirds, waterfowl, and migratory seabirds. More than 240 bird species are seen regularly; 365 species have been sighted over the past 20 years. Rare red crossbills and peregrine falcons are occasionally spotted in the marsh. Eastern North America's largest cormorant colony lies offshore on Manawagonish Island. Semipalmated plovers like the reserve's quiet beaches and tidal flats. You can count on sandpiper varieties on the beach in July, greater shearwaters and Wilson's stormy petrels gliding across the water during summer, and a spectacular show of loons, grebes, and scoters during the autumn migration along the Atlantic flyway. Birds are the most noticeable but by no means the only wildlife to be found here. Deer, porcupines, red squirrels, and snowshoe hares inhabit the reserve, and starfish and sea urchins laze in the tidal pools.

Water Sports

The **Dive Shack** (9 Lower Cove Loop, 506/634-8265, Mon. and Wed.-Fri. 10am-6pm, Sat. 10am-3pm) is the city's prime source for dive trips to the Bay of Fundy. The shop also rents equipment, runs courses, and offers weekend charters. Lower Cove Loop is an extension of Water Street south through downtown.

The top-notch facilities at the **Canada Games Aquatic Centre** (50 Union St., 506/658-4715, Mon.-Fri. 6am-9pm, Sat. 6am-midnight, pool access adult $8, senior and child $5.50) include a 50-meter pool with five diving boards, two shallower pools, two waterslides, whirlpools, saunas, a fitness room, and a cafeteria.

You'll find supervised swimming at Fisher Lake in **Rockwood Park,** at **Dominion**

Park in Saint John West, and at **Little River Reservoir** off Loch Lomond Road in the city's eastern area. **Mispec Beach** at Saint John Harbour's eastern edge is unsupervised, and the water is cold, but it's a nice spot on a warm day and provides close-up views of ships from around the world entering and leaving the harbor. To get there, take Union Street and make a sharp right turn to Bayside Drive, and then turn onto Red Head Road.

ENTERTAINMENT AND EVENTS
Nightlife

Saint John may seem historic and charming during the day, but remember that it's primarily an international port. Be careful after dark, especially at the south end of downtown. That said, bars and restaurants along Market Square have a beautiful outlook, with lots of outdoor tables that stay full with locals and visitors well into the night on summer weekends, when musicians take to an outdoor stage. **Grannan's** (1 Market Sq., 506/634-1555, daily from 11:30am) forms a hub for the many nearby bars of many moods, and its indoor lounge has an inviting pub ambience. Adjacent **Cougar's Lounge** (1 Market Sq., 506/693-6666, daily 11am-2am) and **Saint John Ale House** (1 Market Sq., 506/657-2337, Sun.-Thurs. 11:30am-11pm, Fri.-Sat. 11:30am-2am) also have wide portions of Loyalist Plaza packed with outdoor furniture, with the former offering live music many nights. Toward the water, **York Bistro Pub** (Hilton Saint John, Market Sq., 506/632-8564, daily 11:30am-midnight) is less pretentious than you might expect and has outside tables facing the harbor.

The historic Trinity Royal area, bounded by Prince William, Princess, King, and Germain Streets, is another nightlife center, with nightclubs, pubs, lounges, and sports bars. One of the more welcoming places is **O'Leary's** (46 Princess St., 506/634-7135, Mon.-Tues. 11:30am-11pm, Wed.-Fri. 11:30am-2am, Sat. 3pm-2am), a convivial Irish pub with the obligatory Guinness on tap and the sound of Celtic musicians filling the room Thursday-Saturday.

Performing Arts

The city's pride and joy is the immaculately restored 1913 **Imperial Theatre** (12 King Square S., 506/674-4100, www.imperialtheatre.nb.ca). In its heyday, the theater hosted performances by the likes of Ethel Barrymore, John Philip Sousa, and Harry Houdini. After closing in the 1950s, it was reopened and used by the Full Gospel Assembly Pentecostal Church for 25 years. In 1994, decade-long renovations to restore the theater to its former glory were completed. Today it's once again the star venue of Saint John's performing arts scene, hosting concerts by Symphony New Brunswick, stage productions of Theatre New Brunswick, and a variety of touring performers.

Festivals and Events

On the second Saturday in May, the Marco Polo Cruise Terminal (111 Water St.) fills with the smells of the best in local cooking for the **Fundy Food Festival** (www.fundyfoodfestival.com). Admission is $75, which includes a book of tickets that can be redeemed for food and drink from over 30 local pubs and restaurants.

In addition to free evening entertainment in Loyalist Plaza, summer brings the **Buskers on the Bay** (www.marketsquaresj.com) festival to Market Square and the boardwalk during the second weekend of July.

Saint John Ex finishes the summer with a super-size county fair geared to families. It runs for five days in late August at the Exhibition Grounds (McAllister Dr., 506/633-2020, www.exhibitionparksj.com). Expect all the usual carnival rides as well as agricultural demonstrations and musical performances.

SHOPPING

The city's main shopping district—along Charlotte, Union, Princess, Germain, and Prince William Streets—is filled with interesting outlets selling everything from Inuit art

to Irish tartan. The local penchant for high-quality weaving and handmade apparel is particularly evident at **Handworks Gallery** (12 King St., 506/631-7626, Mon.-Sat. 10am-5:30pm). In the vicinity is one of Atlantic Canada's preeminent antiques dealers, **Tim Isaac Antiques** (213 Wentworth St., 506/652-3222, Mon.-Fri. 10am-4pm).

FOOD

Market Square is the most obvious and convenient choice for visitors looking for a meal, but head uphill into the heart of downtown and you'll come across restaurants that trade on good food and prices alone.

For gourmet coffee-lovers, Saint John doesn't have a great number of choices, but the owners of **Java Moose** (84 Prince William St., 506/657-7283, Mon.-Fri. 7am-5pm, Sat. 8am-3pm, Sun. 9am-3pm) do an excellent job of sourcing high-quality beans to roast. Java Moose also has an outlet in the Saint John City Market (see below). Looking for gourmet teas? Try **Infusion Tea Room** (41 Charlotte St., 506/613-8327, daily 8am-6pm, lunches $7-10), which also has simple soup and sandwich offerings.

Market and Deli

You won't know which way to turn once you've walked through the doors of the ★ **Saint John City Market** (47 Charlotte St., 506/658-2820, Mon.-Thurs. 7:30am-6pm, Fri. 7:30am-7pm, Sat. 7:30am-5pm), a city institution. Choose from a couple of old-fashioned cafés, a seafood market with live lobsters (they'll box them for you) and mussels for just $3 per pound, a delicatessen with sliced meats and gourmet cheeses, and Wild Carrot Café, boasting healthy juices and muffins.

If you're looking for something a little more sophisticated for lunch than the offerings at Saint John City Market, head over to **Urban Deli** (68 King St., 506/652-3354, Mon.-Sat. 11:45am-3pm, lunches around $12), where lunches such as Montreal-style smoked meat sandwiches and quinoa salads cost under $15.

Seafood

Grannan's (1 Market Sq., 506/634-1555, Mon.-Wed. 11am-11pm, Thurs.-Sat. 11am-midnight, Sun. noon-10pm, $19-38) is one of the Market Square restaurants with as many tables outside as in. The specialty is seafood, and everything is good. The chowder is expensive but delicious, while mains include blackened Creole salmon, seafood casserole, and snow crab.

★ **Billy's** (49 Charlotte St., 506/672-3474, Mon.-Thurs. 11am-10pm, Fri.-Sat. 11am-11pm, Sun. 4pm-9pm, $16-33) is tucked away at the back of the Saint John City Market. It's part fish market, part restaurant, so you know everything will be fresh. Everything is good—Atlantic Canada delicacies include Malpeque oysters served raw in their shells, fish cakes, seafood chowder, lobster-stuffed haddock, Digby scallops sautéed in a pesto sauce, blackened salmon with an apple-cinnamon glaze, and a creamy shrimp risotto.

Bistro and Burgers

If you have only one night in Saint John, my pick for eating out is ★ **East Coast Bistro** (60 Prince William St., 506/696-3278, Mon. 11am-3pm, Tues.-Fri. 11am-9pm, Sat. 11am-10pm, $16-29), in the heart of downtown one block uphill from the waterfront in a long, narrow space with exposed brick on one side and local artwork and a bar on the other. Ingredients are sourced locally, which leads to an ever-changing menu of simple yet tasty dishes.

For the city's best burgers, head to **Burgerology** (26 Germain St., 506/646-9100, Mon.-Sat. 7:30am-9pm, Sun. 8am-2pm, $4-14), a modern space where burger options are as simple as the Classic Simple for $5, as unique as the Skippy Rooster (a beef burger with peanut butter), and as creative as The Decadent (comes with chocolate-covered bacon). Delicious milk shakes and enthusiastic service are bonuses.

Thai

Saint John proves it's up on restaurant trends at ★ **Lemongrass** (1 Market Sq., 506/657-8424, daily 11:30am-10pm, $19-26), a warmly decorated Thai-influenced dining room in the bustling Market Square complex. You can't miss with *tod mun pla* (fish cakes infused with red curry and coriander) and either *phad yum* (seafood curry with lime leaves) or *hor neing pla* (steamed haddock with lemongrass and other herbs wrapped in a banana leaf) as a main.

Market Square

Central American

Just a block off King Street, the city hustle and bustle drops off dramatically. Small, bright, and casual ★ **Taco Pica** (96 Germain St., 506/633-8492, Mon.-Sat. 10am-10pm, $18-24) is a real find on a quiet side street in the Trinity Royal historic area, away from the tourist traffic. The Guatemalan proprietor offers a mouthwatering menu of recipes from his homeland, as well as dishes from Mexico and Spain. Try the *pepian* (a spicy Guatemalan beef stew) or Spanish paella, washed down with a Mexican beer.

Hotel Dining

The dining rooms in the major hotels are also safe bets, though pricier. Contemporary **Mix Resto Bar** (Delta Hotels Saint John, 39 King St., 506/649-0731, daily 7am-midnight, $15-34) offers tempting selections such as grilled Fundy Bay salmon fillet grilled on a cedar plank.

The sleek **York Bistro + Pub** (Hilton Saint John, Market Sq., 506/693-8484, daily 6:30am-midnight, $16-32) opens to a dockside patio. Menu highlights include thin-crust pizzas, mussels steamed in wheat beer, and mushroom-crusted rack of lamb.

ACCOMMODATIONS AND CAMPING

Ideally, you'll want to be within walking distance of historic old Saint John and the harbor. The area's B&Bs often provide sumptuous accommodations for lower cost than many hotels. Lodgings beyond walking distance include the Fort Howe-area hotels, with great harbor vistas at reasonable prices, and the many budget choices on Manawagonish Avenue in Saint John West.

$50-100

Of the B&B lodgings clustered near King's Square, none are better value than **Earle of Leinster** (96 Leinster St., 506/652-3275, www. earleofleinster.com, $89-160 s or d), with congenial hosts and a very central location. This gracious brick Victorian townhouse has 12 rooms with private baths. All have Wi-Fi and TVs, and some have basic cooking facilities. Other amenities include laundry facilities, a game room with a pool table, and a courtyard. Rates include a full breakfast.

Around five kilometers from downtown, Manawagonish Avenue is lined with inexpensive motels—a reminder of the time when this was the main route west out of the city. To get there from the west, take Exit 100 from

waterside dining at the York Bistro + Pub

Highway 1 and follow Ocean Westway toward the city; from downtown, take Exit 119 and follow Catherwood Street north. Best choice under $100 is the Hillcrest Motel (1315 Manawagonish Ave., 506/672-5310), around seven kilometers from downtown, which has views of the Bay of Fundy.

$100-150

★Homeport Historic Bed & Breakfast (80 Douglas Ave., 506/672-7255 or 888/678-7678, www.homeport.nb.ca, $109-175 s or d) is arguably the best B&B in Saint John. Set high on the hill overlooking the harbor and city, this lodging combines two mansions dating from the mid-1800s. From the impressive collection of antiques to the super-comfortable beds to the decanter of port left in the lobby for guests returning from dinner, it is obvious hosts Ralph and Karen Holyoke know how to make their guests feel like they're paying a lot more than they really are. Standard rooms are $109 s or d, but the luxury rooms from $149 are well worth the extra money. Rates include a full breakfast.

Travelodge Suites (1011 Fairville Blvd., 506/635-0400 or 800/578-7878, www.travelodge.com, from $120 s or d) is your typical midrange roadside motel, with clean, comfortable, and practical guest rooms that were last renovated in 2013. Standard rooms are $120 s or d, but the much larger suites, with separate bedrooms and king beds, are a good value at $145. A complimentary light breakfast is laid out for guests. Take Exit 117 from Highway 1.

Over $200

Occupying a prime waterfront locale and linked to Market Square by an elevated walkway is ★ Hilton Saint John (1 Market Sq., 506/693-8484 or 800/561-8282, www.hilton.com, $225 s or d), a 12-story high-rise dating to the mid-1980s. Most of its 200 rooms have water views and windows that open. They come with all the usual niceties—daily newspaper, coffeemaker, hair dryer, and more—while a waterfront restaurant, a fitness room,

The Hilton Saint John enjoys a waterfront location.

and an indoor pool are downstairs. Check online for packages that include a buffet breakfast.

Rack rates at the Delta Hotels Saint John (39 King St., 506/648-1981 or 888/890-3222, www.marriott.com, $235 s or d) may be on the high side, but reserve online and you'll pay less. Part of the Brunswick Square Mall and one block back from the harbor, this modern hotel has 254 elegant rooms, as well as an indoor pool, a fitness room, and a restaurant and lounge.

Campgrounds

A five-minute drive from downtown, Rockwood Park Campground (142 Lake Drive S., 506/652-4050, www.rockwoodparkcampground.com, May-Oct., $29-39) has more than 200 sites, most with electricity and water. Amenities include big communal bathrooms, kitchen shelters, fireplaces, and a campers' canteen. Available recreation includes golfing at the nearby course, swimming, boating at the lake, and hiking on trails around the lake. The easiest way to get to the campground is to take Exit 121 or 125 from Highway 1 and follow the signs north. No reservations are taken, but the sites rarely fill.

INFORMATION AND SERVICES

Tourism Saint John (506/658-2855 or 866/463-8639, www.discoversaintjohn.com) does a great job of promoting the city, and its helpful website should be your first point of contact in planning your trip. It operates the city's main **Visitor Information Centre** (15 Market Square, daily 9am-6pm, in summer daily until 8pm) at the eastern entrance to Market Square; it faces the corner of St. Patrick and King Streets. If you are coming into the city from the west along Highway 1, stop at the Saint John Throughway Visitor Information Centre (1509 Saint John Throughway West, 506/658-2940, May-Oct. daily 10am-5pm, longer hours in summer).

Saint John Regional Hospital (400 University Ave., 506/648-6000) is on the university campus near Rockwood Park. For the police or other emergencies, call 911. Convenient pharmacies include **Lawton's Drugs** (Brunswick Sq., 39 King St., 506/634-1422) and **Guardian Drugs** (114 River Valley Dr., 506/738-8406).

GETTING THERE
Car

From Bangor, Maine, Saint John is a 170-kilometer (around three-hour) drive east along Highway 9 to the New Brunswick border, and then via Highway 1 into the city.

Saint John is 110 kilometers (over an hour) south of Fredericton and 155 kilometers (1.5 hours) southwest of Moncton.

Air

Saint John Airport is 16 kilometers east of downtown. The airport is served by **Air Canada** (888/247-2262) from Halifax, Toronto, and Montréal. Car rental companies represented are Avis, Budget, Hertz, and National, while other airport services include a restaurant and gift shop.

Taxis wait outside the airport for flight arrivals; the 25-minute cab ride to Market Square costs about $40.

Bus

Saint John Bus Terminal (125 Station St., 506/672-2055) is the arrival and departure point for **Maritime Bus** (www.maritimebus.com) service to and from Fredericton (three buses daily, 1.5 hours, $31) and Moncton (three buses daily, two hours, $39).

Ferry

Bay Ferries (902/245-2116 or 888/249-7245, www.ferries.ca) sails the *Princess of Acadia* between Saint John and Digby (Nova Scotia) year-round, up to three times daily in summer. It's a good option if you've driven through New Brunswick and want to explore Nova Scotia's Fundy Coast. The crossing is 3.5 hours (adult $46, senior and youth $36, child $31, vehicle $92 plus a $20 fuel surcharge). To get to the terminal from Highway 1, take Exit 120 and follow the signs south along Market Street. The terminal has no café, so if you're looking for a snack while waiting in line, stop at the Tim Hortons along Market Street.

GETTING AROUND

Saint John is a walking town in the historic area, but beyond there you'll need wheels. Highway 1 serves as the city's high-speed expressway and routes east-west traffic through Saint John from St. Stephen and Moncton. Highway 100 is the city's local traffic route, and it serves as a feeder route for Highway 7 to and from Fredericton. Driving is slow going most everywhere in Saint John, but it's worst during the 7am-9am and 4:30pm-6pm rush hours.

Parking garages and lots in the historic area are plentiful and inexpensive. Outdoor lots cost $1 an hour; indoor lots are slightly higher. Coming off Highway 1 at Exit 122, take the first right and you'll pass outdoor pay parking on your right, or continue to the bottom of the hill and turn left for underground parking.

Bus

Saint John Transit (506/658-4700, $2.50-3.50 per sector) buses run throughout the city (Mon.-Fri. 6am-midnight, with limited service on weekends). The company also offers two-hour guided bus tours (adult $20, child $5) of Saint John twice daily (10am and 12:30pm) late June-September.

Taxi

Cabs wait in front of the Delta and Hilton hotels, or call **Saint John Taxi** (506/693-0000), **Diamond Taxi** (506/648-8888), or **Royal Taxi** (506/652-5050). Fares are based on 14 city zones; expect to pay around $10 from Market Square to Fort Howe and $40 to the airport.

SAINT JOHN TO ST. ANDREWS

In addition to the intrinsic beauty of the coast—with thick forests growing right down to the rocky shoreline—several detours spice up the 90-kilometer drive west to St. Andrews. For the first 40 kilometers out of Saint John there is little reason to detour from Highway 1, but at Lepreau the original coastal route (now known as Highway 175) spurs south to **Lepreau Falls,** a picturesque stop with a few picnic tables set on their own personal decks overlooking the falls.

Lepreau and Vicinity

From Lepreau Falls, Highway 175 continues west, although there is the option to head south on Highway 790 to **Point Lepreau Nuclear Generating Station.** It opened in 1980 as Canada's first nuclear power station and currently supplies 30 percent of New Brunswick's power needs.

Backtracking to Lepreau Falls, Highway 175 heading west quickly reaches **New River Beach Provincial Park** (506/755-4046, mid-May-late Sept.), one of the best beaches along the entire Fundy Coast. Walk along the beach back toward Saint John to explore rock pools, laze on the sand, or have a picnic high above the ocean in the cliff-top day-use area. Unfortunately, there is a downside: Access costs $10 per vehicle per day. Across the road from the beach is a large provincial park campground (506/755-4046, mid-May-late Sept., $28-43) with forested sites, many with power hookups.

A good-value accommodation along this

Lepreau Falls is between Saint John and St. Andrews.

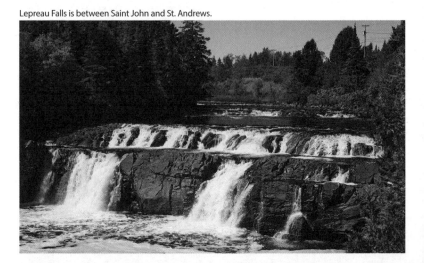

stretch of highway is the **Clipper Shipp Beach Motel** (1312 Highway 175, Pocologan, 506/755-2211, www.clippershipp.com, Mar.-Nov., $95-150 s or d). The rooms are very basic—you're paying for a stunning waterfront location.

GETTING THERE
Lepreau is about 40 kilometers southwest of Saint John on Highway 1 (take Exit 86).

St. George
The most impressive sight at St. George, 32 kilometers before reaching St. Andrews, is the thundering granite gorge of **Magaguadavic Falls.** Visitors can park and walk down a staircase beside the falls to watch salmon swimming upstream past a viewing window. The

specialty at **Oven Head Salmon Smokers** (101 Ovenhead Rd., 506/755-2507, Mon.-Fri. 8am-7pm, Sat.-Sun. 9am-7pm) is, of course, Atlantic salmon, cold-smoked to perfection over hickory and oak chips. The smokehouse wholesales to upscale restaurants throughout the province, although it's much cheaper if purchased directly from the on-site shop.

St. George is also the place to turn off Highway 1 for the short drive to the Deer Island ferry terminus at Letete. Highways 772 and 776 lead to Black Bay, picturesque **Blacks Harbour** (terminus for the Grand Manan Island ferry), and a welter of other islets.

GETTING THERE
St. George is 70 kilometers (one hour) west of Saint John on Highway 1.

St. Andrews and Vicinity

St. Andrews by the Sea, as it is marketed by the local tourism authority, is an immensely attractive seaside town (pop. 1,800) 90 kilometers west of Saint John. New Brunswick's first—and now definitive—resort town, St. Andrews sits at the end of a peninsula dangling into tranquil Passamaquoddy Bay, sheltered from the tumultuous Fundy by Deer Island and Letang Peninsula. The resort crowd revels in St. Andrews's version of old-time velvet-glove Canadiana, especially visible at the many upscale lodgings.

HISTORY
The town has a special, almost sacred historic status among New Brunswickers. It was founded by Loyalists who sailed into the Fundy and followed the coastal curve to the peninsula's tip in 1783. The courageous journey was a technical wonder. The settlers, originally from England's former colonies farther south, had moved to what they believed was Canada at Castine, Maine. But a subsequent international boundary decision forced them to relocate once again. The

pro-Crown settlers reloaded convoys with all their possessions, disassembling houses and reloading the structures on barges, and set sail for a safe homeland. St. Andrews was their creation. Most every street is named for George III or one of his kin. A few Loyalist houses remain and sit cheek-by-jowl with similar New England-style houses fronting narrow residential streets.

SIGHTS
For a town that encourages relaxation, there's a lot to see and do. Many historic attractions are within walking distance of downtown accommodations, while others are just a short drive away. You could easily spend two days in town and still not have time to golf the hallowed fairways of the Algonquin Golf Course or go whale-watching. One of the most interesting things to do in St. Andrews is to watch the effect of the tide. I'm not suggesting you sit at the end of the Town Wharf for six hours, but take a peek at low or high tide, and then return six hours later—the difference is amazing.

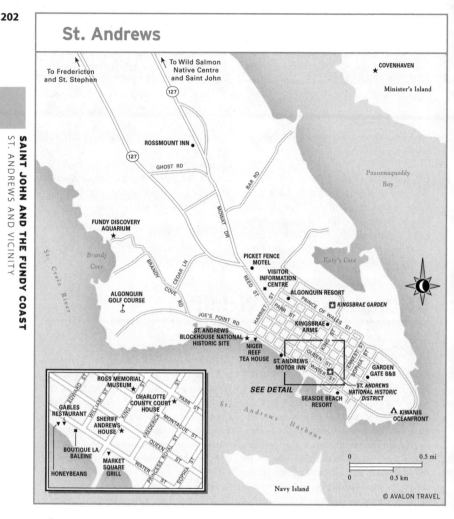

★ St. Andrews National Historic District

As one of the best-preserved Colonial towns in North America (nearly half the buildings in the town core date back more than 100 years), the heart of **St. Andrews** is preserved as a national historic site. Adding to the charm, most buildings have been restored to their original condition. Those along Water Street, the main downtown thoroughfare that follows the shoreline for five blocks, have been brightened up with a variety of pastel-colored paints, creating a resort vibe that extends into the many boutiques and restaurants.

One block back from Water Street, **Sheriff Andrews House** (63 King St., 506/529-5080, late June-early Sept. Mon.-Sat. 9:30am-4:30pm, Sun. 1pm-4:30pm, donation) offers an attractive visual insight into the early Loyalist era. Costumed guides will show you around the county sheriff's neoclassical-style 1820 house, which is simply but elegantly furnished in local period style.

The whitewashed **Charlotte County Court House** (Frederick St., 506/529-3843, July-Aug. Mon.-Sat. 9:30am-noon and 1pm-4:30pm, free) dates to 1840 and is thought to be the country's oldest courthouse in continuous use.

Ross Memorial Museum (188 Montague St., 506/529-5124, early June-early Oct. Tues.-Sat. 10am-4:30pm, donation), in an early 19th-century neoclassical brick home, preserves the furniture, porcelains, rugs, mirrors, paintings, and other items of Henry and Sarah Ross, discerning collectors of antiques and objets d'art.

★ Kingsbrae Garden

Kingsbrae Garden (220 King St., 506/529-3335, mid-May-mid-Oct. daily 9am-6pm, adult $16, senior and child $12) incorporates gardens that were once part of the Kingsbrae Arms estate, as well as additional land, to create 11 hectares of tranquility on the hill above downtown. It is home to more than 2,000 species—a place to feast your eyes on rhododendrons, roses, an orchard, a working windmill, an Acadian coastal forest, and a children's garden featuring miniature houses. The complex also includes a shop selling floral-themed gifts and a **café** (mid-May-mid-Oct. daily 10am-4:30pm) overlooking the garden.

St. Andrews Blockhouse National Historic Site

A pleasant walk along Water Street from downtown will lead you to **St. Andrews Blockhouse National Historic Site** (454 Whipple St., 506/529-4270, June-Aug. daily 10am-6pm, adult $1, child $0.40). The fortification, the last survivor of 12 similar structures, was intended to protect the town from attack in the War of 1812, but nary a shot was fired in battle at this site. The interior depicts the War of 1812 era with re-created soldiers' quarters.

Even if you're not hot on history, the site is worth exploring for the wide grassy expanse out front, which edges the St. Croix River. Time your visit for the ebb (receding) tide, and you'll watch the revealing of a rocky peninsula and pools that are fully submerged at high tide.

Minister's Island Historic Site

The 200-hectare **Minister's Island Historic Site** in Passamaquoddy Bay was where Canadian Pacific Railway magnate William Van Horne built his summer retreat, **Covenhoven** (506/529-5081, $10 pp over age eight, cash only). Completed in 1903, the 50-room home was built of locally quarried

St. Andrews National Historic District

St. Croix Island

In 1604, a French exploration party of 79 led by Samuel de Champlain sailed into the Bay of Fundy and named the Saint John River. After rejecting the site of the present city of Saint John as an improper spot for a settlement, the group spent the bitterly cold winter of 1604-1605 on Douchet's Island in the St. Croix River. The settlement marked the beginning of a French presence in North America. After a bitter winter in which hunger and scurvy claimed 35 lives, the remaining settlers packed up and headed for Nova Scotia's more agreeable side of the Fundy. There they established Port-Royal, the early hub of "Acadia," the name they gave this part of eastern Canada.

The St. Croix River, which drains into the Bay of Fundy at St. Andrews, forms the international border, and the site of the settlement is now protected as **St. Croix Island International Historic Site.** Beside Highway 127, nine kilometers north of St. Andrews, where views extend over the island, interpretive boards tell the story of the settlement. On the U.S. side, there's a viewing platform 13 kilometers south of Calais.

sandstone, and it, a windmill, a tidal swimming pool, and a barn remain. The island is only accessible at low tide, so the two daily tours depart at different times each day (ask at the St. Andrews Visitor Information Centre for times or check the website at www.ministersisland.net). You will be asked to meet at the end of Bar Road, two kilometers northeast of town, from where you follow a lead vehicle across a strip of sand that is exposed only at low tide. The entry fee includes a guided tour.

Fundy Discovery Aquarium

Beyond the golf course, **Fundy Discovery Aquarium** (Brandy Cove Rd., 506/529-1200, mid-May-mid-Oct. daily 10am-5pm, adult $14.25, senior $11.75, child $10) is part of the Huntsman Marine Science Centre, a nonprofit marine biology study facility drawing researchers from far and wide. The aquarium is stocked with hundreds of local fish, crustaceans, mollusks, and marine plant species. A touch tank gives children gentle access to intertidal critters, while seals cavort in the outdoor pool. The center also offers environmental classes with guest lecturers and field and lab work (around $1,000 per week).

Atlantic Salmon Interpretive Centre

On the road back to Saint John, the **Wild Salmon Nature Centre** (24 Chamcook Lake Rd., 506/529-1384, mid-May-mid-Oct. daily 9am-5pm, adult $7, senior $6, child $3.50) is part of a much larger research facility. Displays describe the life cycle of Atlantic salmon and breeding techniques. From the sun-filled room, paths lead upstream to Chamcook Lake and downstream to Passamaquoddy Bay.

SHOPPING

Craft and gift shops abound here. Whether you're looking for sweaters, souvenir T-shirts, locally produced pottery, or what have you, one of the de rigueur activities in St. Andrews is strolling along Water Street and drifting in and out of the shops. One of the nicest is **Boutique la Baleine** (173 Water St., 506/529-3926), which has a wide range of whale- and nautical-oriented souvenirs.

RECREATION
On the Water

Whale-watching is a popular activity here, and several companies offer cruises in search of finback, minke, and humpback whales. In addition to whales, you'll see harbor seals and lots of seabirds. All tours depart from the wharf at the foot of King Street.

Quoddy Link Marine (6 King St., 506/529-2600, www.quoddylinkmarine.com) has a stable covered boat that takes visitors on three-hour naturalist-narrated cruises. Light snacks and beverages and the use of binoculars and foul-weather gear are included in the price (adult $58, senior $52, child $38). For the more adventurous, **Fundy Tide Runners** (16 King St., 506/529-4481, www.fundytiderunners.com, June-Sept., adult $60, child $45) runs out to the whale-watching area in large inflatable Zodiacs, which reach the whale-watching area more quickly than Quoddy Link.

Eastern Outdoors (165 Water St., 506/529-4662, www.easternoutdoors.com) offers a three-hour kayak paddle around Passamaquoddy Bay from the St. Andrews waterfront, with an emphasis on wildlife and human history. The cost is a reasonable $50 per person.

Golf

St. Andrews may not have the history of its Scottish namesake, but golfers have been drawn to the scenic fairways of the **Algonquin Golf Course** (Brandy Cove Rd., 506/529-8165, Apr.-Oct.) for more than 100 years. The course was thoroughly modernized in 2000, with a complete redesign that highlights the sparkling Bay of Fundy at every turn, and then redesigned again in 2017. Summer greens fees are an excellent value at

$95, with discounts early and late in the season. Rates include access to the driving range and a power cart.

FOOD

While St. Andrews has cafés and restaurants to suit all tastes and budgets, seafood dominates local menus.

Toward the entrance to town, **Honeybeans** (157 Water St., 506/529-4888, Mon. and Wed.-Sat. 7:30am-5pm, Sun. 10am-5pm) is a small space serving up great coffee as well as muffins and other pastries. Free Wi-Fi and a few outdoor tables are a bonus.

Overlooking Blockhouse National Historic Site, **Niger Reef Tea House** (1 Joe's Point Rd., 506/529-8005, May 11am-3pm, June-Sept. 11am-9pm daily, lunches $12-15) is in a small waterfront cabin built in 1926 as a chapter house for the Imperial Order of the Daughters of the Empire, a Canadian women's organization that dedicated itself to charity work. Today the setting is almost folksy, with views out across green space to the water of St. Andrews Harbour. The seafood chowder is an excellent choice, or go for the richness of a lobster salad sandwich. Still hungry? Try the strawberry rhubarb crumble.

Algonquin Golf Course

If you're after casual seafood dining with water views, look no farther than ★ **Gables Restaurant** (143 Water St., 506/529-3440, July-Aug. daily 8am-11pm, Sept.-June daily 11am-9pm, $15-27), which occupies a choice spot right on the bay. The waterfront wooden deck out back is a great place for lunch, and couldn't be more romantic in the evening—a great spot for sipping an after-dinner cognac and watching the lights shimmer across the water. The menu stays the same for lunch and dinner, with blackboard specials your best bet. Last time I was through, the seafood pie was delicious. The entrance is down an alleyway (if you pass a massive lobster wood carving, you've found the right spot).

You don't need to be a guest at The Algonquin Resort (184 Adolphus St., 506/529-8823) to take advantage of the in-house restaurant **Braxton's** (summer daily 7am-9pm, the rest of the year Sun.-Wed. 7am-11am, Thurs.-Sat. 7am-11am and 5pm-9pm, $22-48), which specializes in modern presentations of regional game and produce. It's also a good place to come for breakfast, with hot dishes such as eggs Benedict on a lobster cake.

ACCOMMODATIONS AND CAMPING

St. Andrews has a wealth of options, ranging from the family-friendly (Seaside Beach Resort) to the extravagant (take your pick). Always make reservations for July and August.

$50-100

A couple of inexpensive but clean and comfortable motels are along the road into town, including the **Picket Fence Motel** (102 Reed Ave., 506/529-8985, www.picketfencenb.com, $90-110 s or d), where the pricier units have basic cooking facilities.

$100-150

Garden Gate Bed and Breakfast (364 Montague St., 506/529-4453, www.bbgardengate.com, $120-150 s or d) is a lovely late 19th-century home surrounded by mature gardens. Each of the four rooms has an en suite or private bathroom, and rates include a cooked breakfast.

Views from the sweeping lawns of **Rossmount Inn** (4599 Hwy. 127, 506/529-3351 or 877/529-3351, www.rossmountinn.com, Apr.-Dec., $129-138 s or d) extend unimpeded across Passamaquoddy Bay. The three-story mansion holds a dining room, a lounge, an outdoor pool, and 18 guest rooms decorated in soothing cream colors and furnished with Victorian antiques. Outdoors, guests congregate on the patio or use the walking trails to explore the expansive 35-hectare grounds. The lodge is six kilometers northeast of town along the highway to Saint John.

$150-200

For no-frills waterfront accommodations, it's difficult to recommend anywhere but ★ **Seaside Beach Resort** (339 Water St., 506/529-3846 or 800/506-8677, www.seaside.nb.ca, $155-255 s or d). Within walking distance of downtown, this complex comprises a collection of buildings dating back to the mid-1800s. There are over 20 units, some of which are self-contained cabins; others are larger structures complete with slanted floors and handmade windows. My favorite is Harbourview Two, which is right on the water and has two bedrooms and a small deck with a barbecue. All units have kitchens and older televisions.

Right on the edge of the bay and 200 meters from the heart of the village, **St. Andrews Motor Inn** (111 Water St., 506/529-4571, www.standrewsmotorinn.com, $160-230 s or d) is a modern three-story motel. The rates are high for a reason—most rooms have balconies with magnificent water views.

Over $200

The Algonquin Resort (184 Adolphus St., 506/529-8823 or 855/529-8693, www.algonquinresort.com, $220-415 s or d) is a classy Canadian resort with manicured grounds dominating the hill above St. Andrews. Everything about it bespeaks gentility and class—verdant lawns dotted with flowerbeds, gardens, young couples in tennis whites leisurely sipping cool drinks on the veranda—and the tinkling of crystal is the loudest noise you'll hear in the upscale dining room. The original resort opened as a Canadian Pacific Railway hotel in 1889, but burned down in 1914. The Tudor-style replacement that opened the following year is what remains to this day, although it has undergone many expansions and improvements, most recently during 2012-2014, when it was closed for two years for a massive renovation that included giving all guest rooms a modern yet elegant makeover. Amenities include **Braxton's Restaurant and Bar** (the $24.95 Sunday brunch, 11am-1pm, is an excellent value), a large outdoor pool complex, an indoor pool and waterslide, tennis courts, day spa services, and a fitness center.

A member of the prestigious Relais & Chateaux group, the **Kingsbrae Arms** (219 King St., 506/529-1897, www.kingsbrae.com, $379-649 s or d) features eight of the most luxurious guest rooms you'll find anywhere in Atlantic Canada. From the marble bathrooms to the refined room service, this is the place for a serious splurge.

Campgrounds

Through town to the east, and a 10-minute walk to downtown, ★ **Kiwanis Oceanfront Camping** (550 Water St., 506/529-3439 or 877/393-7070, www.kiwanisoceanfrontcamping.com, early Apr.-late Oct., $36-52) lives up to its name, with a front row of campsites that enjoy unimpeded water views. Amenities include showers, a playground, a grocery store, a kitchen shelter, wireless Internet access, and a laundry.

INFORMATION

As you enter town from the west, the **St. Andrews Visitor Information Centre** (24 Reed St., 506/529-3556, www.standrewsbythesea.ca, early May-early Oct. daily 9am-6pm) is tucked away in the trees on the left side of the road beyond the Picket Fence Motel.

GETTING THERE

To get to St. Andrews, head west on Highway 1 out of Saint John for just over 80 kilometers, then go south on Highway 127 for about 20 kilometers. Allow 1.5 hours without stops for this drive.

The Algonquin Resort

Fundy Isles

The Fundy Isles are a world away from mainland living, an archipelago of islands spread across the New Brunswick side of the Bay of Fundy. Four islands—Deer, Campobello, Grand Manan, and White Head—are populated and are linked to the mainland by ferry. They make an interesting diversion from coastal cruising and are little known outside Atlantic Canada.

DEER ISLAND

The sea swirls mightily around Grand Manan but diminishes in intensity as the currents spin off around the coast of Maine to Deer Island, which lies closer to the United States than the Canadian mainland. Sovereignty of Deer and Campobello Islands was disputed for decades after the American Revolution; a treaty gave the islands to New Brunswick in the 1840s.

Sights and Recreation

Wilder and with a lower profile than Campobello, Deer Island is nevertheless reached first from the New Brunswick mainland. It's devoted to fishing and is encircled with herring weirs (stabilized seine nets); other nets create the "world's largest lobster pounds." The **Old Sow,** the largest tidal whirlpool in the Western Hemisphere, can be viewed three hours before high tide from **Deer Island Point Park,** at the island's south end.

Accommodations

A great place to stay is **Deer Island Inn** (272 Route 772, 506/747-1998, www.deerislandinn.com, $85-105 s or d), a grand Victorian-era residence overlooking the village of Lord's Cove. The five rooms have en suite bathrooms, and rates include breakfast.

Getting There

Ferries to Deer Island depart year-round from Letete, 15 kilometers from Highway 1 (turn off at Exit 56, four kilometers west of St. George). Ferries depart up to 20 times daily from 7am. The government-run service is free, and no reservations are taken. Between late June and early September, Deer Island is linked by ferry to Eastport, Maine, by **East Coast Ferries** (506/747-2159, www.eastcoastferriesltd.com, vehicle and driver $13, $3 per extra passenger). Departures are hourly in each direction. Note that this service did not operate in 2016, but was scheduled to return for the 2017 summer season.

CAMPOBELLO ISLAND

Linked by a bridge to Lubec, Maine, Campobello is inextricably linked to the United States, but in summer a ferry links the island to Deer Island, making it a natural extension of your travels through the Fundy Isles.

Campobello, cloaked in granite, slate, and sandstone, was a favorite retreat of U.S. president Franklin Delano Roosevelt. The shingled green and bell-pepper-red family vacation home is now the main attraction at the **Roosevelt Campobello International Park** (459 Route 774, Welshpool, 506/752-2922, mid-May-mid-Oct. daily 10am-6pm, free). The 34-room interior is furnished with authentic family trappings, made somehow all the more poignant because FDR was stricken with polio while on vacation here.

East-facing, 425-hectare **Herring Cove Provincial Park** (136 Herring Cove Rd., 506/752-7010, late May-late Sept., $28-43) has a long stretch of beach, six hiking trails, and a nine-hole golf course (506/752-7041, greens fee $35). Around half of the campground's 88 sites come with electricity, and all have picnic tables and fire pits.

Getting There

Aside from driving to the island from Maine, between late June and September you can reach Campobello by ferry from Deer Island in about 20 minutes. **East Coast Ferries** (506/747-2159, www.eastcoastferriesltd.com, vehicle and driver $16, $3 per extra passenger) schedules hourly crossings 9am-6pm.

★ GRAND MANAN ISLAND

As the Fundy Isles' largest and most southerly island, Grand Manan (pop. 2,700) gets the brunt of the mighty Fundy high tide. Pity the centuries of ships that have been caught in the currents during malevolent storms. Near the island, shipwrecks litter the seafloor and pay homage to the tide's merciless power.

The most photogenic of the island's four lighthouses is **Swallowtail Lighthouse,** which can be seen atop North Head as you approach the island by ferry. Illuminating the sea lanes and warning ships off the island's shoals since 1860, Swallowtail and its surrounding grassy headland provide a wonderful introduction to the island.

Apart from the surging tide, Grand Manan is blissfully peaceful. White, pink, and purple lupines and dusty-pink wild roses nod with the summer breezes. Windswept spruce, fir, and birch shade the woodland pockets. Amethyst and agate are mixed with pebbles on the beaches at **Whale Cove, Red Point,** and **White Head Island** offshore. Dulse, a nutritious purple seaweed rich in iodine and iron, washes in at **Dark Harbour** on the western coast, and islanders dry and package the briny snack for worldwide consumption.

Offshore, every species of marine life known to the Bay of Fundy congregates in the bay's nutrient-rich mouth. Whales in pursuit of herring schools swim in on incoming currents, cavorting in the tempestuous seas—the right, finback, humpback, and minke whales are at their most numerous when the plankton blooms, mid-July-September.

Bird-Watching

Birds of almost 350 species flutter everywhere in season, and each species has a place on this rock in the sea. Seabirds and waterfowl nest at the **Castalia Marsh** on the island's eastern side. Ducks and geese by the thousands inhabit the **Anchorage Beach** area, where a wet-heath bird sanctuary is speckled with ponds that attract many other species, including great blue herons. Expect to see bald eagles and other raptors on the southern cliffs mid-August-November. The eider, storm petrel, and Atlantic puffin prefer offshore islets.

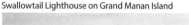

Swallowtail Lighthouse on Grand Manan Island

Fundy Birding

In the Upper Fundy, where the tides are at their most dramatic, the setting belongs to a few remote villages and one of North America's most spectacular shows of migratory birds. The American bittern, Virginia rail, short-eared owl, marsh wren, and hundreds of other species soar across the wide stage. The bird-watching season varies according to species, but it generally runs late March-late May and August-September.

One of the best bird-watching spots is **Grand Manan Island.** On the mainland, bird sanctuaries are scattered from upper Chignecto Bay's western coast across Shepody Bay to the Dorchester Peninsula and the Chignecto Isthmus. They are easily missed—signs are often obscure, and numbered roads may be the only landmarks. Many are managed by **Ducks Unlimited Canada** (506/458-8848), a nonprofit environmental group that manages around 20,000 hectares of wetlands in New Brunswick alone. Another good source of information is the **Canadian Wildlife Service,** which has its Atlantic head office at **Sackville Waterfowl Park** (17 Waterfowl Ln., Sackville, 506/364-5044, Mon.-Fri. 8am-4pm). At this location, there is a display room with details of species you're likely to spot in the adjacent wetland as well as down the road at the **Tintamarre Sanctuary,** a national wildlife area. A similar reserve is **Shepody National Wildlife Area** between Alma and Hopewell Cape.

Bird populations are thickest early April-June and late summer-autumn. A great way to see the birds is by hiking one of the 18 trails (totaling 70 kilometers) that crisscross the headland. Many wind through bird sanctuaries. Another incredible place for bird-watching is **Machias Seal Island,** the outermost bird sanctuary island. Boat tours, restricted to a limited number of passengers, depart Grand Manan to see the archipelago's highest concentration of exotic bird species, including razorbill auks, arctic terns, and 900 pairs of nesting Atlantic puffins.

Tours

While you can take whale- and bird-watching trips from St. Andrews, Grand Manan is where serious nature lovers base themselves. Space is limited and always in demand on the following tours, so make reservations.

One of the finest, most well-established sightseeing outfits in town is **Sea Watch Tours** (North Head, 506/662-8552, www.seawatchtours.com), which runs tour boats ($115 for a six-hour trip) to Machias Seal Island late June-early August. Whale-watching tours ($66) are scheduled July-September.

Food

North Head Bakery (199 Route 776, North Head, 506/662-8862, May-Oct. Tues.-Sat. 7:30am-5:30pm) has a great selection of cookies and cakes, plus bread baked daily from organic ingredients. Also along the main road through North Head, **Harbour Grille** (1140 Route 776, North Head, 506/662-3103, Mon.-Sat. 7am-9pm, Sun. noon-9pm, $11-18) is a small restaurant that is a popular gathering spot for locals. Don't expect anything too creative—come here for simple meals such as burgers, pizza, and fish-and-chips at reasonable prices.

Accommodations and Camping

Though lodgings can be found across the island, it's smart to book ahead. **Compass Rose** (83 Route 776, North Head, 506/662-3563, www.adventurehigh.com, mid-Apr.-Oct., $99-165 s or d) sits atop a headland in the village of North Head, at the island's north end. Its six comfortable guest rooms are spread through two buildings, one of which was the island's original post office. Breakfast (included in the rates) is served in a sunny dining room, and seafood-oriented dinners are available with advance notice. The inn is operated by a local tour company, so this is the place to stay if you are planning on kayaking or biking while on the island.

Also recommended at North Head is **Inn at Whale Cove Cottages** (120 Whistle Rd., 506/662-3181, www.whalecovecottages.ca, June-mid-Oct., $140-180 s, $150-180 d), which combines three guest rooms in a renovated 1816 residence and five cabins with a restaurant open daily for dinner through the summer season. The rooms each have private bathrooms and frilly fabrics and wallpaper, while the cottages are self-contained, including the Willa Carter Cottage, perched on an oceanfront cliff.

You'll need a vehicle to get to **Anchorage Provincial Park** (Seal Cove, 506/662-7022, May-Oct., $26-43), at the south end of the island. The park contains 100 unserviced or serviced campsites with toilets, hot showers, and kitchen shelters. Reservations are not accepted, so it's wise to call ahead to check on availability.

Getting There

Coastal Transport Ltd. (506/662-3724, www.coastaltransport.ca) operates ferries between Blacks Harbour (11 km south of Exit 60 from Highway 1) and North Head. The 27-kilometer crossing takes about 90 minutes. The car/passenger ferries sail daily year-round, with up to seven departures scheduled daily July-early September. The round-trip fare (adult $12, child $6, vehicle from $36) is collected when leaving the island. Reservations are by phone or online; you can also check online for real-time sailing information, including how full each ferry is.

Upper Fundy Coast

The impact of tidal action is extraordinarily dramatic on the Upper Fundy's coastline. The sea floods into the bay and piles up on itself, ravaging the shore at Mispec—where it has clawed into the land's edge to reveal gold veins—and pocking the coastline with spectacular caves at St. Martins. St. Martins also marks the starting point for the region's most challenging trek, to Fundy National Park. The backpacking trip involves just 40 kilometers, but expect to spend 3-5 days. In places the high tide washes out all beach access and forces hikers back inland.

Beyond the national park, the tide's strength increases as the bay forks into the narrow Chignecto Bay and Cumberland Basin. No place is safe during an incoming tide, especially the stretch of coast from Saint John to Hopewell Cape. At Alma, the village at the park's eastern edge, the sea rises waist-high in a half hour and continues rising to a height of 14 meters.

The Fundy orchestrates its final swan song at Hopewell Cape. Beyond the cape, its tidal impact is exhausted; some of the sea moves inland as a tidal bore and flows up the Petitcodiac River to Moncton, and the remainder washes Dorchester Peninsula's coastal marsh edges.

SAINT JOHN TO FUNDY NATIONAL PARK

From Saint John, it's about 90 kilometers northeast along Highway 1 to Exit 211, from which the boundary of Fundy National Park is 22 kilometers southeast.

St. Martins

St. Martins, founded in 1783 as Quaco, became one of the busiest shipbuilding centers in the Maritimes in the 1800s, turning out more than 500 ships over the course of the 19th century. Today the handsome little village is a fishing port, as evidenced by the stacks of lobster traps on the quay. At the harbor, two covered wooden bridges stand within a stone's throw of one another. The local tourist information office is housed in the lighthouse close by.

Some of the great attractions in the vicinity are the **seaside caves** scooped out of the red sandstone cliffs by the Fundy tides. The caves can be explored at low tide.

ACCOMMODATIONS

The village has two excellent accommodations, and being just a 40-minute drive from downtown Saint John, it's worth considering staying an extra night and using St. Martins as a base for a day trip to the city. The historic **Tidal Watch Inn** (16 Beach St., 506/833-4772 or 888/833-4772, www. tidalwatchinn.ca, $110-225 s or d) has comfortable beach house quarters with 15 guest rooms, a dining room open daily for dinner, and a hot tub housed outdoors in a gazebo. Overlooking the Bay of Fundy, the Victorian Gothic ★ **St. Martins Country Inn** (303 Main St., 506/833-4534 or 800/565-5257, www.stmartinscountryinn.ca, $135-165 s or d), former home of one of the seaport's most prosperous shipbuilding families, has aptly been dubbed "the Castle" by locals. The beautifully restored mansion has 16 antiques-furnished rooms, each with private bath and some with canopied beds. Rates include a cooked breakfast; the in-house restaurant is also open for dinner daily.

GETTING THERE

The Highway 1 route to Fundy National Park misses St. Martins. Reach St. Martins from Saint John by following Highway 111 east from the Saint John Airport for 30 kilometers. To continue on to Fundy National Park, take Highway 111 north until you rejoin Highway 1 about 50 kilometers later.

★ FUNDY NATIONAL PARK

The magnificent **Fundy National Park** is a bit out of the way, but well worth the effort to get to. The 206-square-kilometer park encompasses a cross section of Fundy environments and landforms: highlands; deeply cut valleys; swampy lowlands; dense forests of red and sugar maple, yellow birch, beech, red spruce, and balsam fir; and a shoreline of dizzying cliffs and sand and shingle beaches. For all its wilderness, though, Fundy National Park has a surprising number of civilized comforts, including rustic housekeeping chalets, a motel, a restaurant, and a golf course.

a quiet pond in Fundy National Park

From Saint John, Highway 1 feeds into the TransCanada Highway, and the backcountry Highway 114 branches off east of Sussex, peels over the Caledonia Highlands, and plummets through woodlands to sea level. Thick woods rise on one side and conceal the park's deep valleys sown with rivers and waterfalls. Glimpses of the sea, cradled by beaches, appear on the road's other side; most of the 13-kilometer shoreline is wrapped with formidably steep sandstone cliffs.

Park Entry

The park is open year-round, though full services operate and entry fees are charged only mid-May-mid-October. A one-day pass (adult $8, senior $7, child $4) is valid until 4pm the following day.

Hiking

Two dozen hiking trails wander the coastline or reach up into the highlands. The highlands hikes are easy-to-moderate treks, while the toughest trails lie along the coast, impeded by cliffs, ridges, fern glades, and thick forests.

Shorter, easier trails include the **Caribou Plain,** a 3.4-kilometer loop on flat terrain through forest and bog, and **Dickson Falls,** a 1.5-kilometer loop that offers views above and below the waterfall via a system of boardwalks and stairs. The moderately difficult **Goose River Trail** is 7.9 kilometers each way, along an old cart track to a wilderness campground at the mouth of the Goose River in the park's southwestern corner. The 10-kilometer (each way) **Coastal Trail** is graded as difficult, but the rewards include lush fern glades and forest and great ridgetop views over the bay and coastal sea stacks. You can get more detailed information at park headquarters or the Wolfe Lake information center, both of which sell the useful *Fundy National Park Trail Guide.*

Other Recreation

Beyond the grassed meadow below the Visitor Reception Centre is the **Saltwater Pool** (Point Wolfe Rd., late June-early Sept., 11am-7pm, adult $4, senior $3.50, child $2), which is filled with heated saltwater piped in from the Bay of Fundy. If you prefer to be on the water rather than in it, head to **Bennett Lake,** where canoe, kayak, and rowboat rentals are $10 per hour.

Fishing is good for the plentiful trout found in the lakes and rivers; a national park fishing license, available at either visitor center, is required ($10 per day, $35 for an annual pass valid in all national parks).

Fundy National Park

Fundy National Park Golf Course (506/887-2970, mid-May-mid-Oct.) is a fun, old-fashioned nine-hole layout that tumbles down the hillside near the administration building and slices through the coastal forest like a green velvet glove whose fingers reach into the woodlands. The greens fee is $19 for nine holes, or you can play all day for $34. Adjacent to the golf course are **tennis courts** and **lawn bowling;** rental equipment is available at the pro shop.

Food

For locally harvested seafood to take back and cook at your campsite, head for ★ **Butland's** (8607 Main St., Alma, 506/887-2190, early May-early Sept. daily 10am-6pm, early Sept.-Dec. Sat.-Sun. noon-5pm), which sells live and cooked lobsters, scallops, salmon, and haddock. Also in Alma is **Tides** (Parkland Village Inn, 8601 Main St., 506/887-2313, daily for breakfast, lunch, and dinner, $15-28), a casual dining room overlooking the Bay of Fundy that not surprisingly serves lots of local seafood; it's best sampled on the Seafood Platter.

Accommodations

Lodging within the park and in the adjacent fishing village of **Alma** is well priced. The best deal is at **Vista Ridge Cottages** (41 Foster Rd., 506/887-2808, www.fundyparkchalets.com, $145 s or d), which are within walking distance of most park attractions. Each cabin has three bedrooms, a small kitchen, an electric fireplace, and satellite TV.

Fundy Highlands Inn and Chalets (8714 Hwy. 114, 506/887-2930 or 888/883-8639, www.fundyhighlandchalets.com, $95-115 s or d) is two kilometers from the main facility area and enjoys a lofty location high above the bay in the Caledonia Highlands. Choose between comfortable rooms in the main lodge or chalets with water views. All units have cooking facilities.

Parkland Village Inn (8601 Main St., 506/887-2313 or 866/668-4337, www.parklandvillageinn.com, Apr.-Oct., $135-165 s or d) is a 50-year-old three-story motel with a waterfront location along Alma's main street. The rooms are simple but modern, and most have water views. The two-bedroom suites ($165) are a steal.

Parkland Village Inn

Camping

The park has four campgrounds. Reservations can be made through the **Parks Canada Campground Reservation Service** (450/505-8302 or 877/737-3783, www.pc-camping.ca) for $11 per booking, but they are only really necessary for July and August.

Headquarters Campground (mid-May-Oct., $26-36) is within walking distance of the Visitor Reception Centre, the swimming pool, the golf course, and Seawinds Dining Room. Facilities include showers, playgrounds, and full hookups. Back up Highway 114 a little way is **Chignecto North Campground** (mid-May-mid-Oct., $26-36), with similar facilities.

At the end of Point Wolfe Road, six kilometers southwest of the Visitor Reception Centre, ★ **Point Wolfe Campground** (late June-Aug., $26) has a delightful beachside location and is linked to coastal hiking trails. It has showers but no hookups.

In the park's northwest corner, **Wolfe Lake Campground** (mid-May-mid-Oct., $17) has basic facilities such as pit toilets and fire pits.

Information

The main **Visitor Reception Centre** (506/887-6000, www.pc.gc.ca, spring and fall daily 10am-5:45pm, mid-June-early Sept. daily 8am-9:45pm) is on the park's eastern edge, just across the river from the village of Alma. In addition to handing out general park information, the center is home to various natural history displays and holds a bookstore.

Entering from the northwest, you'll find a small **visitor center** (Hwy. 114, late May-early Oct. daily 10am-5:45pm) beside picturesque Wolfe Lake.

Getting There

Fundy National Park is about 130 kilometers (1.5 hours) from Saint John via Highway 1, then Highway 114.

ALMA TO HOPEWELL CAPE

It's 40 kilometers from Alma, the town just east of Fundy National Park, to Hopewell Cape. For bird-watchers there is one important detour, to New Horton Marsh.

Shepody National Wildlife Area

Shepody National Wildlife Area—New Brunswick's stellar bird-watching sanctuary—is made up of three different habitat areas. **Germantown/Beaver Brook Marshes,** 14.7 kilometers northeast of Alma, is the reserve's only inland area and spreads out on 686 hectares on Highway 114's east side. As you approach the area, look for Midway Road, the reserve's southern boundary. Turn right on Midway, cross the covered bridge, and park beyond it at the second path. The nine-kilometer trail follows the marsh's edge alongside woodlands and fields rich with ducks and herons.

The 185-hectare **New Horton Marsh** attracts ducks and herons to a coastal setting. At Alma, take coastal Highway 915 for a 30-kilometer drive to the mudflats. The reserve's northern tip is situated where the road divides; one branch leads to inland Riverside-Albert, the other to Mary's Point Road farther out on the coast. A four-kilometer trek through the marsh starts on a dike off the latter road. Be wary of the tides: The mudflats reach almost to the sea and quickly flood.

A few kilometers beyond New Horton Marsh, Mary's Point Road leads to **Mary's Point,** Canada's only shorebird reserve. Shorebirds by the hundreds of thousands set down on the 109-hectare coastal reserve, their numbers peaking mid-July-mid-August. Among the onslaught are about 9,000 blue herons and an uncountable number of cormorants, all of which swarm over the intertidal zone.

GETTING THERE

Shepody National Wildlife Area is about 20 kilometers (15 minutes) north of Alma via Highway 114.

HOPEWELL CAPE

The great Fundy tides have created a curiously compelling scene at Hopewell Cape, 45 kilometers northeast of Alma and 35 kilometers south of Moncton.

★ Hopewell Rocks

Hopewell Cape is the place-name, and **Hopewell Rocks** (Hwy. 114, 506/734-3534, mid-May-June and Sept.-mid-Oct. daily 9am-5pm, July-Aug. daily 9am-8pm, adult $10, senior $8, child $7.25) is the name of the natural attraction. You pay the entry fee at the tollgate and then are directed to the main Interpretive Centre, where interesting displays describe the geology of the cape and its relationship to the Fundy tides.

Trails lead to a number of cliff-top lookouts, but the vast majority of visitors make a beeline for the **Flowerpot Rocks.** The walking trail takes around 20 minutes, or you can pay $2 each way to ride the oversized golf cart shuttle. Either way, next up is a steep descent down a stairway to the ocean floor.

At the staircase's first landing, you overlook an otherworldly collection of giant natural arches and mushroom-shaped pillars jutting up from the seafloor. Known as "flowerpots," these sea-sculpted red shale and conglomerate sea stacks have been separated from the mainland cliffs by the abrasive tide. Many of the flowerpots are "planted" with stunted black spruce and balsam fir, looking somewhat like clipped haircuts stuck atop the stacks. At low tide, sightseers—dwarfed by the enormous pillars—roam the beach and retrieve seashells left by the tide. Be wary of falling rocks; the pillars and cliffs are continually eroding, and there's always a chance that rocks will loosen and tumble, as happened in March 2016, when one of the best known of the formations, Elephant Rock, collapsed.

It's only possible to "walk on the ocean floor" (as it's promoted) around the flowerpots from three hours before low tide to two hours after. Catch the scene again at high tide and you'll understand why. The tide rises 16 meters here, fully flooding the area. All you'll see are the pillars' tree-covered crowns. Information centers in Fundy National Park and Moncton can tell you when the tide is low at Hopewell Rocks, or

Flowerpot Rocks

check the website (www.thehopewellrocks.ca). When low tide falls during the middle of the day in July and August, the "ocean floor" gets extremely crowded.

Food and Accommodations

Near the access road is **Hopewell Rocks Motel** (Hwy. 114, 506/734-2975 or 888/759-7070, www.hopewellrocksmotel.com, May-mid-Oct., $110-135 s or d, includes a light breakfast), which has 33 rooms with water views, an outdoor swimming pool, and a restaurant with lots of seafood and dishes such as roast beef dinners.

Getting There

Hopewell Cape is 45 kilometers (40 minutes) northeast of Alma on Highway 114. To get to Hopewell Cape from Moncton, it's a 35-kilometer (30-minute) drive south along Highway 114.

Saint John River Valley

Tumbling along, over riverbed boulders and through glistening pools frequented by moose and white-tailed deer, the Saint John River originates in remote northern Maine near the Québec border.

It flows through Edmundston and then curves southeast through the French-flavored towns and villages of Madawaska until it's squeezed into a spuming torrent at the stony gorge at Grand Falls. The rest of the river's journey grows increasingly placid. It's tamed by hydro dams at Beechwood and Mactaquac, and it flows under the world's longest covered bridge at Hartland before draining into the Bay of Fundy at Saint John. The river's interior course splits the inland provincial capital of Fredericton in two. This city of just 56,000 is a sightseer's delight, with an appealing historic downtown core, riverfront walking paths, and tree-lined streets feeding back to quiet residential areas of historic homes with open porches, bay windows, and gardens of pearl-colored peonies and scarlet poppies.

PLANNING YOUR TIME

The majority of travelers who traverse the length of the Saint John River arrive overland through Québec and make the northwestern region of New Brunswick their first stop, with the more adventurous visitors detouring to the remote lakes and forests of **Mount Carleton Provincial Park**. If you've flown into Halifax and caught the ferry across the Bay of Fundy, it will take a little over an hour to reach Fredericton, which should be your focus for a day of sightseeing. This will give you enough time to explore the **Historic Garrison District**, walk through **Beaverbrook Art Gallery**, and marvel at **Christ Church Cathedral. Kings Landing Historical Settlement** is only a short drive from the capital, but it would make for a long day to lump it in with the other city attractions in a single day. Besides, you'll want to continue upriver beyond Kings Landing to **Hartland** to drive across the world's longest covered bridge.

Previous: Saint John River; Legislative Assembly Building. **Above:** bridge that serves as a walking path over the Saint John River.

Look for ★ to find recommended sights, activities, dining, and lodging.

Highlights

★ **Historic Garrison District:** Filling two blocks of downtown Fredericton, this wide-open attraction lets visitors step back in time—while surprising them with quirky attractions, including a 17-kilogram frog (page 222).

★ **Beaverbrook Art Gallery:** Atlantic Canada's finest art gallery holds an impressive collection of Canadian work, as well as paintings by notables like Salvador Dalí (page 224).

★ **Christ Church Cathedral:** In a land of grandiose churches, this is one of the most impressive. Come for summer music recitals, or simply wander through the gardens (page 225).

★ **Kings Landing Historical Settlement:** Loyalist history comes alive at this outdoor museum that will easily fill a full day (page 233).

★ **Hartland Covered Bridge:** The most memorable way to reach the quiet village of Hartland is by crossing the Saint John River via the world's longest covered bridge (page 234).

★ **Mount Carleton Provincial Park:** This remote park takes some effort to reach, but hardy travelers will be rewarded with empty hiking trails leading to beautiful lakes, mountaintops, and waterfalls (page 236).

Saint John River Valley

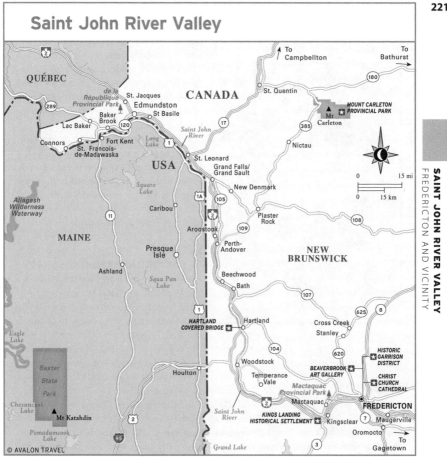

© AVALON TRAVEL

Fredericton and Vicinity

Fredericton (pop. 56,000), in the southwestern heart of the province, is New Brunswick's legislative, cultural, and educational center, and it's one of the country's oldest settlements. The city is the exception to the usual rule of thumb that a province's busiest and largest city is the logical choice for the capital. Fredericton is hardly a metropolis. Rather, it's of modest size, elegant, picture-book pretty, and very Anglo in tone and shape. "There is something subtle and elusive about it," Michael Collie wrote of Fredericton, "like a person who has had long sessions of psychoanalysis and has become more sophisticated and charming in the course of them."

Visitors flying to New Brunswick will find Fredericton makes a good introduction to the province and a good sightseeing base. Roads lead from here to every part of the province. St. Andrews and Saint John on the Fundy are each just over an hour's drive south, and Moncton is 180 kilometers east. And it's

Fredericton

always nice to return to Fredericton, the province's quintessential hometown.

HISTORY

In 1783, the British created a settlement beside the Saint John River and named it Frederick's Town, in honor of King George III's second son. Two years later the little river town was designated the colonial capital—the government had grand plans for Fredericton. Surveyor Charles Morris drew up the first street grid between University Avenue and Wilsey Road. By 1786 the population center had shifted, and central Fredericton as you see it today was redrawn by another surveyor and extended from the riverfront to George Street, bounded by University Avenue and Smythe Street. Space was set aside for the Church of England sanctuary and King's College, now the University of New Brunswick. Public commons were marked off between the riverfront and Queen Street, except for two blocks earmarked for the British Army garrison. By 1800, wharves lined the riverfront from

Waterloo Row to Smythe Street, and sloops, schooners, and brigantines sped between the capital and Saint John. Shipping lumber was a profitable early business, and Fredericton added foundry products, processed leather, carriages, and wagons to its economy in the 1800s. The city was incorporated in 1848, and in 1873 the city limits were extended to nearby towns, doubling the population.

England's plan for Fredericton as a miniature London was never fulfilled. Shipping and manufacturing diminished in the early 1900s, and Fredericton settled into a prosperous, genteel government town, university center, and haunt of the Anglo establishment, roles that continue to this day.

SIGHTS

★ Historic Garrison District

The **Historic Garrison District** (Queen St., 506/460-2129), a national historic site, dominates downtown, encompassing two long city blocks between the modern city to the south and the Saint John River to the north. A military compound built in 1784 as headquarters for the British army, it is enclosed by a curlicue wrought-iron black fence that contains a variety of attractions.

At the corner of Queen and Carleton Streets, the stone **Officers' Quarters** was built in 1827. One street-level room (July-Aug. daily 10am-6pm, free) is open to the public, while around the back, low-ceilinged rooms once used to store ammunition now provide a home for vendors selling arts and crafts. Across the courtyard is the **Guard House** (July-Aug. daily 10am-6pm, free), a simple stone building that looks much like it would have in the mid-1800s, complete with costumed guards out front in summer.

FREDERICTON REGION MUSEUM

Facing the Parade Square at the east end of the Historic Garrison District, the **Fredericton Region Museum** (571 Queen St., 506/455-6041, May and Sept. Tues.-Sat. 1pm-4pm, June-Aug. daily 10am-5pm, adult $5, child $2) is housed within the former Officers' Quarters

Downtown Fredericton

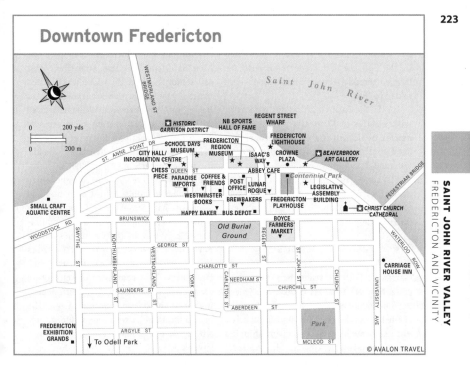

(1825), a three-story stone building designed by the Royal Engineers and unusually styled with a ground-level colonnade of white pillars and an iron handrail. The museum is devoted to provincial history from early Malecite and Mi'kmaq to contemporary events. The unlikely surprise is the Coleman Frog, a 17-kilogram, 1.6-meter-long amphibian stuffed for posterity and squatting inside a glass showcase on the second floor. The believe-it-or-not frog was found a century ago by local Fred Coleman, who developed a friendship with the frog and fattened it up by feeding it rum pudding and June bugs in honey sauce—or so the story goes.

SCHOOL DAYS MUSEUM

Step back into the classroom at the **School Days Museum** (corner of Queen and York Sts., 506/459-3738, mid-June-Aug. Mon.-Fri. 10am-4pm, Sat. 1pm-4pm, free), across York Street from City Hall. In addition to a reconstructed classroom, you'll find an interesting display on one-room schools, textbooks and training manuals, and furniture from as early as the mid-1800s.

NEW BRUNSWICK SPORTS HALL OF FAME

The John Thurston Clark Memorial Building is an impressive 1881 Second Empire French Revival edifice that once served as customs house and post office. The building now provides a home for the **New Brunswick Sports Hall of Fame** (503 Queen St., 506/453-3747, June-early Sept. Tues.-Fri. noon-5pm, Sat. 10am-5pm, adult $3, child $2), with exhibits highlighting the province's best sporting men and women.

City Hall

The red-brick **City Hall,** at the corner of Queen and York Streets and across from the Historic Garrison District, is central to everywhere downtown. The elegant 1876 building has housed city offices, a jail, a farmers market, and an opera house. Its high tower showcases the city's copper clock, and the decorative fountain in front—crowned by the figurine that Frederictonians have dubbed "Freddie, the little nude dude"—was added in 1885.

Inside, the **Council Chamber** is adorned with a series of 27 locally produced tapestries depicting the city's history. The **Fredericton Visitor Information Centre** (506/460-2129), in the building's front vestibule, conducts chamber tours (mid-May-early Oct. daily 8:15am-7:30pm, early Oct.-mid-May Mon.-Fri. by appointment 8:15am-4:30pm).

Fredericton Lighthouse

Cross Regent Street from the Historic Garrison District to reach the privately operated **Fredericton Lighthouse** (615 Queen St., 506/460-2939, mid-June-mid-Sept. daily 10am-10pm, adult $2). The interior consists of 13 separate landings exhibiting shipping and river-sailing artifacts. The top level commands a magnificent riverfront view. At ground level, you'll find a gift shop and outdoor café serving light lunches and delicious ice cream.

★ Beaverbrook Art Gallery

On the east side of downtown is **Beaverbrook Art Gallery** (703 Queen St., 506/458-2028, Mon.-Sat. 10am-5pm, Sun. noon-5pm, adult $10, senior $8, child $5), which was donated to the city by New Brunswick art maven Lord Beaverbrook, also known as William Maxwell Aitken. The gallery boasts an impressive 2,000-piece collection—the most extensive British fine arts collection in Atlantic Canada, if not the nation. Among the British painters represented are Thomas Gainsborough, Sir Joshua Reynolds, John Constable, and Walter Richard Sickert. You'll find Graham Sutherland's sketches of Winston Churchill—drawn in preparation for Churchill's official portrait—and works by Atlantic Canada's Miller Brittain, Alex Colville, and Jack Humphrey. Also central to the collection are the oils of Cornelius Krieghoff, depicting social and domestic scenes of early life in Acadia. Lord Beaverbrook could not resist the European masters—Salvador Dalí's large-scale *Santiago El Grande* and Botticelli's *Resurrection* are prominently displayed.

Legislative Assembly Building

The splendidly regal **Legislative Assembly Building** (706 Queen St., 506/453-2527,

Historic Garrison District

Christ Church Cathedral

★ Christ Church Cathedral

Gothic-styled cathedrals were designed to soar grandiosely toward heaven, and this storied stone cathedral is no exception. With a lofty copper-clad central spire and elegant linear stone tracery, **Christ Church Cathedral** (506/450-8500) rises from a grassy city block at Church and Brunswick Streets. Begun in 1845 and consecrated in 1853, this was the first entirely new cathedral founded on British soil since the Norman Conquest way back in 1066. It was rebuilt after a fire in 1911 and is still the place where the city's nabobs go to pay their respects to the benevolent powers that be. It's open year-round, with recitals taking place in summer on Friday 12:10-12:50pm.

Historic Cemeteries

The **Old Burial Ground** is bounded by Regent, Brunswick, George, and Sunbury Streets. The site—spliced with walkways beneath tall trees—is one of two historic burial grounds in town. This spread of greenery was the final resting place for Loyalist notables.

The **Loyalist Cemetery** (formerly the Salamanca graveyard), on an unmarked gravel road off Waterloo Row at the riverfront, is simpler and marks the final resting place of the founding Loyalists who died in the town's first winter of 1783-1784.

Odell Park

Of the 355 hectares of lush parkland throughout the city, **Odell Park** (Rockwood Ave., 506/460-2038) is the choice spread, holding 16 kilometers of trails, formal lawns, duck ponds, a deer pen, barbecue pits, and picnic tables. The park is Fredericton's largest, covering 175 hectares. It is best known for an arboretum holding every tree species in the province; a 2.8-kilometer walking trail divided into three loops wanders through the shady expanse. To get there from downtown, head south on Rockwood Avenue.

RECREATION

The riverfront **Small Craft Aquatic Centre** (Woodstock Rd., 506/460-2260, July-Aug.

mid-June-Aug. daily 9am-5pm, Sept-mid-June Mon.-Fri. 8:30am-4pm, free) lies kitty-corner from the Beaverbrook Art Gallery. The sandstone French Revival building spreads across a manicured lawn, its massive wings pierced with high arched windows, and the upper floor and tower rotunda are washed in glistening white. The building was completed in 1882 at a cost of $120,000, including construction and furnishings. The front portico entrance opens into an interior decorated in high Victorian style—the apex of expensive taste at the time. Glinting Waterford prisms are set in brass chandeliers, and the spacious rooms are wallpapered in an Oriental design. The interior's pièce de résistance is the **Assembly Chamber,** centered around an ornate throne set on a dais and sheltered with a canopy.

John James Audubon's *Birds of America* is kept in the **Legislative Library.** One of four volumes is on display in a climate-controlled exhibit, and pages are periodically turned to show the meticulous paintings.

daily 6:30am-9am and noon-8:30pm, shorter hours in spring and fall) rents recreational rowing shells, canoes, and kayaks; gives lessons; and leads kayak tours.

ENTERTAINMENT AND EVENTS
Nightlife
Locals love their low-key pubs, and you will find many around the downtown core. The **Lunar Rogue** (625 King St., 506/450-2065, Mon.-Sat. 11am-1am, Sun. 11am-10pm) heads the list with English pub ambience, Canadian and British draft beer, and live music—usually with a Celtic flavor—several nights a week. A cluster of pubs surrounds Pipers Lane, an alley that connects the 300 blocks of King and Queen Streets. **Dolan's Pub** (349 King St., 506/454-7474, Mon.-Sat. 11:30am-2am) offers an excellent menu of pub grub and slightly fancier fare, as well as live entertainment Thursday-Saturday.

Performing Arts
Fredericton specializes in entertaining summertime visitors. Outdoor festivities center around the Garrison Historic District, where **Theatre-in-the-Park** (www.calithumpians.com) takes to the boards July-early

September. Its humorous and historical productions take place Monday-Friday at 12:15pm and on weekends at 2pm. In summer, musicians—pipe bands and folk, country, and bluegrass groups—perform outdoors in Officers' Square every Tuesday and Thursday at 7:30pm, in front of the Guard House on Wednesday at 12:30pm, and in the Main Street Amphitheatre on Wednesday at 7pm. Classic movies are screened outdoors every Sunday at 9pm. Storytellers weave local history into interesting yarns every Wednesday at 3pm in Barracks Square. Best of all, this entire program is presented free of charge.

Theatre New Brunswick (55 Whiting Rd., 506/460-1381, www.tnb.nb.ca), the province's only professional English-speaking theater company, operates full-tilt during the autumn-spring theater season. **The Playhouse Fredericton** (686 Queen St., 506/458-8344, theplayhouse.ca), right downtown, is a stylish venue that hosts touring artists and local theater companies year-round.

Festivals and Events
Festival Francophone, for three days late in May, celebrates Acadian language and culture with concerts, dancing, and children's activities. The festivities take place at

the Old Burial Ground

By Any Other Name

Fredericton is known by many names. New Brunswickers have dubbed the city "North America's Last Surviving Hometown." You could debate the claim, perhaps, but it nonetheless does sum up local priorities.

The naming trend goes back to the 1800s, when locals ruefully joked that the city had a fire every Saturday night and dubbed it the "City of Fires." In 1911, one such fire destroyed the Christ Church Cathedral. The sanctuary was quickly rebuilt, its grandiose silhouette on the skyline leading to the moniker "Cathedral City."

Another Fredericton nickname, "City of Stately Elms," is a testament to Fredericton's leafy ambience. The quiet streets are lined mainly with elms, a choice that goes back to founding Loyalist times. They've survived centuries, even beating Dutch elm disease, which the city quelled in the 1960s and 1970s.

Fredericton's reputation as "Canada's Poets' Corner" is a tribute to native sons Bliss Carmen, Sir Charles G. D. Roberts, and Francis Joseph Sherman. And finally, the nickname "Canada's Pewtersmith Capital" singles out the city's preeminent craft, developed here first by pewtersmith Ivan Crowell in the 18th century.

Centre Communautaire Sainte-Anne (715 Priestman St., 506/453-2731, www.centre-sainte-anne.nb.ca).

The **New Brunswick Highland Games** (506/452-9244, www.highlandgames.ca), a three-day Celtic tribute featuring pipe bands, highland dancing, Gaelic singing, heavy sports, clan booths, and more, takes over the city the last weekend of July.

Fredericton had its first fall fair in 1825, and the tradition continues at the **New Brunswick Provincial Exhibition** (361 Smythe St., 506/458-8819, www.nbex.ca, adult $10, senior $9, child $5), with six days of country fair trappings, including harness racing, lawn mower races, tractor pulls, chainsaw carving, and stage shows. It's held

at the Fredericton Exhibition Grounds during early September.

The summer season finishes in a clamor of music as the outdoor **Harvest Jazz and Blues Festival** (506/455-4523, www.harvestjazzandblues.com) takes over the downtown streets for five days the second week of September. It's billed as the biggest jazz and blues fest east of Montréal, and it features musicians from all over North America.

SHOPPING

Shopping areas are concentrated downtown, mainly along Regent, Queen, York, and King Streets as well as the adjacent side streets, plus on Woodstock Road and at the malls.

Arts and Crafts

Several shops are known for craft specialties. **Aitkens Pewter** (408 Queen St., 506/453-9474, Mon.-Wed. 9am-5:30pm, Thurs.-Fri. 9am-8pm, Sat. 9am-5pm) stocks handcrafted pewter hollowware, jewelry, and decorative pieces. **Cultures Boutique** (383 Mazzuca Ln., 506/462-3088, Mon.-Sat. 9am-5pm, Fri. 9am-8pm) is a nonprofit operation featuring crafts produced by third-world artisans. It is located off York Street between King and Queen Streets.

Connexion (65 York St., 506/454-1433, Fri.-Sat. noon-6pm or check www.connexion-arc.org for special events) is a nonprofit artists' outlet with an eminent reputation for the province's arts. In a stylishly renovated residence, **Gallery 78** (796 Queen St., 506/454-5192, Tues.-Fri. 10am-5pm, Sat. 10am-3pm, Sun. 1pm-4pm) is a stylish space within a grand residence on the east side of downtown that represents the province's very best artists.

FOOD

Fredericton has a reputation for so-so dining. Don't believe it. True, you won't find tony dining rooms by the dozens, and aside from at a few fine restaurants, the cooking is less than fancy. Nonetheless, you can sample virtually all the capital's fare without a qualm, and your dining dollar will go a long way, too.

Cafés and Cheap Eats

Beside City Hall in the heart of downtown, **Chess Piece** (361 Queen St., 506/459-1969, Mon.-Fri. 7am-9pm, Sat. 8am-9pm, Sun. 10am-4pm) is a handy location to pick up freshly made croissants, sandwiches to go, and European-inspired cakes and pastries.

★ **Happy Baker** (520 King St., 506/454-7200, Mon.-Sat. 7:30am-10pm, Sun 8am-10pm, lunches $7-10) is worth searching out in the bowels of the HSBC Building. In addition to the usual array of coffee concoctions, you can purchase a wide array of European-style breads, pastries, and desserts. Continental breakfasts and lunches, including the very best sandwiches I've found in the city, round out this excellent little spot. In the vicinity, **Coffee & Friends** (415 King St., 506/455-4554, Mon.-Sat. 10am-10pm, Sun 11am-6pm, lunches $6-10) has a smaller selection of similar lunches, but it also has a wide selection of teas, as well as a few outdoor tables.

Coffee-loving locals will tell you that the best coffee is poured at **Paradise Imports** (95 York St., 506/455-1711, Mon.-Fri. 7:30am-4pm, Sat. 8:30am-2pm), a funky jewelry store with an espresso bar in one corner. The coffee is roasted in-house daily and served with muffins and cakes.

Year-round **Boyce Farmers' Market** (665 George St., between Regent St. and Saint John St., 506/451-1815, Sat. 6am-1pm) lures *everybody* with stalls heaped with baked goods, homemade German sausage, other local delicacies, and crafts.

Abbey Cafe (546 Queen St., 506/455-6368, Mon.-Fri. 9am-9pm, Sat. 11am-9pm, $9-16) is a small restaurant offering simple vegetarian and vegan cooking in a casual atmosphere. Local art on the walls brightens up the room.

Pubs

The **Lunar Rogue** (625 King St., 506/450-2065, Mon.-Sat. 11am-1am, Sun. 11am-10pm, $12-24), one of Fredericton's most popular pubs, offers dining indoors or alfresco. The same menu is offered throughout the day and has something to suit everyone—sandwiches, salads, soups, stir-fries, pastas, and a decent selection of seafood such as haddock fish cakes for $12 and a seafood platter for $24.

Pizza

Anyone hankering for pizza can step into **BrewBakers** (546 King St., 506/459-0067, Mon. 11:30am-9pm, Tues.-Thurs. 11:30am-10pm, Fri. 11:30am-11pm, Sat. 5pm-11pm, Sun. 5pm-9pm, $15-29), where the pizzas are baked in a wood-fired oven and accompanied by pastas and salads in a contemporary setting.

Mexican

Mexicali Rosa's (304 King St., 506/451-0686, daily 11:30am-10pm, $13-22) is part of an eastern Canadian chain of colorful Mexican restaurants. Expect all the usual Americanized food at reasonable prices. It's a long way from Mexico, but the recipes nonetheless come off quite well. Margaritas and cold cerveza are available.

Contemporary

Enthusiastic local owners, a funky ambience in an 1855 courthouse, and well-priced meals make ★ **Isaac's Way** (649 Queen St., 506/474-7222, Mon.-Fri. 11:30am-10pm, Sat.-Sun. 10am-10pm, $17-27) a solid choice for lunch or dinner. Game and produce are sourced from within the province, and everything is made from scratch—right down to the sauces and desserts. Sample dinner mains include maple curry salmon (using local maple syrup, of course) and chicken breast stuffed with goat cheese and cranberries.

Hotel Dining

The dining rooms at the major hotels are good bets for fancier fare. At the Crowne Plaza (659 Queen St., 506/451-1804), **The Terrace** (daily for breakfast, lunch, and dinner, $16-26), with city and river views, offers breakfast and lunch at moderate prices and dinner items using regional produce. You'll need reservations for the Friday evening seafood buffet. The adjacent ★ **Maverick Room** (daily 5pm-10pm,

The Diplomat Restaurant

$20-42) serves a more upscale menu of steak and seafood.

At the Delta Fredericton, **Catch Urban Grill** (225 Woodstock Rd., 506/457-7000, daily 7am-9pm, $25-38) lures crowds for fare such as chicken saltimbocca—a sautéed stuffed chicken breast basted with white wine and served on linguine—and seafood, beef, and pasta. Look for cooked breakfasts under $15 and the ever-popular Sunday brunch buffet ($29). Also at the Delta is **The Dip** (June-Aug. daily 11am-11pm), an outdoor poolside restaurant with tables and chairs spread across a terrace where the views extend across the river. The menu covers all bases, from simple sandwiches to a lobster boil.

Although it's not actually within a hotel, **Diplomat Restaurant** (253 Woodstock Rd., 506/454-2400, 24 hours daily, $13-24) is across the parking lot from the Delta Fredericton on the west side of downtown. This family-style restaurant has well-priced breakfasts served throughout the day and a mix of Canadian

and Chinese dishes that aren't a bargain, but portions are generous.

ACCOMMODATIONS AND CAMPING

In keeping with its status as a provincial capital, Fredericton has a choice of downtown chain hotels, each offering a wide range of modern services aimed at business travelers. Other options are historic inns dotted around the outskirts of downtown and regular motels along major arteries. The main concentration of the latter is three kilometers south of downtown at the junction of Regent and Prospect Streets (Exits 6A and 6B off Hwy. 8).

$50-100

Across the river from downtown, the **Fort Nashwaak Motel** (15 Riverside Dr., 506/472-4411 or 800/684-8999, www.fortnashwaak.com, $75-102 s, $85-102 d) and, four kilometers downstream, the **Norfolk Motel** (815 Riverside Dr., 506/472-3278 or 800/686-8555, www.norfolkmotel.ca, $80-100 s or d) are basic cheapies with free Internet access and a number of kitchenettes.

$100-150

The three-story Queen Anne Revival **Carriage House Inn** (230 University Ave., 506/452-9924 or 800/267-6068, www.carriagehouse-inn.net, $120 s, $130 d) is a restored 1875 home southeast of downtown but still within walking distance. The 10 guest rooms are furnished with antiques; guests have use of a solarium and laundry. Breakfasts are a real treat.

None of the motels around the junction of Regent and Prospect Streets offer anything extraordinary. Instead, you get the reliability of chains such as the **Comfort Inn** (797 Prospect St., 506/453-0800 or 800/228-5150, www.choicehotels.ca, $120 s, $135 d). In the vicinity, and one of the largest motels in the city, is the four-story **Fredericton Inn** (1315 Regent St., 506/455-1430 or 800/561-8777, www.frederictoninn.nb.ca, $125 s or d), between the Regent and Fredericton shopping malls. It has 200 guest rooms, two restaurants (one open for dinner buffets and summer lobster suppers), a lounge, and an indoor pool.

Around 20 kilometers west of downtown along Highway 102 (at Exit 274), **Riverside Resort** (35 Mactaquac Rd., 506/363-5111 or 800/561-5111, www.riversidefredericton. com, from $150 s or d) has a very un-city-like location within striking distance of Kings Landing. It's a sprawling property with a restaurant and lounge and a fitness center with a heated indoor pool, a hot tub, and an exercise deck. It features 85 motel-like rooms in the three-story main building, and six two-bedroom chalets ($280 s or d) are also on the manicured grounds.

$150-200

★ **On the Pond** (Rte. 615, Mactaquac, 506/363-3420 or 800/984-2555, www.onthe-pond.com, from $175 s or d) is a grandiose country inn where the emphasis is on being pampered in a back-to-nature environment. Guests enjoy a wide variety of spa services, proximity to Mactaquac Provincial Park and its golf course, and a fitness center. The eight guest rooms have an earthy old-world charm, with little niceties such as plush robes and inviting living areas. Bed-and-breakfast rates start at $170 per person, but also check the website for spa and golf packages.

Along the river, within striking distance of downtown attractions, is the ★ **Delta Fredericton** (225 Woodstock Rd., 506/457-7000 or 888/890-3222, www.marriott.com, from $199 s or d), which has an agreeable resort-style atmosphere centering on a large outdoor pool complex, complete with resort furniture and a poolside bar. It also has an indoor pool, a fitness room, two restaurants, and a lounge. Check the website for discounted rooms, and maybe consider a splurge on a suite that will cost the same as a regular room in a big-city hotel.

Over $200

One of Fredericton's better lodgings is the **Crowne Plaza Fredericton Lord**

Crowne Plaza Fredericton Lord Beaverbrook

Beaverbrook (659 Queen St., 506/455-3371 or 866/444-1946, www.cpfredericton.com, $230-460 s or d), aimed squarely at those in town on government business. Don't let the dowdy exterior of this bulky hotel put you off—the 165 guest rooms are thoroughly modernized. Amenities include an indoor pool and fitness complex, two dining rooms, and a lounge.

Campgrounds

The closest camping to Fredericton is at **Hartt Island RV Resort,** seven kilometers west of town on the TransCanada Highway (2475 Woodstock Rd., 506/462-9400, www.harttisland.ca, May-Oct., $40-60), which is a great spot to enjoy river sports like canoeing and kayaking. Amenities include a huge outdoor pool complex, mini-golf, and kayak tours.

On the same side of the city, but on the north side of the river, **Mactaquac Provincial Park Campground** (Hwy. 105, 506/363-4747, mid-May-mid-Oct., $33-40) is a huge facility 24 kilometers from downtown. In addition to 305 campsites, there's a golf course, hiking, biking, swimming, and fishing.

INFORMATION AND SERVICES

The main **Visitor Information Centre** (397 Queen St., 506/460-2129, mid-May-late June and Sept.-mid-Oct. daily 8am-5pm, late June-Aug. daily 8am-8pm) is right downtown, inside the lobby of City Hall. For advance information, contact **Fredericton Tourism** (506/460-2041 or 888/888-4768, www.tourismfredericton.ca).

In an emergency, call 911 or the **RCMP** (1445 Regent St., 506/452-3400). For medical emergencies, contact the **Dr. Everett Chalmers Hospital** (700 Priestman St., 506/452-5400) or **Regent Street After Hours Clinic** (1015 Regent St., 506/458-0200).

GETTING THERE

Fredericton is in the south-central portion of New Brunswick along the TransCanada Highway (Highway 2). From Bangor, Maine, it's around three hours via Highway 95, then Highway 2 to Fredericton. It's 110 kilometers (over an hour) to Fredericton from Saint John via Highway 7 and 180 kilometers (two hours) from Moncton via Highway 2. If you are driving from Halifax to Fredericton, allow around 4.5 hours for the 440-kilometer drive via Moncton.

Fredericton Airport (2570 Hwy. 102, 506/460-0920, www.frederictonairport.ca), 14 kilometers southeast of downtown off Highway 102, is served by daily **Air Canada** (506/458-8561 or 888/247-2262) flights from Montréal, Toronto, Ottawa, and Halifax. Avis, Hertz, Budget, and National have counters near the baggage carousels. Other airport facilities include a café, a gift shop, free wireless Internet, and a business center. A cab to downtown costs $22.

Maritime Bus (105 Dundonald St., 506/455-2049, www.maritimebus.com) has daily bus service from Fredericton to Saint John, Moncton, and Edmundston. The small terminal is open daily 8am-8:30pm.

GETTING AROUND

Fredericton Transit (506/460-2200) has a web of nine bus routes connecting downtown with outlying areas (Mon.-Sat.). Fare is $2.75 per sector.

Look for cabs cruising downtown streets and waiting at major hotels, or call **Trius Taxi** (506/454-4444).

Car rental firms are plentiful. Chains in town include **Avis** (506/446-6006), **Budget** (506/452-1107), **Hertz** (506/446-9079), and **National** (506/453-1700).

Metered parking is plentiful in parking lots behind sights and curbside on Queen, King, upper York, Carleton, Regent, and Saint John Streets. The city provides free three-day parking passes for out-of-province visitors; the passes are available at City Hall and the Legislative Assembly Building, both on Queen Street.

GAGETOWN AND VICINITY

The Saint John River downstream of Fredericton is dotted with islands, around which a skein of twisting channels is braided. It's beautiful countryside, and a delightful drive, with Gagetown, 60 kilometers from the capital, a good turnaround point. Quite a bit goes on in this little town of 600 over the course of the season. Look for the four-day **Queens County Fair** (www.queenscountyfair.com) in mid-September, which features lots of agricultural attractions and competitions.

Sir Leonard Tilley House (69 Front St., 506/488-2966, mid-June-mid-Sept. daily 10am-5pm, adult $3) is in a handsome white wooden house that was the birthplace of Sir Leonard Tilley, one of the "Fathers of Confederation." The first floor is dutifully furnished with Loyalist antiques, and upstairs holds vintage county exhibits.

The riverfront town of **Oromocto**, halfway to Gagetown, is built around Canadian Forces

Base Gagetown, a military training installation located near the town center off Broad Road. On the base itself, the **New Brunswick Military History Museum** (506/422-1304, Mon.-Fri. 8am-4pm, $2) has exhibits on the past and present of the Canadian armed forces since the late 18th century, with weapons, uniforms, and other memorabilia.

Getting There

To get to Oromocto from Fredericton, follow Highway 102 east along the river for just over 20 kilometers. Continue on to Gagetown on Highway 102, cross divided Highway 2 (the TransCanada Highway), and, 60 kilometers later, you'll find yourself in the pretty riverfront town of Gagetown.

Up the Saint John River

From Fredericton, Highway 2 (the TransCanada Highway) wends north along the Saint John River, crossing it numerous times before reaching Edmundston after 270 kilometers. As part of the transcontinental highway, it's easy, smooth driving, but leave the main route and you'll find beautiful rural scenery and a region dotted with small towns. The region's highlights are within day-tripping distance of Fredericton, so you could travel as far as Hartland to see the world's longest covered bridge and then spend the afternoon at Kings Landing.

MACTAQUAC AND VICINITY

Stemming the flow of the Saint John River is **Mactaquac Dam,** part of a massive hydroelectric scheme 20 kilometers west of Fredericton that supplies power to 10 percent of New Brunswick residences. Completed in 1968, the dam rerouted the river and raised the water level 60 meters, flooding the valley and creating Mactaquac Lake Basin. Historic buildings from the flooded area found a new home at the Kings Landing Historical Settlement, a provincial heritage park that opened in 1974.

the Saint John River

Mactaquac Provincial Park

Not all New Brunswickers were pleased with this massive river alteration, but the creation of 525-hectare **Mactaquac Provincial Park,** which opened the following year, was a sweetener. It's beside Highway 105 on the north side of the river, 24 kilometers upriver from Fredericton.

The park ($8 per vehicle per day) offers hiking trails, supervised beaches, bike rentals, picnic areas, and bass fishing, but its pièce de résistance is the 18-hole **Mactaquac Golf Course** (506/363-4926, greens fee $58), a challenging tree-lined layout considered one of Atlantic Canada's top public courses.

The wooded campground has more than 300 sites ($29 unserviced, $36 with electrical hookups) with kitchen shelters, hot showers, a launderette, and a campers' store fronting the Mactaquac Lake Basin. The park and campground are open mid-May-mid-October, and a day pass is $8 per vehicle.

Getting There

Mactaquac is 25 kilometers (20 minutes) west of Fredericton via Highway 102. You can also reach Mactaquac from Fredericton by using Highway 105, making for a 30-kilometer (30-minute) drive.

★ KINGS LANDING HISTORICAL SETTLEMENT

A marvelous counterpoint to Caraquet's Village Historique Acadien, the **Kings Landing Historical Settlement** (5804 Rte. 102, 506/363-4999, mid-June-Sept. daily 10am-5pm, adult $18, senior $16, child $13)—a grand-scale living museum—is in a beautiful setting alongside the Saint John River, 35 kilometers west of Fredericton. The river valley was settled by Loyalists who arrived in New Brunswick in 1783, and it is this era through to the early 1900s that the village represents. Bring comfortable walking shoes, since the site spreads across 120 hectares with 70 houses and buildings—among them a sawmill, farmhouses, a school, a forge, and a printing office. Informative costumed "residents" depict rural New Brunswick life as it was lived in the 1800s. One of many interesting links to the past is an orchard where hybrid apples developed by Francis Peabody Sharp in the mid-1800s are grown. Demonstrations include horseshoeing, metal forging, cloth spinning and weaving, and farming. Special events include live theater, an agricultural fair in late August, the Provincial Town Criers' Competition in early

Kings Landing Historical Settlement

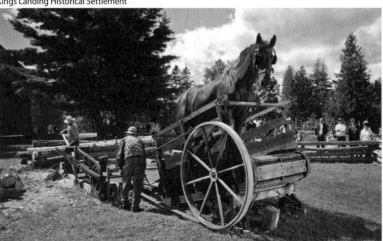

September, and a Harvest Festival in early October to close out the season.

No one ever leaves the **Kings Head Inn** (506/363-4950, late May-mid-Oct. daily 11:30am-4:30pm, lunches $7-14) complaining about being hungry. At the riverside end of the village, this restaurant serves up hearty fare like salmon chowder, crunchy almond fish cakes, and divine desserts that include maple-brandy squash pie.

Getting There

Kings Landing is about 35 kilometers (30 minutes) west of Fredericton via Highway 2 (take Exit 253).

TO GRAND FALLS

West from Kings Landing, the TransCanada Highway follows the Saint John River along one of its loveliest stretches. Tourism New Brunswick refers to this stretch of highway, the 200 kilometers between Fredericton and Grand Falls, as the **River Valley Scenic Drive.** To fully appreciate the forested scenery and the wide and blue river, bounded by green fields and forests of maple and hemlock, is to detour from the Trans-Canada Highway and take secondary roads such as Highway 105 through the riverside communities of Woodstock and Hartland. Allow four hours to travel between Fredericton and Grand Falls along these roads.

Woodstock

Around 100 kilometers west then north from Fredericton, Woodstock is a charming riverside town with paths and parkland along the Saint John River. The gracious 1884 redbrick **courthouse** is a dominant feature of the main street, but **The River** (558 Main St., 506/325-2829, Sun.-Wed. 10am-10pm, Thurs.-Sat. 11am-11pm, $11-21) is where you'll find the law-abiding locals. The most sought after tables on a warm day are those out on the riverside deck, but inside is also welcoming at this part pub, part restaurant. The food is typical pub fare, with a few Irish favorites thrown in—cottage pie and meatloaf are both reasonably priced.

GETTING THERE

Following Highway 2, it's 100 kilometers (one hour) from Fredericton to Woodstock.

★ Hartland Covered Bridge

North from Woodstock, give the TransCanada Highway a miss and stick to Highway 103, which hugs the west bank of the Saint John River for 30 kilometers, from where it makes a sharp right turn and crosses the world's longest covered bridge before emerging in the village of Hartland. The **Hartland Covered Bridge** is only wide enough for one-way traffic, so make sure no one else is driving toward you before entering the bridge. Built in 1901, covered in 1921, and now protected as a national historic site, it stretches 391 meters over the Saint John River. On the east side is an information center (summer daily 9am-6pm) with displays on the bridge's history and on other covered bridges in New Brunswick. From this point, a walking trail leads upstream and then along the Becaguimac Stream.

Grand Falls (Grand-Sault)

The otherwise placid Saint John River becomes a frothing white torrent when it plunges 23 meters over the stony cataract that gave Grand Falls, or Grand-Sault, its name. Below the falls, which have been harnessed to produce hydroelectric power, the tremendous force of the river has worn a two-kilometer-long, horseshoe-shaped gorge through 70-meter-high rock walls. Here the river is at its narrowest, and the gorge's bottleneck impedes the water's force. The river pushes through the narrows in tumultuous rapids, like pent-up champagne bursting from the bottle.

Grand Falls Visitor Information Centre (25 Madawaska Rd., 506/475-7788, early May-June and Sept.-mid-Oct. daily 9am-6pm, July-Aug. daily 9am-9pm) makes a convenient starting point for exploring the area. From the center's rear windows, you'll see the thundering cataracts tumbling through the gorge. A two-kilometer-long path leads along the gorge to **La Rochelle.** From there, a rock staircase leads down to the cataract edge, where the agitated river swirls in the rocky wells. The river is most spectacular during spring runoff.

Several well-priced lodgings in Grand Falls make the town all the more appealing for overnight stays. The best choice is the **Quality Inn** (10039 Route 144, 506/473-1300, www.choicehotels.ca, $120-175 s or d), on the north side of town. It has 100 well-appointed rooms, an indoor pool, and a small fitness room, and a light breakfast is included.

GETTING THERE
It's nearly 200 kilometers (under two hours) from Fredericton to Grand Falls via Highway 2.

EDMUNDSTON AND VICINITY
Originally settled by Acadian refugees on the site of a Malecite village, Edmundston boasts 16,000 residents, over 90 percent of whom are French speakers, a higher percentage than any other North American city outside Québec.

Sights and Recreation
For an insight into the area's checkered history and "mythical Madawaska," stop in at the **Madawaska Museum** (195 Blvd. Hébert, 506/737-5282, July-Aug. Mon.-Fri. 10am-5pm, Sat.-Sun. 1pm-5pm, Sept.-June Mon.-Thurs. 10am-3pm, Sat.-Sun. 1pm-5pm, adult $5, child $3.50). But to truly experience the local Acadian-flavored culture, come for the five-day **Foire Brayonne** (506/739-6608, www.foirebrayonne.com), on the weekend closest to August 1. More than 100,000 people show up for the celebration of Brayon foods, music, dance, sports, and other entertainment.

Accommodations
Edmundston's ritziest lodging is the large **Four Points Edmundston** (100 Rice St., 506/739-7321 or 800/576-4656, www.starwoodhotels.com, from $135 s or d), which has over 100 spacious and elegantly decorated guest rooms, an indoor pool, hot tub, sauna, restaurant, lounge, and free wireless Internet throughout. With similar facilities is **Quality Inn Edmundston** (919 Canada Rd., 506/735-5525 or 800/563-2489, www.choicehotels.ca, $115-125 s or d). Both are accessed from Exit 18 of the TransCanada Highway.

Hartland Covered Bridge

Getting There

From Fredericton, it's 270 kilometers (under three hours) northwest along Highway 2 to Edmundston.

Saint-Jacques

North of Edmundston, about halfway to the Québec border, is the town of Saint-Jacques, home of **de la République Provincial Park,** where the highlight is the **New Brunswick Botanical Garden** (Exit 8 of the TransCanada Hwy., 506/737-5383, May-June and Sept. daily 9am-5pm, July-Aug. daily 9am-8pm, adult $15, senior $13, child $7.50). The formal garden complex on 17 hectares was designed by the skilled Michel Marceau (who also designed the famous Montreal Botanical Garden). It brims with 60,000 plants of 1,500 species. Roses, perennials, and rhododendrons bloom among the prolific posies in nine gardens, all orchestrated with classical music in a romantic vein. **Butterflies of the World** (included in admission fee) is a glass pavilion filled with butterflies from Central and South America. Other park facilities include an outdoor heated swimming pool ($2.50 pp), tennis courts, and a campground (506/735-2541, May-Sept., $28-36) beside the Madawaska River.

Targeted at visitors entering New Brunswick from Québec, the **Provincial Visitor Information Centre** (17412 Route 2, 506/735-2747, late May-June and Sept.-early Oct. daily 9am-6pm, July-Aug. daily 9am-7pm) is alongside the TransCanada Highway, nine kilometers south of the border.

GETTING THERE

Saint-Jacques is about 10 kilometers (10 minutes) north of Edmundston via Highway 2. It's 280 kilometers (three hours) northwest from Fredericton, also along Highway 2.

Lac-Baker

Lac-Baker is in New Brunswick's remote northwestern corner, near where the Saint John River flows into the province from the northern reaches of Maine. Here you'll find all the quiet woodlands you could ever want, as well as the rustic **Camping Plein Air Lac Baker** (510 Church Rd., 506/992-2136, www.campinglacbaker.com, mid-May-mid-Sept.). The lakeshore complex lies several kilometers north of the river and has eight cabins ($85-105 s or d), campsites ($28-40), a dining room and canteen, and swimming, canoeing, and kayaking.

GETTING THERE

Lac-Baker is about 35 kilometers (30 minutes) west of Edmundston via Highway 120. From Fredericton, head northwest on Highway 2, then west from Edmundston on Highway 120, for a total of 300 kilometers (over three hours).

★ Mount Carleton Provincial Park

The 17,000-hectare **Mount Carleton Provincial Park,** in the remote interior of New Brunswick, is far from the normal tourist route but well worth searching out if you are looking for a true wilderness experience. The park centers around a string of unspoiled lakes surrounded by dense forest and the province's highest peaks. Wildlife such as deer, moose, lynx, porcupines, and over 100 species of birds are present. Access to the park costs $10 per vehicle per day.

Get a feeling for the park by driving around the road that encircles Big and Little Nictau Lakes, although be warned that the gravel road is narrow and very winding in places. Along the way are numerous lake access points, including short stretches of beach. Hiking trails leading from the road are as short as a 300-meter path to photogenic **Williams Falls,** but keen hikers will want to reach the summit of the Maritimes' highest point of land, **Mount Carleton** (820 meters). If you go, wear sturdy shoes and bring a jacket to combat the winds. The easiest, marked ascent goes up a 4.4-kilometer trail through a spruce, fir, and yellow birch forest. The mountain's peak rises above the tree line, and the view is marvelous, overlooking the adjacent mountains and lakes from a summit strewn with mountain cranberries and wild blueberries.

Within the park are three auto-accessible campgrounds (506/235-0793, mid-May-mid-Sept., $28), of which only one, **Armstrong Campground,** is suitable for RVs and campers. It has 88 campsites, flush toilets, showers, kitchen shelters, a playground, a small beach, and a concession (July and Aug. only). Another option are older cabins on the south side of Nictau Lake and the southeast side of Bathurst Lake ($70-100 s or d). They require guests to supply their own sleeping bags and cooking utensils, but are otherwise a great way to experience the park. Along with campsites, the cabins can be booked online (https://parc-snbparks.ca).

The entrance to the park is 50 kilometers east of Saint-Quentin along Highway 180. Saint-Quentin is roughly halfway between Grand Falls and Campbellton, so if you're looping around the province by road, you'll pass within 50 kilometers of the park. For travelers northbound along Highway 2, take Exit 115 at Perth-Andover (halfway between Hartland and Grand Falls) and follow Highway 109 and the Mamazekel River through Plaster Rock to reach the park via a more direct route than continuing north to Grand Falls.

GETTING THERE

Mount Carleton is about 150 kilometers (two hours) east of Edmundston. To get there, take Highway 2 east, Highway 17 northeast, and Highway 180 east, then follow signs for the park. To get there from Fredericton, allow at least 3.5 hours for the 245-kilometer journey northwest via Highways 2, 17, and 180.

Williams Falls

Acadian Coast

Along the eastern edge of New Brunswick is the Acadian Coast—a French-flavored realm of seaports, barrier beaches, sand dunes, salt marshes, sandy pine-clad shores, and rocky coastline.

Northumberland Strait is the shallow, narrow sea strip between New Brunswick's southeastern coast and Prince Edward Island. Here the coastline attracts summertime sunbathers, swimmers, and windsurfers to welcoming beaches and waters warmed by the Gulf Stream. Farther north, the warm sea mixes with the cooler Gulf of St. Lawrence. Here the Labrador Current swirls in the open gulf, and the swift currents arrive ashore with low rolls of surf. Offshore, barrier islands hold sheltered seaports. Farthest north, the Baie des Chaleurs ("Bay of Warmth") is the shallow sea pocket between northern New Brunswick and Québec's Gaspé Peninsula.

The essence of French-speaking Acadia is entwined in its dining and festivals. To understand the region's cultural roots, visit the Village Historique Acadien at Caraquet, where early Acadian life has been re-created with authentic buildings and costumed reenactors. In the south, Moncton, northern

New Brunswick's trendy urban commercial and educational center, is Caraquet's bustling modern counterpoint—a very successful Acadia of the new millennium. Acadian pride runs high, and everywhere in the region the Acadian flag—the red, white, and blue French tricolor with a single gold star—is displayed prominently. But other ethnic groups are represented here as well, most notably the Irish.

Stretched-out distances notwithstanding, getting around is easy and very manageable. Highway 11 lopes along most of the three coasts from seaport to seaport, with the sea almost always within view. End to end, it's an easygoing 10-hour one-way drive between Campbellton and Shediac, if you take your time. But by all means, take the side roads branching off the main route and amble even closer to the water to explore the seaports and scenery. For example, Highway 11 diverges from the

Previous: Kelly's Beach in Kouchibouguac National Park; the world's largest lobster in Shediac. **Above:** Confederation Bridge.

Look for ★ to find recommended sights, activities, dining, and lodging.

Highlights

★ **Bore Park:** This is a good place to watch the tidal bore, and it's home to the region's main information center (page 242).

★ **Sackville Waterfowl Park:** Bird-watchers will be enthralled with the many and varied bird species that call this reserve home (page 252).

★ **Parlee Beach:** Buff—and not so buff—bods flock to Parlee Beach for its long expanse of sand, warm swimming water, and holiday vibe. Long after the crowds have left, the evening sunset is sublime (page 254).

★ **Le Pays de la Sagouine:** The literary world learned about Acadian life from the novels of Antonine Maillet. This energetic historical park in her hometown brings her writing to life (page 256).

★ **Kouchibouguac National Park:** This coastal park is laced by hiking trails leading through wetlands, across coastal bays via boardwalk, and along extended stretches of sand (page 257).

★ **Village Historique Acadien:** Experience Acadian life up close and personal at this outdoor museum (page 263).

© AVALON TRAVEL

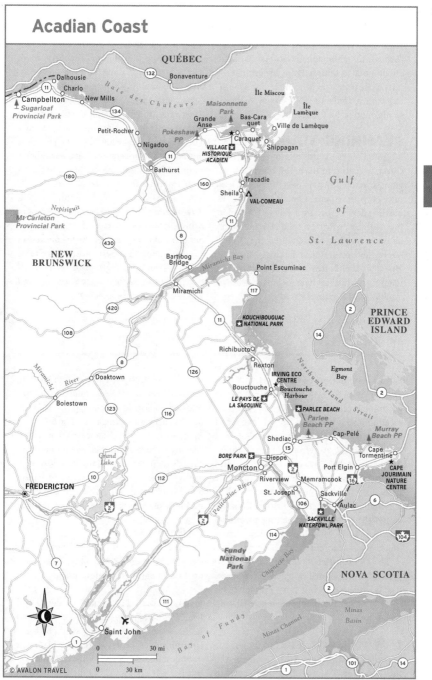

Acadian Coast

QUÉBEC

Baie des Chaleurs

Dalhousie
Charlo
Campbellton
New Mills
132
Bonaventure
Île Miscou
11
Maisonnette Park
Île Lamèque
134
Sugarloaf Provincial Park
Grande Anse
Bas-Caraquet
Ville de Lamèque
Petit-Rocher
Pokeshaw PP
Caraquet
Nigadoo
11
VILLAGE HISTORIQUE ACADIEN
Shippagan
Bathurst
160
Tracadie
180
Sheila
VAL-COMEAU
Nepisiguit
Mt Carleton Provincial Park
8
11
Gulf
of
St. Lawrence
430
NEW BRUNSWICK
Bartibog Bridge
Miramichi Bay
420
Miramichi
Point Escuminac
117
108
11
KOUCHIBOUGUAC NATIONAL PARK
2
PRINCE EDWARD ISLAND
14
8
Doaktown
126
Richibucto
Rexton
Egmont Bay
Miramichi River
IRVING ECO CENTRE
Northumberland
2
Boiestown
123
116
Bouctouche
Bouctouche Harbour
LE PAYS DE LA SAGOUINE
Strait
Murray Beach PP
PARLEE BEACH
Parlee Beach PP
Cap-Pelé
Shediac
Grand Lake
15
10
112
BORE PARK
Dieppe
2
Moncton
Port Elgin
Cape Tormentine
CAPE JOURIMAIN NATURE CENTRE
FREDERICTON
2
Riverview
Memramcook
16
St. Joseph
106
Sackville
6
114
Aulac
104
SACKVILLE WATERFOWL PARK
Petitcodiac River
7
Fundy National Park
NOVA SCOTIA
2
111
Minas Basin
Saint John
1
Bay of Fundy
Minas Channel
Chignecto Bay
101
14
1
0   30 mi
0   30 km

© AVALON TRAVEL

coast and cuts an uninteresting beeline between Miramichi and Bouctouche. Coastal Highway 117 is far more scenic, running through Kouchibouguac National Park and curling out to remote Point Escuminac—a lofty shale plateau at Miramichi Bay's southeastern tip, frequented, in season, by thousands of migratory seabirds.

PLANNING YOUR TIME

Moncton, at the south end of the Acadian Coast, is central to the entire Maritimes region, so you'll probably pass through at least once on your Atlantic Canada vacation. The bustling downtown core is well worth exploring, with **Bore Park** a good starting point. (If you're traveling with children, they'll definitely want you to stop at the city's **Magnetic Hill** commercial attractions). Getting back to nature, a nearby highlight for bird-watchers is **Sackville Waterfowl Park.**

If you look at a map of New Brunswick, you'll see that the Acadian Coast extends the entire length of the province (it's 320 kilometers from Moncton to Campbellton), so to avoid returning along the coastal highway, plan on combining time along the Acadian Coast with the drive down the Saint John River valley to Fredericton—in effect, two of three legs of a loop around the entire province. This circuit will take four days at an absolute minimum, and preferably six. If the weather is warm, factor in some beach time, and there's no better place for this than **Parlee Beach,** just a short drive from Moncton. As you drive north, passing the coastal wilderness of **Kouchibouguac National Park,** it is impossible not to be intrigued by the pockets of Acadian culture. The best places to learn more about this culture's tragic history and revitalized present are **Le Pays de la Sagouine** and **Village Historique Acadien.**

Moncton

With a population of 65,000 (135,000 in Greater Moncton), this bustling city is the geographic center of the Maritimes. It does an admirable job of promoting its many and varied attractions, and it exudes a vitality and energy unlike anywhere else in the province. Visitors can take in two very different natural attractions—one related to the colossal Fundy tides, the other to a quirk of nature—while children will be attracted to Atlantic Canada's largest theme park. The bustling downtown core is packed with well-priced accommodations, good restaurants, and a lively nightlife.

The city is officially bilingual. About 30 percent of the population speaks French as a first language. So while most everyone also speaks English, knowledge of French will help the visitor.

DOWNTOWN SIGHTS

Downtown Moncton is centered on the north side of "The Bend," a sharp turn in the Petitcodiac River. The busy and bustling **Main Street,** a block in from the river, has brick sidewalks, old-time lampposts, and park benches beneath sapling trees. The following sights are ordered by distance from the water, starting at the riverfront and moving outward. There's no parking on Main Street. Instead, use one of the adjacent side streets and deposit a loonie ($1 coin) for an hour in a metered parking slot, or park in one of the nearby lots.

★ Bore Park

The huge Bay of Fundy tides reach Moncton twice daily, when the tidal bore, a lead wave up to 60 centimeters high, pulses up the Petitcodiac River. Within an hour or so, the muddy bed of the Petitcodiac—locally dubbed the "Chocolate River"—will be drowned under some 7.5 meters of water. The tourist information center at Resurgo Place can provide a tidal schedule. While the Moncton tourism folks put watching the tidal bore on their list of must-see attractions, many locals call it the Total Bore. In any case, the sight is most impressive at those times of the month when the tides are highest—around the full and new moons.

The best place to witness the tidal phenomenon is off Main Street at **Bore Park,** which is dotted with shade trees and park benches, and even has tiered seating overlooking the river. This is also the site of a riverside boardwalk.

Resurgo Place

Artifacts from the city's history—from the age of the Mi'kmaq to World War II—and touring national exhibits are displayed in the modern, architecturally stunning **Resurgo Place** (20 Mountain Rd., 506/856-4383, June-Aug. Mon.-Wed. and Fri.-Sat. 10am-5pm, Thurs. 10am-8pm, Sun. noon-5pm, adult $10, senior $8, child $5), which opened in 2014. Although the building is new, the architect concocted an interesting arrangement that combined the original native sandstone facade of the original city hall, which stood on the site, inside the building. Also within the building are the Transportation Discovery Centre, where the focus is on interactive displays; the Moncton Museum, telling the city's story; Moncton's main visitor center; and a gift shop.

Adjacent to Resurgo Place, the tidy, small **Free Meeting House**—Moncton's oldest building—dates to 1821 and served as a sanctuary for religious groups as diverse as Anglicans, Adventists, Jews, and Christian Scientists.

Thomas Williams House

A century ago, the Intercolonial Railroad brought the movers and shakers to town. Among them was Thomas Williams, the railroad's former treasurer. His 12-room Second Empire-style mansion, the **Thomas Williams House** (103 Park St., 506/857-0590, late June-late Aug. Wed.-Sun. 10am-5pm, donation) was built in 1883 and is now open to the public. Elegantly furnished with period pieces, it's a showpiece of the good old days. The Tea Room serves tea, coffee, and muffins in summer.

Galerie d'Art et Musée Acadien

The Acadian region is as creatively avant-garde as it is historic. At the Université de Moncton in the Clément Cormier Building, the **Galerie d'Art et Musée Acadien** (off Wheeler Blvd., 506/858-4088, June-Sept. Mon.-Fri. 10am-5pm, Sat.-Sun. 1pm-5pm, the

Bore Park

rest of the year Sat.-Sun. 1pm-4pm, adult $2), a gallery and museum, touches upon numerous aspects of Acadian culture in the combined exhibits. The university itself spreads across a large campus north of downtown. It is Atlantic Canada's sole French-speaking university and grants degrees in business, fine arts, science, education, nursing, and law.

MAGNETIC HILL

Magnetic Hill is an attraction in itself, but the surrounding area (generally also called Magnetic Hill) is dotted with commercial attractions, and if you're traveling with children, this part of the city will be the focus of your time in Moncton.

The namesake **Magnetic Hill** (506/853-3540, mid-May-early Sept. daily 8am-8pm) is just a hill, but if you believe your eyes, you'll agree it's one of the world's oddest. Is Magnetic Hill magnetic? It must be. The unassuming dirt road, which seems to defy the rules of logic, is said to be Canada's third most popular natural tourist attraction, behind Niagara Falls and the Canadian Rockies.

The hill's slope plays tricks on anything with wheels. Set your car at the hill's "bottom," shift into neutral, and release the brake. The car appears to coast backward *up* the hill.

Cars aren't the only things that defy gravity here. A stream alongside the road seems to flow uphill, too.

The illusion baffled Monctonians for decades. Before the 1900s, the local farmers fought the incline when they tried to haul wagons "down" the hill. Several decades later, reporters from Saint John discovered Magnetic Hill. Their newspaper coverage of the "natural phenomenon" brought a slew of spectators, and the stream of nonbelievers hasn't stopped since.

If you think a strange and otherworldly force powers Magnetic Hill, think again. For the record, the whole countryside hereabouts is tilted. Magnetic Hill forms the southern flank of 150-meter-high Lutes Mountain, northwest of Moncton. The hill is an optical illusion, and believe it or not, the hill's top crest is lower than the hill's "bottom." Try to walk the hill with your eyes closed. Your other senses will tell you that you are traveling down rather than up. To get there from downtown, follow Mountain Road northwest; from the TransCanada Highway, take Exit 488.

Attractions

So many tourists arrived to observe the illogical hill that an adjacent gift shop was opened

Resurgo Place

Moncton

in the 1970s, and the area quickly grew into a concentration of family-oriented attractions.

Magnetic Hill Zoo (125 Magic Mountain Rd., 506/877-7718, Apr.-June and Sept.-Nov. daily 10am-4pm, July-Aug. daily 9am-7pm, adult $15, senior $13, child $11) bills itself as the largest zoo in Atlantic Canada. It houses some 100 animal species, including zebras, reindeer, tigers, camels, wolves, and gibbons. A petting zoo entertains the wee ones, and the crowds gather daily at 2:30pm for Meet the Ranger.

Magic Mountain Waterpark (2875 Mountain Rd., 506/857-9283, late June-mid-Aug. daily 10am-7pm, mid-Aug.-end of Aug. daily 10am-6pm, $28 for those over 48 inches tall, $21 for between 42 and 48 inches, seniors $9.50) has an outdoor wave pool, numerous chutes, tube rides, and mini-golf.

The Boardwalk (506/852-9406, summer daily 9am-dusk) offers go-kart rides, mini-golf, batting cages, a driving range, and a playground. The adjacent **Wharf Village** (506/858-8841) is a shopping area featuring arts and crafts and a family-style restaurant overlooking an artificial pond.

ENTERTAINMENT AND EVENTS
Nightlife

Most of the drinking and dancing action happens along Main Street, where the college crowds gather at bars and nightclubs and tables spill onto the streets. The **Pump House Brewery** (5 Orange Ln., 506/855-2337, Mon.-Wed. 11am-midnight, Thurs. 11am-1am, Fri.-Sat. 11am-2am, Sun. noon-midnight) is a little quieter than most and

Downtown Moncton

has a sun-drenched patio out front. It brews its own beer, which is available on draught and in bottles.

Live music at the **Tide and Boar** (700 Main St., 506/857-9118, Mon.-Wed. 11am-midnight, Thurs.-Sat. 11am-2am, Sun. noon-midnight, $13-20) every Friday and Saturday night could be anything from up and coming Halifax bands to the most popular Canadian indie groups. At any time, it's a good place to sample craft beers from across North America and some of the most creative pub cooking in town.

For a quiet drink, **Le Galion,** in Château Moncton (100 Main St., 506/870-4444, daily from 11am) is a good choice. With seating inside and out, you get to enjoy the river scenery up close and can sip a beer while waiting for the tidal bore in a bright,

contemporary setting. In the Crowne Plaza Moncton Downtown, **Bin 1005** (1005 Main St., 506/854-6340, daily from 11am) is a typical upscale hotel lounge, with the bonus of an excellent wine list.

Oxygen (125 Westmorland St., 506/854-0265, daily from 9pm) is generally regarded as one of the province's hottest destinations for dance parties, with DJs spinning discs on weekends.

Theater

The Capitol (811 Main St., 506/856-4379, www.capitol.nb.ca) has been transformed from a 1920s vaudeville theater to a gracious symbol of the past. Today this lovely old grande dame, ornately decorated with frescoes and murals, glitters with concerts, ballets, shows, and film festivals.

Festivals and Events

Moncton hosts the **World Wine & Food Festival** (506/532-5333, www.wineexpo.ca) over the first week of November. It brings together wine representatives from around the world with celebrity chefs, but the ambience is anything but pompous as the general public gathers to soak up the worldly atmosphere at seminars, tastings, and dinners.

The mid-November **Festival International du Cinéma Francophone en Acadie** (506/855-6050, www.ficfa.com) is a major French-language film festival.

RECREATION
Centennial Park

At the western side of town, the 180-hectare **Centennial Park** (St. George Blvd., 506/853-3516, daily 9am-11pm) makes a pleasant place to picnic and relax amid woodlands, and offers hiking trails and a lake with a sandy beach. Summer activities include lawn bowling, swimming, tennis, and canoeing and paddling on the lake. In winter, lighted trails invite cross-country skiers, skaters, and hockey players to take to the frozen lake.

SHOPPING

Major shopping malls in the area include Dieppe's **Champlain Place** (corner of Paul St. and Champlain St., Mon.-Sat. 10am-9pm, Sun. noon-5pm), Atlantic Canada's largest mall, and **Northwest Centre Plaza** (1380 Mountain Rd.), a typical North American strip mall, but to sample the local flair for arts and crafts, you'll need to look elsewhere.

If you're in town on the weekend, head to **Moncton Market** (120 Westmorland St., www.marchemonctonmarket.ca, Sat. 7am-2pm) for local arts and crafts, as well as delicious foods from local farmers and suppliers. It's difficult to miss the bright pink facade of **Gifts Galore** (569 Main St., 506/857-9179, Mon.-Fri. 10am-9pm, Sat. 10am-5pm, Sun. noon-5pm), which carries a little bit of everything—glass, pottery, pewter, T-shirts, and more. It helps to speak French at some shops, such as **Galerie Sans Nom** (140 Botsford St.,

506/854-5381, Tues.-Wed. 10am-5pm, Thurs.-Fri. 11am-7pm), a cooperative where the emphasis is on contemporary arts and crafts.

FOOD

You might stumble on a few Acadian dishes, but most local restaurants keep it simple and straightforward, appealing to the college crowd with cheap food and energetic service.

Cafés

Main Street is the place to head for a coffee at a street-side table, and no one pours better drinks than **Cafe C'est la Vie** (785 Main St., 506/854-0994, Mon.-Wed. 7:30am-6pm, Thurs.-Fri. 7:30am-8pm, Sat. 9am-6pm, lunches under $10), where, in addition to the usual choices, the menu includes a mint latte and a caramelized macchiato brule. The food is also delicious and inexpensive, including soups, salads, and sandwiches. In the vicinity, **Calactus** (125 Church St., 506/388-4833, daily 11am-10pm, $11-17) is a vegetarian restaurant, but the coffee is excellent.

In a red-brick heritage building two blocks east of Café C'est la Vie, **Café Cognito** (700 Main St., 506/854-4888, Mon.-Fri. 7:30am-4:30pm, lunches $7-10) also has excellent coffee, along with chai lattes, daily-made soups, grilled sandwiches made to order, and baked pastries and treats. Outdoor tables add to the appeal.

Although it's away from downtown, to the northwest toward Magnetic Hill, **Café Codiac** (666 St. George Blvd., 506/854-7100, Mon.-Fri. 7am-6pm, Sat. 8am-5pm, Sun. 9am-5pm, lunches $5.50-8) is worth searching out for excellent coffee, delicious soups made daily, and a wide range of baked goodies.

Pubs

Most of the pubs along Main Street serve food, but the offerings at **Tide and Boar** (700 Main St., 506/857-9118, Mon.-Wed. 11am-midnight, Thurs.-Sat. 11am-2am, Sun. noon-midnight, $14-24) are a notch above the rest. The platters to share are a good way to start (or the Boar Poutine for the brave), before moving

ACADIAN COAST
MONCTON

on to parmesan-crusted haddock, beer-battered cod, or pizza with caramelized plums and goat cheese. Wash your meal down with a beer from the long list of choices or a house-made ginger beer and rum.

Pump House Brewery (5 Orange Ln., 506/855-2337, Mon.-Wed. 11am-midnight, Thurs. 11am-1am, Fri.-Sat. 11am-2am, Sun. noon-midnight, $12-22) has been around since the late 1990s, and it remains popular both for its handcrafted beer and well-priced food. Highlights are the wood-fired pizzas, including such varieties as roast vegetable and bacon cheeseburger.

Steak and Seafood

Stylish ★ **Maverick's** (Future Inns, 40 Lady Ada Blvd., 506/855-3346, Mon.-Thurs. 6:30am-10pm, Fri. 6:30am-11pm, Sat. 7:30am-11pm, Sun. 7:30am-10pm, $23-36) is out on the main highway through town. All the favorites are offered—an extra-thick cut of prime rib, tender rib eye, and a variety of strip loins—and they all come exactly how you ordered them. The menu also offers top-notch seafood, including boiled lobster. A well-rounded wine list adds to the appeal.

T-bones (Crowne Plaza Moncton, 1005 Main St., 506/854-6340, daily 6am-2pm and 5pm-10pm, $18-40) has a predictable wide-ranging menu that doesn't offend anyone, with choices that include everything from vegetarian fettuccine to 16-ounce namesake T-bone steaks.

Vegetarian

Along the main street, ★ **Calactus** (125 Church St., 506/388-4833, daily 11am-10pm, $11-17) is a cheery little vegetarian restaurant with a few outdoor tables on a patio. Ingredients are sourced locally, but cooking styles are taken from around the world, including in the selection of delicious pizzas (Indian, Greek, Mexican, and more). One of the favorites is the veggie burger with roasted potatoes and Caesar salad for just $15. House-made desserts and a drink list that varies from

organic wines to fruit smoothies rounds out this excellent choice for lunch or dinner.

Magnetic Hill

Overlooking the pond at Wharf Village is **Wharf Village Restaurant** (50 Magic Mountain Rd., 506/859-1812, May-Oct. daily 10am-8pm, lunches $8-13), which does a fine job feeding Magnetic Hill visitors familiar family fare at good value for the dollar. Seating is outside on a covered deck or inside with basic decor and air-conditioning. On the right side of the restaurant is a self-service counter hawking soup and sandwiches to go.

ACCOMMODATIONS AND CAMPING

Lodgings are conveniently concentrated in two main areas—downtown and at the city's northwestern corner, near Magnetic Hill. Overall, prices are reasonable, especially for the larger downtown properties.

$100-150

The three-story **Rodd Moncton** (434 Main St., 506/382-1664 or 800/565-7633, www.roddvacations.com, $135 s or d, extra for river views) overlooks Bore Park with 97 guest rooms and an outdoor pool (summer only). The rooms aren't particularly large, but are clean and comfortable, and the location still makes this place a good value, especially since a light breakfast is included.

On the eastern edge of downtown, ★ **Château Moncton** (100 Main St., 506/870-4444 or 800/576-4040, www.chateaumoncton.ca, $140-190 s or d) is a distinctive red-roofed chateau-style lodging overlooking the tidal bore. Guests enjoy 97 modern and spacious rooms and suites with wireless Internet access, an exercise room, voice mail, free local calls, and daily newspapers. Rates include a cooked breakfast. The hotel also has a riverside deck and a pleasant lounge.

The motels clustered around Magnetic Mountain (take Exit 488 from the

Château Moncton has a prime riverfront location.

$150-200

My pick for downtown accommodations is the ★ **Residence Inn** (600 Main St., 506/854-7100 or 888/236-2427, www.residenceinnmoncton.com, from $165 s or d), with 133 modern and spacious guest rooms in the heart of the city. Many units have one or two bedrooms, and all have kitchens. Other amenities include a surprisingly large indoor pool and a fitness room. Adding to the appeal, rates include a hot breakfast buffet.

Crowne Plaza Moncton (1005 Main St., 506/854-6340 or 866/854-4656, www.ihg.com, $189 s or d) comes complete with contemporary decor, the best beds in town, CD clock radios, and many other niceties. The in-house steakhouse and lounge save leaving the property in the evening. Other amenities include an indoor pool and a large fitness room.

Delta Beauséjour (750 Main St., 506/854-4344 or 888/890-3222, www.marriott.com, from $189 s or d) is equal to the Crowne Plaza in style, service, and facilities, but everything is a little less new. On the plus side, the 310 guest rooms are very spacious. Other facilities include a café, two restaurants, a lounge, and an indoor pool with a waterslide.

TransCanada Highway) are mostly within this price range. **Holiday Inn Express** (2515 Mountain Rd., 506/384-1050 or 800/465-4329, www.hiemoncton.com, $135 s or d) has the most facilities, with an indoor pool, hot tub, sauna, restaurant, lounge, business center, and family suites with bunk beds.

The folks at **Nor-West Motel** (1325 Mountain Rd., 506/384-1222 or 800/561-7904, www.norwestmotel.com, from $120 s or d) have done a great job of upgrading an older motel out near Magnetic Hill, with colorful flower arrangements out front adding to the appeal. A hot breakfast is included in the rates.

Travelodge Suites (2475 Mountain Rd., 506/852-7000 or 800/525-4055, www.travelodge.com, from $145 s or d) has 77 spacious, nicely appointed guest rooms with free in-room movies, work desks, and small fridges. A daily newspaper, wireless Internet access, and a hot buffet breakfast are included in the rates.

INFORMATION AND SERVICES

The city's main **Tourist Information Centre** (20 Mountain Rd., 506/8564383, www.moncton.ca, mid-May-early Sept. daily 8:30am-5:30pm) is in Resurgo Place, on the north side of downtown.

Both the **Moncton Hospital** (135 Macbeath Ave., 506/857-5111) and **Dr. Georges-L.-Dumont University Hospital Centre** (330 University Ave., 506/862-4000) are between Magnetic Hill and downtown. For the **RCMP,** call 911 or 506/857-2400.

GETTING THERE

Moncton lies in the geographic heart of the three Maritimes provinces, so even if you don't make the city a destination in itself, you will probably pass through on your travels.

Car

Driving time to Moncton from Saint John (155 kilometers to the southwest) is around 80 or 90 minutes. From the provincial capital of Fredericton (180 kilometers west), the drive is slightly longer. For those continuing to Prince Edward Island, allow an hour to reach the Confederation Bridge, 92 kilometers to the east.

Air

Greater Moncton Airport (777 Aviation Ave., Dieppe, 506/856-5444, www.cyqm.ca) is 10 kilometers from downtown Moncton on Champlain Street/Highway 132 (a continuation of Main Street in Moncton) in adjacent Dieppe. The airport has a food court, a lounge, wireless Internet, and car rental desks (Avis, Budget, Hertz, and National). A metered taxi ride with **Air Cab** (506/857-2000) to Main Street in Moncton costs about $20 one-way.

The airport is served by **Air Canada** (888/247-2262) from Halifax, Montréal, and Toronto and by **WestJet** (800/538-5696) from Toronto, Hamilton, and Calgary.

From **Halifax Stanfield International Airport,** allow around two hours for the 230-kilometer trip north along Highway 102 and then west along the TransCanada Highway to Moncton (without a single traffic light en route).

Train and Bus

Moncton is served by **VIA Rail** (1240 Main St., 506/857-9830 or 800/561-3952, www.viarail.ca) on its route between Montréal and Halifax (four hours, $30). The railway station is behind Highfield Square on Main Street.

By virtue of its central location, Moncton is a hub for **Maritime Bus** (1240 Main St., 506/854-2023, www.maritimebus.com). Services run to Saint John, Fredericton, Charlottetown, Halifax, and along the Acadian Coast to Campbellton from the Maritime Bus Terminal, which is part of the main railway station on the west side of downtown. Buses depart three times daily for Saint John (two hours, $34). From Halifax, the thrice-daily service takes around four hours to reach Moncton ($49).

GETTING AROUND

Codiac Transit (506/857-2008) operates local bus service (Mon.-Wed. and Sat. 6:20am-7pm, Thurs.-Fri. 6:20am-10:15pm). Fare is $2.25 per sector.

Air Cab (506/857-2000) charges $3.85 to start and about $1.75 per kilometer.

Major car rental companies with downtown and airport desks are **Avis** (506/855-7212), **Budget** (506/857-3993), **Hertz** (506/858-8525), and **National** (506/382-6114).

Southeast from Moncton

Geologically, the area southeast of Moncton is related to the Bay of Fundy, but as it is separated from the rest of the Fundy Coast, it is covered here. Driving nonstop, you'll cross over to Nova Scotia in a little over 30 minutes and be in Halifax in three hours.

MEMRAMCOOK

Take Highway 106 southeast from Moncton for 20 kilometers to reach the village of Memramcook and **Monument-Lefebvre National Historic Site** (488 Centrale St., 506/758-9808, June-mid-Oct. daily 9am-5pm, mid-Oct.-May Mon.-Sat. 9am-5pm, adult $4, senior $3.50, child $2), which is dedicated to the memory of Father Camille Lefebvre, founder of Canada's first French-language university. Within the historic Monument-Lefebvre building on the Memramcook Institute campus, the **Acadian Odyssey** exhibit explains Acadian survival with a series of displays.

Getting There

Memramcock is just over 20 kilometers (20 minutes) southeast of Moncton via Highway 106. To get there from Fredericton, take Highway 2 east for 180 kilometers, then Highway 106 southeast for 20 kilometers (2.5 hours).

SACKVILLE

The 17th-century settlers who founded Sackville, 45 kilometers southeast of Moncton, emigrated from around the estuaries of western France, so they were experienced in wresting tidelands from the sea. By creating an extensive system of dikes called *aboideaux,* they reclaimed thousands of acres of Chignecto Isthmus marsh and brought the extremely fertile alluvial lands into agricultural production. Their raised dikes can be seen around Sackville and into Nova Scotia.

Mount Allison Academy (later University) was founded here in 1843; a "Female Branch" was opened 11 years later. In 1875, the university gained the distinction of being the first in the British Empire to grant a college degree to a woman.

The beautiful campus, surrounded by stately houses and tree-shaded streets, is still

Sackville Waterfowl Park

at the heart of this town. A number of artists have chosen Sackville as their home, and one of the best places to see their work is at Mount Allison University's **Owens Art Gallery** (61 York St., 506/364-2574, Mon.-Fri. 10am-5pm, Sat.-Sun. 1pm-5pm, free). The Owens ranks as one of the major galleries in the province and emphasizes avant-garde work by local, regional, and national artists.

★ Sackville Waterfowl Park

If you're short on time and can stop at only one of the area's several wildlife sanctuaries, make it the **Sackville Waterfowl Park** (daily dawn-dusk), a 22-hectare reserve where more than 170 bird species have been recorded. The main entrance, just a few blocks north of downtown, is easy to miss but offers interesting park displays. From this point, the sanctuary spreads out, with trails routed through bush and bleached wooden walkways crossing wetlands. Over 150 bird species have been recorded in the park; ducks, great blue herons, teals, and bitterns are common, while spotting loons, Canada geese, sandpipers, and peregrine falcons is possible. At the entrance to the park is **Sackville Visitor Information Centre** (34 Mallard Dr., 506/364-4967, May-mid-Oct. daily 9am-5pm, until 7pm in summer), with displays related to the surrounding bird-rich environment.

Food and Accommodations

For a place to stay, consider ★ **Marshlands Inn** (55 Bridge St., 506/536-0170, www.marshlands.nb.ca, $135-155 s or d), among the province's best-value historic lodgings. The inn, built in the 1850s, got its name from an early owner, who christened the mansion in honor of the adjacent Tantramar Marshes. The resplendent white wooden heritage inn sits back from the road under shady trees and offers 20 guest rooms furnished with antiques and a dining room of local renown. Open daily for guests and nonguests, the dining room is smart and elegant, with many steak and seafood choices ($17-30), including crepes filled with lobster, shrimp, and scallops.

Dorchester Peninsula

Another prime birding site is not far from Sackville. From Dorchester, 14 kilometers west of Sackville on Highway 106, turn off on Highway 935. The backcountry gravel road loops south around the **Dorchester Peninsula**—the digit of land separating Shepody Bay from the Cumberland Basin. Some 50,000 semipalmated sandpipers nest mid-July-mid-September between Johnson Mills and Upper Rockport, where the road loops back toward Sackville. Roosting sites lie along pebble beaches and mudflats, and the birds are most lively at feeding time (low tide). Smaller flocks of dunlins, white-rumped sandpipers, and sanderlings inhabit the area late September-October.

Getting There

To get to Sackville from Moncton, take Highway 2 southeast for about 50 kilometers (30 minutes). From Fredericton, take Highway 2 east for 230 kilometers (2.5 hours).

AULAC AND VICINITY

The last town before crossing into Nova Scotia is Aulac, on the Bay of Fundy side of the TransCanada Highway at the turnoff to the Confederation Bridge.

Fort Beauséjour

Eight kilometers east of Sackville, a signpost marks the turnoff from the TransCanada Highway to the **Fort Beauséjour National Historic Site** (111 Fort Beauséjour Rd., 506/364-5080, June-mid-Oct. daily 9am-5pm, adult $4, senior $3.50, child $2), overlooking the Cumberland Basin just west of the Nova Scotia border. Continue on the road to the fort ruins, which mark France's last-ditch military struggle against the British, who threatened Acadia centuries ago. France lost the fort in 1755 after a two-week siege. The Brits renamed it Fort Cumberland and used it in 1776 to repel an attack by American revolutionaries. The fort stood ready for action in the War of 1812, though no enemy appeared. Fort Cumberland was abandoned in the 1830s, and nature soon reclaimed the site. Some of the ruins have since been restored. Facilities include a picnic area and a museum-visitors center with exhibits on life in the old days.

Tintamarre Sanctuary
Tintamarre National Wildlife Area fans out beyond the fort ruins. Continue on Highway 16 for about 10 kilometers to Jolicure, a village at the reserve's edge. No trails penetrate the 1,990-hectare mix of marshes, uplands, old fields, forests, and lakes. A few dikes provide steady ground through some of the terrain, but you are asked to stay on the roads encircling the area to do your bird-watching. Amid the cattails, sedges, and bulrushes, sightings include migratory mallards, grebes, red-winged blackbirds, yellow warblers, swamp swallows, common snipes, black ducks, Virginia rails, and bitterns; short-eared owls take wing at dusk. Bring binoculars—and insect repellent. The area can be thick with mosquitoes.

Getting There
Aulac is 55 kilometers (30 minutes) southeast of Moncton via Highway 2. From Fredericton, take Highway 2 east for 235 kilometers (2.5 hours).

Getting There

Cape Tormentine is just over 50 kilometers (45 minutes) northeast of Aulac via Highway 16. From Fredericton, it's 280 kilometers (3.5 hours) via Highways 2 and 16.

West to Shediac

A few fine, quiet beaches dot the Cap-Pelé area, farther west on Highway 15. At Gagnon Beach, **Camping Gagnon Beach** (506/577-2519 or 800/658-2828, www.gagnonbeach. com, late May-mid-Sept., $27-45) has 208 sites with full hookups plus a separate wooded tenting area.

SHEDIAC

The self-proclaimed "Lobster Capital of the World," 20 kilometers northeast of Moncton, Shediac backs up its claim with the **world's largest lobster**—an 11-meter-long, cast-iron sculpture by Winston Bronnum sitting beside the road into town. For the real stuff, head for the town's restaurants, which have a reputation for some of the province's best lobster dinners.

★ Parlee Beach

This is *the* beach getaway for Moncton residents, and it can be crowded on weekends.

Parlee Beach Provincial Park (506/533-3363) protects one of many beaches strung out to the east. This placid three-kilometer-long beach is popular for the warmth of the water, which reaches 24°C (75°F) in summer. The entrance is from the eastern edge of Shediac, along an access road that ends at a massive parking lot behind low sand dunes. Behind the beach are changing rooms, a café, and a restaurant, while down on the beach swimming is supervised by trained lifeguards. Access is $13 per vehicle per day (collected in summer only).

Food

Overlooking the water near the end of the road out to Pointe-de-Chene Marina (turn off the highway on the east side of town), you'll find ★ **Captain Dan's** (506/533-2855, daily 11am-10pm, $12-27), a super-casual, perennially crowded bar and grill with a beachin' atmosphere and great food. Hang loose, watch the boats, and feel your blood pressure drop.

Accommodations and Camping

The beautiful white **Auberge Inn Thyme** (310 Main St., 506/532-6098 or 877/466-8496,

looking out across Cape Jourimain

www.innthyme.com, $120-145 s, $125-165 d) was built in 1911 for a Shediac dentist, but it has been thoroughly modernized, with seven contemporary guest rooms and amenities like wireless Internet and a small café. The inn sits back from the road beneath stately trees. It's near the western edge of town, just a quick stroll from the beach.

In the heart of Shediac, ★ **Tait House** (293 Main St., 506/532-4233 or 888/532-4233, www.maisontaithouse.com, from $169 s or d) is a beautifully restored 1911 mansion with historic guest rooms complemented by contemporary features, such as polished hardwood floors and plush mattresses topped with white linens. The in-house restaurant offers a menu of local ingredients prepared with cooking styles from throughout Europe. Rates include a continental breakfast.

Parlee Beach Provincial Park (45 Parlee Beach Rd., 506/533-3363, June-Aug., $28-38) is within walking distance of the beach. It has hot showers, a playground, and more than 165 sites. It's also very popular, so make reservations as far ahead as possible through the government website https://parcsnbparks.ca.

Getting There

Shediac is a little more than 20 kilometers (25 minutes) northeast of Moncton via Highway 11/Highway 15. To get there from Fredericton, head east on Highway 2 for 180 kilometers, then northeast for 20 kilometers on Highway 11/Highway 15. Allow just over two hours.

BOUCTOUCHE

North of Shediac, Highway 11 zips through a wooded corridor, sacrificing scenery for efficiency. For a taste of the slower pace of rural coastal Acadia, strike out on any of the local highways (such as 530, 475, or 505) to the east, which hug the coast and lead to quiet beaches at Saint-Thomas, Saint-Edouard-de-Kent, and Cap-Lumière. Along the way, the routes come together at Bouctouche, 30 kilometers north of Shediac. You can learn about two centuries of Acadian culture at **Le Musée de Kent** (150 Chemin du Couvent, 506/743-5005, July-early Sept. Mon.-Sat. 9am-5:30pm, Sun. noon-6pm, adult $4, senior $3, child $2), in a restored 1880 convent two kilometers east of downtown, but the two main local attractions are Le Pays de la Sagouine and Irving Eco-Centre.

ACADIAN COAST
STRAIT COAST

sunset over Parlee Beach Provincial Park

★ Le Pays de la Sagouine

Author Antonine Maillet is renowned in the literary world for her colorful descriptions of Acadian life, and so there is no better place to re-create the ambience of her work than this lively outdoor theme park in her hometown of Bouctouche. **Le Pays de la Sagouine** (57 Acadie St., 506/743-1400, late June-early Sept. daily 10am-4:30pm, adult $20, senior and child $15) is on a peninsula and islet with a hamlet of houses and other buildings, a reception center, and a craft shop. The highly recommended guided tour (included in admission) leaves daily at 11am and 3pm. Evening dinner theater (in French) is the site's big draw; you'll have a choice of seafood, Canadian, or—the best bet—traditional Acadian fare. And your meal will be accompanied by Acadian music, which might be in any number of styles. The show only is adult $60, child $30, or pay $70 and $40, respectively, for park admission, dinner, and show.

Irving Eco-Centre

Continue through town beyond Le Musée de Kent and turn north up the coast to reach **Irving Eco-Centre** (Hwy. 475, 506/743-2600, June and Sept. daily 10am-5pm, July-Aug. daily 10am-6pm, free), which preserves the ecosystem surrounding a 12-kilometer-long sand dune along Bouctouche Bay. The ecosystem was created as a public relations gesture by New Brunswick megacorporation J. D. Irving Ltd. (which conducts petroleum, logging, you name it). A two-kilometer-long wheelchair-accessible boardwalk leads from an interpretive center through the dunes. Other trails traverse forest and marshland. Naturalists work on-site May-November, doing ecology research and leading school field trips. Bird-watchers will spot great blue herons, piping plovers, and long-winged terns, among other species.

Getting There

Bouctouche is about 35 kilometers (25 minutes) north of Shediac along Highway 11. To get there from Fredericton, drive east on Highway 2 for 180 kilometers, northeast on Highway 11/Highway 15 for 20 kilometers, then northwest on Highway 11 for 35 kilometers. Allow 2.5 hours.

Le Pays de la Sagouine

★ KOUCHIBOUGUAC NATIONAL PARK

The Northumberland Strait coast ends at **Kouchibouguac National Park,** a 238-square-kilometer gem of a park that takes its name from the Mi'kmaq word for "river of the long tides"—a reference to the waterway that meanders through the midsection of the low-lying park. Some pronounce it "KOOSH-ee-buh-gwack," others say "kee-gee-boo-QUACK," and Parks Canada says it's "kou-she-boo-gwack." You'll hear many other variations.

Slender barrier islands and sandy beaches and dunes, laced with marram grass and false heather, face the gulf along a 25-kilometer front. A gray seal colony occupies one of the offshore islands. In the park's interior, boardwalks ribbon the mudflats, freshwater marshes, and bogs, and nature trails probe the woodlands and fields.

Park Entry

Entry fees are charged mid-May-mid-October. A one-day pass is adult $8, senior $7, child $4 (to a maximum of $20 per vehicle).

Recreation

The land and coast are environmentally sensitive; park officials prefer that you stay on the trails and boardwalks or use a bike to get around on the 30 kilometers of biking and hiking trails. Naturalist-led programs and outings are organized throughout summer. Check at the Visitor Reception Centre and campgrounds for a schedule.

If time is limited, my suggestion is to head straight for the **Kelly's Beach Boardwalk** trail, which leads from a large parking lot over shallow channels and across sand dunes to a beautiful stretch of beach, from where you can take off your shoes and head in either direction for as long as you like. Other trails that explore the park's varied ecosystems include the **Pines** and **Salt Marsh** trails, and the 1.8-kilometer **Bog** trail. You can take longer hikes on the **Clair-Fontaine** (3.4 kilometers), **Osprey** (5.1 kilometers), and **Kouchibouguac** (14 kilometers; allow five hours) trails.

The Black, St. Louis, Kouchibouguac, and other rivers that weave through the park are wonderful to explore by canoe, kayak, rowboat, or pedal boat. Those watercraft, as well as fishing equipment and bicycles, are available at **Ryan's Rental Centre** (506/876-3733, mid-June-early Sept. daily 8am-9pm). Fishing in the national park also requires a license:

Kouchibouguac National Park

$10 per day or $35 for an annual license. Swimming is supervised at **Kelly's Beach** in summer, while swimming at Callander's and other beaches is unsupervised.

Camping

Within the park are two campgrounds. Finding a site shouldn't be a problem, except in July and August. At these times, reservations through the **Parks Canada Campground Reservation Service** (877/737-3783, www.pccamping.ca) are wise. The cost is $12 per booking plus the campsite fee.

South Kouchibouguac Campground (mid-May-mid-Oct., $28-33) offers 265 unserviced sites and 46 sites with power hookups. Civilized comforts include showers, flush toilets, kitchen shelters, firewood ($7 per bundle), launderettes, and a campers' store near the beach.

Côte-à-Fabien Campground (mid-June-early Sept., $16) has 32 primitive campsites but few facilities and no hookups.

Information

Make your first stop the **Visitor Reception Centre** (1 km inside the main entrance off Hwy. 134, 506/876-2443, www.pc.gc.ca, mid-May-mid-June and early Sept.-mid-Oct. daily 9am-5pm, mid-June-early Sept. daily 8am-8pm). For a memorable introduction, be sure to see the 20-minute slide presentation, *Kouchibouguac*. Campsite registration is handled at the center, and information on activities, outdoor presentations, and evening programs is posted here, too.

Getting There

Kouchibouguac National Park is nearly 100 kilometers (one hour) north of Shediac via Highway 11. From Fredericton, drive east on Highway 2 for 180 kilometers, northeast on Highway 11/Highway 15 for 20 kilometers, then northwest for 100 kilometers on Highway 11. Allow at least three hours.

Miramichi River

The gorgeous Miramichi (meer-ma-SHEE) River and its myriad tributaries drain much of the interior of eastern New Brunswick. The river enjoys a wide reputation as one of the best (if not *the* best) Atlantic salmon waters in the world.

Leaving the conurbation of Miramichi near the river's mouth, Highway 8 follows the river valley southwest for most of its length. Most of the valley is lightly populated.

MIRAMICHI

Don't get too confused if that old road map of New Brunswick you're using doesn't seem to jibe with the signs you're seeing out the car window. No, the cities of Chatham and Newcastle didn't disappear; in 1995 they amalgamated into a single municipal entity called Miramichi. The former Chatham

is now Miramichi East, and the former Newcastle is Miramichi West.

Old French maps of this area show the Miramichi River as the Rivière des Barques, the "River of Ships." From as early as the last quarter of the 18th century, the locally abundant timber and the deepwater estuary made this an excellent location for the shipbuilding industry. The Cunard brothers began their lucrative shipbuilding empire at Chatham in 1826 and built some of the finest vessels of their day. The industry thrived for half a century and then faltered and faded, leaving no physical evidence—outside of museums—that it ever existed.

Sights

At Miramichi East, before Highway 11 crosses to the north side of the river, **St. Michael's Basilica** (10 Howard St., 506/778-5150, daily

8am-4pm, free) is a distinctive 1920 sandstone church overlooking the river.

Across the river and farther southwest along Highway 8 is **Miramichi West** (formerly Newcastle), a pleasant river town with lots of old buildings that center on a small square hosting a memorial to Lord Beaverbrook. One of the most powerful newspapermen in British history, he was raised at what is now known as **Beaverbrook House** (518 King George Hwy., 506/622-5572, June-early Sept. Mon.-Sat. 9am-5pm, Sun. 1pm-5pm, adult $5), a small museum dedicated to his life and links to New Brunswick. If it's a warm sunny day, head down to **Ritchie Wharf Park** (Ledden St.), a former shipbuilding yard that has been spruced up with riverfront shops and cafés, a nautically themed playground, and a gazebo where live music is performed on Sunday evenings.

Festivals and Events

In the mid-19th century, Middle Island, a river island just east of town, was the destination of thousands of Irish emigrants, many of them fleeing the catastrophic potato famine of the 1840s. Their descendants are still in the region, and since 1984 the area has celebrated its Irish heritage with **Canada's Irish Festival** (506/778-8810, www.canadasirishfest.com). The three-day event in mid-July includes concerts, dances, a parade, lectures and music workshops, booths selling Irish mementos and books, and the consumption of a good deal of beer.

The first week of August is the five-day **Miramichi Folksong Festival** (506/622-1780, www.miramichifolksongfestival.com), which opens with an outdoor gospel concert and continues with a shindig of traditional and contemporary singing, dancing, and fiddling.

Food

1809 Restaurant (Rodd Miramichi River, 1809 Water St., Miramichi East, 506/773-3111, Sun.-Thurs. 7am-10pm, Fri.-Sat. 7am-11pm, $15-26), on the south side of the river, has a dependable breakfast, lunch, and dinner menu, with lots of outdoor riverside seating in summer and an indoor log fireplace to keep diners warm during winter. Salmon is the specialty, and rather than including it in specific dishes, you can order it cooked in one of six ways (poached, grilled, blackened, etc.) with a variety of sauces (pineapple mango chutney, mayonnaise, and more), all for $24 with accompaniments.

Some of the oldest Miramichi buildings lie on the south side of the river.

Salmon Fishing on the Miramichi

Fly-fishing is the only method allowed for taking Atlantic salmon. Fish in the 13- to 18-kilogram range are not unusual; occasionally, anglers land specimens weighing up to 22 kilograms. The salmon season runs mid-May-mid-October. Nonresidents are required to hire guides, who are plentiful hereabouts.

Riverside fishing resorts, which let you drop a line in rustic elegance, are a popular way to enjoy the piscatorial experience. They're not cheap, however. One of the best and most historic is **Upper Oxbow Outdoor Adventures** (2260 Route 420, near Trout Brook, 506/622-8834 or 888/227-6100, www.upperoxbow.com), which has been in operation since 1823 through five generations of the same family. The company offers day trips ($210 pp, guides and equipment included), but most anglers stay overnight on packages that typically cost from $350 per person per day, including meals, accommodations, and guiding.

A more luxurious option is **Pond's Resort** (Porter Cove Rd., Sillikers, 506/369-2612 or 877/971-7663, www.pondsresort.com), which charges $475 per person per day for lodging in a riverside log cabin, meals, and guided fishing.

Accommodations and Camping

Step back in time at the **Governor's Mansion Inn** (62 St. Patrick's Dr., 506/622-3036 or 877/647-2642, www.governorsmansion.ca, $89-159 d), which dates to the 1860s and was once used as the official residence of New Brunswick's lieutenant governor. This historic home is in a quiet out-of-town setting across the road from the Miramichi River. The four rooms have en suite bathrooms, and two have river views and king beds. Breakfast is extra and dinner is available on weekends.

At the upper end of the price range is the **Rodd Miramichi River** (1809 Water St., Miramichi East, 506/773-3111 or 800/565-7633, www.roddvacations.com, $135-165 s or d), a modern riverside complex where rooms are painted in warm heritage colors. Amenities include a restaurant and an indoor pool.

Enclosure Campground (8 Enclosure Rd., 506/622-0680, www.enclosurecampground.com, $28-32) is in a pleasant riverside location 10 kilometers south of town along Highway 8. It offers over 100 campsites, hiking trails, a heated pool and hot tub, kitchen shelters, a café with Wi-Fi Internet access, and a playground.

Information

Miramichi Visitor Information Centre (199 King St., 506/778-8444, www.discovermiramichi.com, June-Aug. daily 10am-5pm) is beside Highway 11 as it enters town from the south. Wi-Fi Internet access is free, and there's a short trail for walking your dog.

Getting There

Miramichi is 130 kilometers (1.5 hours) north of Shediac via Highway 11. From Fredericton, Mirimichi is 175 kilometers (2-2.5 hours) northeast on Highway 8.

MIRAMICHI TO FREDERICTON

From Miramichi, it's 175 kilometers southwest along the Miramichi River to Fredericton, the capital of New Brunswick. The route is a handy highway if you're planning to drive a loop around the province, but aside from the rural scenery, the drive's biggest draw is salmon fishing.

Doaktown

Crossing through the deep interior of the province, Highway 8 runs alongside the famed salmon-rich Miramichi River to Doaktown, 86 kilometers southwest of Miramichi. Squire Robert Doak from Scotland founded the town and gave it a boom start with gristmills and paper mills in the early 1800s. The squire's white wooden house (with some original furnishings) and nearby barn have been set aside as **Doak Historic Site** (386 Main St., 506/365-2026, July-Sept. Mon.-Sat. 9am-5pm, Sun. noon-5pm, donation).

Also in town, the **Atlantic Salmon Museum** (263 Main St., 506/365-7787, June-Sept. Mon.-Sat. 9am-5pm, Sun. noon-5pm, adult $5, senior $4, child $3) will be especially interesting to anglers. Exhibits depict the life cycle and habitat of this king of game fish, as well as the history of the art of catching it (including a collection of rods, reels, and gaudily attractive flies). Live salmon specimens at various stages of development swim in the aquariums.

GETTING THERE

Doaktown is about 80 kilometers (1.5 hours) southwest of Miramichi via Highway 8. Coming from Fredericton, it's a 50-kilometer (45-minute) drive northeast along Highway 8.

Boiestown

Another well-conceived museum is the **Central New Brunswick Woodmen's Museum** (6342 Hwy. 8, 506/369-7214, June-mid-Oct. daily 9:30am-5pm, adult $6, senior $5, child $3), which spreads over 15 acres along Highway 8 near Boiestown. The museum's exhibits explain forestry's past and present. Among the buildings are replicas of a sawmill and a blacksmith shop, wheelwright shop, trapper's cabin, bunkhouse, and cookhouse. A Forestry Hall of Fame remembers the Paul Bunyans of New Brunswick's timber industry, and a miniature train makes a 15-minute loop through the grounds.

GETTING THERE

Boiestown is about 110 kilometers (1.5 hours) southwest of Miramichi via Highway 8 and 65 kilometers (1 hour) northeast of Fredericton on Highway 8.

Baie des Chaleurs

North of Miramichi Bay, the Acadian peninsula juts northeast into the Gulf of St. Lawrence. One side of the peninsula faces the Gulf of St. Lawrence, while the other side fronts the Baie des Chaleurs. In contrast to the wild Gulf of St. Lawrence, the shallower Baie des Chaleurs is warm and calm. Busy seaports dot the eastern coast of the bay—the region's commercial fishing fleets lie anchored at Bas-Caraquet, Caraquet, and Grande-Anse. Interspersed between the picturesque harbors are equally beautiful peninsulas, coves, and beaches. Swimming is especially pleasant along the sheltered beaches, where the shallow sea heats up to bathtub warmth in summer. Across the bay, Québec's Gaspé Peninsula is usually visible, sometimes with startling clarity when conditions are right. From Bathurst west, the fishing villages give way to industrial towns.

ACADIAN PENINSULA
Bartibog Bridge

It's a 10-minute drive on Highway 11 from Miramichi to this bayside town, where **MacDonald Farm Heritage Site** (600 Hwy. 11, 506/778-6085, late June-early Sept. Tues.-Sun. 10am-4pm, adult $4, senior $3, child $2) re-creates a Scottish settler's life in 1784. Guides take visitors through the two-story stone farmhouse, fields, orchards, and outbuildings.

Val-Comeau

Farther north on Highway 11, straddling a narrow peninsula jutting into the Gulf of St. Lawrence, **Camping Plage Val-Comeau**

Acadian Deportation

After the signing of the Treaty of Utrecht in 1713, England had demanded but not enforced an oath of allegiance from the Acadians who lived under its jurisdiction. By the 1750s, however, the British decided to demand loyalty. Those who refused to sign the oath of allegiance were rounded up and deported, and their villages and farmlands burned.

The Acadians being deported were herded onto ships bound for the English colonies on the Eastern seaboard or any place that would accept them. Some ships docked in England, others in France, and still others in France's colonies in the Caribbean. As the ports wearied of the human cargo, many of them refused the vessels entry, and the ships returned to the high seas to search for other ports willing to accept the Acadians.

In one of the period's few favorable events, the Spanish government offered the refugees free land in Louisiana, and many settled there in 1784, where they became known as Cajuns. Many Acadians fought the British in guerrilla warfare or fled to the hinterlands of Cape Breton Island, Prince Edward Island, New Brunswick, and Québec.

Exact deportation numbers are unknown. Historians speculate that 10,000 French inhabitants lived in Acadia in 1755; by the time the deportation had run its course in 1816, only 25 percent of them remained. The poet Longfellow distilled the tragedy in his *Evangeline,* a fictional story of two lovers divided by the events.

(506/393-7150, June-mid-Sept., $28-38) is a large campground with spacious sites, beach swimming, and a playground. The peninsula itself is interesting for lush sphagnum bogs, formed when the last ice sheet melted and pooled without a place to drain on the flat terrain. Seabirds inhabit the surrounding nutrient-rich marshes, and birdlife is prolific.

Shippagan

New Brunswick's largest commercial fishing fleet is based in this sheltered bay at the tip of the Acadian Peninsula, 110 kilometers northeast of Miramichi (allow at least 90 minutes). **New Brunswick Aquarium and Marine Centre** (100 Aquarium St., 506/336-3013, June-late Sept. daily 10am-6pm, adult $9, senior and child $7) opens up the world of gulf fishing with exhibits and viewing and touch tanks holding over 100 native fish species.

Camping Shippagan (4 km west of town, 506/336-3960, www.camping.shippagan.com, June-Sept., $25.50-35) enjoys a great location, right on the water with a nice beach. Amenities include firewood, showers and washrooms, kitchen shelters, a picnic area, a launderette, and organized activities through July and August.

Getting There

Continuing north from Miramichi, the options are to take Highway 8 directly north to Bathurst (75 kilometers, well under one hour) or detour along the Acadian Peninsula (via Highway 11) to Shippagan and rejoin the main highway at Bathurst. Total distance for this second option is around 200 kilometers, but you should allow at least three hours since the road passes through many towns.

ÎLE LAMÈQUE

Offshore of Shippagan, Île Lamèque noses into the gulf at the brow of the Acadian Peninsula. Connected to the mainland by a bridge, the island changes with the seasons: Spring brings a splendid show of wildflowers; summer brings wild blueberries ripening on the barrens; autumn transforms the landscape to a burnished red. The spruce trees here are bent and dwarfed by the relentless sea winds, but oysters, moon snails, blue mussels, and jackknife clams thrive along the beautiful white-sand beaches.

Lamèque International Baroque Music Festival

Île Lamèque is best known for the late July

Lamèque International Baroque Music Festival (506/344-3261, www.festivalbaroque.com), as unlikely as that may seem out here among the peat bogs and fishing villages. It is the only festival in North America dedicated to the celebration of music from the baroque period (1600-1760) and has been attracting the world's best early music performers since the early 1970s. The setting is superb—almost divine—within the acoustically perfect 1913 Church Sainte-Cecile.

Accommodations

The fanciest digs on the island are at **Auberge des Compagnons** (11 rue Principale, Lamèque, 506/344-7766 or 866/344-7762, $125-190), a modern 16-room lodge with sweeping water views. The restaurant serves a buffet-style breakfast, which is extra.

Getting There

Île Lamèque is 125 kilometers (two hours) north of Miramichi via Highway 11, then Highway 113 into and through Shippagan. From Fredericton, head 175 kilometers northeast on Highway 8 to Mirimichi and on to Île Lamèque, for a 300-kilometer, four-hour drive.

CARAQUET

From the south, Highway 11 lopes into town and turns into a boulevard lined with shops, lodgings, and sights. Established in 1758, picturesque Caraquet (pop. 4,200), 32 kilometers west of Shippagan, is northern New Brunswick's oldest French settlement and is known as Acadia's cultural heart.

Sights and Recreation

★ **VILLAGE HISTORIQUE ACADIEN**
Ten kilometers west of Caraquet, **Village Historique Acadien** (14311 Rte. 11, Rivière du Nord, 506/726-2600, mid-June-late Sept. daily 10am-6pm, adult $20, senior $16, families $45) provides a sensory journey through early Acadia. To re-create the period 1780-1890, more than 40 rustic houses and other authentic buildings were transported to this 1,133-hectare site and restored. The buildings—including a church, smithy, school, printing shop, carpenter's shop, gristmill, farmhouses, and others—are spread across woods and fields along the North River. You walk the dusty lanes or hop aboard a horse-drawn wagon to get from one building to the next, where costumed "residents" describe their daily lives, jobs, and surroundings in French and English. Out in the park, two "post

ACADIAN COAST
BAIE DES CHALEURS

Village Historique Acadien

houses" serve sandwiches, snacks, and drinks. The site also holds **La Table des Ancetres,** which serves typical hearty Acadian dishes at reasonable prices.

THE ACADIAN MUSEUM
The **Acadian Museum** (15 St-Pierre Blvd., 506/726-2682, June-mid-Sept. Mon.-Sat. 10am-6pm, Sun. 1pm-6pm, adult $4, child $1.50) is a less ambitious look at local history than the waterfront Village Historique Acadien, but it's still a worthwhile stop. The adjacent **Carrefour de la Mer** (51 St-Pierre Blvd., 506/726-2688), whose name translates to "Crossroads of the Sea," encompasses the local information center, an art gallery, a playground, and a restaurant.

Festivals and Events
Caraquet is the place to be for early August's two-week **Festival Acadien** (www.festivalacadien.ca), one of the province's best-attended events. It includes the blessing of the huge fishing fleet by the local Roman Catholic clergy; jazz, pop, and classical music concerts ($16-26); live theater; food and drink; and the Tintamarre, a massive street celebration on Acadia Day (Aug. 15).

Food and Accommodations
The distinctive three-story, crisply colored red-and-green ★ **Hotel Paulin** (134 St-Pierre Blvd. W., 506/727-9981 or 866/727-9981, www.hotelpaulin.com, $195-315 s or d) is a family-run boutique hotel that has been entertaining guests since 1901. The 12 guest rooms have hardwood floors, comfortable beds, and a low-key but stylish decor. The top-floor Waterfront Suites are huge. The downstairs restaurant oozes charm and opens nightly for creative table d'hôte dining.

Getting There
Caraquet is about 110 kilometers (1.5 hours) north of Miramichi via Highway 11. From Fredericton, head 175 kilometers northeast on Highway 8 to Mirimichi and on to Caraquet for a 285-kilometer, four-hour drive.

GRANDE-ANSE AND VICINITY
From Caraquet, Highway 11 heads west, then jogs north at Bertrand to reach the shoreline of Baie des Chaleurs. For a swim in the warm bay, take Highway 320, the narrow road that diverges to the right, to **Maisonnette Park,** an exquisite spread of beach overlooking Caraquet across Baie Caraquet. The warm-water beach is a favorite, especially when the tide retreats to reveal sand dune fingers washed by shallow, sun-heated waters.

Take a left turn where Highway 11 hits the coast and you'll quickly reach Grand-Anse, where **Musée des Papes** (184 Acadie St., 506/732-3003, mid-June-Sept. daily 10am-5pm, adult $6, senior and child $3) commemorates the visit of Pope John Paul II to New Brunswick in 1985. Exhibits include vestments, chalices, and other ecclesiastical paraphernalia, plus a detailed scale replica of St. Peter's Basilica.

Getting There
Grande-Anse is about 20 kilometers (20 minutes) west of Caraquet along Highway 11. From Fredericton, head northeast on Highway 8 for 260 kilometers, then northeast on Highway 11 for 50 kilometers. Allow four hours.

BATHURST AND VICINITY
The town of Bathurst (pop. 12,000) sits by its own fine natural harbor at the vertex of Nepisiguit Bay, a broad gulf on the Baie des Chaleurs. It's 75 kilometers west of Caraquet, or 75 kilometers north of Miramichi as you shoot up Highway 8. All routes into town converge downtown at the pleasant **La Promenade Waterfront,** where you'll find a boardwalk, local **visitor center** (86 Douglas Ave., 506/548-0418, summer daily 9am-5pm), shops selling local arts and crafts, cafés, an ice cream shop, and a gazebo that hosts musicians throughout summer.

Daly Point Nature Reserve spreads across 40 hectares of salt marshes, woodlands, and fields northeast of town; an observation tower provides views of nesting ospreys, various seabirds, and songbirds. To get there, take Bridge Street (the Acadian Coastal Drive) east from Bathurst, then turn left on Carron Drive. Bring insect repellent.

Bathurst to Campbellton

Highway 11 stays inland for the scenically dull 85-kilometer stretch between Bathurst and Charlo. Far preferable is coastal Highway 134, which runs through the fishing villages of Nigadoo, Petit-Rocher, Pointe-Verte, and Jacquet River. The coast between Bathurst and Dalhousie is famed for sightings of a phantom ship. Numerous witnesses over the years have described a ship under full sail engulfed in flames on the bay; sometimes the vision includes a crew frantically scurrying across the deck. Some say the vision dates from the Battle of Restigouche (1760)—the last naval engagement between France and England in this part of eastern Canada—when France's fleet was destroyed by the British.

At the end of a narrow, private wooded road, ★ **La Fine Grobe Sur-Mer** (289 Rue Principale, Nigadoo, 506/783-3138, daily 5pm-10pm, $18-53) enjoys a delightful setting overlooking Chaleur Bay. One of the region's finest

and most respected restaurants, La Fine Grobe Sur-Mer has been in the business of serving French-inspired dishes like chateaubriand, herb-crusted rack of lamb, and seafood pancakes for decades. Set three-course menus ranging $27-$50 are the best value, but dining here is a memorable experience regardless of how you order your meal.

Getting There

Bathurst is about 75 kilometers (under an hour) north of Miramichi via Highway 8. To get there from Fredericton, head northeast on Highway 8 for 260 kilometers (three hours).

CAMPBELLTON

At the head of the Baie des Chaleurs, the New Brunswick and Gaspé coastlines meet near Campbellton (pop. 7,400), the area's largest town. A bridge here spans the broad mouth of the Restigouche River to connect with Québec's Highway 132. Highway 17 plunges deep into the unpopulated interior of New Brunswick, across the Restigouche Uplands. Along this route, it's 92 kilometers to Saint-Quentin, where you can veer east to Mount Carleton Provincial Park or continue another 80 kilometers to join the Saint John River valley at Saint-Léonard.

ACADIAN COAST
BAIE DES CHALEURS

La Promenade Waterfront, Bathurst

Sights and Recreation

Restigouche Gallery (39 Andrew St., 506/753-5750, summer Mon.-Sat. 9am-5pm, the rest of the year Tues.-Sat. 10am-4pm, adult $2) is a public art gallery displaying works by local, national, and international artists, as well as natural history and science exhibits.

Sugarloaf Park (Exit 415 off Hwy. 11, 506/789-2366) overlooks the whole region. A year-round chairlift offers views to the 305-meter gumdrop-shaped peak of Sugarloaf Mountain. The park also has hiking trails, chairlift-assisted mountain biking ($25 per day), tennis courts, and supervised swimming. In winter, the park is popular for snowmobiling, skating, and cross-country skiing. The park campground is open mid-May-mid-October and has 76 wooded sites for $28-36.

Accommodations

Campbellton's most interesting accommodation is also the least expensive. **HI-Campbellton** (1 Ritchie St., 506/759-7044, www.hihostels.ca, mid-June-late Aug., $21-25) is in an old red-and-white lighthouse along the Restigouche River. It has 16 beds in two dormitories (one for males and one for females), a small kitchen, Wi-Fi Internet access, and a common area.

The centrally located **Super 8** (26 Duke St., 506/753-7606 or 877/582-7666, www.super8campbellton.com, $115-145 s or d) has a small indoor swimming pool and a complimentary breakfast.

Getting There

Campbellton is a 115-kilometer (1.5-hour) drive northwest of Bathurst via Highway 11. The most direct route to Campbellton from Fredericton is to follow Highway 2 then Highway 17 from Saint-Léonard. The drive is 390 kilometers (four hours).

La Fine Grobe Sur-Mer

Prince Edward Island

Charlottetown and Queens County

A

s Canada's smallest provincial capital, Charlottetown (pop. 34,500)—the island's governmental, economic, cultural, and shopping center—makes no pretense of being a big city.

Rather, this attractive town is walkable, comfortable, and friendly. Its major attractions include a beautiful harborside location, handsome public and residential architecture, sophisticated art and cultural happenings, and plentiful lodgings and appealing restaurants.

The city also makes a good sightseeing base for exploring surrounding Queens County, which is the definitive Prince Edward Island as you imagined the province would be. The region is temptingly photogenic, a meld of small seaports with brightly colored craft at anchor and farmland settings with limpid ponds and weathered barns. Along the Gulf of St. Lawrence is Cavendish, the island's most popular tourist destination. Cavendish was the childhood home of Lucy Maud Montgomery, who created perfection on earth within the pages of her books, which centered on the spunky heroine Anne of Green Gables.

HISTORY

In the late 1750s, English surveyor Samuel Holland surveyed all of Prince Edward Island, recommending that the main settlement be established on a peninsula within Hillsborough Bay. He named it Charlotte, for the consort of King George III. The town had its grid laid out in 1764 and was named the island's capital the next year. Charlottetown's development paralleled the island's development. A road network was laid out by 1850. And by 1860, some 176 sawmills were transforming forests into lumber, greasing the island's economy and providing the raw materials for a thriving shipbuilding industry. As the center of government and commerce, the town was enriched with splendid stone churches and public buildings, many of which date to the mid-1800s and stand to this day.

Look for ★ to find recommended
sights, activities, dining, and lodging.

Highlights

★ **Province House:** This historic sandstone building in the heart of Charlottetown hosted the Fathers of Confederation in 1864 and continues today as the provincial seat of government (page 273).

★ **Victoria Park:** Take a break from the relative bustle of downtown with a walk through this waterfront park, home to the impressive Fanningbank residence (page 276).

★ **International Shellfish Festival:** You can feast on seafood year-round in Charlottetown, but this late-September festival is the place to try all your favorites at once (page 279).

★ **Prince Edward Island National Park:** Stretching along the Gulf of St. Lawrence, this park is one of the island's few undeveloped tracts of land. Warm water, beaches, and red cliffs are the main draws (page 289).

★ **North Rustico Harbour:** It's just a dot on the map, but this small fishing village is particularly photogenic. A lighthouse, kayak tours, and an excellent restaurant add to the appeal (page 293).

★ **Green Gables Heritage Place:** Northern Queens County is lovingly known as "Anne's Land," for Anne of Green Gables, one of the world's best-known literary characters (page 295).

Charlottetown and Queens County

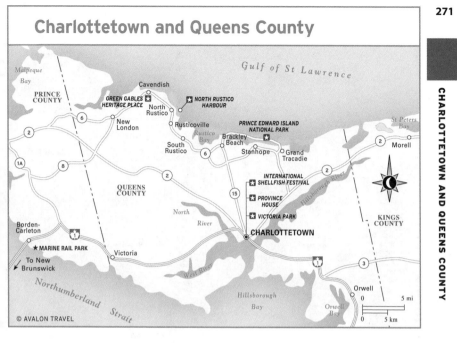

© AVALON TRAVEL

PLANNING YOUR TIME

For many visitors, Queens County *is* Prince Edward Island. A typical itinerary would be to catch the ferry to Wood Islands, spend one day in the capital, Charlottetown, and another in Cavendish before driving off the island via the Confederation Bridge. This is enough time in the capital to visit major attractions such as **Province House** while having enough time to end the day with an evening walk through **Victoria Park.** If your travels coincide with the late September **International Shellfish Festival,** you may want to stay longer.

Cavendish, the most popular destination on all of Prince Edward Island, is just an hour's drive from the capital. This makes a day trip possible and means you can settle yourself into Charlottetown for two or more nights, taking advantage of the theater and many restaurants. Cavendish does have many accommodations, but good dining rooms are severely lacking. Regardless of where you stay, your trip to Cavendish should include a drive through **Prince Edward Island National Park,** the short detour to **North Rustico Harbour,** and a visit to **Green Gables Heritage Place.**

ORIENTATION

The city, small as it is, may be baffling for a new visitor because of the way historic and newer streets converge. The town began with a handful of harbor-front blocks. The centuries have contributed a confusing jumble of other roads that feed into the historic area from all sorts of angles.

From either direction, the **TransCanada Highway** (Route 1) will take you right into the heart of town. From the west, it crosses the North River, turns south at the University of Prince Edward Island campus, and becomes University Avenue. From the east, take the Water Street exit to reach the visitors information center.

Extending from the harbor to Euston Street, the commercial area is pleasantly compact, attractive, and easily covered on foot. **Old Charlottetown** (or Old Charlotte Town,

Charlottetown

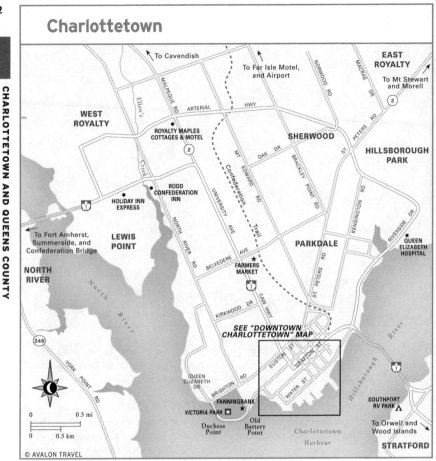

© AVALON TRAVEL

depending on who's describing the area) has been restored with rejuvenated buildings and brick walkways, lighted at night with gas lamps.

The most sought-after residential areas, with large stately houses, rim Victoria Park and North River Road. Working-class neighborhoods fan out farther north beyond Grafton Street and are marked with small, pastel-painted houses set close to the streets.

Sights and Recreation

Downtown Charlottetown is compact; plan on parking and exploring on foot. The waterfront area is the best place to leave your vehicle. Not only is it central, but you can make the provincial **Visitor Information Centre** (178 Water St., 902/370-2842, www.discover-charlottetown.com, May daily 9am-5pm, June daily 9am-6pm, July-Aug. daily 8:30am-6pm, Sept. daily 8:30am-5pm, Oct. daily 9am-4pm) your first stop.

DOWNTOWN

Most visitors to Prince Edward Island arrive by road, traveling either across the Confederation Bridge or on the ferry. You can also fly to Charlottetown.

Confederation Players

The **Confederation Players** are keen local historians who dress in period costume to conduct walking tours ($15 pp) of downtown Charlottetown mid-June-August. The Great George Street walking tour departs Tuesday-Saturday at 10am and 3:30pm from the Visitor Information Centre at 178 Water Street, taking in all the historical highlights along one of Canada's best known boulevards. The Historic Queen Square tour departs from its namesake in the heart of downtown Tuesday-Saturday at 2:30pm, focusing on Province House and the Confederation Centre of the Arts.

Downtown Waterfront

A rejuvenation project has resulted in much improvement in the downtown waterfront precinct. The adjacent **Confederation Landing Park** is rimmed by a seaside boardwalk and filled with pleasant gardens and well-trimmed grass. The park is integrated with **Peake's Wharf,** where the Fathers of Confederation arrived on the island. This is now a tourist hub of sorts, with restaurants and shops, and tour boats line the docks waiting to take interested visitors on sightseeing trips.

★ Province House

The nation of Canada began at **Province House** (corner of Grafton St. and Great

Province House

Downtown Charlottetown

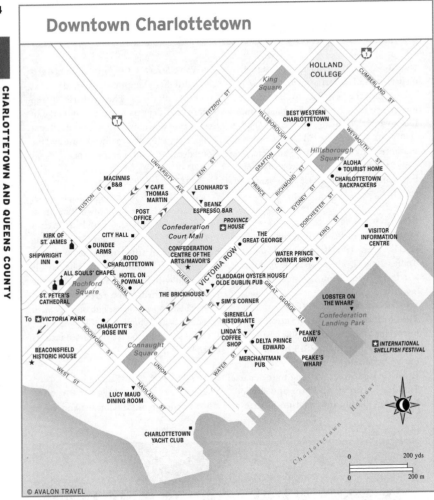

George St., 902/566-7626, June-Sept. daily 9am-5pm, Oct.-May Mon.-Fri. 9am-5pm, free), four blocks up Great George Street from the harbor. Now protected as a national historic site, the buff sandstone neoclassical edifice at the high point of downtown was erected in 1847 to house the island's colonial legislature. It quickly became the center of public life on the island. It was the site of lavish balls and state functions, including the historic 1864 conference on federal union. The provincial legislature still convenes here; meetings are in session between mid-February and early May for 5-17 weeks, depending on how much provincial government haggling is underway.

In the late 1970s, Parks Canada undertook restoration of the age-begrimed building, a five-year task completed in 1983. Layers of paint came off the front columns. The double-hung windows throughout were refitted with glass panes from an old greenhouse in New Brunswick. About 10 percent of the original furnishings remained in the building before restoration and were retained. Most of the rest

Getting to Prince Edward Island

CONFEDERATION BRIDGE

The impressive **Confederation Bridge** (902/437-7300 or 888/437-6565, www.confederationbridge.com) is Prince Edward Island's most important transportation link to the rest of Canada. From Cape Jourimain (New Brunswick), 80 kilometers east of Moncton, the bridge stretches across Northumberland Strait to Borden-Carleton, which is in Prince County, 60 kilometers west of Charlottetown. Driving across the impressive 12.9-kilometer span takes about 10 minutes (views are blocked by concrete barriers erected as a windbreak).

The round-trip bridge toll is $46 per vehicle, including passengers. Payment (credit card, debit card, or cash) is collected at Borden-Carleton upon leaving the island.

Confederation Bridge

BY FERRY

Prince Edward Island is also linked to the rest of Atlantic Canada by ferry. The mainland departure point is Caribou (Nova Scotia), near Pictou, a two-hour drive from Halifax. The ferry docks at Wood Islands, a scenic 62-kilometer drive southeast from Charlottetown. The 75-minute crossing is operated by **Northumberland Ferries** (902/566-3838 or 800/565-0201, www.ferries.ca) May-mid-December, with up to nine crossings in each direction daily during peak summer season. The round-trip fare is $71 per vehicle, regardless of the number of passengers. As with the bridge crossing, payment is made upon leaving the island, so to save a few bucks, take the ferry to PEI and return on the Confederation Bridge.

BY AIR

Air Canada (888/247-2262, www.aircanada.com) has direct flights to Charlottetown from Halifax, Montréal, Ottawa, and Toronto. **WestJet** (403/250-5839 or 888/937-8538, www.westjet.com) flies in from Toronto.

were replaced by period antiques obtained in the other provinces and the northeastern United States. A flowered rug was woven for Confederation Chamber, where the Fathers of Confederation convened. Every nook and corner was refurbished and polished until the interior gleamed. Today, Province House is one of Atlantic Canada's most significant public buildings.

Confederation Centre of the Arts

Confederation Centre of the Arts (145 Richmond St., 902/628-1864, www.confederationcentre.com) is the other half of the imposing complex shared by Province House. The promenades, edged with places to sit, are great places for people-watching, and kids like to skateboard on the walkways.

The center opened in 1964 to mark the centennial of the Charlottetown Conference, as the confederation meeting became known in Canadian history. It's a great hulk of a place, compatible with its historic neighbor in its design and coloring. The center houses an art gallery, the provincial library, four theaters, and a café. The emphasis at the **Confederation Centre Art Gallery** (mid-May-Oct. daily 9am-5pm, Nov.-mid-May Wed.-Sat. 11am-5pm, Sun. 1pm-5pm, free) is the work of Canadian artists—expect to see some of island artist Robert Harris's paintings and Lucy Maud Montgomery's original manuscripts. A gift shop stocks wares by the cream of PEI's artisans.

All Souls' Chapel

A few blocks west of Queen Street, the remarkable **All Souls' Chapel** next to **St. Peter's Cathedral** (Rochford St., 902/566-2102, daily 8am-6pm, free) was a joint Harris family creation. The architect William Harris styled it in island sandstone with a dark walnut interior. His brother Robert painted the murals and deftly mixed family members and friends among the religious figures.

Beaconsfield Historic House

A bright yellow, 25-room mansion, **Beaconsfield Historic House** (2 Kent St., 902/368-6603, tours summer daily 10am-4:30pm, spring and fall Mon.-Fri., adult $5, senior and child $4) was built in 1877 from a William Critchlow Harris design. The building has survived more than a century of varied use as a family home, a shelter for "friendless women," a YWCA, and a nurses' residence. It

was rescued in 1973 by the PEI Museum and Heritage Foundation, which turned it into foundation headquarters and a heritage museum. A good bookstore is on the first level, and genealogical archives are kept across the hall and upstairs. The wide front porch overlooking the harbor across a long lawn is a great place to have tea and scones.

★ Victoria Park

Victoria Park, adjacent to Beaconsfield House, reigns as one of Charlottetown's prettiest settings, with 16 wooded and grassy hectares overlooking the bay at Battery Point. The greenery spreads out across the peninsula tip; to get there, follow Kent Street as it turns into Park Roadway. The park's rolling terrain is built of moraines, heaps of gravelly deposits left behind by ice-age glaciers.

Joggers like the park's winding paths, and birders find abundant yellow warblers, purple finches, and downy woodpeckers nesting in the maples, firs, oaks, pines, and birches. The white palatial mansion overlooking the water is **Fanningbank** (Government House), the lieutenant governor's private residence—nice to look at, but it's closed to the public.

Fanningbank is home to the lieutenant governor.

BEYOND DOWNTOWN
Charlottetown
Farmers Market

The **Charlottetown Farmers Market** (100 Belvedere Ave., 902/626-3373, Sat. 9am-2pm and summer Wed. 9am-2pm) is across from the university campus. The indoor market holds about 40 vendors selling everything from flowers and crafts to baked goods, produce, and fish.

Fort Amherst-Port-la-Joye National Historic Site

Just four kilometers across the harbor from downtown but a 35-minute drive via Routes 1 and 19, **Fort Amherst-Port-la-Joye National Historic Site** protects the island's first European settlement. It all began in 1720, when three French ships sailed into Port-la-Joye (today's Charlottetown Harbour) carrying some 300 settlers. Most of them moved to the north shore and established fishing villages, but the rest remained here at the military outpost.

Within just four years, adverse conditions had driven out most of the French. The British burned Port-la-Joye in 1745 and took control of the island. The French later returned to rebuild their capital, but were compelled to surrender Port-la-Joye to a superior British force in 1758. The British renamed the post Fort Amherst. After the British established a new capital at Charlottetown, Fort Amherst fell quickly into disrepair, and now no buildings remain. The grounds, which have picnic tables, are open June-August.

RECREATION

Those looking for easy walking gravitate to the waterfront at the southwestern end of downtown. This is the starting point for a **paved trail** that extends to Old Battery Point and Victoria Park. While this area is also popular for biking, cyclists looking for longer rides will be impressed at how easy it is to reach the rural landscape beyond city limits. From downtown, the ride out to Brackley Beach (45 kilometers) is a good full-day ride.

MacQueen's Bike Shop (430 Queen St., 902/368-2453, Mon.-Sat. 8:30am-5:30pm, Sun. 10am-2pm) provides complete bike and accessory rental and repairs and can also arrange island cycle-touring packages. **Smooth Cycle** (330 University Ave., 902/569-5690, Mon.-Thurs. 9am-5:30pm, Fri. 9am-6pm, Sat. 9am-5pm) also offers rentals and repairs, as well as drop-offs for the Confederation Trail. Both companies charge from $30 per day for a road bike.

Entertainment and Events

Charlottetown once rolled up the sidewalks at night, but in recent years a rousing nightlife and pub scene has emerged centered on drinking and dancing. Last call for drinks is at 1:30am; the doors lock at 2am. For complete listings of all that's happening around the city, pick up the free weekly *Buzz* (www.buzzon. com) or the weekend editions of *The Guardian* (www.theguardian.pe.ca).

NIGHTLIFE

Peake's Quay (1 Great George St., 902/368-1330, daily from 11am) has a prime waterfront location, making it popular with both locals and visitors. While the service is often indifferent, it's a good family-friendly environment with inexpensive food and lots of outdoor seating. Look for live music most weekends after 9pm. **Olde Dublin Pub** (131 Sydney St., 902/892-6992, Mon.-Wed. 11am-midnight, Thurs.-Sat. 11am-2am, Sun. 4pm-11pm) has a popular deck and offers Celtic and Irish music Thursday-Saturday for a small cover charge.

Mavor's (145 Richmond St., 902/628-6107, Mon.-Wed. 11am-9pm, Thurs.-Sat. 11am-midnight), in the Confederation Centre of the Arts, is a colorful space with more than 40 wines by the glass, top-notch martinis, and a thoughtful menu of light meals under $25.

Water's Edge Bar (Delta Prince Edward, 18 Queen St., 902/894-1208, Sun.-Thurs. 11am-11pm, Fri.-Sat. 11am-midnight) is a sophisticated space within one of the city's top hotels. The highlight for beer-lovers is a long list of regional brews.

The Brickhouse (125 Sydney St., 902/566-4620, Sun.-Thurs. 11am-10pm, Fri.-Sat. 11am-11pm) is another good choice for a quiet drink and conversation. Located in an 1850s building where the timber-frame and red brick is exposed, it's a stylish space that is best known as a restaurant, but there's no problem stopping by for a quiet drink at the bar or heading upstairs to the more private lounge (Thurs.-Sat. from 6pm).

A mainstay of the live music scene is **Baba's Lounge** (upstairs at 81 University Ave., 902/892-7377, Mon.-Thurs. 11am-11pm, Fri.-Sat. 11am-midnight, Sun. 5pm-midnight), a popular hangout with the younger set since the earlier 1990s. "Intimate" is an understatement here; bodies writhe to the rhythm on a dance floor about the size of a postage stamp. Expect live music ranging from slightly alternative to modern rock.

PERFORMING ARTS

The **Confederation Centre of the Arts** (145 Richmond St., 902/566-1267) is the performing arts capital of the province and the site of the **Charlottetown Festival** (www.confederationcentre.com), which runs mid-June-late September. The festival is best known for the *Anne of Green Gables* musical (July and August daily at 1:30pm and 7:30pm); tickets cost $50-70. Also on the bill are repertory productions in the center's main theater and cabaret-style productions at the **MacKenzie Theatre,** the festival's second stage (University Ave. and Grafton St.).

FESTIVALS AND EVENTS
June

The mid-June-late September **Charlottetown Festival** (902/566-1267, www.confederationcentre.com) presents musical theater and cabaret at the Confederation Centre of the Arts and the nearby MacKenzie Theatre. Two musicals are presented, including one centering on *Anne of Green Gables.*

judging at the International Shellfish Festival

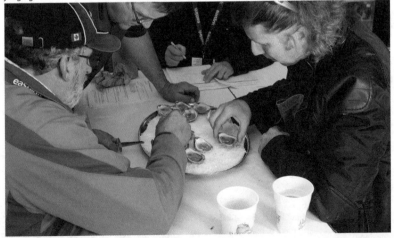

July

The **Canada Day** long weekend (first weekend in July) is celebrated on the waterfront with a food fair, nationalistic displays, buskers, island music, and the **Festival of Lights** fireworks display.

Organized by the Charlottetown Yacht Club, **Race Week** (902/892-9065, www.cyc.pe.ca) runs Wednesday-Saturday in the middle of July. The program revolves around yacht races for various classes of boats, with other scheduled activities including shore games and nightly entertainment. Even if you're not involved in the event, watching the yachts racing across the harbor is a sight to behold.

August

The mid-August **Old Home Week** (902/629-6623, www.oldhomeweekpei.com), Atlantic Canada's largest agricultural exposition, centers on Charlottetown Driving Park, northeast of downtown along Kensington Road. The city unofficially shuts down for the festival-ending **Gold Cup Parade** (www.goldcupparade.ca) through the streets of Charlottetown—said to be Atlantic Canada's biggest and best-attended parade. Daily grounds admission is a reasonable adult $12, child $5.

September
★ INTERNATIONAL SHELLFISH FESTIVAL

Summer ends with the **International Shellfish Festival** (www.peishellfish.com), over the third weekend of September. Festivities along the waterfront include an oyster-shucking contest, a Chowder Challenge, "touch tanks," cooking classes, the World Is Your Oyster children's program, sock-hanging, and chefs from the local culinary institute sharing their cooking skills with the public.

Shopping

Centrally located and PEI's largest city by far, Charlottetown is the island's shopping hub. Downtown is a pleasant blend of old and new shopping experiences, although the main concentration of shopping malls is north of downtown along University Avenue. Stores catering to islanders are normally open Monday-Saturday about 9am-5pm, while touristy ones stay open later in July and August and also operate on Sunday.

ARTS AND CRAFTS

Local artists capture the island in masterful watercolors, acrylics, oils, and sculpture. Local crafts include finely made quilts, knits and woolens, stained glass, jewelry, pewter, pottery, and handsome furniture. The Anne doll is the most popular souvenir, and it's produced in innumerable variations for as little as $20 to as much as $800.

An exquisite handmade quilt costs $400-800—seldom a bargain. But well-crafted quilts are sturdily constructed and will last a lifetime with good care. Sweaters ($75-300) are especially high quality. One of the best sources is **Northern Watters Knitwear,** which operates a downtown factory outlet (150 Richmond St., 902/566-5850, Mon.-Fri. 9am-6pm, Sun. 11:30am-5pm).

The **PEI Crafts Council** (www.pei-craftscouncil.com) is a driving force behind local arts and crafts. It counts about 100 provincial craftspeople among its esteemed ranks. A visit to their website shows all members and the variety of their products (quilts, glassware, sculpture, clothing, knitted apparel, and jewelry ad infinitum), and provides a list of markets and craft shows they attend.

Food

Island fare is *good,* and while it centers on homegrown produce and seafood from the surrounding ocean, everything comes together in the capital, where you'll find an excellent array of dining opportunities for all budgets. The center of the eating action is **Victoria Row,** a block of vintage buildings along Richmond Street between Queen and Great George Streets. The street is pedestrian-only through summer. The restaurants set up outdoor tables while musicians play to the assembled crowd of diners.

Even if you're not in town for the **International Shellfish Festival** (third weekend of Sept.), you'll find local delicacies such as lobster and Malpeque oysters on menus throughout the city. Local produce and dairy products are delicious. Chefs make the most of island-grown succulent berries, locally produced maple syrup, and thick, sweet honey.

CAFÉS

What began with a German couple selling homemade bread to a local farmers market has morphed into **Leonhard's** (42 University Ave., 902/367-3621, daily 9am-5pm, lunches $6.50-13), a cozy café where the emphasis is on hearty yet healthy European-style cooking. Look for mouthwatering French toast and Bavarian-style omelets for breakfast; at lunch, the delicious gluten-free soups are made from scratch, or choose the smoked turkey focaccia.

A couple of doors down from Leonhard's, **Beanz Espresso Bar** (38 University Ave., 902/892-8797, Mon.-Sat. 6:30am-6pm, Sun. 9am-5pm, lunches $7-12) gets rave reviews for its coffee, but the soups, salads, sandwiches, and old-fashioned pastries draw me back every time I'm in Charlottetown.

One block north of the two places recommended above, **Cafe Thomas Martin** (98 Fitzroy St., 902/892-0809, Mon.-Fri. 8am-3pm, lunches $6-10) is a friendly place far enough away from the main tourist attractions that it is missed by most tourists. On the menu are dozens of hot drink choices, light lunches such as chowders and sandwiches, and a tempting array of sweet treats.

Beanz Espresso Bar

At the Confederation Centre of the Arts, ★ **Mavor's** (145 Richmond St., 902/628-6107, daily 8am-8pm, lunches $8-15) is a striking room where you can get your fill of Starbucks coffee. The kitchen opens daily (except Sunday) at 11am, serving up fresh and wholesome food, with ethnic influences showing through in dishes such as blue mussels steamed in Thai curry broth. Also good: the thin-crust smoked salmon pizza and sweet potato wedges with a side of sour cream.

If you like old-fashioned diners with menus to match the era, sidle up to a booth or the counter at **Linda's Coffee Shop** (32 Queen St., 902/892-7292, daily 8am-2pm, lunches $6-11).

SEAFOOD

★ **Water Prince Corner Shop** (141 Water St., 902/368-3212, May-Oct. daily 11am-10pm, $16-32) looks like a regular convenience store from the outside, but inside the ocean-blue clapboard building is a casual dining space where the emphasis is on fresh seafood at reasonable prices. It's all good—lobster burgers, lobster dinners with potato salad and mussels, Malpeque oysters, seafood chowder, steamed clams, and more.

For its harbor-front location alone, **Lobster on the Wharf** (2 Prince St., 902/368-2888, May-Oct. 11:30am-10pm, $17-36) is a longtime favorite with visitors and locals alike. It has well over 300 seats, with more than 100 of these outside on multi-tiered decks built over the water. As the name suggests, lobster is the specialty (the two-person Lobster Feed is a local favorite), but the fish-and-chips and baked halibut are also excellent.

Fishbones (136 Richmond St., 902/628-6569, May-Oct. daily 11am-midnight, $14-28) is a fresh, casual restaurant along pedestrian-only Victoria Row. Start at the oyster bar before moving on to a set menu of contemporary creations, such as butter salmon curry. Other highlights include lobster mac and cheese, grilled halibut with mango salsa, and a wide selection of local beers and creative cocktails.

The ★ **Claddagh Oyster House** (131 Sydney St., 902/892-9661, Mon.-Sat. 5pm-10pm, Sun. 5pm-9pm, $27-34) is authentically Irish, starting with owner Liam Dolan from County Galway. Local oysters dominate the menu and come in many forms (including a tasting platter of 10 for $29). Seafood is the specialty on the main menu, with choices such as lobster risotto—a rich-tasting splurge.

PUBS

Taking full advantage of its harbor-front locale is the upstairs **Peake's Quay** (1 Great George St., 902/368-1330, daily from 11am, $13-24), with informal indoor and outdoor dining and an enviable seafood selection; try the scallops sauced with honey butter. Peake's Quay is also arguably the hottest nightspot in town, drawing locals, landlubber tourists, and yachties (who tie up at the adjacent marina) alike to see and be seen while listening or dancing to top touring bands, so plan on dining early.

The **Merchantman Pub** (23 Queen St., 902/892-9150, daily 11am-10pm, $16-28) has a nice atmosphere, a wide-ranging menu that includes some Thai and Cajun dishes, and a good beer selection. But the place seems a little overpriced, probably because of its location across the street from the upscale Delta Prince Edward.

CANADIAN

The **Lucy Maud Dining Room** (4 Sydney St., 902/894-6868, summer Tues.-Sat. 5:30pm-8:30pm, the rest of the year Tues.-Fri. 11:30am-1pm and 5:30pm-8:30pm, Sat. 5:30pm-8:30pm, $22-35) is the training restaurant for the Culinary Institute of Canada, a respected school that attracts students from across the country. Turn a blind eye to the rather institutional room, concentrate on the water views, and sit back to enjoy enthusiastic service and well-priced meals that blend contemporary and Continental cuisine.

Take a break from seafood by making reservations at ★ **Sims Corner** (86 Queen St., 902/894-7467, daily 11:30am-10:30pm,

$18-35), the island's only true steakhouse. Ensconced in a historic 1860s red-brick building, the subtle setting is the perfect place to indulge in island-raised beef cooked exactly as ordered. For the full effect, choose a robust red from the extensive wine list and end your meal with a slab of dark chocolate brownie parfait.

If you want to dine in one of the city's best restaurants, but don't want to pay for an expensive dinner, eat breakfast at **Water's Edge** (Delta Prince Edward, 18 Queen St., 902/894-1208, daily 7am-11pm, $24-39). The buffet is $19, or try dishes as traditional as blueberry muffins or as creative as lobster eggs Benedict. Things go upscale in the evening: That's when you can order beet salad or seafood chowder, followed by pan-seared halibut with a side of curried mussels.

The **Griffon Room** (Dundee Arms, 200 Pownal St., 902/892-2496, daily for breakfast, lunch, and dinner, $22-33) is away from the tourist crush within a restored three-story manor that combines an old-fashioned setting with elegantly conceived fine cuisine emphasizing red meats and seafood. If you feel like a break from seafood, you won't regret the mint-rubbed rack of lamb.

ITALIAN

Sirenella Ristorante (83 Water St., 902/628-2271, Mon.-Fri. 11:30am-2pm and 5pm-10pm, Sat. 5pm-10pm, $17-28) serves up traditional northern Italian food in the simple surrounds of a small yellow building set back from busy Water Street. The veal dishes are tempting, but order the scallop and wild mushroom pappardelle for your fill of local produce. The wine list is dominated by Italian reds and whites.

ICE CREAM

Dairy fanciers whoop it up at ★ **Cow's**, a local ice cream company that is renowned as much for its creamy treats wrapped in handmade waffle cones as for its colorful merchandise. Downtown outlets include one opposite the Confederation Centre (corner of Queen St. and Grafton St., 902/892-6969, daily 10am-6pm) and at Peake's Quay (902/566-4886, May-Oct. daily 10am-10pm). On your way off the island, you can also indulge at Gateway Village (126 Abegweit Blvd., 902/437-6883, daily 9am-9pm) or aboard the ferry.

Accommodations and Camping

You'll find every kind of lodging, from plain budget places to sumptuous expensive rooms, in Charlottetown's 100-plus lodgings. Also, unlike elsewhere in the province, most are open year-round.

Unless noted otherwise, prices given are for a double room; sales tax is not included.

DOWNTOWN
Under $50

The city's lone hostel is the HI-affiliated **Charlottetown Backpackers** (60 Hillsborough St., 902/367-5749, www. charlottetownbackpackers.com, dorm beds $29-33, $72-80 d), a converted residential home two blocks east of Province House. Facilities include a living room with a fireplace, bike rentals, a recreation room, and wireless Internet.

$50-100

In the vicinity of the hostel is another cheapie—**Aloha Tourist Home** (234 Sydney St., 902/892-5642 or 855/892-5642, www.alohaamigo.com, $89-225 s or d), an inexpensive downtown accommodation for those looking for private rooms. The renovated home has six guest rooms with single or double beds, two shared bathrooms, a shared kitchen, a lounge area, and free wireless Internet throughout. The least expensive rooms share bathrooms, while the others have en suites.

One of the least expensive of Charlottetown's historic accommodations with en suite bathrooms is **MacInnis Bed and Breakfast** (80 Euston St., 902/892-6725), a homey, centrally located choice with a veranda that overlooks pleasant gardens. It offers two regular guest rooms ($85 s or d) and a top-floor one-bedroom suite ($135 s or d), all decorated in a distinctive Victorian style.

$100-150

The elegant 1860s ★ **Shipwright Inn** (51 Fitzroy St., 902/368-1905 or 888/306-9966, www.shipwrightinn.com, $149-299 s or d) was originally the home of shipbuilder James Douse. The inn has eight rooms and suites, all with private baths and furnished in richly colored nautical themes (my favorite is the Chart Room, with an 1830s four-poster walnut bed, heavy drapes, and historic sea charts on the walls). Rates include a full breakfast.

What makes **Elmwood Heritage Inn** (121 North River Rd., 902/368-3310 or 877/933-3310, www.elmwoodinn.pe.ca, $179-279 s or d including breakfast) stand out is the setting. Still within easy walking distance of downtown, its parklike grounds are surrounded by mature gardens; a row of stately elm trees leads up from the wrought-iron entry gates to the front door. Built for the grandson of Samuel Cunard in 1889, the mansion boasts 28 very Victorian guest rooms, many with jetted tubs and fireplaces.

Best Western Charlottetown (238 Grafton St., 902/892-2461 or 800/528-1234, www.bestwesternatlantic.com, $145-185 s or d including a hot breakfast) is a three-block jaunt from Province House. It has 143 mid-size rooms fronting both sides of the street. Facilities include an indoor pool, fitness center, hot tub, and launderette.

$150-200

A restored Queen Anne Revival mansion awash with antiques, **Dundee Arms** (200 Pownal St., 902/892-2496 or 877/638-6333, www.eden.travel, $165-220 s, $175-230 d) has been taking in guests since the early 1970s. Conveniently located between downtown and Victoria Park, its other pluses include a good restaurant and comfortable beds. Note that half the 22 rooms are in a modern addition behind the original home, but these are still stylishly decorated and come with wireless Internet, bathrobes, and more.

Charlotte's Rose Inn (11 Grafton St., 902/892-3699 or 888/237-3699, www.charlottesrose.com, Apr.-Oct., $150-205 s or d) is a three-story 1884 home on a quiet residential street. Original hardwood floors, high ceilings, and Victorian-era furnishings add to the charm of guest rooms in the main house. Rates include a hot breakfast, wireless Internet, and use of bikes.

Over $200

A few steps from Province House, ★ **The Great George** (58 Great George St., 902/892-0606 or 800/361-1118, www.thegreatgeorge.com, $225-375 s or d) comprises 60 guest rooms spread through 15 beautifully restored buildings from as early as 1811. The lobby is in a building that was originally known as the Pavilion Hotel, at the corner of Great George and Sydney Streets. It was here that the Fathers of Confederation stayed during the 1864 Charlottetown Conference. This building also has a large lounge area and a fine-dining restaurant. Rooms in this and buildings running up Great George Street and beyond have been beautifully restored, with the addition of modern amenities like air-conditioning and wireless Internet.

Extensive renovations have transformed the old Islander motel into the ★ **Hotel on Pownal** (146 Pownal St., 902/892-1217 or 800/268-6261, www.thehotelonpownal.com, $240 s or d), offering chic boutique lodging. The 45 guest rooms are smartly decorated and filled with modern amenities, including extra-large wall-mounted TVs, iPod docking stations, and wireless Internet. Comfortable beds, luxurious bathrooms, and a free continental breakfast round out this popular downtown lodging.

Rodd Charlottetown (75 Kent St., 902/894-7371 or 800/565-7633, www.roddvacations.com, from $245 s or d) is a grand red-brick 1931 Georgian gem with magnificent woodwork and furnishings made by island craftspeople. It offers 115 rooms and suites and a restaurant, whirlpool, indoor pool, and rooftop patio. As always with these top-end properties, check the website for the best deals.

Like the nearby Confederation Centre of the Arts, the **Delta Prince Edward** (18 Queen St., 902/566-2222, www.marriott.com, $250 s or d) stands out for its boxy look amid the gracious buildings of downtown. Inside are 211 well-decorated rooms. The more expensive Delta Rooms have king beds and water views. It offers all the amenities of a full-service hotel, including underground valet parking, a day spa, a fitness room, an indoor pool, a lounge, and a restaurant. Disregard the rack rates and check online—you should find packages that include accommodations and either theater tickets or greens fees for around $200 d.

NORTH OF DOWNTOWN

Staying downtown has its perks, but if you're looking for a well-priced motel room or are traveling with a family, staying on the north side is a good alternative.

$50-100

Out near the airport, **Fair Isle Motel** (Rte. 2, 902/368-8259 or 800/309-8259, www.fairislepei.com, Apr.-Nov., $85-135 s or d) is an old roadside motel where rooms overlook landscaped gardens and a small playground. All rooms have wireless Internet and basic cooking facilities. If you've picked up fresh seafood at Lobster on the Wharf, take advantage of this motel's barbecues for a great outdoor dinner.

Rodd Charlottetown

I doubt too many Canadian capitals boast a cottage complex surrounded by expansive lawns within city limits, but Charlottetown does, in the form of ★ **Royalty Maples Cottages & Motel** (Rte. 2, 902/368-1030 or 800/831-7829, www.royaltymaples.com, May-Nov., $109-149), which is one kilometer north of the junction of Routes 1 and 2. The 10 one- and two-bedroom cottages each have a full kitchen, living area, and air-conditioning. Six motel rooms also go for $80-120 s or d per night.

$150-200

At the busy intersection of Routes 1 and 2, north of downtown along University Avenue, is **Rodd Royalty** (14 Capital Dr., 902/894-8566 or 800/565-7633, www.roddvacations.com, $145-190 s or d). This spread-out property features 119 standard rooms and suites (the latter are a better value). Other facilities include an indoor pool with a long waterslide, a fitness room, and a restaurant.

The **Holiday Inn Express** (200 TransCanada Hwy., 902/892-1201 or 800/465-4329, www.ihg.com, $165-210 s or d) maintains the same standards and facilities expected of this worldwide chain. The modern rooms have air-conditioning and high-speed Internet access, and rates include a continental breakfast. Families can take advantage of children's suites, complete with Nintendo systems and bunk beds separate from the main bedroom. Other amenities include an indoor pool and a sundeck.

CAMPGROUNDS
West
★ **Cornwall/Charlottetown KOA** (208 Ferry Rd., off Rte. 248, 2 km east of Cornwall, 902/566-2421, www.koa.com, mid-May-early Oct., $32) spreads across 25 beautiful hectares along the West River. Amenities include an outdoor swimming pool, a playground, hayrides, showers, a launderette, and a kitchen shelter.

Transportation and Services

Charlottetown Visitor Information Centre (178 Water St., 902/370-2842, May daily 9am-5pm, June daily 9am-6pm, July-Aug. daily 8:30am-6pm, Sept. daily 8:30am-5pm, Oct. daily 9am-4pm) is inside a restored 1876 railway building. The staff answers questions and stocks a good supply of literature about the city, as well as the province.

Queen Elizabeth Hospital is on Riverside Drive (902/894-2200). For **police** call 902/566-7112.

GETTING THERE
Air
Charlottetown Airport (250 Maple Hills Ave., 902/566-7997, www.flypei.com) is eight kilometers north of downtown along Brackley Point Road. The airport has a restaurant, gift shop, seasonal visitor center, and wireless Internet (for a fee). Taxis wait outside during flight arrivals and charge $12 for one person or $16 for two for the 15-minute drive to town. Avis, Budget, Hertz, and National rent vehicles at the airport, but their counters are not staffed between flights. **Air Canada** (888/247-2262) has direct flights from Toronto, Montréal, Ottawa, and Halifax, while **WestJet** (888/937-8538) flies in from Toronto.

Car
From Moncton, it's a little more than 160 kilometers (two hours) to Charlottetown via Route 15 and the Confederation Bridge.

Ferry
From Caribou, a short drive north of Pictou, **Northumberland Ferries** (902/566-3838 or 800/565-0201, www.ferries.ca) operates 5-9 sailings May-mid-December daily to the eastern side of Prince Edward Island. The trip takes just over an hour, and the fare is $71 round-trip per vehicle, regardless of the number of passengers (you pay when leaving the island).

GETTING AROUND
Use **Charlottetown Transit** (902/566-9962) to get anywhere in Greater Charlottetown for adult $2.50, child $1.25; buses run weekdays only.

Charlottetown taxis are plentiful; you'll pay $8-10 to get almost anywhere downtown. Taxis cruise the streets or wait at major downtown hotels. Taxi companies include **City Cab** (902/892-6567), **Co-op** (902/892-1111), and **Yellow Cab** (902/566-6666).

Local rental car agencies include **Avis** (902/892-3706), **Budget** (902/566-5525), **Hertz** (902/966-5566), and **National** (902/628-6990).

Boat Tours

Peake's Wharf Boat Tours (1 Great George St., 902/629-1864, www.charlottetownboattours.com) operates a covered 42-foot boat from Peake's Wharf, at the foot of Great George Street. Options include a 2.5-hour seal-watching cruise (2:30pm, adult $55) and 70-minute evening and sunset cruises (6:30pm and 8pm, both adult $39). The tours run June-early September, with children half the adult price.

The South Shore

From Charlottetown, Route 1 (TransCanada Highway) whisks travelers 56 kilometers southwest to Borden-Carleton, where the Confederation Bridge provides a link to the rest of Canada. If you're arriving on the island via the bridge, consider veering off Route 1 at DeSable and following scenic Route 19 along the South Shore to Rocky Point and Fort Amherst-Port-la-Joye National Historic Site for views of the city skyline across sparkling Charlottetown Harbour.

VICTORIA

Victoria (pop. 200), 35 kilometers west of Charlottetown, marks Queens County's southwestern corner. The town owed its start to shipbuilding, and by 1870 Victoria ranked as one of the island's busiest ports. As the demand for wooden ships faded, the seaport turned to cattle shipping—herds of cattle were driven down the coastal slopes to water's edge, where they were hoisted with slings onto waiting ships.

Today Victoria shows just a spark of its former luster. The seaport slipped off the commercial circuit decades ago, and the settlement shrank to a handful of waterfront blocks. Happily, island craftspeople discovered the serene setting. It's still a quiet place where the fishing fleet puts out to sea early in the morning as the mist rises off the strait. But now the peaceful seaport also holds a modest arts colony, with outlets along the main street.

Victoria Playhouse

If an evening at the theater sounds good, make plans to attend the **Victoria Playhouse** (Howard St., 902/658-2025, www.victoriaplayhouse.com, adult $32.50, senior $30.50, child $20.50), a repertory theater that showcases historically themed comedy and drama, as well as concerts of jazz and folk music.

Food and Accommodations

Next to the Victoria Playhouse, **Victoria Village Inn** (Howard St., 902/658-2483 or 866/658-2483, www.victoriavillageinn.com, $100-155 s or d) is an 1870s inn that was originally built for a sea captain. Awash with lustrous antiques, it offers four comfortable guest units—one with three bedrooms.

Kitty-corner to the theater, the **Orient Hotel** (34 Main St., 902/658-2503 or 800/565-6743, www.theorienthotel.com, mid-May-mid-Oct., $95-160 s or d) has been taking in guests since 1900. It features a few smallish guest rooms and three larger suites (from $125). Rates include a delicious breakfast and tea and coffee throughout the day.

Enterprising locals remodeled the old general store and post office and opened ★ **Landmark Café** (12 Main St., 902/658-2286, June-Sept. daily 11:30am-2:45pm and 5pm-9:30pm, $11-22). You can't go wrong with any of the fresh seasonal cooking, but the soups and meat pies are especially good.

Getting There

To get to Victoria from Charlottetown, it's a 35-kilometer (25-minute) drive along Route 1.

BORDEN-CARLETON

The twin villages of Borden-Carleton, 55 kilometers west of Charlottetown, are the closest point of the island to mainland Canada, and so have always been an important transportation hub. Back in the late 1700s, iceboats carrying mail and passengers crossed Northumberland Strait when the island was icebound from December to early spring. The voyages generated hair-raising tales of survival, and the iceboats—rigged with fragile sails and runners—were often trapped in the strait's ice. It wasn't until 1916 that the first vehicle ferry made the crossing. In 1997, the Confederation Bridge opened and the ferry service was discontinued. Since the opening of the bridge, Borden-Carleton has seen much development, as thousands of travelers peeling off the bridge come looking for food and information, and those leaving stop to stock up on last-minute souvenirs.

Gateway Village

As you descend the final span of Confederation Bridge, 12-hectare **Gateway Village** soon comes into view down on the right. It is designed especially for bridge travelers, but it's worth visiting even if you're on your way back to the mainland. Designed on the theme of an island streetscape of the early 1900s, the shops are filled with island souvenirs, some tacky (T-shirts, Christmas decorations), some tasty (fresh lobster), and some trendy (wine from Rossignol Estate Winery). The epicenter for new arrivals is the cavernous **Gateway Village Visitor Information Centre** (902/437-8570, winter daily 9am-6pm, spring and fall daily 9am-8pm, summer daily 9am-10pm), where friendly staff will help sort out the best way to spend your time on the island. Displays focus on various island experiences. Outside, amid the café tables and wandering visitors, free musical performances and crafts demonstrations add to the appeal.

Marine Rail Park

From the heart of Gateway Village, head south toward Northumberland Strait on Carleton Street and turn right on Borden Avenue to reach **Marine Rail Park.** Until the bridge was completed in 1997, this was where ferries from the mainland docked, and today the area has been converted to a green space. Interpretive boards tell the story of the former ferry service, but the best reason to visit the park is for unobstructed views of the Confederation Bridge.

Accommodations

A few kilometers east of Borden-Carleton toward Charlottetown, **Carleton Motel** (TransCanada Hwy., 902/437-3030, www.carletonmotelpei.com, $89-119 s or d) offers 22 basic rooms, some with cooking facilities; a small adjacent café is open daily 7am-around 3pm.

★ **Lord's Seaside Cottages** (Bells Point Rd., off Rte. 10, 902/437-2426 or 888/228-6765, www.lordsseasidecottages.com, June-Sept., $165 s or d per night in spring and fall, $1,075 per week in July-Aug.) is well worth the extra money. Sitting on Bells Point, a few kilometers west of Borden-Carleton, the eight simple cottages each have 1-3 bedrooms, a TV, and a deck with a barbecue—an excellent deal for families or couples traveling together.

Getting There

From Charlottetown, it's 55 kilometers (40 minutes) to Borden-Carleton via Route 1.

CROSSING THE CONFEDERATION BRIDGE

If you arrived in Borden-Carleton via the Confederation Bridge, you enjoyed a free ride. If you're leaving the island, it's time to pay. The toll is $46 per departing vehicle, including passengers. Payment is collected at toll booths on the island side of the bridge. Have cash, a credit card, or a debit card ready.

Charlottetown to Cavendish

The most direct route between Charlottetown and Cavendish is to take Route 2 west from the capital for 25 kilometers, and then head north from Hunter River on Route 13. It takes less than one hour to reach the coast. A more leisurely alternative (1.5 hours) begins by taking Route 2 northeast from Charlottetown to Grand Tracadie and then following Route 6 west along the coast to Cavendish. If you've been traveling through Kings County (on eastern Prince Edward Island), Tracadie Cross, the turnoff for the coastal route, is just seven kilometers west of Mount Stewart.

GRAND TRACADIE

Grand Tracadie is about 20 minutes from Charlottetown. It is the eastern gateway to Prince Edward Island National Park, but it is best known for a historic inn that lies within the park, two kilometers from the town center.

Food and Accommodations

Elegant green roofed ★ **Dalvay by the Sea** (16 Cottage Ln., 902/672-2048 or 888/366-2955, www.dalvaybythesea.com, mid-June-early Oct., $200-400 s or d, including breakfast) appeals to guests who like an old-money ambience. The rustic mansion was built in 1895 by millionaire American oil industrialist Alexander MacDonald, who used the lodging as a summer retreat. Today the hotel, its antiques, and its spacious grounds are painstakingly maintained by the national park staff. Eight three-bedroom cottages on the grounds ($400-420 d, including breakfast) are most popular with families.

The hotel's dining room is locally renowned, and nonguests are welcome with advance reservations. Entrées ($24-42) feature formal Canadian cuisine prepared with a French flair. The emphasis is on the freshest produce, best seafood, and finest beef cuts. Mains include rack of lamb crusted with hazelnut and grainy mustard; the sticky date pudding topped with toffee sauce is an easy choice for dessert. Other hotel facilities include a well-stocked gift shop, a nearby beach, a tennis court, bike rentals, a lake with canoes, and nature trails.

Dalvay by the Sea is one of the island's premier lodgings.

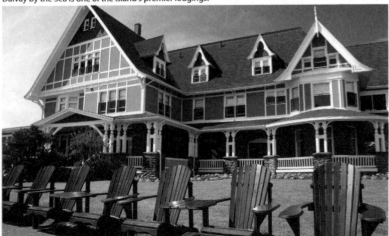

Getting There

Grand Tracadie is a little over 25 kilometers (20 minutes) northeast of Charlottetown via Route 2 and Route 6.

BRACKLEY BEACH

With its proximity to the national park, excellent beaches, golf, deep-sea fishing, and other attractions, Brackley Beach is a popular base.

Just south of town is **Dunes Studio Gallery and Cafe** (Brackley Point Rd., 902/672-2586, June-Oct. daily 9am-9pm), an architecturally distinctive building with the ocean-facing wall composed almost entirely of windows. Inside, a wide spiral walkway passes the work of some 70 artists, including island craftspeople who create stoneware, framed photography, gold jewelry, pottery, watercolors, woodcarvings, oils, and sculptures. It's worth browsing just for porcelains crafted by owner Peter Jansons. Make sure you find your way up to the rooftop garden.

Food

For its stylish setting, sweeping views, and creative dishes, the restaurant within the ★ **Dunes Cafe** (Brackley Point Rd., 902/672-2586, June-Sept. daily 11:30am-9pm, Oct. daily 11:30am-2:30pm, $27-38) is one of the best places to eat on Prince Edward Island. Seating choices are in a sunken area at the rear of the gallery or on a higher level overlooking the garden. Regardless of your preference, you will most definitely need reservations for either lunch or dinner any time through July and August. Lunches are priced $9-16 and include a cold-water seafood stew and a grilled lamb burger. In the evening, both the seafood chowder and brie and pear pizza can't be faulted as starters, while for a main, the banana bread-crumbed halibut is hard to pass up.

Accommodations and Camping

Distinctive red-and-white ★ **Shaw's Hotel** (99 Apple Tree Rd., 902/672-2022, www.shaws-hotel.ca, June-mid-Oct., $145-240 s or d) overlooks the bay from a 30-hectare peninsula at the edge of Prince Edward Island National Park. This was the Shaw family's homestead in the 1860s, and it's still in the family, now protected as a national historic site. The property has 16 antiques-furnished guest rooms in the main house, 25 adjacent historic cottages, and 15 newer upscale waterfront chalets. In high season, rates start at $145 s or d for a room only; in the off-season, you can pay from $120 per person to include breakfast and dinner. The ambience is informal and friendly—a nice place for meeting islanders and other visitors. The hotel dining room (June-mid-Oct., daily 8am-10am and 6pm-9pm, $24-36) is consistently good; start with a chowder appetizer and stick to the chef's daily choices, prepared from whatever seafood is in season.

Camping is available nearby at the 12-hectare **Vacationland Travel Park** (east of Rte. 15, overlooking Brackley Bay, 902/672-2317 or 800/529-0066, www.vacationlandrv.pe.ca, mid-May-mid-Sept., $35-42). Facilities include a convenience store, a launderette, a heated pool, hot showers, mini-golf, and other recreational activities.

Getting There

Brackley Beach is about 15 kilometers (10 minutes) west of Grand Tracadie via Route 6. To get there directly from Charlottetown, take Route 15 north from the Charlottetown Airport for about 15 kilometers (10 minutes).

★ PRINCE EDWARD ISLAND NATIONAL PARK

The sandy beaches, dunes, sandstone cliffs, marshes, and forestlands of **Prince Edward Island National Park** represent the island as it once was, unspoiled by 20th-century development.

The park protects a slender 40-kilometer-long coastal slice of natural perfection, extending almost the full length of Queens County, as well as a 6-square-kilometer spit of land farther east, near Greenwich on the North Shore of eastern Prince Edward

Island. The park also extends inland at Cavendish to include Green Gables Heritage Place and Green Gables Golf Course. The main body of the park is bookended by two large bays. At the eastern end, Tracadie Bay spreads out like an oversized pond with shimmering waters. Forty kilometers to the west, New London Bay forms almost a mirror image of the eastern end. In between, long barrier islands define Rustico and Covehead Bays, and sand dunes webbed with marram grass, rushes, fragrant bayberry, and wild roses front the coastline.

Sunrise and sunset here are cast in glowing colors. All along the gulf at sunrise, the beaches have a sense of primeval peacefulness, their sands textured like herringbone by the overnight sea breezes.

Getting around is easy. Route 6 lies on the park's inland side, connecting numerous park entrances, and the Gulf Shore Parkway runs along the coast nearly the park's entire length. You can drive through the park year-round. Cyclists will appreciate the smooth wide shoulders and light traffic along the Gulf Shore Parkway.

Park Entry

Between early June and mid-September, a one-day pass is adult $8, senior $7, child $4, to a maximum of $16 per vehicle. Before purchasing a pass, check with your Cavendish accommodation, as some local lodgings include a park pass in their rates.

Environmental Factors

The national park was established in 1937 to protect the fragile dunes along the Gulf of St. Lawrence and cultural features such as Green Gables Heritage Place. Parks Canada walks a fine line, balancing environmental concerns with the responsibilities of hosting half a million park visitors a year. Boardwalks route visitors through dunes to the beaches and preserve the fragile landscape.

Bird-watchers will be amply rewarded with sightings of some of the more than 100 species known to frequent the park. Brackley Marsh,

Orby Head, and the Rustico Island Causeway are good places to start. The park preserves nesting habitat for some 25 pairs of endangered piping plovers—small, shy shorebirds that arrive in early April to breed in flat, sandy areas near the high-tide line. Some beaches may be closed in spring and summer when the plovers are nesting; it's vital to the birds' survival that visitors stay clear of these areas.

Recreation

The park's unbroken stretches of sandy beaches—some white, others tinted pink by iron oxide—are among the best in Atlantic Canada. On warm summer days, droves of sunbathers laze on the shore and swim in the usually gentle surf. The busier beaches have a lifeguard on duty, but always be aware of undertows.

Stanhope Beach, opposite the Stanhope Campground, is wide and flat and remains relatively busy throughout summer. Next up to the east, **Brackley Beach** is backed by higher sand dunes. The adjacent visitors center has changing rooms and a snack bar. **Cavendish Beach** is the busiest of all; those toward Orby Head are backed by steep red-sandstone cliffs.

Established **hiking trails** range from the 0.5-kilometer wheelchair-accessible **Reeds and Rushes Trail,** beginning at the Dalvay Administration Building near Grand Tracadie, to the 8-kilometer **Homestead Trail** beginning near the entrance to Cavendish Campground. The latter wends inland alongside freshwater ponds and through woods and marshes, and is open to both hikers and bikers. Be wary of potentially hazardous cliff edges and of the poison ivy and ticks that lurk in the ground cover.

If you'd like to learn more about the park's ecology, join one of the **nature walks** led by Parks Canada rangers. The treks lead through white spruce stunted by winter storms and winds, to freshwater ponds, and into the habitats of such native animal species as red fox, northern phalarope, Swainson's thrush, and junco.

Camping

The park's two campgrounds are distinctly different from one another. A percentage of sites can be reserved through the **Parks Canada Campground Reservation Service** (877/737-3783, www.pccamping.ca) for $12 per reservation. During July and August, especially for weekends, reservations are recommended. The remaining sites are offered on a first-come, first-served basis.

Stanhope Campground (north of Stanhope, early June-early Oct.) is across the road from the ocean and has 95 unserviced sites ($28), 16 sites with two-way hookups ($33), and 14 sites with full hookups ($36). Amenities include showers, a playground, a grocery store, laundry facilities, and wooded tent sites.

Closest to Cavendish and the center of the park's summer interpretive program is **Cavendish Campground** (early June-early Oct.). This, the most popular of the two campgrounds, has 230 unserviced sites ($28) and 78 hookup sites ($36). Campground facilities include a grocery store, kitchen shelters, launderettes, flush toilets, and hot showers.

Information

The main **Cavendish Visitor Information Centre** (902/672-6350, mid-May-June and Sept.-mid-Oct. daily 9am-5pm, July-Aug. daily 8am-9pm) is combined with the province's Visitor Information Centre, 50 meters north of the Route 6 and Route 13 intersection in Cavendish. As well as offering general park information, displays depict the park's natural history, and a small shop sells park-related literature and souvenirs. Another source of information is Parks Canada (www.pc.gc.ca).

Getting There

The Gulf Shore Parkway runs along the coast nearly the park's entire length, with four access points along a 12-kilometer stretch of Route 6 between Cavendish and North Rustico. You can drive through the park year-round.

The closest entrance to Charlottetown is at North Rustico, 30 kilometers (30 minutes) north of the capital along Routes 2, 7, and 6. Continuing north for 4 kilometers from North Rustico you can access the park along Cape Road. This access point is 34 kilometers (32 minutes) north of Charlottetown via Routes 2, 7, and then 6. The main park entrance is at Cavendish, 40 kilometers (40 minutes) north of Charlottetown via Routes 2 and 13. Less than 1 kilometer west of this entrance

Cavendish Beach

Lucy Maud Montgomery

Lucy Maud Montgomery, known and beloved around the world as the creator of *Anne of Green Gables,* was born at New London, Prince Edward Island, in 1874, a decade after the Charlottetown Conference. When she was only two, her mother died and her father moved to western Canada. Maud, as she preferred to be called, was left in the care of her maternal grandparents, who brought her to Cavendish.

Cavendish, in northern Queens County, was idyllic in those days, and Montgomery wrote fondly about the ornate Victorian sweetness of the setting of her early years. As a young woman, she studied first at the island's Prince of Wales College and later at Dalhousie University in Halifax. She then returned to the island as a teacher at Bideford, Lower Bedeque, Belmont, and Lot 15. In 1898, her grandfather's death brought her back to Cavendish to help her grandmother.

The idea for *Anne of Green Gables* dated to her second Cavendish stay, and the book was published in 1908. In 1911, Montgomery married the Reverend Ewen MacDonald at her Campbell relatives' Silver Bush homestead overlooking the Lake of Shining Waters. (The Campbell descendants still live in the pretty farmhouse and have turned their home into a museum.) The couple moved to Ontario, where Montgomery spent the rest of her life, returning to PEI only for short visits. But Maud never forgot Prince Edward Island. Those brief revisitations with her beloved island must have been painful; after one trip, she wistfully recalled in her journal:

is Grahams Lane, which leads to the park's most popular beach. This access point is 41 kilometers (40 minutes) north of Charlottetown via Routes 2 and 13 to Cavendish and then west on Route 6.

RUSTICO BAY

A decade after the French began Port-la-Joye near Charlottetown, French settlers cut through the inland forest and settled Rustico Bay's coastline. England's Acadian deportation in 1755 emptied the villages, but not for long. The Acadians returned, and the five revived Rusticos—Rusticoville, Rustico, Anglo Rustico, North Rustico, and North Rustico Harbour—still thrive and encircle Rustico Bay's western shore.

Sights and Recreation

For a glimpse at Acadian culture, check out the imposing two-story **Farmers' Bank of Rustico Museum** (Church Rd., Hunter River, 902/963-3168, June-Sept. Mon.-Sat. 9:30am-5:30pm, Sun. 11am-5pm, adult $6, senior $4.50, child $3.50). Built in 1864 as Canada's first chartered people's bank (the precursor of today's credit unions), the building served as the early Acadian banking connection, then as

a library. Exhibits at this national historic site include heritage displays plus artifacts from the life of the Reverend Georges-Antoine Belcourt, the founder.

Half a dozen charter fishing operators tie up at Rustico Harbour (along the wharf behind Fisherman's Wharf Lobster Suppers). The average cost is a remarkably low $40 per person for a three-hour outing or $180 for a full day's charter; the catch includes cod, mackerel, flounder, and tuna. Most charters operate July-mid-September. The crew will outfit you in rain gear if needed, provide tackle and bait, and clean and fillet your catch. **Aiden's Deep-sea Fishing** (902/963-3522, www.peifishing.com) has been in business for decades and has three excursions (adult $45, child $35) scheduled daily mid-June-mid-September.

Food

Fisherman's Wharf Lobster Suppers (7230 Rustico Rd., North Rustico, 902/963-2669, mid-May-mid-Oct. daily 11am-8pm) is a cavernous 500-seat restaurant that attracts the tour bus crowd from Cavendish and Charlottetown. Although it's open for lunch, the lobster supper doesn't start until 4pm.

This evening I spent in Lover's Lane. How beautiful it was—green and alluring and beckoning! I had been tired and discouraged and sick at heart before I went to it—and it rested me and cheered me and stole away the heartsickness, giving peace and newness of life.

Montgomery died in 1942 and was buried in Cavendish Cemetery. She left 20 juvenile books and myriad other writings. Her works have been published worldwide, translated into 16 languages. In Japan, Montgomery's writings are required reading in the school system, which accounts for the island's many Japanese visitors.

Montgomery wrote for children, and she viewed Cavendish and Prince Edward Island with all the clarity and innocence that a child possesses. Her books are as timeless today as they were decades ago. Some critics have described Montgomery's writings as mawkish. Contemporary scholars, however, have taken a new look at the author's works and have begun to discern a far more complex style. The academic community may debate her literary prowess, but no matter—the honest essence of Montgomery's writings has inspired decades of zealous pilgrims to pay their respects to her native Cavendish. To islanders, she is Lucy Maud, their literary genius, on a first-name basis.

Choose from three different sizes of lobster ($34-42), pay your money, and join the fray. The cost includes one full lobster and unlimited trips to the super-long buffet counter, including chowder, mussels, hot entrées, salad, dessert, and hot drinks.

If your accommodation has cooking facilities, head to **Doiron Fisheries** (North Rustico dock, 902/963-2442, May-early Oct. daily 8am-8pm) for lobsters, mussels, clams, fish, and delicious Malpeque oysters.

Accommodations and Camping

Accommodations at **Rustico Resort** (corner of Rte. 6 and Rte. 242, Rustico, 902/963-2357, www.rusticoresort.com, May-Oct., $145-410 s or d) are usually filled with golfers, who stay in the cottages (from $215 s or d, including breakfast and unlimited golf on the adjacent 18-hole course). Other amenities include motel-style rooms, grass tennis courts, a heated pool, paddleboard rentals and lessons, and a restaurant with tasty pizzas from $14.

The 1870 **Barachois Inn** (2193 Church Rd., Rustico, 902/963-2194 or 800/963-2194, www.barachoisinn.com, May-Oct., $165-295 s or d) overlooks Rustico Bay from just

off Route 243. The main house holds four historically themed guest rooms, while the adjacent McDonald House contains four larger, more modern rooms. Rates include a full breakfast.

Cymbria Tent and Trailer Park (729 Grand Pere Point Rd., Cambria, 902/963-2458, www.cymbria.ca, June-early Sept., tent sites $30, hookups $35-40) occupies a quiet 12-hectare location close to the beach, four kilometers east of Rustico. Facilities include a store, game room, playground, dump station, and hot showers.

Getting There

Rustico is 10 kilometers (10 minutes) west of Brackley Beach along Route 6. To get to Rustico Bay directly from Charlottetown, go north on Routes 2 and 7, then west on Route 6, for a total of 30 kilometers (30 minutes).

★ NORTH RUSTICO HARBOUR

The tiny village of North Rustico Harbour, on the north side of Rustico Bay, is one of my favorite spots on Prince Edward Island. It's around 1.5 kilometers east of North Rustico by road, but a more enjoyable way to get there is to walk along the harbor-front boardwalk from North Rustico. The village itself has only a few homes, built on a slight rise sloping down to the water. At the end of the road you'll find a restored wharf with shops and cafés, sea kayak rentals, and a few shops. Add to the scene an old wooden lighthouse, a beach that is used as a parking lot at low tide, and one of the region's best restaurants, and you have a destination as far removed from nearby commercial Cavendish as you could imagine. Although it's out of sight from the harbor, make sure to wander across the dunes behind the lighthouse to **North Rustico Beach** (which is within Prince Edward Island National Park).

North Rustico Harbour is the push-off point for kayak tours operated by **Outside Expeditions** (370 Harbourview Dr., 902/963-3366, mid-May-mid-Oct.). A 90-minute paddle around the bay is $45 per person; a three-hour trip, with the chance of seeing abundant bird life, is $65; and a six-hour trip across to Robinsons Island is $125, including lunch.

Food

A shack on the main dock has been converted to the ★ **Blue Mussel Café** (Harbourview Dr., 902/963-2152, mid-June-mid-Sept. Mon.-Thurs. 11:30am-9pm, Fri.-Sun. 11:30am-10:30pm, $15-28), where many of the tables are outside on a private corner of the wharf. The menu reads like a list of what fisherfolk haul in from local waters—salmon, haddock, mackerel, oysters, mussels, and lobster—and unlike at most other island restaurants, there's not a deep fryer in sight.

Getting There

To get to North Rustico Harbour from North Rustico, go east on Harbourview Drive for two kilometers. North Rustico Harbour is about 30 kilometers (30 minutes) northwest of Charlottetown via Routes 2, 7, and 6.

North Rustico Harbour

Cavendish

Thanks to Lucy Maud Montgomery and a certain fictional character named Anne, Cavendish, 40 kilometers northeast of Charlottetown, is Prince Edward Island's most popular tourist destination. Unfortunately, those who come here expecting to find a bucolic little oasis of tranquility will be sorely disappointed. The once rural Cavendish area has become a maze of theme parks, fast-food outlets, and souvenir shops in parts, and the village has repositioned itself as an official resort municipality to try to grapple with fame. To dedicated readers of Montgomery's sentimental books, the village's lure is emotional. For others—those who don't know Anne of Green Gables from Anne Frank—it might best be avoided. Still, if you end up here and are looking for something to do, you'll have a multitude of choices—including heading into adjacent Prince Edward Island National Park, golfing at Green Gables Golf Course, or browsing through craft shops.

Montgomery portrayed rural Cavendish as an idyllic "neverland" called Avonlea, imbued with innocence and harmony. Beyond the crass commercialism, as you drive the rambling red-clay lanes and walk the quiet woods, meadows, and gulf shore, you'll have to agree that the lady did not overstate her case. The most pastoral and historic places are preserved as part of **Prince Edward Island National Park.** Cavendish itself is home to two important Anne attractions, while others dot the surrounding countryside.

★ GREEN GABLES HERITAGE PLACE

Located on the west side of the Route 6 and Route 13 intersection, **Green Gables Heritage Place** (902/963-7874, May-Oct. daily 9am-5pm, adult $8, senior $7, child $4) reigns as the idyllic hub of a Montgomery sightseeing circuit. The restored 19th-century farmhouse, once home to Montgomery's elderly cousins and the setting for her most famous book, *Anne of Green Gables,* is furnished simply and stolidly, just as it was described in the novel. A fire in 1997 badly damaged portions of the house, but repairs commenced immediately, and within a couple of weeks the landmark was back in perfect

Green Gables Heritage Place

Cavendish and Vicinity

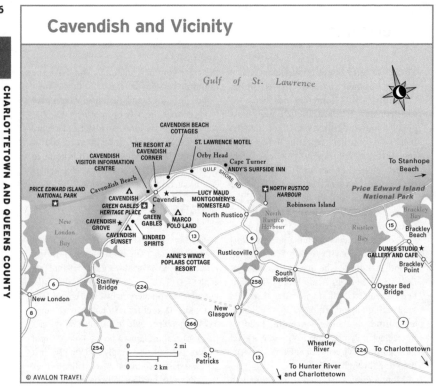

Gulf of St. Lawrence

CAVENDISH BEACH COTTAGES

THE RESORT AT CAVENDISH CORNER

ST. LAWRENCE MOTEL

CAVENDISH VISITOR INFORMATION CENTRE

Orby Head

Cape Turner

ANDY'S SURFSIDE INN

GULF SHORE RD

PRICE EDWARD ISLAND NATIONAL PARK

Cavendish Beach

CAVENDISH

Cavendish

NORTH RUSTICO HARBOUR

Price Edward Island National Park

LUCY MAUD MONTGOMERY'S HOMESTEAD

Robinsons Island

CAVENDISH GREEN GABLES HERITAGE PLACE

North Rustico

North Rustico Harbour

Rustico Bay

Brackley Bay

CAVENDISH GROVE

GREEN GABLES

MARCO POLO LAND

15

Brackley Beach

New London Bay

CAVENDISH SUNSET

KINDRED SPIRITS

DUNES STUDIO GALLERY AND CAFE

ANNE'S WINDY POPLARS COTTAGE RESORT

13

Rusticoville

6

Brackley Point

Stanley Bridge

224

258

South Rustico

Oyster Bed Bridge

6

New London

8

New Glasgow

266

7

254

0   2 mi
0   2 km

St. Patricks

13

Wheatley River

224

To Charlottetown

To Hunter River and Charlottetown

To Stanhope Beach

© AVALON TRAVEL

condition. Among other memorabilia in the pretty vintage setting are artifacts such as the author's archaic typewriter, on which she composed many well-loved passages. Period-style gardens, farm buildings, and an interpretive center and gift shop complete the complex. From the grounds, the Balsam Hollow and Haunted Woods trails feature some of Montgomery's favorite woodland haunts, including Lover's Lane.

LUCY MAUD MONTGOMERY HOMESTEAD

Montgomery spent much of her childhood living with her grandparents in a small home one kilometer east of Green Gables Heritage Place. "I wrote it in the evenings after my regular day's work was done," she recalled of her most famous novel, "wrote most of it at the window of the little gable room that had been mine for

many years." While the main building is long gone, the stone cellar remains. Surrounded by a white picket fence and apple trees, it has been converted to a **small museum and bookstore** (Rte. 6, 902/963-2231, mid-May-June and Sept.-mid-Oct. daily 9am-5pm, July-Aug. daily 9am-6pm, adult $3, child $1) operated by Montgomery's descendants, who live at the end of the road.

Montgomery is buried in the nearby **Cavendish Cemetery,** at the corner of Route 6 and Route 13.

RECREATION

The focus of most visitors to Cavendish are the beaches of **Prince Edward Island National Park,** which parallel the main highway through town and are within easy walking and biking distance of many accommodations. In the heart of the commercial strip, **Cavendish Grove** was once the site of a fun park, but upon its closing, the land was incorporated into the national park. Today, it's a pleasant green space with artificial ponds, manicured lawns, and paths leading to the beach.

Golf

Little known outside Canada, Stanley Thompson was one of the world's great 20th-century golf course architects. His best-known courses are those within the country's national park system. **Green Gables Golf Course** (Rte. 6, 902/963-4653 (greens fees $105 including cart, $60 after 3pm) may not be as revered as Thompson-designed Highland Links (Cape Breton Highlands National Park) or Banff Springs (Banff National Park), but this old-fashioned layout within Prince Edward Island National Park is a gem of composition defined by water views and deep bunkers.

Amusement Parks and Museums

The only theme park with any relationship to Anne of Green Gables is **Avonlea Village** (Rte. 6, 902/963-3050, www.avonlea.ca, mid-June-early Sept. daily 10am-6pm, free), which used to be a full-blown amusement park, but now offers free admission. Instead of Anne's world being brought to life through musical shows and costumed interpreters, you'll find a number of cafés and restaurants, as well as occasional live music performances.

You'll see the rides of **Sandspit Amusement Park** (8986 Cavendish Rd., 902/963-3939, www.sandspit.com, last two weeks of June daily 10am-6pm, July-Aug. daily 10am-10pm), east of the junction of Routes 6 and 13, long before arriving at the front gate. The huge park, a magnet for kids on vacation, features a roller coaster (The Cyclone, billed as the largest in the Maritimes), a carousel, and other rides, rides, rides. It's free to get in, but each ride costs a small amount. All-day ride packages cost $13.50-25, depending on your height.

And what tourist town would be complete without a **Ripley's Believe It or Not! Museum** (Rte. 6, 902/963-2242, June and Sept. daily 10am-6pm, July-Aug. daily 9am-9pm, adult $15, senior $11.50, child $9) or a wax museum—in this case, the adjacent **Wax World of the Stars** (Rte. 6, 902/963-3444, early June and early Sept. 10am-4:30pm, July-Aug. 9am-7:30pm, adult $15, senior $11.50, child $9), which is exactly as the name suggests.

Green Gables Golf Course

FOOD
Lobster Supper

Lobster suppers are casual good-value gatherings held across the island. They can be very commercial or simply an annual gathering of locals in a church basement. A great compromise is the ★ **New Glasgow Lobster Suppers** (Rte. 258, 902/964-2870, June-mid-Oct. 4pm-8:30pm), eight kilometers southeast of Cavendish along Route 13. In operation since 1958, this one fills a cavernous hall with up to 500 diners at a time. It even has its own lobster holding pond, allowing the tradition to continue beyond lobster fishing season. Choose the size of lobster and pay at the front desk, then feast on limitless mussels, clam chowder, salad, and bread until your lobster is brought to your table. Options range from a one-pound lobster ($35) to a four pounder ($75), or share a four-pound lobster for $100. If lobster isn't your thing, many other options are offered, ranging from vegetarian to scallops ($25-30).

Other Dining Options

Man cannot live on lobster alone, so if you're in town more than one night, you'll need to find somewhere else to eat. If you have cooking facilities at your accommodation (even just a barbecue), pick up fresh seafood at **Doiron Fisheries** (North Rustico dock, 902/963-2442, May-early Oct. daily 8am-8pm).

For do-it-yourself meals, take your choice of markets along major highways; shops at **Cavendish Beach Shopping Plaza** answer most needs. The main excuse to stop at **Cavendish Boardwalk**, another mall, is for an ice cream at **Cow's** (9139 Rte. 6, 902/963-2692, mid-June-mid-Sept. daily 10am-6pm).

ACCOMMODATIONS AND CAMPING

While accommodations in Cavendish are plentiful, they book up well in advance for July and August. No place in Atlantic Canada sees a more dramatic drop in room rates for the shoulder seasons (mid-May-June and

Sept.-mid-Oct.), while the rest of the year, most accommodations close completely.

Under $50

★ **Andy's Surfside Inn** (Gulf Shore Rd., 902/963-2405, June-Nov., $55-85 s or d) is a big old whitewashed home right on the ocean, a few kilometers east of Cavendish along the coastal road. The rooms and facilities are older, but the setting can't be beat. Only one room has its own bathroom; other amenities include a deck, bikes, and a barbecue.

$50-100

The **St. Lawrence Motel** (351 Gulf Shore Rd., 902/963-2053 or 800/387-2053, www.stlawrencemotel.com, mid-May-early Oct., $80-178 s or d) is within Prince Edward Island National Park between Cavendish and North Rustico. Set on eight hectares, this 16-room property overlooks the gulf, a short walk from the water. All but one of the units has a kitchen, and the largest have three bedrooms. The beach is a short walk down the road, and on-site amenities include an outdoor swimming pool, a recreation room, barbecues, and lawn games such as horseshoes and croquet.

Silverwood Motel (Rte. 6, 902/963-2439 or 800/565-4753, www.silverwoodmotel.com, June-Sept., $99-159 s or d) has regular motel rooms as well as one- and two-bedroom units with kitchens. There's also a heated outdoor pool and adjacent restaurant.

Over $100

The Resort at Cavendish Corner (corner of Rte. 6 and Rte. 13, 902/963-2251 or 877/963-2251, www.resortatcavendishcorner.com, May-Oct., $120-320 s or d) offers more than 100 rooms and cottages spread across a three-hectare site, across from the main visitor center and within walking distance of the beach. Amenities include barbecues, two outdoor heated pools, two playgrounds, a restaurant, and wireless Internet throughout.

From ★ **Kindred Spirits Country Inn and Cottages** (Memory Ln., off Rte. 6, 902/963-2434 or 800/461-1755, www.

kindredspirits.ca, mid-May-mid-Oct., $135-375 s or d), guests can stroll along Lover's Lane to Green Gables Heritage Place, just the way Lucy Maud Montgomery described in *Anne of Green Gables*. This grandly Victorian estate is handy to the golf course as well, but it's also very private and far removed from busy Route 6. Bed-and-breakfast rooms in the main inn ($135-180 s or d) are decorated with stylish antiques. Some have balconies and fireplaces. Surrounding the inn are 14 kitchen-equipped cottages, each surrounded by green space. Rates range from $205 for a one-bedroom unit to $375 for a three-bedroom cottage with a whirlpool bath.

Overlooking the Gulf of St. Lawrence from within Prince Edward Island National Park is **Cavendish Beach Cottages** (1445 Gulf Shore Rd., 902/963-2025, www.cavendish-beachcottages.com, early May-Sept., $169-229 s or d), a complex of 13 simply furnished yet modern cottages, each with a deck offering ocean views. The cottages, set back 200 meters from the beach, are just a few steps from the park's jogging and hiking trails. Off-season rates (May and Sept.) start at $120.

The price may seem a little high considering its location more than two kilometers from the beach, but **Anne's Windy Poplars Cottage Resort** (Rte. 1, 902/963-2888 or 800/363-5888, www.anneswindypoplars.com, late Apr.-mid-Oct., $200-380 s or d) has many things going for it—spacious and immaculate cottages, a pleasant pool complex with a hot tub and sauna, and well-tended gardens dotted with playgrounds. The cottages all come with kitchens, decks, up to three bedrooms, and wireless Internet.

Campgrounds

What ★ **Cavendish Campground** (late May-early Oct., $28-36) lacks in facilities it makes up for in location, close to the ocean within Prince Edward Island National Park and just a few kilometers from downtown Cavendish. Amenities include showers, kitchen shelters, and fire pits (firewood $8 per bundle). Even with more than 300 campsites, it fills most summer days, so plan on arriving before noon or booking a site in advance. These can be made through the **Parks Canada Campground Reservation Service** (877/737-3783, www.pccamping.ca) for $12 per reservation.

Marco Polo Land (Rte. 13, 902/963-2352 or 800/665-2352, www.marcopololand.com, late May-mid-Sept., $34.50-45) is the island's definitive commercial campground, replete

Kindred Spirits Country Inn and Cottages

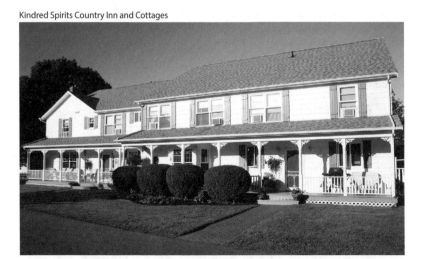

with resort trappings. Facilities at the 40-hectare park include more than 400 campsites ($24-31), tennis courts, mini-golf, a full-size outdoor pool, a street hockey rink, a petting zoo, a wading pool, a restaurant, and a grocery store.

The 465-site **Sunset Campground** (Rte. 6, 902/963-2440 or 800/715-2440, www.cavendishsunsetcampgropund.com, June-early Sept., $34.50-45) is big, bold, and very family-friendly. It has many of the same amenities as Marco Polo Land, although on a smaller scale. Its selling point is its location within walking distance of Cavendish's many commercial attractions.

INFORMATION AND SERVICES

Cavendish has no downtown. Instead, services such as restaurants and gas stations are scattered along a five-kilometer stretch of Route 6 southeast from the junction with Route 13. Plan on doing chores such as grocery shopping, banking, and posting mail back in Charlottetown.

Cavendish Visitor Information Centre (902/963-2391, mid-May-June and Sept.-mid-Oct. daily 9am-5pm, July-Aug. daily 8am-9pm) is combined with the provincial Visitor Information Centre, 50 meters north of the Route 6 and Route 13 intersection, and represents local operators and accommodations. Tourism Prince Edward Island shares the building with Parks Canada (902/963-2391), which hands out national park information.

GETTING THERE

From North Rustico Harbour, it's about 15 kilometers (10 minutes) northwest to Cavendish via Route 6. To get to Cavendish directly from Charlottetown, go north on Route 2 and Route 13. The trip is about 40 kilometers (40 minutes).

VICINITY OF CAVENDISH

Hamlets encircle Cavendish. The rural scenery is lovely, and exploring the beaches and back roads should help you sharpen your appetite for a night at one of PEI's famed lobster-supper community halls, which are scattered hereabouts.

Stanley Bridge

For seaworthy sightseeing, check out **Stanley Bridge Marine Aquarium** (32 Campbellton Rd., 902/886-3355, mid-June-early Oct. daily 9:30am-8pm, adult $9, child $7), five kilometers southwest of Cavendish. The privately operated aquarium has a limited number of fish species in viewing tanks and exhibits on natural history (lots of stuffed birds) and oyster cultivation. Part of the complex is a café with a waterfront deck.

In the vicinity, shoppers like the **Stanley Bridge Studios** (Rte. 6, 902/886-2800, daily 10am-5pm), where shelves and floor space overflow with woolen sweaters, quilts, apparel, stoneware, porcelain, jewelry, and Anne dolls.

GETTING THERE

It's seven kilometers to Stanley Bridge from Cavendish west along Route 6. From Charlottetown, take Route 2 west then Route 230 north, then 254 north, for a total distance of 45 kilometers (50 minutes).

New London

The **Lucy Maud Montgomery Birthplace** (corner of Rte. 6 and Rte. 20, 902/886-2099, mid-May-mid-Oct. daily 9am-5pm, adult $4, child $2) lies 10 minutes from Cavendish, at what was once Clifton. The author was born in the unassuming house in 1874. The exhibits include her wedding dress, scrapbooks, and other personal items.

Old-fashioned tearooms dot the countryside around Cavendish, and none are more welcoming than ★ **Blue Winds Tea Room** (10746 New London Rd., 902/886-2860, late May-mid-Oct. Fri.-Wed. 11:30am-5pm, Thurs. 2pm-5pm), on the south side of the village. Here the soups are made from scratch, breads and pastries are baked daily, and recipes for treats such as New Moon Pudding are taken from historic cookbooks. On Thursday, afternoon tea is served for $14 per person.

GETTING THERE

New London is about 12 kilometers west of Cavendish via Route 6. From Charlottetown, take Route 2 west then Route 8 north, a total distance of 45 kilometers (50 minutes).

Park Corner

Anne of Green Gables Museum (Rte. 20, 902/436-7329, www.annemuseum.com, mid-May-June and Sept.-mid-Oct. daily 11am-4pm, July-Aug. daily 9am-5pm, adult $5.50, child $2), eight kilometers northwest of New London, is another Montgomery landmark and the ancestral home of the author's Campbell relatives. The estate spreads out in a farmhouse setting in the pastoral rolling countryside, with the Lake of Shining Waters, described in *Anne of Green Gables,* in front of the main buildings. Montgomery described the house as "the big beautiful home that was the wonder castle of my dreams," and here she was married in 1911. The museum's exhibits include Montgomery's personal correspondence and first editions of her works.

GETTING THERE

Park Corner is 22 kilometers (25 minutes) northwest of Cavendish. Get there by taking Route 6 west, then Route 20 north. The village is 70 kilometers (one hour) northwest of Charlottetown via Routes 2, 8, and 20.

the Lucy Maud Montgomery Birthplace

Prince County

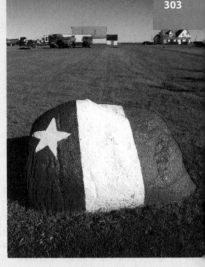

Prince County encompasses the western third of Prince Edward Island. Like Kings County in the east, it is well off the main tourist path.

Along the southern portion of Prince County, the land is level, and the pastoral farmlands flow in gentle, serene sweeps to the strait coastline.

Thick woodlands span the county's midsection, and you'll see fields of potatoes that blossom in July and green carpets of wheat nodding in the summer breezes. The northern tip is a remote and barren plain with a windswept coast, where farmers known as "mossers" use stout draft horses to reap Irish moss (a seaweed) from the surf.

Summerside, the province's second-largest town, boasts an ample supply of lodgings, restaurants, and nightlife. Just west of there is the province's largest Acadian area, the Région Évangéline. Count on high-quality crafts and wares at town boutiques and outlying shops throughout the region; the region's craftspeople are renowned for quilts, knitted apparel, Acadian shirts, and blankets.

Route 2, PEI's main expressway, enters Prince County at the town of Kensington, glides past the seaport of Summerside on a narrow isthmus, and leads inland for 100 kilometers to finish at the village of Tignish, near the island's northwestern tip. The highways up and down the east and west coasts come together as Lady Slipper Scenic Drive, one of the provincial scenic sightseeing routes (it's signposted with a red symbol of the orchid-like flower). The county's most idyllic scenery—and some of the island's most spectacular sea views—lie along this route, at the sea's edges of Northumberland Strait and the Gulf of St. Lawrence. About 50 meandering side roads lead off the coastal route to connect with Route 2 and others. You may become temporarily lost on the roads, but not for long—the blue sea invariably looms around the next bend.

PLANNING YOUR TIME

It's possible to reach the northern tip of Prince County on a day trip from Charlottetown, but a more sensible option if you have just one day would be to concentrate on the southern half of the county. A suggested route would be to

---

Previous: Summerside Harbour; Spinnakers' Landing. **Above:** the Acadian flag painted on a rock in Région Évangéline.

Highlights

★ **College of Piping:** Students from around the world gather at this school to learn the art of bagpiping and Highland dancing. Visitors are more than welcome to watch (page 306).

★ **Green Park Shipbuilding Museum and Yeo House:** An attraction that is as scenic as it is historic, this waterfront estate was once the center of a thriving shipbuilding industry (page 310).

★ **Our Lady of Mont-Carmel Acadian Church:** This magnificent church rises high above the trim Acadian homes of Mont-Carmel (page 312).

★ **Canadian Potato Museum:** Learn about the province's main agricultural crop at this museum; it is more interesting than the name might suggest (page 314).

★ **North Cape:** Drive to the end of the road on Prince Edward Island and you'll find yourself in the middle of a wind farm with panoramic ocean views in all directions (page 317).

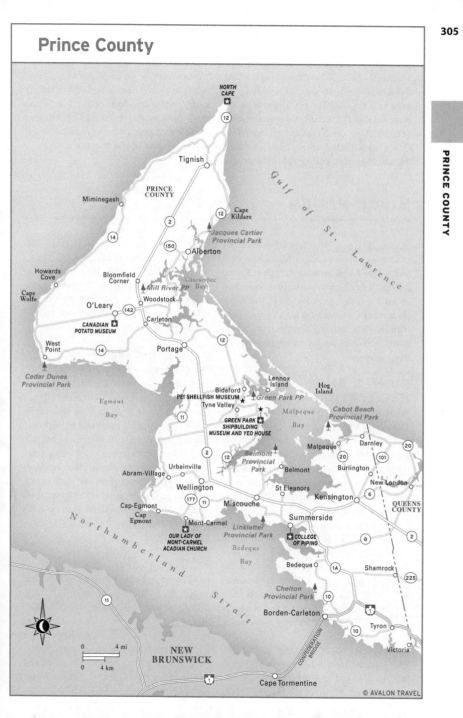

Prince County

NORTH CAPE
12

Tignish

PRINCE COUNTY

Miminegash

12   Cape Kildare

Jacques Cartier Provincial Park

2

14

150

Alberton

Howards Cove

Bloomfield Corner

Mill River PP

Cascumpec Bay

Cape Wolfe

Woodstock

O'Leary   142

Carleton

CANADIAN POTATO MUSEUM

West Point

14   Portage   12

Cedar Dunes Provincial Park

Egmont Bay

Gulf of St. Lawrence

Lennox Island

Bideford

PEI SHELLFISH MUSEUM

Tyne Valley

Green Park PP

Hog Island

GREEN PARK SHIPBUILDING MUSEUM AND YEO HOUSE

11

Malpeque Bay

Cabot Beach Provincial Park

Belmont Provincial Park

Malpeque   Darnley   20

2

12

Belmont

20

Burlington   101

New London

Abram-Village

Urbainville

Wellington

6

Kensington

St Eleanors

QUEENS COUNTY

Cap-Egmont

177 11   Miscouche

Cap Egmont

Mont-Carmel

OUR LADY OF MONT-CARMEL ACADIAN CHURCH

Linkletter Provincial Park

Summerside

COLLEGE OF PIPING

8

2

Bedeque Bay

Bedeque   1A   Shamrock

Chelton Provincial Park   10   225

Northumberland Strait

11

NEW BRUNSWICK

0   4 mi
0   4 km

Borden-Carleton

CONFEDERATION BRIDGE

1

Cape Tormentine

10   Tyron

Victoria

© AVALON TRAVEL

stop in Summerside to visit the **College of Piping**, drive through Région Évangéline past the spectacular **Our Lady of Mont-Carmel Acadian Church,** and jog north to the **Green Park Shipbuilding Museum and Yeo House.** The main reason to explore further is for the coastal scenery, especially along the Northumberland Strait. Other attractions include the **Canadian Potato Museum,** golfing at Mill River, and the feeling of accomplishment of driving to the end of the road at **North Cape.**

Tourist services are more limited in Prince County than elsewhere in the province. You should be able to find somewhere to stay with a few days' notice, but for top picks such as **West Point Lighthouse** (West Point), plan on being disappointed if you arrive without reservations.

Summerside

Summerside (pop. 14,500), 60 kilometers west of Charlottetown and 30 kilometers northwest of the Confederation Bridge, is Prince Edward Island's second-largest town and its main shipping port. It's got all the bustle yet none of the seaminess usually associated with seaports. Stately old homes anchor wide lawns, and quiet streets are edged with verdant canopies.

SIGHTS AND RECREATION
Along the Harbor

The tourist's Summerside lies along Heather Moyse Drive, where **Spinnakers' Landing** was developed after a military base was phased out. The complex comprises numerous shops and restaurants, an outdoor stage built over the water, a nautical-themed playground, and a lighthouse.

Taking its name from the Mi'kmaq word for "hot spot," **Eptek Art & Cultural Centre** (130 Heather Moyse Dr., 902/888-8373, July-Aug. Mon.-Fri. 9am-4pm, Sat. noon-4pm, the rest of the year Tues.-Fri. 10am-4pm, admission varies) has a spacious main gallery hosting touring national fine arts and historical exhibits.

Wyatt Historic House Museum

The home of Wanda Lefurgey Wyatt until her death at 102 in 1998, the grandly restored **Wyatt Historic House** (85 Spring St., 902/432-1327, July-Aug. Mon.-Sat. 10am-5pm, adult $6, child $4.50) allows you to step back into the lives of a well-to-do family with long ties to the Summerside community. Adding to the charm are guided tours of the 1867 home led by costumed guides.

★ College of Piping

The **College of Piping** (619 Water St. E., 902/436-5377, www.collegeofpiping.com), affiliated with Scotland's College of Piping in Glasgow, attracts students from around the world to its teaching programs of Highland dancing, step dancing, fiddling, and bagpiping. Students perform for the public at a series of summer concerts that take place weekdays on the hour between 11am and 3pm in July and August ($7 pp). Another program open to the public is the Highland Storm ceilidh (July-Aug. Tues.-Thurs. 7pm, adult $35, senior $29, child $23).

FOOD

At the west end of the original main street (uphill from the waterfront), **Samuel's Coffee House** (4 Queen St., 902/724-2300, Mon.-Fri. 7:30am-7pm, Sat.-Sun. 8am-5pm, lunches $7-10) pours the best coffee in town within a stylish room at street level of a historic red-brick bank building. A coffee and muffin before 9am is just $3, but the breakfast sandwiches are also good. The rest of the

Summerside

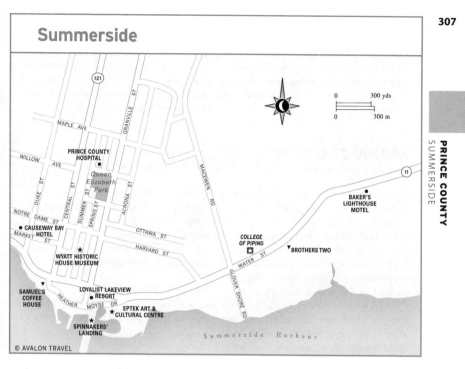

© AVALON TRAVEL

day, expect soups, sandwiches, and muffins, all freshly made and delicious.

Away from the water, **Brothers Two** (618 Water St. E., 902/436-9654, Mon.-Thurs. 11:30am-9pm, Fri. 11:30am-10pm, Sat. 4pm-10pm, Sun. 4pm-8pm, $16-25) has been Summerside's social hub for decades. It's no-frills family-style seafood dining at its best. Mains come as simple as meatloaf and as fancy as scallops poached in white wine. If it's a warm evening, talk your way into a table on the rooftop patio.

ACCOMMODATIONS AND CAMPING

Summerside's least expensive motel is **Baker's Lighthouse Motel** (802 Water St., 902/436-2992, $70 s, $80-90 d), two kilometers east of downtown. The rooms are plain but clean and comfortable. There's also wireless Internet access and air-conditioning.

The 108-room **Causeway Bay Hotel** (311 Market St., 902/436-2157 or 800/565-7829, www.causewaybayhotels.ca, $135-195) is centrally located and offers large rooms (some with kitchenettes), an indoor pool, a restaurant, a lounge, and amenities for the physically challenged.

Across the road from Spinnakers' Landing, **Loyalist Lakeview Resort** (195 Heather Moyse Dr., 902/436-3333 or 877/355-3500, www.lakeviewhotels.com, $155-205 s or d) features 103 spacious motel rooms decorated with a distinct country inn-style decor. It offers a good range of amenities—tennis, an indoor pool, a fitness room, bike rentals, a pub, and a restaurant—making it a good choice for those looking for city-type accommodations.

Summerside's closest campground is in beachside **Linkletter Provincial Park,** eight kilometers west of town (Rte. 11, 902/888-8366, early June-late Sept., $27-36). This 30-hectare park on Bedeque Bay has 84 serviced and unserviced sites, hot showers, and a launderette, dump station, kitchen shelter, and nearby store.

INFORMATION

In the heart of harbor-front Spinnakers' Landing, the **Visitor Information Centre** (124 Heather Moyse Dr., 902/888-8364, www.exploresummerside.com, late June-early Sept. daily 9:30am-9:30pm) is well signposted as you come into town.

GETTING THERE

Summerside is 60 kilometers (45 minutes) west of Charlottetown via Route 2. To get to Summerside from the Confederation Bridge, take Route 10 north from Borden-Carleton, then go west on Route 11, for a total of 30 kilometers (20 minutes).

Malpeque Bay

Sheltered from the open gulf by the long, narrow sandbar of Hog Island, the shallow waters of broad Malpeque Bay are tranquil and unpolluted. The bay's long fretted coastline is deserted, nearly bereft of development apart from three small provincial parks. Conditions are perfect for the large oyster fishery that thrives here. Ten million Malpeque oysters—Canada's largest source of the shellfish—are harvested each year. The purity of the bay water in part accounts for the excellent flavor of the oysters, which has made them famed worldwide as a gustatory treat. You'll find them served in a variety of ways at restaurants in the region.

KENSINGTON

Kensington lies at the intersection of five roads, including the trans-island Route 2. Summerside is 15 kilometers to the southwest, Charlottetown is 48 kilometers to the east, and Cavendish is 38 kilometers to the northeast.

Sights

Make your first stop **Kensington Railyards**, where you'll find the **Kensington Welcome Centre** (902/836-3031, www.kensington.ca, mid-May-Sept. daily 9am-9pm) and a **farmers market** (July-Sept. Sat. 10am-2pm), a good place to come for fresh produce, baked goods, snacks, and crafts.

On the main road through town, **Haunted Mansion** (81 Victoria St. W., 902/836-3336, mid-June and early Sept. daily 10am-5pm, July-Aug. daily 9am-7pm, adult $15, senior $13, child $9) is a popular spot with children. This imposing Tudor-style mansion was built in the 1890s by a homesick Englishman and has been reinvented as a tourist attraction, with access to the labyrinth of underground rooms and extensive gardens.

Getting There

Kensington is about 15 kilometers (15 minutes) northeast of Summerside via Route 2. It's 48 kilometers (40 minutes) northwest of Charlottetown via Route 2.

CABOT BEACH PROVINCIAL PARK

From Kensington, Route 2 loops around the head of Malpeque Bay to the Tyne Valley, but **Cabot Beach Provincial Park** (902/836-8945, late June-early Sept.) is worth the 10-minute detour.

This 140-hectare park, 30 kilometers north of Summerside on Route 20, is the most worthwhile attraction along the east side of Malpeque Bay. It occupies a gorgeous setting on a peninsula tip just inside the bay, including a coastline of sandy beaches broken by rocky headlands. At the park's day-use area is **Fanning School** (mid-June-mid-Sept. daily 10am-dusk, free), a schoolhouse built in 1794 and unique (for the time) for having two stories. Finally closed in 1969, it's now open to the public. Facilities at the park campground include more than 150 sites (unserviced sites $27, hookups $33), a supervised ocean beach, a launderette, hot showers, kitchen shelters, and a nearby general store.

Getting There

Cabot Beach is 15 kilometers (15 minutes) north of Kensington via Route 20. It's 60 kilometers (one hour) northwest of Charlottetown via Routes 2 and 20.

WEST SIDE OF MALPEQUE BAY
Tyne Valley

Quiet and bucolic, the crossroads hamlet of Tyne Valley (pop. 200), at the intersection of backcountry Routes 12, 178, and 167, lies on the west side of Malpeque Bay, a 50-minute drive from Summerside and uncountable kilometers from the rest of the modern world.

In the 1800s, Tyne Valley began as a Green Park suburb. Two generations of the Yeo family dominated the island's economy with their shipbuilding yards on Malpeque Bay, and the empire begun by James Yeo—the feisty, entrepreneurial English merchant who arrived in the 1830s—spawned the next generation's landed gentry.

The empire's riches are gone, but the lovely landscape remains, like a slice of Lucy Maud Montgomery's utopian Avonlea, transplanted from Cavendish to this corner of Prince County. To get there, follow Route 12 around Malpeque Bay, or from Route 2, turn east on Route 132 or 133. The paved and red-clay roads ripple across the farmlands like velvet ribbons on plump quilts.

The quiet village stirs to life in the first weekend of August with the **Tyne Valley Oyster Festival** (www.peioysterfest.com), a three-day tribute to Malpeque oysters. Daytime oyster-farming exhibits and evening oyster and lobster dinners are accompanied by talent shows, oyster-shucking demonstrations, fiddling and step-dancing contests, a parade, and a dance.

GREEN PARK PROVINCIAL PARK

Take Route 12 east from Tyne Valley and continue north through the hamlet of Port Hill to reach the beautiful **Green Park Provincial Park,** protecting a peninsula that juts into Malpeque Bay. From the end of the road (at the Shipbuilding Museum), a three-kilometer hiking trail brings you as deep into the bay as you can go without getting your feet wet. (Wear sneakers anyway, and bring insect repellent; mosquitoes flourish in the marsh pools.) The trail starts among white birches, short and stunted because of the bay's winter winds and salt. Beyond there, the path wends through hardwood groves, brightened with a ground cover of pink wild roses, bayberries,

Tyne Valley is a picturesque village on the west side of Malpeque Bay.

and goldenrod. Eventually the trail gives way to marshes at the peninsula's tip. The small inland ponds at the bay's edge are all that remain of a local effort to start oyster aquaculture decades ago. Marsh hay and wild grasses bend with the sea winds. Minnows streak in tidal pools, and razor clams exude continuous streams of bubbles from their invisible burrows beneath the soggy sand.

A 58-site campground (902/831-2370, late June-early Sept., $27-33) fronts the bay beneath tree canopies on a sheltered coastal notch. It offers a launderette, kitchen shelters, hot showers, a riverside beach, and summer nature programs.

★ GREEN PARK SHIPBUILDING MUSEUM AND YEO HOUSE

The **Green Park Shipbuilding Museum and Yeo House** (902/831-7947, June Mon.-Fri. 9am-5pm, July-Aug. daily 9am-5pm, adult $5, child $3.50) lies on the edge of the provincial park. The Yeo House sits back on a sweep of verdant lawn. It's a gorgeous estate, fronted by a fence that rims the curving road. Inside, rooms are furnished with period antiques. Up four flights of stairs, the cupola—from which James Yeo would survey his shipyard—overlooks the grounds and sparkling Malpeque Bay. Behind the house, the museum has exhibits explaining the history and methods of wooden shipbuilding, Prince Edward Island's main industry in the 19th century. From these buildings, it's a short walk through a meadow to the water, where outdoor displays include a partially finished vessel cradled on a frame, plus historic shipbuilding equipment.

PEI SHELLFISH MUSEUM

North of Tyne Valley, turn onto Route 166 to reach the modest **PEI Shellfish Museum** (166 Bideford Rd., Bideford, 902/853-2181, late June-early Sept. Mon.-Sat. 9am-5pm, Sun. 1pm-5pm, adult $5, child $2.50). Everything you could ever want to know about oysters and mussels is explained. A small aquarium contains mollusks, lobsters, snails, and inshore fish; outside, experimental farming methods are underway in the bay.

GETTING THERE

Tyne Valley is about 45 kilometers (45 minutes) northwest of Kensington via Routes 2, 132, then 178. It's 90 kilometers (1.5 hours) northwest of Charlottetown via Routes 2, 132, then 178.

artifacts at the Green Park Shipbuilding Museum and Yeo House

Lennox Island

A causeway off Route 163 brings you to this small island, home to 250 people of Mi'kmaq ancestry intent on cultivating oysters, spearing eels, trapping, and hunting while pursuing recognition of the 18th-century treaties with England that entitled them to their land. The province's Mi'kmaq are said to have been the first native Canadians converted to Christianity. Their history is kept alive at the **Mi'kmaq Cultural Centre** (8 Eagle Feather Trail, 902/831-3109, summer Mon.-Sat. 10am-7pm, Sun. noon-6pm, donation). The 1895 **St. Anne's Roman Catholic Church,** a sacred tribute to their patron saint, grips the island's coastline and faces the sea. A craft shop just north of the church markets Mi'kmaq baskets, silver jewelry, pottery, and other wares.

GETTING THERE

Lennox Island is about 15 kilometers (15 minutes) northeast of Tyne Valley via Route 12 and Route 163. It's 100 kilometers (1.5 hours) northwest of Charlottetown via Routes 2, 133, 12, then 163.

Région Évangéline

The bilingual inhabitants of the Région Évangéline, the province's largest Acadian area, date their ancestry to France's earliest settlement efforts. The region offers French-flavored culture at more than a dozen villages spread west of Summerside between Route 2 and the strait seacoast. Miscouche, the commercial center, is a 10-minute drive west of Summerside on Route 2, and Mont-Carmel, the region's seaside social and tourist hub, is 30 minutes from the seaport along coastal Route 11.

MISCOUCHE

As you approach from the east, the high double spires of **St. John the Baptist Church** announce from miles away that you've left Protestant, Anglo Prince Edward Island behind and are arriving in Catholic territory.

The village of 700 inhabitants at the intersection of Routes 2 and 12 began with French farmers from Port-la-Joye in the 1720s, augmented by Acadians who fled England's Acadian deportation in 1755. The settlement commands a major historical niche among Atlantic Canada's Acadian communities and was the site of the 1884 Acadian Convention, which adopted the French tricolor flag, with the single gold star symbolizing Mary.

Musée Acadien

On the east side of town, **Musée Acadien** (Rte. 2, 902/432-2880, mid-May-mid-Oct. Mon.-Sat. 9am-5pm, adult $4.50, student $3.50) is a genealogical resource center and also has exhibits of early photographs, papers, and artifacts, as well as a book corner (mainly in French) with volumes about Acadian history and culture on Prince Edward Island since 1720. Don't miss the documentary on events leading up to the 1755 Acadian deportation; it's screened on demand.

Getting There

Miscouche is 20 kilometers west of Kensington via Route 2, a 15-minute drive. It's 65 kilometers (one hour) northwest of Charlottetown, also via Route 2.

MONT-CARMEL

Two kilometers south of Miscouche and 24 kilometers west of Summerside, the backcountry Route 12 meets the coastal Route 11 (Lady Slipper Scenic Drive), which lopes south and west across Acadian farmlands to this hamlet, best known for Le Village, a complex of lodgings with a restaurant. Mont-Carmel, 16 kilometers from Miscouche, makes a handy sightseeing base for touring the Région Évangéline.

★ Our Lady of Mont-Carmel Acadian Church

The magnificent **Our Lady of Mont-Carmel Acadian Church,** between Route 11 and the red cliffs fronting Northumberland Strait, reflects the cathedral style of France's Poitou region, which is renowned for its Romanesque churches featuring elaborate exteriors. The cathedral is open Sunday during Mass. For permission to enter at other times, ask at the **Musée Religieux** (902-854-2260, July-Aug. daily 1pm-5pm, donation), across the road.

Getting There

Mont-Carmel is 25 kilometers west of Summerside. It's a 30-minute drive along Route 11. Head northwest from Charlottetown to Summerside on Route 2, then west on Route 11, for a total distance of 85 kilometers (1.5 hours).

CONTINUING ALONG ROUTE 11
Cap-Egmont

A few kilometers west of Mont-Carmel is the village of Cap-Egmont, best known for the very un-Acadian **Bottle Houses** (Rte. 11, 902-854-2987, mid-May-June and Sept.-early Oct. daily 9am-6pm, July-Aug. daily 9am-8pm, adult $7, senior $6.50, child $2). They are the work of Edouard Arsenault, who in the 1970s mortared together 25,000 glass bottles of all colors, shapes, and sizes to form three astonishing buildings—a chapel with an altar and pews, a tavern, and a six-gabled house. The structures qualified for inclusion in *Ripley's Believe It or Not.*

Turn off on the west side of the village to reach **Cape Egmont Lighthouse.** Although it's not open to the public, this light sits in a commanding position overlooking Northumberland Strait. Built in 1884, it is the same design as the one at Wood Islands (where the ferry from Nova Scotia docks), and like other lighthouses around the island, it has been moved back from the ocean edge as erosion has taken its toll on surrounding cliffs.

Our Lady of Mont-Carmel Acadian Church

GETTING THERE

Cap-Egmont is about five kilometers west of Mont-Carmel via Route 11. From Charlottetown, head northwest on Route 2 to Summerside, then west on Route 11, for a total distance of 90 kilometers (1.5 hours).

Abram-Village

From Cap-Egmont, the scenic coastal Route 11 wends north for 10 kilometers and turns inland to this hamlet known for crafts. **La Co-op d'Artisanat d'Abram Village** (Abram's Village Handcraft Co-op, 2181 Cannontown Rd., 902-854-2096, mid-June-Sept. Mon.-Sat. 9:30am-5:30pm), at the intersection of Routes 11 and 124, is the area's definitive craft source, with weavings, rugs, Acadian shirts, pottery, and dolls.

GETTING THERE

To get to Abram-Village from Mont-Carmel, take Route 11 west, then north, for a total of 15 kilometers (15 minutes). From Charlottetown, it's 90 kilometers (1.5 hours) northwest on Route 2, then west on Route 124.

Western Prince County

Beyond Summerside and the Région Évangéline, Route 2 cuts into the interior, out of sight of the seas. Nonetheless, most backcountry roads off the main route eventually finish at the water. To the west, the Northumberland Strait is the pussycat of summer seas, and the warm surf laps peacefully along the southern and western coastlines. The Gulf of St. Lawrence, however, is more temperamental, with a welter of rolling waves breaking onto the north shore.

For sightseeing information, stop at the provincial **Visitor Information Centre** (Rte. 2, 902/831-7930, June and Sept. daily 9am-4:30pm, July-Aug. daily 9am-7pm) in Portage, which is 43 kilometers north of Summerside.

MILL RIVER PROVINCIAL PARK

As you exit Route 2 at Woodstock, you enter a wooded realm on a ribbon of a road into **Mill River Provincial Park.** The park meshes lush landscapes with contemporary resort trappings and full recreation facilities, including the championship-quality Mill River Golf Course.

Recreation

The 18-hole, par-72 **Mill River Golf Course** (902/859-8873 or 800/377-8339, greens fees $70-85) is generally regarded as one of Canada's top 100 courses and has hosted many national events through the years. The course spans 6,747 yards and is open May-October. During July and August, you'd be wise to make reservations 48 hours in advance.

On warmer days, **Mill River Fun Park** (902/859-3915, July-Aug. daily 11am-7pm, $9 pp, child under 6 free), offering waterslides and outdoor pools, is a good place for families looking for watery fun.

Food and Accommodations

The three-story **Rodd Mill River** (Rte. 2,

902/859-3555 or 800/565-7633, www.roddvacations.com, Jan.-Oct., $155-295 s or d) is a sleek wood-sided hotel with 90 spacious and modern rooms and suites. Guests are attracted to the resort-style activities—golf, tennis, canoeing, biking, swimming in the indoor pool, and more. The resort's **Hernewood Dining Room** (daily 7am-9pm, $21-29) boasts regionally renowned dining that draws an appreciative clientele from Summerside; expect a reasonably priced menu featuring seafood specialties, with a dish-of-the-day emphasis on salmon, halibut, or lobster.

The park's riverfront campground (902/859-8790, mid-June-late Sept.) has 72 sites: 18 unserviced ($28), 18 with two-way hookups ($33), and 36 with full hookups ($36). Amenities include kitchen shelters, hot showers, a launderette, and summer interpretive programs.

Getting There

Mill River Provincial Park is 60 kilometers (50 minutes) northwest of Summerside along Route 2. It's 120 kilometers (1.5 hours) northwest of Charlottetown via Route 2.

O'LEARY

On Prince Edward Island, O'Leary is synonymous with potatoes. Legend has it that the hamlet took its name from an Irish farmer who settled here in the 1830s. By 1872, rail service connected the hamlet with the rest of the island, and with that link in place, O'Leary was on its way to becoming Canada's largest potato producer.

O'Leary straddles backcountry Route 142, a five-minute drive from Route 2 and 50 minutes from Summerside. You might expect mountains of potatoes; rather, O'Leary (pop. 900) is a tidy place, nestled in the midst of surprisingly attractive fields of low-growing potato plants. If you're in the area during the autumn harvest, you'll see the fields lighted by tractor headlights as the farmers work late at night to harvest the valuable crop before the frost.

★ Canadian Potato Museum

Don't be put off by the name; the **Canadian Potato Museum** (1 Dewar Ln., off Rte. 142, 902/859-2039, mid-May-mid-Oct. daily 9:30am-5:30pm, adult $10, senior $9, family $20.50) is an interesting stop that depicts the history of Prince Edward Island's most famous crop. The museum explains the story of the potato's humble beginnings in South America, the way the crop is grown and harvested, and how science has played a hand in the potatoes we eat today. A barn, a schoolhouse, and a chapel are out back. Within the museum is the **Potato Country Kitchen** (mid-May-mid-Oct. Mon.-Sat. 11am-3pm, Sun. 1pm-4pm), with rotating daily specials such as potato oyster stew and cottage pie. You can order a loaded potato (including one topped with a lobster hollandaise sauce), potato soup, and poutine (fries topped with gravy and cheese curds). Save room for a slice of seaweed pie, which is actually a slice of cake made with locally harvested seaweed and topped with strawberry sauce and whipped cream.

Getting There

O'Leary is 60 kilometers (50 minutes) northwest of Summerside via Routes 2 and 142. It's 120 kilometers (1.5 hours) northwest of Charlottetown via Routes 2 and 142.

WEST POINT AND VICINITY

Route 14 exits Route 2 at Carleton, eight kilometers west of Portage, doglegs west across the verdant farmlands, and heads to West Point at the island's western tip. From there, the scenic coastal route hugs the strait shore and brings some of the island's most magnificent sea views—a total distance of 80 kilometers to Tignish. Potato fields peter out at the strait coastline, which is definitely off the beaten tourist route. The coast's long stretches of beach are interspersed with craggy red cliffs.

Cedar Dunes Provincial Park

Cedar Dunes Provincial Park fronts Northumberland Strait 30 kilometers from Route 2. It's only a small park, but it has a sandy beach backed by sand dunes and a small campground (902/859-8785, late June-early Sept., $29-33) with around 60 campsites, a supervised beach, an activities program, a

Canadian Potato Museum

nature trail, kitchen shelters, a nearby store, and hot showers.

Within the park is one-of-a-kind ★ **West Point Lighthouse** (Cedar Dunes Park Rd., 902/859-3605, www.westpointharmony.ca, mid-June-mid-Sept., $150-170 s or d), the only place in Canada where you can stay overnight in a lighthouse. There's just one guest room in the actual lighthouse ($170 s or d), but others are spread through adjacent buildings. The complex also has a small museum and a gift shop.

West Point to Miminegash

Beyond West Point, Route 14 cleaves to the coastline and heads north, first to **Cape Wolfe** (where British general James Wolfe is said to have stepped ashore on the way to battle the French in 1759) and then to **Howards Cove,** fronted with precipitous cliffs of burnished red. The distance from West Point to Miminegash is 36 kilometers.

Getting There

To get to West Point from Summerside, take Route 2 west and north, then Route 14 west, for a total of 75 kilometers (just over an hour). To get there from Charlottetown, take Route 2 west and north and then Route 14 west for 135 kilometers (1.5 hours).

MIMINEGASH

Nestled beside a body of water protected from the winds of Northumberland Strait by low dunes, Miminegash is renowned as the home of people who earn a living from collecting seaweed. Storm winds whip the sea on this side of the island into a frenzy, churning seafloor plants into a webbed fabric that floats to the surface and washes to shore. This seaweed, known as **Irish moss,** was traditionally used as a stabilizer in ice cream and toothpaste (a practice that continues, though to a much smaller degree than in years past). It is harvested from the sea by boat, as well as from along the shore—after a storm you may see locals raking the beach north of the harbor, reaping the Irish moss and hauling it away with the help of draft horses.

Getting There

Miminegash is 36 kilometers (40 minutes) north of West Point via Route 14. To get to Miminegash from Charlottetown, head west then north on Route 2, northwest on Route 145, then north on Route 14. Total driving time for this 140-kilometer trip is 1.5 hours.

the beach at Miminegash

ROUTE 12 NORTH TO TIGNISH

None of the three highways that lead north through Prince County to Tignish are particularly busy, but Route 12, along the Gulf of St. Lawrence, is the least traveled. It branches off Route 2 just beyond the village of Portage, 42 kilometers from Summerside.

Alberton

The seaport of Alberton (pop. 1,200) is the northern area's largest town. Named for Albert, Prince of Wales, the town began in 1820 with 40 families who worked at the shipyards in nearby Northport. Deep-sea fishing aficionados will readily find charter boats here. The **Alberton Museum** (457 Church St., 902/853-4048, June-Sept. Mon.-Sat. 9:30am-5:30pm, donation) is in a historic stone building that was originally a courthouse and jail. Exhibits delve into the town's history with antiques, clothing, and farm tools. The fox farming display is particularly interesting.

JACQUES CARTIER PROVINCIAL PARK

It's only a short hop from Alberton back to Route 2, then 16 kilometers north to Tignish, but a worthwhile detour is to continue north on Route 12 to the coastal **Jacques Cartier Provincial Park** (902/853-8632, mid-June-early Sept., $29-33), occupying the site where explorer Cartier is believed to have stepped ashore in 1534. The campground rims the gulf. It offers a sandy beach, over 50 campsites (many with water views), hot showers, a launderette, and a summer interpretive program.

GETTING THERE

Alberton is about 65 kilometers (one hour) north of Summerside via Route 2 and Route 12. From Charlottetown, head west then north on Route 2, then take Route 150 east, for a total distance of 125 kilometers (1.5 hours).

Rail to Trail

A joy for hiking and biking, the **Confederation Trail** spans Prince Edward Island, extending from Tignish in the west to Elmira in the east, a distance of 279 kilometers. Spur trails, including those leading to Charlottetown's downtown waterfront and the Confederation Bridge, add an additional 80 kilometers.

The trail was developed on a decommissioned rail line. The advantages of creating the trail on a rail line were twofold—there are no hilly sections, and the route passes through dozens of towns and villages. Add a base of finely crushed gravel, extensive signage, picnic tables, benches, and lookouts, and you get one of the finest opportunities for outdoor recreation in all of Atlantic Canada.

The Confederation Trail is well promoted by both the provincial tourism authority and **Island Trails** (www.islandtrails.ca), a nonprofit organization that manages the system. Accommodations in villages along the route provide a handy base for traversing sections of the trail or as an overnight stop for those traveling longer distances. Some, such as the **Trailside Café & Inn** (Mount Stewart, 902/394-3626, www.trailside.ca), have been specifically developed for trail travelers, offering beds and meals.

TIGNISH AND VICINITY

Tignish (pop. 1,300) is simply laid out, with Church Street/Route 2 as the main street. The town is 20 minutes from Alberton, a half hour from O'Leary, and 80 minutes from Summerside. Stories of legendary riches and the fur that created a haute-couture sensation over a century ago embellish the lore of Tignish and the northern peninsula. The world's first successful silver fox breeding began in the Tignish area in 1887. Charles Dalton—later knighted by the queen—was the innovator; he joined with Robert Oulton from New Brunswick to breed the foxes. The pelts sold for thousands of dollars in fashion salons worldwide. From 1890 to 1912, the

Tignish Heritage Inn

features 1,118 pipes, from six inches to 16 feet in length. It was installed in 1882, and until the 1950s the organ was pumped by hand.

Food and Accommodations

M.J.'s Bakery (300 Church St., 902/882-2454, Mon.-Sat. 11am-5pm, lunches $5-8) has a small but tasty selection of sandwiches, bread baked daily, and sweet treats like blueberry pinwheels. The bakery has a small dining area, or purchase to go.

Right in town, an old red-brick convent has been converted to the **Tignish Heritage Inn** (Maple St., 902/882-2491, www.tignishheritageinn.ca, mid-June-mid-Oct, $100-145 s or d). The 17 guest rooms are basic but adequate, and the inn has amenities such as a lounge area, a laundry, wireless Internet, and a kitchen, as well as continental breakfast. A highlight is relaxing in the extensive garden out front. The inn is set back from Route 14, the main road through town; access it from Church Street or down beside St. Simon and St. Jude Church.

Getting There

Tignish is 85 kilometers north of Summerside via Route 2, a 70-minute drive. To get to Tignish from Alberton, it's a 20-kilometer, 20-minute drive along either Route 2 or Route 12. From Charlottetown, head west then north on Route 2 for 140 kilometers (two hours).

★ North Cape

Some 15 kilometers north of Tignish, Route 12 ends at **North Cape,** the northern tip of Prince County. The dominant artificial feature, the **Wind Energy Institute of Canada,** juts up from the windy headland with a federal project complex that tests and evaluates wind turbines. There's no access to the main site, although interpretive panels along its fence set the scene. Better still, make time to visit the adjacent **North Cape Wind Energy Interpretive Centre** (21817 Rte. 12, 902/882-2991, May-June and Sept.-Oct. daily 10am-6pm, July-Aug. daily 9am-8pm, adult $6, senior and child $3), which describes the

Dalton and Oulton partnership kept a keen eye on the venture and the number of silver fox breeding pairs. As luck would have it, generosity was their downfall: Their empire fell apart when one of the partners gave a pair of the breeding foxes to a relative. The cat—the fox, that is—was out of the bag. That single pair begat innumerable descendants that were sold worldwide, and breeding became an international business.

Sights

Make your first stop the **Tignish Cultural Centre** (Maple St., 902/882-1999, mid-June-mid-Sept. daily 10am-4pm, free), which offers a small display on the natural and human history of the area, holds the usual array of tourism brochures, and offers public Internet access. Nearby, the **St. Simon and St. Jude Church** (902/882-2049, daily 8am-7pm) is the town's stellar attraction (and the island's largest church), notable for its frescoes of the apostles and its mighty pipe organ. The organ, built by Louis Mitchell of Montréal, science behind the wind turbines and also has a small aquarium. The center is also the starting point for the 5.5-kilometer (round-trip) **Black Marsh Nature Trail.** This easy path passes under a windmill, over marshland, and along the rugged coastline.

When you've finished exploring the cape, head back to the interpretive center, where the **Wind and Reef Restaurant** (21817 Rte. 12, 902/882-3535, May-June and Sept.-Oct. daily 10am-6pm, July-Aug. daily 9am-8pm, lunches $9-16) has priceless views across the Gulf of St. Lawrence. Seafood dominates the menu of this casual eatery, but there's also salads and burgers.

Four kilometers before the cape, the low-slung **Island's End Motel** (42 Doyle Rd., Sea Cow Pond, 902/882-3554, www.islandsendmotel.com, $85-95 s or d) overlooks the Gulf of St. Lawrence and is within walking distance of a beach. Some units have full kitchens.

GETTING THERE

North Cape is about 15 kilometers (15 minutes) north of Tignish along Route 12. To get there from Charlottetown, head west then north on Route 2 to Tignish, then north on Route 12, for a total of 155 kilometers (just over two hours).

Eastern Prince Edward Island

Look for ★ to find recommended
sights, activities, dining, and lodging.

Highlights

★ **Belfast Corn Maze:** If you can drag your children away from the coastline, encourage them to get lost in this country-style attraction that will (hopefully) keep them busy for hours (page 323).

★ **Rossignol Estate Winery:** The vineyard at Rossignol is perched atop red cliffs high above Northumberland Strait—and the wine isn't bad either (page 325).

★ **Seal-Watching:** Seal colonies inhabit islands along the southeast coast, but none are more accessible than those near Montague (page 328).

★ **Basin Head Provincial Park:** The unlikely combination of a fascinating fisheries museum and silica-filled sand that "sings" as you walk across it makes for a stop that all ages will enjoy (page 332).

★ **Prince Edward Island National Park, Greenwich Unit:** The Greenwich Unit of the island's only national park protects a moving sand dune system that is slowly burying a coastal forest (page 335).

★ **Crowbush Cove:** Prince Edward Island is dotted with golf courses, but the best is the oceanfront Links at Crowbush Cove (page 335).

The eastern third of Prince Edward Island, much of it within Kings County, is cut off geographically from the rest of the province by the Hillsborough River. One of this region's main attractions is the lack of crowds.

It has none of the hype of Cavendish, and its activities and sights are more limited. If you're looking for sightseeing and recreation combined with natural attractions—coastal windswept peninsula beaches, seal colonies, sand dunes, and, inland, an improbable herd of provincial bison—you'll find that and more.

A two-lane highway circumnavigates the entire region, with farmland laid out on the intensely red earth on one side, and the sea and sapphire-blue sky on the other. The eastern shore, from Cardigan through to Murray Harbour, is tattered with little offshore islands and dozens of deeply indented bays and river estuaries. The southern region's climate is warm, humid, and almost tropical; islanders refer to this region as the "banana belt," and even such crops as wine grapes and tobacco thrive here. The long northern coast is nearly straight and uninterrupted, except at large St. Peters Bay, where a tract of coast is protected as part of Prince Edward Island National Park. The northeast area is relatively remote, lightly populated and developed, and, inland, thickly wooded. As any islander will tell you, the county's northern portion is "far out"; that is, far out of sight and out of mind from mainstream Prince Edward Island. But the pastoral inland countryside is beautiful. It is cultivated in farms of corn, berries, grains, potatoes, and tobacco and rimmed on the north by forests and tracts of provincial woodlot plantations.

PLANNING YOUR TIME

Distances throughout the eastern portion of the island are much shorter than they may first appear when poring over the provincial road map. It is possible to drive around the entire region (under 400 kilometers) in one day from Charlottetown, and you can reach Souris, in the far eastern corner, in

Eastern Prince Edward Island

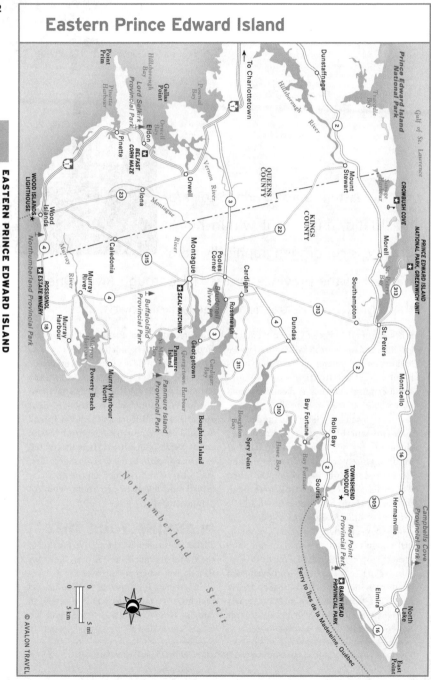

© AVALON TRAVEL

one hour from the capital. Visitors arriving on the island by ferry land at Wood Islands. Most make a beeline for the capital, less than an hour's drive to the west (unless you have children that demand a stop at the **Belfast Corn Maze**), but this is also a good starting point for exploring the region by heading in the opposite direction to Murray Harbour and beginning the convoluted coastal route north and then west along the North Shore. Aside from exploring the provincial parks and admiring the coast-meets-farmland scenery, the three highlights of the drive are taking a **seal-watching trip** from Montague, visiting the beach and museum at **Basin Head Provincial Park,** and admiring the coastal wilderness of **Prince Edward Island National Park.**

Even though Prince Edward Island is tiny, the eastern portion of the province is well off the main tourist route. This means you will find well-priced accommodations. For this reason, it's a good place to take a break from touring. An ideal scenario would be to book a cabin for a couple of days and plan on spending time exploring the surrounding area, relaxing on the beach, strolling through the surrounding towns, golfing at one of the top-notch golf courses such as **Crowbush Cove,** or doing nothing at all. Larger villages have seafood markets, so plan on doing your own cooking, then kick back in the evening with a glass of wine from **Rossignol Estate Winery,** which you pass right near the Wood Islands ferry terminal.

Along Northumberland Strait

The TransCanada Highway (Highway 1) extends southeast from Charlottetown for 62 kilometers to Wood Islands. This small village is the termination point for ferries from Nova Scotia, and also the starting point for touring through Kings County.

ORWELL

The small village of Orwell, 27 kilometers east of Charlottetown, has a couple of interesting historic attractions; it is also the turnoff for those cutting across Kings County to Montague.

Sights

Orwell Corner Historic Village (98 Macphail Park Rd., 902/651-8515, July-Aug. daily 9:30am-5pm, Sept.-Oct. Mon.-Fri. 9:15am-4:45pm, adult $6, child $4.25) is a restored Scottish village representing the 1890s. Buildings include the farmhouse, general store, dressmaker's shop, blacksmith's shop, church, and barns. In summer, there's a ceilidh (Celtic music and dancing) Wednesday at 8pm.

Beyond the historic village is the **Sir Andrew MacPhail Homestead** (271 Macphail Park Rd., 902/651-2789, July-mid-Sept. daily 9am-5pm, donation), the summer home of a doctor of national renown who was involved in developing the island's potato industry. Three walking trails lead through the 57-hectare grounds, and afternoon tea is served Wednesday-Sunday 11:30am-2:30pm.

Getting There

Orwell is 25 kilometers (25 minutes) southeast of Charlottetown on Route 1.

ORWELL TO WOOD ISLANDS

Eldon

★ **BELFAST CORN MAZE**

When the corn reaches a height of six feet, the four-hectare **Belfast Corn Maze** (5265 Hwy. 1, Eldon, 902/659-2246, Aug. daily 10am-7pm, Sept.-Oct. Sat.-Sun. 10am-7pm, $13) fills with children and adults trying to find their way out. Cut into a different design each year, it's one of the few such mazes in Atlantic Canada, and takes at least an hour to get through. The destination is more than a maze, with a petting zoo, a giant sandbox, "corn cannons," a jumping pillow, and a rope climbing wall adding to the appeal.

The maze is part of the family-operated **Chuck Wagon Farm Market** (Aug.-early Sept. daily 10am-7pm, early Sept.-Oct. Sat.-Sun. 10am-7pm), where produce is picked daily for the public. In addition to locally grown fruit and vegetables, you can buy jams and preserves, treat the kids to an ice cream (if they make it out of the maze), or enjoy barbecue lunch at an outdoor table.

LORD SELKIRK PROVINCIAL PARK

Tucked on the eastern shore of Orwell Bay, an inlet off the larger Hillsborough Bay, is beachfront **Lord Selkirk Provincial Park** (142 Selkirk Park Rd., 902/659-2794, late June-early Sept.). The park, named for the Scottish leader of one of the early immigrant groups, is right off the TransCanada Highway, a stone's throw west of Eldon, 10 kilometers south of Orwell. Although the beach here isn't good for swimming, it's great for walking, beachcombing, and clam digging. The park's campground has unserviced sites ($26) and hookups ($33), an outdoor swimming pool, a nine-hole golf course, mini-golf, laundry, kitchen shelters, fireplaces, and a nearby campers' store.

A naturalist program runs throughout summer, and the first weekend of August, the park is the site of the annual **Highland Games,** which include piping, dancing competitions, Scottish athletic competitions, and lobster suppers.

GETTING THERE

Eldon is nine kilometers south of Orwell along Highway 1. It's 35 kilometers southeast of Charlottetown on Route 1.

Point Prim

Point Prim Lighthouse (902/659-2768, July-Aug. daily 10am-6pm, adult $3.50, child

lost in Belfast Corn Maze

$2) is at the end of Route 209, which peels off the TransCanada Highway and runs 10 kilometers down the long, slender peninsula jutting into Hillsborough Bay. Built in 1845, it's Prince Edward Island's oldest lighthouse and Canada's only circular brick lighthouse tower. The view overlooking the strait from the octagonal lantern house at the top is gorgeous.

The **Chowder House** (2150 Point Prim Rd., 902/659-2187, July-Aug. daily 11am-8pm, first two weeks of Sept. Tues.-Sun. noon-8pm, lunches $7-14) serves fresh local clams and mussels, chowder, sandwiches, and homemade breads and pastries.

GETTING THERE

Point Prim is about 20 kilometers (20 minutes) southwest of Orwell, via Routes 1 and 209. To get there from Charlottetown, head east then south on Routes 1 and 209, for a total distance of 45 kilometers (45 minutes).

tending grapes at Rossignol Estate Winery

WOOD ISLANDS

Not an archipelago of islands at all, but a little village 60 kilometers southeast of the capital, this is where the ferry service from Nova Scotia unloads its cargo of vehicles and people.

Along the main highway through town is the **Plough the Waves Centre** (13056 Shore Rd., 902/962-3761, mid-May-mid-Oct. daily 9am-6pm), which holds the local information center.

Wood Islands Lighthouse

Ferry travelers will spot the traditional red-and-white **Wood Islands Lighthouse** (173 Lighthouse Rd., 902/962-3110, early June-late Sept. daily 9:30am-5:30pm, adult $6, senior $5, child $4) long before arriving at Wood Islands (stand on the starboard side for the best views). Dating to 1876, it is part of a small provincial park right beside the ferry dock. You can climb to the top of the lighthouse and admire displays that tell the story of the ferry service and rum running.

Getting There

CAR

Wood Islands is about 35 kilometers (30 minutes) south of Orwell and 60 kilometers (one hour) southeast of Charlottetown via Route 1.

FERRY

Between May and mid-December (the rest of the year, ice in Northumberland Strait restricts shipping), ferries depart Wood Islands 5-9 times daily for Caribou, Nova Scotia. The crossing takes 75 minutes, but expect to wait at least that long during peak travel periods (July and August weekends). The round-trip fare is $71 per vehicle, including passengers. For a schedule, contact **Northumberland Ferries** (902/566-3838 or 877/635-7245, www.ferries.ca).

WOOD ISLANDS TO MURRAY HARBOUR

From Wood Islands, Route 4 continues into Kings County, making a sharp left inland to Murray River. Route 18 sticks to the coast, wrapping around Murray Head before leading into the town of Murray Harbour and then into Murray River.

Northumberland Provincial Park

Just three kilometers from Wood Islands, **Northumberland Provincial Park** (Rte. 4, 902/962-7418, late June-late Aug.) fronts the ocean, near enough to the terminal to see the ferries coming and going to Caribou. The park offers rental bikes, hayrides, a nature trail, a stream for fishing, an ocean beach with clam digging, and mini-golf. Facilities at the well-equipped campground include 60 sites (tent sites $28, hookups $33-36), a launderette, kitchen shelters, a nearby campers' store, and hot showers.

★ Rossignol Estate Winery

Beyond Northumberland Provincial Park, the highway crosses into Kings County and quickly reaches Prince Edward Island's only commercial winery, **Rossignol Estate**

Winery (11147 Shore Rd., 902/962-4193, www.rossignolwinery.com, May-Oct. Mon.-Sat. 10am-5pm, Sun. 1pm-5pm, tastings free). Try not to let the glorious ocean views distract you from the task at hand—tasting a wide range of reds and whites (including chardonnay and pinot cabernet), along with fruit wines and deliciously sweet blackberry mead. The winery produces 45,000 bottles annually and does everything right, including using oak barrels for aging. No tours are offered, but you are free to wander down the red-dirt path leading to the ocean cliffs.

Murray Harbour to Souris

From Wood Islands, you'll pass through tiny hamlets like Little Sands and White Sands, marked more by road signs than clusters of houses as Route 18 approaches Murray Harbour. An enormous number of seals live in this well-sheltered harbor, and they love to loll about on offshore islands.

The Murray family settled the area and has namesakes everywhere: The Murray River flows into Murray Harbour, whose entrance is marked by Murray Head; seal colonies cluster on the harbor's Murray Islands; and the three seaport villages are Murray Harbour, Murray River, and Murray Harbour North.

MURRAY HARBOUR

On the south side of the bay is the small village of Murray Harbour. Beyond town to the east is **Beach Point Lighthouse,** from where seals are often visible.

Set on a waterfront property between Murray Harbour and the Murray River, ★ **Ocean Acres** (247 Fox River Rd., 902/962-3913, www.oceanacres.ca, cottages $160 s or d, camping $40) offers five two-bedroom cottages. Each unit has modern furnishings, a flat-screen TV, wireless Internet, and a deck with private barbecue. The property also has an outdoor pool, bike and kayak rentals, and a small café. In Murray Harbour itself, **Harbour Motel** (174 Mill Rd., www.harbourmotelpei.com, 902/962-3660, $95 s or d) has seven kitchen-equipped units within walking distance of town.

Easily the best place to eat in town, **Brehauts Restaurant** (7 Mariners Ln., 902/962-3141, Apr.-late Sept. Mon.-Sat. 8am-9pm, Sun. 10am-9pm, $12-21) has a big deck overlooking the river. The menu is strong on seafood, simply prepared and well priced.

Getting There

To get to Murray Harbour from Wood Islands, take Route 4 east then Route 18A north for 20 kilometers (20 minutes). From Charlottetown, take Route 1 west to Wood Islands, then Routes 4 and 18A, for a total distance of 80 kilometers (1.5 hours).

MURRAY RIVER

The oval-shaped harbor is centered on the town of Murray River, hub of the island's southeast corner.

Sights and Recreation

Children will love **King's Castle Provincial Park** (1887 Gladstone Rd., 902/962-7422, mid-June-mid-Sept. daily 9am-9pm, free) on the banks of the Murray River east of town. A grassy meadow is filled with concrete storybook characters, trails lead through the woods, and there's a riverside beach (complete with hot showers). A covered picnic shelter is the perfect spot for lunch.

If you like woodland walking, stretch your legs at **Murray River Pines,** a provincial woodlot near town. The site, off Route 4, is remote. Look for an abandoned mill, the former provincial Northumberland Mill and Museum, now closed; the woodlot is inland behind the site. A 30-minute hike on the red-clay road leads to dense groves of red and white pines abutted by stands of balsam, red maple, and red spruce. The largest pines date to the 1870s, when England's Royal Navy cut down most of the forest for masts. Somehow these trees survived, and they have become havens for birds of all kinds, including blue herons, kingfishers, swallows, blue jays, and chickadees.

The **Old General Store** (9387 Main St., 902/962-2459, July-Aug. Mon.-Sat. 10:30am-5:30pm, Sun. noon-5pm, shorter hours in spring and fall) ranks as one of the island's best crafts sources, and stocks folk art, linens, and domestic wares.

Accommodations and Camping

On a small lake east of town, **Forest and Stream Cottages** (446 Fox River Rd., 902/962-3537 or 800/227-9943, www.forestandstreamcottages.com, mid-June-Oct., $115-125 s or d) comprises six simple but tidy cottages, each with a kitchen, a bedroom, and a covered porch. Rowboats are supplied, and there's a playground.

Continue through town to the northeast to reach ★ **Seal Cove Campground** (87 Mink River Rd., 902/962-2745, www.sealcovecampground.ca, mid-May-Sept., $27-44), which overlooks offshore seal colonies. When you're done watching seals, there's a nine-hole golf course ($20 greens fee for a full day), an outdoor pool, kayak rentals, and a playground to keep everyone busy.

Getting There

Murray River is 10 kilometers northwest of Murray Harbour via Route 18. From Charlottetown, take Route 1 west to Wood Islands and then Route 4 east and north, for a total of 80 kilometers (1.5 hours).

MURRAY RIVER TO MONTAGUE

Route 4 is the most direct road between Murray River and Montague, but Route 17 is more scenic.

Through the village of Murray Harbour North, **Poverty Beach,** at the end of a spur off Route 17, is a long, narrow sandbar that separates the sea from the harbor. It's quiet, remote, and wrapped in a sense of primeval peacefulness. The peninsula is worth a trek, but think twice about swimming in the surf; powerful sea currents here can be dangerous, and no lifeguards are around to rescue foundering bathers.

Panmure Island

Panmure Island, a remote and windswept wilderness, lies 15 kilometers north of Poverty Beach. It is linked to the mainland by a narrow strip of land, traversed by Route 347, which rambles out along the flag-shaped peninsula that wags between St. Mary's Bay, Georgetown Harbour, and the sea. A supervised beach fronts the strait, and a wisp of a road angles into the interior and emerges at the waterfront with views of Georgetown across the harbor. Back on the mainland is **Panmure Island Provincial Park** (902/838-0668, late June-early Sept.). A campground here has 22 unserviced sites and 16 two-way hookup sites ($27-33), supervised ocean swimming off a beautiful white-sand beach, a launderette, a campers' canteen, fireplaces, and hot showers.

GETTING THERE

Via Route 17, Panmure Island is about 25 kilometers (25 minutes) north of Murray River. To get there from Charlottetown, take Route 1 southwest to Wood Islands, then Route 4 east and north, then Route 17 east and north, then Route 347 north, for a total of 105 kilometers (1.5 hours).

Buffalo Park

Halfway between Murray River and Montague along Route 4, the 40-hectare **Buffalo Provincial Park** (year-round, free) may seem deserted at first glance. If you look closely, though, you'll spot bison (historically known as buffalo) and white-tailed deer roaming the woodlands. The namesake herd began with 14 bison imported from Alberta in 1970 as part of a federal experiment to help preserve the almost-extinct species. There's still no population explosion, but the herd numbers around 25 bison now. No guarantees, but in mid-afternoon the bison herd often emerges to feed near the Route 4 fence.

MONTAGUE

Montague, 46 kilometers east of Charlottetown and 25 kilometers north of Wood Islands, is the largest town in Kings County, yet the population is under 2,000. The town is defined by the Main Street bridge over the Montague River. In fact, the town began as Montague Bridge in 1825, when the bridge was made of logs and the area had just four farms. Shipbuilding brought riches to the town, and many a schooner or other sailing craft was launched here on the broad river.

The town is uncomplicated, pretty, clean, and friendly. Everything important lies along Main Street, which slices through town and proceeds up, over, and down the bridge.

Sights and Recreation
GARDEN OF THE GULF MUSEUM
The **Garden of the Gulf Museum** (564 Main St., 902/838-2467, mid-June-late Sept. Mon.-Sat. 9am-5pm, adult $5, cash only) is housed in an old post office overlooking the Montague River at the bridge. The building is an impressive hulk of red brick with a steeply pitched roof, showing its French architectural influence. The collection includes exhibits on local history, including the colorful story of Trois Rivières, which was established nearby in 1732 by French entrepreneur Jean Pierre de Roma.

★ SEAL-WATCHING
Tightline Tours (1 Station St., 902/969-0412, adult $50, child $35) offers two-hour seal-watching tours from the town's marina just off Route 4. Departure times are tide-dependent (so call ahead), but typically head downstream toward the ocean. The experienced captain knows the most likely places harbor seals will be sunning themselves along the shoreline, but you may also see them swimming near the boat. Birdlife includes great blue herons, gulls, and ospreys. On the return journey, freshly harvested mussels are boiled up on board for a memorable feast.

Accommodations
Overlooking the water, **Lanes Riverhouse Inn** (33 Brook St., 902/838-2433 or 800/268-7532, www.lanesriverhouseinn.com, $109-189 s or d) combines a newer 30-room hotel with

Harbor seals are often sighted on boat tours from Montague.

a pleasant cluster of older cottages that have basic cooking facilities. The hotel rooms are spacious and have river-facing balconies, air-conditioning, and the most comfortable beds in this part of the province.

Getting There

Via Route 315, Montague is 25 kilometers (25 minutes) north of Wood Islands. Via Routes 1 and 3, then Route 4 south, Montague is 46 kilometers (50 minutes) east of Charlottetown.

VICINITY OF MONTAGUE
Brudenell River Provincial Park

The 30-hectare park-cum-resort called **Brudenell River Provincial Park** occupies a gorgeous pastoral setting on the peninsula that juts out into Cardigan Bay between the Brudenell and Cardigan Rivers. You enter the park from Route 3, five kilometers north of Montague and then three kilometers east of Pooles Corner, and the road winds through manicured grounds to Brudenell River Resort.

RECREATION

Golfers enjoy walking the fairways of two golf courses, **Brudenell River** and the newer **Dundarave** (902/652-8965 or 800/377-8336, May-Oct., greens fees $85-95), which plays to a challenging 7,300 yards from the back tees. The courses both rank among Atlantic Canada's superior golf greens and have been the site of various national and Canadian Professional Golfers' Association tournaments.

Other park activities include canoeing (rentals $38 per day), horseback riding (902/652-2396, $40 for a one-hour beach ride), indoor and outdoor pools, tennis, and boat tours. All park activities are open to campers, resort guests, and day visitors alike.

FOOD AND ACCOMMODATIONS

The epicenter of the resort complex is **Rodd Brudenell River** (902/652-2332 or 800/565-7633, www.roddhotelsandresorts.com,

May-mid-Oct., $180-280 s or d). Dating from the early 1990s, the resort holds two distinct types of rooms: contemporary and spacious hotel rooms in the main lodge and two-bedroom Echelon Gold Cottages with kitchens and fireplaces. Check the website for deals and packages. The resort's riverfront **Gordon on the River** dining room is casually upscale and specializes in seafood entrées ($19-33); try the haddock stuffed with spinach and Italian Bocconcini cheese, and, for dessert, shortbread squares topped with lemon meringue or the homemade parfait.

The 15 modern units at ★ **Brudenell Chalets** (Rte. 3, 902/652-2900 or 866/652-2900, www.brudenellchalets.com, $225-350 s or d) are more like mini houses than chalets. Each has 2-4 bedrooms, a well-designed kitchen, a lounge with TV, washing and drying facilities, and a deck with a barbecue. On the edge of the park, the place is close to the golf courses and also has its own outdoor swimming pool and playground.

CAMPING

The park isn't all resort. Continue beyond the main entrance to reach **Brudenell River Provincial Park Campground** (902/652-8966, mid-May-late Sept.). Tent sites are spread through a wooded area ($27), while hookup sites ($31-36) have plenty of room to maneuver big rigs. Amenities include hot showers, kitchen shelters, a launderette, interpretive programs, a riverfront beach, and a walking trail that links the campground to the resort.

Georgetown

Located at the end of Route 3, beyond Brudenell River Provincial Park, Georgetown was once a major shipbuilding center. The naming of Georgetown was surveyor Samuel Holland's tribute to George III of England. The port boasted one of the island's most perfectly created deepwater harbors. Its early economy was built with British money, however, and when England's economy had a short-lived collapse, Georgetown lost its economic edge and never regained it. The town slid into the shadows, replaced by Montague first as a shipbuilding and shipping center and then as the area's principal market town. Georgetown is now best known for the **King's Playhouse** (65 Grafton St., 902/652-2053, www.kingsplayhouse.com, June-mid-Sept., $15-20), a repertory company that stages dramas and comedies in a downtown theater year-round.

Cardigan

At the hamlet of Cardigan, five kilometers north of Brudenell River Provincial Park, **Cardigan Lobster Suppers** (4557 Wharf Rd., 902/583-2020, late June-early Oct. daily 4pm-9pm) are well worth partaking in. Seating is inside, or outside on a deck with sweeping water views. The full lobster supper is $39 per person (including all-you-can-eat seafood chowder), or there's other choices aimed at children.

BAY FORTUNE

About 30 kilometers northeast of Cardigan, the Fortune River flows into Bay Fortune, which was named long before the fortunes of Broadway fueled the local retreats of producer David Belasco and playwright Elmer Harris. Upriver six kilometers is the hamlet of Dingwells Mills, where *Johnny Belinda*, one of Harris's most successful Broadway plays and later a movie, was set.

Food and Accommodations

The ★ **Inn at Bay Fortune** (Rte. 310, 902/687-3745, www.innatbayfortune.com, late May-mid-Oct., $225-425 s or d) has earned an international reputation, thanks to the care lavished on the property by innkeeper David Wilmer. The estate was once the summer home of renowned playwright Elmer Harris, who designed the 19th-century version of a motel to house the entourage of thespians who traveled with him. The 17 guest rooms (14 with fireplaces) are impeccably furnished and filled with natural light. The most sought-after is the two-level Tower Suite, which has sweeping water views from the upstairs lounge. Rates include a cooked breakfast.

A strong sense of conviviality pervades the inn's dining room, which is regarded as one of Canada's finest restaurants. Meals are served on the front enclosed porch during summer or inside with tables arranged before the fireplace when the weather is cooler. The creative menu features entrées emphasizing local products from both the land and the sea (try scallops topped with strawberry and balsamic salsa), accompanied by a sophisticated wine list. Although you don't need to be a guest to dine here, many are, staying as part of a package.

Getting There

Bay Fortune is 30 kilometers (30 minutes) northeast of Cardigan via Routes 4 and 332. To get there from Charlottetown, head east and northeast on Routes 1, 3, 4, and 332 for 70 kilometers (1.5 hours).

Souris and Vicinity

Any islander will tell you that the fishing town of Souris is "far out," the end of the line on the beaten tourist track. The town (pop. 1,150), notched on the strait seacoast 80 kilometers northeast of Charlottetown and 45 kilometers northeast of Montague, garners unqualified raves for its setting. Consider Souris as a base for touring throughout the northeast. The location translates as good value for the dollar in lodgings and dining. The restaurants are plainly furnished and specialize in seafood platters, ranked by islanders as among the province's best and freshest.

SIGHTS AND RECREATION

The town overlooks Northumberland Strait from sloping headlands, bounded in part by grasslands that sweep down to the water and in other parts by steeply pitched red cliffs. On the southern boundary, the Souris River rushes toward the sea in a gush of red water and pours into the blue strait, like a palette of blended watercolor pigments.

Townshend Woodlot

Townshend Woodlot is a 106-hectare spread that closely resembles the island's original Acadian forest. In 1970, the International Biological Program designated the setting as one of the island's finest examples of old-growth hardwood groves. To get there, take Route 305 three kilometers north to the hamlet of Souris Line Road. The woodlot plantation lies off the road, fairly well hidden and obscurely marked—you may want to ask for directions in Souris. Acquired by the province in 1978, the woodlot lacks a clear hiking route, but it's easily walkable on a level grade of sandy loam. The groves meld beech trees—a species that once dominated half the island's forests—with yellow birch, red maple, and sugar maple, whose dark brown trunks stretch up as high as 32 meters. Eastern chipmunks nest in underground tunnels. Dwarf ginseng—rare on the island—and nodding trillium thrive.

The beach at Basin Head is famous for its "singing sands."

★ Basin Head Provincial Park

Formed by the winds, most sand dunes grow and creep along, albeit at a snail's pace. At **Basin Head Provincial Park,** off Route 16, 13 kilometers east of Souris, the dunes are known as "walking" dunes for their wind-blown mobility. The high silica content of the sand here and at nearby Red Point Provincial Park causes it to squeak audibly when crunched underfoot; islanders poetically describe the phenomenon as "singing sands." At Basin Head, the dunes are high and environmentally fragile; visitors should stay off the dunes and tread instead along the beach near the water's edge. But the beach is most popular simply for being somewhere to sunbathe and swim throughout summer, and it can get very busy.

Access to the beach is from the end of Basin Head Road, which is also home to the **Basin Head Fisheries Museum** (Rte. 16, 902/357-7233, mid-June-late Sept. daily 9am-5pm, adult $4, child $3.50), which sits high on the headland overlooking the beach and an inlet you must cross to reach the sand. Here you'll

find boats, nets, and a museum with expertly conceived exhibits detailing the historic inshore fishing industry and local coastal ecology.

FESTIVALS AND EVENTS

In early July, musicians from across the island and beyond gather southeast of town at Rollo Bay for the **Prince Edward Island Bluegrass & Old Time Music Festival** (www.bluegrasspei.com), where a weekend ticket costs $65. The highlight of the local event calendar is the late July **Mermaid Tears Sea Glass Festival** (www.peiseaglassfestival.com), which, as the name suggests, features sea glass art in a variety of forms, as well as family-friendly events throughout the town.

FOOD

If it's a warm, sunny day, plan on eating at the ★ **Lobster Shack** (8 Main St., 902/743-3347, June daily 10am-6pm, July-mid-Sept. daily 10am-7pm, $12-18), beautifully located along the boardwalk overlooking the beach and ocean. Choices are very simple: shucked oysters or lobster rolls; seating is on adjacent picnic tables.

The **Blue Fin** (10 Federal Ave., 902/687-3271, daily 8am-8pm, $9-18) is partly protected from the tourist crowd by its tucked-away location off the main street. But for well-priced, simple seafood dishes, it's well worth searching out. The seafood chowder and the fish-and-chips are both excellent.

ACCOMMODATIONS AND CAMPING

Fronting the ocean and within walking distance of a beach, **Lighthouse and Beach Motel** (51 Sheep Pond Rd., off Rte. 2, 902/687-2339 or 800/689-2339, www.lighthouseandbeachmotel.ca, mid-June-mid-Sept., $80-115 s or d) offers 20 regular motel rooms with a light breakfast included in the rates. An old lighthouse on the property is rented by the week ($700) and has a jetted tub, separate bedrooms, and a kitchen. This lodging is two kilometers west of town.

A further six kilometers west is **Rollo Bay Inn** (Rte. 2, 902/687-3550 or 877/687-3550, www.therollobayinn.com, $105 s or d). This lodging combines a re-created Georgian setting with 15 rooms, housekeeping units, and suites on spacious grounds with a restaurant serving basic island cuisine.

Red Point Provincial Park (13 km east of Souris, off Rte. 16, 902/357-2463, late June-early Sept.) has a campground with 32 tent sites ($29) and 58 powered sites ($33). Amenities include kitchen shelters, fireplaces, and hot showers.

INFORMATION

Souris Visitor Information Centre (95 Main St., 902/687-7030, June-Sept. daily 9am-6pm) is in a historic building in the middle of town.

GETTING THERE

Souris is 45 kilometers (40 minutes) northeast of Montague via Route 4 and Route 2. From Charlottetown, it's an 80-kilometer (1.5-hour) drive northeast to Souris along Route 5 and 4, then Route 2.

North Shore

If you like photogenic landscapes, windy seacoasts washed with tossing surf, and weathered seaports, consider northeastern Kings County for a revealing glimpse of this seafaring island as it once was. Beyond Souris, the strait seacoast stretches 25 kilometers to windswept East Point, the island's easternmost point. On the equally remote gulf coast in this region, you'll find few tourists, a dozen tiny seaports, and a handful of lonesome lighthouses that stand as sentinels along the 75-kilometer-long coastline, strewn with centuries of shipwrecks.

FAR EAST
East Point

At the northeastern tip of Prince Edward Island, 25 kilometers northeast of Souris, Northumberland Strait and the Gulf of St. Lawrence meet in a lathered flush of cresting seas, sometimes colored blue and often tinged with red from oxide-colored silt. Here stands the 20-meter-high octagonal tower of **East Point Lighthouse** (404 Lighthouse Rd., off Rte. 16, 902/357-2106, June-Sept. daily 9am-6pm, guided tours adult $3, senior $2, child $1), which is still in use. The first lighthouse at this spot was built in 1867, but erosion has

forced subsequent structures to be moved farther back from the cliff edge.

GETTING THERE
East Point is 100 kilometers (two hours) northeast of Charlottetown via Route 5, 4, and 2, then Route 16. From Souris, it's about 25 kilometers (25 minutes) northeast on Route 16 to East Point.

Elmira
Elmira Railway Museum (Rte. 16A, 902/357-7234, June-late Sept. Mon.-Fri. 9am-5pm, daily in July-Aug., adult $5) is the end of the line—literally. This is where a rail line that once spanned Prince Edward Island came to an end. The original station now serves as a testament to the island railroad's halcyon years, with the province's only exhibits and documentation on rail service. The museum is on the **Confederation Trail,** the old rail bed, which has been converted to a walking and bike path that extends 279 kilometers to the west end of the island.

GETTING THERE
Elmira is about 20 kilometers (20 minutes) northeast of Souris, just off Route 16. From

Charlottetown, it's about 95 kilometers (1.5 hours) via Souris on Routes 5, 4, and 2, then 16.

North Lake and Vicinity

North Lake harbor is one of four departure points for deep-sea fishing; anglers try for trophy catches of giant bluefin tuna, which can grow to 500 kilograms. Expect to pay up to $1,250 for a full-day charter for up to six anglers. Trips depart daily during the July-early October season from the North Lake, Naufrage, Launching, and Red Head harbors. **Tony's Tuna Fishing** (902/357-2055, www.tonystunafishing.com), at North Lake harbor, is among the most respected operators.

Points East Beach Motel (7 Cape Rd., 902/357-2228, www.peimotel.com, July-Sept., $120-140 s or d) has 10 above-average motel rooms right on the beach.

Campbells Cove Campground (Rte. 16, 3 km west of North Lake, 902/357-3080, www.campbellscovecampground.com, late June-early Sept., campsites $26-38, cabins $53-87 s or d) fronts the gulf and a long stretch of beautiful sandy beach that is rarely crowded. In addition to campsites and basic cabins, facilities include kitchen shelters, a launderette, and a convenience store.

GETTING THERE

North Lake is about eight kilometers (10 minutes) west of East Point via Route 16. It's about 100 kilometers (1.5 hours) to get to North Lake via the northern route (northeast on Route 2 and Route 16) from Charlottetown. Or use the southern route (east on Route 5, northeast on Route 4, east on Route 2 and then 16), also 100 kilometers, but a slightly longer driving time (1.5 hours).

GULF SHORE
St. Peters Bay

If you're in the area the first week of August, check out the port's **Wild Blueberry Festival** (www.stpetersblueberryfestival.com), an islander favorite with concerts, entertainment, blueberry dishes, lobster and beef barbecue, and a pancake brunch.

At **St. Peters Campground** (5930 St. Peters Rd., 902/961-2786, www.stpeterspark.ca, mid-June-late Sept., $25-33), you have a choice of 11 unserviced sites and more than 70 full-hookup sites. Amenities include a launderette, kitchen shelters, free firewood, two swimming pools, mini-golf, and hot showers.

A hiking trail in Prince Edward Island National Park

GETTING THERE

St. Peters Bay is about 30 kilometers (25 minutes) northwest of Souris via Route 2. It's 50 kilometers (50 minutes) northeast of Charlottetown, also on Route 2.

★ Prince Edward Island National Park, Greenwich Unit

Take Route 313 west from St. Peters along the north side of St. Peters Bay to reach the easternmost of three units that comprise **Price Edward Island National Park.** Known as the **Greenwich Unit,** this six-square-kilometer tract of land encompasses a fragile dune system and wetlands. Near the end of the park access road is **Greenwich Interpretation Centre** (902/963-2391, mid-June-mid-Sept. 10am-4pm, until 6pm July-Aug., adult $8, senior $7, child $4). From the interpretive center, a boardwalk leads across the dunes to the beach, but the hiking trails starting from the very end of the road are the highlight. The 4.8-kilometer (round-trip) **Greenwich Dunes Trail,** which leads through a coastal forest and across the dunes, typifies the coastal habitat best. Wind is slowly pushing the dunes here back into the forest, burying trees that over time become bleached skeletons—an intriguing and unique sight.

MORELL AND VICINITY

Berries are the focus at Morell, 40 minutes from Charlottetown. The St. Peters Bay seaport makes much of the harvest at mid-July's six-day **Morell River Run Festival,** with a parade, concerts, dances, barbecues, strawberry desserts, and other community events.

★ Crowbush Cove

Along the coast just west of Morell is the **Links at Crowbush Cove** (902/368-5761, May-Oct., greens fees $95-115), a highly acclaimed, 18-hole, par-73 golf course. A links course in the Scottish tradition, Crowbush challenges players with nine water holes and nine holes surrounded by dunes. Overlooking the golf course is ★ **Rodd Crowbush Golf & Beach Resort** (902/961-5600, www.rodd-vacations.com, mid-May-mid-Oct.), comprising contemporary rooms in the main lodge and two-bedroom cottages spread along the course. Amenities include spa services, a fitness center, an indoor pool, tennis courts, and a restaurant overlooking the course. Most guests stay as part of golf packages, from $230 per person per night.

Links at Crowbush Cove

Ferries to Îles de la Madeleine

Souris is the departure point for ferries to Québec's Îles de la Madeleine (Magdalen Islands), in the Gulf of St. Lawrence, 105 kilometers from the northern tip of Prince Edward Island and 215 kilometers from the closest point of Québec. This remote archipelago comprises 12 islands, 6 of which are linked by rolling sand dunes, and totals 200 square kilometers. The islands are renowned as a remote wilderness destination, featuring great beaches and abundant birdlife. Villages dot the islands, and each has basic tourist services.

CTMA Ferry (418/986-3278 or 888/986-3278, www.ctmatraversier.ca/en) operates a vehicle/passenger ferry between Souris and the islands year-round. The 134-kilometer crossing takes five hours, with a schedule that includes 6-8 sailings weekly in each direction. Most runs leave Souris at 2pm and leave Cap-aux-Meules for the return at 8am. One-way passenger fares are adult $52, senior $42, child $26, vehicle from $100.

For information on the Magdalens, contact the local **tourism office** (128 Chemin Débarcadère, Cap-aux-Meules, 418/986-2245). This office also maintains an excellent website, www.ilesdelamadeleine.com, with detailed island information and links to accommodations.

Getting There

Morell is about 40 kilometers (40 minutes) northwest of Souris via Route 2, and about 40 kilometers (40-minute drive) northeast of Charlottetown via Route 2.

MOUNT STEWART

Located on the Hillsborough River, 30 kilometers northeast of Charlottetown, Mount Stewart grew as a shipbuilding center in the second half of the 19th century. Today, instead of shipyards, the draw is the **Confederation Trail,** a rail bed that has been converted to a hiking and biking trail that spans the entire island. Mount Stewart is a good place to base yourself for a day or overnight trip along a short section of the trail.

The main attraction in town is the **Hillsborough River Eco-Centre** (104 Main St., 902/676-2050, July-Aug. daily 10am-6pm, free), which has displays on the river and its ecosystem, public Internet access, and a gift shop. Make sure to climb the tower out back for sweeping views up and down Prince Edward Island's major river.

The ★ **Trailside Music Café & Inn** (109 Main St., 902/394-3626, www.trailside.ca, Apr.-Nov., $115 s or d) is named for the Confederation Trail, which passes through town. Located in a restored general store, the four rooms have private bathrooms, hardwood floors, and televisions. For those looking at traveling the trail, this is a handy place to base yourself. The in-house café is renowned across the island for musical performances (check the website for a schedule). The Trailside often hosts local musicians, including every Sunday at 11am through summer, when brunch and live music costs just $22 per person.

Getting There

Mount Stewart is on Route 2, 15 kilometers (10 minutes) southwest of Morell and 30 kilometers (35 minutes) northeast of Charlottetown.

Background

The Landscape

Nova Scotia is predominantly rocky and thinly covered with soil, making it less conducive to farmland than to forests, and thick woodlands blanket the province. The Atlantic coast is rugged, edged with granite, and flanked with sandy beaches, salt marshes, and bogs. The Fundy Coast, from Yarmouth to Cape Split, is rimmed by basalt bedrock mixed with tidal flats. Along this coast, Annapolis Valley, famed for its fruit orchards, is a geological oddity; scoured out by glaciers at the end of the last ice age, the valley is sheltered by mountains north and south, creating a hothouse of warmth and humidity. Along the Northumberland Strait seacoast, rolling terrain with fertile farmlands rises to picturesque high hills and plateaus in Pictou and Antigonish Counties.

Cape Breton Island is joined to mainland Nova Scotia by the 1.4-kilometer Canso Causeway. Cape Breton's smaller, eastern section consists of lowlands and rolling hills, with deeply indented Sydney Harbour on its northern coast. The western part of the island rises gradually from sea level to soaring headlands and highlands, culminating at Cape Breton Highlands National Park near the northern tip. Much of the island's center is taken up by the expansive saltwater Bras d'Or Lakes.

Known as the Graveyard of the Atlantic, the province's shores and treacherous shoals are littered with scores of shipwrecks.

In the Beginning

Nova Scotia was under a shallow sea until 500 million years ago. Then pressurized sand and clay oozed to the surface, where it cooled and hardened to create a landscape of sandstone, quartzite, and slate. Molten

granite later emerged the same way, heaved, and broke apart. You can see these primordial extrusions at Peggy's Cove near Halifax, where the coast is strewn with oddly placed mammoth boulders.

As the earth's surface heaved and shuddered, the land's contours and seacoasts were formed. Between 405 million and 190 million years ago, the turbulent earth devoured its own creations; evidence is visible at Joggins on the upper Fundy's Chignecto Bay, where upright trees were enfolded into cliff edges. Archaeologists date these fossils at 280 million to 345 million years old.

Glaciation

Glaciation and eons of erosion, however, ground down the once-mammoth summits, such as 532-meter **White Hill,** in Cape Breton Highlands National Park, which is Nova Scotia's highest point. One of the reasons for this was glacial ice, uncountable trillions of tons of it, formed in the last four ice ages. Glaciers up to an estimated three kilometers thick weighed down on the elastic bedrock as recently as 14,000 years ago, submerging the coasts and counteracting the inexorable thrust of tectonic uplift.

The last ice sheet retreated and took what remained of prehistory with it. The ice had scoured the earth's surface as it raked back and forth, and this too can be seen at Peggy's Cove, where the ancient scratches are etched in the granite boulders.

As the ice sheet moved, it bulldozed glacial debris into drumlins, large islands of fine soil piled up in places on the predominantly rocky land. The best known of these drumlins is the steep hill upon which the Halifax Citadel sits, but to see drumlins

---

Previous: fishing boat at Brier Island; Black bears are widespread in all Atlantic Canada provinces except Prince Edward Island.

without the man-made distractions, plan to visit Kejimkujik National Park.

Water

More than any other province, Nova Scotia is defined by water—it is nearly completely surrounded by ocean. The 7,400-kilometer-long coastline is a study in contrasts. While the Atlantic Ocean laps the entire east coast, the planet's mightiest tides surge through the Bay of Fundy; the unexpectedly warm Northumberland Strait creates a broad blue parenthesis dividing Prince Edward Island from Nova Scotia; and the wild and woolly Cabot Strait separates Nova Scotia's Cape Breton Island and the island of Newfoundland.

CLIMATE
Nova Scotia

The province has a pleasant, modified continental climate, moderated by air and water currents from the Gulf Stream and the Arctic. Summers are warm and winters are mild. Cape Breton is subject to more extreme weather than the mainland. Precipitation province-wide averages 130 centimeters annually, falling mainly as rain during autumn and as snow in winter.

Spring high temperatures range -2.5-9°C (28-48°F), though the days begin to warm up toward the end of March. Summer weather has a reputation for changing from day to day; daytime highs range up to 30°C (86°F), while nights are cool, averaging 12°C (54°F). Inland areas are generally 5°C (41°F) warmer during the day. The coasts often bask in morning fog. Caribbean hurricanes, having spent their force farther south, limp through the region, bringing to the northwestern Atlantic short spells of rain and wind.

In autumn, the evenings start to cool, but pleasant days continue through September at up to 18°C (64°F). The days are cool and frosty October-mid-November. Winter lasts late November-early March, with temperatures averaging -10-4°C (14-39°F).

New Brunswick

New Brunswick's continental climate contrasts hot summers with cold winters. Extremes are moderated by the surrounding seas, more so near the coast than in the interior. Summer means warm days and cool nights, with an average daytime high temperature of 23°C (73°F) in June, 26°C (79°F) in July, and 25°C (77°F) in August. July is the sunniest month. September and October are

The Bay of Fundy experiences the world's highest tides.

pleasantly warm, with increasingly cool days toward November. Winter is cold.

Precipitation throughout the province averages 115 centimeters annually. The Bay of Fundy coast is steeped in dense fog about 70 days a year.

Prince Edward Island

The island basks in a typical maritime climate, with one major exception: Its growing season of 110-160 days is Atlantic Canada's longest. The island also gets more than its share of year-round breezes, pleasant and warm in summer but fiercer come fall. Spring is short, lasting early-mid-May until mid-June. Summer temperatures peak in July and August, when temperatures range 18-23°C (64-73°F); an unusually warm day can reach 35°C (95°F), while the other extreme can be quite cool at just 5°C (41°F). Autumn brings with it Atlantic Canada's brightest and most dramatic fall foliage. Winter temperatures can dip below 0°C (32°F) in December and January.

Annual precipitation amounts to 106 centimeters, with approximately half of that falling May-October.

Water Temperatures

The ocean water off Nova Scotia is far from hot, but water temperatures in some areas can be pleasantly warm. Conditions vary on the four seas and in each region. The warmest seas during August are found along the Northumberland Strait, where water temperatures reach 18°C (64°F). The Atlantic is a cool 10-15°C (50-59°F) at Mahone Bay and warms a bit as you head up the coast to the northeast—hence the popularity of swimming and surfing at Martinique and Lawrencetown Beaches. Generally, Cape Breton's coastal waters range 14-17°C (57-63°F). The Bay of Fundy is always cool to cold, although it becomes bearable where low tide leaves shallow pools that warm up.

ENVIRONMENTAL ISSUES

Humans have been exploiting Nova Scotia's abundant natural resources for thousands of years. Indigenous hunting and fishing had little effect on ecological integrity, but the arrival of Europeans, who came especially to harvest cod in local waters as early as the 1500s, did. Today, the state of local fisheries, most notably the collapse of cod stocks, is the most important environmental issue facing the province. The beginning of the end was the arrival of "factory ships" in the 1960s, which could harvest up to 200 tons of cod per hour. By the late 1980s, the cod stock had been mostly obliterated, and in the early 1990s a moratorium was put in place until the fishery had recovered. Unfortunately, what was not fully understood at that time was that overfishing was only a part of the problem. Cod are a groundfish, and the factory ships had been bottom-trawling—scooping up the cod in nets with an opening up to one kilometer wide that dragged along the seafloor and devastated the very ecosystem that was a breeding ground for the fish. It is widely thought that the cod stock will never fully recover, although it is currently in better shape here than in the waters off Newfoundland.

Contacts

An excellent website for learning more about sustainable seafood is www.seachoice.org. For information on general environmental issues in Nova Scotia, contact the following organizations: **Canadian Parks and Wilderness Society Nova Scotia** (www.cpawsns.org), **Greenpeace** (www.greenpeace.ca), and **Ecology Action Centre** (www.ecologyaction.ca).

Plants and Animals

To a great extent, it was the land's natural resources—and the potential riches they represented—that attracted Europeans to Canada over the centuries. Since time immemorial, mammals, fish, and varied plant species had, of course, fed and clothed the indigenous peoples of Nova Scotia, who harvested only enough to sustain themselves. But the very abundance of the wildlife seemed to fuel the rapacity of the newcomers, driving them to a sort of madness of consumption—and hastening the exploration and settlement of the newfound continent. Luckily for today's visitor, much remains, in sometimes astonishing abundance and variety, thanks to each species' own unique genius for survival, blind luck, the shifting vagaries of public tastes, and even the occasional glimmer of human enlightenment.

PLANTS

The receding glaciers of the last ice age scoured the land and left lifeless mud and rubble in their wake. Overall, the climate then was considerably cooler than it is today, and the first life forms to recolonize in the shadow of the glaciers were hardy mosses, lichens, and other cold-tolerant plants. Junipers and other shrubs later took root, and afterward came coniferous trees—hardy, fast-growing spruce and fir—that could thrive here despite the harsh climate and relatively brief growing season. In the boggy interior sprouted moisture-loving willows and tamaracks. As the climate warmed and the soil grew richer, broadleaf deciduous trees arrived. Today, 80 percent of Nova Scotia is thickly blanketed by a typical Acadian forest of mixed hardwoods and conifers. Common trees include hemlock, spruce, balsam fir, yellow and paper birches, cedar, maple, ash, and oak. In autumn, the brilliant hues of the changing leaves are one of the province's most cherished attractions.

Large tracts are set aside in the province at Kejimkujik and Cape Breton Highlands National Parks, which protect areas of unique plant habitat. In the Cape Breton Highlands, for example, stands of 300-year-old maples (believed to be the oldest in the country) have survived, and unusual wild orchid species thrive as well. In the highlands' highest elevations, the stunted taiga and alpine-arctic plant communities have been included in an international biological preserve. Bogs in the national parks nourish insectivorous pitcher plants, more orchids, and other specially adapted species.

Forests

Maritime Canada's forests abound with ash, balsam fir, birch, beech, cedar, hemlock, maple, oak, pine, and spruce. Thick woodlands now blanket over 81 percent of Nova Scotia and 93 percent of New Brunswick, whose interior conifer forests in places resemble vast impenetrable fields of dark green wheat. Prince Edward Island, by contrast, is the country's least-forested province, with its land area about equally divided between farmlands and woodlands.

Wildflowers and Other Plants

Trees, of course, are only part of the picture. Along the forest margins, raspberry and blackberry thickets proliferate, providing, among other benefits, welcome snacks for summertime hikers. Throughout the spring and summer months, the Maritimes host magnificent wildflower shows that change subtly week by week. Common wildflowers throughout New Brunswick and Nova Scotia—seen especially along roadsides in summertime—include lupine, Queen Anne's lace, yarrow, pearly everlasting, and daisies. The showy spikes of purple loosestrife, a pretty but aggressive and unwelcome pest, can be seen everywhere.

Bayberries and wild rose bloom on the Chignecto Isthmus during June. The

Was That a Cougar?

Probably not. Cougars (called mountain lions or pumas elsewhere in North America) may still live in Canada's western provinces, but in Nova Scotia their presence is a bit of a mystery.

These large members of the cat family can grow to more than two meters in length and weigh up to 90 kilograms. Elsewhere in Canada, their fur varies in color from light brown to a reddish-tinged gray, but one thing many local sightings have in common is reports of much darker fur. They are incredibly agile creatures. They can spring forward more than 8 meters from a standstill, leap 4 meters into the air, and safely jump from a height of 20 meters.

Once widespread through the province, they were hunted to supposed extinction by 1900, and the most recent confirmed sighting was all the way back in the 1930s. Today there are a few unconfirmed sightings every year, usually in or around Kejimkujik National Park and in the remote backcountry of the Marine Drive. But researchers do not believe there are any wild cougars in the province.

bayberry bush grows clusters of dimpled fruits close along woody stems and releases a pleasant spicy aroma, popular in potpourri and Christmas candles. The yellow beach heather colors the Northumberland Strait dunes and sandy plains, and the rhodora (miniature rhododendron) brightens coastal marshes. Another dune resident, the beach plum, grows snowy white to pinkish flowers in June, which produce fruit welcomed by birds, beasts, and man in late summer and early fall. Nutrient-rich bogs in northeastern New Brunswick nurture plant exotics, especially at Lamèque and Miscou Islands, where wild cranberry and sundew grow among peat moss beds. Prince Edward Island is like one large garden when late spring and summer's warm temperatures urge columbines, bachelor's buttons, pansies, lilacs, wild roses, pink clover, and the delicate lady's slipper (the provincial flower) into blossom.

You may encounter poison ivy. Mushrooms are everywhere; be absolutely certain you know the species before sampling—the chanterelles are culinary prizes, but the amanitas deadly poison.

LAND MAMMALS

Nova Scotia is home to 70 different mammals. Some, such as beavers, are common. Others, such as the lynx, are endangered, while the presence of cougars is unproven, and species such as woodland caribou have disappeared completely. But it's not all bad news—wildlife-viewing opportunities present themselves throughout the province.

Moose

The giant of the deer family is the moose, an awkward-looking mammal that appears to have been designed by a cartoonist. It has the largest antlers of any animal in the world, stands up to 1.8 meters at the shoulder, and weighs up to 500 kilograms. Its body is dark brown, and it has a prominent nose, long spindly legs, small eyes, big ears, and an odd flap of skin called a bell dangling beneath its chin. Apart from all that, it's good-looking. Each spring the bull begins to grow palm-shaped antlers that by August will be fully grown. Moose are solitary animals, preferring marshy areas and weedy lakes, but they are known to wander to higher elevations searching out open spaces in summer. They forage in and around ponds on willows, aspen, birch, grasses, and all aquatic vegetation. Although they may appear docile, moose will attack humans if they feel threatened.

Moose are present in Nova Scotia and New Brunswick. Ironically, they are not native to the island. The estimated 150,000 or so that thrive in the province today are descended from a handful of individuals introduced in 1878 and 1904 as a source of meat. On the mainland, they are most common in Cape Breton Highlands National Park (Nova Scotia).

White-Tailed Deer

Populations of deer are not particularly high in Nova Scotia; they were practically nonexistent by the late 1800s but came back in the ensuing years. The color of the white-tailed deer varies with the season, but it is generally light brown in summer, turning dirty gray in winter. The white-tailed deer's tail is dark on top, but when the animal runs, it holds its tail erect, revealing an all-white underside. Whitetails frequent thickets along the rivers and lakes of interior forests.

Black Bears

Black bears are the only bears present in Nova Scotia. But black bears are not always black (they can be brown), causing them to be called brown bears when in fact they are not. Black bears are widespread through the province but are not particularly common, estimated to number about 8,000 of Canada's total estimate of 380,000. Their weight varies considerably; males average 150 kilograms and females 100 kilograms. Their diet is omnivorous,

consisting primarily of grasses and berries and supplemented by small mammals. They are not true hibernators, but in winter they can sleep for up to a month at a time before changing position. During this time, their heart rate drops to 10 beats per minute, their body temperature drops, and they lose up to 30 percent of their body weight. Females reach reproductive maturity after five years; cubs, usually two, are born in late winter while the mother is still asleep.

Lynx

The elusive lynx is an endangered species. It is present in low numbers in all provinces except Prince Edward Island. Easily identifiable by its pointy black ear tufts and an oversized tabby cat appearance, the animal has broad, padded paws that distribute its weight, allowing it to float on the surface of snow. It weighs up to 10 kilograms but appears much larger because of its coat of long, thick fur. The lynx is a solitary creature that prefers the cover of forest, feeding mostly at night on small mammals.

Beavers

One of the animal kingdom's most industrious mammals is the beaver. Growing to a length of 50 centimeters and tipping the

white-tailed deer

scales at around 20 kilograms, it has a flat, rudder-like tail and webbed back feet that enable it to swim at speeds of up to 10 kilometers per hour. Once hunted for their fur, beavers can be found in flat, forested areas throughout the province. They build their dam walls and lodges of twigs, branches, sticks of felled trees, and mud. They eat the bark and smaller twigs of deciduous plants and store branches underwater near the lodge as a winter food supply.

SEA LIFE

The ocean water that surrounds the provinces nurtures an astonishing abundance and variety of sea creatures, from tiny, uncounted single-celled organisms up through the convoluted links of the food chain to the Earth's largest beings—whales.

Tidal Zones

Along the shores, the same conditions that provide for rich and diverse plants—rocky indented coasts, dramatic tidal variations—also create ideal habitats for varied animal communities in the tidal zone. Between the highest and lowest tides, the Maritime shore is divided into six zones, each determined by the amount of time it is exposed to air. The black zone, just above the highest high-water mark, gets its name from the dark band of primitive blue-green algae that grows there. The next zone is called the periwinkle zone, for the small marine snails that proliferate within it. Able to survive prolonged exposure to air, periwinkles can leave the water to graze on the algae. The barnacle zone, encrusted with the tenacious crustaceans, while also exposed several hours daily during low tides, receives the brutal pounding of breaking waves. Next is the rockweed zone—home to mussels, limpets, and hermit crabs (which commandeer the shells of dead periwinkles)—and the comparatively placid Irish moss zone, which shelters and feeds sea urchins, starfish, sea anemones, crabs, and myriad other animals familiar to anyone who has peered into the miniature world of a tide pool. Last is the laminarian zone, where lobsters, sponges, and fishes thrive in the forests of kelp growing in the deep, churning water.

Fish

Beyond the tidal zones lie the waters of the continental shelf and then the open sea. Flowing south from the Arctic, cold oxygen-laden currents also carry loads of silica, ground out of the continental granite by the glaciers and poured into the sea by coastal rivers. Oxygen and silica together create an ideal environment for the growth of diatoms, the microscopic one-celled plants that form the bedrock of the ocean's food chain. In the sunlight of long summer days in these northern latitudes, the numbers of diatoms increase exponentially. They are the food source for shrimp and herring, which in turn support larger fish, such as mackerel, Atlantic salmon, and tuna.

Fisheries have been the economic engine driving exploration and development of these northeastern Atlantic coasts for centuries. In days past, codfish were said to carpet the seafloor of the shallow Grand Banks, and the men who caught them—first with lines from small dories, then with nets, and finally from great trawlers that scour the sea—have hauled in untold millions of tons of not only cod but also flounder, salmon, pollack, haddock, anchovies, and dozens of other species. But the fish are in serious trouble, and so, too, inexorably, are the people and communities whose lives have revolved around them.

Whales

The whales that frequent Nova Scotia arrive from the Caribbean between June and mid-July and remain through October. Watching the whales cavort is one of summer's great visitor delights; whale-watching boats leave from Brier Island on the Bay of Fundy and Cape Breton's Chéticamp. The Fundy is especially rich in whales, and the fast incoming tides bring in the mammoth mammals in pursuit of herring schools. Among the 20 species that summer offshore, the most frequently sighted are minkes, pilots, fins, orcas, and humpbacks. The Atlantic right whale is a treasured August visitor.

Seals

Gray and harbor seals inhabit Nova Scotian waters at various times of the year. Whale-watching tours often include a stop at an offshore seal colony, although you may also spot one unexpectedly, such as while dining at a waterfront restaurant in Halifax or in the ocean far below while walking the trail to Cape Chignecto. Harp seals, Arctic dwellers that fatten themselves on fish off the Labrador and Greenland coasts, are occasionally sighted around Cape Breton Island.

BIRDS

About 280 bird species have been reported in Nova Scotia. The province is best known for its bald eagles; about 250 pairs nest here, the second-largest population on North America's east coast after Florida. The season for eagle-watching is July and August. Some of the prime viewing areas are the Lake Ainslie and St. Ann's Bay coastlines; the village of Iona, where Bras d'Or Lakes meets St. Andrews Channel on Cape Breton Island; and the St. George's Bay coastline. Ospreys nest on McNabs Island in Halifax Harbour. Other raptors may be seen at Brier Island on the Bay of Fundy.

As Nova Scotia lies on the Atlantic flyway, many migratory species can be spotted, including common and arctic terns, kittiwakes, great and double-crested cormorants, Leach's storm petrels, Atlantic puffins, guillemots, and various gulls, ducks, and geese.

Bird-Watching

The **Nova Scotia Bird Society** (www.ns-birdsociety.ca) can direct you to prime birding sites and answer even the most esoteric questions about the province's many and varied species. Its website has bird lists, a schedule of field trips, and links to local contacts.

In New Brunswick's interior, crossbills, varied woodpecker species, boreal chickadees, and gray jays nest in the spruce and fir forests. Ibises, herons, and snowy egrets wade among lagoons and marshes. Among Nova Scotia's 300 or so bird species, the best known is the bald eagle. About 250 pairs nest in the province, concentrated on Cape Breton—the second-largest population on North America's east coast after Florida. The season for eagle watching is July and August. Other birds of prey include red-tailed, broad-winged, and other hawks; owls; and the gyrfalcon in Newfoundland and Labrador. Peregrine falcons were reintroduced to Fundy National Park in 1982. They nest in seaside cliffs and attack their prey in "stoops," kamikaze dives in which the falcon can reach speeds of over 300 kilometers per hour.

The noisy blue jay, Prince Edward Island's official provincial bird, is at home throughout the province, but the island's showiest species is the enormous, stately great blue heron, which summers there May-early August. The rare piping plover may be seen (but not disturbed) on the island's national park beaches, and arctic terns nest along the coast near Murray Harbour.

History

THE EARLIEST INHABITANTS

The earliest evidence of human habitation in Nova Scotia dates from about 8600 BC and is found at the present site of Debert, northwest of Truro. Here, at one of the northernmost Paleo-Indian sites in North America, archaeologists have uncovered a wealth of artifacts, including telltale Clovis-like spear tips. The people who once set up camp here were descendants of *Homo sapiens* who migrated from northeast Asia across a land bridge spanning the Bering Strait starting 15,000 years ago. At the time, the northern latitudes of North America were covered by an ice cap, forcing them to travel south down the west coast before fanning out across the ice-free southern latitudes. As the ice cap receded northward, the people drifted north also, perhaps only a few kilometers in an entire generation, and began crossing the 49th parallel, which roughly follows the present U.S.-Canadian border, about 12,000 years ago.

Mi'kmaq

Culturally and linguistically related to Algonquian people, the largest language group in Canada, the Mi'kmaq made a home throughout present-day Nova Scotia as well as northern New Brunswick and as far west as Québec. They were coastal dwellers who fished with spears and hook and line while also collecting shellfish from the shoreline. Hunting was of lesser importance for food but earned one a great degree of status among other members of the group. Canoes with sails were built for summer travel, while in winter toboggans ("toboggan" originates from the Mi'kmaq word *topaghan*) and snowshoes were essential.

Like other aboriginal peoples across North America, the Mi'kmaq practiced a kind of spiritual animism, deeply tied to the land. The trees, animals, and landforms were respected and blessed. Before food could be consumed or a tree felled, for example, it was appreciated for its life-sustaining sacrifice. Mythology also played an important part in spiritual life, along with rituals, shamanism, and potlatch ceremonies.

The name Mi'kmaq (also Micmac) is thought to have derived from the word *nikmaq,* meaning "my kin-friends," which early French settlers used as a greeting for the tribe. Mi'kmaq historically referred to themselves as Lnu (meaning "human being" or "the people").

ACADIA

Nova Scotia's tie to Europe began in 1497, when the explorer John Cabot sighted Cape Breton Island and claimed it for England. A few decades later, French explorer Jacques Cartier also claimed much of the same coastline. For France, the region was choice property, a potential New France in the New World. On the other hand, England's colonial aspirations centered farther south, where colonization had begun at Virginia and Massachusetts. England didn't *need* what is now Nova Scotia, though the region offered much with its rich fisheries, but it was a place to confront the expansion of the French, England's most contentious enemy in Europe.

Colonization

England's claim notwithstanding, France eyed the area for colonization and dispatched explorer Samuel de Champlain to the region in 1604. After a tough winter on an island on the St. Croix River (which today forms the New Brunswick-Maine border), the encampment moved across the Bay of Fundy, where the fortified Port-Royal was established near what is now Annapolis Royal. The French named the region—encompassing what is now Nova Scotia, New Brunswick, and Prince Edward Island—Acadia (Peaceful Land). Not to be outdone, England's James I named the same region Nova Scotia (New Scotland) and granted it to Sir William Alexander in 1621.

After a 1632 peace treaty forced England to surrender Nova Scotia to the French, Acadian settlements quickly spread beyond the Port-Royal area to the Fundy and Minas Basin coastlines. The merchant Nicholas Denys, whose name is entwined with France's early exploration, established a fortified settlement on Cape Breton Island at St. Peters and also at Guysborough in 1653. So many Acadians settled at Grand-Pré that it became the largest settlement and hub of villages along the Fundy Coast. Other settlements were established across Acadia on Cape Breton Island, the Cobequid Bay and Cape Chignecto coastlines, and in what is now New Brunswick. The villagers cultivated grains and forage crops on wetlands reclaimed by dikes and planted the region's first orchards.

Through Acadian expansion, bitter military confrontations continued. The two powers had different strategies: France first built settlements, then used its military to defend them. England, boasting a superior military savvy, fought its battles first, then used settlements to stabilize areas. As it turned out, England had the edge, and it was on this advantage that Nova Scotia's history frequently turned during the following century and a half.

Treaty of Utrecht

Hostilities between England and France in the New World mirrored political events in Europe. Fighting ebbed and flowed across the region as the powers jockeyed for control on the European continent. Queen Anne's War (1701-1713), the War of Austrian Succession (1745-1748), and the Seven Years' War (1756-1763) were all fought in Europe, but corresponding battles between the English and French took place in North America as well (where they were known collectively as the French and Indian Wars).

The Treaty of Utrecht in 1713 settled Queen Anne's War in Europe. Under the terms of the treaty, England fell heir to all of French Acadia (though the borders were vague), which became an English colony. Nova Scotia (New Scotland) rose on the ashes of New France and the fallen Port-Royal; the British took the fort in 1710, renamed it Fort Anne, and renamed the settlement Annapolis Royal. The town was designated the colony's first capital, remaining as such until Halifax was established and became the capital in 1749.

Port-Royal National Historic Site, the first permanent settlement north of Florida

Acadian Deportation

In the mid-1700s, decades of war between England and France were winding down in England's favor. The British demanded unqualified oaths of allegiance from the Acadians, who refused and claimed neutrality. Rather than compromise their principles, they fled Nova Scotia for Acadia's more peaceful north. The British followed, burning villages and crops as they went. The Acadian deportation began in 1755, when about 1,100 Acadians were deported to England's other colonies in South Carolina, Georgia, and Pennsylvania. Guerrilla warfare raged as the Acadians fought for their lives and then fled to the hinterlands.

Refugee camps sprang up, the most well-known of which were Beaubears Island, now a national historic site on the Miramichi River, and the nearby swatch of land today home to Enclosure Park (at Derby Junction, five kilometers west of Miramichi), one of the province's most important archaeological sites. Many Acadians died of scurvy and starvation.

The Peace of Paris in 1763 ushered in an uneasy truce. France surrendered its mainland possessions, but during the ensuing decades about 3,800 Acadians returned to the region. The deportation officially finished in 1816.

ONGOING CONFLICT

The French military regrouped after the fall of Port-Royal. It fled from the region and began to build the Fortress of Louisbourg on Cape Breton Island in 1719. Once again, the French envisioned the fortification as a New Paris and France's major naval base, port city, and trading center in North America.

The British quickly responded. A fort at Grassy Island on Chedabucto Bay was their first effort, a site close enough to the Fortress of Louisbourg to watch the arrivals and departures of the French fleets. By 1745, Louisbourg represented a formidable threat to England, so the Brits seized the fortress and deported the inhabitants. But no sooner had they changed the flag than the French were moving back in again. The War of Austrian Succession in Europe ended with the Treaty of Aix-la-Chapelle in 1748, which, among other things, returned Louisbourg to France.

Full-Fledged War

In 1749 a British convoy sailed into Halifax Harbour, established England's military hub in the North Atlantic in the capacious harbor, and named Halifax the capital of Nova Scotia. Seven years later, the Seven Years' War broke out in Europe, and once more both powers geared for confrontation across the Atlantic Ocean. In 1758 the British again seized the Fortress of Louisbourg and toppled Port la Joye, renaming it Fort Amherst. In the ultimate act of revenge, the British troops returned to Louisbourg in 1760 and demolished the fortress stone by stone so it would never rise again against England.

Fort Edward, on the Fundy Coast, went up in the midst of an Acadian area and guarded the overland route from Halifax. Fort Lawrence on the Chignecto Isthmus, between Nova Scotia and New Brunswick, was built to defend the route to the mainland.

BRITISH SETTLEMENT

After the Acadian deportation, the British began peopling the territory with pro-Crown settlers. Lunenburg began with 2,000 German, Swiss, and French "foreign Protestants." In 1760 England resettled the prime Fundy Coast once farmed by the Acadians with 12 shiploads of farmers from its colonies farther south. The Crown officially regained the region, including Cape Breton Island, with the Peace of Paris in 1763. After the American Revolution, 25,000 British Loyalists poured into Nova Scotia.

Cable to Canso

On the outskirts of tiny Canso, at the northeastern end of the Marine Drive, is **Hazel Hill Cable Station,** an imposing but crumbling brick building that has important ties to the history of communications. The first cable link between Europe and North America came ashore in Newfoundland, and the company that established the link was given landing rights for 50 years. With problems providing a reliable link between Newfoundland and New York, the Commercial Cable Company laid its own cable, which came ashore at Canso and then continued south to Boston and New York. Completed in 1884, the Hazel Hill Cable Station was a state-of-the-art facility, helping transmit messages from one side of the Atlantic to the other in less than one minute. The distress signal from the sinking *Titanic* and news of the 1929 stock market crash were transmitted through the station; the final message was sent in 1962.

SCOTTISH HERITAGE

Nova Scotia's Scottish heritage originated with a shipload of immigrants who arrived at Pictou in 1773, followed by hundreds of settlers to New Glasgow in the 1780s and the Arisaig area in the next decade.

It was during the early 1800s, however, that the region's decidedly Scottish complexion was firmly established. England and France were engaged in the Napoleonic War, and the French had blocked British ports. England desperately needed food and began the Highland Clearances, in which poor tenant farmers in Scotland were turned off their land, their homes burned, and the farmlands converted to sheep and cattle pastures. The

Clearances continued for almost two decades. Thousands of Scots died of starvation and disease, while thousands more took the Crown up on its offer of free land in Nova Scotia. They left their beloved Highlands forever and re-created their old homes in a new land. Intense emotional ties to the region remain to this day, and the Scots' heritage is kept alive with festivals commemorating their history and culture.

NOVA SCOTIA TAKES SHAPE

In the late 18th century, Nova Scotia was defined as a distinct colony. Cape Breton Island, for a while a separate colony, was reannexed to

Nova Scotia in 1820. Fortunes were founded on trade. Halifax's Samuel Cunard started a shipping empire based on steamship service to England in 1839. During the Great Age of Sail, shipbuilding seaports thrived. In 1878 Yarmouth ranked as Canada's second-largest port. Coal mining began in 1872 at Springhill, near Amherst, where the 1,220-meter shaft was Canada's deepest.

Confederation

In 1864, Nova Scotia sent five delegates across to neighboring Prince Edward Island for a landmark event in Canada's history. The "Fathers of the Confederation"—from Nova Scotia as well as New Brunswick, Prince Edward Island, Ontario, and Québec—met at Province House in Charlottetown to discuss the joint dominion that followed. England gave the union its blessing and signed the British North America Act (now known as the Constitution Act). Confederation was not popular with all Nova Scotians, but it offered economic inducements, including the rail connections to central Canada that Nova Scotia wanted. Finally, the Dominion of Canada was born on July 1, 1867, as a confederation of Québec, Ontario, New Brunswick, and Nova Scotia united under a parliamentary government, with the other provinces of today joining between 1870 and 1949 (neighboring Newfoundland and Labrador was last to join).

Government and Economy

GOVERNMENT

Canada is a constitutional monarchy. The federation of 10 provinces and three territories operates under a parliamentary democracy in which power is shared between the federal government, based in Ottawa, and the provincial governments. Canada's three nonprovincial territories, Nunavut, Yukon, and the Northwest Territories, exercise delegated—rather than constitutionally guaranteed—authority. The power to make, enforce, and interpret laws rests in the legislative, executive, and judicial branches of government, respectively.

The Federal Government

Under Canada's constitutional monarchy, the formal head of state is the queen of England, who appoints a governor-general to represent her for a five-year term. The governor-general stays out of party politics and performs largely ceremonial duties, such as opening and closing parliamentary sessions, signing and approving state documents on the queen's behalf, and appointing a temporary replacement if the prime ministry is vacated without warning. The head of government is the prime minister, who is the leader of the majority party or party coalition in the House of Commons.

The country's legislative branch, the Parliament, comprises two houses. The House of Commons, with 308 members, is apportioned by provincial population and elected by plurality from the country's districts (11 members are from Nova Scotia). The Senate comprises 105 members appointed by the governor-general on the advice of the prime minister. Legislation must be passed by both houses and signed by the governor-general to become law.

National elections are held whenever the majority party is voted down in the House of Commons or every five years, whichever comes first. Historically, it has been unusual for a government to last its full term.

Provincial and Local Governments

Whereas the federal government has authority over defense, criminal law, trade, banking, and other affairs of national interest, Canada's 10 provincial governments bear responsibility for civil services, health, education, natural resources, and local government. As in the other provinces, Nova Scotia's Legislative Assembly consists of a one-house legislative body with members elected every four years. The nominal head of the provincial government is the lieutenant governor, appointed by the governor-general of Canada. Executive power, however, rests with the cabinet, headed by a premier, the leader of the majority party.

As elsewhere, local government in Nova Scotia has always been top-heavy with bureaucracy, and so in the 1990s the number of incorporated towns was trimmed by creating regional municipalities. One of these was Cape Breton Regional Municipality, formed by amalgamating six incorporated towns and one existing county. The main population base lives in Halifax Regional Municipality, which was created through the amalgamation of the cities of Halifax and Dartmouth and the town of Bedford.

ECONOMY

Traditionally, Nova Scotia's economy revolved around resource-based industries such as fishing, forestry, and mining. Although communities established around fishing and farming areas continue to thrive, the economy today is a lot more diverse. In addition to the stalwarts discussed below, other growing sectors include information technology, the medical field (Nova Scotia is a world leader in multiorgan transplants), and the film industry.

In 2014, Nova Scotia's gross domestic product was a little more than $39 billion, with ocean industries generating the largest segment ($3.1 billion). Second most important to the economy is manufacturing ($2.1 billion).

Ocean Industries

Fishing, the traditional stalwart of the Nova Scotia economy, has decreased greatly in importance dollar-wise in the last two decades. Poor resource management and overfishing have destroyed its once-bounteous supplies. Cod stocks especially have declined greatly,

and quotas have been put in place in an effort to protect and rebuild existing stocks. Even so, fisheries and fish-processing remain an important contributor to Nova Scotia's gross domestic product, and cod, haddock, herring, and lobster are caught inshore and off the Atlantic's Scotian Shelf. The province is the world's largest lobster exporter.

New Brunswick's fisheries produce groundfish, lobster, crab, scallops, and herring. The newest aquaculture developments are Atlantic salmon farms and blue mussel beds. Blacks Harbour-area canneries on the Bay of Fundy rank first in Canadian sardine production.

Prince Edward Island also has an important fishing industry, especially in lobster and shellfish such as farmed mussels.

The government has put a positive spin on the decline of the fishing industry by claiming that the "ocean industries" sector is growing. It may be, but only because other industry is being added to the fishing equation, including aquaculture, boatbuilding, offshore gas and oil drilling, ocean-related tourism, sea-based government services, and transportation. Regardless of how you approach the issue, the ocean is extremely important to the Nova Scotian economy, generating $3.1 billion dollars annually. Actual annual fish and seafood exports are worth $1.3 billion to the provincial economy, with lobster leading the way ($580 million).

Tourism

Tourism ranks as the third most important component of the provincial economic pie, generating $2 billion annually. It is also the fastest-growing sector of the economy, having doubled in worth during the last decade and currently employing over 45,000 people. Most visitors (36 percent) are from the neighboring provinces, while the rest of Canada contributes 30 percent, and the United States adds almost 25 percent. Of the 2.1 million people who arrive annually, around three-quarters are returning visitors.

Agriculture and Forestry

Although just 8 percent of Nova Scotia's land is arable, agriculture contributes heavily to the economy, producing fruits (including Annapolis Valley apples), dairy products, poultry, hogs, and the world's largest share of blueberries.

Fishing gets all the attention, but forestry has historically been an important component of the provincial economy. In the 1800s, local lumber was used in shipbuilding, but today the pulp and paper industries use the great majority of harvested wood. About 37,000 square kilometers of Nova Scotia is deemed to be productive forest, and most of it is owned by private companies. Nova Scotia also exports 1.7 million Christmas trees each year, which are worth $30 million to the local economy.

Diminutive Prince Edward Island ranks first in Canada's potato production. Half of the crop is grown in Prince County, and the remainder is produced by farms scattered across the province. The province harvests 12 million oysters annually, and most are exported. The island's beauty may be attributed to its investment in agriculture, which contributes about 9.5 percent to the gross domestic product. The sector yields $120 million a year and employs 4,000 islanders on 2,200 farms, each of which averages 140 hectares. Grains, fruit, beef, pigs, sheep, and dairy products are other components of mixed farming production.

Military

Nova Scotia is the region's federal civil service and military center. Halifax has served as a naval center since its founding in 1749 as headquarters for the Royal Navy. The city is now Maritime Command headquarters for the Canadian Armed Forces. Other in-province military installations are at Shearwater, Cornwallis, and Greenwood; training stations are at Barrington, Mill Cove, Shelburne, and Sydney.

Mining

Offshore deposits of oil and gas below the Scotian Shelf near Sable Island, 250 kilometers from the mainland, have been drilled since the early 1990s. It is estimated that two billion barrels of oil and up to 40 trillion cubic feet of natural gas remain. Important salt deposits are mined along the Northumberland Strait, including at Pugwash. Nova Scotia is the leading Canadian supplier of gypsum, which is exported to the United States. Historically, coal was the most important mineral product, with mines on Cape Breton Island supplying coal to power stations and used to produce iron and steel. Today, a small coal mine near Steallarton is coming to the end of its life, although there has been talk of reopening an abandoned mine at Donkin, on Cape Breton Island.

People and Culture

While the rugged topography of Nova Scotia has tended to separate people and isolate them in scattered settlements, centuries of sometimes turbulent history have bound the Nova Scotians together: the mutual grief of the early wars, the Acadian deportation, immigration upheavals, and the abiding hardships common to resource-based economies.

DEMOGRAPHY

A few statistics say much about the region. The entire population of the country numbers some 35.2 million—smaller than California's population. Atlantic Canada's four provinces make up 14.8 percent of Canada's total population, with a combined total of 2,371,000 people.

Nova Scotia

Nova Scotia's population is 943,000. It is the seventh most populous province and is home to 2.3 percent of Canada's total population. Distribution is closely divided between urban and rural, with a full third of Nova Scotians concentrated in and around Halifax.

Almost four of five Nova Scotians trace their lineage to the British Isles. Some 49 original Scottish families, from Archibald to Yuill, are still on the rolls of the Federation of Scottish Clans in Nova Scotia (www.scotsns.ca), which does genealogical surveys.

After the American Revolution, 25,000 United Empire Loyalists poured into Nova Scotia. Several thousand African Americans arrived during the War of 1812, followed by Irish immigrants from 1815 to 1850. Recent worldwide immigration has added more than 50 other ethnic groups (including Poles, Ukrainians, Germans, Swiss, Africans, and Lebanese) to the province's cultural milieu, making it the most cosmopolitan in the region. About 8,000 Black people live in Nova Scotia today, many of them descendants of immigrants from the colonial United States.

New Brunswick

The province, with a population of 755,000, is in a sense a miniature Canada, a provincial composite of Anglophones and Acadian Francophones who harmoniously coexist—the exception rather than the rule in a nation whose two dominant cultures are so often at odds. One suspects the harsh history that divided New Brunswick at its inception has run its course and mellowed. As Canada's only officially bilingual province, it steps to an agreeable duple beat.

The duality repeats itself in numerous ways. New Brunswick has an Anglophone region and another equally distinctive Acadian Francophone counterpart. The distinctions were set in stone centuries ago when the British evicted the Acadians from their original settlements and resettled the Loyalists. The Anglophone cities, towns, and settlements lie along the Fundy seacoast and throughout most of the Saint John River valley. The French-speaking Acadian region lies beyond, on the province's outer rim in the northwestern woodlands along the Saint John River and on the coastlines of the Baie des Chaleurs, the open gulf, and the sheltered strait. Today, English is the first language of about 65 percent of New Brunswickers, while French is the mother tongue for about 33 percent.

Prince Edward Island

Although it's anything but crowded, Prince Edward Island (PEI, population 148,000) is Canada's most densely populated, with around 24 people per square kilometer. At the same time, Prince Edward Island is the most rural province, with fewer than two in five residents living in urban areas. PEI's people are also said to be Canada's most homogeneous. The province's ancestry is 80 percent Anglo—a third Irish and the remainder Scottish. Acadians represent 17 percent of the population (5 percent of them speak French). Southeast Asians, Germans, and a thriving population of about 500 Mi'kmaq (most living on Lennox Island on the north shore and at Scotchfort) together constitute about 2 percent of the population. PEI still lures immigrants, mainly from other Atlantic Canada provinces and Ontario.

Mi'kmaq

For thousands of years before the arrival of Europeans, the Mi'kmaq people had lived off the land's abundant natural resources. As the Mi'kmaq were forced to sign treaties, they gave up traditional land and settled on reserves (known as reservations in the United States). They were no longer free, they no longer hunted or fought, their medicine men could do nothing to stop the spread of the white man's diseases, and, slowly, they lost their pride. The first Indian Act, drafted in 1876, attempted to prepare natives for "European" society, but it only ended up isolating them from the rest of society.

Today, a total of 45 reserves and bands create affiliation for 6,000 Mi'kmaq. The total number of aboriginal people in Nova Scotia is quoted at 26,000; many of the remaining 20,000 live off reserves but on traditional lands.

Various names are used to describe aboriginal Canadians, and all can be correct in context. The government still uses the term "Indian," despite its links to Christopher Columbus and the misconception that he had landed in India. "Native" is generally considered acceptable only when used in conjunction with "people," "communities," or "leaders." "Indigenous" or "aboriginal" can have insulting connotations when used in certain contexts. The Mi'kmaq themselves most often refer to themselves and others by none of the above, preferring to use band names.

Métis

The progeny of native people and Caucasians, the Métis (named for an old French word meaning "mixed") form a diverse and complex group throughout Canada. They date from the time of earliest European contact; in Nova Scotia, unions between European fishermen and Mi'kmaq women—sometimes casual, sometimes formal—produced Métis offspring by the early 1600s. In the 17th century, the French government encouraged this mixing, seeing it as conducive to converting the native people to Christianity and to more speedily increasing the population of New France. Samuel de Champlain said, "Our young men will marry your daughters, and we shall be one people." That policy had changed by the 1700s, however, and France then *discouraged* mixed unions, in part because of the increased presence of white women in North America.

Today, Métis culture in Nova Scotia remains strongest along the Fundy Coast.

LANGUAGE AND RELIGION

Although Canada is constitutionally bilingual, English is the language of choice for the majority of Nova Scotians. (French is the mother tongue of about 22 percent of Canadians, while the figure in Québec is 88 percent.) The Official Languages Acts of 1969 and 1988 established French and English as equal official languages and designated rights for minority-language speakers throughout the country. Still, there has been no shortage of acrimony between francophone Québec and the rest of the country over the issue of language (as well as broader cultural distinctions), which has led to constitutional crisis and nearly to the secession of Québec from the confederation.

English is spoken by 94 percent of Nova Scotians, while 6 percent are bilingual. French has gained appeal as a second language, and one in four primary schoolchildren in Halifax is enrolled in French immersion classes. Francophones are a small minority in Nova Scotia (4 percent). The French spoken here is not a patois; it's closely tied to the language that was brought to the continent by the original settlers from France. Visitors who have studied standard Parisian French may have a little trouble with the accent, syntax, and vocabulary (the differences are not unlike those between American and British English).

Canada, Eh!

Canadian English is subtly different from American English, not only in pronunciation but also in lexicon. For instance, Canadians may say "serviette," "depot," and "chesterfield" when Americans would say "napkin," "station," and "couch." Spelling is a bit different as well, as Canadians have kept many British spellings—for example, *colour, kilometre, centre, and cheque.* "Eh?" is a common lilt derived from British and Gaelic, in which each sentence ends on a high note, as though a question had been asked. At the same time, Canadian English has been profoundly influenced by its neighbor to the south. Nevertheless, language variations pose no serious threat to communication.

Religion

Although the domination of organized religions over the lives of Canadians has waned substantially since the 1960s, church affiliation in Nova Scotia is higher than elsewhere in the country.

Nova Scotia's cultural diversity is reflected in religion. Protestants and Roman Catholics make up 58 and 37 percent of the mainland population, respectively, while on Cape Breton Catholics are in the majority. Anglicans account for almost 16 percent of the mainland and 10 percent of Cape Breton. Other denominations include the United Church of Canada and the Baptist and Presbyterian churches, as well as small populations of Jews, Buddhists, and Hindus, living mainly in Halifax.

THE ARTS

The Canada Council gives grants to theaters, dance troupes, orchestras, and arts councils to promote and keep the arts alive. The **provincial tourism office** (902/425-5781 or 800/565-0000, www.novascotia.com) can tell you what's going on, or you can check out the local paper. See each travel chapter for specific listings detailing nightlife, theater, dance, and music options.

Halifax attracts concerts and major events to the Halifax Metro Centre. Farther up the hillside, the Neptune Theatre hosts year-round repertory theater, as does Dalhousie University's Rebecca Cohn Auditorium, which doubles as the home of the Symphony of Nova Scotia. Dozens of nightclubs and other venues around the capital city showcase established and up-and-coming local bands, such as Sloan, which are earning the province, and especially Halifax, a reputation as an influential breeding ground for pop, rock, and alternative music.

Cape Breton is renowned for its contributions to folk music. Not surprisingly, Scottish and Irish fiddle tunes form much of the source material, but Cape Breton musicians have taken that extremely rich foundation and made something with a uniquely Maritime flavor: frisky jigs and reels for dancing, as well as ballads, often centering on the theme of fishing and the ubiquitous sea.

Museums

With an ethnic heritage as varied as Nova Scotia's, it's no wonder that its museums are among the country's best. Some museums are moving tributes to the people, such as the Grand Pré National Historic Site, while others, such as the Fortress of Louisbourg National Historic Site, re-create early Anglo years with authentic buildings and demonstrations.

On a smaller scale, county and town museums document regional historical, cultural, and economic subjects. Municipal or privately operated museums in towns and villages put the emphasis on local history or specialties.

Dancing the Jig

Through the first half of the 18th century, life in the northeast and Highlands of Scotland was becoming more and more difficult. Not only was there discontent over the union with England, but the Scots also were facing ever-decreasing resources, the dismantling of clans, and the confiscation of property. After the defeat of Bonnie Prince Charlie in 1745, thousands of these Gaelic speakers migrated to the New World, with many of them settling in Nova Scotia. They brought with them their farming skills, their language, and their music. Centuries later, these Celtic traditions remain a strong part of life in Nova Scotia.

Music is the best-known part of the Celtic culture, especially fiddle music, which creates the perfect rhythm for step dancing. While this style of music is all but forgotten in Scotland, it thrives in Nova Scotia. Many cherished songs describing life on the land have been passed down through the generations, while a new wave of lively tunes (known as jigs and reels) creates a spirited mix of music heard throughout the region and beyond.

Cape Breton-born **Natalie MacMaster** has the highest profile of Nova Scotia's fiddlers. Her energetic performances, in which she steps the dances while playing, bring crowds around the world to their feet. Born and raised on the west coast of Cape Breton Island, five siblings make up **The Rankins,** who infuse a variety of musical styles into their music. The fiddle, mandolin, and percussion instruments keep the traditional vibe going, while the songs vary from country to folk. The fiddle is central to the music performed by **Ashley MacIsaac,** but his shows are anything but traditional. Described by some as "grunge fiddle," his music crosses from Celtic to garage rock to heavy metal, and he's a unique nonconformist who performs in sold-out shows across North America. In addition to the big names, bands such as the **Irish Descendants** (from Newfoundland, but often performing in Nova Scotia) are worth watching for, while bands churning out lively foot-stomping, beer-drinking tunes can be heard in pubs throughout the province.

Essentials

Air Taxes

The Canadian government collects a variety of "departure taxes" on all flights originating from Canada. These taxes are generally not in the advertised fare, but they will all be included in the ticket purchase price. First up is the **Air Travellers Security Charge,** $7-14 each way for flights within North America and $25 round-trip for international flights. **NAV Canada** also dips its hand in your pocket, collecting $10-20 per flight for maintaining the country's navigational systems. Additionally, passengers departing Halifax International Airport must pay an **Airport Improvement Fee** of $25, while those departing Sydney also pay $25 (these are among the highest AIFs in Canada). Additionally, if your flight transits through Toronto, you pay a $4 improvement fee for that airport.

Getting There

Visitors have the option of arriving by road, rail, ferry, or air. The main gateway city for flights from North America and Europe is the capital, Halifax. Ferries cross to Yarmouth from Maine and to Digby from New Brunswick, while the main rail line enters the region from New Brunswick and terminates at Halifax.

Unless otherwise noted, telephone numbers given in this section are the local (North American) contacts.

AIR

Most long-haul international and domestic flights into eastern Canada set down at Toronto, Ottawa, or Montréal, with connecting or ongoing flights to Halifax.

Air Canada

Air Canada (888/247-2262, www.aircanada. com) is one of the world's largest airlines, serving five continents. The company has one of the world's easiest-to-understand fare systems, with five fare levels and multiple ways of searching for online flights and fares. It offers direct flights to Halifax from Fredericton, Saint John, Moncton, St. John's, Montréal, Ottawa, Toronto, Calgary, and Boston. All other flights from North America are routed through Toronto, Ottawa, or Montréal, where connections can be made to Halifax. From Europe, Air Canada flies from London to Halifax. From the South Pacific, Air Canada operates flights from Sydney to Vancouver for onward connections to Halifax. Asian cities served by direct Air Canada flights include Beijing, Hong Kong, Nagoya, Osaka, Seoul, Shanghai, Taipei, and Tokyo. All terminate in Vancouver. Air Canada's flights originating in South America are all routed through Toronto.

WestJet

Canada's second-largest airline, WestJet (403/250-5839 or 888/937-8538, www.westjet. com), is the main competition to Air Canada. Based in Calgary, its flights extend as far east as St. John's, with flights routed through Toronto to Halifax.

U.S. Airlines

Air Canada offers direct daily flights from Boston to Halifax, but the city is also served by Delta (800/221-1212, www.delta.com)

Previous: Halifax International Airport; oceanfront camping at Rissers Beach Provincial Park.

Cutting Flight Costs

Ticket structuring for air travel is so complex that finding the best deal requires some time and patience (or a good travel agent). In the first place, to get an idea of what you will be paying, call the airlines or check their websites and compare fares. Air Canada (www.aircanada.com) has a streamlined fare structure that makes it easy to find the fare that serves your needs and budget. Also look in the travel sections of major newspapers—particularly in weekend editions—where budget fares and package deals are frequently advertised. While the Internet has changed the way many people shop for tickets, having a travel agent that you are comfortable with—who takes the time to call around, does some research to get you the best fare, and helps you take advantage of any available special offers or promotional deals—is an invaluable asset in starting your travels off on the right foot.

Within Canada, Travel Cuts (866/246-9762, www.travelcuts.com) and Flight Centre (888/967-5302, www.flightcentre.ca), both with offices in all major cities, including Halifax, consistently offer the lowest airfares available, with the latter guaranteeing the lowest. Flight Centre offers a similar guarantee from its U.S. offices (866/967-5351, www.flightcentre.us), as well as those in the United Kingdom (tel. 0870/499-0040, www.flightcentre.co.uk), Australia (tel. 13-31-33, www.flightcentre.com.au), and New Zealand (tel. 0800/24-35-44, www.flightcentre.co.nz). In London, Trailfinders (215 Kensington High St., Kensington, tel. 0845/058-5858, www.trailfinders.com) always has good deals to Canada and other North American destinations. Reservations can be made directly through airline or travel agency websites, or use Internet-only companies such as Travelocity (www.travelocity.com) or Expedia (www.expedia.com).

When you have found the best fare, open a frequent flyer membership with the airline—Air Canada has a very popular reward program that makes rewards easily obtainable (www.aeroplan.com).

Edward Hasbrouck's *The Practical Nomad Guide to the Online Travel Marketplace* (Avalon Travel) is an excellent resource for working through the web of online travel planning possibilities.

from New York (LGA), American (800/433-7300, www.aa.com) from Philadelphia, and United (800/538-2929, www.united.com) from Chicago and Newark.

RAIL

Amtrak (800/872-8725, www.amtrak.com) has service from New York City to Toronto (via Buffalo), and from New York City to Montréal.

VIA Rail

Once you're in Canada, rail travel is handled by VIA Rail (416/366-8411 or 888/842-7245, www.viarail.ca). Best known for the transcontinental rail route, the spectacular journey from Vancouver to Toronto through the Canadian Rockies. VIA Rail has replicated that route's deluxe trappings and service with its Sleeper Plus class aboard the Ocean. The Ocean departs Montréal, follows the St.

Lawrence River's southern shore to northern New Brunswick, cuts across the province to Moncton, speeds into Nova Scotia via Amherst and Truro, and finishes at Halifax. The trip takes 21 hours. The train has a variety of classes, but it is the Sleeper Plus class that gets all the attention. These luxuriously appointed carriages include a domed car with three small salons (one of which is a replica of the transcontinental's mural lounge), a dining car with art deco trappings, and a more informal car designed for lighter dining. Fares from Montreal to Halifax range from $180 each way in Economy class to $625 in Sleeper Plus class, the latter including sleeping-car accommodations and all meals.

BUS

North America's main bus line, Greyhound (800/231-2222, www.greyhound.ca or www.greyhound.com), doesn't provide service to

Nova Scotia. Instead, you will need to get yourself to Riviere-du-Loup in Quebec and connect with Maritime Bus (902/429-2029 or 800/575-1807, www.maritimebus.com), which provides service to and from locations throughout Nova Scotia.

Car

The majority of visitors drive to Atlantic Canada. From the United States, Highway 9 heads east from Bangor, Maine, and enters New Brunswick—Atlantic Canada's principal land gateway—at St. Stephen, near the Fundy coast. The TransCanada Highway from central Canada (another main entry route) is more roundabout, following the St. Lawrence River through Québec to enter northwestern New Brunswick at Saint-Jacques near Edmundston. Once in New Brunswick, you can take the Confederation Bridge to Prince Edward Island or continue driving east into Nova Scotia.

FERRY

From Toronto, the most direct driving route to Halifax includes a ferry trip across the Bay of Fundy.

From New Brunswick

Bay Ferries (902/245-2116 or 888/249-7245, www.ferries.ca) handles the busy Bay of Fundy crossing between Saint John (New Brunswick) and Digby (a three-hour drive from Halifax), a shortcut that saves drivers a few hours of driving time. Operating once or twice daily year-round, one-way high-season fares are adult $46, senior and youth $36, child under five free, vehicle $92 plus a $20 fuel surcharge. Reservations are essential through summer.

TO PRINCE EDWARD ISLAND

Northumberland Ferries (902/566-3838 or 877/762-7245, www.ferries.ca) operates 5-9 sailings daily between Caribou (Nova Scotia) and Wood Islands in eastern Prince Edward Island. The crossing takes just over one hour. The fare is $71 per vehicle, regardless of the number of passengers. Motorcycles are $40, and those on bicycles pay $20. You pay when leaving the island, so take the ferry to PEI and return on the Confederation Bridge to save a few bucks.

From Maine

Yarmouth, 310 kilometers southwest of Halifax, is the Canadian terminus for CAT (877/762-7245, www.ferries.ca, adult $107, senior $102, child $65, vehicle under 6.6 feet $199), which departs Portland, Maine, daily for the 5.5-hour crossing.

Getting Around

Driving, whether with your own vehicle or a rental car, is by far the best way to get around Nova Scotia. This section talks about driving in Canada as well as the public transportation options.

AIR

While Halifax International Airport, 35 kilometers from Halifax, serves as Atlantic Canada's principal air hub, there is a just a single intraprovincial flight within Nova Scotia—the daily Air Canada (888/247-2262, www.aircanada.com) link between Halifax and Sydney.

BUS

Getting around Nova Scotia by bus is made possible by Maritime Bus (902/429-2029 or 800/575-1807, www.maritimebus.com), which links all major cities and towns as well as many minor ones (although there is no service along the South Shore or Fundy Coast). It operates seven days a week year-round.

Halifax has an extensive public transportation system that revolves around scheduled bus service. If you have a day on your hands and no other plans, consider an early morning bus to an unexplored area and a late afternoon or early evening return to the city. Few outsiders do it, but mixing among the locals on a bus circuit is a terrific way to explore the capital.

DRIVING IN CANADA

U.S. and international driver's licenses are valid in Canada. All highway signs give distances in kilometers and speeds in kilometers per hour. Unless otherwise posted, the maximum speed limit on the highways is 100 kilometers per hour (62 miles per hour).

Infants weighing up to nine kilograms must be strapped into a "bucket"-style car seat. Use of a child car seat for larger children weighing 9-18 kilograms is also required. Before venturing north of the 49th parallel, U.S. residents should ask their vehicle insurance company for a Canadian Non-resident Inter-provincial Motor Vehicle Liability Insurance Card. You may also be asked to prove vehicle ownership, so be sure you have your vehicle registration form.

If you're a member in good standing of an automobile association, take your membership card—the Canadian AA provides members of related associations full services, including free maps, itineraries, excellent tour books, road- and weather-condition information, accommodations reservations, travel agency services, and emergency road services. For more information, contact the **Canadian Automobile Association** (613/247-0117, www.caa.ca).

Note: **Drinking and driving** (with a blood alcohol level of 0.08 percent or higher) in Nova Scotia can get you imprisoned for up to five years on a first offense and will cost you your license for at least 12 months. Those caught driving with a blood alcohol level between 0.05 and 0.08 percent automatically lose their license for seven days.

Additionally, like most Canadian provinces, Nova Scotia has a **distracted driving** law that prohibits drivers from using handheld cell phones while operating a motor vehicle.

Highways and Byways

Long distances notwithstanding, the province has a superb system of roads, classified by numbers. For example, the TransCanada (Highway 104) enters at Amherst, zips east across the mainland, and finishes at North Sydney. The highway is one of the new 100-series roads designed for rapid transit. Similar highways connect major towns in the central region and rim the heavily traveled southwest region's seacoast along the Fundy.

The highways numbered 1-99 often parallel the 100-series expressways and connect major cities and towns. Roads numbered 200-399 are paved, rambling, two-lane routes that take visitors to all the interesting out-of-the-way places. These roads often work as diversionary routes off major sightseeing highways, such as Highway 316, which departs the Marine Drive's Highway 7 and meanders through Canso and Guysborough on its way to the Canso Strait. The Cabot Trail around western Cape Breton is the exception. It is unnumbered and ranks as a special scenic highway.

Car Rental

All major car rental companies have outlets at Halifax International Airport, in downtown Halifax, and in major towns across the province. Try to book well in advance, especially in summer. Expect to pay from $50 a day and $250 a week for a small economy car with unlimited kilometers.

Major rental companies with outlets in Halifax include:

- **Avis** (800/331-1212, www.avis.ca)
- **Budget** (800/268-8900, www.budget.ca)
- **Discount** (800/263-2355, www.discount-car.com)
- **Enterprise** (800/261-7331, www.enterprise.com)
- **Hertz** (800/654-3131, www.hertz.ca)

- **National** (877/222-9058, www.national-car.com)
- **Rent-a-Wreck** (800/327-0116, www.rent-awreck.ca)
- **Thrifty** (800/847-4389, www.thrifty.com)

RV and Camper Rental

You might want to consider renting a camper-van or other recreational vehicle for your trip. With one of these apartments-on-wheels, you won't need to worry about finding accommodations each night. Even the smallest units aren't cheap, but they can be a good deal for longer-term travel or for families or two couples traveling together. The smallest vans, capable of sleeping two people, start at $185 per day with 100 free kilometers (62 miles) per day. Standard extra charges include insurance, a preparation fee (usually around $60-80 per rental), a linen/cutlery charge (around $60 per person per trip), and taxes. Major agencies with rental outlets in Halifax include Cruise Canada (800/671-8042, www.cruisecanada. com) and Canadream (888/480-9726, www. canadream.com). Both of these companies also have rental outlets across the country.

Recreation

In Atlantic Canada's great outdoors, just about every form of recreation is feasible and first-rate: bicycling, hiking, scuba diving, canoeing, sea kayaking, stand-up paddleboarding, sailing, rockhounding, bird-watching, surfing, fishing, golfing, and downhill skiing—you name it. Many outfitters around the province rent bikes, boats, and other equipment and can equip you for wilderness expeditions and all sorts of other activities.

PARKS

The province's national and provincial parks come in a wide range of personalities and offer an equally eclectic array of activities and facilities, from searching for gemstones at Blomidon Provincial Park to lounging in luxury at Cape Breton Highlands' Keltic Lodge resort.

National Parks

Atlantic Canada has 9 of Canada's 45 national parks. **Cape Breton Highlands National Park,** in Nova Scotia, is one of the most spectacular, but it is also very accessible: ocean panoramas, abundant wildlife, and an extensive network of hiking trails are the highlights. Best known for its wild horses, **Sable Island National Park,** off the Nova Scotia coast, is much more remote and requires an air charter to access. In the same province, **Kejimkujik National Park** is the only one not on the ocean, which means visitors trade kayaks for canoes to explore the extensive system of freshwater lakes. In New Brunswick, **Fundy National Park** is renowned for the world's highest tides, while **Kouchibouguac National Park** fronts the calm waters of Northumberland Strait. The beaches of **Prince Edward Island National Park** are a popular destination for vacationing families.

For more information on park passes, check the **Parks Canada** website (www. pc.gc.ca).

Provincial Parks

Protecting areas of natural, historical, and cultural importance, Atlantic Canada's many hundreds of provincial parks also provide a wide variety of recreational opportunities. All provide day-use facilities such as picnic areas and washrooms, while many also have playgrounds, canoe rentals, and concessions. A good number also have campgrounds and summer interpretive programs.

You'll find lots of information about provincial parks at local information centers and in general tourism literature. You can also contact the following:

A Photographer's Dream

Peggy's Cove

Nova Scotia has incredible light for photography. The sky turns from a Wedgwood color to sapphire blue—a beautiful background for seacoast photographs. Rise at dawn to take advantage of the first rays of sunlight hitting picturesque east coast villages such as popular **Peggy's Cove** and **Fisherman's Cove,** both within an hour's drive of Halifax, as well as delightful seaside gems such as **Blue Rocks,** beyond Lunenburg. The town of Lunenburg itself attracts photographers for its harbor-front panorama of colorful buildings (best in the late afternoon).

While photography is simplest when the weather is favorable—and that's more often than not—don't pass up a morning basking in thick mist, as bright sun illuminates the sky behind the thick clouds. The fog breaks apart gradually, and when it does, the sun radiates like a spotlight, illuminating the sparkling dampness that briefly clings to the landscape.

- **Nova Scotia:** Department of Natural Resources, 902/662-3030, http://parks.novascotia.ca

- **New Brunswick:** Department of Tourism and Parks, 506/462-5924, www.tourismnewbrunswick.ca

- **Prince Edward Island:** Prince Edward Island Tourism, 902/368-4444, www.tourismpei.com

HIKING AND WALKING

Hiking is one of the most popular activities in Nova Scotia. Not only are there hundreds of trails to explore, but it's free and anyone can do it. The hiking season spans spring-fall. Coastal areas are generally free of pesky insects, but insect repellent is wise inland May-September. As national and provincial parks protect the most spectacular scenery, it'll be no surprise that this is where you find the best hiking. One standout is Cape Breton Highlands National Park on Cape Breton Island. Here you can find anything from short interpretive trails along raised boardwalks to strenuous slogs that end at high ocean lookouts. Nova Scotia's provincial parks generally lack long trails, but short walks often lead to local natural landmarks. Brochures on these walking trails are widely available at information centers, or check the Department of Natural Resources website (http://parks.novascotia.ca).

FISHING

Neighboring New Brunswick and Newfoundland and Labrador get most of the attention by anglers, but Nova Scotia has a wide range of fishing experiences and a diverse number of species.

Salmon

Just one species of salmon is native to the tidal waters of Nova Scotia—the Atlantic salmon. It is anadromous, spending its time in both freshwater and saltwater. The fish spend up to three years in local rivers before undergoing massive internal changes that allow them to survive in saltwater. They then spend between two and three years in the open water, traveling as far as Greenland. After reaching maturity, they begin the epic journey back to their birthplace, to the exact patch of gravel on the same river from where they emerged. It is the returning salmon that are most sought after by anglers, with Cape Breton Island's Margaree River the focus for serious anglers. Atlantic salmon grow to 36 kilograms, although their landlocked relatives rarely exceed 10 kilograms.

Deep-Sea Fishing

Deep-sea fishing's star attraction is the giant bluefin tuna; its season runs September-November. In 1979, a bluefin weighing a record 679 kilograms was caught off St. Georges Bay. The bay ranks as the top tuna area, while the Fundy Coast off Yarmouth from Cape St. Mary to Wedgeport is another prime fishing area. Expect to pay $160-300 per person per day for a tuna charter. In addition to tuna, other deep-sea catches include pollack, mackerel, striped bass, sea trout, and bottom dwellers such as haddock, cod, and halibut.

Freshwater Fish

Speckled trout (also known as brook trout) are widespread throughout the region and are fun to catch and tasty to eat. They tend to gravitate to cooler water, such as spring-fed streams, and can be caught on spinners or flies. A 3.4-kilogram specimen, one of the largest ever caught, is on display in Halifax's Museum of Natural History (the record is one that weighed in at 4.1 kilograms, which was reeled in from Porters Lake, east of Halifax). Introduced in the late 1800s, rainbow trout are in lakes and rivers across Nova Scotia. Sherbrooke Lake and Dollar Lake, both near Halifax, have healthy populations of lake trout. Brown trout are found in some streams and larger lakes.

Fishing is a popular activity throughout the province.

Long and lean, **striped bass** inhabit rivers and estuaries throughout the region. There is a definite art to catching the species—it is estimated it takes an average of 40-50 hours of fishing to catch one. **Smallmouth bass** are a popular sport fish introduced to the waterways of southwestern Nova Scotia. They live in clear, calm water that usually has a gravelly bottom. Common throughout North America, **whitefish** are easily caught in most rivers and lakes, although they rarely exceed 15 centimeters in length. **Atlantic whitefish** (also called Acadian whitefish) are endemic to southwestern Nova Scotia. As they are a protected species, angling for them is prohibited, so carry an identification chart if fishing these waters. **Yellow perch** (also known as lake perch) are identified by wide vertical stripes. Most often caught in shallow rivers and lakes throughout Nova Scotia, they are great fun for children to reel in.

Around 1.7 million fingerlings from two hatcheries are released at 400 easily accessible lakes and rivers across the province each year. Most are speckled trout because they are easy to raise and adapt to varying conditions; other stocking fish are rainbow and brown trout. You can catch them on artificial flies, small spinners, or spoons.

Fishing Licenses and Regulations

Before casting a line, make yourself aware of provincial regulations. The recreational fishery is managed by the Department of Fisheries and Aquaculture (www.novascotia.ca/snsmr/paal/ndxfish.asp). A freshwater license for nonresidents costs $13 for one day, $34 for seven days, or $64 per year. Residents pay $28 for an annual license. No license is required for ocean fishing.

Fishing in national parks requires a separate license, which is available from park offices and some sports shops ($9.80 for a seven-day license, $34.30 for an annual license).

CYCLING AND MOUNTAIN BIKING

Reasonably good roads and gorgeous scenery make Nova Scotia excellent road-biking territory, while mountain biking has caught on among the adventurous as a way to explore more remote areas of the region. Except on main arteries, particularly the TransCanada Highway, car traffic is generally light. Cyclists, nonetheless, should remain vigilant: Narrow lanes and shoulders are common, and in some areas, drivers may be unaccustomed to sharing the road with bicycles. The premier bike-touring route is the Cabot Trail through Cape Breton Highlands National Park.

Many shops rent decent- to good-quality road and mountain bikes. But if you plan to do some serious riding, you'll probably want to bring your own; most airlines will let you bring a bike for little or no extra charge. An outstanding information resource is **Bicycle Nova Scotia** (902/425-5454, www.bicycle.ns.ca), which handles cycling information and publishes *Nova Scotia by Bicycle,* detailing 4,000 kilometers of roads along 20 detailed routes. Also contact **Atlantic Canada Cycling** (902/423-2453, www.atlanticcanadacycling.com), which publishes extensive information on cycling routes (including descriptions and ratings of highways and byways throughout the province), tours, races, clubs, and equipment.

Guided Tours

Halifax-based **Freewheeling Adventures** (902/857-3600 or 800/672-0775, www.freewheeling.ca) leads agreeable arrangements of guided trips in small groups, each accompanied by a support van to carry the luggage and, if necessary, the weary biker. Owners Cathy and Philip Guest plan everything—snacks, picnics, and meals at restaurants en route, as well as overnight stays at country inns. Expect to pay around $300-400 per person per day for the all-inclusive tour. The trips pass through some of Nova Scotia's prettiest countryside, including the South Shore, the Annapolis Valley, and Cape Breton Island.

ESSENTIALS
RECREATION

GOLFING

Nova Scotia has more than 80 golf courses and a season that extends mid-April-late October. Greens fees are generally very reasonable, with rates at less than $20 at some municipal courses. Where you really see a difference in fees is at better courses such as Chester Golf Club, a mature seaside layout kept in pristine condition, where the high-season rate is just $63, and $40 after 3pm. The best-known Nova Scotia courses are on Cape Breton Island, including Highlands Links, considered one of the world's finest, yet costing just over $100 per round, while nearby Cabot Links (2012) and adjacent Cabot Cliffs (2016) both opened to rave reviews as two of the best new golf courses in North America. A limited number of resort-style courses have been developed in the last decade, with the most upscale being Fox Harb'r Golf Resort and Spa, along Northumberland Strait, where greens fees are over $200.

The provincial governing body is the **Nova Scotia Golf Association** (902/468-8844, www.nsga.ns.ca), which provides a listing of all courses with contact numbers and fees. **Golf Nova Scotia** (877/894-3982, www.golf-novascotia.com) promotes a selection of the province's better courses.

WATER SPORTS

This ocean-bound province has no shortage of beaches, and most waterside provincial parks have a supervised swimming area. The warmest beaches are found along the Northumberland Strait. The Bay of Fundy and Atlantic shores tend to be much cooler, although conditions vary considerably throughout the region.

With so much water surrounding and flowing through the province, **boating** opportunities are nearly infinite. Sailing is popular in the Bay of Fundy, in spacious Halifax and Sydney harbors, and in protected inland areas such as Bras d'Or Lakes.

Canoeing, Kayaking, and Stand-up Paddleboarding

If you bring your own canoe, kayak, or stand-up paddleboard, you can slip into any body of water whenever you please, taking in the scenery and viewing wildlife from water level. Canoeing is a traditional form of transportation that remains extremely popular throughout Nova Scotia. You can rent canoes at many of the more popular lakes, including those protected by Kejimkujik National Park.

Coastal kayaking is another adventure, especially around picturesque South Shore

Highlands Links ranks as one of Canada's best golf courses.

fishing villages, along the remote coast near Tangier, and along Cape Breton Island's Atlantic coast. Expect to pay around $100 per person for a full day of kayaking. The tour cost always includes kayak and wetsuit rental, and usually also lunch.

Tidal-Bore Rafting

Instead of white-water rafting, Nova Scotia is known for wild and woolly trips on the tidal bore created by the world's highest tides in the Bay of Fundy. Between May and October, Tidal Bore Rafting Park (902/758-4032, www.tidalboreraftingpark.com) offers trips for varying levels of adrenaline rushes in motorized Zodiacs, riding the bore as it rushes upriver before blasting back across its face. Trips last two or four hours and cost from $60 and $95 per person, respectively. This company is based a one-hour drive north of Halifax.

Whale-Watching

Today's lucrative whaling industry is based not on butchering but on simply bringing curious onlookers to observe the wonderful animals up close. Prime whale-watching areas are the Bay of Fundy (commercial operators are based along Digby Neck and on Brier Island) and off the west coast of Cape Breton Island. Minke, pilot, finback, orca, and humpback whales are the most populous species, and Atlantic right whales are spotted during a short window of time (August) in the Bay of Fundy.

Surfing

Nova Scotia is home to a small but dedicated population of surfers who hit the waves of the province's east coast year-round. Lawrencetown Beach, less than an hour's drive north of Halifax, is the best-known spot, with beach breaks along the long stretch of sand and a right-hander breaking off the rocky point. Other surf spots are scattered along the province's east coast. Water temperatures rarely rise above 16°C (61°F), meaning a

4/3 mm or 3/2 mm wetsuit is necessary, even in midsummer.

Boards and wetsuits can be rented from **Kannon Beach** (4144 Lawrencetown Rd., 902/471-0025, Mon.-Fri. 9am-6pm, Sat. 9am-5pm), ideally located within walking distance of Lawrencetown Beach, and from **Rossignol Surf Shop** (White Point Beach Resort, 902/354-7100, www.surfnovascotia. com) on the South Shore.

WINTER SPORTS

Winter is definitely low season for travel to Nova Scotia. Outdoor recreation is severely limited by the weather, although snow-related sports are popular with the locals. In addition to downhill skiing and boarding, skating on frozen ponds is a hit, while locals cheer for minor-league ice-hockey teams scattered throughout the region.

Skiing and Snowboarding

The alpine resorts of Atlantic Canada may lack the vertical rise of their western counterparts, but snowfall is high and outsiders will be greeted with open arms wherever they choose to ski. Day passes top out at $40, and each resort has day lodge facilities and rentals. Vertical rises range 180-300 meters, and the season generally runs from Christmas to late March.

Nova Scotia has three downhill resorts. Closest to Halifax is **Ski Martock,** south of the Annapolis Valley; **Wentworth** is near the New Brunswick border; and **Cape Smokey** has spectacular ocean views from its Cape Breton Island location.

In New Brunswick, **Crabbe Mountain,** west of Fredericton, and **Ski Mont-Farlagne,** near Edmundston, have loyal followings.

Cross-Country Skiing

The province's two mainland national parks stay open year-round. In winter, hiking routes are transformed by snow into excellent cross-country ski trails, many of which are groomed by local ski clubs that charge a nominal fee for their use. Ski Tuonela (902/929-2144, www.

skituonela.com), on Cape Breton Island, is one of North America's only lift-served telemark hills. In addition to a rope tow, the resort has 20 kilometers of groomed trails, a day lodge, and overnight accommodations.

Organizations with handy websites loaded with information and links to ski clubs are **Canada Trails** (www.canadatrails.ca) and **Cross Country Canada** (www.cccski.com).

SPECTATOR SPORTS

Windsor, Nova Scotia, claims its place in history as the birthplace of ice hockey (known simply as "hockey" in Canada). Although the region is home to no National Hockey League (NHL) teams, the exploits of the Toronto Maple Leafs, Montréal Canadiens, and other NHL franchises are passionately followed here. You can also see lively play from the Québec Major Junior Hockey League's Halifax Mooseheads (www.halifaxmooseheads.ca), as well as high-quality college and amateur teams in cities and towns throughout the region. The season runs October-March; check with local tourist information offices for game schedules and ticket information.

Accommodations and Food

Nova Scotia has all the chain hotels you know, as well as a range of accommodations that showcase the region—historic B&Bs, grand resorts, waterfront cottage complexes, and rustic campgrounds. This section will give you a taste of the choices and some hints on reserving a room. (Throughout the travel chapters of this book, I detail my favorites in all price ranges.)

To make reservations at any of the chain properties, simply phone their toll-free reservation centers or book online using their websites. Another option is a province-sponsored free reservation system, which is online at www.novascotia.com.

HOTELS, MOTELS, AND RESORTS

International, Canadian, and regional lodging chains are represented in Nova Scotia. At the more expensive properties, expect all the requisite amenities and services—swimming pools, air-conditioning, high-speed Internet access, room service, toiletries, restaurants, and bars. This type of accommodation can be found in central locations in Halifax, Sydney, and major tourist areas. Rates at four-star hotels start at $180 s or d in high season. Prices for a basic motel room in a small town start at $70 s, $80 d, rising to $120 for a room in a chain hotel within walking distance of a major city's downtown core.

The chains you know are represented in Nova Scotia, as well as the following you may not be familiar with.

Best Western

Presumably you have heard of the world's largest motel chain, but the website www.bestwesternatlantic.com is helpful in providing direct links to local properties.

Choice Hotels Canada

Over 300 properties across Canada are marketed under the Choice Hotels (800/424-6423, www.choicehotels.ca) banner. It operates 10 brands, including Sleep, with smallish but clean, comfortable, and inexpensive rooms; Comfort, where guests enjoy a light breakfast and newspaper with a no-frills room; Quality, a notch up in quality with a restaurant and lounge; and Econo Lodge, older properties that have been renovated to Choice's standard and often have a pool and restaurant.

Delta Hotels and Resorts

Owned by the Marriott company but still branded by their Canadian name, at Delta Hotels and Resorts you can expect fine hotels with splendid facilities in notable downtown

Getting a Good Deal on Accommodations

Rates quoted through this guidebook are for a standard double room in the high season (usually July and August, but sometimes as early as June and as late as September). Almost all accommodations are less expensive outside of these busy months, with some discounting their rates by up to 50 percent. You'll enjoy the biggest seasonal discounts at properties that rely on summer tourists, such as those in Lunenburg or along the Northumberland Strait. The same applies in Halifax on weekends—many of the big downtown hotels rely on business and convention travelers to fill the bulk of their rooms; when the end of the week rolls around, the hotels are left with rooms to fill at discounted rates Friday, Saturday, and Sunday nights.

While you have no influence on the seasonal and weekday/weekend pricing differences detailed above, *how* you reserve a room *can* make a difference in how much you pay. First and foremost, when it comes to searching out actual rates, the Internet is an invaluable tool. All hotel websites listed in *Moon Nova Scotia* show rates, and many have online reservation forms. Use these websites to search out specials, many of which are available only on the Internet. Don't be afraid to negotiate during slower times. Even if the desk clerk has no control over rates, there's no harm in asking for a bigger room or one with a better view. Just look for a vacancy sign hanging out front.

Most hotels offer auto association members an automatic 10 percent discount, and whereas senior discounts apply only to those older than 60 or 65 on public transportation and at attractions, most hotels offer discounts to those ages 50 and older, with chains such as Best Western also allowing senior travelers a late checkout. "Corporate Rates" are a lot more flexible than in years past; some hotels require nothing more than the flash of a business card for a 10-20 percent discount.

When it comes to frequent-flyer programs, you really do need to be a frequent flyer to achieve free flights, but the various loyalty programs offered by hotels often provide benefits simply for signing up.

settings. Locations include downtown Halifax. Reservations can be made by calling 888/236-2427 or online at www.marriott.com. Check the Marriott website for package deals offered year-round.

Maritime Inns and Resorts

With package deals and locations in Antigonish, Port Hawkesbury, and the Cape Breton resort town of Baddeck, these properties (902/863-4001 or 888/662-7484, www.maritimeinns.com) are popular with holidaying locals. Generally, packages include meals and activities such as golfing from about $120 per person per day.

Signature Resorts

Nova Scotia's provincial government owns two stunning resorts. They appeal to the carriage trade—travelers who like the understated ambience of a resort lodge with a tony rustic setting and furnishings, gourmet dining, a remote location with manicured grounds, and the genteel sports of golf or fly-fishing. Provincial resorts in Nova Scotia are the Pines Resort at Digby and Liscombe Lodge at Liscomb Mills. The website www.signatureresorts.com has links to both.

BED-AND-BREAKFASTS

Nova Scotia is blessed with hundreds of B&Bs. Concentrations are in Halifax, Mahone Bay, Lunenburg, the Annapolis Valley, and Baddeck. Styles run the gamut from historic mansions to rustic farmhouses, and as a result, amenities can also vary greatly. Regardless, guests can expect hearty home cooking, a peaceful atmosphere, personal service, knowledgeable hosts, and conversation with like-minded travelers. B&Bs are usually private residences, with hosts who live onsite and up to eight guest rooms. As the name suggests, breakfast is included in quoted rates; ask before booking whether it is a cooked or continental breakfast. Rates fluctuate enormously—from $60 s, $70 d for a spare room in an otherwise regular family home to $200 in a grandly restored Victorian mansion.

Finding and Reserving a Room

My favorite B&Bs are recommended throughout the travel chapters of this book. You can also use the provincial accommodations guide (www.novascotia.com) and local information centers to find out about individual properties. Select Atlantic Inns (www.selectinns.ca) is an organization of mid- to top-end B&Bs, with online reservations and lots of information on specific properties. The Canadian Bed and Breakfast Guide (www.canadianbandbguide.ca) is a regularly updated database, although listings aren't recommendations as such. Finally, Bed and Breakfast Online (www.bbcanada.com) doesn't take bookings, but links are provided and its search engine helps you find the accommodation that best fits your needs.

Before reserving a room, it is important to ask a number of questions of your hosts. The two obvious ones are whether or not you'll have your own bathroom and how payment can be made (many establishments don't accept debit cards or all credit cards).

Tracing Family Roots

If you are interested in tracing family ties, the place to start is with **Nova Scotia Archives** (6016 University Ave., Halifax, 902/424-6060, https://archives.novascotia.ca, Mon.-Fri. 8:30am-4:30pm, Sat. 9am-5pm). It's possible to take advantage of the department's resources without visiting in person. Its website is an excellent starting point—helpful for everyone from those searching out long-lost relatives to professional genealogists.

Ancestries originating on Cape Breton can be traced at the **Beaton Institute** (Cape Breton University, Glace Bay, 902/563-1329, www.cbu.ca/campus/beaton-institute).

BACKPACKER ACCOMMODATIONS

As accommodation prices are reasonable throughout Nova Scotia, there is less of a need to find a dorm bed than in other parts of North America. Privately operated backpacker lodges are limited (those at Mahone Bay and Brier Island are both excellent), and

Garrison House, at Annapolis Royal, is just one of hundreds of historic homes that provide visitors with overnight accommodations.

Hostelling International operates five hostels around the province.

Hostelling International

The curfews and chores are long gone in this worldwide nonprofit organization of over 4,000 hostels in 60 countries. Hostelling International Canada has hostels in Nova Scotia at Halifax, Springhill, Wentworth, and two on Cape Breton Island. For a dorm bed, members of Hostelling International pay $22-30 per night, nonmembers pay $26-34. Generally, you need to provide your own sleeping bag or linens, but most hostels supply extra bedding (if needed) at no charge. Accommodations are in dormitories (2-10 beds), although single and double rooms are often available for an additional charge. All also offer a communal kitchen, lounge area, and laundry facilities, while some have Internet access, bike rentals, and organized tours.

You don't *have* to be a member to stay in an affiliated hostel of Hostelling International, but membership pays for itself after only a few nights of discounted lodging. Aside from discounted rates, benefits of membership vary from country to country but often include discounted air, rail, and bus travel; discounts on car rental; and discounts on some attractions and commercial activities. For Canadians, the membership charge is $35 annually, or $175 for lifetime membership. For more information, contact **HI-Canada** (800/663-5777, www.hihostels.ca). Joining the Hostelling International affiliate of your home country entitles you to reciprocal rights in Canada, as well as around the world; click through the links at www.hihostels.com to your country of choice.

CAMPING

Camping out is a popular summer activity across Nova Scotia, and you'll find campgrounds in both national parks, many provincial parks, on the outskirts of cities and towns, and in most resort areas. Facilities at park campgrounds vary considerably, but most commercial operations have showers and water, electricity, and sewer hookups.

National parks provide some of the nicest surroundings for camping. All sites have picnic tables, fire grates, toilets, and fresh drinking water, although only some provide showers. Prices range $18-38, depending on facilities and services. A percentage of sites can be reserved through the **Parks Canada Campground Reservation Service** (877/737-3783, www.pccamping.ca). Backcountry camping in a national park costs $8 per person per night.

Online reservations for **provincial park campgrounds** (https://secure.camis.com/nsdnr) open in early April. The reservation fee is $9 per booking. Most provincial parks, however, do not accept reservations, but instead assign sites on a first-come, first-served basis. At those parks, it's best to arrive before noon to ensure yourself a spot. Most provincial parks are open mid-May-mid-October.

Most privately owned campsites ($20-60 per night) accept reservations, although some have started to charge up to $10 for the privilege of reserving a site.

FOOD AND DRINK

Thankfully, the Nova Scotian cuisine promoted today is very different from what locals traditionally dined on. In what was a difficult environment, generations past were happy eating salt pork, salt cod, hardtack (a type of vegetable), and vegetables that were boiled longer than necessary. Locals have traditionally shunned hot spices and go lightly on other condiments. While country-style cooking embodies the essence of provincial style in the smaller towns and seaports, dining in Halifax offers more sophisticated global fare.

If you travel on your stomach, look for the **Taste of Nova Scotia** (www.tasteofnovascotia.com) emblem affixed to restaurants' front windows or doors. The emblem is awarded to dining places judged noteworthy by the province.

Highlights

Regardless of cooking styles, seafood, red meat, and produce abound. Local lamb originates in Pictou County. Fruits and vegetables are fresh and often picked from backyard inn and restaurant gardens. Local delicacies include wild chanterelle mushrooms, smoked mackerel pâté, and seafood ranging from lobster to locally caught Digby scallops and Solomon Gundy (pickled herring). Preserves are generally homemade. Soups vary from lobster chowder thickened with whipped cream to pea soup brimming with corned-beef chunks.

Salmon is often cooked on a cedar plank before an open fire, as the Mi'kmaq historically prepared it. Desserts know no limit and vary from trifles rich with raspberry jam and sherry, to cheesecakes concocted of local cheese and cream, to molded flans embellished with fruit toppings.

Acadian

While Anglo cuisine features red meats, Acadian fare is based on seafood. Common Acadian-style dishes include seafood chowder, shellfish (shrimp and crab), and fish (especially mackerel, herring, and cod). For variety, Acadian menus might offer chicken fricot (chicken stew), poutine râpé (boiled or deep-fried pork and grated raw potatoes, rolled into a ball and dipped in corn or maple syrup or molasses), and rappie pie (filled with a mixture of clams or chicken with grated potatoes as translucent as pearls). Desserts include sugar pie, apple dumplings, and cinnamon buns. Acadian cooking may be terribly hard on the waistline, but it's delicious. The best places to sample Acadian cuisine are along La Côte Acadienne (Fundy Coast) and in Chéticamp (Cape Breton Island).

Drinks

All the popular Canadian and American beers are available at bars and liquor stores, but you should be drinking the Halifax-brewed Keith's if you want to look like a local. Halifax also has a number of microbreweries.

Nova Scotia has 70 grape growers and 320 hectares of commercially harvested grapes. Local wines are prominently displayed on wine lists throughout the province, especially those from Jost Vineyards, along the Northumberland Strait. Most grapes are French hybrids, but the local specialty is **ice wine,** made by a process in which the grapes aren't harvested until *after* the first frost; the

traditional rappie pie

Two Traditional Acadian Recipes

RAPPIE PIE

This traditional recipe is unique for the texture of the potato filling, and one succulent bite will make you a convert. (For best results, read the recipe all the way through before starting.)

> 5-6 lbs. chicken
> 6 large onions
> 2 tsp. salt, or 2 tbsp. salted (preserved) onions
> 1 tsp. pepper
> 1 pail (10 lbs.) of big potatoes

1. Cut chicken in pieces, place in a large pot, and cover with water. Bring to a boil. Add three large chopped onions, salt (or salted onions), and pepper. (While chicken is cooking, continue with the following steps.) When chicken is cooked, remove it from the pot, remove meat from the bones, and tear pieces into desired size. Keep broth simmering to be used later.

2. Chop the remaining onions and sauté in butter or margarine until tender but not brown. Set aside to be used later.

3. Peel, rinse, and grate potatoes into a large bowl. Take note of how much grated potato you have, because later you will use this same large bowl to scald the potatoes after they are squeezed, and you should have the same amount of potato mixture then as you have grated potatoes now.

4. Squeeze potatoes (about two cups at a time) in a fine cotton bag or cloth until quite dry. Place the squeezed potatoes in a second bowl as you go, and transfer them back into the large bowl when done. Add the sautéed onions.

5. Scald the squeezed potatoes by adding the boiling chicken broth gradually and stirring constantly. Remember, you must end up with the same amount of scalded potato mixture in this bowl as you had grated potatoes before. If you do not have enough broth, add boiling water. When you're through scalding, the mixture should be slightly thicker and darker. Add salt and pepper to taste.

6. Grease a 17-by-12-inch pan and dust with flour. Spread half of the potato mixture in the pan. Spread chicken meat evenly over this. Cover with other half of potato mixture. Bake at 400°F for 2.5 hours. It should come out brown, crusty, and delicious! The more often you make it, the better it gets.

CHICKEN FRICOT

A cross between a soup and a stew, this dish is especially appreciated on a cold winter evening.

> 2 lbs. chicken (cut in small pieces)
> 2 large onions, diced
> 2 tsp. salted (preserved) onions, or 1 tsp. salt
> ½ tsp. pepper
> 8 medium-size potatoes, diced and rinsed
> 2 medium-size potatoes, grated

In a soup pot, put chicken pieces, diced onions, salted onions (or salt), and pepper. Add 12 cups of water and bring to a boil. Cook for 30 minutes on medium heat. Add diced potatoes and continue to boil until cooked. To thicken *fricot,* lower heat to simmer and add grated potatoes. Cook a few minutes more. Serve hot in bowls.

Courtesy of Imelda Chiasson, lifetime resident of Nova Scotia, from the village of Concession, La Côte Acadienne.

frost splits the skins and the fermentation process begins with the grapes still on the vine. These concentrated juices create a supersweet wine. Ice wine is generally marketed in a distinctively narrow 375-milliliter bottle and promoted as a dessert wine. The website www.winesofnovascotia.ca is a good source of information.

The legal drinking age in Nova Scotia is 19, the same as all other Canadian provinces except Québec, Manitoba, and Alberta (where it is 18).

Tips for Travelers

EMPLOYMENT AND STUDY

International visitors wishing to work or study in Canada must obtain authorization before entering the country. Authorization to work will only be granted if no qualified Canadians are available for the work in question. Applications for work and study are available from all Canadian embassies and must be submitted with a nonrefundable processing fee. The Canadian government has a reciprocal agreement with Australia for a limited number of holiday work visas to be issued each year. Australian citizens aged 30 and younger are eligible; contact your nearest Canadian embassy or consulate. For general information on immigrating to Canada, check the Citizenship and Immigration Canada website (www.cic.gc.ca).

VISITORS WITH DISABILITIES

A lack of mobility should not deter you from traveling to Nova Scotia, but you should definitely do some research before leaving home.

If you haven't traveled extensively, start by doing some research at the website of the Access-Able Travel Source (www.accessable.com), where you will find databases of specialist travel agencies and lodgings in Canada that cater to travelers with disabilities. Flying Wheels Travel (612/381-1622 or 877/451-5006, www.flyingwheelstravel.com) caters solely to the needs of travelers with disabilities. The Society for Accessible Travel and Hospitality (212/447-7284, www.sath.org) supplies information on tour operators, vehicle rentals, specific destinations, and companion services. For frequent travelers, the membership fee (US$49 per year) is well worth it. Emerging Horizons (www.emerginghorizons.com) is a U.S. quarterly online magazine dedicated to travelers with special needs.

Access to Travel (www.accesstotravel.gc.ca) is an initiative of the Canadian government that includes information on travel within and between Canadian cities. For vision-impaired visitors, CNIB (www.cnib.ca) offers a wide range of services from its Halifax office (902/453-1480 or 800/563-2642). Finally, Spinal Cord Injury Canada (www.spinalcordinjurycanada.ca) is another good source of information; the provincial head office is in Halifax (www.thespine.ca).

FAMILY TRAVEL

Regardless of whether you're traveling with toddlers or teens, you will face decisions affecting everything from where you stay to your choice of activities. Luckily for you, Nova Scotia is very family-friendly, with a variety of indoor and outdoor attractions aimed specifically at the younger generation, such as Shubenacadie Wildlife Park, north of Halifax, and Upper Clements Parks, near Annapolis Royal. The Annapolis Valley is also home to a number of campgrounds where the emphasis is on keeping the kids busy rather than being simply somewhere to stay the night. The best of these are South Mountain Park and Look-Off Family Camping.

Admission prices for children are included throughout the travel chapters of this book.

What to Take

You'll find little use for a suit and tie in Nova Scotia. Instead, pack for the outdoors. At the top of your must-bring list should be walking shoes or **hiking boots.** Even in summer you should be geared up for a variety of weather conditions, especially at the change of seasons or if you'll be spending time along the coast. Do this by preparing to **dress in layers,** including at least one pair of fleece pants and a heavy long-sleeved top. For breezy coastal sightseeing, a sweater or windbreaker, hat, sunscreen, and comfortable shoes with rubber soles will come in handy. For dining out, **casual dress** is accepted at all but the most upscale restaurants.

Electrical appliances from the United States work in Canada, but those from other parts of the world will require a **current converter** (transformer) to bring the voltage down. Many travel-size shavers, hair dryers, and irons have built-in converters.

As a general rule, reduced prices are for 6- to 16-year-olds. For two adults and two-plus children, always ask about family tickets.

Children younger than six nearly always get in free. Most hotels and motels will happily accommodate children, but always try to reserve your room and let the reservations desk know the ages of your brood. Often, children stay free in major hotels, and in the case of some major chains—such as Holiday Inn—eat free also. Generally, B&Bs aren't suitable for children and in some cases don't accept kids at all. Ask ahead.

When it comes to traveling with children, let them help you plan the trip, looking at websites and reading up on Nova Scotia together. To make your vacation more enjoyable if you'll be spending a lot of time on the road, rent a minivan (all major rental agencies have a supply). Don't forget to bring along favorite toys and games from home—whatever you think will keep your kids entertained when the joys of sightseeing wear off.

The **provincial tourism website** (www.novascotia.com) has a section devoted to children's activities. Another handy source of online information is **Traveling Internationally with Your Kids** (www.travelwithyourkids.com).

Health and Safety

Nova Scotia is a healthy place. To visit, you don't need to get any vaccinations or booster shots. And when you arrive, you can drink the water from the faucet and eat the food without worry.

If you need an ambulance, call 911 or the number listed on the inside front cover of local telephone directories. Halifax and most of the large towns have hospitals (look in the travel chapters of this book for locations and telephone numbers).

INSURANCE AND PRESCRIPTIONS

Intraprovincial agreements cover the medical costs of Canadians traveling across the nation.

As a rule, the usual health insurance plans from other countries do not include medical-care costs incurred while traveling; ask your insurance company or agent if supplemental health coverage is available, and if it is not, arrange for coverage with an independent carrier before departure. Hospital charges vary from place to place but can be as much as $3,000 a day, and some facilities impose a surcharge for nonresidents. Some Canadian companies offer coverage specifically aimed at visitors.

If you're on medication, bring adequate supplies with you, and get a prescription from your doctor to cover the time you will be away. You may not be able to get a prescription filled at Canadian pharmacies without visiting a Canadian doctor, so don't wait till you've almost run out. If you wear glasses or contact lenses, ask your optometrist for a spare prescription in case you break or lose your lenses, and stock up on your usual cleaning supplies.

SEXUALLY TRANSMITTED DISEASES

AIDS and other venereal and needle-communicated diseases are as much of a concern here as anywhere in the world today. Take exactly the same precautions you would at home—use condoms, and don't share needles.

GIARDIA

Giardiasis, also known as "beaver fever," is a real concern for those who drink water from backcountry water sources. It's caused by an intestinal parasite, Giardia lamblia, that lives in lakes, rivers, and streams. Once ingested, its effects, although not instantaneous, can be dramatic: severe diarrhea, cramps, and nausea are the most common. Preventive measures should always be taken and include boiling all water for at least 10 minutes, treating all water with iodine, or filtering all water using a filter with a small-enough pore size to block the Giardia cysts.

WINTER TRAVEL

Although distances are not great, travel through Nova Scotia during winter should not be undertaken lightly. Before setting out in a vehicle, check antifreeze levels, and always carry a spare tire and blankets or sleeping bags.

Frostbite can occur in a matter of seconds if the temperature falls below freezing and if the wind is blowing. Layer your clothing for the best insulation against the cold, and don't forget gloves and, most important, a warm hat, which can offer the best protection against heat loss. Frostbite occurs in varying degrees. Most often it leaves a numbing, bruised sensation and the skin turns white. Exposed areas of skin such as the nose and ears are most susceptible, particularly when cold temperatures are accompanied by high winds.

Hypothermia occurs when the body fails to produce heat as fast as it loses it. Cold weather combined with hunger, fatigue, and dampness creates a recipe for disaster. Symptoms are not always apparent to the victim. The early signs are numbness, shivering, slurring of words, dizzy spells; in extreme cases, these can progress to violent behavior, unconsciousness, and even death. The best treatment is to get the patient out of the cold, replace wet clothing with dry, slowly give hot liquids and sugary foods, and place the victim in a sleeping bag. Prevention is a better strategy; dress for cold in layers, including a waterproof outer layer, and wear a warm wool cap or other headgear.

CRIME

Nova Scotia enjoys one of the country's lowest crime rates. Violent crimes are infrequent; the most common crime is petty theft. If you must leave valuable items in your car unattended, keep them out of sight, preferably locked in the vehicle's trunk. Women have few difficulties traveling alone throughout the region.

Remember that Halifax is an international port with seamy (albeit interesting) bars and taverns at or near the working area of the waterfront; keep your wits about you here, especially late at night. Better yet, leave these night scenes to the sailors and others who frequent the areas.

Both possession and sale of illicit drugs are considered serious crimes and are punishable with jail time, severe fines, or both. Furthermore, Canadians consider drinking while driving equally serious; the penalty on the first conviction is jail, a heavy fine, or both. A conviction here or in your home country can even be grounds for exclusion from Canada.

Royal Canadian Mounted Police (RCMP)

Despite the romantic image of the staid

red-jacketed officer on horseback, Mounties (as they are most often called) nowadays favor the squad car as their mount of choice and a less colorful uniform. They are as ubiquitous a symbol of the country as the maple leaf and are similar to the highway patrol or state police in the United States. They operate throughout all the country's provinces and territories (except Ontario and Québec), complementing the work of local police.

Information and Services

MONEY

Unless noted otherwise, prices quoted in this guide are in Canadian currency.

Canadian currency is based on dollars and cents, with 100 cents equal to one dollar. Coins come in denominations of 1, 5, 10, and 25 cents, and one and two dollars. The 11-sided, gold-colored, one-dollar coin is known as a "loonie" for the bird featured on it. The unique two-dollar coin is silver with a gold-colored insert. The most common notes are $5, $10, $20, and $50. A $100 bill does exist but is uncommon.

Credit and debit cards are readily accepted throughout Atlantic Canada. By using these cards you eliminate the necessity of thinking about the exchange rate—the transaction and rate of exchange on the day of the transaction will automatically be reflected in the bill from your bank or credit-card company. On the downside, you'll always get a better exchange rate when dealing directly with a bank. You should always carry some cash, as places like farmers' markets and some bed and breakfasts do not accept debit or credit cards.

Costs

The cost of living in Nova Scotia is similar to that in the surrounding provinces but lower than elsewhere in the country. By planning carefully, having a tent, or traveling in the shoulder seasons, it is possible to get by on about $120 per person per day or less. If you will be staying in hotels or motels, accommodations will be your biggest expense. Gasoline is sold in liters (3.78 liters equals one U.S. gallon) and is generally $1.20-1.40 per liter for regular unleaded.

Tipping charges are not usually added to your bill. You are expected to add a tip of 15 percent to the total amount for waiters and waitresses, barbers and hairdressers, taxi drivers, and other such service providers. Bellhops, doormen, and porters generally receive $1 per item of baggage.

Harmonized Sales Tax (HST)

The 15 percent Harmonized Sales Tax is a tax levied on most goods and services purchased in Nova Scotia. All residents must pay the tax, as must visitors.

SHOPPING
Export Details

Americans can bring $400 worth of duty-free goods back into the United States after a 48-hour stay in Canada; $25 is the duty-free limit after stays of less than 48 hours. Gifts sent by mail and worth a total of $50 or less are duty-free also.

If you are interested in shopping for exotic wares, such as whalebone carvings or bearskin rugs, beware of customs regulations prohibiting the export of these types of items; hundreds of animals and their by-products are on the Convention on International Trade in Endangered Species of Wild Fauna and Flora list, which is online at www.cites.org. For a list of imports banned in your home country, contact your nearest customs office before departure.

Business Hours

Shopping hours are generally Monday-Saturday 9am-6pm. Late shopping in most areas is available until 9pm on Thursday and

Friday, and supermarkets open 24 hours have begun to appear in a few towns. Generally, banks are open Monday-Wednesday 10am-4pm and Thursday-Friday 10am-5pm A few banks may open on Saturday, but all are closed on Sunday. Nova Scotia is the only Canadian province that disallows Sunday shopping, although exceptions are made for essential services such as gas stations and in "tourist areas" such as the Halifax waterfront.

MAPS AND INFORMATION
Maps

Driving maps such as those published by MapArt (www.mapart.com) and Rand McNally (www.randmcnally.com) are available at bookstores, gas stations, and even some grocery stores across the province. In Halifax, Maps and Ducks (1601 Lower Water St., 902/422-7106, www.maps-and-ducks.com) and the Trail Shop (6210 Quinpool Rd., 902/423-8736, www.trailshop.com) are specialty map stores. The most detailed atlas to the province is the Nova Scotia Atlas, produced by Formac Publishing.

Nautical maps are handled by the **Canadian Hydrographic Service,** a division of Fisheries and Oceans Canada, but it doesn't sell directly to the public. To request a map catalog and a list of dealers, call 613/995-4413 or check www.charts.gc.ca. This department also distributes *Sailing Directions,* a composite of general navigational information, port facility descriptions, and sailing conditions (in English or French) for Nova Scotia and the Gulf of St. Lawrence.

Tourism Information

Begin planning your trip by contacting the government tourist office: Tourism Nova Scotia (902/425-5781 or 800/565-0000, www.novascotia.com). Its literature and a provincial map can be downloaded from the website or ordered by phone. This organization also operates Provincial Visitor Centres at major gateways, including one at Halifax

National Holidays

- **New Year's Day:** January 1
- **Good Friday:** late March-mid-April
- **Easter Monday:** late March-mid-April
- **Victoria Day:** third or fourth Monday in May
- **Canada Day:** July 1
- **Labour Day:** first Monday in September
- **Thanksgiving Day:** second Monday in October
- **Remembrance Day:** November 11
- **Christmas Day:** December 25
- **Boxing Day:** December 26

International Airport (902/873-1223, daily 9am-9pm) and another along the downtown waterfront (1655 Lower Water St., 902/424-4248, daily 9am-5pm, until 8pm in summer). Other locations are Yarmouth (mid-May-Oct.) and Amherst (year-round).

Every town of any size in Nova Scotia has a locally operated **Visitor Information Centre** (hours vary, but most are open mid-May-mid-Oct.).

COMMUNICATIONS
Postal Services

Canada Post (www.canadapost.ca) issues postage stamps that must be used on all mail posted in Canada. First-class letters and postcards sent within Canada are $1, to the United States $1.20, to other foreign destinations $2.50. Prices increase with the weight of the mailing. You can buy stamps at post offices (closed weekends), some hotel lobbies, airports, many retail outlets, and some newsstands.

Phone

The country code for Canada is 1, the same as the United States, and the area code for all

Heading Farther Afield?

- **Tourisme Québec** (514/873-2015 or 877/266-5687, www.quebecoriginal. com)

- **Newfoundland and Labrador Tourism** (709/729-2830 or 800/563-6353, www.newfoundlandlabrador.com)

- **Maine Office of Tourism** (888/624-6345, www.visitmaine.com)

of Nova Scotia is 902. This prefix must be dialed for all long-distance calls. Toll-free numbers have the 800, 888, 877, or 866 prefix and may be good for Nova Scotia, the Maritimes, Canada, North America, or, in the case of major hotel chains and car rental companies, will work worldwide.

To make an international call from Canada, dial the prefix 011 before the country code or dial 0 for operator assistance.

Public phones accept 5-, 10-, and 25-cent coins; local calls are $0.35-0.50, and most long-distance calls cost at least $2.50 for the first minute. The least expensive way to make long-distance calls from a public phone is with a **phone card.** These are available from convenience stores, newsstands, and gas stations.

Internet Access

If your Internet provider doesn't allow you to access your email away from your home computer, open an email account with Gmail (www.gmail.com), Hotmail (www.hotmail. com), or Yahoo! (www.yahoo.com)—or use Facebook (www.facebook.com) to keep in touch with friends and family.

Free public Internet access is available throughout Nova Scotia through the **Community Access Program (CAP).** To find out addresses and hours of the 400-odd locations across the province, call 866/569-8428 or go to www.nscap.ca.

Almost all hotels and motels and most B&Bs have wireless access from guest rooms. You'll also find wireless access at most libraries, visitors centers, and cafés.

WEIGHTS AND MEASURES

Canada uses the **metric system,** with temperature measured in degrees Celsius, liquid measurements in liters, solid weights in kilograms and metric tons, land areas in hectares, and distances in kilometers, meters, and centimeters. This system hasn't completely taken hold everywhere, and many Nova Scotians still think in terms of the imperial system; expect to hear a lobster described in pounds, local distances given in miles, and the temperature expressed in Fahrenheit degrees.

The electrical voltage is **120 volts.** The standard electrical plug configuration is the same as that used in the United States—two flat blades, often with a round third pin for grounding.

Time Zones

Even though Nova Scotia was home to Sir Sandford Fleming, the man who devised time zones, the province didn't receive any special favors. It is on Atlantic Standard Time (AST), the same as New Brunswick and Prince Edward Island.

Atlantic Standard Time is one hour ahead of Eastern Standard Time and four hours ahead of Pacific Standard Time.

Resources

Suggested Reading

NATURAL HISTORY

Aldersey-Williams, Hugh. *The Tide: The Science and Stories Behind the Greatest Force on Earth.* New York: W.W. Norton, 2016. This hardcover book covers a lot of ground, but there is much space devoted to the Bay of Fundy's Nova Scotia coast, home to the world's largest tides, both the science behind them and the impacts on the human population.

Billard, Allan, and Donna Barnett. *Beaches of Nova Scotia.* Halifax: Formac Publishing, 2015. The subtitle of this book, *Discovering the Secrets of Some of the Province's Most Beautiful Beaches* sums up what you find within the pages—information and color photos on beaches throughout the province.

Dawson, Joan. *The Mapmaker's Eye: Nova Scotia Through Early Maps.* Halifax: Nova Scotia Museum, 1988. Nova Scotia evolved through the centuries, as did the art of mapping. This illustrated book is a cartographer's dream.

Grescoe, Taras. *Bottomfeeder.* Toronto: HarperCollins, 2008. Although now a decade old, the insights into the fisheries industry, made more readable by the author's firsthand accounts of visits to the world's most important fisheries (including Nova Scotia), are still relevant.

Hare, F. K., and M. K. Thomas. *Climate Canada.* Toronto: John Wiley & Sons, 1974. One of the most extensive works on Canada's climate ever written. Includes a chapter on how the climate is changing.

MacAskill, Wallace R. *MacAskill Seascapes and Sailing Ships.* Halifax: Nimbus Publishing, 1987. Cape Breton's famed photographer captures the misty moods of fishermen, schooners, seaports, and seacoasts. Look for this book in used bookstores throughout the region.

Natural History of Nova Scotia. Halifax: Departments of Education and Lands and Forests, two volumes. Everything on land or beneath the nearby seas is comprehensively detailed here with illustrations.

Primrose, Mary, and Marian Munro. *Wildflowers of Nova Scotia, New Brunswick & Prince Edward Island.* Halifax: Formac Publishing, 2006. A glorious combination of text by Munro and stunning color photography by Primrose—a must for every naturalist who revels in wildflowers.

Saunders, Gary. *Discover Nova Scotia: The Ultimate Nature Guide.* Halifax: Nimbus Publishing, 2001. Perfect for a daypack, this handy guide includes maps, trail descriptions, and the natural wonders of Nova Scotia's parks.

Thurston, Harry. *Tidal Life: A Natural History of the Bay of Fundy.* Halifax: Nimbus Publishing, 1998. The lavishly illustrated contents describe natural habitats formed by the Fundy.

Towers, Julie, and Anne Camozzi. *Discover Nova Scotia: Wildlife Viewing Sites.* Halifax: Nimbus Publishing, 1999. Another of Nimbus's popular "Discover Nova Scotia" titles, this one gives detailed directions to more than 100 sites where you're likely to spot wildlife.

Tufts, Robbie. *Birds of Nova Scotia.* Halifax: Nimbus Publishing, 2007. The authoritative guide since 1961. The most recent edition includes color plates, detailed illustrations, a provincial map, and all the descriptive information bird-watchers will need to find and identify species across the province.

Wagg, Len (photographer). *Nova Scotia Landmarks.* Halifax: Formac Publishing, 2004. Filled with stunning aerial photography, this coffee-table book pinpoints natural highlights across the province. A great souvenir.

HUMAN HISTORY

Boileau, John. *Half-Hearted Enemies.* Halifax: Formac Publishing, 2005. Examines the intriguing story of how Nova Scotia and New England continued to trade through the War of 1812.

Brasseaux, Carl A. *The Founding of New Acadia.* New Orleans: Louisiana State University Press, 1997. A little academic, but this book will make interesting reading for anyone from the South who wants to learn about the links between Cajuns and the Acadians of Nova Scotia.

Bruce, Harry. *An Illustrated History of Nova Scotia.* Halifax: Nimbus Publishing, 1998. Primarily aimed at the younger set, this book is highly readable and well worth a look, even for adults.

Campey, Lucille H. *After the Hector: The Scottish Pioneers of Nova Scotia and Cape Breton 1733–1852.* Edinburgh: Birlinn Publishing, 2005. An account of those who arrived in Pictou aboard the *Hector* and how their Scottish Highlands heritage helped them adapt and thrive in the New World.

Crooker, William. *Oak Island Gold.* Halifax: Nimbus Publishing, 2011. One of many books devoted to the world's longest treasure hunt, this one does a noble job of unraveling the story—and even suggests an explanation to the secrets of the island.

Crowell, Clement W. *Novascotiaman.* Halifax: Nova Scotia Museum, 1979. A sea captain's correspondence forms the basis for a retelling of the story of Nova Scotia's Great Age of Sail.

Daigle, Jean, ed. *Acadians of the Maritimes.* Moncton, New Brunswick: Chaire d'Études Acadiennes, Université de Moncton, 1995. The history of the Acadians in Atlantic Canada is a tangled tale of upheaval and survival, cultural clashes and passions. Daigle's collection of Acadian literature is among the best on the bookshelves.

Duivenvoorden Mitic, Trudy. *Pier 21: Gateway that Changed Canada.* Halifax: Nimbus Publishing, 2011. As a child of parents who emigrated through Pier 21 and then was employed as a director with Employment and Immigration Canada, Duivenvoorden Mitic is well qualified to author a book on this important Halifax site.

Faragher, John Mack. *A Great and Noble Scheme: The Tragic Story of the Expulsion of the French Acadians from Their American Homeland.* New York: W. W. Norton, 2005. In this hefty 560-page book, Faragher describes the evolution of Acadia, the horrors of the deportation, and the resulting pockets of Acadian culture that thrive to this day.

Hamilton-Barry, Joann. *Oak Island and the Search for Buried Treasure*. Halifax: Nimbus Publishing, 2015. Designed for children but interesting for all ages, this book tells the story of one of the world's great treasure hunts using maps and photographs.

Irwin, Rip. *Lighthouses and Lights of Nova Scotia*. Halifax: Nimbus Publishing, 2011. Nova Scotia is renowned for its photogenic lighthouses—and this new edition details all 164, complete with historical facts.

Lawrence, Ian. *Historic Annapolis Royal*. Halifax: Nimbus Publishing, 2002. Filled with historical photographs, this book details the history of the oldest town north of St. Augustine, Florida.

Ledger, Don. *Swissair Down*. Halifax: Nimbus Publishing, 2000. The story of the September 1998 crash of a Swissair jetliner off the village of Peggy's Cove from a pilot's point of view.

Lyell, Charles. *Travels in North America in the Years 1841–2*. New York: Arno Press, reprinted 1978. The author included Nova Scotia in his 19th-century travel observations.

Nunn, Bruce. *History with a Twist*. Halifax: Nimbus Publishing, 2002. Light yet interesting reading that covers a few dozen tales from Nova Scotia's past. And if you're looking for more, there's *More History with a Twist* by the same author, as well as a third volume released in 2008.

Poliandri, Simone. *First Nations, Identity, and Reserve Life: The Mi'kmaq of Nova Scotia*. Lincoln, Nebraska: University of Nebraska Press, 2011. A big, beautiful book that tells the story of the Mi'kmaq starting from their arrival in the province.

Raddall, Thomas. *Halifax: Warden of the North*. Halifax: Nimbus Publishing, 2007.

One of the best historical accounts of the provincial capital, although the focus is on its military past.

Vacon, Shirley Irene. *Giants of Nova Scotia: The Lives of Anna Swan and Angus McAskill*. East Lawrencetown, Nova Scotia: Pottersfield Press, 2008. The remarkable story of two Nova Scotians who toured the world as the "world's tallest couple" in the 1800s.

SPORTS, CULTURE, AND CRAFTS

Buist, Ron. *Tales from Under the Rim: The Making of Tim Hortons*. Fredericton, New Brunswick: Goose Lane Editions, 2011. Although non-Canadians may not be familiar with the Tim Hortons chain of fast-food restaurants, you'll see them everywhere on your Nova Scotia travels, which makes this book an interesting read for those interested in a local marketing success story.

Elliot, Elaine. *The Chowder Trail Cookbook*. Halifax: Formac Publishing, 2014. One of the best-loved meals in Atlantic Canada is seafood chowder. This hardcover book takes readers on a journey through Nova Scotia, searching out the best ingredients and recipes.

Harper, Marjory. *Myth, Migration and the Making of Memory: Scotia and Nova Scotia*. Halifax: John Donald Publishers, 2000. Explores Nova Scotia's Scottish heritage and the importance of the province's links to Scotland through the years.

Hollingsworth, Paul. *Sidney Crosby: The Story of a Champion*. Halifax: Nimbus Publishing, 2011. Hockey's current superstar has already been the subject of many books, but this one, published by a local company, includes much detail of his growing up in Nova Scotia's Cole Harbour.

Lief, Charles. *Taste of Nova Scotia Cookbook*. Halifax: Nimbus Publishing, 2011. An in-depth look at local cuisine, including many traditional dishes, with recipes supplied by local restaurants, inns, and bed and breakfasts.

Nightingale, Marie. *Out of Old Nova Scotia Kitchens.* Halifax: Nimbus Publishing, 2011. Beloved by Nova Scotians for decades, this is a reprint of a classic known for its simple approach to preparing comfort food with locally available ingredients.

Parsons, Catriona. *Gaidhlig Troimh Chomhradh (Gaelic Through Conversation).* South Gut St. Ann's, Nova Scotia: Gaelic College of Celtic Arts and Crafts. The college's mission is to keep the language alive, and it does so with this text and accompanying cassette tapes, as well as a number of other books and varied literature.

Penney, Allen. *Houses of Nova Scotia: An Illustrated Guide to Architectural Style Recognition.* Halifax: Nova Scotia Museum and Formac Publishing, 1989. Penney, a professor of architecture, sums up provincial architectural styles and explains how to identify styles by dates, similarities, and differences.

Pilsworth, Graham. *Nova Scotia Drink-o-pedia.* Halifax: Nimbus Publishing, 2008. Local author Pilsworth takes a detailed yet humorous look into the culture of drinking in Nova Scotia, from the days of rum running to the success of Alexander Keith's brewery.

Rhindress, Charlie. *I'm Not What I Seem.* Halifax, Nova Scotia, 2016. A biography of Rita McNeil, a folk singer-songwriter who represented the working-class of Cape Breton Island through her music that is beloved worldwide, even after her 2013 passing.

Sawler, Sarah. *100 Things You Don't Know About Nova Scotia.* Halifax, Nova Scotia,

2016. Exactly as the name suggests, this easy-to-read book is filled with unique and eccentric facts about the province.

RECREATION GUIDES AND GUIDEBOOKS

Doers and Dreamers Guide. Free online download from Tourism Nova Scotia. Lists accommodations, campgrounds, and some attractions. Go to www.novascotia.com.

Haynes, Michael. *Hiking Trails of Cape Breton.* Fredericton, New Brunswick: Goose Lane Editions, 2012. The second edition of this reliable hiking guide details 40 trails, and although emphasis is on the national park, all regions of the island are covered. Includes maps and trailhead GPS directions.

Haynes, Michael. *Hiking Trails of Mainland Nova Scotia.* Fredericton, New Brunswick: Goose Lane Editions, 2012. The ninth edition of this comprehensive yet compact guide details about 50 trails throughout the province. Each description, up to five pages long, is accompanied by a map.

Haynes, Michael. *Trails of Halifax Regional Municipality.* Fredericton, New Brunswick: Goose Lane Editions, 2010. This comprehensive guide to hiking trails in and around Halifax includes maps, photos, GPS coordinates, and useful offerings such as cellphone coverage for each trail.

Hempstead, Andrew. *Moon Atlantic Canada.* Berkeley, California: Avalon Travel, 2017. For those traveling beyond Nova Scotia.

MAGAZINES, MAPS, AND ATLASES

Canadian Geographic. Ottawa: Royal Canadian Geographical Society (www.canadiangeographic.ca). Bimonthly publication pertaining to Canada's natural and human histories and resources.

Explore. Toronto. Bimonthly publication of adventure travel throughout Canada (www. explore-mag.com).

Hamilton, William B. *Place Names of Atlantic Canada.* Toronto: University of Toronto, 1996. Although no book is devoted to the toponymy of Nova Scotia, this tome includes definitions of all the province's most unusual and interesting place-names.

MapArt. Driving maps for all of Canada, a Halifax-Dartmouth street atlas, and folded maps of Atlantic Canada and Nova Scotia (www.mapart.com).

Nature Canada Newsletter. Ottawa. Seasonal e-newsletter of Nature Canada (www.naturecanada.ca).

Nova Scotia Atlas. Halifax: Formac Publishing, 2006. This comprehensive atlas breaks the province down into 90 topographical-style maps, including geographical features and all public roads. The back matter includes an index of 14,500 place-names and a short description of all provincial and national parks.

Rand McNally. Products include the *Atlantic Canada Road Atlas* and *Halifax* and *Nova Scotia Communities StreetFinder,* as well as folded maps of Nova Scotia, Halifax, and Cape Breton Island (www.randmcnally. com).

Internet Resources

TRAVEL PLANNING
Canadian Tourism Commission
www.canadatourism.com
Official tourism website for all of Canada.

Destination Halifax
www.destinationhalifax.com
In addition to all the usual travel information, use this website to order free literature, learn about current festivals and events, and read up on Halifax trivia.

Economic and Rural Development and Tourism
www.novascotia.com
The first place to go when planning your trip to Nova Scotia. This site includes a distance calculator, order forms for brochures, and detailed events calendars.

PARKS
Nova Scotia Provincial Parks
http://parks.novascotia.ca
This government website details seasons, fees, and the campsite reservation process, and has a handy search tool to help make finding parks easy.

Parks Canada
www.pc.gc.ca
Official website of the agency that manages Canada's national parks and national historic sites, of which two and 16, respectively, are located in Nova Scotia.

Parks Canada Campground Reservation Service
www.pccamping.ca
Use this website to make reservations for campsites in Kejimkujik and Cape Breton Highlands National Parks.

GOVERNMENT

Citizenship and Immigration Canada
www.cic.gc.ca
Check this government website for anything related to entry into Canada.

Environment Canada
www.weather.gc.ca
Seven-day forecasts from across Canada, including over 50 locations in Nova Scotia. Includes weather archives such as seasonal trends, hurricane history, and sea ice movement.

Government of Canada
www.gc.ca
The official website of the Canadian government.

Halifax Regional Municipality
www.halifax.ca
Official website of the Halifax Regional Municipality. Has links to transit schedules as well as information on visiting the city for business and local government issues.

Nova Scotia Museum
https://museum.novascotia.ca
A network of museums managed by the Nova Scotia Department of Communities, Culture, and Heritage. This website includes details on each site, as well as passes for those planning on extensive touring.

ACCOMMODATIONS

Bed and Breakfast Online
www.bbcanada.com
Easy-to-use tools for finding and reserving B&Bs that suit your budget and interests.

Hostelling International–Canada
www.hihostels.ca
Canadian arm of the worldwide organization.

Select Atlantic Inns
www.selectinns.ca
A loosely affiliated group of mid- to top-end B&Bs use this online presence to promote their properties and take bookings.

Signature Resorts
www.signatureresorts.com
Upscale lodging chain owned and operated by the government of Nova Scotia. Locations include Digby and Liscomb Mills.

TRANSPORTATION

Air Canada
www.aircanada.ca
Canada's national airline.

Halifax International Airport
www.hiaa.ca
The official airport website, which includes images of departure and arrival boards, tools to help reach Halifax using the most direct flights, and virtual flight maps that show the location of all incoming and outgoing flights.

Maritime Bus
www.maritimebus.com
Where Greyhound buses terminate, Maritime takes over, with inexpensive service throughout Nova Scotia.

Northumberland Ferries
www.ferries.ca
Provides a link between Saint John, New Brunswick, and Digby, Nova Scotia.

VIA Rail
www.viarail.ca
Passenger rail service across Canada, including Montreal to Halifax.

WestJet
www.westjet.com
Before booking with Air Canada, check out this airline for flights into Halifax from throughout Canada.

CONSERVATION

Canadian Parks and Wilderness Society (Nova Scotia Chapter)
www.cpawsns.org
Particularly active local chapter of a non-profit organization that is instrumental in highlighting conservation issues throughout Canada.

Ducks Unlimited Canada
www.ducks.ca
Respected organization responsible for the protection of over 30,000 hectares of wetland throughout Nova Scotia.

Nova Scotia Nature Trust
www.nsnt.ca
Provincial nonprofit organization that has been instrumental in land protection through the purchase and donation of land.

Sable Island Green Horse Society
www.greenhorsesociety.com
A group of individuals interested in Sable Island and its unique environmental issues.

OTHER INTERNET RESOURCES

Dill's Atlantic Giant
www.howarddill.com
Dill, the world's preeminent super-sized pumpkin grower, sells his record-breaking seeds through this website. He also gives growing tips and uploads photos of his massive vegetables.

Nimbus Publishing
www.nimbus.ca
While all the best books on Nova Scotia are detailed under *Suggested Reading,* check the website of this prolific Nova Scotia publisher for the latest titles.

Pugwash Conferences on Science and World Affairs
www.pugwash.org
This is the official website of a Nobel Prize-winning peace movement that had its beginnings in Pugwash, Nova Scotia.

Titanic in Nova Scotia
www.novascotia.ca/titanic
Maintained by the government of Nova Scotia, this website includes everything from full passenger lists to local links as obscure as a plaque in the Halifax YMCA that commemorates the sinking with the wrong date.

Index

List of Maps

Photo Credits

Title page photo: © Wally Hayes | Tourism Nova Scotia
page 6 © Katyenka | Dreamstime.com; page 7 © Andrew Hempstead; page 8 (top left) © Andrew Hempstead, (top right) © Andrew Hempstead, (bottom) ©Tourism Nova Scotia; page 9 (top) © Andrew Hempstead, (bottom left) © Andrew Hempstead, (bottom right) © Tourism Nova Scotia; page 10 © Andrew Hempstead; page 11 (top) © Andrew Hempstead, (bottom left) © Wally Hayes | Tourism Nova Scotia; (bottom right) © Andrew Hempstead; page 14 (bottom left) © Andrew Hempstead; (bottom right) © Dean Casavechia | Tourism Nova Scotia; page 15 © Andrew Hempstead; page 16 © Andrew Hempstead; page 17 © Andrew Hempstead; page 19 © Andrew Hempstead; page 18 (top) © Andrew Hempstead, (bottom) © Andrew Hempstead; page 21—57 © Andrew Hempstead; page 62 (top) © Andrew Hempstead, (bottom) © Andrew Hempstead; page 63—93 © Andrew Hempstead; page 94 (top) © Andrew Hempstead, (bottom) © Tom Goodwin; page 93—105 © Andrew Hempstead; page 106 © Tom Goodwin; page 108—120 © Andrew Hempstead; page 123 (top) © Andrew Hempstead, (bottom) © Andrew Hempstead; page 125—151 © Andrew Hempstead; page 153 (top) © Andrew Hempstead, (bottom) © Andrew Hempstead; page 155 —175 © Andrew Hempstead; page 179 © Wally Hayes/Tourism Nova Scotia; page 181 © Graça Victoria | 123rf.com; page 182 (top) © Robert R. Williams, (bottom) © Andrew Hempstead; page 183—207 © Andrew Hempstead; page 209 © New Brunswick Tourism; page 212—214 © Andrew Hempstead; page 216 © New Brunswick Tourism; page 218 (top) © Andrew Hempstead, (bottom) © Andrew Hempstead; page 219—232 © Andrew Hempstead; page 233 © New Brunswick Tourism; page 235—237 © Andrew Hempstead; page 238 (top) © Andrew Hempstead, (bottom) © Andrew Hempstead; page 239— 243 © Andrew Hempstead; page 244 © Resurgo Place; page 249—255 © Andrew Hempstead; page 256 © Dolores Breau/Le Pays de la Sagouine; page 257— 259 © Andrew Hempstead; page 263 © Village Historique Acadien; page 265 — 266 © Andrew Hempstead; page 267 © V. J. Matthew/123rf.com; page 268 (top) © Andrew Hempstead, (bottom) © Andrew Hempstead; page 269 —276 © Andrew Hempstead; page 278 © Martin Caird, Sandpiper Studios; page 280—301 © Andrew Hempstead; page 302 (top) © Andrew Hempstead, (bottom) © Andrew Hempstead; page 303—317 © Andrew Hempstead; page 319 (top) © Andrew Hempstead, (bottom) © Andrew Hempstead; page 321 —324 © Andrew Hempstead; page 325 © Emily Louise Photography; page 328 —335 © Andrew Hempstead; page 337 (top) © Andrew Hempstead, (bottom) © Andrew Hempstead; page 339— 356 © Andrew Hempstead; page 357 (top) © Andrew Hempstead, (bottom) © Andrew Hempstead; page 363 — 372 © Andrew Hempstead.

Also Available

ONTARIO
CAROLYN B. HELLER

MONTRÉAL &
QUÉBEC CITY
SACHA JACKSON

VERMONT
JEN ROSE SMITH

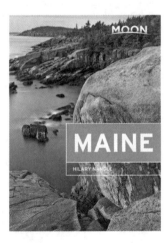

MAINE
HILARY NANGLE

MAP SYMBOLS

≈≈≈≈ Expressway	○ City/Town	✈ Airport	⚲ Golf Course
━━━━ Primary Road	◉ State Capital	✕ Airfield	▣ Parking Area
━━━━ Secondary Road	⊛ National Capital	▲ Mountain	⬟ Archaeological Site
⋯⋯ Unpaved Road	★ Point of Interest	✦ Unique Natural Feature	⛪ Church
━━━━ Feature Trail	• Accommodation		
------ Other Trail	▾ Restaurant/Bar	⟋ Waterfall	⛽ Gas Station
⋯⋯⋯ Ferry	■ Other Location	▲ Park	Glacier
≈≈≈ Pedestrian Walkway	Λ Campground	◫ Trailhead	Mangrove
▪▪▪▪▪ Stairs		✕ Skiing Area	Reef
			Swamp

CONVERSION TABLES

°C = (°F - 32) / 1.8
°F = (°C x 1.8) + 32
1 inch = 2.54 centimeters (cm)
1 foot = 0.304 meters (m)
1 yard = 0.914 meters
1 mile = 1.6093 kilometers (km)
1 km = 0.6214 miles
1 fathom = 1.8288 m
1 chain = 20.1168 m
1 furlong = 201.168 m
1 acre = 0.4047 hectares
1 sq km = 100 hectares
1 sq mile = 2.59 square km
1 ounce = 28.35 grams
1 pound = 0.4536 kilograms
1 short ton = 0.90718 metric ton
1 short ton = 2,000 pounds
1 long ton = 1.016 metric tons
1 long ton = 2,240 pounds
1 metric ton = 1,000 kilograms
1 quart = 0.94635 liters
1 US gallon = 3.7854 liters
1 Imperial gallon = 4.5459 liters
1 nautical mile = 1.852 km

MOON NOVA SCOTIA, NEW BRUNSWICK & PRINCE EDWARD ISLAND

Avalon Travel
An imprint of Perseus Books
A Hachette Book Group company
1700 Fourth Street
Berkeley, CA 94710, USA
www.moon.com

Editor: Kimberly Ehart
Series Manager: Kathryn Ettinger
Copy Editor: Ann Siefert
Production Designer: Sarah Wildfang
Cover Design: Faceout Studios, Charles Brock
Interior Design: Domini Dragoone
Moon Logo: Tim McGrath
Map Editor: Albert Angulo
Cartographers: Austin Ehrhardt and Brian Shotwell
Proofreader: Rachael Sablik
Indexer: Greg Jewett

ISBN-13: 978-1-63121-4875

Printing History
1st Edition — 2006
5th Edition — June 2017
5 4 3 2 1

Front cover photo: Mira / Alamy Stock Photo
Back cover photo: Andrew Hempstead

Printed in Canada by Friesens